Marx and the Political Economy of the Media

D1641150

Studies in Critical Social Sciences Book Series

Haymarket Books is proud to be working with Brill Academic Publishers (www.brill.nl) to republish the *Studies in Critical Social Sciences* book series in paperback editions. This peer-reviewed book series offers insights into our current reality by exploring the content and consequences of power relationships under capitalism, and by considering the spaces of opposition and resistance to these changes that have been defining our new age. Our full catalog of *SCSS* volumes can be viewed at https://www.haymarketbooks .org/series_collections/4-studies-in-critical-social-sciences.

Marx and the Political Economy of the Media

Edited by
Christian Fuchs
Vincent Mosco

Haymarket
Books
Chicago, IL

First published in 2015 by Brill Academic Publishers, The Netherlands.
© 2016 Koninklijke Brill NV, Leiden, The Netherlands

Published in paperback in 2017 by
Haymarket Books
P.O. Box 180165
Chicago, IL 60618
773-583-7884
www.haymarketbooks.org

ISBN: 978-1-60846-708-2

Trade distribution:
In the U.S. through Consortium Book Sales, www.cbsd.com
In Canada, Publishers Group Canada, www.pgcbooks.ca
In the UK, Turnaround Publisher Services, www.turnaround-uk.com
In all other countries by Publishers Group Worldwide, www.pgw.com

Cover design by Jamie Kerry of Belle Étoile Studios and Ragina Johnson.

This book was published with the generous support of Lannan Foundation
and the Wallace Action Fund.

Printed in Canada by union labor.

10 9 8 7 6 5 4 3 2 1

Library of Congress Cataloging-in-Publication Data is available.

Contents

List of Figures and Tables

Figures

Tables

About the Authors

Editors

Christian Fuchs

is Professor at and Director of the University of Westminster's Communication and Media research Institute (CAMRI). He is co-editor of the open access online journal tripleC: Communication, Capitalism & Critique (http://www.triple-c.at). His research interests lie in the fields of Critical Information Society Studies, Critical Internet Research, critical social theory, media & society and the Critical Political Economy of Media, Communication & Society. He is author of numerous publications on these topics, including the monographs "Reading Marx in the Information Age: A Media and Communication Studies Perspective on Capital Volume 1" (Routledge 2016), "Digital Labour and Karl Marx" (Routledge 2014), "Social Media: A Critical Introduction" (Sage 2014), "Culture and Economy in the Age of Social Media" (2015), "OccupyMedia! The Occupy Movement and Social Media in Crisis Capitalism" (Zero Books 2014), "Foundations of Critical Media and Information Studies" (Routledge 2011), "Internet and Society: Social Theory in the Information Age" (Routledge 2008).

Vincent Mosco

is Professor Emeritus of Sociology at Queen's University where he was Canada Research Chair in Communication and Society and head of the Department of Sociology. His most recent books include To the Cloud: Big Data in a Turbulent World (2014), The Laboring of Communication (with Catherine McKercher, 2008), The Political Economy of Communication, second edition (2009), Getting the Message: Communication Workers and Global Value Chains (edited with Ursula Huws and Catherine McKercher, 2010), and Critical Studies in Communication and Society (with Cao Jin and Leslie Regan Shade, 2014).

Authors

Lee Artz

Ph. D., University of Iowa, teaches media studies and international communication at Purdue University Calumet. Artz, a former steelworker, has edited and published eight books, including Global Media Entertainment: A Critical Introduction (2015) and dozens of articles on social change, hegemony, popular culture, and international media.

Pablo Castagno

holds a PhD in Cultural Studies from George Mason University and is currently Professor of Political Science at Universidad Nacional de La Matanza, Argentina, where he teaches on cultural and political theory. His research on culture, media and critical political economy has appeared in *Mediations, tripleC: Communication, Capitalism & Critique, Historical Materialism*, and *Cultural Studies*. He is working on a comparative study of the political manifestations of the global capitalist crisis in Southern Europe and South America.

Nicole S. Cohen

is an assistant professor in the Institute of Communication, Culture, Information and Technology and the Faculty of Information at the University of Toronto. She researches in political economy of communication and labour, particularly freelance media workers and, along with Greig de Peuter and Enda Brophy, cultural workers' collective responses to precarity (culturalworkersorganize.org).

İrfan Erdogan

is Professor and Head of the Department of Public Relations and Advertising, Faculty of Management at Atilim University, Ankara, Turkey. He has published 16 books, 9 chapters in edited books and over 30 methodological, ideological, cultural and political economy aspects of mass communication. Currently he is conducting research about the mode of representation of social life by television programmes in Turkey.

Christian Garland

is a writer and theorist; he is also a PhD candidate at the University of Warwick and Fellow of the Institut für Kritische Theorie, Freie Universität Berlin. His research interests include the original Frankfurt School and critical media theory. His publications include *Refusing the terms of non-existence, breaking their constraints: John Holloway, cracking capitalism and the meaning of revolution today*, which is forthcoming in *Journal of Classical Sociology* (12.2) and, also forthcoming in 2012, *Negating that which Negates us: Marcuse, Critical Theory and the New Politics of Refusal* in *Radical Philosophy Review*.

Richard Hall

is Professor of Education and Technology at De Montfort University, Leicester, UK. At DMU he is Head of Enhancing Learning through Technology and leads the Centre for Pedagogic Research. Richard is a National Teaching Fellow and a co-operator at the Social Science Centre in Lincoln, UK. He writes about life in higher education at: http://richard-hall.org.

Stephen Harper
is Senior Lecturer in Media Studies at the University of Portsmouth, UK. His research interests span political and social issues in British television, critical theory and cultural geopolitics. He has written academic articles on a wide range of subjects including British television drama and documentary, dramatic representations of war and media representations of mental distress. He is also the author of *Madness, Power and the Media* (Palgrave, 2009) and *Beyond the Left: The Communist Critique of the Media* (Zero Books, 2012).

William H.J. Hebblewhite
is currently a PhD Student in the Philosophy department of Macquarie University, Sydney. His MA from La Trobe University examined the work of post-Althusserian Marxism. His current work looks at the paradox of emancipation from Kant to contemporary political philosophy. His interests revolve around broadly, contemporary Marxist theory, Post-Marxism, Liberal Political Philosophy and European Philosophy.

Peter Ludes
was the 1973–75 Fulbright Scholar at Brandeis. 1978 PhD, thesis "Towards a Sociology of Alternatives"; (visiting) positions at Memorial University of Newfoundland, Wuppertal, Amsterdam, Harvard, Siegen, Mannheim, Constance; since 2002 a Professor of Mass Communication, Jacobs University Bremen. He initiated the Project News Enlightenment in 1997 and international cooperation on Key Visuals: http://www.keyvisuals.org and http://www.nachrichtenaufklaerung.de. Co-chair of the Research Network Sociology of Communications and Media Research, European Sociological Association (2008–2011); http://www.jacobs-university.de/directory/pludes.

Jim McGuigan
is Professor of Cultural Analysis in the Department of Social Sciences at Loughborough University, UK. His most recent books are *Cool Capitalism* (Pluto, 2009) and *Cultural Analysis* (Sage, 2010).

Brice Nixon
is a visiting assistant professor in the Communications Department at the University of La Verne. His research is in the areas of the political economy of communication, digital media studies, media history, journalism studies, communication law and policy, and critical theory. His primary interest is in analysing how communication industries from the print era to today have sought to determine the conditions of cultural consumption in order to turn communicative practices into the business of media and culture. Recent work in this

area includes an article on the "old media" business of Google, in *Media, Culture & Society*.

Wilhelm Peekhaus

is Assistant Professor in the School of Information Studies, University of Wisconsin-Milwaukee. He has published a variety of research articles on a range of topics, including the privacy of medical/genetic information, the political economy of intellectual property, social media use by capital, access to government information, open access, and the labour of academic publishing. His book, *Resistance is fertile: Canadian biotechnology policy and struggles on the biocommons*, employs Marxist political economic theory to interrogate the ways in which agricultural biotechnology has been appropriated by capital as an element of broader accumulation strategies. The monograph similarly emphasises the major instances of social resistance that are being mobilised against particular aspects of agricultural biotechnology in Canada.

George Pleios

is Professor and Head of the Faculty of Communication and Media Studies at the University of Athens, Greece, and director of the Laboratory for Social Research in Mass Media. He is author of 5 books, co-author of 1 book, author of 17 chapters in Greek and international edited books, editor of 1 book, co-editor of 1 book and author of more than 40 articles which have been published in Greek and internationally. In his recent work "Social media in time of crisis" he examines the social, cultural, economic and political uses of Facebook in countries in crisis and in contemporary capitalism as well. In his recent book (ed.) "The media and the crisis" it is analyzed the impact of crisis on the media's economic model and content as well as the relations between the media and the political system. He has been primary investigator in more than 20 research projects and has presented about 50 papers in national and international conferences. His interests are focusing on the relations between capitalism, ideology and the media.

Michelle Rodino-Colocino

is Associate Professor of Film, Video and Media Studies in the College of Communications and is an affiliate faculty member in the Department of Women's Studies at The Pennsylvania State University. Dr. Rodino-Colocino taught for three years as assistant professor at the University of Cincinnati before coming to Penn State. Her research, teaching and service work spans feminist media and critical cultural studies, with special interest in labor, new media, and activism. Dr. Rodino-Colocino's work has appeared in *Communication, Culture & Critique, Communication and Critical/Cultural Studies, Critical Studies in Media Communication, Democratic Communiqué, Feminist Media Studies, New Media and Society, Work Organization, Labour and Globalization* and more. Dr. Rodino-Colocino serves on the editorial boards of *Communication, Culture & Critique, tripleC: Communication, Capitalism & Critique,* and *Ada: A Journal of Gender, New Media, and Technology* and serves on the steering committee of the Union for Democratic Communications (UDC) and on the legislative assembly of the National Communication Association (NCA) as Vice Chair of the Critical and Cultural Studies Division.

Padmaja Shaw

Graduated with a Master's degree in Journalism from Osmania University, India and a Master's in Telecommunications from Michigan State University, USA. She completed a PhD in Development Studies and has been teaching at the Department of Communication and Journalism, Osmania University, India, since 1988. She has two tracks of interest: Broadcast production and political economy of communication. She contributes regularly to a media watch website, The Hoot, and writes a regular column in a local English-language daily newspaper, The Hans India.

Bernd Carsten Stahl

is Professor of Critical Research in Technology and Director the Centre for Computing and Social Responsibility at De Montfort University, Leicester, UK. His interests cover philosophical issues arising from the intersections of business, technology, and information. This includes the ethics of ICT and critical approaches to information systems.

Gerald Sussman

is Professor of Urban Studies and International Studies at Portland State University, where he teaches graduate courses in international development, political economy, political communication, and media studies. His latest book (as editor) is: *The Propaganda Society: Promotional Culture and Politics in Global Context* (Peter Lang, 2011). He is also the author of *Branding Democracy: u.s. Regime Change in Post-Soviet Eastern Europe* (Peter Lang, 2010), *Global Electioneering: Campaign Consulting, Communications, and Corporate Financing* (Rowman & Littlefield, 2005), and *Communication, Technology, and Politics in the Information Age* (Sage, 1997), and editor of two other books.

CHAPTER 1

Introduction: Marx is Back – The Importance of Marxist Theory and Research for Critical Communication Studies Today

Christian Fuchs and Vincent Mosco

'Marx is fashionable again', declares Jorn Schutrumpf, head of the Berlin publishing house Dietz, which brings out the works of Marx and his collaborator Friedrich Engels. Sales have trebled – albeit from a pretty low level – since 2005 and have soared since the summer. [...] The Archbishop of Canterbury, Rowan Williams, gave him a decent review last month: 'Marx long ago observed the way in which unbridled capitalism became a kind of mythology, ascribing reality, power and agency to things that had no life in themselves'. Even the Pope has put in a good word for the old atheist – praising his 'great analytical skill'.

THE TIMES, *Financial crisis gives added capital to Marx's writings. October 20, 2008*

No one claims that we're all Marxists now but I do think the old boy deserves some credit for noticing that 'it's the economy, stupid' and that many of the apparently omniscient titans who ascend the commanding heights of the economy are not so much stupid as downright imbecilic, driven by a mad exploitative greed that threatens us all. Marx's work is not holy writ, despite the strivings of some disciples to present it as such.

THE EVENING STANDARD, *Was Marx Right All Along? March 30, 2009*

Karl Marx is back. That, at least, is the verdict of publishers and bookshops in Germany who say that his works are flying off the shelves.

THE GUARDIAN, *Booklovers Turn to Karl Marx as Financial Crisis Bites in Germany. October 15, 2008*

Policy makers struggling to understand the barrage of financial panics, protests and other ills afflicting the world would do well to study the works of a long-dead economist: Karl Marx. The sooner they recognize we're facing a once-in-a-lifetime crisis of capitalism, the better equipped they will be to manage a way out of it.

BLOOMBERG BUSINESS WEEK, *Give Karl Marx a Chance to Save the World Economy. August 28, 2011*

Time Magazine showed Marx on its cover on February 2nd, 2009, and asked in respect to the crisis: "What would Marx think?" In the cover story, Marx was presented as the saviour of capitalism and was thereby mutilated beyond recognition: "Rethinking Marx. As we work out how to save capitalism, it's worth studying the system's greatest critic."

TIME MAGAZINE EUROPE, *February 2, 2009*

In the golden, post-war years of Western economic growth, the comfortable living standard of the working class and the economy's overall stability made the best case for the value of capitalism and the fraudulence of Marx's critical view of it. But in more recent years many of the forces that Marx said would lead to capitalism's demise – the concentration and globalization of wealth, the permanence of unemployment, the lowering of wages – have become real, and troubling, once again.

NEW YORK TIMES ONLINE, *March 30, 2014*

These news clippings indicate that with the new global crisis of capitalism, we seem to have entered new Marxian times. That there is suddenly a surging interest in Karl Marx's work is an indication for the persistence of capitalism, class conflicts, and crisis. At the same time, the bourgeois press tries to limit Marx and to stifle his theory by interpreting him as the new saviour of capitalism. One should remember that he was not only a brilliant analyst of capitalism, he was also the strongest critic of capitalism in his time: "In short, the Communists everywhere support every revolutionary movement against the existing social and political order of things. In all these movements, they bring to the front, as the leading question in each, the property question, no matter what its degree of development at the time. Finally, they labour everywhere for the union and agreement of the democratic parties of all countries. The Communists disdain to conceal their views and aims. They openly declare that their ends can be attained only by the forcible overthrow of all existing social conditions. Let the ruling classes tremble at a Communistic revolution. The proletarians have nothing to lose but their chains. They have a world to win. Proletarians of all lands unite!" (Marx and Engels 1848/2004, 94).

In 1977, Dallas Smythe published his seminal article "Communications: Blindspot of Western Marxism" (Smythe 1977), in which he argued that Western Marxism had not given enough attention to the complex role of communications in capitalism. 35 years have passed and the rise of neoliberalism resulted in a turn away from an interest in social class and capitalism. Instead, it became fashionable to speak of globalization, postmodernism, and, with the fall of Communism, even the end of history. In essence, Marxism became the blindspot

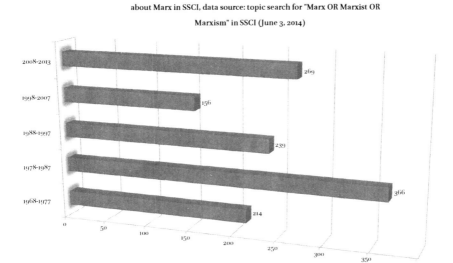

Average annual number of articles
about Marx in SSCI, data source: topic search for "Marx OR Marxist OR
Marxism" in SSCI (June 3, 2014)

FIGURE 1.1   *Articles published about Marx and Marxism in the Social Sciences Citation Index*

of all social science. Marxist academics were marginalized and it was increasingly career threatening for a young academic to take an explicitly Marxist approach to social analysis.

The declining interest in Marx and Marxism is visualized in Figure 1.1 that shows the average annual number of articles in the Social Sciences Citation Index that contain one of the keywords Marx, Marxist or Marxism in the article topic description and were published in the five time periods 1968–1977, 1978–1987, 1988–1997, 1998–2007, 2008–2013. Choosing these periods allows observing if there has been a change since the start of the new capitalist crisis in 2008 and also makes sense because the 1968 revolt marked a break that also transformed academia.

Figure 1.1 shows that there was a relatively large academic article output about Marx in the period 1978–1987: 3659. Given that the number of articles published increases historically, also the interest in the period 1968–1977 seems to have been high. One can observe a clear contraction of the output of articles that focus on Marx in the periods 1988–1997 (2393) and 1998–2007 (1563). Given the historical increase of published articles, this contraction is even more severe. This period has also been the time of the intensification of neoliberalism, the commodification of everything (including public service communication in many countries) and a strong turn towards postmodernism and culturalism in the social sciences. One can see that the average number of annual articles published about Marxism in the period 2008–2013 (269) has increased in comparisons to the periods 1988–2007 (156 per year) and 1988–1997 (239 per year). This circumstance is an empirical indicator for a renewed interest in Marx and Marxism in the social sciences as effect of the new capitalist crisis. The question is if and how this interest can be sustained and materialised in institutional transformations.

Due to the rising income gap between the rich and the poor, widespread precarious labour, and the new global capitalist crisis, neoliberalism is no longer seen as common sense. The dark side of capitalism, with its rising levels of class conflict, is now recognized worldwide. Eagleton (2011) notes that never has a thinker been so travestied as Marx and demonstrates that the core of Marx's work runs contrary to common prejudices about his work. But since the start of the global capitalist crisis in 2008, a considerable scholarly interest in the works of Marx has taken root. Moreover, Žižek (2010) argues that the recent world economic crisis has resulted in a renewed interest in the Marxian critique of political economy.

Communism is not a condition in a distant future, it is rather present in the desires for alternatives expressed in struggles against the poverty in resources, ownership, wealth, literacy, food, housing, social security, self-determination, equality, participation, expression, healthcare, access, etc. caused by a system of global stratification that benefits some at the expense of many. It exists wherever people resist capitalism and create autonomous spaces. Communism is "not a state of affairs which is to be established, an ideal to which reality [will] have to adjust itself," but rather "the real movement which abolishes the present state of things" (Marx and Engels 1844, 57). It is a revolution of the propertyless, by those who do not own and control the economy, politics, culture, nature, themselves, their bodies, their minds, their knowledge, technology, etc. Communism needs spaces for materializing itself as a movement. The contemporary names of these spaces are not Facebook, YouTube or Twitter, but rather Tahrir Square, Syntagma Square, Puerta del Sol, Plaça Catalunya, and Zuccotti Park. The context of contemporary struggles is the large-scale colonization of the world by capitalism. A different world is necessary, but whether it can be created is uncertain and only determined by the outcome of struggles.

The capitalist crisis and the resulting struggles against the poverty of everything are the context for the two books. We have set ourselves the aim to contribute with this issue to the discussion about the relevance of Marx for analyzing communication and knowledge in contemporary capitalism. Robert McChesney (2007, 235-236, fn 35) has accurately noted that while Marx has been studied by communication scholars, "no one has read Marx systematically to tease out the notion of communication in its varied manifestations." He also notes that he can imagine that Marx had things to say on communication that are of considerable importance. The task of the two books is to contribute to overcoming this lack of systematic reading of Marx on communication and media.

The chapters in the two books "Marx and the Political Economy of the Media" and "Marx in the Age of Digital Capitalism" make clear that Baudrillard was wrong to claim that "the Marxist theory of production is irredeemable partial, and cannot be generalized" to culture and the media and is also incorrect to insist that "the theory of production (the dialectical chaining of contradictions linked to the development of productive forces) is strictly homogenous with its object – material production – and is non-transferable, as a postulate or theoretical framework, to contents that were never given for it in the first place" (Baudrillard 1981, 214). Marshall McLuhan (1964/2001, 41) was wrong when he argued that Marx and his followers did not "understand the dynamics of the new media of communication." The two books demonstrate the enormous importance of Marx's theory for Critical Communication Studies today (see also Fuchs & Sandoval 2014, Fuchs 2016). If one wants to critically study communication and to use that research for social change, then the work of Marx provides an essential building block. Moreover, the chapters maintain that to critically examine communication we need to engage with the analysis and critique of capitalism, class, exploitation and with practical struggles for emancipation.

Most of the chapters in the two books are revised and updated editions of the special issue Marx is Back: The Importance of Marxist Theory and Research for Critical Communication Studies Today that was published in 2012 in the open access online journal tripleC: Communication, Capitalism & Critique (Vol. 10, No. 2, pp. 127–632, http://www.triple-c.at). The 28 updated chapters from the special issue are accompanied by updated version of three further articles published in tripleC (by Dal Yong Jin, Marisol Sandoval, and Christian Fuchs' Dallas Smythe article) as well as a new chapter by Vincent Mosco ("Marx in the Cloud").

When putting together the tripleC special issue, we published a Call for Papers that much reflects the topics of the contributions in the two books and the special issue. It asked these questions:

> * What is Marxist Media and Communication Studies? Why is it needed today? What are the main assumptions, legacies, tasks, methods and categories of Marxist Media and Communication Studies and how do they relate to Karl Marx's theory? What are the different types of Marxist Media/Communication Studies, how do they differ, what are their commonalities?

* What is the role of Karl Marx's theory in different fields, subfields and approaches of Media and Communication Studies? How have the role, status, and importance of Marx's theory for Media and Communication Studies evolved historically, especially since the 1960s?

* In addition to his work as a theorist and activist, Marx was a practicing journalist throughout his career. What can we learn from his journalism about the practice of journalism today, about journalism theory, journalism education and alternative media?

* What have been the structural conditions, limits and problems for conducting Marxian-inspired Media and Communication Research and for carrying out university teaching in the era of neoliberalism? What are actual or potential effects of the new capitalist crisis on these conditions?

* What is the relevance of Marxian thinking in an age of capitalist crisis for analyzing the role of media and communication in society?

* How can the Marxian notions of class, class struggle, surplus value, exploitation, commodity/commodification, alienation, globalization, labour, capitalism, militarism and war, ideology/ideology critique, fetishism, and communism best be used for analyzing, transforming and criticizing the role of media, knowledge production and communication in contemporary capitalism?

* How are media, communication, and information addressed in Marx's work?

* What are commonalities and differences between contemporary approaches in the interpretation of Marx's analyses of media, communication, knowledge, knowledge labour and technology?

* What is the role of dialectical philosophy and dialectical analysis as epistemological and methodological tools for Marxian-inspired Media and Communication Studies?

* What were central assumptions of Marx about media, communication, information, knowledge production, culture and how can these insights be used today for the critical analysis of capitalism?

* What is the relevance of Marx's work for an understanding of social media?

* Which of Marx's works can best be used today to theorize media and communication? Why and how?

* Terry Eagleton (2011) maintains that the 10 most commonly held prejudices against Marx are wrong. What prejudices against Marx can be found in Media and Communication Studies today? What have been the consequences of such prejudices? How can they best be contested? Are there continuities and/or discontinuities in prejudice against Marx in light of the new capitalist crisis?

Thomas Piketty's (2014) book *Capital in the Twenty-First Century* shows empirically that the history of capitalism is a history of inequality and capital concentration. It has resulted in many responses and a public discussion of capitalism's
problems (for an analysis of the reception of the book and its relevance for the
political economy of the Internet see Fuchs 2014). Piketty's book is certainly not
the 21st century equivalent of Marx's Capital because it lacks solid theoretical
foundations. Piketty also misinterprets Marx (see Fuchs 2014), which is not a surprise because when being asked about Karl Marx, Piketty said: "I never managed
really to read it."[1] Piketty's book has however stressed the importance of political
measures that weaken capitalist interests and the capitalist class and especially
the role that global progressive tax on capital and wealth could play in this context. This political debate should be welcomed by Marxists because Marx and
Engels themselves called in the Communist Manifesto for a "heavy progressive or
graduated income tax" (Marx and Engels 1968, 51). Marx and Engels would today
embrace and radicalise the idea of a global progressive tax on capital.

A Marxist theory of communication should "demonstrate how communication and culture are material practices, how labor and language are mutually
constituted, and how communication and information are dialectical instances
of the same social activity, the social construction of meaning. Situating these
tasks within a larger framework of understanding power and resistance would
place communication directly into the flow of a Marxian tradition that remains
alive and relevant today" (Mosco 2009, 44). A Marxist theory of communication sees communication in relation to capitalism, "placing in the foreground
the analysis of capitalism, including the development of the forces and relations of production, commodification and the production of surplus value,
social class divisions and struggles, contradictions and oppositional movements" (Mosco 2009, 94). Marxist Media and Communication Studies are not
only relevant now, but have been so for a long time because communication
has always been embedded into structures of inequality in class societies. With
the rise of neoliberalism, Marxist communication theory has suffered a set-
back because it had become common to marginalise and discriminate against
Marxist scholarship and to replace Marxism with postmodernism. So Marx
was always relevant, but being Marxist and practicing Marxism were always
difficult, in part because Marxist studies have lacked a solid institutional base.
What we can see today is a rising interest in Marx's work. The question is whether
it will be possible to channel this interest into institutional transformations

---

1   Chotiner, Isaac. 2014. "Marx? I never really managed to read it" – an interview with Thomas
    Piketty. *New Statesman Online* May 6, 2014: http://www.newstatesman.com/politics/2014/05/
    marx-i-never-really-managed-read-it-interview-thomas-piketty.

TABLE 1.1   *A systematic account of the role of media in the Marxian circuit of capital*

Circulation	Production	Circulation	Consumption
M – C (Mp, L)	.. P.. Media Technology as Means of Rationalization: $s/v\uparrow$ The process of capital concentration and centralization in the realm of the media	C' – M'	

Knowledge workers as wage labourers in media corporations

Media as means of inter-organizational corporate communication and co-ordination: $v\downarrow, c\downarrow$

Media for the spatial distribution and extension of capitalism

Media as carriers of advertisements
Transmission media as forms of capital
Media and trade globalization
Media and spatial centralization of capital
Media as carriers & diffusion channels of ideologies

Alternative media as negating forces in media production, circulation, and consumption

that challenge the predominant administrative character of media institutions and (see: Fuchs 2016, 2011, 2010) strengthen the institutionalization of critical studies of communication.

Table 1.1 shows how various aspects of media and communications are related to the capital accumulation cycle M – C .. P – C' – M' that Marx has elaborated. We can summarise the following areas of production, usage, and effects of media as they are found in Marx's works (for a detailed discussion of

Marx on media communication in capitalism and explanation of a theoretical model, see: Fuchs 2010, 2011).
In commodity production:

- Specific: Media technology as rationalization technology in the media industry
- Specific: The process of capital concentration and centralization in the media sector
- Specific: The production of media capital, knowledge workers as wage labourers in media corporations
- General: Communication technologies for the spatial and temporal co-ordination of production in order to reduce constant and variable capital shares
- General: Communication technologies as means for the spatial expansion of capitalist production

In commodity circulation:

- Specific: Transmission technologies as means of accumulating media infra-structure capital
- Specific: Media as carriers of advertisements
- General: Communication technologies as means for reducing the circula-tion and turnover time of capital
- General: Media as means and outcomes of the globalization of world trade
- General: Media as means of the spatial centralization of capital

In the circulation and reception of ideas:

- Media as carriers and circulators of ideologies

In the production, circulation, and reception of alternative media:

- Alternative media that are alternatively produced, distributed, and interpreted and function as means of class struggle and means of circulation of critical ideas

The model in Figure 1.2 summarises the connection of four aspects of the media, i.e., four roles of the media in the capitalist economy:

    1) the commodity form of the media,
    2) the ideological form of the media,
    3) media reception, and
    4) alternative media.

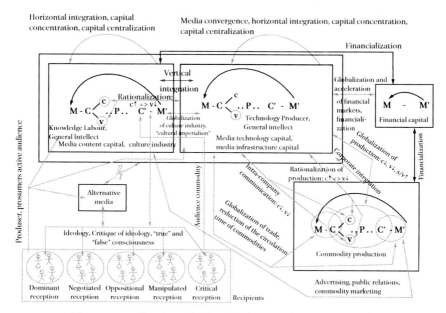

FIGURE 1.2   *The processes of media production, circulation, and consumption in the capitalist economy*

It focuses on the role of the media in the production, circulation, and consumption processes of the economy, not on the relations to the political system (state, civil society, laws, etc.) and cultural institutions (education, family, religion, etc.). Capital accumulation within the media sphere takes place in both the media content sphere and the media infrastructure sphere. These two realms together form the sphere of media capital. The Marxian circuit of capital is shown for each of the two realms, which indicates that they are oriented to capital accumulation.

The commodity hypothesis can be visualized as the following processes that are shown in Figure 1.2: vertical and horizontal integration, media concentration, media convergence, media globalization, the integration of media capital and other types of capital, the rationalization of production, the globalization of production, circulation, and trade, and intra-company communication, advertising and marketing. The production of media content and the production of media technologies are shown as two different systems. They both belong to the media industry, but create different products. Processes of vertical integration make the boundaries between the two systems fuzzy. Concentration processes and horizontal integration, which are inherent features of capital accumulation, shape each of the two spheres. Media convergence is a specific feature of media infrastructure capital. The two realms together are factors that influence the globalization of the culture industry. The realm of the economy that is shown at the bottom right of Figure 1.2 represents capital accumulation in non-media industries and services. It is partly integrated with the media sector due to corporate integration processes. Media technologies advance the rationalization of production in this realm as well as in the media content industry. Furthermore, they advance the globalization of production, circulation, and trade. These globalization processes are also factors that, in return, promote the development of new media technologies. Media technologies are also used for intra-company communication. Rationalization, globalization, and intra-company communication are processes that aim at maximizing profits by decreasing the investment cost of capital (both constant and variable) and by advancing relative surplus value production (more production in less time). The media content industry is important for advertising and marketing commodities in the circulation process of commodities, which is at the same time the realization process of capital in which surplus value is transformed into money profit.

The ideology hypothesis is visualized in Figure 1.2 by media content capital and its relation to recipients. Media content that creates false consciousness is considered as ideological content. Media content depends on reception. The reception hypothesis is visualized in the lower left part of Figure 1.2. Reception is the realm wherein ideologies are reproduced and potentially challenged.

Alternative media is a sphere that challenges the capitalist media industry. The alternative media hypothesis is visualized in Figure 1.2 by a separate domain that stands for alternative ways of organizing and producing media whose aim is to create critical content that challenges capitalism. Media content depends on reception. Five forms of reception are distinguished in the left lower left part of Figure 1.2. Reception is the realm where ideologies are reproduced and potentially challenged. In some types and parts of media content capital, capital is accumulated by selling the audience, at a rate determined by its demographic characteristics, as a commodity to advertising clients. Dallas Smythe (1977) spoke in this context of the audience commodity. As advertising profits are not a general feature of all media capital, there is a dotted line in Figure 1.2 that signifies the audience commodity. In recent times, recipients have increasingly become an active audience that produces content and technologies, which does not imply a democratisation of the media, but mainly a new form of exploitation of audiences and users.

The use value of media and media technologies lies primarily in their capacity to provide information, enable communication, and advance the creation of culture. In capitalist society, use value is dominated by the exchange value of products, which become commodities. When the media take on commodity form, their use value only becomes available for consumers through exchanges that accumulate money capital in the hands of capitalists. Media and technologies as concrete products represent the use value side of information and communication, whereas the monetary price of the media represents the exchange value side of information and communication. The commodity hypothesis addresses the exchange value aspect of the media. The ideology hypothesis shows how the dominance of the use value of the media by exchange value creates a role for the media in the legitimatization and reproduction of domination. The two hypotheses are connected through the contradictory double character of media as use values and as exchange values. The media as commodities are in relation to money use values that can realize their exchange value, i.e., their price, in money form. Money is an exchange value in relation to the media. It realizes its use value – i.e. that it is a general equivalent of exchange – in media commodities. Consumers are interested in the use value aspect of media and technology, whereas capitalists are interested in the exchange value aspect that helps them to accumulate money capital. The use value of media and technology only becomes available to consumers through complex processes in which capitalists exchange the commodities they control with money. This means that the use value of media and technology is only possible through the exchange value that they have in relation to money. Commodification is a basic process that underlies media and technology in capitalism. Use value and exchange value are "bilateral polar opposites" (MECW 29, 326) of media and technology in capitalist society. By the time media and technology reach consumers, they have taken on commodity form and are therefore likely to have ideological characteristics. The sphere of alternative media challenges the commodity character of the media. It aims at a reversal so that use value becomes the dominant feature of media and technology by the sublation of their exchange value. Processes of alternative reception transcend the ideological character of the media – the recipients are empowered in questioning the commodified character of the world in which they live.

Marx's analysis of the media in capitalism visualized in Figure 1.2 can be summarized in the form of four major dimensions. The chapters in our two books reflect a categorisation of the role of the media in capitalism and study these dimensions each to a specific extent.

1) Media and commodities:
capital accumulation, media technology industry, media content industry/cultural industry, digital media industry, media and financialization, media and globalization, audience commodification, media concentration, media convergence, etc

2) Media and ideology:
media manipulation, media propaganda filters, advertising, public relations, commodity marketing, cultural imperialism, etc

3) Media reception and use:
ideological reception, critical reception, critical media use, etc

4) Alternative media:
alternative media production spheres, alternative public spheres, media and social struggles, etc

The published and submitted contributions are predominantly in the areas of media and commodification, media and ideology, and alternative media. Media reception studies are not as well represented. This means that topics like the audiences' interpretation of reality TV, popular music, soap operas, sports, movies, quiz shows, or computer games are not so important for most contemporary Marxist media and communication scholars in comparison to topics like the exploitation of free labour on the Internet, the commodification of research and education, Internet ideologies, socialist struggles about the role of the media in various countries, the marginalization and discrimination of Marxists and Marxism in Media and Communication Studies, capitalist crisis and the media, communication labour, critical journalism, the socialist open access publishing, or alternative social networking sites. This demonstrates three key points:

* In the current situation of capitalist crisis and exploding inequality, a focus on political economy topics, class struggle issues, the role of alternatives seems to be more important than the focus on cultural studies topics (like fan culture) that can easily be accommodated into capitalist interests and do not deal with the pressing problems such as precarious living conditions and inequalities in the world.
* Classical audience studies has to a certain extent been transformed into the study of the political economy of mediated play labour and media prosumption, which is an area in which the study of production, consumption and advertising converge. Marxist Media and Communication Studies have, as the two books show, welcomed this convergence and related topics have become an important topic of this approach. An important implication of this development is that the classical criticism that Marxist Media and Communication Studies is not particularly interested in reception and media consumption does not hold because the issue has been taken up to a great degree with

the rise of consumption becoming productive, a development that has been started by the audience commodification typical of the broadcasting area and lifted to a new dimension of analysis by the rise of Internet prosumption.

* There is a pressing need for engaging with Marx and the critique of class and capitalism in order to interpret and change the contemporary world and contemporary media. The chapters in the two books show a deep engagement with and care about Marx's theory and it is natural that they do not align themselves with research streams that are critical of or ignore Marxist studies. They are predominantly grounded in Critical Political Economy and Critical Theory.

The chapters published in the 2 books *Marx and the Political Economy of the Media* and *Marx in the Digital Age* show the crucial relevance of Marx today for coming to grips with the world we live in, the struggles that can and should be fought, and the role of the media in capitalism, in struggles against it, and in building alternatives. It is encouraging to see that there is a growing number of scholars, who make use of Marx's works in Media and Communication Studies today. Whereas Marx was always relevant, this relevance has especially not been acknowledged in Media and Communication Studies in recent years. It was rather common to misinterpret and misunderstand Marx, which partly came also from a misreading of his works or from outright ignorance of his works. Terry Eagleton (2011) discusses ten common prejudices against Marx and Marxism and shows why Marx was right and why these prejudices are wrong. We have added to the following overview a media and communication dimension to each prejudice. This communication dimensions point towards common prejudices against Marx within Media and Communication Studies. The chapters in the two books show that these prejudices are wrong and that using Marx and Marxian concepts in Media and Communication Studies is an important and pressing task today. As a summary of the results provided by the chapters in the two books, we counter each of the anti-Marxian prejudices with a counter-claim that is grounded in the analyses presented in the two books show the importance of Marx for understanding society and the media critically.

1a) *Marxist Outdatedness!*
Marxism is old-fashioned and not suited for a post-industrial society.

1b) *Marxist Topicality!*
In order to adequately and critically understand communication in society, we need Marx.

2a) *Marxist Repression!*
Marxism may sound good in theory, but in practice it can only result in terror, tyranny and mass murder. The feasibility of a socialist society and socialist media are illusionary.

2b) *Capitalist Repression!*
Capitalism neither sounds like a good idea/theory nor does it work in practice, as the reality of large-scale inequality, global war, and environmental devestation shows. The feasibility of socialism and socialist media arises out of the crises of capitalism.

3a) *Marxism = Determinism!*
Marx believed in deterministic laws of history and the automatic end of capitalism that would also entail the automatic end of capitalist media.

3b) *Marxism = Dialectics and Complexity!*
Marxian and Hegelian dialectics allow us to see the history of society and the media as being shaped by structural conditioning and open-ended struggles and a dialectic of structure and agency.

4a) *Marxist Do-Goodism!*
Marx had a naïve picture of humanity's goodness and ignored that humans are naturally selfish, acquisitive, aggressive and competitive. The media industry is therefore necessarily based on profit and competition; otherwise it cannot work.

4b) *Capitalist Wickedness!*
The logic of individualism, egoism, profit maximization, and competition has been tried and tested under neoliberal capitalism, which has also transformed the media landscape and made it more unequal.

5a) *Marxist Reductionism!*
Marx and Marxism reduce all cultural and political phenomena to the economy. They do not have an understanding of non-economic aspects of the media and communication.

5b) *Marxist Complexity!*
Contemporary developments show that the economy in capitalism is not determining, but a special system that results in the circumstance that

all phenomena under capitalism, which includes all media phenomena, have class aspects and are dialectically related to class. Class is a necessary, although certainly not sufficient condition for explaining phenomena of contemporary society.

6a) *Marxist Anti-Humanism!*
Marx had no interests in religion and ethics and reduced consciousness to matter. He therefore paved the way for the anti-humanism of Stalin and others. Marxism cannot ground media ethics.

6b) *Marxist Humanism!*
Marx was a deep humanist and communism was for him practical humanism, class struggle practical ethics. His theory was deeply ethical and normative. Critical Political Economy of the Media necessarily includes a critical ethics of the media.

7a) *The Outdatedness of Class!*
Marxism's obsession with class is outdated. Today, the expansion of knowledge work is removing all class barriers.

7b) *The Importance of Class!*
High socio-economic inequality at all levels of societal organisation is indicative of the circumstance that contemporary society is first and foremost a multi-levelled class society. Knowledge work is no homogenous category, but rather a class-structured space that includes internal class relations and stratification patterns (both a manager and a precariously employed call centre agent or data entry clerk are knowledge workers)

8a) *Marxists Oppose Democracy!*
Marxists favour violent revolution and oppose peaceful reform and democracy. They do not accept the important role of the media for democracy.

8b) *Socialism=Democracy!*
Capitalism has a history of human rights violations, structural violence, and warfare. In the realm of the media, there is a capitalist history of media support for anti-democratic goals. Marxism is a demand for peace, democracy, and democratic media. Marx in his own journalistic writings and practice struggled for free speech, democratic journalism, democratic media, and the end to censorship.

9a) Marxist Dictatorship!
Marxism's logic is the logic of the party that results in the logic of the state and the installation of monstrous dictators that control, monitor, manipulate and censor the media.

9b) Capitalist Dictatorship!
Capitalism installs a monstrous economic dictatorship that controls, monitors, manipulates and censors the media by economic and ideological means. Marxism's logic is one of a well-rounded humanity fostering conditions that enable people to be active in many pursuits and includes the view that everyone can become a journalist.

10a) Non-class-oriented New Social Movements!
New social movements (feminism, environmentalism, gay rights, peace movement, youth movement, etc) have left class and Marxism behind. Struggles for alternative media are related to the new social movements, not to class struggles.

10b) Class-oriented New New Social Movements!
The new movements resulting from the current crisis (like the Occupy movement) as well as recent movements for democratic globalization are movements of movements that are bound together by deep concern for inequality and class. Contemporary struggles are class struggles that make use of a multitude of alternative media.

Overview of the Book *Marx and the Political Economy of the Media*

Vincent Mosco argues that the crisis of capitalism has resulted in a renewed interest in Marx and that it is therefore crucial to engage thoroughly with all of his work and to pay special attention to how it can help to illuminate a blindspot of Critical Media and Communication Studies, i.e., knowledge labour and media practice. He points out the importance of the discussion of information and the means of communication in the *Grundrisse* as well as the significance of Marx's journalistic practice as a political calling of considerable relevance for contemporary communication students and scholars, journalists, and knowledge workers.

Nicole Cohen analyses the exploitation of freelancers in the cultural industries. She does not share the analysis that cultural work is beyond Marxian analysis, but rather argues that one needs Marx's theory for understanding precarious cultural labour. She maintains that cultural work in capitalism should not be separated analytically from capitalism's universal structures of exploitation and from other forms of work. Moreover, exploitation and class are at the heart of labour process theory that remains well suited for understanding labour today. Concretely, she explores the role of unpaid and precarious labour in journalism.

Richard Hall and Bernd Stahl discuss how innovations in the realm of digital technology impact the university. The authors stress that in neoliberal cognitive capitalism, the university has become an important site of production of surplus value and struggles. The context of the analysis is the intensified commodification of the university from the start of the current capitalist crisis. Emerging technologies are increasingly embedded, interconnected, invisible, adaptive, personalized, and pervasive and advance commodification and fetishization in the university.

George Pleios focuses on how to conceptualize Marxist communication theory in the information society. He emphasizes that for Marx, communication in capitalism has a commodity aspect and ideological qualities and that communication is a productive force. Communication is not simply part of a superstructure, but integrated into class relations and the base. He observes this phenomenon in relation to *laissez faire* capitalism, monopoly capitalism, and symbolic capitalism. The convergence of leisure and work would further erase the boundaries between base and superstructure and between production and communication.

Irfan Erdogan analyses the role of communication in Marx's work and the role of Marx in communication studies. He conducted an empirical study of the role of Marx and Marxism in communication journals. He found that Marxian thinking has been systematically distorted and marginalized. One result is that while mainstream research tends to gently ignore Marx, alternative research traditions such as Cultural Studies tend to attack Marx and make uninformed claims. Erdogan's close study of Marx's writings shows that Marx considered communication as a crucial means of human life that has a class character in capitalism.

Christian Garland and Stephen Harper reflect on the role of the critique of neoliberalism and the critique of capitalism in Media and Communication Studies: They argue that there has been a shift from a conflict between Marxism and liberalism towards a dominance of liberal pluralism and a marginalization of Marxism. The critique of capitalism has been replaced by a critique of neoliberalism that can be accommodated with liberal pluralism. The authors outline the limits of the critique of neoliberalism with two examples:

the News of the World scandal and discussions about the causes of the economic crisis.

Jim McGuigan reviews the debate between Critical Political Economy and Cultural Studies in light of contemporary changes in capitalism. The author stresses that by criticizing economism, Cultural Studies has often eliminated economic criticism. He points out the role of "cool" in capitalist ideology. Consumer culture would be a particularly important expression of cool capitalism. The "coolness" of communication technology is especially important. The need for a Marxist analysis of contemporary culture and the media is ascertained in order to understand their ideological and economic roles.

Brice Nixon discusses the role of dialectical thinking for a critical political economy of the media and communication. The author argues that consciousness is a crucial issue for a critical political economy. He emphasizes the role of dialectical thinking for Marx as the foundation for Marx's opposition to classical political economy. Nixon points out that a dialectical method can be incorporated into Critical Media and Communication Studies through engagement with the works of critical theorists like Georg Lukács, Herbert Marcuse, Max Horkheimer, Henri Lefèbvre, Jean-Paul Sartre, and Raymond Williams.

Michelle Rodino-Colocino analyses Sarah Palin's politics and ideology from a Marxist-Feminist perspective. She argues that as part of the revival of Marxism, a revival of Marxist Feminism is needed. She maintains that there has been insufficient engagement with Marx and Marx's ideology concept in Media and Communication Studies. An engagement with Marx's ideology critique is needed today in Critical Media and Communication Studies as well as in Feminist Theory. The author shows how Palin appropriates and inverts the contents of Feminism for her own ideological political goals that serve anti-feminist purposes.

Gerald Sussman discusses the role of ideology and propaganda in the contemporary capitalist media economy. He argues that ideology and propaganda have become central productive forces and that we live in a propaganda society. The author describes the transformation of ideology under the neoliberal regime and in that part of the economy based on unpaid prosumer labour. The exploitation and surveillance of prosumers makes a Marxist theory of value crucial today. Digital media environments could also enable collective activities that resist capitalism.

Peter Ludes discusses the relevance of Marx's notion of a classless society. Based on a review of Marx's use of the term, he draws conclusions about the development of 20th century capitalism. He argues that the establishment of alternatives requires the networking of projects that start in the here and now. Ludes suggests updating Marx's notion of a classless society by engaging with the works of Norbert Elias. This would especially require taking into account the role of communication as well as civilizing and decivilizing processes when thinking about how to establish alternatives.

Wilhelm Peekhaus analyses the political economy of academic journal publishing. He demonstrates how the exploitation of the free labour of academics, monopolization and capital concentration tendencies, and high journal prices coupled with declining library budgets shapes this industry. He interprets capitalist academic publishing as a form of primitive accumulation and points out that open access publishing can pose a viable alternative. Open access would however have today certain limits that could only be overcome by an anti-capitalist open access movement that questions the capitalist character of academic publishing.

Padmaja Shaw analyses the role of Marx's works on the press for contemporary politics in India. The author discusses the relevance of three aspects of Marx's works on the press: freedom of speech and censorship, the press as a part of free trade, and the role of media in bourgeois democracies. He stresses that on the one hand, there is a broad diffusion of left-wing voices in the Indian press and that, on the other hand, censorship and repression against the Left and Left journalism reign in the insurgent Red Corridor areas. The institutionalized Left would benefit by reflecting on Marx's press politics to better respond to this situation.

Pablo Castagno provides a Marxist framework for understanding the development of Argentina's political system and the role of media and media policies in various stages of this development. The author describes how the fascist military junta implemented neoliberalism that was later deepened by the Menem government (1989–2999). The author shows how political developments over the years influenced the role of the media in Argentina (fascist media control, neoliberal media privatization under Menen, Kirchnerismo's state-commercial nexus for establishing a national culture industry).

William Hebblewhite discusses Raymond Williams' paper "Means of Commnication as a Means of Production." The author argues that Williams established a reductionist culturalist concept of the relation of base and superstructure and maintains that for overcoming the flaws identified in Williams' and Marx and Engels' concepts of base and superstructure, an engagement with Louis Althusser's theory is needed. Based on this theoretical framework, the author argues that the Internet is a means of production and communication and introduces the notion of promunication (production and communication).

Lee Artz analyses how 21st century socialism works in Venezuela and what the role of communication is in it. The public has the opportunity to discuss and influence all government proposals in public debates and social services were set up across the country. The author argues that Venezuela is a capitalist state with a socialist government. He analyzes the Venezuelan political economy of the media: More than 80% of the media are commercial in character. Community media and public service media oppose them. The author shows that Venezuela and Venezuelan media are in transition and have great potential for socialism.

Christian Fuchs discusses the relevance of Dallas Smythe's works today. Dallas Smythe was one of the founders of the field of the Marxist political economy of media and communication. Fuchs points out commonalities and differences between Smythe's approach and the Frankfurt School and argues that they are complementary. He especially gives attention to Smythe's notions of the audience commodity and audience labour that Smythe used for analysing the political economy of commercial media. Fuchs shows that this concept has gained new importance in the age of commercial social media such as Facebook, YouTube, Weibo and Twitter.

References

Baudrillard, Jean. 1981. *For a Critique of the Political Economy of the Sign.* St. Louis: Telos Press.

Eagleton Terry. 2011. *Why Marx Was Right.* London: Yale University Press.

Fuchs, Christian. 2016. Reading Marx in the Information Age: A Media and Communication Studies Perspective on "Capital, Volume 1". New York: Routledge.

Fuchs, Christian. 2014. Thomas Piketty's Book "Capital in the Twenty-First Century," Karl Marx and the Political Economy of the Internet. *tripleC: Communication, Capitalism & Critique* 12 (1): 413–430.

Fuchs, Christian. 2011. *Foundations of Critical Media and Information Studies.* New York: Routledge.

Fuchs, Christian. 2010. Grounding Critical Communication Studies: An Inquiry into the Communication Theory of Karl Marx. *Journal of Communication Inquiry* 34 (1): 15–41.

Fuchs, Christian and Marisol Sandoval, eds. 2014. *Critique, Social Media and the Information Society.* New York: Routledge.

Marx, Karl and Friedrich Engels. 1844. *The German Ideology.* Amherst, NY: Prometheus Books.

Marx, Karl and Friedrich Engels (MECW). 1975–2005. *Collected Works.* New York: International Publishers.

Marx, Karl and Friedrich Engels. 1848/2004. *The Communist Manifesto.* Peterborough: Broadview.

Marx, Karl and Friedrich Engels. 1968. *Selected Works in One Volume*. London: Lawrence & Wishart.

McChesney, Robert W. 2007. *Communication Revolution. Critical Junctures and the Future of Media*. New York: The New Press.

McLuhan, Marshall 1964/2001. *Understanding Media: The Extensions of Man*. New York: Routledge.

Mosco, Vincent. 2009. *The Political Economy of Communication*. London: Sage. 2nd edition.

Piketty, Thomas. 2014. *Capital in the Twenty-First Century*. Cambridge, MA: Belknap Press.

Smythe, Dallas W. 1977. Communications: Blindspot of Western Marxism. *Canadian Journal of Political and Social Theory* 1 (3): 1–27.

Žižek, Slavoj. 2010. *Living in the End Times*. London: Verso.

CHAPTER 2

Marx is Back, But Which One? On Knowledge Labour and Media Practice

Vincent Mosco

1   Marx is Back

The global economic crisis that filled the headlines beginning at the end of 2008 led to a resurgence of popular interest in the work of Karl Marx. Those who made use of this body of thought for many years questioned whether he had ever left, but that was beside the point, as the media were filled with anecdotal accounts of strange sightings and even stranger sound bites. The *Times* of London led the charge on October 21, 2008 when, as capitalism appeared to be crumbling, the normally stodgy newspaper declared in a headline: "Marx is Back." The *Times* of India wrote about "Marx in the time of pink slips" (Saxena 2008). *Das Kapital* rose up the best seller list in Germany and, across the border, Nicholas Sarkozy, never one to miss a photo opportunity, was snapped leafing through a copy. Even Pope Benedict, an otherwise deeply conservative thinker, was quoted as praising Marx's "great analytical skill" (Kapital Gains 2008). Not to be outdone, the Archbishop of Canterbury praised Marx for demonstrating that "capitalism became a kind of mythology," charging that its boosters were engaging in nothing short of "idolatry" (Gledhill 2008). This strange dalliance with the theorist of revolution continued well into 2011 as evidenced by a story in *Bloomberg Businessweek* which declared in a story "Marx to Market" that "The Bearded One has rarely looked better" (September 14, 2011). Indeed a headline in Canada's national newspaper declared that it was "Springtime for Marx" (Renzetti 2011). The UK's *Guardian* newspaper tried to explain this seemingly strange phenomenon with a 2012 piece on "Why Marxism is on the Rise Again" (Jeffries 2012).

Marxist scholars, accustomed to toiling in relative obscurity, were courted by mainstream media to explain these developments. *Foreign Policy* magazine featured Leo Panitch's article "Thoroughly Modern Marx" on its cover (Panitch 2009). Invited to lunch with George Soros, Eric Hobsbawn worried about whether he would have to tiptoe around radical talk, only to have one of the world's leading financiers admit that Marx "discovered something about capitalism 150 years ago that we must take notice of" (Renzetti 2011). Even as coverage of the economic crisis diminished, the beat went on. Once again *Foreign Policy* took up the theme in 2014 even returning to the title "Marx is Back," that concludes the coming years "might put a ghostly smile on Karl's face" (Kenny 2014).

One can certainly make too much of all this Marx talk. As government bailouts calmed the markets, the homage to Marx diminished. But it still resonates enough to turn attention to the relevance of Marx's thought for communication theory. Specifically, this chapter focuses on two neglected dimensions of Marx's work that are of particular relevance to media and communication scholars.

2   But Which One?

One of the first thoughts on facing the prospect of writing about Marx is to wonder about which of the many persona of Marx one should emphasize. It is clear that the media care about Marx the political economist and revolutionary who provided at least some food for thought about what was for them the shocking meltdown of financial markets, the continued stagnation, and the deepening fears for the future of capitalism. This is certainly understandable and critical scholars are no strangers to the task of documenting the importance of this Marx, the Marx of *Capital* and political economy, for understanding global communication. Yet there is another Marx not unrelated to the first whose writing about culture and ideology featured in *The German Ideology*, *The Economic and Philosophical Manuscripts*, and other works of the younger Marx have inspired analysis and critique in cultural studies. It is not an exaggeration to conclude that the Marx of political economy and of cultural studies form pillars of critical communication study (Dyer-Witheford 2014; Fuchs 2014; Huws 2014).

Nevertheless, an exclusive emphasis on this bifurcated "young Marx/culture – old Marx/political economy" risks missing two other key elements of Marx that are vital to contemporary communication studies. Indeed, although there are many ways to divide Marx, one particularly useful one is to see him in four parts- and no, not just Groucho, Harpo, Chico and Zeppo. In addition to the Marx of political economy and the Marx of cultural studies, there is the Marx of his famous, and also infamous, notebooks *The Grundrisse* and the work of Marx the professional journalist. Indeed, although Marx practiced journalism throughout his life, both *The Grundrisse* and the best of Marx's journalism bridged the critical period between the earlier and later years of his career.

3   The Grundrisse

What has come to be called the *Grundrisse* is actually a collection of seven notebooks written over the period 1857–58, midway between the *Manifesto* and the first volume of *Capital*. They were produced in the midst of one of capitalism's first great economic crises, certainly its first crisis of overproduction. The notebooks have been depicted conventionally, by Martin Nicolaus (1973), as the precursor to *Capital*. They also have been described less conventionally by Nick Dyer-Witheford as "the delirious notebooks" which "Marx used to prophesy a moment when capital's development would depend not on the direct expenditure of labour power in production but rather on the mobilization of social and scientific knowledge."[1] I encountered the *Grundrisse* as a graduate student when the first English translation appeared and joined the applause of young Marxists who were now offered fresh material to digest, debate and use. It did not dim my enthusiasm when former Marxists like my thesis supervisor Daniel Bell rejected the new work as of little use for understanding Marxist thought.

There are good reasons to see the *Grundrisse* as anticipating key arguments in *Capital* and in other later works. But it also explores themes that Marx would not have the time to develop in a sustained fashion and some of these have been taken up in contemporary Marxist scholarship. As he would do in *Capital*, Marx acknowledges the contribution of technology and especially that of new communication media like the telegraph for the expansion of global capitalism. For Marx, "Capital by its nature drives beyond every spatial barrier. Thus the creation of the physical conditions of exchange – of the means of communication and transport the annihilation of space by time – becomes an extraordinary necessity for it. Only in so far as the direct product can be realized in distant markets in mass quantities in proportion to reductions in the transport costs, and only in so far as at the same time the means of communication and transport themselves can yield spheres of realization for labor, driven by capital; only in so far as commercial traffic takes place in massive volume – in which more than necessary labour is replaced – only to that extent is the production of cheap means of communication and transport a condition for production based on capital, and promoted by it *for that reason*" (Marx 1973, 524).

This passage captures the dual nature of communication in capitalism. Communication contributes to the commodification of all productive forces

1   http://www.fims.uwo.ca/peopleDirectory/faculty/fulltimefaculty/full_time_faculty_profile
.htm?PeopleId=3667; see also Piccone 1975.

and it also becomes a commodity in its own right. In the process, communication technology serves as a key tool, along with the development of the means of transportation, in the spatial expansion of capitalism, what we now call globalization, perhaps better put as spatialization (Mosco 2009). At another point in this work, Marx makes clear that commodification and spatialization are intimately connected to the process of structuration, the development of social relations, including new forms of communication: "Not only do the objective conditions change in the act of reproduction, e.g., the village becomes a town, ..., but the producers change too, in that they bring out new qualities in themselves, develop themselves in production, transform themselves, develop new powers and ideas, new modes of intercourse, new needs and new language" (Marx 1973, 494).

These ideas are central to developing a Marxist theory of communication. They both build upon the early work and prepare the way for *Capital*. But the *Grundrisse* is much more than a way station on the long march to *Capital*, a point missed by one of the first scholars to bring the *Grundrisse* to an English-speaking world. The critical difference between this work and *Capital* is not the difference between the creative display of a work in progress and a fully formed creation, as Nicolaus maintains. Rather, the *Grundrisse* is, however dishevelled or even delirious, a substantive creation in its own right and a touchstone for vital developments in critical communication research. It contains ideas that *Capital* never got around to addressing but which matter considerably to scholarship and politics today.

In the *Grundrisse*, Marx focuses explicit attention on the significance of information for capital. This is expressed in numerous different ways roughly signifying, at different times, social knowledge, the state of scientific and artistic research, and the general intellect. In essence, one of the most important consequences of a developing capitalist economy is that it provides free time to think, create, and advance the general state of scientific, technical and artistic information. Capitalism aims to incorporate this expansion of individual and social capacity into the production process, but faces the resistance of increasingly knowledgeable and empowered workers. In the very process of its development capitalism produces the conditions for its own expansion but also lays the groundwork for resistance from workers who increasingly have the opportunity to advance their own creative ability. In the emphasis on technology, on the material machinery of production that is understandably derived from a reading of *Capital*, one can miss a central point made in the notebooks: the most important embodiment of fixed capital is not the assembly line but "man himself."

In the Grundrisse, as nowhere else, the source of value is information, the creative worker, what some would today call human capital: "Nature builds no machines, no locomotives, railways, electric telegraphs, self-acting mules etc. ...They are organs of the human brain, created by the human hand; the power of knowledge, objectified" (Marx 1973, 706). The determination of value, a concept central to Marx's political economy, comes to be based firmly on the creative individual: "it is neither the direct human labour he himself performs, nor the time during which he works, but rather the appropriation of his own general productive power, his understanding of nature and his mastery over it by virtue of his presence as a social body – it is, in a word, the development of the social individual which appears as the great foundation-stone of production and of wealth" (Marx 1973, 705).

As capitalism comes to be based increasingly on control over creative ability, and therefore over information, it must mobilize all social institutions involved in producing information. Hence the need for the commodification of the entire creative apparatus, something that can only be achieved "when large industry has already reached a higher stage, and all the sciences have been pressed into the service of capital." As result, "Invention then becomes a business, and the application of science to direct production itself becomes a prospect which determines and solicits it" (Marx 1973, 704).

Because information grows increasingly central to capitalist development, it is important to consider what Marx means by information. This is difficult because he uses a multiplicity of expressions to encompass it. Nevertheless, it is clear that Marx means more than merely technical knowledge because he uses words that connote both artistic and experiential knowledge. For example, in discussing the contradiction between capital's need to reduce labour time and the need to use it as a measure of social wealth, he refers to the importance for capital of the "artistic, scientific etc. development of individuals in the time set free" (Marx 1973, 706). Again, in a rousing conclusion to a section on economic history, Marx asks what is left of the bourgeois concept of wealth once its limited form is stripped away: "...the universality of individual needs, capacities, pleasures, productive forces, etc. created through universal exchange. ... The absolute working-out of his creative potentialities, with no presupposition other than the previous historic development, which makes the totality of development, i.e., the development of all human powers as such, the end in itself, not as measured on a predetermined yardstick" (Marx 1973, 488).

This and the accompanying passages demonstrate that while scientific and technical knowledge are important components of an expanding sphere of information, the point of raising its significance does not end there. That is because information is more significantly a marker for the development of full human capacities, including the scientific but also the artistic, the experiential and, certainly, the creative.

Undoubtedly those familiar with Marx's *Economic and Philosophical Manuscripts*, will note distinct similarities to the notebooks. But a key difference in the *Grundrisse* is that the discussion of the full development of human powers is now presented within a well-grounded materialist theory of capitalism. The bourgeois world makes it essential that people develop their capacities, but it is so constrained by its own needs for self and social class preservation that it has to restrict this process or be overrun by its consequences. Subsequent work of Marx would provide a more thorough understanding of capitalism, but it does so without returning to the full consideration of the consequences of its own creation. It is the *Grundrisse* that holds out the potential of actually building on the forces of that creation: information, knowledge, creativity, and experiential capability.

The focus on social information or the general intellect has significant implications for the study of labour and especially for labour in the communication industries. First, in the *Grundrisse* Marx acknowledges that however new the industrial world might be, it too was rapidly changing. Just as capitalism needs to commodify all of the creative industries, including science, to accomplish its goals, it must extend the commodification process to every individual's general productive capacity: "No longer does the worker insert a modified natural thing as middle link between the object and himself; rather, he inserts the process of nature, transformed into an industrial process, as a means between himself and inorganic nature, mastering it. He steps to the side of the production process instead of being its chief actor. In this transformation, it is neither the direct human labour he himself performs, nor the time during which he works, but rather the appropriation of his own general productive power, his understanding of nature and his mastery over it by virtue of his presence as a social body – it is, in a word, the development of the social individual which appears as the great foundation-stone of production and of wealth" (Marx 1973, 705).

Nevertheless, as Marx describes it, the process of commodifying labor, including both intelligence and affect, demonstrates the need to expand these very human capacities. Capital no longer needed just the laborer as appendage to a machine; it needed then and needs now the full "social body" of the individual. This passage and others like it acknowledge, at a remarkably early stage in capitalist development, the requirement for both knowledge and affective labor. Capital needs to create the worker in its fullest subjectivity and then make it part of a process that channels that subjectivity into productivity. On the one hand such a process holds great potential for expanding capitalism into what we now call the knowledge, culture, and information industries. On the other hand, controlling such labour is far more challenging than it is to control and channel manual labour whose knowledge and affect were less consequential to meet the needs of capital. In essence, the *Grundrisse* suggests that understanding the labour of knowledge, cultural, and creative workers is central to understanding the future of capitalism. What is capital's capacity to control these workers? What are their capacities for resistance? What is capital's ability to control their labour process and what is their ability to give it new direction? It is the very utopian quality of many of the notebooks' passages, ("the absolute working-out of his creative potentialities"), that makes it so powerful because it acknowledges just how important are the stakes in this struggle. It is not just a matter of understanding or even of dismantling capitalism, topics which fill the pages of *Capital*, it is also a matter of appreciating what is to be won, i.e., full control over one's humanity, including the creative potential of both intellect and affect.

This brief overview could only paint a picture in the broadest strokes, suggesting why it is absolutely vital for communication scholars to make use of the *Grundrisse* in research on communication labour and in the wider political economy of communication. There is much more to be addressed in the notebooks themselves as well as in interpretations offered by Piccone (1975), Hardt and Negri (2004), (Negri 1991), Terranova (2004), Gorz (2010), and others. It is now important to turn to another facet of Marx that is intimately related to the theoretical questions raised in the *Grundrisse*: the life of Marx as a journalist or professional knowledge worker.

4   Marx the Journalist

Scholars who teach about Marx in communication programs focus exclusively on his theoretical writing and tend not to have much to say about Marx as a journalist. There are exceptions, particularly in the work of the critical journalism scholar Hanno Hardt (2001). On the other hand, professors who teach journalism practice exclude Marx completely. When academic journalism instructors do address Marx, it is typically by equating his views with the totalitarian Marxism of Soviet and Chinese communism. This is unfortunate because there is a great deal to learn about journalism from an analysis of Marx's career as a professional communicator. A genuine appreciation of Marx the theorist is significantly diminished without consideration of his journalism. Indeed the eminent political philosopher Isaiah Berlin maintains that it was in the course of putting together a story in 1843 that Marx came to recognize "his almost total ignorance of history and principles of economic development" and leapt into the formal study of political economy (Berlin 1970, 12). Moreover, there is a close connection between Marx's *Grundrisse* and his journalism. Although he practiced journalism throughout his life, arguably Marx's best journalism came in the "middle" period of his life, as he was producing the notebooks. In essence, Marx's most interesting theoretical reflections on what we have come to call knowledge and immaterial labour were penned at about the same time that Marx engaged in his most mature work of knowledge labour as a journalist.

It is a remarkable fact, one passed over all too casually, that one of the most profound social theorists of the nineteenth century, someone whose work continues to resonate powerfully today, also practiced the craft of journalism throughout his life. It is all the more stunning that his journalism takes up a full seven volumes of the fifty that comprise his collective works. Marx's journalism was most intensive in two periods, in the early years when at age 24 he wrote for and soon thereafter took on the job of editor in chief of the *Rheinische Zeitung* and then again as writer and editor for the *Neue Rheinische Zeitung* in Prussia. He decided to pursue journalism because, like so many new PhDs today, he could not find an academic job, particularly under the stifling controls over the university that the Prussian government fiercely enforced. His journalism work in this period focused on investigations into the authoritarian political establishment of Prussia and included numerous articles on censorship and freedom of the press, which landed him in constant difficulties with the authorities, ultimately leading to his banishment from Prussia. Marx produced his most mature journalism in the period 1852–62 when he became a foreign correspondent for the *New York Tribune*, a newspaper founded by Horace Greeley, a leader in the American anti-slavery movement. Greeley's goal was to counter the dominant sensationalist press with in-depth coverage of news and public affairs. Marx wrote from London, where he spent the last half of his life.

Marx's journalism consistently follows principles that provide valuable lessons for any journalist, but especially for those learning about what it means to practice journalism. Moreover, they are principles that also begin to emerge in the *Grundrisse* and which might apply in varying degrees to all knowledge workers. Throughout his career in journalism Marx was consistently opposed to all forms of censorship and regularly made the case for free expression. Consider this assessment of a proposed new censorship law in Prussia: "Censorship brings us all into subjection, just as in a despotism everybody is equal, if not in worth, then in unworthy; it's a kind of press freedom that wants to introduce oligarchy into the mind. At best, censorship declares a writer to be inconvenient, unsuitable within the boundaries of its domain. Freedom of the press proceeds on the presumption of anticipating world history, sensing in advance the voice of the people which alone has hitherto judged which writer was 'competent' which 'incompetent'" (Marx 1974, 43).

When Americans like Thomas Jefferson wrote lines like this, they were venerated as champions of freedom. Marx typically does not enjoy the same praise, not when he wrote them and not now. Harassed by the censor and ultimately the police and government officials, he was made to resign from the newspaper, which itself was disbanded by the authorities.

Nevertheless, Marx followed this principle throughout the rest of his life, but in the 1850s focused more of his critical attention on the growing tendency of self-censorship in the media. The *Tribune* was widely read throughout the United States and its editors, although progressive and generally supportive, would engage in their own forms of harassment. For example, they would sometimes refuse to publish an article because of its political tone, would soften the content and lift his byline. Even worse, his editors would often insert remarks that distanced the paper from Marx's ideas, like this one that appeared after his byline in one piece: "Mr. Marx has very decided opinions of his own, with some of which we are far from agreeing" (Ledbetter 2007, xx). Not one to back down, he consistently fought with his own editors to resist their editorial censorship which often made for colourful comments such as this one to Engels in 1857: "It's truly nauseating that one should be condemned to count it a blessing when taken aboard by a blotting-paper vendor such as this" (ibid.).

In spite of working in a pressure cooker, Marx continued to practice journalism because of his commitment to the principle that journalism was not just a vocation or even a calling, but a *political* calling. He recognized that a newspaper like the *Tribune* did more than help to pay his bills; it provided him with a platform to reach a wide audience which, at the time he wrote for it, counted 200,000 in its circulation, including Abraham Lincoln who read it avidly (Nichols 2011, 61–100). Marx had his own outlets in what we would today call "alternative" media, but these reached far fewer people. In essence, radical though he was, Marx recognized the importance of working for a mainstream publication to widely circulate his central ideas. There is no doubt that his struggles to use journalism to help bring about political change, including walking a tightrope with a mainstream newspaper, took its toll on his spirit and on his writing. Again, complaining to Engels: "To crush up bones, grind them and make them into soup like paupers in the workhouse- that is what the political work to which one is condemned in such large measure in a concern like this (the *Tribune*) boils down to" (Ledbetter 2007, xx). Although the counter-revolution of 1848 left him less hopeful that revolution was imminent, Marx's journalism continues to reveal the urgency of his political mission. As one recent commentator notes in an insightful assessment: "And yet, reading through Marx's *Tribune* dispatches, you can't help but see an urgency, an excitement – almost an impatience – in his portrayals of some insurrections and crises in Europe and India. At times he wrote as if this particular rise in corn prices, or this little dust-up with authorities in Greece, was going to be THE spark that would ignite revolution. And it's not as if one can fault Marx for feeling that way; after all, during this period crowned heads of Europe were toppling and certainly at least liberal revolutions seemed likely in a number of settings. But there are times when his discipline of thought appears to leave him, and he is also prone to the tautology that revolution can only occur when the masses are ready, but we can't know for certain if the masses are ready until they create a revolution" (Sherman 2011).

In addition to holding fast to the principles of free expression and journalism as a political calling, Marx used his journalism to give attention to the critical issues facing the world. His was certainly not the journalism of on scene reporting and of interviews with official and unofficial sources. On the latter, the popular American journalist Murray Kempton wrote of Marx: "Of all the illusions one brought to journalism, the one most useful to lose is the illusion of access to sources. ...Persons privy to events either do not know what is important about them or, when they do, generally lie. ...Marx had neither the temptation nor the opportunity of access" (Ledbetter 2007, xix). Rather, his approach was to take an event in the news such as the second Opium War in China or the American Civil War and, using the most up-to-date material, address its political economic significance. In this respect he did not disappoint. His writing for the *Tribune* covered imperialism, including major work on China and India, free trade, war and revolution in Europe, British politics and society, the changing world of economics and finance, and the slave question in America.

Marx's writing on China and India in the context of British domination and the mythology of free trade was among the best of the time and is well worth reading today in light of the West's increasingly uncomfortable relationship with these two Asian powers. As one commentator has put it: "With the possible exception of human slavery, no topic raised Marx's ire as profoundly as the opium trade with China" (Ledbetter 2007, 1). This passage conveys some of its depth and passion:

> The Indian finances of the British Government have, in fact, been made to depend not only on the opium trade with China, but on the contraband character of that trade. Were the Chinese Government to legalize

the opium trade simultaneously with tolerating the cultivation of the poppy in China, the Anglo-Indian exchequer would experience a serious catastrophe. While openly preaching free trade in poison, it secretly defends the monopoly of its manufacture. Whenever we look closely into the nature of British free trade, monopoly is pretty generally found to lie at the bottom of its 'freedom'. (Marx 2007b, 31)

And where is the allegedly free Western media in all of this? His response is worth citing at length:

How silent is the press of England upon the outrageous violations of the treaty daily practiced by foreigners living in China under British protection! We hear nothing of the illicit opium trade, which yearly feeds the British treasury at the expense of human life and morality. We hear nothing of the constant bribery of sub-officials, by means of which the Chinese Government is defrauded of its rightful revenue on incoming and outgoing merchandise. We hear nothing of the wrongs inflicted 'even unto death' upon misguided and bonded emigrants sold to worse than Slavery on the coast of Peru and into Cuban bondage. ...Thus, the English people at home, who look no farther than the grocer's where they buy their tea, are prepared to swallow all the misrepresentations which the Ministry and the Press choose to thrust down the public throat. insert (Marx, 2007a, 23-4)

Marx's journalism provides a central example of his praxis, the unity of theory and practice, that animated his life. It is also full of examples of what journalism can be when it rises above the conventions that sometimes contribute to good writing but often make it difficult to practice the principles that might advance democracy. These include complete commitment, whatever the cost, to freedom of expression and opposition to censorship, complete belief in journalism as a political calling, and an unrelenting focus on the major issues facing the world. It does not surprise me to read one journalist's assessment: "Even if he had done nothing else, Marx would deserve to be remembered as one of the great nineteenth-century journalists" (Wheen 2007, xiii).

5   Conclusion

This chapter has taken up two facets of Marx's writing, the *Grundrisse* and his journalism, that have heretofore not been presented together. The former was a work of Marx's middle years bridging and moving beyond the early writing on ideology and culture and his later work on political economy. Marx practiced journalism throughout his life but the middle years were also a time of his strongest journalism when he served as foreign correspondent for the *New York Tribune*. Whereas the *Grundrisse* suggested ways to theorize knowledge and communication labor, his journalism demonstrated how to practice it with passion and intelligence. These are lessons that all scholars but especially those interested in media and communication, would do well to learn.

References

Berlin, Isaiah. 1970. *Karl Marx: His Life and Environment*. Oxford: Oxford University.

Dyer-Witheford, Nick. 2014. *Cyber-Proletariat: Global Labor in the Digital Vortex*. Chicago, IL: University of Chicago Press.

Fuchs, Christian. 2014. *Culture and Economy in the Age of Social Media*. London: Routledge.

Gledhill, Ruth. 2008. The Archbishop of Canterbury Speaks in Support of Karl Marx. *Times Online*, September 24. Accessed December 14, 2011. http://www.timesonline .co.uk/tol/comment/faith/article4819605.ece.

Gorz, André. 2010. *The Immaterial*. London: Seagull.

Hardt, Hanno. 2001. *Social Theories of the Press*. Lanham, MD: Rowman and Littlefield.

Hardt, Michael and Negri, Antonio. 2004. *Multitude: War and Democracy in the Age of Empire*. New York: Penguin.

Huws, Ursula. 2014. *Labor in the Global Digital Economy: The Cybertariat Comes of Age*. New York: Monthly Review Press.

Jeffries, Stuart. 2012. Why Marxism is on the Rise Again. *The Guardian*, July 4. Accessed October 21, 2014. http://www.theguardian.com/world/2012/jul/04/the-return-of -marxism.

Kapital Gains, 2008. *Times Online*, October 20. Accessed December 14, 2011. http:// www.timesonline.co.uk/tol/comment/leading_article/article/4974195.ece.

Kenny, Charles. 2014. Marx is Back. *Foreign Policy*. January 21. Accessed October 21, 2014. http://www.foreignpolicy.com/articles/2014/01/21/marx_is_back_global_working _class.

Ledbetter, James. Ed. 2007. *Karl Marx: Dispatches for the New York Tribune*. London: Penguin.

Marx, Karl. 1973. *The Grundrisse*. Trans. by Martin Nicolaus. London: Penguin.

Marx, Karl. 1974. Debates on Freedom of the Press and Publication. In *Karl Marx on Freedom of the Press and Censorship*, edited by Saul K. Padover, 3–47. New York: McGraw Hill.

Marx, Karl. 2007a. English Atrocities in China. In *Karl Marx: Dispatches from the New York Tribune*, edited by James Ledbetter, 20–24. London: Penguin.

Marx, Karl. 2007b. History of the Opium Trade (II). In *Karl Marx: Dispatches from the New York Tribune*, edited by James Ledbetter, 28–31. London: Penguin.

Mosco, Vincent. 2009. *The Political Economy of Communication*. 2nd edition. London: Sage.

Negri, Antonio. 1991. *Marx beyond Marx*. London: Pluto.

Nicolaus, Martin. 1973. Foreword. *Grundrisse*, 5–66. London: Penguin.

Nichols, John. 2011. *The "S" Word: The Short History of an American Tradition...Socialism*. London: Verso.

Panitch, Leo. 2009. Thoroughly Modern Marx. *Foreign Policy*, April 15. Accessed December 14, 2011. http://www.foreignpolicy.com/articles/2009/04/15/thoroughly_modern_marx.

Piccone, Paul. 1975. Reading the Grundrisse: Beyond Orthodoxy. *Theory and Society* 2 (2): 235–255.

Renzetti, Elizabeth. 2011. Springtime for Marx. *The Globe and Mail*, March 26, F5.

Saxena, Shobhan. 2008. Marx in the Time of Pink Slips. *Times of India*, 2 November.

Sherman, Steve. 2011. Marx as Journalist: An Interview with Jim Ledbetter. Accessed December 14, 2011. http://www.marxsite.com/Marx%20as%20a%20Journalist.html.

Terranova, Tiziana. 2004. *Network Culture: Politics for the Information Age*. London: Pluto.

Wheen, Francis. 2007. Foreward. In *Karl Marx: Dispatches for the New York Tribune*, edited by James Ledbetter, ix–xiii. London: Penguin.

CHAPTER 3

Cultural Work as a Site of Struggle: Freelancers and Exploitation

Nicole S. Cohen

1   Introduction: Missing Marx

Although once considered a blind spot of communication studies (Mosco and McKercher 2006, 493), cultural work has become a growing site of inquiry as scholars from a range of perspectives consider the work that goes into producing media, culture, and communication.[1] Marx, however, is largely missing from these studies. On the surface, Marx's inquiry into the characteristics of nineteenth-century industrialized production seems an outdated approach for understanding cultural work in the post-Fordist era. In *Capital* ([1867] 1990), Marx described conditions on the factory floor: the wage labourer with nothing to sell but that most peculiar of commodities, labour power, enters into a

---

[1] Definitions are contentious in studies of work and labour in the communication and cultural industries. In this chapter, by cultural workers, I refer to people who work in the cultural industries, or those industries that generate and circulate commodities that "influence on our understanding of the world" and "produce social meaning" (Hesmondhalgh 2007, 3, 12). Banks (2007, 2) defines the cultural industries as "those involved in the production of 'aesthetic' or 'symbolic' goods and services; that is, commodities whose core value is derived from their function as carriers of meaning in the form of images, symbols, signs and sounds." I use the term culture in order to speak to the issues that arise from the association of this work with creativity and art. Precisely which sectors count as cultural industries varies. Statistics Canada (2012), for example, includes a range of occupations, from librarians and curators to writers, artists, and technical occupations in film and broadcasting. This perspective, while still somewhat broad, is useful because it views the character of cultural work through an understanding of the specificities of the industries in which it is performed rather than through the content of the work. There is something distinctive about cultural goods and their consumption that can explain why cultural production is organized in particular ways (Hesmondhalgh 2007, 101; Miège 1989; Garnham 1997). This avoids, for example, attributing experiences of cultural workers to personal character traits, which is part of the argument I develop in this chapter. The term "creative labour," for example, draws attention to qualities specific to a person (Smith and McKinlay 2009a, 3), whereas I argue that the organization of cultural production has a structural effect on workers' experiences, and freelance writers' labour experiences flow directly from the logics of the industry in which they work.

"free" relationship of exploitation with an employer, who sets the worker to work. Under the capitalist's control, the worker toils for a long stretch of the day. After earning more than what is necessary to reproduce her labour power, she generates surplus value, or profit, for capital. In the process, the worker becomes part of a generalized class of labourers. Her concrete labour is made abstract as it is sunk into standardized commodity production. Marx describes a subjugated, alienated worker who is interchangeable with other workers, rendered an anonymous input for production.

As work has moved out of the physical factory and into the studios, offices, and home-based workplaces of the creative economy, Marx's account has either been ignored or deemed outmoded. In many cases, cultural workers are understood to be unique kinds of workers and cultural work radically different from other kinds of work, removed from traditional labour-capital antagonisms (Caves 2000; Florida 2002; Deuze 2007; Christopherson 2009). In more critical accounts, Marx is dismissed as reductive because he does not attend to workers' agency or subjectivity (Banks 2007; Conor 2010; Hesmondhalgh and Baker 2011). The most prevalent critique is of Marx's theory of alienation, which describes the worker as separated from control of the labour process, from the products she creates, from other workers, and from her own human essence (Marx [1844] 1978a). For example, Mark Banks (2007, 11) critiques a vision of cultural workers as "condemned to serve as alienated labour [...] assumed to be devoid of active subjectivity and suppressed 'from above' by managers and owners." Cultural work is more often described as the antithesis of alienation: as social and collaborative work that grants workers relative autonomy in the labour process and facilitates self-expression and opportunities to engage in total human activity. Cultural workers feel great attachment to the products they create, particularly when these products carry a worker's name, such as a novel or a film. It is difficult to reconcile Marx's interpretation of work as an alien power, "not voluntary, but coerced" (Marx [1844] 1978a, 74), with conceptions of cultural work as highly desirable and glamourous.[2]

In a position I review in greater detail below, critical scholars of cultural work argue that that the specificities of cultural commodities require that workers at the idea-creation stage of production be granted relative autonomy in the labour process (Ryan 1992; Banks 2010). Relative autonomy enables some cultural workers to enjoy more time, autonomy, and resources than other workers

---

2 In *Capital*, Marx describes alienation not as a subjective experience, but in an objective sense, as a way of being under a mode of production organized around private property and waged labour. For Marx, workers are alienated because they do not own the means of production and must sell their labour power to survive.

are granted, which diminishes experiences of alienation (Hesmondhalgh 2007, 70). Although relative autonomy is always tenuous and negotiated, this arrangement has led to arguments that cultural work should be understood as a potential site of "good work" or as work that grants opportunities to produce "'radical' autonomous critique" even within the confines of capitalism (Hesmondhalgh and Baker 2011; Banks 2010, 252). Contemporary conditions of cultural production, however, are undermining relative autonomy. Cultural workers are experiencing declining material conditions and intensifying precarity, defined as "intermittent employment and radical uncertainty about the future" or "financial and existential insecurity" (Ross 2009, 4; Brophy and de Peuter 2007, 180). Indeed, precarity has become a central feature of cultural work. Although a variety of interdisciplinary approaches are necessary for thinking through the complexities of cultural work – which can be simultaneously precarious and satisfying, risky and rewarding – Marx's understanding of the inner logic of work provides a foundational understanding of the structural forces giving form to cultural work.

Marx's foundational concepts[3] bring useful insights to bear on investigations of the transformations in work and workers' lives. In what follows, I argue that a dynamic Marxist political economy approach can account for the processes, practices, and structures that have resulted in the increasing precarization of cultural work. In particular, exploitation remains the key process driving transformations in the cultural industries and can account for the ways cultural workers' relative autonomy is being undermined. To demonstrate this, I draw on examples from an ongoing case study of freelance writers, a growing segment of the Canadian media labour force.[4] As freelancers are increasingly learning, refusing an employment relationship (or being denied one, as is rapidly becoming the norm) does not mean an escape from exploitation or labour-capital antagonisms. Whereas capital has historically increased surplus value by extending the working day and intensifying production (Marx [1867] 1990, 645), corporations that rely on freelance labour have developed alternate methods of extracting surplus value from workers. For writers, these methods

---

3   Other aspects of Marx's thought are useful for understanding the character of cultural labour, particularly his writing in *The Grundrisse*, which has been taken up by autonomist Marxists to interrogate the way contemporary capital incorporates general intellect, and workers' affect and personalities into the accumulation process on an unprecedented scale. In this chapter, however, I want to focus on Marx's "old" concepts (Huws 2003, 135), which receive less attention in communication and cultural studies.

4   This study is based on a qualitative survey of 200 freelance writers across Canada and interviews with representatives of freelance writer organizations. Unless otherwise cited, all quotes in this chapter are from freelancers who participated anonymously in my survey.

include an increase in unpaid labour time and the aggressive pursuit of copyrights.

A Marxist political economy that is process-oriented, historical, and attentive to workers' agency and desires for autonomy provides insights into current conditions. Studies of cultural work can benefit from a materialist approach that understands work in these industries in relation to dynamics of capitalism and an approach that positions cultural work as a site of struggle. Many accept precarious conditions as the new reality that media workers in volatile industries must consent and adapt to, including industry, the state, training institutes, scholars, and workers themselves (McRobbie 2002; Deuze 2007; Hesmondhalgh 2007, 207). A Marxist approach disrupts this mindset to uncover dynamic processes that reveal a deeper understanding of the nature of cultural work and how it has evolved. In what follows, I outline a Marxist approach to cultural work and discuss the challenges and possibilities for considering cultural work through the lens of labour process theory. I then introduce a case study of freelance writers and examine dynamics of exploitation of unpaid labour time and copyright. I conclude with a discussion of how positioning cultural work as a site of struggle points to possibilities for transformation.

2   Back to Marx: A Political Economy of Cultural Work

A Marxist political economy of cultural work is concerned with the dynamics of the labour-capital relation, tensions and contradictions that structure this relationship, struggles over control and exploitation, and with questions of power and resistance. This approach flows from an understanding that these practices and processes are situated within a particular historical context: capitalist commodity production, under which those who do not own the means of production must sell their labour power to earn a living, thus engaging in a consensual relationship of exploitation of surplus value. Countering the rejection of Marxism as reductive, David Harvey (1996, 49) argues that Marx must be understood as a dialectical thinker concerned with "processes, flows, fluxes, and relations" rather than an analyst of structures and things. Marx uncovers the processes that constitute and sustain capitalism (ibid., 50) and accounts for "unfolding and dynamic relations between elements within a capitalist system" (Harvey 2010, 12). His concepts capture the dynamic relations and contradictions propelling the change and instability inherent to the process of capital accumulation (Harvey 1996, 54).

A Marxist political economic analysis of cultural work speaks to the historical developments of cultural industries, which did not emerge fully formed but rather are the result of contestation about how to produce culture and how to organize work. A historical, process-oriented perspective reveals how taken-for-granted characteristics of cultural work – its volatile, project-based, precarious nature – are often the result of transformations in media and cultural industries that have occurred alongside shifting dynamics of capitalism. Most recently, this shift has been a transformation from Fordist mass production to a flexible accumulation regime[5] organized around lean production, information communication technologies, and deregulated and flexible labour markets (Moody 1997; Albo 2010). In this context, cultural industries have undergone significant change, which shapes workers' experiences (ILO 2000; Gough-Yates 2003; Hesmondhalgh 2007; Deuze and Fortunati 2011). For example, it is widely accepted that workers in cultural industries have "boundaryless" or "portfolio careers," which means they perform work for multiple engagers on a project basis, often simultaneously (Leadbeater and Oakley 2005; Hartley 2005). However, the portfolio nature of careers is more often described as an inherent trait of cultural workers themselves and less often as a coping strategy to deal with work made intermittent and precarious – a decidedly less glamorous view, but one that links work arrangements to broader political economic dynamics. The role of capitalism in shaping cultural work and the resulting power relations are obscured in many accounts of cultural work and directly situating cultural work in capitalist production relations reaffirms a materialist approach to the study of media, culture, and communication.

Marx is often overlooked in studies of cultural work because he did not attend to workers' subjectivity, and subjectivity is a key component of cultural work, which "is first and foremost about communicating meaning and very often also about identification and pleasure" (McGuigan 2010, 326). Indeed, subjectivity is a crucial component of all types of work, especially now that contemporary capitalism increasingly requires the incorporation of workers' subjectivities into production (Dyer-Witheford and de Peuter 2009, 4). Subjectivity is important for considering the limits of capital's ability to contain cultural workers' resistance and for considering how and why cultural workers

---

5   Harvey (1990, 147) uses the term flexible accumulation to describe the regime of accumulation that has followed the gradual shift from Fordism in the early 1970s, characterized by flexible labour markets, labour processes, and consumption patterns, as well as the emergence of new technologies and financial services. Vosko (2010, 89) argues that this concept is preferable to terms such as post-Fordism because it emphasizes "continuity through change," or the "continuation of aspects of the system of mass production associated with Fordism alongside the expansion of new productive technologies and greater specialization" (Vosko 2000, 27).

choose to collectively organize in particular ways (de Peuter 2011; Cohen 2011). However, as Harvey (2006, 113) argues, it is difficult to understand current experiences of cultural work *primarily* through workers' subjective experiences of labour. It is first critical to understand the objective conditions of that labour, or, "what it is that workers are being forced to cope *with* and to defend *against*; to come to terms with the manifest forces that impinge upon them at every turn" (ibid., emphasis in original).

This approach stems from Marx's ([1852] 1978b, 595) assertion that people "make their own history, but they do not make it as they please; they do not make it under circumstances of their own choosing, but under circumstances existing already, given and transmitted from the past." Of course cultural work holds potential to be fulfilling and provide a sense of creative autonomy, if indicated just by the increase in numbers of cultural workers, the expansion of education and training programs, and fierce competition for work that is generally insecure and low paid, or not paid at all (Hill and Capriotti 2009; Perlin 2011; Lacey 2011). To understand why work is experienced in particular ways requires broadening the focus from individual experiences to consider cultural workers as part of a class of workers struggling over the terms of the commodification of their labour power. The Marxist approach positions workers as active subjects engaged in a dynamic process of production with contested power relations, not simply as "brutalized and exploited workers" (Conor 2010, 31).

To maintain a connection to the broader social totality and the conditions of labour under capitalism, Marxist political economy avoids setting cultural workers apart as wholly unique. Mike Wayne (2003), for example, draws out Marx's relational conception of the connections between all workers under capitalism, conceived through the lens of class as a social relationship. Wayne acknowledges the "wider social conditions of creative and intellectual labour as a collective relationship occupying a contradictory position between capital and the 'traditional' working class" (7). He draws on Erik Olin Wright's (1978) theorization of the class character of intellectuals – defined as "a category of people...whose activity is primarily that of elaborating and disseminating ideas" (192) – in advanced capitalist societies. Wright argues that because intellectual workers do not control the labour of others nor maintain "real control over much of their own labour process," these workers "typically occupy a contradictory class location between the working class and the petty bourgeoisie at the economic level and between the working class and the bourgeoisie at the ideological level" (106, 204). Cultural workers occupy a contradictory class location because they are integrated into capitalism yet differentiated from the working class by "cultural privileges, relative workplace independence and (usually) by remuneration levels," but they are not capitalists: their "status as

labour reasserts itself whenever [these workers] are subject to similar processes of exploitation and proletarianization as the working class below them"
(Wayne 2003, 23). As I will demonstrate, cultural workers' status as labour is
rapidly reasserting itself.

Although there are important differences between workers, these differences are not absolute. Rather, workers in various sectors and occupations can
be understood as different parts of a social and economic class that must sell
its labour power to survive (Wayne 2003; Smith and McKinlay 2009a). Whereas
capital seeks to establish a hierarchy between mental and manual labour, Marx
emphasized the process "by which capital develops a socially unified labour
capacity in which particular roles represent only a limb of the total labourer,"
while all work under capitalism is submitted to generalized exploitation (Wayne
2003, 15). This understanding of cultural work retains a notion of labour-capital
antagonisms and of class struggle, and so can account for transformations in
media forms, technology, and business models. Capital's "immanent drive" to
increase surplus value by cheapening the cost of labour (Marx [1867] 1990, 437)
clashes with workers' desires to pursue meaningful work, to be paid decently
for their labour power, and to be able to sustain themselves.

A Marxist conception of class avoids setting cultural workers apart as exceptional types of workers. It refuses the tendency to understand cultural workers'
actions as motivated by artistic temperament, personality, and by an insatiable
"desire to create," making links instead to the political economic context in
which they work (Caves 2000, 3; Christopherson 2009, 74). The nature of the
market economy, regulatory frameworks, state and employer policies, the
organization of industries, wages, and access to union protection, for example,
influence workers' actions and experiences. For a full understanding of cultural work, research should integrate an understanding of "enduring features"
of cultural work, such as risk and uncertainty, with historical analysis of the
political economic context structuring these dynamics (Christopherson 2009;
Hesmondhalgh 2007; Miège 1989).

Key to this analysis is Marx's concept of exploitation, which occurs when
one group (workers) produces a surplus that is controlled by another (capitalists) (Himmelwit 1983a, 157). Under capitalism, exploitation occurs through
the extraction of surplus value, which Marx viewed as arising from the division
of the working day into two parts: during the first part, the worker spends
socially necessary labour time producing the equivalent of her wage; during
the second, the worker spends surplus labour time producing profit for the
capitalist (1983b, 474). It is this process of exploiting surplus value that drives
capital accumulation and class conflict. As Susan Himmelwit (ibid.) writes:
"the history of capitalist production can be seen as the history of struggle over

attempts by capital to increase, and attempts by the working class to resist increases in, the rate of surplus value."

Exploitation is a dynamic concept. It links antagonism and resistance: those who exploit workers are also dependent on workers to realize surplus value, which gives workers power, an "inherent capacity to resist" (Wright 1997, 35). The process of exploitation includes worker agency, resistance, and a desire for autonomous forms of work. Autonomist Marxism, which theorizes capital as always confronting and reacting to workers' resistance, provides a framework for this approach (Cleaver 2000). Under this view, capitalist cultural production is not a top-down process of domination, but dynamic and constitutive, reacting to workers' agency and, often, militancy. However, as Marx demonstrates in *Capital*, "capitalism is characterized by fetishisms that obscure, for both capitalist and worker alike, the origin of surplus value in exploitation" (Harvey 2006, 113). The labour-capital relations in cultural work can be obscured for a variety of reasons, including the fact that choosing to pursue cultural work despite the risks can be empowering, that an ideology of enterprise increasingly underscores cultural work, and that cultural work is based on personal relationships that can mask economic relations (Lorey 2009; Neff, Wissinger and Zukin 2005; Ekinsmyth 2002). Relations of exploitation can be so obscured that it often seems as if cultural work is not really work at all, giving rise to a "labour of love" discourse that preempts discussions of power relations (Beck 2003, 3). A return to Marx uncovers the antagonisms and social relations of capitalism that pervade cultural work. Traditionally, labour process theory has been at the core of Marxist studies of work.

3   Labour Process Theory and Cultural Work

As a body of scholarship, labour process theory emerged from Harry Braverman's ([1974] 1998) critique of the organization of work under capitalism and its deleterious effects on workers' skills. Drawing on Marx, Braverman sought to understand the contradiction of modern work, which required increasing training and skill yet produced greater dissatisfaction. Braverman describes how the labour process is subsumed under and shaped by processes of capital accumulation: work is continually brought under capitalists' control in order to extract value from workers, and the labour process is rationalized, first in the factory, then in the office, transforming the labour process from an activity that creates something useful into a process explicitly designed to expand capital. Structural dynamics of competition and accumulation push capitalists to constantly revolutionize the process of production to increase productivity and lower labour costs. This impels capitalists to obtain control over the labour process. As Marx ([1867] 1990, 436–437) writes, "capital...has an immanent drive, and a constant tendency, towards increasing the productivity of labour, in order to cheapen commodities and, by cheapening commodities, to cheapen the worker himself." This process is carried out by applying new technologies and principles of scientific management to the labour process, dividing work into its constituent parts, deskilling workers, separating conception from execution, and bringing work under management's control (Braverman [1974] 1998, 49, 118).

Braverman argued that capitalism tends to reduce the majority of workers to a homogeneous group of interchangeable labourers who require little specialized training. In some cases, his vision of degraded work has been carried into the digital age. Consider, for example, the growing market for digital piecework, where mental labour such as research, translation, and design are broken into small tasks and farmed out to people working remotely for alarmingly low pay on websites like Mechanical Turk, ODesk, and Microtask. Yet labour process theory has some limits in the context of cultural work, particularly the creative aspects of cultural work. For one, labour process theory has been predominantly workplace focused and concerned with workers in employment relationships, and cultural work is increasingly situated outside of these structures. In addition, cultural workers seem to need no coercion to fully invest themselves in their work or to work long hours for low pay (Ursell 2000; McRobbie 2002). Finally, the argument that cultural workers have been granted relative autonomy at the point of production seems to challenge the relevance of labour process theory.

Michael Chanan (1976; 1983) and Bill Ryan (1992) trace a lineage from art and artistic practice to labour in the commercialized cultural industries, drawing on Marx to outline a conception of aesthetic labour – forms of labour in which, unlike in other commodity production, it is difficult to completely separate the author from her work. As artistic practice is brought under the logic of capitalist commodity production, the "art-capital contradiction" emerges, defined as a source of conflict inherent to the transformation of culture into capital (Ryan 1992, 34). Historically, for cultural commodities to have use values, these commodities must retain a trace of the person who created them, especially in instances of "person-specific" or personalized labour, where the creator's name is attached to the work (Smith and McKinlay 2009a, 12; Ryan 1992, 136). As Ryan (45) writes, "every book must have an author, every score a composer, every film a writer, director [...] unlike cans of peaches, lines of cars [...] where the direct producers of these commodities are entirely unknown to their purchasers. Artists must be engaged as named, concrete labour." Even

cultural producers who are not "stars" – that small group for whom name recognition fetches high remuneration (Hesmondhalgh 2007, 199) – are valued
because "of the identifiable, expressive abilities attributable to and inseparable
from each and each alone" (Ryan 1992, 44).

The requirement for concrete labour limits the extent to which the idea creation process in cultural work can be broken down and divided into constituent tasks, and so cultural industries have tended to grant relative autonomy to
workers at the point of creation (idea and symbol generation), while tightening control over reproduction, distribution, and circulation of cultural commodities (Chanan 1976; Miège 1989; Ryan 1992; Hesmondhalgh 2007). As Chanan
(1983, 318) writes, "the content of cultural forms cannot, in the last instance, be
mechanized." Workers who create originating texts cannot be replaced with
machines or with other people without altering the text.[6] This complicates the
production process for capitalists. Usually, capital's compulsion to lower the
costs of production has required that concrete labour – specific skills or tasks
performed by a particular worker – be reduced to average levels so that it does
not matter who performs the work. Ideally, individual workers are transformed
into abstract labour: interchangeable inputs for production, their particular
contributions congealed in and disguised by the commodity form. Capital's
compulsion is to separate conception from execution and to reduce workers'
specialized knowledge and heterogeneous skills to simple labour (Braverman
[1974] 1998; Harvey 2006, 57).

Recognition of the structural tendency to grant cultural workers relative
autonomy at the point of production has served to eject labour process analysis from studies of cultural work (notable exceptions include Murphy 1991; Im
1997; Ursell 2000; Smith and McKinlay 2009a). For if it is true that cultural
workers have control over the process and products of their work, then it seems
labour process theory and its Marxist heritage are no longer relevant. Many
cultural workers are so self-motivated that they "set themselves" to work, working excessively long hours for little pay, embracing uncertainty and risk in
order to pursue careers in culture (McRobbie 2002, 101; Ursell 2000). From this
view, managers are not required to motivate cultural workers or increase productivity, and cultural workers are considered to self-exploit. But identifying

---

6   This argument is perhaps best demonstrated by the embodied nature of performing arts
    work. As William Baumol and William Bowen (1966, 164) write, changes in the training or
    specificities of a performer "affects the nature of the service he supplies." Unlike manufactur-
    ing workers, "performers are not intermediaries between raw material and the completed
    commodity – their activities are themselves the consumers' goods" and therefore the specific
    worker cannot be separated from the work of performing.

self-exploitation, while key to uncovering the myriad ways power operates, can mask true relations of exploitation, almost letting capital off the hook.

For Sheila Cohen (1987), labour process theory cannot be so easily side-stepped. She argues that the post-Braverman labour process debate was too focused on questions of control, neglecting the process of exploitation that is at the core of the capitalist labour process. It is not control that "constitutes the principal dynamic at work in the capitalist labour process," but rather exploitation, ownership over the means of production, and class (ibid., 35, 66). Cohen recasts the focus of labour process theory on valorization and exploitation, which is the motor of capitalist accumulation and production, fundamentally structured around the extraction of surplus value from workers. The labour process is political not because of an "ongoing power struggle over managerial domination," but because it is "the site of the central dynamic of [...] exploitation and the generation of surplus value" (39). This means that control over production can be surrendered if it is not an impediment to exploitation. Indeed work is constantly reorganized to suit capitalism's overall objective of valorization (Braverman [1974] 1998), and ceding control over the labour process to certain workers is exactly in line with some needs of accumulation. This ranges from empowerment strategies on the factory floor (Moody 1997) to "fun" environments in the permissive offices of new media firms designed to capture workers' creative and emotional potential; their "freest thoughts and impulses" harnessed for productivity (Ross 2003, 19; Dyer-Witheford and de Peuter 2009). In some ways, this loosening of control is a descendent of the age-old strategy of lengthening the working day. Pondering the playful offices of amenity-packed new media firms, Andrew Ross (2001, 78) asks, "who would ever want to go home?"

More overt attempts to rationalize production are evident in forms of cultural work that have previously seemed impervious to organizing the author out of production. Consider Alloy Entertainment, a company that generates book projects for publishers, pumping out thirty books per year targeted to teen girls. What is unusual about this "book factory" (Semuels 2008) is not the formulaic plots and generic tropes Alloy relies on for mass-market appeal, but the way labour is organized in the production of each book: ideas are brainstormed at a meeting, an editor composes a story, and a writer is hired on spec to draft a chapter. The writer works closely with editors to develop the plot and produce more chapters. Alloy pitches the chapters, a book synopsis, and a cover image to publishers, retaining all rights to the intellectual property. Often, company-owned pseudonyms are used instead of real writers' names, and some names represent a team of ghostwriters (Mead 2009). Perhaps an extreme case of rationalizing literary production, yet Alloy offers an example of how capital finds ways around the need to grant creative workers relative autonomy if and when it is required for profitable production. Under Alloy's model, it does not matter who writes a particular book. Authors, formerly assured the privilege of being named labour, are interchangeable and often not credited for their work.

Labour process analysis that draws on dynamic concepts from Marx remains a relevant method for researching cultural work, providing a theoretical foundation for an investigation of cultural work in its various and specific forms. Labour process theory centres on processes of capital accumulation and opens a critical line of inquiry: if the continuity of capitalist production has thoroughly penetrated the cultural industries and if exploitation is fundamental to the capitalist labour process, how does this dynamic manifest in cultural work? If cultural workers have been granted relative autonomy at the point of idea creation, how then does capital respond? In most instances, firms tighten control over workers who do not require relative autonomy in production, creating divisions in status, job quality, and material conditions between workers in cultural industries. Increasingly, and as technologies change, however, cultural workers' relative autonomy is being further encroached upon. This is especially the case for writers who pursue freelance work in order to claim some autonomy over their craft. A case study of freelancers reveals these tensions.

4   Case Study: Freelance Writers

On the surface, freelance writers seem removed from the capitalist labour process. Legally classified as independent contractors, freelancers work for multiple clients to produce one-off pieces or are hired for short-term projects. They write for magazines, newspapers, books, and produce content for corporations, governments, and NGOs.[7] The labour-capital relations that underscore freelance cultural production are often obscured: because freelancers are not engaged in an employment relationship and are not paid a salary, it appears that they sell simply a finished piece of work, or "labour already objectified in the product" (Marx [1867] 1990, 692), not the labour time required to produce that piece. However, Marx argues that piece wages are a form of time wages

---

7   The freelancers I study are primarily freelance journalists who write for newspapers, magazines, and online journalistic outlets. However, because it is so difficult to earn a living solely from freelance journalism, many freelancers have expanded the types of work they perform to include a range of industries and formats. For this reason, I use the broader term freelance writer.

and that the existence of this form of payment "in no way alters [its] essential nature," which is "the general relation between capital and wage-labour" (693, 696). Freelance cultural work has relations of exploitation at its core.

Historically, piecework has been a method of lowering wages and lengthening the working day (698). For cultural workers, however, freelancing provides an escape from the employment relationship, a way to gain some control over where and when they work, what they work on, with whom, and how work is performed. But despite writing for profitable media industries (Winseck 2010), Canadian freelance writers' incomes have been stagnant for over three decades, averaging $24,000 before tax (PWAC 2006).[8] In a survey I conducted of 200 freelance writers across Canada, 45 percent of respondents reported earning under $20,000 (before tax) from freelance writing in 2009, and 71 percent of these writers say that freelance writing is their main job.

While freelancing is presented as the ultimate freedom for workers (Pink 2001), it is also an ideal arrangement for capital. Freed from the burden of employment, relieved of the costs of training, overhead, benefits, and paying for unproductive time, firms can hire someone for a short-term project or purchase only completed works: an article, a piece of research, a design. The risks and costs of production are downloaded onto workers who, motivated by the relentless search for work and increasing competition, strive to produce their best works, providing capital ample choice from a pool of skilled workers bargaining down the costs of their labour power. This arrangement allows for relative autonomy in creative production yet impels firms to develop alternate methods of extracting surplus value. For publishers, exploitation is made easier by the casualization of media work, which has increased competition for work, made workers insecure, and pressured wages down.

Marx's ([1867] 1990, 697) observations on piece wages point to the contradictions of freelance work:

> the wider scope that piece-wages give to individuality tends to develop both that individuality, and with it the worker's sense of liberty, independence and self-control, and also the competition of workers with each other. The piece-wage therefore has a tendency, while raising the wages of individuals above the average, to lower this average itself.

This demonstrates the dialectical nature of the labour-capital relation: workers constantly seek to resist exploitation and capital constantly reorganizes to

---

8   The Professional Writers Association of Canada surveyed 858 freelance writers, most of whom are full-time writers, meaning that writing is their sole source of income (PWAC 2006).

address workers' resistance. As Harvey (2006, 116) writes, "if the value productivity of labour can be better secured by some reasonable level of worker autonomy, then so be it. Capital is, presumably, indifferent to how the value productivity of labour is preserved and enhanced." Increasingly, capital secures the value productivity of labour through exploiting freelancers' unpaid labour time and copyrights to their works. I examine each example in turn.

5   Labour Casualization and Exploitation of Unpaid Labour Time

Working as a freelancer has traditionally provided journalists a way out of the strictures of an employment relationship and the limitations of routinized news production to pursue more creative, experimental, or interesting writing. However, what was once a strategy available to a small segment of journalists who could leverage a monopoly over their skills to build freelance careers has become a core business model as the media workforce is casualized. As companies download more of the risk and costs of doing business onto workers, the autonomy freelancers have enjoyed, even in the face of low pay, is being undermined.

By now the shift to precarious forms of employment is well documented (Vosko 2006; Standing 2011). In line with the neoliberal transformation of capitalist economies and the resulting re-structuring of work and employment dating from the 1970s (Vosko 2000; Albo 2010), cultural industries have moved from production based on full-time, steady employment to more precarious forms: part-time, temporary, casual, contract, and freelance (Murdock 2003; Nies and Pedersini 2003; Walters, Warren and Dobbie 2006; Smith and McKinlay 2009b). Typically, this work has low wages, no benefits, little job and social security, limited access to union protections, and long working hours. Cultural work has been casualized, transformed from "internal and regulated labour markets" to networks of individuals providing specialized services on an as-needed basis (Smith and McKinlay 2009b, 29; Hill and Capriotti 2009). These changes are linked to firm strategies such as concentration, convergence, and outsourcing, the erosion of union power, and the spread and acceptance of precarious forms of employment. They are also made possible by a restructured global division of labour that harnesses information and communication technologies to establish chains of flexible accumulation spanning the globe, chains that begin from the outsourcing of components of the production process to the low-waged regions of the world and link to the outsourced work now performed in the homes of knowledge, information, and cultural workers in western capitalist states (Huws 2007). Although cultural industries have a history of non-standard forms of work,[9] accepting freelance, contract, or temporary employment is no longer a choice as firms shed their workforces, flooding the labour market with freelancers (Nies and Pedersini 2003; PWAC 2006; Walters et al., 2006; McKercher 2009). Rather than continuously employing people, cultural industries maintain loose affiliations with networks of cultural producers constantly developing ideas from which firms can pick and choose.

This "reserve army" of cultural workers (Murdock 2003, 22) absorbs cultural firms' financial risk, which is offloaded onto individuals. Because the creative stage of production cannot be completely rationalized, companies trade relative autonomy for the ability to extract higher value through contract and freelance status, protecting capital from risk, lowering labour costs, and intensifying competition for work (Ryan 1992, 48; Hesmondhalgh 2007; Smith and McKinlay 2009b, 40). Project-based work, short-term contracts, and freelance arrangements demonstrate some of the underlying contradictions of cultural work: these relationships grant workers the relative autonomy and flexibility required to develop creative works, but absolve firms of paying a salary and the benefits associated with secure employment. The benefits of autonomy are often undermined by precarity. This arrangement, despite having roots in political economic dynamics, has perpetuated the notion that to be a cultural worker one must accept and adapt to intermittent employment, low wages, and precarity, drawing out the romanticized notion of suffering for one's art into industrialized, highly capitalized cultural industries (Menger 1999; Ross 2000).

As pieceworkers, freelance writers are usually paid per word or per article (or, as the unfortunate joke goes, "perhaps").[10] By purchasing finished stories from freelancers; publishers do not pay for time spent developing and researching ideas, pitching stories, conducting interviews, or for time spent editing and rewriting. The arbitrary per-word form of payment, popular among magazines and newspapers, obscures a large portion of the labour that goes into the writing of those words. As one freelance writer explains: "The pay often does not reflect the work you put into a piece. You are expected to come up with ideas, research and pitch without pay, yet are not adequately compensated when your story ideas are accepted." Added to this are the crucial tasks of sourcing and securing work, self-promotion, training and skills development, invoicing and chasing payments, and the various other tasks involved in maintaining a

---

9   Indeed, cultural industries are credited with serving as a model of flexible, project-based, work for other industries (Ross 2009, 18–19; McRobbie 2004).

10   Kingston and Cole 1986. For corporate and non-journalism contracts, freelancers are usually paid per hour.

freelance career. As I discuss below, once an article is written, the costs of reproduction for companies is minimal, yet writers are often not paid for multiple use of their works in various formats, or "the labour power that is still latent within the article" (D'Agostino 2010, 238).

As Marx explained, unpaid labour that contributes to the generation of surplus value for capitalists is exploited labour.[11] And exploitation is spreading throughout the cultural industries, thanks to the casualization of the labour force, which leaves a growing number of workers stitching work together to earn a living, paid for far less than the time required for production of their works. This glut of freelance and un- and under-employed workers represents huge value for companies, as competition for work pressures wages downwards. New forms of temporal exploitation are made possible by processes of spatialization, or extending the capacities for value extraction into new spaces – in this case, workers' homes (Mosco 2009). Media corporations capitalize on this arrangement, building business models on access to flexible, cheap, or free labour they need not employ. For example, firms are replacing paid workers with unpaid internships; writers are increasingly paid in "exposure" on profitable websites such as The Huffington Post, and skilled employees are laid off because major news networks such as CNN can increasingly rely on volunteer-submitted content, or exploit "citizen" journalism through "crowdsourcing" (Perlin 2011; Guthrie 2011; Kperogi 2011). These strategies are complemented by the intensifying exploitation of copyrights.

6   Copyright as Exploitation

Freelance writers' livelihoods in a digital age are built on the shaky foundations of copyright protection, which are being eroded by corporations' tightening grip on intellectual property rights. Unlike employees, who in exchange for salaries give up ownership of works they produce to employers (D'Agostino 2010, 4), freelance writers in Canada are legally classified as independent contractors and therefore own copyrights to the articles they write. Publishers are granted a limited licence to publish articles in designated publications for specified periods of time (Canada 1985, s.13; D'Agostino 2004, 6). Traditionally,

---

11   Feminist activists and political economists have long been arguing that unpaid labour time is valuable for capitalism, particularly the unpaid labour performed by women in the home. See, for example Waring 1999 and Dalla Costa and James 1972. McKercher (2009) makes important links between women's unpaid household labour and the precarious work of freelance writing.

this has been a benefit of working freelance, enabling writers to re-sell articles and in some way compensating for low rates of pay (Lorinc 2005, 37; PWAC 2006, 41). However, traditional practices are being undermined by uses of new technologies and aggressive publishing strategies.

The growth and consolidation of media and entertainment firms over the past few decades has been enabled by technological development, especially digital communications and digitization, a process that provides a universal language for media content and has led to convergence across media platforms, allowing corporations to deepen the exploitation of labour (Mosco 2003). Digitization enables quick transmission of information and simplifies duplication, especially online, which means publishers can repackage information for publication in multiple formats.

Most periodical and newspaper publishers in Canada are part of large media chains that control a range of integrated media properties and are hungry for content that can be re-purposed for various platforms. Digitization helped corporations realize their ambitions of concentration and convergence, aided by and fuelling the push to obtain copyrights (D'Agostino 2010, 20). These rapid shifts in corporate media organization have directly affected freelance writers' earnings, initially by shrinking the number of markets in which writers can re-sell work (PWAC 2006, 35).

These practices have grown more pervasive as they have moved online. For example, in Fall 2010, Rogers Media, a division of the massive media conglomerate Rogers Communications, began syndicating articles written for its magazines by freelancers to other websites without alerting writers, let alone paying them for extra use (Scott 2010; Story Board 2010). Unbeknownst to writers, executives began syndication as an initiative of Rogers Digital Media, which promotes access to its content to advertisers. Rogers Digital Media claimed the syndication was covered under the "promotions" clause in Rogers' new standard contract all writers must sign, which states that Rogers can "publish the Work and/or an edited version thereof in any promotion of the publication and/or its brand in all forms of media" (ibid.). Writers' organizations, however, claim that this is a broad interpretation of the contract: "most contributors would not read 'promotion' as syndication on [websites] many months after their story first appears in a Rogers publication," argued freelance writer agent Derek Finkle (Scott 2010).

This example demonstrates publishers' growing desire to own outright the rights to writers' works, which are cheap to "digitally recycl[e]" into new profit (D'Agostino 2010, 239). This strategy aligns with Marx's ([1867] 1990, 325) explanation of surplus value: after a worker earns enough to reproduce her labour power, the capitalist owns the rest of the value she produces, which "for the capitalist has all the charms of something created out of nothing." Most large publishers now present writers with "streamlined" contracts that claim all copyrights for writers' works at once (D'Agostino 2005, 166). Contracts can demand, for example, "all rights, in perpetuity, throughout the universe" in any form, including rights for media formats yet to be invented. These contracts are generally non-negotiable and do not offer extra payment for extra rights (PWAC 2006, 35). Depending on the company and its media holdings, rights demanded can include translations, digitizing, adaptations and performances, reprints, relicensing, promotions, and storage of articles in electronic databases.

Current contracting regimes have effectively expanded possibilities for exploitation of surplus value indefinitely (D'Agostino 2010, 241). Economists view copyright primarily as providing economic incentive for creators to produce intellectual and artistic works (Bettig 1996, 7; Towse 2003). However, under the capitalist mode of cultural production, copyright's primary function is to guarantee its owner exclusive right to exploit the work and to extract surplus value from workers who have been granted relative autonomy at the point of production. With workers providing services on a one-off basis, companies need not be concerned with *how* works are created, as the real value for corporations lies in the continued exploitation of completed works. Notes one freelance writer, "No one cares where I am, just as long as I get the work done." What matters to firms is not the time spent on a project or the pace of work – control over the labour process – but ownership over the final product, which can be re-published, re-licensed, and re-purposed, generating surplus value from the works themselves and lowering labour costs.

Capitalism developed by generating technological methods of extracting knowledge from workers to control production and increase efficiency and exploitation (Braverman [1974] 1998), and continues this trajectory by claiming ownership of the information workers produce (May 2002, 318). This is a crucial, under-examined link between cultural work and capital, obscured either by a focus solely on the autonomy of cultural workers or by a failure to acknowledge that it is labour that creates the texts, images, ideas, and symbols that are transformed into private property (Rossiter 2006, 145).

Copyright has become a high-stakes site of struggle in Canada and beyond. Freelance journalists in North America have won class action lawsuits against publishers for using works without acknowledgement or extra payment (D'Agostino 2010). Film and television writers struck for three months in 2007–2008 to win a greater share of residual money from DVD sales and revenues from digital downloads (Klowden and Chatterjee 2008) Freelance photographers effectively delayed the launch of *People* magazine's iPad app over its licensing agreement, as photographers demanded payment for use of their photos beyond the pages of the magazine (Wallenstein 2010). Book producers such as Alloy Entertainment and Full Fathom Five[12] are transforming copyright relations between writers and publishers by hiring authors to write prefabricated books, often under a pseudonyms, and retaining all rights to their works, generating licensing deals for film and television while contractually barring writers from claiming authorship (Mozes 2010). These struggles will become more charged as we move deeper into the digital age.

7 Conclusion: Cultural Work as a Site of Struggle

A Marxist political economy approach to cultural work identifies the links between precarious working conditions and broader transformations underway in the cultural industries while also recognizing workers as agents who resist, struggle over, and negotiate their labour conditions. Without this powerful tool of analysis, based on Marx's foundational understanding of the labour process under capitalism, the manifestations of capitalist social relations in old and new forms can be obscured, especially as labour is casualized and digital technologies are used to transform production. As Marx argued, "capitalism is unique in hiding its method of exploitation behind the process of exchange" (Himmelwit 1983a, 158). Key to understanding the full experience of cultural work is discovering how exploitation shapes work and workers' lives.

   In the case of freelance writers, exploitation is at the core of the casualization of work and the aggressive pursuit of copyrights. For freelancers, control over the labour process is traded for increased flexibility for employers and a greater extraction of surplus value from writers who are working harder for longer hours and earning lower wages (PWAC 2006). Although the market has long played a role in influencing the type of material writers could sell

---

12   Frey, a controversial writer, launched Full Fathom Five to tap into the commercial young
      adult fiction market. Frey hires newly minted (and indebted) MFA graduates to write novels for $250 (some writers earn an additional $250 upon completion of the book). The writer earns a percentage of all revenue the book generates (30 percent if the idea came from Frey, 40 percent if the idea was the writer's), including revenue from TV, film, and merchandise licensing. The writer does not own copyright to the book yet is responsible for any potential legal action. Full Fathom Five has the right to decide to use the author's name or a pseudonym, even if the writer is no longer involved in the project. The writer has no say in the use of his or her image in publicity photos or biographies and must sign a confidentiality agreement, risking a $50,000 penalty for "admit[ing] to working with Full Fathom Five without permission." The terms of copyright on Frey's projects are nonnegotiable (Mozes 2010).

(Mills 1956; Kingston and Cole 1986), this pressure has intensified as publishers seek "content" that can be syndicated for use across multiple platforms. These new publishing practices limit the possibilities for writers to produce certain kinds of work, including longer pieces that require research, investigative journalism, and creative or challenging works that take time to produce. These limitations are reflected in Canadian freelance writers' experiences. Just over half of the writers I surveyed would most like to write long-form narrative features, creative non-fiction, essays, and investigative journalism. However, few find opportunities to pursue this type of work and to be compensated adequately for it. Other reports reveal a discrepancy between the type of writing freelancers most want to pursue (periodicals, books, and American magazines, which pay more) and the type of writing most do: writing for corporate clients and shorter magazine pieces that are faster to produce (PWAC 2006). As one writer says, "I've built my career on the 'service' journalism industry. It's paid my bills and helped establish my reputation and skills, but I would like to do more meaningful, issues-related writing. I do some, but there are probably three or four bill-payers for every piece I'm truly proud of." Increasingly, freelancers view their journalistic work, which motivated them to become freelancers in the first place, as a luxury to indulge in when time and money permit. These experiences trouble the concept of relative autonomy.

Because antagonism lies at the core of Marx's concept of exploitation and because capitalist production is "inherently, structurally a site of contestation" (Wayne 2003, 13), it is useful to conceive of cultural work as a site of struggle (see also Artz 2006). This conception is acknowledged in some studies of cultural work, where struggle manifests as tension between "artistic desires for creative autonomy" and the requirements of profit-oriented cultural production (Banks 2007, 6; Ryan 1992). A broader conception, however, views this struggle as labour-focused, as contestation over the terms of commodification and exploitation of labour power. Autonomist Marxist theorizing is useful here, as this approach begins from the notion that workers actively resist capitalist exploitation and enclosure, and that capital reacts to worker resistance, which always has the potential to escape capital's control. This cycle, in turn, generates new strategies and tactics of struggle among workers that threatens capitalism anew (Cleaver 2000; Brophy and de Peuter 2007, 178). As capital extends relations of exploitation, workers seek meaningful and autonomous forms of work. Autonomists view the move toward flexible work as partly motivated by workers themselves. For example, in his schema of the "precarious labour personas" found along a continuum of precarity in contemporary capitalism, Greig de Peuter (2011, 419, 420) argues that "the autonomous worker" – typified in freelance cultural workers – is subject to flexibility "instituted from above" but also desires this type of labour arrangement (see also Ross 2009; Vosko 2010; Hesmondhalgh and Baker 2011). As de Peuter (2011, 420) writes, "the autonomous worker is immanent to a genealogy in which the pursuit of flexible work in immaterial production is a decision taken in an act of self-determination and as a conscious rejection of standard work."

It is useful to consider freelance writers in this way. As journalism developed into a mass industry in the late nineteenth century, journalists were proletarianized, or brought under a system of wage labour, which standardized the labour of reporting (Smythe 1980). The introduction of formulaic news writing geared toward a mass audience challenged writers' independence and degraded the craft of writing (Carey 1965). Even as journalists gained professional status through unionization, many grew frustrated with anonymity, wage dependency, and routine conditions of work (Smythe 1980). Freelancing offered escape from reporters' descent into "a white collar proletariat" (Kaul 1986, 47) and the newsroom grind. Although the decision to work freelance is no longer a choice for most, many freelancers retain this spirit, seeking autonomy, the ability to pursue interesting and creative work, flexibility, and control over the terms of commodification of their labour power. Freelancing can also represent a more politicized conception of work and how it should be organized, hinting at a radical conception of a "refusal of work" and escape from the wage relation (Weeks 2005). As Andrew Beck (2003, 4) notes, freelance cultural work can be viewed simultaneously as "labour at the margins" and as "a last space of resistance."

As media industries continue to contract out work, as states envision entrepreneurial, creative cities populated with self-employed workers, with the rise of co-working spaces to absorb office-less workers, and with no shortage of work to be done, it would seem that the time of the freelancer has arrived (Horowitz 2011). However, freelance wages are generally low, incomes are intermittent, and workers are experiencing intensified precarity. These conditions demonstrate that in response to worker resistance, capital adjusts its strategies to exploit those who have seemingly escaped the wage relation, a continuation of labour-capital antagonisms.

The struggle takes on new dimensions as workers begin collectively organizing to address and resist precarious conditions. Alongside established unions in the film and television industries, workers in sectors not often considered sites of labour, such as modelling, art, and writing, are identifying and challenging conditions of their exploitation. Cultural workers in a range of sectors are reaffirming their status as workers by embracing the term "precariat," whose roots lie in European social and protest movements (Prickett 2012; Standing 2011; de Peuter 2011). Canadian freelance writers, who have historically organized in professional associations, are turning to union models to collectively improve low wages and exploitative contracts (Cohen 2011). The US-based National Writers Union has launched a "Pay The Writer!" campaign to protest free labour online and to set a fair wage scale for online freelance journalists. Canadian Artists' Representation/le Front des artistes Canadiens (CARFAC), which represents visual artists in Canada, is demanding payment for artists when paintings are re-sold, as the labour power embedded in their work generates surplus value for sellers (CBC News 2011). Building on CARFAC's model, artists in New York City formed Working Artists in the Greater Economy (W.A.G.E.) to organize around the demand that artists be paid for their labour in gallery shows. Also in New York, The Model Alliance was formed to recognize modelling as work and to challenge the exploitative relations that underpin models' affective labour (de Peuter 2012). Key to these initiatives is that cultural workers are naming and addressing the precise conditions of their exploitation.

Emergent efforts by cultural workers to collectively organize are significant for those concerned with labour movement renewal. These initiatives are attempting to organize the unorganized, often through experimental formations that could serve as "test cases" for how to organize precarious workers in a flexible economy (de Peuter 2014). These initiatives are raising awareness of labour struggles and power relations in industries that are generally under the labour movement's radar, either by establishing alliances with trade unions or by organizing outside of union structures. Underpinning these efforts are not demands to return to standard forms of employment, but rather policy proposals and demands that can build worker power outside of any particular workplace; demands that aim to reclaim non-standard work as a viable option for autonomous, flexible, yet secure work (de Peuter 2011; Vosko 2010). It remains to be seen if these efforts can build solidarity with the labour movement and politicize cultural workers, or if organizations will reinforce the individualism and entrepreneurialism underscoring cultural work under neoliberalism (Abrahamian 2012; Cohen 2011). Yet these initiatives signify changes underway that could have implications for labour politics and the way culture is produced.

As the growth of cultural worker organizing demonstrates, it is crucial to identify the processes, practices, and social relations that undermine autonomy in cultural work so that they can be interrupted. The need to disrupt the feelings of inevitability and self-responsibility that still pervade many cultural workers' outlooks is urgent, and requires a critical political economy approach that understands material conditions as "always active, always unsettled, always subject to change" (Artz 2006, 45). After all, in some of Marx's most famous words ([Marx, 1888] 1978c), the point is not just to interpret the world, but to change it.

References

Abrahamian, Atossa Araxia. 2012. The 'I' in Union. *Dissent.* Accessed May 16, 2012. http://dissentmagazine.org/article/?article=4094.

Albo, Gregory. 2010. The "New Economy" and Capitalism Today. In *Interrogating The New Economy: Restructuring Work in the 21st Century*, edited by Norene J. Pupo and Mark P. Thomas, 3–20. Toronto: University of Toronto Press.

Artz, Lee. 2006. On The Material and The Dialectic: Toward a Class Analysis of Communication. In *Marxism and Communication Studies: The Point Is to Change It*, edited by Lee Artz, Steve Macek, and Dana L. Cloud, 5–51. New York: Peter Lang.

Banks, Mark. 2007. *The Politics of Cultural Work.* London: Palgrave Macmillan.

Banks, Mark. 2010. Autonomy Guaranteed? Cultural Work and the 'Art – Commerce Relation'. *Journal for Cultural Research* 14 (3): 251–269.

Baumol, William J., and William G. Bowen. 1966. *Performing Arts: The Economic Dilemma.* New York: The Twentieth Century Fund.

Beck, Andrew. 2003. Introduction: Cultural Work, Cultural Workplace – Looking at the Cultural Industries. In *Cultural Work: Understanding the Cultural Industries*, edited by Andrew Beck, 1–6. London: Routledge.

Bettig, Ronald V. 1996. *Copyrighting Culture: The Political Economy of Intellectual Property.* Boulder, CO: Westview Press.

Braverman, Harry. (1974) 1998. *Labor and Monopoly Capital: The Degradation of Work in the Twentieth Century.* New York: Monthly Review Press.

Brophy, Enda, and Greig de Peuter. 2007. Immaterial Labor, Precarity and Recomposition. In *Knowledge Workers in the Information Society*, edited by Catherine McKercher and Vincent Mosco, 191–207. Lanham, MD: Lexington.

Canada. 1985. Copyright Act. Department of Justice. Accessed May 16, 2012. http://laws-lois.justice.gc.ca/eng/acts/C-42/.

Carey, James W. 1965. The Communications Revolution and the Professional Communicator. In *The Sociology of Mass Media Communications*, edited by Paul Halmos, 23–38. Keele: University of Keele.

Caves, Richard E. 2000. *Creative Industries: Contracts between Art and Commerce.* Cambridge, MA: Harvard University Press.

CBC News. 2011. Visual Artists Vie for a Cut of Resale Profits. *CBC News.* November 28, 2011. http://www.cbc.ca/news/business/story/2011/11/28/art-resale-right-carfac-auction-gallery.html.

Chanan, Michael. 1976. *Labour Power in the British Film Industry.* London: British Film Institute.

Chanan, Michael. 1983. Labour Power and Aesthetic Labour in Film and Television in Britain. In *Communication and Class Struggle: Liberation, Socialism*, edited by Armand Mattelart and Seth Siegelaub, 317–332. New York: International General.

Christopherson, Susan. 2009. Working In The Creative Economy: Risk, Adaptation, and the Persistence of Exclusionary Networks. In *Creative Labour: Working in the Creative Industries*, edited by Alan McKinlay and Chris Smith, 72–90. London: Palgrave Macmillan.

Cleaver, Harry. 2000. *Reading Capital Politically*. Leeds and Edinburgh: Anti/Theses and AK Press.

Cohen, Nicole S. 2011. Negotiating Writers' Rights: Freelance Cultural Labour and the Challenge of Organizing. *Just Labour: A Canadian Journal of Work and Society* 17 & 18: 119–138.

Cohen, Sheila. 1987. A Labour Process To Nowhere? *New Left Review* 165 (October): 34–50.

Conor, Bridget. 2010. 'Everybody's a Writer' Theorizing Screenwriting as Creative Labour. *Journal of Screenwriting* 1 (1): 27–43.

D'Agostino, Giuseppina. 2004. Should Freelancers Keep Their Copyrights in the Digital Era? *Copyright & New Media Law Newsletter* 8 (4): 6–8.

D'Agostino, Guiseppina. 2005. Freelance Authors For Free: Globalisation of Publishing, Convergence of Copyright Contracts and Divergence of Judicial Reasoning. In *New Directions in Copyright Law*, edited by Fiona Macmillan, 1: 166–215. Northampton, MA: Edward Elgar.

D'Agostino, Guiseppina. 2010. *Copyright, Contracts, Creators: New Media, New Rules.* Cheltenham, UK: Edward Elgar.

Dalla Costa, Mariarosa, and Selma James. 1972. *The Power of Women and the Subversion of the Community*. Bristol: The Falling Wall Press.

de Peuter, Greig. 2011. Creative Economy and Labor Precarity: A Contested Convergence . *Journal of Communication Inquiry* 35 (4): 417–425.

de Peuter, Greig. 2012. Modelling Workers' Rights. *Shameless.* http://www.shameless-mag.com/stories/2012/04/modelling-workers-rights/.

de Peuter, Greig. 2014. "Beyond the Model Worker: Surveying a Creative Precariat." *Culture Unbound* 6: 263–284.

Deuze, Mark. 2007. *Media Work*. London: Polity.

Deuze, Mark, and Leopoldina Fortunati. 2011. Atypical Newswork, Atypical Media Management. In *Managing Media Work*, edited by Mark Deuze, 111–120. London: Sage.

Dyer-Witheford, Nick, and Greig De Peuter. 2009. *Games of Empire: Global Capitalism and Video Games*. Minneapolis: University of Minnesota Press.

Ekinsmyth, Carol. 2002. Project Organization, Embeddedness and Risk in Magazine Publishing. *Regional Studies* 36 (3): 229–243.

Florida, Richard L. 2002. *The Rise of the Creative Class: And How It's Transforming Work, Leisure, Community and Everyday Life*. New York: Basic Books.

Garnham, Nicholas. 1997. Concepts of Culture – Public Policy and the Cultural Industries. In *Studying Culture*, 2nd ed., edited by Ann Gray and Jim McGuigan, 54–61. London: Arnold.

Gough-Yates, Anna. 2003. *Understanding Women's Magazines: Publishing, Markets and Readerships*. London: Routledge.

Guthrie, Marissa. 2011. CNN Cuts 50 Staff Members. *The Hollywood Reporter*, November 11. http://www.hollywoodreporter.com/news/cnn-cuts-50-staff-members-260737.

Hartley, John. 2005. Creative Industries. In *Creative Industries*, edited John Hartley, 1–40. Malden, MA: Blackwell.

Harvey, David. 1990. *The Condition of Postmodernity: An Enquiry into the Origins of Cultural Change*. Malden, MA: Blackwell.

Harvey, David. 1996. *Justice, Nature and the Geography of Difference*. Malden, MA: Blackwell.

Harvey, David. 2006. *The Limits to Capital*. London: Verso.

Harvey, David. 2010. *A Companion to Marx's Capital*. London: Verso.

Hesmondhalgh, David. 2007. *The Cultural Industries*. 2nd ed. London: Sage.

Hesmondhalgh, David, and Sarah Baker. 2011. *Creative Labour: Media Work in Three Cultural Industries*. London: Routledge.

Hill, Kelly, and Kathleen Capriotti. 2009. *A Statistical Profile of Artists in Canada*. Hill Strategies Research Inc., February.

Himmelwit, Susan. 1983a. Exploitation. In *A Dictionary of Marxist Thought*, edited by Tom Bottomore, Laurence Harris, V.G. Kiernan and Ralph Miliband, 157–158. Cambridge, MA: Harvard University Press.

Himmelwit, Susan. 1983b. Surplus Value. In *A Dictionary of Marxist Thought*, edited by Tom Bottomore, Laurence Harris, V.G. Kiernan and Ralph Miliband, 472–475. Cambridge, MA: Harvard University Press.

Horowitz, Sara. 2011. The Freelance Surge Is the Industrial Revolution of Our Time. *The Atlantic*, September 13. http://www.theatlantic.com/business/archive/2011/09/the-freelance-surge-is-the-industrial-revolution-of-our-time/244229/.

Huws, Ursula. 2003. *The Making of a Cybertariat: Virtual Work in a Real World*. New York: Monthly Review Press.

Huws, Ursula. 2007. Defragmenting: Towards a Critical Understanding of the New Global Division of Labour. *Work Organisation, Labour & Globalisation* 1 (2): 1–4.

ILO [International Labor Office]. 2000. *Symposium on Information Technologies in the Media and Entertainment Industries: Their Impact on Employment, Working Conditions and Labour-management Relations*. Geneva: ILO. http://www.ilo.org/public/english/dialogue/sector/techmeet/smei00/smeir.htm.

Im, Yung-Ho. 1997. Towards a Labour-Process History of Newsworkers. *Javnost/The Public* 41 (1): 31–48.

Kaul, Arthur J. 1986. The Proletarian Journalist: A Critique of Professionalism. *Journal of Mass Media Ethics* 1 (2): 47–55.

Kingston, Paul William, and Jonathan R. Cole. 1986. *The Wages Of Writing: Per Word, Per Piece, or Perhaps*. New York: Columbia University Press.

Klowden, Kevin, and Anusuya Chatterjee. 2008. *Writers' Strike of 2007–2008 The Economic Impact of Digital Distribution*. Santa Monica, CA: Milken Institute.

Kperogi, Farooq A. 2011. Cooperation with the Corporation? CNN and the Hegemonic Cooptation of Citizen Journalism Through iReport. *New Media & Society* 13 (2): 314–329.

Lacey, Liam. 2011. Screenwriting: It's a Terrible Job But Everybody Wants To Do It. *The Globe and Mail*, July 7, R1.

Leadbeater, Charles, and Kate Oakley. 2005. Why Cultural Entrepreneurs Matter. In *Creative Industries*, edited by John Hartley, 299–311. Malden, MA: Blackwell.

Lorey, Isabell. 2009. Governmentality and Self-Precarization: On The Normalization of Cultural Producers. In *Art and Contemporary Critical Practice: Reinventing Institutional Critique*, edited by Gerald Raunig and Gene Ray, trans. Lisa Rosenblatt and Dagmar Fink, 187–202. London: MayFly Books.

Lorinc, John. 2005. *Creators and Copyright in Canada. The Working Conditions of Creators in Quebec and Canada*, Report prepared for Creators' Copyright Coalition and Droit d'auteur / Multimédia-Internet / Copyright. Accessed May 16, 2012. www.creatorscopyright.ca/documents/lorinc-beaulieu.html.

Marx, Karl. (1844) 1978a. Economic and Philosophic Manuscripts of 1884. In *The Marx-Engels Reader*, 2nd ed., edited by Robert C. Tucker, 594–617. New York: Norton.

Marx, Karl. (1852) 1978b.The Eighteenth Brumaire of Louis Bonaparte. In *The Marx-Engels Reader*, 2nd ed., edited by Robert C. Tucker, 66–135. New York: Norton.

Marx, Karl. (1888) 1978c. Theses on Feuerbach. In *The Marx-Engels Reader*, 2nd ed., edited by Robert C. Tucker, 143–145. New York: Norton.

Marx, Karl. (1867) 1990. *Capital: A Critique of Political Economy, Volume 1*. London: Penguin Books.

May, Christopher. 2002. The Political Economy of Proximity: Intellectual Property and the Global Division of Information Labour. *New Political Economy* 7 (3): 317–342.

McGuigan, Jim. 2010. Creative Labour, Cultural Work and Individualization. *International Journal of Cultural Policy* 16 (3): 323–335.

McKercher, Catherine. 2009. Writing On The Margins: Precarity and the Freelance Journalist. *Feminist Media Studies* 9 (3): 370–374.

McRobbie, Angela. 2002. From Holloway to Hollywood: Happiness at Work in the New Cultural Economy? In *Cultural Economy: Cultural Analysis and Commercial Life*, edited by Paul du Gay and Michael Pryke, 97–114. London: Sage.

McRobbie, Angela. 2004. 'Everyone Is Creative': Artists as Pioneers of the new Economy? In *Contemporary Culture in Everyday Life*, edited by Tony Bennett and Elizabeth Silva, 186–202. Durham, UK: Sociologypress.

Mead, Rebecca. 2009. The Gossip Mill: Alloy, the Teen-Entertainment Factory. *The New Yorker*, October 19: 62–71.

Menger, Pierre-Michel. 1999. Artistic Labor Markets and Careers. *Annual Review of Sociology* 25: 541–574.

Miège, Bernard. 1989. *The Capitalization of Cultural Production*. New York: International General.

Mills, C. Wright. 1956. *White Collar: The American Middle Classes*. New York: Oxford University Press.

Moody, Kim. 1997. *Workers in a Lean World*. London: Verso.

Mosco, Vincent. 2003. The Transformation of Communication in Canada. In *Changing Canada: Political Economy as Transformation*, edited by Wallace Clement and Leah F. Vosko, 287–308. Montreal and Kingston: McGill-Queen's University Press.

Mosco, Vincent. 2009. *The Political Economy of Communication*, 2nd ed. London: Sage.

Mosco, Vincent, and Catherine McKercher. 2006. Editorial. *Canadian Journal of Communication* 31 (3): 493–497.

Mozes, Suzanne. 2010. James Frey's Fiction Factory. *New York*, November 12. http://nymag.com/arts/books/features/69474/.

Murdock, Graham. 2003. Back To Work: Cultural Labor in Altered Times. In *Cultural Work: Understanding the Cultural Industries*, edited by Andrew Beck, 15–36. London: Routledge.

Murphy, David. 1991. Journalists and the Labour Process: White-Collar Production Workers. In *White-collar Work: The Non-Manual Labour Process*, edited by Chris Smith, David Knights, and Hugh Willmott, 139–161. London: Macmillan.

Neff, Gina, Elizabeth Wissinger, and Sharon Zukin. 2005. Entrepreneurial Labor among Cultural Producers: 'Cool' Jobs in 'Hot' Industries. *Social Semiotics* 15 (3): 307–334.

Nies, Gerd, and Roberto Pedersini. 2003. *Freelance Journalists in the European Media Industry*. European Federation of Journalists. http://www.ifj-europe.org/pdfs/FinalReportFreelance.pdf.

Perlin, Ross. 2011. *Intern Nation: How to Earn Nothing and Learn Little in the Brave New Economy*. London: Verso.

Pink, Daniel H. 2001. *Free Agent Nation: How America's New Independent Workers are Transforming the Way We Live*. New York: Warner.

Prickett, Sarah Nicole. 2012. SNP's Word of the Day: Precariat. *Fashion*. January 13. http://www.fashionmagazine.com/blogs/society/2012/01/13/snps-word-of-the-day-precariat/.

PWAC [Professional Writers Association of Canada]. 2006. *Canadian Professional Writers Survey: A Profile of the Freelance Writing Sector in Canada*. Toronto. http://www.pwac.ca/files/PDF/PWACsurvey.pdf.

Ross, Andrew. 2000. The Mental Labor Problem. *Social Text* 18 (2): 1–31.

Ross, Andrew. 2001. No-Collar Labor in America's 'New Economy'. *Socialist Register* 37: 76–87.

Ross, Andrew. 2003. *No Collar: The Human Workplace and its Hidden Costs*. Philadelphia: Temple University Press.

Ross, Andrew. 2009. *Nice Work If You Can Get It: Life and Labor in Precarious Times*. New York: New York University Press.

Rossiter, Ned. 2006. *Organized Networks: Media Theory, Creative Labour, New Institutions*. Rotterdam: NAi Publishers.

Ryan, Bill. 1992. *Making Capital From Culture: The Corporate Form of Capitalist Cultural Production*. Berlin: Walter de Gruyter.

Scott, D.B. 2010. Rogers Syndication Practices Called Into Question by Canadian Writers Group. *Canadian Magazines*. October 2. http://canadianmags.blogspot.com/2010/10/rogers-syndiction-practices-called-into.html.

Semuels, Alana. 2008. Book Publisher Finds Teen Lit Adapts Well in Hollywood. *Los Angeles Times*, August 2. http://articles.latimes.com/2008/aug/02/business/fi-alloy2.

Smith, Chris and Alan McKinlay. 2009a. Creative Industries and Labour Process Analysis. In *Creative Labour: Working in the Creative Industries*, edited by Alan McKinlay and Chris Smith, 3–28. London: Palgrave Macmillan.

Smith, Chris and Alan McKinlay. 2009b. Creative Labour: Content, Contract and Control. *Creative Labour: Working in the Creative Industries*, edited by Alan McKinlay and Chris Smith, 29–50. London: Palgrave Macmillan.

Smythe, Ted Curtis. 1980. The Reporter, 1880–1900: Working Conditions and Their Influence on the News. *Journalism History* 7 (1): 1–10.

Standing, Guy. 2011. *The Precariat: The New Dangerous Class*. London: Bloomsbury.

Statistics Canada. 2012. Occupations in Art, Culture, Recreation and Sport. National Occupational Classification (NOC) 2011. http://www.statcan.gc.ca/cgi-bin/imdb/p3VD.pl?Function=getVDDetail&db=imdb&dis=2&adm=8&TVD=122372&CVD=122373&CPV=5&CST=01012011&MLV=4&CLV=1&CHVD=122374.

Story Board. 2010. Rogers Refuses to Remove Writer's Work From Yahoo. *Story Board*. November 30. http://www.thestoryboard.ca/?p=142.

Towse, Ruth. 2003. Copyright Policy, Cultural Policy and Support for Artists. In *The Economics of Copyright*, edited by Wendy J. Gordon and Richar Watt, 66–80. Cheltenham, UK: Edward Elgar.

Ursell, Gillian. 2000. Television Production: Issues of Exploitation, Commodification and Subjectivity in UK Television Labour Markets. *Media, Culture & Society* 22 (6): 805–825.

Vosko, Leah F. 2000. *Temporary Work: The Gendered Rise of a Precarious Employment Relationship*. Toronto: University of Toronto Press.

Vosko, Leah F. 2006. *Precarious Employment: Understanding Labour Market Insecurity in Canada*. Montreal and Kingston: McGill-Queen's University Press.

Vosko, Leah F. 2010. *Managing the Margins: Gender, Citizenship, and the International Regulation of Precarious Employment*. New York: Oxford University Press.

Wallenstein, Andrew. 2010. People Magazine iPad App Delayed by Paparazzi. *The Hollywood Reporter*. Accessed October 14, 2010. http://www.hollywoodreporter.com/news/exclusive-people-magazine-ipad-app-26788.

Walters, Emma, Christopher Warren, and Mike Dobbie. 2006. *The Changing Nature of Work: A Global Survey and Case Study of Atypical Work in the Media Industry.* Switzerland: International Federation of Journalists. http://www.ifj.org/pdfs/ILOReport070606.pdf.

Waring, Marilyn. 1999. *Counting For Nothing: What Men Value and What Women Are Worth*, 2nd ed. Toronto: University of Toronto Press.

Wayne, Mike. 2003. *Marxism and Media Studies: Key Concepts and Contemporary Trends.* London: Pluto.

Weeks, Kathi. 2005. The Refusal of Work as Demand and Perspective. In *The Philosophy of Antonio Negri: Resistance in Practice*, edited by T.S. Murphy and A-K. Mustapha, 109–135. London: Pluto Press.

Winseck, Dwayne. 2010. Financialization and the 'Crisis of the Media': The Rise and Fall of (Some) Media Conglomerates in Canada. *Canadian Journal of Communication* 35 (3): 365–393.

Wright, Erik Olin. 1978. Intellectuals and the Class Structure of Capitalist Society. In *Between Labor and Capital*, edited by Pat Walker, 191–211. Montreal: Black Rose Books.

Wright, Erik Olin. 1997. *Class Counts: Comparative Studies in Class Analysis.* New York: Cambridge University Press.

CHAPTER 4

Against Commodification: The University, Cognitive Capitalism and Emergent Technologies

Richard Hall and Bernd Stahl

1   Introduction

Emergent technologies, represented below in the four manifestations of affective computing, augmented reality, cloud-based systems, and human machine symbiosis, serve as examples of how technological innovation is commodified and fetishised within the University, and how it thereby enables capital to reproduce itself. Marx (2004, 493) understood and described this in terms of technology's place inside a historical totality: "Technology discloses man's mode of dealing with Nature, the process of production by which he sustains his life, and thereby also lays bare the mode of formation of his social relations, and of the mental conceptions that flow from them." Thus, emergent technologies that are produced at the limits of "man's modes" of recasting and reforming social relationships offer a critical insight into how capital co-opts research and development inside the University, in order to restructure higher education for value formation and accumulation (Hall 2014a).

The argument outlined herewith will develop this idea of co-option through an analysis of how technological developments are underpinned by commodification and fetishisation. A focus on emergent technologies enables an exploration of the possible ways in which technological innovation may affect power struggles and resistance in the academy, in particular where these are still being embedded in the academic practices of the University. However, they demonstrate the potential to change significantly *both* the ways in which education is conceived and delivered, *and* through which its institutions reproduce capitalist social relationships, in order to re-inscribe the history of labour-in-capitalism (Postone 1996, Winn 2014). Thus at the core of the argument lies an engagement with the mechanisms through which these emergent technologies reproduce hierarchical power inside the University. In analysing the interstices between commodity fetishism, emergent technologies and higher education, the relationships between emerging technologies, academic activism, and the possibilities for student/worker protests inside and beyond the academy will be addressed (Amsler and Neary 2012, Thorburn 2012).

The domain of the University is important here as a site of cognitive or knowledge capital. Under modes of cognitive capitalism (Dyer-Witheford 1999, Virno 2004), these social relationships are constructed out of the compression and enclosure of time and space themselves wrought by technologically-transformed capital (Lebowitz 2003, Marx 2004, Postone 2009). This process of transforming the University into an active site of struggle over the value produced by cognitive capitalism is accelerated through the commodification of emergent technologies and their subsequent fetishisation. This process amplifies how capital manoeuvres for power inside the academy, and promotes an instrumentalism of academic practice that is related through immaterial labour and class struggles to critiques of academic activism and cybernetic control of knowledge production (Holloway 2002, Tiqqun 2001, Virno 2004).

One result is that an engagement with autonomous Marxism's critique of power relations can enable an argument *for* the development of emergent technologies as spaces for dissent. Here the co-operative conquest of power might be developed as a step towards the abolition of power relations (Holloway 2002, Dyer-Witheford 2004), in order to re-inscribe a different set of possibilities upon the world, and to critique how *our* technologically-enabled global webs of social relations contribute to the dehumanisation of people, where they are treated as means in a production/consumption-process rather than as ends in themselves able to contribute to a common wealth. At issue is whether students and teachers are able to recapture the production and distribution of emergent technologies, in order to dissolve the symbolic power of the University into the actual, existing reality of protest and negation (Hall 2014b). Moreover, in Harvey's (2010, 46) terms, can a critique of emergent technologies enable those who work in higher education "to find an alternative value-form that will work in terms of the social reproduction of society in a different image"?

1.1 *A Note on Technology*

The historical development of technology inside capitalism has served as a means for reproducing biopower (Feenberg 1999, Foucault 1977, Noble 1998, Weber 1969), and for systematising the control of labour through socio-technical routines, procedures and cultures (Postone 1996). This enculturation is a key point for the Ethical Issues of Emerging ICT Applications (ETICA) project's scoping of the interplay between ethics and technology. The argument detailed below builds on some of the findings of this project. The project team argue that a technology is a high level system that affects the way humans interact with the world. This means that one technology in most cases can comprise numerous artefacts and be applied in many different situations. It needs to be associated with a vision that embodies specific views of humans and their role in the world.

IKONEN ET AL. 2010, 3–4

This role in the world is underpinned by a range of socio-technical characteristics. Thus, in an analysis of ambient technologies, these characteristics are revealed by the actors engaged with them as embeddedness, interconnectedness, invisibility, adaptivity, personalisation, and pervasiveness. As a result, the ETICA project defined a socio-technical view of the world, in which human enterprise, or labour, requires and desires technological support that is increasingly seamlessly connected, and which is increasingly adaptive, through the systemic integration of artifacts such as sensors, networks, algorithms and grids.

The emerging and everyday reality of adaptive technologies shaping and redefining the relationship between humanity, nature or the world and power emerges as a central thread inside a Marxist analysis of the relationships between machines and humanity. Marx (1993, 594) argued that technologies in the form of machines "are the products of human industry, natural materials transformed into instruments of the human domination of Nature, or of its activity in Nature...they are the materialised power of knowledge." This materialised power then reflects the relationships that exist between those who use those technologies to create, repurpose and reproduce society, and *both* those who innovate around those specific technologies *and* those who use them in their labour. For Feenberg (1999, 83) this means that "technology is a site of social struggle," through which hegemonic positions are developed, legitimated, reproduced and challenged, and he argues (1999, 87) for "[a] critical theory of technology [that] can uncover that horizon, demystify the illusion of technical necessity, and expose the relativity of the prevailing technical choices."

This view of technology as a critical site of struggle reflects the amplified alienation of labour inside the social factory, achieved through the symbiosis of human and machine (Negri 1989, Tronti 1973). As humanity is entwined and embedded with technological appendages, the possibilities for cybernetic control and the further alienation of subjectivity become more apparent (Miller Medina 2005, Tiqqun 2001). Harvey (1990) argues that such objectification is a function of the incorporation of the flesh and blood of humanity inside the machines of capital as one response of neoliberalism to the economic and political crises of the 1970s. In this view, capital actively sought new strategies that "put a premium on 'smart' and innovative entrepreneurialism" (Harvey 1990, 157). Such entrepreneurialism was in part realised in emergent technologies that incorporate humanity inside the reality of fixed capital (Davies 2014). This fusion of dead and living labour from which new forms of value can be extracted, is a critical way in which the circulation costs of capital can be reduced (Marx 2006). For Hardt and Negri (2000, 406) this is a deeply political antagonism for "machines and technologies are not neutral and independent entities. They are biopolitical tools deployed in specific regimes of production, which facilitate certain practices and prohibit others."

Here it is the productive power of socio-technical systems and the creation of cybernetic systems that enable humanity or its life-world to become increasingly machinic, so that humanity's everyday existence is incorporated inside the means of re-production of capital (Habermas 1987, Hardt and Negri 2000, Marx 2004, Tiqqun 2001). In Marxian terms this further objectifies social relationships as commodities from which value can be extracted through, for instance, the monitoring and harvesting of personal data, the enclosure and control of spaces or applications of consumption, the use of venture capitalism to support specific social networks, and the technological augmentation and capture of affectivity. This real subsumption of everyday activity then ensures that for the individual

> the creative power of his labour establishes itself as the power of capital, as an *alien power* confronting him...Thus all the progress of civilisation, or in other words every increase in the *powers of social production*...in the *productive powers of labour itself* – such as results from science, inventions, divisions and combinations of labour, improved means of communication, creation of the world market, machinery etc., enriches not the worker, but rather *capital*; hence only magnifies again the power dominating over labour.. the *objective power* standing over labour.
> MARX 1993, 307

Thus, technologies are deployed by capital as revolutionary forces that enable it to destroy "all the barriers which hem in the development of the forces of production, the expansion of needs, the all-sided development of production, and the exploitation and exchange of natural and mental forces" (Marx 1993, 409). This exploitation is constantly seeking to overcome the barriers that result from physical limitations, and increasingly rests on the fusion of the human as social being with technology, in order to create new commodities and forms of fetishisation. The University is one socio-technical space in which capital develops this process of overcoming (Hall 2014a, Winn 2014).

2   On the Commodification of Technologies, Immateriality
        and the University

The period of global austerity politics signalled by the collapse of Lehman
Brothers in 2008 has witnessed a neoliberal backlash against state-subsidized
public assets, as a form of economic shock therapy (Basu and Vasudevan 2011,
Lapavitsas 2012). In the United Kingdom, this process has led to the incorporation of higher education inside the market logic of capitalism, with a concomitant transfer of the idea of higher education as a public good to become one
where it is produced as an individual good to be serviced through private debt
on a North American model (Hall 2014a, McGettigan 2013). This subsumption
of the life of the University inside the market reflects the systemic logic of capital, which aims to totalise itself (Hardt and Negri 2000). As Meiksins Wood
(1997, 1) noted

> we're living in a moment when, for the first time, capitalism has become
> a truly universal system.... Capitalism is universal also in the sense that its
> logic – the logic of accumulation, commodification, profit-maximisation,
> competition – has penetrated almost every aspect of human life and
> nature itself.

One of the ramifications of this process for academics and students is the commodification of their scholarly work, in terms of courses, technologies, knowl-
edges and cultural assets (Ball 2012, Hall 2013). Labour inside the University is
increasingly: driven by efficiency; underpinned by the dictates of key information sets and impact measures, public/private partnerships, knowledge transfer
and external income generation; and disciplined by the logic that if a producer
of educational goods is inefficient it will suffer in the market (McGettigan 2013,
Winn 2014). Thus, higher education has become a site of marketisation in which
knowledge-work as the labour of an individual academic is being brought into
direct competition with that of other academics, across societies and inside
new partnerships between state assets and private corporations.

    Competition between individual academics and these new associations of
which they form a part then forms a way of structuring socially the allocation/
abundance of relevant, academic labour (Marx 2004). The incorporation of
academic work inside the market catalyses the subsequent creation of academic
use-values that can be exchanged, and scholarship that can be commodified.
The nature of exchange, and the attempt to extract surplus value from a co-
opted academic process, means that hierarchical power relations developed
inside universities are re-produced as the relation between those things that

can actually be exchanged. As a result, academic labour is directly subsumed under this drive to extract surplus value (Clarke 1994, Marx 2004).

Knowledge work inside the University is particularly valuable as a result of the amount of socially-necessary labour-time embedded in its products. Marx highlighted that the magnitude of the value of labour, determined by the labour-time socially necessary to produce a specific commodity, is defined as "the labour-time required to produce any use-value under the conditions of production normal for a given society and with the average degree of skill and intensity of labour prevalent in that society" (Marx 2004, 129). Inside higher education, the specialisation of the work and the skill-levels required to innovate promise high rates of surplus value extraction, especially where technological research and development catalyses efficiencies in production and a reduced circulation time for specific capitals. This specialisation and the promise of increased rates of relative surplus value extraction fuels the employability agendas of government educational departments for whom the skills developed at University are framed increasingly by the needs of the labour market (Ball 2012, Jappe 2014), which itself forms a central mechanism for regulating academic labour (Marx 2006).

As technologies inside capitalism are used to deliver systemic efficiency and further valorise value, it becomes difficult to sustain a positivist argument for the emancipatory potential of enhanced technological skills. The logic of technological innovation and deployment is for productivity gains or outsourcing, or for workplace monitoring and surveillance alongside labour management and stratification, or to catalyse the creation of value by opening up/harnessing new markets (Lebowitz 2003, Marx 2004). In the short-term, technological innovation gives capital a high marginal productivity underpinned by and underpinning high levels of demand from both public and private sectors. However, over time "moral depreciation" affects the gains made by technological innovation:

> in addition to the material wear and tear, a machine also undergoes, what we may call a moral depreciation. It loses exchange-value, either by machines of the same sort being produced cheaper than it, or by better machines entering into competition with it. In both cases, be the machine ever so young and full of life, its value is no longer determined by the labour actually materialised in it, but by the labour-time requisite to reproduce either it or the better machine. It has, therefore, lost value more or less. The shorter the period taken to reproduce its total value, the less is the danger of moral depreciation; and the longer the working-day, the shorter is that period. When machinery is first introduced into an industry, new

methods of reproducing it more cheaply follow blow upon blow, and so do improvements, that not only affect individual parts and details of the machine, but its entire build. It is, therefore, in the early days of the life of machinery that this special incentive to the prolongation of the working-day makes itself felt most acutely.

MARX 2004, 528

As a result, the drive under the treadmill logic of competition becomes to deliver constant innovation across a whole socio-technical system, in order to maintain or increase the rate of extraction of relative surplus value, and to tear down the barriers of under-consumption. This has ramifications for academic labour as Newfield (2010, 13) highlights, with an increasing proletarianisation of scholarly work under three types of labour. The first type relates to "commodity skills," which are "readily obtained" and whose possessors are inter-changeable, for instance, back-office or help-desk workers. The second type incorporates those with "leveraged skills," which require advanced education and which offer clear added-value to the University, and yet which are pos-sessed by labour in many universities, for instance, computer programmers or network administrators. The third type includes those with "proprietary skills," defined as "the company-specific talents around which an organization builds a business." University management cultivate and commodify only those with the skills to enhance propriety knowledge, from which rents or profits can be extracted (Hall 2014a).

The first two types of labour noted above can be proletarianised or out-sourced because of the low levels of socially-necessary labour time embedded in the value of their work. However, as proprietary skills are enclosed the com-petitive nature of marketised academic labour ensures that such work becomes increasingly precarious (Neilson and Rossiter 2008, Pusey and Sealey-Huggins 2013). This is because the socially necessary character of the labour-power expended in producing a particular commodity or innovation or technology is diminished over-time and this reduces its value in the market. As a result a persistent demand to innovate becomes essential inside the system. Thus, it is around the holders and management of these proprietary or creative skills, which can be exchanged, where academic work that is congealed in the form of emergent technologies tends to become fetishised in its social form as value (Jappe 2014, Marx 1993).

Fetishisation describes how, in a commodity producing society, the relation-ships that exist amongst producers, mediated socially in the market, take on the form of a "social relation between the products of labour" (Marx 2004, 164). This means that the exchange value of a specific commodity, which is in reality an expression of socially-necessary labour time, appears to be an inherent property of the commodity, as revealed in its market price. In part this is because commodity producing labour does not appear to be directly social as commodities are produced by independent individuals. As a result, labour only appears to be socially-necessary in the process of exchange, rather than in the processes of production and this underpins a reality of alienation.

> [T]he result of the process of production and realization is, above all, the reproduction and new production of the *relation of capital and labour itself*, of *capitalist and worker*. This social relation, production relation, appears in fact as an even more important result of the process than its material results. And more particularly, within this process the worker produces himself as labour capacity, as well as the capital confronting him, while at the same time the capitalist produces himself as capital as well as the living labour capacity confronting him. Each reproduces itself, by reproducing its other, its negation. The capitalist produces labour as alien; labour produces the product as alien.
>
> MARX 1993, 458

The product or commodity has destroyed part of the living labour of the individual labourer and is alienated from her as a fetishised form of value through the process of exchange. Inside the University, where the struggle between labour and capital lies in the creation and commodification of cognitive capital, the notion of fetishism needs to be re-worked and re-analysed because the production and circulation processes are "immaterial" (Hall 2014b, Žižek 2009). For Feenberg (1999, viii) this is the reality of technological essentialism, where "technology reduces everything to functions and raw materials," with the result that individual emotions and affects, cultural cues and mores, and the construction of the relations between individuals "are themselves the very material of our everyday exploitation" (Žižek 2009, 139). From this process, two elements emerge as central in understanding how knowledge work or cognitive capital or the information society becomes fetishised. Firstly, capital finds mechanisms or technologies that enable it to enclose and commodify an increasingly fluid and identity-driven set of social relations, which can form the basis of further exchange (Virno 2001, Virno and Hardt 1996), catalysed by work inside the University and based on mutations of human subjectivity (Berardi 2009, Vercellone 2007). Secondly, capital commodifies and extracts value from everyday experiences and relationships, in order to reduce the unproductive circulation time of capital, and thereby increase the rate of profit and relative surplus value (Jappe 2014, Marx 2006).

In this process of fetishisation, social relations are increasingly structured by technically-mediated organisations, like the University, which then re-inscribe anew socio-political hierarchies that are increasingly technological, coercive and exploitative (Foucault 1977). In part this alienates and separates individuals within a society through an exclusive division of labour (Bologna 2013, Marx 2004). Moreover, as Marx highlights (1993), the development of such technologies that subsume all of human life under capital's logic strengthens the idea that capitalist relations are natural and purely technical. However, this naturalisation process reveals the construction of knowledge through the reproduction of the general intellect, or knowledge as society's main productive force (Marx 1993). On the one hand, capital uses this process to subsume and alienate social relationships further as commodities, in particular through the control of communication and the re-purposing of information (Dyer-Witheford 1999, Negri 1989). On the other hand, the reproduction of the general intellect as mass intellectuality becomes the actual foundation of subversion-through-praxis (Hall 2014a, Neary and Hagyard 2010, Tomba and Bellofiore 2014 Virno 2001).

In part these processes of the production, distribution and consumption of mass intellectuality are amplified by the extreme socialisation of web-based technologies and the ways in which emergent technologies are socialised. Therefore, the research and development of emergent technologies inside the University is a critical site of struggle through which a critical theory of socio-technology and cognitive capitalism might be developed, and against which academic activism might be revealed. For Marx (2004) understanding socio-technical innovation and transformation was important because it highlighted the mechanics of the relationships between labour and capital.

> By means of machinery, chemical processes and other methods, [capital] is continually transforming not only the technical basis of production but also the functions of the worker and the social combinations of the labour process. At the same time, it thereby also revolutionizes the division of labour within society, and incessantly throws masses of capital and of workers from one branch of production to another.
>
> MARX 2004, 617

3 Emergent Technologies and Cognitive Capitalism

The influence of neoliberal ideology on higher education is being increasingly documented and analysed (Ball 2012, McGettigan 2013). There is a pervasive narrative that sees education as primarily concerned with developing students' employability, where science and technology form primary means of fostering economic growth, and where technologies underpin discourses related to value-for-money, commercial efficiency and business process re-engineering. These ideas can be found in high level policy documents such as the European Vision 2020 (European Commission (EC) 2014a) or the Higher Education Funding Council for England's support for technology-enhanced learning (HEFCE 2014), and in the funding protocols for innovation programmes (EC 2014b, Hall 2013). These protocols then shape and legitimise the spaces in which individual universities develop projects, mission statements or strategies, and they connect educational innovation to fiscal "realities."

This ideological positioning is reflected through funding strategies, which focus on innovation and research in the natural sciences and technology, with a concomitant diminishing flow of resources of social sciences and humanities. The use of technology within education amplifies this ideological turn, and further catalyses the commodification and fetishisation of educational practices and institutions (Dyer-Witheford and de Peuter 2009, Feenberg 1999, Hall 2014b), alongside their enclosure (Hall 2013). This thereby undermines education's moral legitimacy (Stahl 2006). At issue here then is to move this argument beyond the critique of established and embedded technologies inside the University, in order to analyse how emergent technologies might impact the forms and content of higher education and thereby enable capitalist social relations to be re-produced (Wendling 2009).

Critical in this process is the organisation, disciplining and exploitation of an increasingly immaterial workforce, through the use of emergent technologies that are inserted into the everyday activities and life-worlds of living human subjects (Davies 2014, Dyer-Witheford 1999, Habermas 1987, Wendling 2009), and which are incubated inside universities as centers of research and development. This is a relentless dynamic, centered on capitalism's constant revolutionizing of the means of production, in order that capital can drive "beyond every spatial barrier...[and the ability to enhance] the creation of the physical conditions of exchange – of the means of communication and transport – the annihilation of space by time – becomes an extraordinary necessity for it" (Marx 1993, 524). In reducing the time of production and circulation, technology is implicated in a totalizing re-production of social relations, which are in constant flux and motion (Postone 2009).

However, in this war on time and production/circulation costs, the fusion of human and machine forms a new front in the use of the machine as a weapon in the struggle of capital against labour. Research, development and implementation inside the University are sites of alienation, and therefore form spaces from which negation and dissent might spring. In developing this position, an analysis of four interconnected examples of emergent technologies enable a clearer understanding of likely future developments to emerge. In the following sub-sections the definition of emergent technologies is outlined alongside a justification for the choice of the four technologies that are discussed in more depth, with a view to understanding their role in future higher education. The technologies in question are: affective computing; virtual and augmented reality; cloud computing; and human-machine symbiosis.

3.1   *Emergent Technologies*

The present discussion explores how emergent technologies that have been identified through horizon-scanning might be expected to influence higher education and contribute to the conceptual issues of fetishisation, commodification and immateriality. The basis on which to discuss such emergent technologies raises issues that are related to historical uncertainties in the future development of capitalism and the fundamental impossibility of predicting the nature and use of those technologies. Despite these future unknowns, humans have developed mechanisms for developing expectations and using these to make decisions that shape the future. One established mechanism in academia is the use of foresight research (Cuhls 2003), which does not claim to know the future but develops visions of possible futures that allow decision-makers to work towards possibilities that are deemed desirable. The argument developed herewith uses this logic and draws on existing research on future and emergent ICTs, which it then uses to explore the possible roles of such technologies in higher education.

The argument draws on the findings of the ETICA project (Ikonen et al. 2010) to clarify the roles that emergent technologies can play in higher education. The ETICA project was a European-funded research project, which ran from 2009–2011, and that could be characterised as a foresight project. It aimed to identify emerging technologies with a view to analyze their ethical consequences and thereby consider governance and policy implications. ETICA defined emergent technologies as those that are likely to change significantly the ways in which humans interact with the world in the near future of 10 to 15 years. These technologies are characterized by the fact that they are subject to intensive research and development, which allows a reasonable prediction of their future shape. It is important to note that whilst they are described as emergent, this does not affect their current status. Some of these emergent technologies are already established, for instance cloud computing, but they are described as emergent because there are significant research and development activities currently going on that are expected to change their shape and possible applications, and thus their socio-political consequences.

The ETICA project did not focus on applications of technology, either in higher education or in any other field, and the project did not apply a specifically Marxist viewpoint. The argument detailed herewith does not claim to represent ETICA in any way, nor does it reflect the position of the ETICA consortium. However, an analysis of the outcomes of first stage of the ETICA project enables the identification of webs of emerging technologies that are particularly pertinent for higher education. Engagement with four interconnected technologies serves as a point of departure for a demonstration of the commodification and fetishisation of the social relations and identities that emerge from inside the University and that underpin the development of mass intellectuality. These technologies are: affective computing; augmented reality; cloud-based systems; and human machine symbiosis.

These four technologies were chosen out of the 11 technologies identified by the ETICA project because they enable an interpretation of early technological adoption inside higher education, and their status as emergent technologies means that they are likely to become even more influential through the premium placed on high-technology (Gartner 2011). Thus, they lend themselves to an analysis of how the University is impacted by emergent technology. They represent a spectrum of technologies that cover the issues discussed here and which then exemplify the re-production of socio-technical systems inside the University, as well as the potential to resist prevailing ideological developments. However, each of the four interacts with at least one of the others, and this offers the possibility that combinations of innovation might impact the relationships that exist between capital and labour inside higher education. Each of the four technologies are discussed in a separate sub-section which defines them, and which then discusses expected uses in higher education, and how utility relates to questions of ideology, fetishisation, commodification and immateriality. Pathways towards resistance, exemplified by these technologies, are then suggested.

3.2   *Affective Computing*

The technology: affective computing, sometimes also called emotional computing, aims to develop artefacts that can perceive, express and model human emotions. Interest in the computational aspects of affects or emotions developed inside research laboratories in the last decade of the 20th century, paralleled by the neoliberal focus on enterprise technologies that could be deployed as innovations in the social factory. A critical development was the increased capabilities of computers to model emotions (Cowie 2005), and to work for embedding emotionality into socio-technical systems that in turn enable capital to use cognition or immateriality to reproduce itself. Such re-production is witnessed in the widening of the definition of such technologies to include emotion-processing or human behavioral modeling.

Thus, this type of research underpins the creation of more responsive applications where human and computers interact, in order to harness the use of emotions in decision-making through data collection for profiling, and brain imaging tools and sensors for the detection of emotions. Whilst Robinson and el Kaliouby's (2009) research discusses a number of application areas related to social inclusion and modeling social cognition, it is clear that affective computing enables the commodification of social cognition. For instance, it is used: in modeling products related to the management of social-emotional intelligence by agents and robots (Tao and Tan 2005); in developing affective games that react to a player's emotional state and enabling the game to deliver content at the most appropriate moment (Sykes and Brown 2003); and generating the ability to communicate the affective state of a game player to third parties (Hudlicka 2009).

For capital, capturing and mining this type of activity is an important field of innovation and value extraction, because "data suggest that less than 10% of human life is completely unemotional. The rest involves emotion of some sort" (Cowie 2005). Thus, capturing emotionality or affect through technology focuses upon enhancing "the quality of human-computer communication and improving the intelligence of the computer" (Tao and Tan 2005, 981). As emotion pervades human interaction, sensitivity to emotions becomes fundamental to communicative action (Habermas 1987). As a result, affective computing influences the ways in which humans interact with the world as it is mediated through feelings and the physical changes associated with them, alongside shifts in perception, judgments, and actions (Brook 2009).

Educational application: the ability to understand and react to the emotional states of users is envisaged through innovations in types of e-teaching related to games-based learning and virtual world simulations, where sensing the learner's mood allows the customization of learning content and presentation (Porto Interactive Center 2014, xDelia 2012). Driven by research and development in affective computing, cognitive and behavioral psychology are further commodified inside capital, in-part through the partnerships between universities and commerce, as affective computing drives the assumption that human emotions are capable of being measured, recognised, classified, produced and valorised (Massachusetts Institute of Technology (MIT) Media Lab 2012). An important aspect of this emergent technology is that there is a direct link between emotions and external actions like consumption.

Similarly an emotional awareness would allow better responses from teachers who are then able to monitor their own and students' emotional states, in order to gather mutual feedback on the success of teaching sessions. Thus, the MIT Media Lab (2014) focuses upon "computing that relates to, arises from, or deliberately influences emotion or other affective phenomena." The growing focus on learning analytics as a means of monitoring and surveillance learning outcomes, in order to commodify them, also connects cognitive and emotional practices and outcomes (Educause 2014), especially where they are connected to the on-going fetishisation of learning delivery through mobile devices (Hall 2013).

The potentially positive outcomes of the use of affective computing in higher education, in particular in work-based and placement learning, and related to simulations, can be contrasted with less beneficial ones, relating to increased manipulation and control. Personal behaviours and characteristics can be more easily inscribed inside teaching programmes by rewarding particular reactions to managed interventions. This is exacerbated by the fact that the use of such technologies in education would likely be designed by private corporations for profit or through rents emerging from application-based interventions. These interventions are likely to be translated into marketised solutions, which in-turn enable students to be more successfully oriented towards employability, rather than a critical questioning of the discourses around the political role of the University.

Resistance: a critical space for resistance related to affective computing is through re-humanisation and the co-operative development of solutions to problems related to gaming, simulations or work-based learning, and the outright refusal to commodify virtual interactions (Hall 2014b). In fact, affective computing offers a clear space for analysing socio-technical systems that are ethically problematic, as users are able to discern the possibility of being manipulated. Moreover, there is good reason to believe that where scholars resist the appearance of emotions in educational machinery, in-part because such emotions appear to be false in the sense that they are fundamentally different from human emotions, they are able to develop an ethical digital literacy. In particular this relies upon the engagement of mutual networks of scholarly critique, in order to connect real-world emotionality to shared problem-solving (Hall 2014a). The hope is that this will overcome the threat of individuated, false or augmented affects, which separate users from each other and enable cognitive capitalism to maintain its power relationships inside the University, for example through the sousveillance (Ganascia 2010) of teachers by students or of management by staff.

3.3   *Virtual and Augmented Reality*

The technology: virtual or augmented reality is closely related to affective computing, It developed from Heilig's (1962) Sensorama Simulator that was designed to mitigate against the risks that came with hazardous jobs by simulating the environments in which capital needed labour to be trained. The history of the development of virtual and augmented reality deeply connects innovation inside the University with commercial enterprise. Thus, applications like Lanier's VPL DataGlove demonstrated that these technologies could be extended beyond head-worn displays to include handheld and LCD displays, and into smart-phones whose applications extend the marketisation of everyday experience, through the enclosure of content and concomitant subscription or rental. This content is then further commodified as virtual information is projected onto the augmented objects or as augmented information is projected onto the real life contexts (Zhou et al 2008).

Advanced computer hardware enables virtual and augmented reality applications to become more immersive and integrated into daily life. Thus, the technology is extendable into the manufacture and repair of complex machinery, in reducing the costs of maintaining fixed labour, alongside its potential to annotate objects and environments, and further fetishises the user's experiences of her life-world and her very identity. Capital uses these techniques to influence the behaviour, interpersonal communication and cognition of labour, and also to enhance the colonisation and enclosure of virtual space, meaning that virtual identities, like avatars, are individuated and commodified beyond the social relationships from which they spring. Thus, virtual objects convey information that enables the real subsumption of labour in its performance of real-world tasks. By supplementing an everyday reality with virtual objects or data the immaterial labourer is able to perceive the environment more comprehensively than with her own senses. Consequently the process of immersion enables the enhancement of labour's perception of and interaction with the real world by capturing and harnessing multiple sensorial channels (Cline 2005). This enables capital to re-produce itself in new forms and through the production of new services that move beyond the barriers of under-consumption.

Educational applications: the use of virtual and augmented reality technologies in higher education is well advanced, and focused on training, discover-based learning, modelling, gaming and extending virtual resources. It has historical links with defense and military training, and with extending opportunities for marketing (Hamilton 2014), and mobile learning (Joint Information Systems Committee (JISC) 2012). For instance, Second Life (Dyer-Witheford and de Peuter 2009) serves as a platform to provide material and interactions inside scholarly communities, and for experimenting with simulations, in-part as a form of play. Universities have used this platform to provide specific training on topics that require more than a textual interface, for instance in the management of schizophrenia or in health sciences where views of bodies or organs may be required, as well as in interacting with remote students through the construction of virtual campuses. While Second Life may be the most prominent example of virtual environments, there is a broader move towards such technologies in higher education (Human Interface Technology Laboratory New Zealand (HIT Lab NZ) 2014), and to some degree Learning Management Systems like Blackboard increasingly seek to incorporate aspects of augmentation and immersion into their virtual environments.

Resistance: augmentation enables the creation of spaces from which rents can be extracted by private corporations operating inside education through in-world or application-based innovation, as a form of entrepreneurialism (Davies 2014). This demonstrates the co-opted inter-relationships between emerging technologies, the labour-in-capitalism and higher education (Dyer-Witheford and de Peuter 2009, Wendling 2009). Virtualisation catalyses significant discussion inside universities and from higher education policy-makers about whether external providers should host educational activities and extract rents as a form of accumulation. This is partly driven by practical considerations such as intellectual property and the security of teaching material in outsourced environments. However, scholarly resistance focuses upon technical and usability issues, alongside the acceptability of engaging in the further enclosure of virtualised space through augmentation technologies (Wake and Stahl 2010). At issue in the educational resistance to augmented technologies is the ways in which scholars are actively encouraged to produce and share open curricula and artifacts in ways that reveal humanising engagements that do not form new commodities, but help maintain a diversity of expertise across communities. Thus, in these mutual spaces, the relevance of marginal developments like application-based, locative and augmented reality services might be questioned through consensus, and related to social need and issues of privacy and identity.

3.4   Cloud Computing

The technology: increasingly the innovative services addressed by affective computing or virtual and augmented reality, are being managed through cloud computing, which promises to deliver computing resources to different locations through globalised circulation networks. It originated with Licklider's work on

ARPANET (Ikonen et al. 2010). Alongside the generation of value for the military, its development was predicated upon its value as a public utility like water or electricity. This became increasingly possible via the growth in bandwidth in the 1990s. As a direct result, its development was able to facilitate remote working, and the separation and surveillance of proletarianised work at a distance from any formal, Taylorised work setting, enabling capital to distribute available commodity and leveraged skills amongst low-wage societies through outsourcing (Newfield 2010). The evolution of cloud computing through phases of grid and utility computing, application service provision, and Software as a Service (Dikaiakos et al. 2009), enables the dynamics of cognitive labour to pervade the social factory and thereby amplify immateriality on a global scale (Hardt and Negri 2000, Virno 2004).

In particular, cloud computing enables capital *both* to extract value from social networks and personal interconnections through the corporate control of systems, networks and data, *and* to reduce the circulation costs of productive capital through scalable and elastic IT-enabled capabilities that are delivered as a service from low wage circuits into those spaces from where high value can be extracted (Marx 2006). As enterprises seek to consume their IT services in the most cost-effective way, interest has grown in drawing a broad range of services, for example, computational power, storage and business applications, from the "cloud" rather than from on-premises equipment. This outsourced approach is focused on reducing the costs of distribution of commodities and labour.

Where cloud services are used to store very personal data, such as photos and videos, data mining and tagging are enmeshed with capitalist accumulation through rental costs, and targeted marketing. In some cases this enables smart consumption, for instance through the data-driven connection between hardware like RFID tags and smart-phones, localisation services, and cloud-based services like customer relationship management systems and payment service providers (The Think-Trust project 2010). It also enables the commodification of data related to medical records between business and insurance partners (Andriole and Khorasani 2010), thereby supporting the further incorporation of bio-power into healthcare. Ease of use of cloud services is emphasized with very fast, optimized connections and enforced terms of service or agreements through which users give away ownership of personal data (Fuchs 2010). The interconnections generated by shared data in these networks are very dynamic and enable the consumers of these services to produce and consume a nomadic lifestyle that is bound less by space than by time. In fact, the permanent immateriality of these services forms an attempt by capital to annihilate space by time.

Educational applications: cloud computing is a technology that is already used in higher education, in particular to share services, like email and back-end information management, and for research processes or data storage (Gartner 2013). It is particularly widespread with regards to social networks and other social media, which tend to be in profit-oriented and which then further reify and objectify human relationships. This is realised in the discourses around words like "follower" and "friend." Inside Universities, attempts are also being made to commodify and sell the idea of cloud computing in terms of green IT or sustainability, despite the lack of evidence that the cloud is "greener," and industry has wrapped itself around this concept as a space for further service-led innovation (Hall and Winn 2011).

A related question is how cloud computing can affect the way in which higher education is structured and organised, and in particular how Universities redesign their teaching design and delivery around the cloud (Das 2012) and services like library provision (Sanchati and Kulkarni 2011). In the United Kingdom there is a debate about the use of technology to decrease the price of education and cloud computing is perceived to be one means by which services can be shared and thus costs can be reduced. This is purely oriented towards the financial cost of education through labour costs, and redesigning the labour market around commodified services (Hall 2014a, Wendling 2009), and does not consider the ways in which pedagogic considerations impact technological deployment.

Resistance: cloud computing highlights the complex entanglements of technology, the social relationships that are revealed in organisational structures, and politics. On the one hand one can see examples of resistance to the extraction of rents and value from the implementation of cloud technologies that are directed at business process re-engineering. This is a form of state-subsidized privatization, and highlights concerns about the continuation and provision of services to students through outsourcing and sharing. This has concomitant data and privacy issues, as well as opening-up educational data for mining by transnational venture capitalists. Such transnational networks also enable governments to use the logic of homeland security to monitor data (Walden 2011).

However, social media also allow the circumvention of control and thereby offer new avenues for subversive collaboration against and resistance to managerial agendas (Thorburn 2012). These uses of cloud computing lead to a blurring of boundaries and higher education institutions which are driven by financial interests and subsequently find it increasingly difficult to legitimise the boundaries between inside and outside the University. This is a problem for capital because its structures cannot control the activities of their employees and students in networks beyond the University, and these can be co-opted to open-up cracks in intellectual property and the production of social relationships for other, mutual interests (Amsler and Neary 2012, Winn 2014). The implementation of cloud technologies thereby contain the seeds of resistance towards the very enclosing motives that promote it.

3.5   *Human-Machine Symbiosis*
The technology: the apogee of this attempt to reduce the costs associated with and emerging from the processes of exchange and the extraction of relative surplus value, and capital's desire to reduce socially-necessary labour time, is human-machine symbiosis or human augmentation. This is a technology in which the connections between affective and augmented technologies for the production of socially-defined, identity-driven commodities, and their development, monitoring and distribution through cloud-based tools are revealed. What is witnessed is the apotheosis of the fetishised form of the human as optimised labour-power; of the human as machine designed, augmented and alienated for the valorisation of value (Marx 1993).

Human-machine symbiosis was originally envisaged by Licklider (1960, 1) as a means by which more efficient co-operative action could be catalysed, through a "very close coupling" between human and machine, in order to increase the efficiency of "formulative thinking" and the control of "complex situations without inflexible dependence on predetermined programs." Licklider (1960, 1) hoped that "the symbiotic partnership will perform intellectual operations much more effectively than man alone can perform them." The premise was that human intellect could be augmented, and that as a result human beings would be able to perform tasks or labour that was beyond their ordinary physical limitations.

This approach led to the development of the mouse, to innovations in human-computer interaction, interactive computing, hypermedia, and video-conferencing, as mediums that enhance the efficiency and value of labour and reduce the circulation time of commodities (Ikonen et al. 2010). For Roy (2004) this meant that human-machine symbiosis could be understood as a technology that enhances and improves human potential where human capacities are restricted. He views the technological machine as an extension of the human, and such symbiosis emerges through wearable technologies, assistive technologies or neural implants (Ikonen et al. 2010).

Pace Marx (1993, 2004), this is one of the logical outcomes of capital's need to enforce co-operation in industrialised labour. This co-operation is dissolved into the fabric of society through: the development of personal consoles; the affective desires integrated into mobile and personal technologies; and the integration of machinery into the labourer's body as an extension of her labour-power. As Greef et al (2007, 1) argue in relation to augmented cognition, the aim is "the creation of adaptive human-machine collaboration that continually optimises performance of the human-machine system." This connects to Marx's (1993) view of the incorporation of labour inside the machinery of capitalist re-production.

> In machinery, objectified labour confronts living labour within the labour process itself as the power which rules it; a power which, as the appropriation of living labour, is the form of capital...The development of the means of labour into machinery is not an accidental moment of capital, but is rather the historical reshaping of the traditional, inherited means of labour into a form adequate to capital. The accumulation of knowledge and of skill, of the general productive forces of the social brain, is thus absorbed into capital, as opposed to labour, and hence appears as an attribute of capital.
>
> MARX 1993, 694–695

Human-machine symbiosis has now permeated society to an extent where technology appears as a fetish or veil, as the social brain appears to be a natural well-spring from capitalism's forces of production, constructed through emergent technologies. Thus, consumers have become dependent and reliant to a large extent on their personal technology, as it extends their role or identity in the social factory. This affects how labour is enabled to access information, to conduct business, and to communicate globally. However, although such symbiosis enables labour *both* to perform more complex computations *and* to reduce the costs of circulation of commodities as information or communication, the impact of moral degradation means that there is a persistent need to innovate.

Educational applications: possible applications relate to the provision of immediate and personalised feedback, as is seen in the work being carried out by the MIT Media Lab (2014), which is designing, developing and evaluating new human machine interfaces that can be applied in haptic user interfaces related to the sense of touch. The lab aims to incorporate psychophysics, biomechanics and neurology in its development of smart and effective haptic interfaces and devices. Elsewhere, the MIT 10x program (2014) continually evaluates a cross-section of applications including aspects of memory, in order to enhance and expand human cognitive abilities. This focuses upon the radical re-structuring of the practices that underpin knowledge work both inside the University and through knowledge exchange into the social factory. Such symbiosis demonstrates a constant striving to commodify and re-produce human experience beyond the limits of human capabilities, as they are organised inside capitalism.

This augmentation of cognitive processing power underpins innovation in brain-machine interfaces, an emerging neuro-technology that translates brain activity into command signals for external devices. Research on these interfaces began in the 1970s at the University of California Los Angeles, with the establishment of a direct communication pathway between the brain and specific devices to be controlled. Whilst these technologies are mainly being developed for medical reasons (Berger 2007, Gasson and Warwick, K, 2007) they also enable different forms of immaterial labour to be imagined inside the University, and as a direct result everyday experience is co-opted for the extraction of surplus value by corporations. This is seen in Human-Systems Integration for Optimal Decision Making, which augments labour in dynamic and complex environments like air traffic control and nurse training (Ikonen et al. 2010). Not only does research inside the University catalyse these innovations in immateriality, but those same University contexts provide work-based spaces in which they can be trialled and then embedded across society.

Thus, there is a focus inside the range of higher education contexts on the amplification of human-systems integration, in order to consider socio-technical issues related to personnel, training, system safety, and health hazards, in the design of the symbiotic technologies that a targeted audience will use. For example, the National ICT Australia projects (NICTA 2014) are modelling human-systems integration to support optimal decision-making in a range of environments. This demonstrates how research that is generated inside the University enables integrated processes and tools to be developed and tested, in order that they revolutionise capitalist work and enable the re-production of capitalist social relations in the spaces beyond higher education. Thus, whilst these projects initially support people's cognitive work-based learning in health and air traffic management environments, the specific intention is to extend this immaterial work to other domains, through the integration of learning and training, people, technologies and the environments in which they work.

Resistance: human-machine symbiosis is a technology that carries the possibility of radical resistance to the incorporation of humanity inside the means of re-production on capitalist social relations, in particular through its impact on what human beings perceive as natural (Miller Medina 2005, Wendling 2009). This is amplified as close relationships between humans and technology are depicted as problematic and undesirable, in particular where a process of dehumanisation is uncovered as labour-power is continually optimised through upgrades. This is a refusal to accept humanity as machine designed, augmented and alienated for the valorisation of value (Hall 2014a, Jappe 2014, Winn 2014). These uses of ICT are therefore be likely to encounter dissent inside higher education environments where one of the traditional aims is that of the development of autonomous individuals, rather than commodified individuality, an aim which is contradicted in the redevelopment of the technology itself.

3.6   Summary: Emergent Technologies in Higher Education

The innovations located in these four emergent technologies enable cognitive labourers to transcend physical barriers through virtual reality, and to consume their educational life-world in new ways. As those experiences are produced and commodified both globally and yet on an individual level, capital is able to capture and harness everyday experiences as commodities for rent, value extraction and profit (Clarke 1994, Marx 2004), and for the subsequent re-production of itself through the development of proprietary skills. The very fact of capital's enclosure of the human body inside its machinery of exploitation is catalysed by research inside the University. However, it is also played out in: the deployment of marketised and cloud-based learning environments and educational services; the application of virtualisation and augmentation to education as a means of maintaining hegemonies; in work-based learning and placement experiences; and through the insertion of emergent machinery directly into the life-world of labour. This means that labour's very educational life-world is a site of surplus value creation and extraction, and accumulation through commodification and rent. As Meiksins-Wood (1997) identified, there is no outside of this system of alienation.

However, for Postone (1996) it is the historic role of labour-in-capitalism that contains revolutionary potential, precisely because its increasing exploitation, alienation and dehumanising mechanisation is persistently revealed in its everyday practices. As education becomes a core site for the re-production of hegemonic discourses and power relationships, this revelation of commodification that is amplified through technological innovation precedes reflexivity and praxis from inside the University. The possibility remains that labour will realise the increasing proletarianisation of its educational practices. Thus, it is possible to sketch and support a flowering of dissent based on the autonomous utilisation of those same emergent hardware, software and networks that are used to immiserate (Colman 2012, Dyer-Witheford 1999, Newfield 2010, Thorburn 2012). At issue here is how the production of emerging technologies inside the University might affect academic labour as a form of activism.

4   For Exodus and the Courage of Academic Activism

Holloway (2002) argues that we deceive ourselves if we believe that the structures which exist in order to reproduce capitalist social relations can be used as
a means to overcome its alienating organisation of work. Whilst he makes this
point for the structure of the democratic state as a symbol of failed revolutionary hope, his point might equally be made about the University.

> In reality, what the state [University] does is limited and shaped by the
> fact that it exists as just one node in a web of social relations. Crucially,
> this web of social relations centres on the way in which work is organised.
> The fact that work is organised on a capitalist basis means that what the
> state [University] does and can do is limited and shaped by the need to
> maintain the system of capitalist organisation of which it is a part.
>   HOLLOWAY 2002, 6

Thus, any institution's room for manoeuvre is constricted by transnational
global capital, and in particular by the compression and enclosure of time and
space wrought by technologically-transformed, finance capital (Ball 2012,
Davies 2014). In this view, working to take control of an institution crushes the
transformatory intent of those who would fight against capitalism, because
this transformation is always about limited manoeuvring for power. In Virno's
(n.d.) terms this is based on "weak thought," or a political philosophy that "was
developed by philosophers with theories that offer an ideology of the defeat
[of the labour movement by neoliberalism] after the end of the "70s." Thus,
educational values are predicated instrumentally on the tenets espoused by
liberal democracy as it is revealed inside capitalism, tied to tropes of equality
or liberty, or on often ill-defined practices/qualities like respect or openness.
Even inside the University it becomes difficult to imagine a different form of
social life beyond the realities of capitalist work (Hall 2014a, Winn 2014).

In this way the fetishisation of emergent technologies risks reinforcing
hegemonies, so that they are seen as revolutionary only in terms of how they
generate individual, user-generated outcomes, rather than in describing new
forms of value. In this view, they re-produce a set of universal, transhistorical
norms, through which it is simply not acceptable to argue for other forms of
value or organisation beyond those imposed by democratic capitalism. Moreover, it no longer becomes possible to address the structural dominance of
educational elites within capitalism, or the limited, procedural definition of
the value of education and educational innovation inside capitalism. Important
here are the mechanisms by which innovation flowing to/from the University

supports the ways in which neoliberal capitalism intentionally designs, promotes and manages forms of democracy and governance that complement its
material objectives (Harvey 2010). This is achieved, in-part, through the implementation of ideological control inside the socio-technical institutions and
cultures of civil society, which in-turn make it impossible to step beyond the
controlling logic of the rights of consumers.

   This is not to say that oppositional forms that are against the University,
and which utilise open and emergent technologies do not exist (Amsler and
Neary 2012, EduFactory 2009, Hall2014a, Neary 2012). The counter-hegemonic
practices of occupation are increasingly being seen as educational, and are
enabling the re-imagining of socio-technical systems and forms of life,
through general assemblies, militant research strategies and activity that is
deliberative and conducted in public. In fact, it is from the activities of these
global movements, arising from indignation, that a critique of the development of emergent technologies inside the University might be situated, in
order to identify opportunities for dissent, negation and pushing back against
the alienating rhetoric of capitalist work (Holloway 2010). This critique
emerges from two strands: firstly, in being *against* pedagogies of consumption
that define the uptake of emergent technologies through the commodification of engagement and activity; secondly, from the recognition that those
technologies help to critique the reality and history of labour-in-capitalism
(Thorburn 2012, Wendling 2009, Winn 2014).

   In some cases these radical education projects are working politically to re-
define issues of power and are an attempt to re-inscribe higher education as
higher learning dissolved into the fabric of society. In most cases they see the
institution of the school or the university as symbolically vital to a societal
transformation. They form a process of re-imagination that risks fetishisation
or reification of radical education, but which offers a glimpse of a different
process that shines a light on the University as one node in a global web of
social relations. This also focuses upon rethinking in public the role of academics in society, facilitated through emergent technologies and where the use of
these technologies for production-in-public is the central organising theme.
One focus is on overcoming individuation through association and embedding
resources in target communities with an academic, co-operative consideration
of the issues involved (Hall 2014a, Winn 2014).

   Thus, where a critique of everyday scholarly activities, related to higher
learning inside and beyond the academy, is folded into the logic of capital's production of these technologies, they become a networked space within which
negation, dissent and revolt can emerge (Holloway 2002). Here, globally-
connected, human-machine symbiosis might become especially important

in overcoming the totalising logic of capitalism where it enables the mutual, co-operative conquest of power as a step towards the abolition of power relations. Critical here is the revelation of the dehumanisation of people as means in a production/consumption-process, for example in the mining of emotions enabled by affective computing or in the virtualisation of educational life, rather than as individuals able to contribute to a common wealth (Hall 2014b). Thus, the use of cloud-based, emergent technologies offers the possibility to connect a global politics of refusal through socio-technological systems. This demands the invocation of a world of disjuncture, disunity, and discontinuity, where academic labour inside capitalism becomes riskier as the repetitive, precarious nature of its alienation and dehumanisation is revealed.

The connection of higher education and society through emergent technologies is important in defining spaces for dissent and pushing-back that are technologically-enabled, because the University remains a symbol of those places where mass intellectuality can be consumed, produced and more importantly contributed to by all. Thus, the revelation of shared experiences of alienation inside the social factory, using emerging technologies that heighten the sensation of oppression and enable them to be shared, offers a possibility that new sites of opposition and critique can be created. In amplifying this process, scholarly practices inside the University offer sites for courageous action against states of exception (Agamben 2005, Amsler 2013) that enclose how and where and why people assemble, associate and organise. However, academics inside the University have little room for manoeuvre in resisting the enclosing logic of competition and in arguing for a socialised role for higher education, given the ideological, political drive towards, for instance, indentured study and debt, internationalisation, privatisation and outsourcing. As a result, the internal logic of the University is increasingly prescribed by the rule of money, which forecloses on the possibility of creating transformatory social relationships as against fetishised products and processes of valorisation.

The idea of exodus is important here, as a form of dissent, revolt or rebellion against capital's exploitation of the entirety of social life, as it is revealed through emergent technologies. This exploitation is witnessed in affective technologies through playbor in games-based industries (Dyer-Witheford and de Peuter 2009), and in the harvesting of cloud-based data for the the subsumption of identities for further accumulation by social networks (Winer 2011), or in the enclosure of the open web through augmentation applications that are designed for profit (Short 2011). Thus, the fetishisation of personalisation, of self-branding, of the emergent technologies through which individuals connect, risks the commodification of each and every action we take in the world. However, this enhanced, connected, semantic web of social relations also offers a crack through which the domination of capital might be opposed. As Illich (1975, 82) argues: "Only among convivially structured tools can people learn to use the new levels of power that modern technology can incorporate in them." Thus, the very automation or human-machine augmentation and symbiosis that capital demands and develops in order to discipline and control labour makes possible an exodus from the society of capitalist work through the radical redisposal of the surplus time that arises as an outcome of that automation, alongside the new ways in which different groups can interconnect in that surplus time (Virno 2004).

Academics then have an important role in amplifying the potentialities for an exodus away from the society of capitalist work. This is more than a series of atomised rearguard actions against capital's cybernetic command (Dyer-Witheford 1999). This role begins in negation or refusal of the starting point for cognitive labour. For Noble (1998), this meant arguing against the conversion of intellectual activity into intellectual capital and hence private property, catalysed through virtualisation that is itself driven by the commodification of research and teaching and the emergence of commercially-viable, proprietary products that can be marketised. The capitalist processes of deskilling and automation, fetishisation of products, and proletarianisation of labour are at the core of this process. Thus, by reconnecting the University life-world that includes research and development to Marx's deeper, structural technological critique, it is possible to legitimise the development-in-public of emergent technologies, and their revelation as a fetishised force of production, as a re-politicised form of activity between students, teachers and public. Moreover, it becomes possible to use this legitimation to catalyse spaces of dissent or protest that underpin new workerist revolts (Colman 2012, Bologna 2014, Tomba and Bellofiore 2014). The workerist nature of these protests is important because of the tendency of capital to subordinate and exploit proletarianised social labour, in order to sustain and enhance the more valuable, cognitive labour of those with proprietary skills (Newfield 2010, Dyer-Witheford 2004).

Thus, in the mass of protests that form a politics of events against austerity academics need to consider their participatory traditions and positions, and how they actively contribute to the dissolution of their expertise as a commodity, in order to support other socially-constructed forms of production. In the critique of knowledge production, revealed through the production/consumption of specific emergent technologies, the University can grow in excess of its symbolic role. As a result, students and teachers might reconsider how they engage with emergent technologies, in order to contribute to a re-formation of their webs of social interaction. How do students and teachers contribute to public dissent against domination and foreclosure? For Marx (1992, 2004), technology is a central strand in the revolutionary transformation of society. This transformation overthrows the capitalist value-form in the construction of an alternative value-structure, and an alternative value-system that does not have the specific character of that achieved under capitalism. *Pace* Marx scholars might consider how their work on and with emergent technologies dissolves the symbolic power of the University into the actual, existing reality of protest, in order to engage with this process of transformation beyond mere commodification

References

Agamben, Giorgio. 2005. *State of Exception.* Chicago: University of Chicago Press.

Amsler, Sarah. 2013. The Fearless University. Accessed November 30, 2014. http://amsler.blogs.lincoln.ac.uk/2013/05/16/the-fearless-university/.

Amsler, Sarah and Mike Neary. 2012. Occupy: a new pedagogy of space and time? *The Journal for Critical Education Policy Studies.* 10 (2): 106–138. Accessed November 30, 2014. http://www.jceps.com/PDFs/10-2-03.pdf.

Andriole, Katherine P., and Ramin Khorasani. 2010. Cloud Computing: What Is It and Could It Be Useful? *Journal of the American College of Radiology* 7 (4): 252–254.

Azuma, Ronald T., Baillot, Yohan, Behringer, Reinhold, Feiner, Steven, Julier, Simon and Blair MacIntyre. 2001. Recent Advances in Augmented Reality. *IEEE Computer Graphics and Applications.* Accessed November 30, 2014. http://www.cs.unc.edu/~azuma/cga2001.pdf.

Ball, Stephen J. 2012. *Global Education Inc. New Policy Networks and The Neo-Liberal Imaginary.* London: Routledge.Basu, Deepankar and Ramaa Vasudevan. 2011. Technology, Distribution and the Rate of Profit in the US Economy: Understanding the Current Crisis. Accessed November 30, 2014. http://people.umass.edu/dbasu/BasuVasudevanCrisis0811.pdf.

Berardi, Franco. 2009. *The Soul at Work: From Alienation to Autonomy.* Translated by F. Cadel and G. Mecchia, with preface by J.E. Smith. Los Angeles, CA: Semiotext(e).

Berger, Theodore W. 2007. Report on International Assessment of Research and Development in Brain-Computer Interfaces. Accessed November 30, 2014. http://www.wtec.org/bci/BCI-finalreport-10Oct2007-lowres.pdf.

Bologna, Sergio. 2014. Workerism: An Inside View. From the Mass-Worker to Self-Employed Labour. In Beyond Marx: Theorising the Global Labour Relations of the Twenty-First Century, edited by Marcel van der Linden, and Karl H. Roth, 121–44. Leiden: Brill.

Brook, Paul. 2009. The Alienated Heart: Hochschild's 'emotional labour' thesis and the anticapitalist politics of alienation. Capital and Class, 33 (2): 7–31. Accessed November

30, 2014. http://www.uk.sagepub.com/edgell/6.1%20Brook%20%282009%29%20 The%20alienated%20heart.pdf.

Clarke, Simon. 1994. *Marx's Theory of crisis*. Basingstoke: Macmillan Press.

Cline, Mychilo S. 2005. *Power, Madness, and immortality: The future of virtual reality*. University Village Press.

Cowie, Roddy. 2005. What are people doing when they assign everyday emotion terms?. *Psychological Inquiry* 16 (1): 11–48.

Cuhls, Kerstin. 2003. From forecasting to foresight processes – new participative foresight activities in Germany. *Journal of Forecasting* 22 (2–3): 93–111. Accessed November 30, 2014.

Das, Gaurav. 2012. 6 universities to teach cloud computing, mobile tech. Accessed November 30, 2014. http://articles.timesofindia.indiatimes.com/2012-02-08/ guwahati/31037183_1_cloud-technology-manipur-university-curriculum Davies, William. 2014. The Limits of Neoliberalism: Authority, Sovereignty and the Logic of Competition. London: SAGE.

Dikaiakos, Marios D., George Pallis, Dimitrios Katsaros, Penkaj Mehra, and Athena Vakali. 2009. Cloud Computing: Distributed Internet Computing for IT and Scientific Research. *IEEE Internet Computing* 13 (5): 10–13.

Dyer-Witheford, Nick. 1999. *Cyber-Marx: Cycles and Circuits of Struggle in High Technology Capitalism*. Chicago, IL: University of Illinois Press.

Dyer-Witheford, Nick. 2004. *Autonomist Marxism and the Information Society*. Canberra: Treason Press. Accessed November 30, 2014. http://libcom.org/library/ autonomist-marxism-information-society-nick-witheford.

Dyer-Witheford, Nick, and Greg de Peuter. 2009. *Games of empire: global capitalism and video games*. Minnesota: University of Minnesota Press.

EduFactory Collective. 2009. Towards a Global Autonomous University. Accessed November 30, 2014. https://libcom.org/library/towards-global-autonomous -university-edu-factory-collective.

EC. 2014a. *Europe 2020 – Europe's growth strategy*. Accessed November 30, 2014. http:// ec.europa.eu/eu2020/.

EC. 2014b. *Research and InnovationFunding 2014–2020*. Accessed November 30, 2014. http://ec.europa.eu/research/fp7/.

Educause. 2014. Learning Analytics. Accessed November 30, 2014. http://www.educause .edu/library/learning-analytics.

Feenberg, Andrew. 1999. *Questioning Technology*. London: Routledge.

Foucault, Michel. 1977. *Discipline and Punish*. New York: Pantheon.

Friedewald, Michael. 2005. The Continuous Construction of the Computer User: Visions and User Models in the History of Human-Computer Interaction. In *Total Interaction: Theory and Practice of a New Paradigm*, edited by Gerhard M. Buurman, 26–41. Basel: Birkhäuser.

Fuchs, Christian. 2010. Labor in Informational Capitalism and on the Internet. *The Information Society* 26 (3): 179–196.

Ganascia, Jean-Gabriel. 2010. The generalized sousveillance society. *Social science information* 49 (3): 489–507.

Gartner. 2011. Gartner's 2011 Hype Cycle Special Report Evaluates the Maturity of 1,900 Technologies. Accessed November 30, 2014. http://www.gartner.com/it/page.jsp?id=1763814.

Gartner. 2013. Gartner Reveals Top Predictions for IT Organizations and Users for 2014 and Beyond. Accessed November 30, 2014. http://gtnr.it/17RLm2v.

Gasson, Mark, and Kevin Warwick, K. 2007. D12.1 Study On Emerging AmI Technologies. *FIDIS – Future of Identity in the Information Society*. Accessed November 30, 2014. http://www.fidis.net/resources/deliverables/hightechid/d122-study-on-emerging-ami-technologies/doc/8/.

Greef de Tjerk. E., Arciszewski Henryk F.R., and Mark A. Neerincx. 2010. Adaptive Automation Based on an Object-Oriented Task Model: Implementation and Evaluation in a Realistic C2 Environment. *Journal of Cognitive Engineering and Decision Making* 4 (2): 152–182.

Habermas, Jürgen. 1987. *Lifeworld and System: A Critique of Functionalist Reason*, volume 2 of *The Theory of Communicative Action*. Boston: Beacon Press.

Hall, Richard. 2013. Educational Technology and the Enclosure of Academic Labour Inside Public Higher Education. Journal for Critical Education Policy Studies 11 (3): 52–82. Accessed November 30, 2014. http://www.jceps.com/PDFs/11-3-03.pdf.

Hall, Richard. 2014a. On the Abolition of Academic Labour: The Realationship Between Intellectual Workers and Mass Intellectuality. *tripleC* 12 (2): 822–837. Accessed November 30, 2014.

Hall, Richard. 2014b. The implications of Autonomist Marxism for research and practice in education and technology. *Learning, Media and Technology*. http://dx.doi.org/10.1080/17439884.2014.911189.

Hall, Richard, and Joss Winn. 2011. Questioning Technology in the Development of a Resilient Higher Education. E-Learning and Digital Media 8 (4): 343–356.

Hamilton, Karen E. 2014. Augmented Reality in Education. Accessed November 30 2014. http://augmented-reality-in-education.wikispaces.com/.

Harvey, David. 1990. *The Condition of Postmodernity: An Enquiry into the Origins of Cultural Change*. Cambridge: Blackwell.

Harvey, David. 2010. *A Companion to Marx's Capital*. London: Verso.

HEFCE. 2014. Technology-enhanced learning. Accessed November 30, 2014November 30, 2014. http://www.hefce.ac.uk/learning/techlearn/.

Heilig, Morton L. 1962. *Sensorama Simulator*. Accessed 14 March, 2012. http://www.mortonheilig.com/SensoramaPatent.pdf.

HIT Lab NZ. 2014. BuildAR. Accessed November 30, 2014. http://www.buildar.co.nz/.

Holloway, John. 2002. *Change the World Without Taking Power*. London: Pluto Press.

Hudlicka, Eva. 2009. Affective Game Engines: Motivation and Requirements. In *Proceedings of the 4th International Conference on Foundations of Digital Games*, 299–306. Orlando, Florida: ACM. doi:10.1145/1536513.1536565.

Ikonen, Veikko, Kanerva, Minni, Kouri, Panu, Stahl, Bernd Carsten & Wakunuma, Kutoma. 2010. ETICA Project Deliverable D.1.2: Emerging Technologies Report. Accessed November 30, 2014. http://cordis.europa.eu/result/rcn/56066_en.html.

Illich, Ivan. 1975. *Tools for Conviviality*, London: Fontana.

Jappe, Anselm. 2014.Towards a History of the Critique of Value. Capitalism, Nature, Socialism 25 (2): 25–37.

JISC. 2014. Mobile Learning. Accessed November 30, 2014. http://www.jiscinfonet.ac .uk/infokits/mobile-learning/.

Lapavitsas, Costas 2010. Financialisation and Capitalist Accumulation: Structural Accounts of the Crisis of 2007–2009. Research on Money and Finance, Discussion paper no 16. Accessed November 30, 2014. http://bit.ly/1locdwA.

Lebowitz, Michael A. 2003. *Beyond Capital: Marx's Political Economy of the Working Class*. Basingstoke: Palgrave Macmillan.

Lepratti, Rafaello. 2006. Advanced Human-Machine System for Intelligent Manufaturing: Some Issues for Employing Ontologies for Natural Language Processing. *Journal of Intelligent Manufacturing* 17 (6): 653–66.

Licklider, Joseph C.R. 1960. Man-Computer Symbiosis. *IRE Transactions on Human Factors in Electronics*, HFE-1: 4–11. Accessed November 30, 2014. http://groups.csail .mit.edu/medg/people/psz/Licklider.html.

Marx, Karl. 1992. *Capital, Volume 3: A Critique of Political Economy*. London: Penguin.

Marx, Karl. 1993. *Grundrisse. Foundations of the Critique of Political Economy*. London: Penguin.

Marx, Karl. 2004. *Capital, Volume 1: A Critique of Political Economy*. London: Penguin.

Marx, Karl. 2006. *Capital, Volume 2: A Critique of Political Economy*. London: Penguin.

Meiksins-Wood, Ellen. 1997. Back to Marx. *Monthly Review* 49 (2): 1–9. Miller Medina, Jessica E. 2005. "The State Machine: Politics, Ideology, and Computation in Chile, 1964–1973." Unpublished PhD thesis, MIT. Accessed November 30, 2014. http:// dspace.mit.edu/handle/ 1721.1/39176.

MIT Media Lab. 2012. Accessed November 30, 2014. www.media.mit.edu.

MIT. 2014. 10x Human-Machine Superperformance. Accessed November 30, 2014. http://10x.media.mit.edu/.

Neary, Mike. 2012. Teaching Politically: Policy, Pedagogy and the New European University. The Journal for Critical Education Policy Studies 10 (2): 233–257. Accessed November 30, 2014. http://www.jceps.com/PDFs/10-2-08.pdf.

Neary, Mike, and Andy Hagyard. 2010. Pedagogy of Excess – an Alternative Political Economy of Student Life. In *The Marketisation of Higher Education: The Student as Consumer*, edited by Mike Molesworth, Richard Scullion and Elizabeth Nixon, 209–24. London: Routledge.

Negri, Antonio. 1989. *The Politics of Subversion: A Manifesto for the Twenty First Century*. Cambridge: Polity Press.

Neilsson, Brett, and Ned Rossiter. 2008. Precarity as a Political Concept, or, Fordism as Exception. *Theory, Culture & Society* 25 (7–8): 51–72.

Newfield, Christopher. 2010. The Structure and Silence of Cognitariat. *EduFactory Webjournal* 0: 10–26. Accessed November 30, 2014. http://www.edu-factory.org/edu15/webjournal/no/Newfield.pdf.

NICTA. 2014. Accessed November 30, 2014. http://www.nicta.com.au/.

Noble, David F. 1998. Digital Diploma Mills: The Automation of Higher Education. *First Monday* 3 (1): Accessed November 30, 2014. http://firstmonday.org/htbin/cgiwrap/bin/ojs/index.php/fm/article/view/569/490.

Postone, Moishe. 1996. *Time, Labour and Social Domination: A Reinterpretation of Marx's Critical Theory*. Cambridge: Cambridge University Press.

Postone, Moishe. 2009. Rethinking Marx's Critical Theory. In *History and Heteronomy: Critical Essays* (UTCP Booklet 12), edited Moishe Postone, Viren Murthy and Yasuo Kobayashi, 31–47. Tokyo: The University of Tokyo Center for Philosophy.

Porto Interactive Center. 2014. LifeisGame Project. Accessed November 30, 2014. http://www.portointeractivecenter.org/lifeisgame/.

Pusey, Andre and Leon Sealy-Huggins. 2013. Transforming the University: Beyond Students and Cuts. *ACME Journal* 12: 443–458. http://www.acme-journal.org/vol12/PuseySealeyHuggins2013.pdf.

Robinson, Peter, and Rana el Kaliouby. 2009. Computation of Emotions in Man and Machines. *Philosophical Transactions of the Royal Society B: Biological Sciences* 364 (1535): 3441–3447. doi:10.1098/rstb.2009.0198.

Roy, Deb. 2004. 10x: Human-Machine Symbiosis. *BT Technology Journal* 22 (4). Accessed November 30, 2014. http://10x.media.mit.edu/10x draft.pdf.

Sanchati, Rupesh, and Gaurav Kulkarni. 2011. Cloud Computing in Digital and University Libraries. *Global Journal of Computer Science and Technology* 11 (12): 36–41. Accessed November 30, 2014. http://globaljournals.org/GJCST_Volume11/6-Cloud-Computing-in-Digital-and-University.pdf.

Short, Adrian. 2011. It's the End of the Web As We Know It. Accessed November 30, 2014. http://adrianshort.co.uk/2011/09/25/its-the-end-of-the-web-as-we-know-it/.

Stahl, Bernd Carsten. 2004. E-Teaching – The Economic Threat to the Ethical Legitimacy of Education? In *Journal of Information Systems Education* 15 (2): 155–66.

Sykes, Jonathan, and Simon Brown. 2003. Affective gaming: measuring emotion through the gamepad. In *CHI '03 extended abstracts on Human factors in computing systems*, 732–733. Ft. Lauderdale, FL: ACM. doi:10.1145/765891.765957.

Tao, Jianhua, and Tieniu Tan. 2005. Affective Computing: A Review. *Lecture Notes in Computer Science* 3784: 981–995.

The Think-Trust Project. 2010. Accessed November 30, 2014. http://www.tssg.org/projects/think-trust/.

Thorburn, Elise. 2012. Actually Existing Autonomy and the Brave New World of Higher Education. *Occupied Studies*. Accessed November 30, 2014. http://bit.ly/xzcPRO.

Tiqqun. 2001. *The Cybernetic Hypothesis*. Accessed November 30, 2014. http://archive.org/details/Tiqqun1.

Tomba, Massimiliano and Riccardo Bellofiore. 2014. The 'Fragment on Machines' and the Grundrisse: The Workerist Reading in Question. In *Beyond Marx: Theorising the Global Labour Relations of the Twenty-First Century*, edited by Marcel. van der Linden and Karl H. Roth, 345–68. Leiden: Brill.

Tronti, Mario. 1973. Social Capital. *Telos* 17: 98–121.

Vercellone, Carlo. 2007. From Formal Subsumption to General Intellect. *Historical Materialism* 15 (1): 13–36.

Virno, Paolo. 2001. General Intellect. *Generation Online*. Accessed November 30, 2014. http://www.generation-online.org/p/fpvirno10.htmVirno, Paolo. 2004. *A Grammar of the Multitude: For an Analysis of Contemporary Forms of Life*. Los Angeles: Semiotext.

Virno, Paolo. 2002. General Intellect, Exodus, Multitude: Interview with Paolo Virno. *Archipélago* (54). Accessed November 30, 2014. http://www.generation-online.org/p/fpvirno2.htm.

Virno, Paolo, and Michael Hardt, eds. 1996. *Radical Thought in Italy: A Potential Politics*. Minneapolis: University of Minnesota Press.

Walden, Ian. 2011. Accessing Data in the Cloud: The Long Arm of the Law Enforcement Agency. *Social Science Research Network*. Accessed November 30, 2014. http://papers.ssrn.com/sol3/papers.cfm?abstract_id=1781067.

Wake, Matthew, and Bernd Carsten Stahl. 2010. Ethical Issues of the Use of Second Life in Higher Education. In *Proceedings of ETHICOMP*, 13 to 16 April 2010, Tarragona, Spain.

Weber, Max. 1969. *The Theory of Social and Economic Organization*. New York: Macmillan.

Wendling, Amy E. 2009. Karl Marx on Technology and Alienation. London: Palgrave Macmillan.

Winer, Dave. 2011. Facebook is scaring me. Accessed November 30, 2014. http://scripting.com/stories/2011/09/24/facebookIsScaringMe.html.

Winn, Joss. 2014. Writing about Academic Labour. *Workplace* 25: 1–15. Accessed November 30, 2014. http://ojs.library.ubc.ca/index.php/workplace/article/view/185095/185275.

xDelia. 2012. Xcellence in Decision-making through Enhanced Learning in Immersive Applications. Accessed November 30, 2014. http://www.xdelia.org.

Zhou, Feng. Duh, Henry Been-Lirn, and Mark Billinghurst. 2008. Trends in Augmented Reality Tracking, Interaction and Display: A Review of Ten Years of ISMAR. In *ISMAR '08: Proceedings of the 7th IEEE/ACM International Symposium on Mixed and Augmented Reality*.

Žižek, Slavoj. 2009. *First As Tragedy, Then As Farce.* London: Verso.

CHAPTER 5

Communication and Symbolic Capitalism – Rethinking Marxist Communication Theory in the Light of the Information Society

George Pleios

1 Methodological Issues

The main purpose of this chapter is not to examine the Marxist theory of communication as a specific social field, but to look into communication as a parameter in general Marxist social theory. In other words, this chapter aims to look into the structural role of communication on the basis of a base – superstructure model of social organization with regard to its historical transformation and to different approaches in Marxist social theory. Therefore, it elaborates the discussion mainly between the approach of traditional Marxism and those of later schools of thought, both Marxist or any influenced by them in an effort to assess the development of the capitalist mode of production as a result of the key role of communication.

In my opinion we can draw a development of the Marxist concept of the relations between the capitalist mode of production and communication, in four steps or moments. At first (e.g. in "The German Ideology"), communication and the relations of production are identical. In the primary formulation, in the "German Ideology" (Marx and Engels 1978a, 67), the relations of production (or property relations) are characterized as "forms of communication." With this term, Marx and Engels aim to explain ideology, which they perceive as being equal to idealism, in relation to the mode of production and class relations. A certain degree or form of division of labour leads to a certain quality and quantity of distribution of the products of labour. In other words, the structure of distribution is connected to the division of labour within the production process. Certain social relations of production and distribution emanate from this division of labour and (Marx and Engels 1978a, 78). Marx and Engels understand relations of production as class/property relations on one hand, and as communication forms on the other.

As they note, "the production of ideas, of conceptions, of consciousness, is at first directly interwoven with the material activity and the material intercourse of men, the language of real life. Conceiving, thinking, the mental intercourse of men, appears at this stage as the direct efflux of their material behavior. The same applies to mental production as expressed in the language of politics, laws, morality, religion, metaphysics, etc., of a people. Men are the producers of their conceptions, ideas, etc. – real, active men, as they are conditioned by a definite development of their productive forces and of the intercourse corresponding to these, up to its furthest forms. Consciousness can never be anything else than conscious existence, and the existence of men is their actual life-process" (Marx and Engels 1978a, 67–68).

Thus they understand relations of production as social relations within a broader context, where social interaction, the use of symbols in it and the ideas that derive from it or refer to that interaction are regarded as a whole. In this formulation, the "forms of communication" become a means of establishing, sustaining and changing the social relations of production, and vice versa, in connection to the division of labour. From this point of view, communication and symbolic structures are not only passive means but also an essential part of the social relations of production, especially in pre-capitalist societies. For example, Marx notes that Moses managed to establish new laws in favor of virtue, justice and morality because he grounded the new principles on land ownership (Marx 1983, 100). In other words, the answer to the question about the importance of forms of communication regarding the social relations of production and social organization depends on the division of labour and the overall mode of production overall.

In a second step/moment, Marx accepts that, communication and especially its ideational content are relatively separated from the relations of production, which are perceived to be class and property relations, and placed within the superstructure. "In the social production of their life, men enter into definite relations that are indispensable and independent of their will, relations of production which correspond to a definite stage of development of their material productive forces. The sum total of these relations of production constitutes the economic structure of society, the real foundation, on which rises a legal and political superstructure and to which correspond definite forms of social consciousness" (Marx and Engels 2001, 39).

Here, communication depends on and reflects what is taking place in the base, in class and property relations. According to Marx and Engels: "The ideas of the ruling class are in every epoch the ruling ideas, i.e. the class which is the ruling material force of society, is at the same time its ruling intellectual force. The class which has the means of material production at its disposal has control at the same time over the means of mental production, so that thereby, generally speaking, the ideas of those who lack the means of mental production are subject to it" (Marx and Engels 1978a, 94). This view can be interpreted, in two ways.

a. In a more instrumental approach, where it is accepted that the means of communication belong to those that own the means of production and thus use them "on purpose" to express their views in order to gain profit from this business or/and justify and maintain social inequality. The communication product (or text with semiotic terms) as merchandise, i.e. a product of commodity production, which is bought for money and is intended to satisfy certain needs. As Marx states: "beyond all commodity is an external object, something which with its attributes satisfies human needs. The nature of these needs, no matter their origin, for example stomach or imagination, does not change the nature of the work" (Marx and Engels 2001, 39–42; Marx 1979, 45). Marx and Engels also assert that those who own the means of production, also own the means of communication, which they use in order to maintain political and ideological control over society and preserve capitalist property and class relations. "The individuals composing the ruling class possess among other things consciousness, and therefore think. Insofar, therefore, as they rule as a class and determine the extent and compass of an epoch, it is self-evident that they do this in its whole range, hence among other things rule also as thinkers, as producers of ideas, and regulate the production and distribution of the ideas of their age: thus their ideas are the ruling ideas of the epoch" (Marx and Engels 1978a, 94).

b. The above mentioned statement can be interpreted in a more structural notion, one that asserts that those who own and control the means of production, may usually see their views being reflected in the products of communication Such an approach focuses mainly on the ideological aspects of communication content. "The ruling ideas are nothing more than the ideal expression of the dominant material relationships, the dominant material relationships grasped as ideas; hence of the relationships which make the one class the ruling one, therefore, the ideas of its dominance. The individuals composing the ruling class possess among other things consciousness, and therefore think. Insofar, therefore, as they rule as a class and determine the extent and compass of an epoch, it is self-evident that they do this in its whole range, hence among other things rule also as thinkers, as producers of ideas, and regulate the production and distribution of the ideas of their age: thus their ideas are the ruling ideas of the epoch" (Marx and Engels 1978a, 94). Communication (of ideas) reflects the social relations that exist in the base of a social structure, an idea supported by positivists according to Williams (Williams 2001, 153). The communication product is examined in its content as a whole of ideas. In this context, communication and communication products/commodities are becoming part of the superstructure.

Overall, in the second step of the evolution of the Marxist theory of communication, the latter is regarded more or less as an autonomous social field. Marx
himself not only separates the superstructure from the structure, but also the
idea of the "relative autonomy" between art and superstructure (Marx and
Engels, 1975). Such a view has long dominated Marxist theory.

Thirdly, other Marxists have developed various notions of communication –
production relations are discussed in phase two in a more systematic way and
often separated from each other. At the same time, their accounts constitute
different types of Marxism or (neo) Marxist communication theory. In my
analysis, it is important to remember that what is under investigation in each
case happens in tandem with the specific historical or spatio-temporal context
of the communicative process.

For a long period of time, a distinct Marxist tradition was developed that
was looking at communication as a cultural field, which reflects the broader
structures of capitalist society in the form of ideas and discourses. Therefore
it focused on the ideological aspects of communication content and practices
(also mainly of the fictional types of content). Such an approach was undertaken by Marxist structuralism (Althusser 1990, 69–95) and, in a different manner, by Soviet Marxism. Marxist structuralism does not focus on the process of
production of cultural products or other goods and their relation to communication content and ideology; rather, it absorbs the relations of production in the
communication content as the ruling classes' view of reality. The two aspects of
cultural production (economic and communicative) were considered as structural parallels, which however are not essentially interconnected. The ideological function of cultural production, even if linked to its commodity character,
preserves its autonomy and depends to a great degree on the cultural rules and
the particular cultural field to which the product belongs – otherwise, the commodity function of the cultural product is absorbed by ideology. Whatever the
case, the ideological function of communication is not connected organically
to its economic role, being a special symbolic process. This particular Marxist
approach is not related to my analysis of communication as a key component
of the social structure.

Besides the above mentioned, mainly cultural approach, a different one has
been developed in the realm of (neo) Marxism. It analyzes, in different ways
and degrees, communication and its content in relation to the process of commodity production of symbolic and non-symbolic products, and the relations
of production. Critical Theory, mostly Adorno, undertook a more structural
socio–philosophical approach and investigated communication as a field
which penetrated the industrial capitalist mode of production (and structures)
that characterizes State Monopoly Capitalism (Horkheimer and Adorno 1986;

Adorno and Horkheimer 1987, 219–243). Industrial production, hand in hand with commoditization, enters the communication field, but the problem is not technology because it is materialization of the capitalist mode of production. This on one hand leads to an extreme commoditization of communication products that eliminates their commercial character and on the other to the embodiment of the ruling classes' ideology in the content. The mass production of communication products leaves little room for alternative ideas. Adorno and Horkheimer underline that "Films and radio no longer need to present themselves as art. The truth that they are nothing but business is used as an ideology to legitimize the trash they intentionally produce. They call themselves industries and the published figures for their directors' incomes quell any doubts about the social necessity of their finished products" (Adorno and Horkheimer 2001, 72).

Beyond that, commoditized communication (e.g. advertisement) became a means that helps the circulation of industrial non-cultural commodities, which also dominate the everyday life of individuals. The consumption of communication products satisfies the needs of the routine reproduction of the labour force like the non-cultural ones. "Entertainment is the prolongation of work under late capitalism. It is sought by those who want to escape the mechanized labor process so that they can cope with it again. At the same time, however, mechanization has such power over leisure and its happiness, determines so thoroughly the fabrication of entertainment commodities, that the off-duty worker can experience nothing but afterimages of the work process itself" (Adorno and Horkheimer 2001, 82). Due to the embodied ideas and the commoditized form of their consumption, this leads to the integration of the working class in the system.

Thus communication serves the sustainment of the (Monopoly State) capitalist mode of production. In this way, Critical Theory does not focus only on the consequences of the capitalist mode of production on the autonomous superstructure, like Marxist structuralism does. Instead, it looks at the penetration of the capitalist mode of production in communication and its ideological and structural consequences, which results in the abolition of the autonomy of the superstructure – the base, thus, conquers and homogenizes the superstructure. For this reason, such an approach in the words of Garnham could be characterized as "economic determinism" in cultural and communication studies (Garnham, 1979) in contrast to the idealism of Marxist structuralism. But Critical Theory does not examine the role of communication in the formation of the State Monopoly Capitalist mode of production itself at the level of production (i.e. the role of consumed symbolic goods at the work place). It only examines the reproductive role of regarding the capitalist base as determining its contestation.

The propaganda model accepts a more instrumental version of the Marxist theory of communication. More precisely it informs the way in which the agents of capitalist cultural production embody the ruling ideas in the content (mainly the factual content) in order to fulfill economic as well as political goals. Thus the propaganda model focuses also on the process of production of communication commodities and their ideological content, on their political consequences, and thus the sustaining of capitalist economic and social relations, in close relation to the activity and objectives of those that own the means of cultural production (Herman and Chomsky 2001). In this manner, communication contributes to the sustaining of the capitalist mode of production not directly, but trough manufacturing consent in the political and ideological arena.

The "encoding/decoding" model connects organically a cultural and economic analysis of communication with the production and consumption (reading) moment of the communication process (Hall 1980). From this starting point, Critical Political Economy of Communication combines the Critical/theoretical analysis with the positive/empirical analysis of economic, cultural and political factors that determine communication products, and the field of communication as such, as part of the capitalist economy (Schiller 1973; Mosco 2009; Curran 1979; Golding and Murdock 2001). The industrial–capitalist manufacturing of communication products is regarded not as the core, but as part of the broader capitalist economy and structure of interests (Golding and Murdock 2001, 26–28). Critical Political Economy examines the consequences of the capitalist mode of production for communication in a more complex and historical way. As Nicolas Garnham put it "...the superstructure/culture is and remains subordinate and secondary and the crucial questions are the relationship between, on the one hand, the mode of extraction and distribution of the material surplus, e.g. class relations and, on the other, the allocation of this material surplus within the superstructure, for instance, the problem of public expenditure among others" (Garnham 1979). Despite the importance of Critical Political Economy in understanding the complex role of economic, political and cultural mechanisms in the production of communication commodities (and their ideology) in lat capitalism, the question about the contribution of communication to the process of production of (non-communication) commodities and to the "division of labour" remains unanswered.

In general, in this third stage, communication is conceived as part of the superstructure and as a field of extension and penetration of the capitalist–industrial mode of production. In a nutshell, in the Marxist theory of communication, while the contribution of the capitalist mode of production in the communication field and the mode of communication has been under examination for long, the significance of (the mode of) communication in the production, not the circulation of commodities, the political, has not been enough analysed.

The later is a key issue in a fourth step or moment in the development of the Marxist Theory of Communication, which is indispensable from those Marxist theories of the third step that connect communication with the production process. Critical Theory is in my view a neomarxist approach that focuses extensively on the role of communication in sustaining and reproducing the (State Monopoly) capitalist mode of production. But, as I already mentioned, this is limited to the simple reproduction of the labour force just before it visits the workplace. Williams tended to treat the "base" as indispensable for certain superstructure elements, especially at the level of the work force (Williams 2001, 154–155). In his view: "If we have the broad sense of forces of production, we look at the whole question of the base differently, and we are then less tempted to dismiss it as superstructural, and in that sense as merely secondary certain vital productive social forces, which are in the broad sense, from the beginning basic" (Williams 2001, 155). Ezensberger investigates the organic role of communication in the sphere of production. It is argued that the means of communication are means of production (Ezensberger 1981). Finally, put in its historical context, one must reconfigure in Marxist terms Baudrillard's idea that the mode of production is a result of the communication mode and not the other way round (Baudrillard 1990, 112; Pleios 1993, 50–64). At this point, one should not leave aside Debord's theory, according to which the spectacle is the superior form of commodity production, exchange and consumption (Debord, 1986).

The connection of communication with the mode of production (and especially the relations of production) in the frame of the Marxist rationale can be seen into two ways. Firstly, communication is regarded as a process which is placed mostly in the sphere of commodity circulation, that is to say that it facilitates the sale of the product for example as it happens with advertising or promoting a consumerist way of life (Marx and Horkheimer 2001; Fuchs 2010a).

Secondly, it can be argued that the economic role of communication is not limited only to the sphere of trade and consumption. In my opinion, communication can be regarded as a process that facilitates, strengthens or changes the capitalist mode of production in its core (the "division of labour"), beyond the sphere of cultural industries or cultural consumption alone. That perhaps could explain the modifications of the capitalist mode of production and the deeper role of communication and cultural industries the development of the capitalist mode of production.

My analysis is situated within this fourth step. I do not examine communication just as form of the superstructure which reflects and reproduces the base or as a field that penetrates the industrial capitalist mode of production or as a means that facilitates the circulation of goods. I explore the role of socially organized communication (including cultural industries) in the core of the capitalist mode of production, namely in the process of the production of goods (of non cultural industries) as well as in the structuration of relations of production. In other words, I examine communication as force of sustaining and changing the mode of production in its core, in the social relations of production at the workplace. This is not something that characterizes every form/stage of capitalism, but it is a historical result of the development of the capitalist mode of production. Hence, I accept that communication contributes not only to the realization of the surplus value that has been created in production, or to the simple reproduction of the workforce. My starting point is that via consumption certain attributes (values and norms) are created among the workforce that renders them more productive, so that surplus value is increased during the process of production under specific organization of the work. This second stance is feasible in the frame of consumer capitalism.

Enlarged consumption does not only help the consumption of commodities, but also reconstructs the labour force in such a way that it becomes more productive and consequently increases its productivity, which in other words decreases the working time needed for its own reproduction and as a result contributes to the increase of surplus value (Pleios 1993, 56–58). This approach is not unknown, but has been proposed with the help of other terms. Human capital theory, for example, which is a functionalist theory, adopts a similar approach (Schultz 1961). In the present article, this second spectrum of analysis is followed, focusing on the social-symbolic construction and not the biological-bodily manufacture and reproduction of the working force via consumption and communication.

2   The Marxist Approach and Its Contestation

In the frame of Marxist tradition, especially as it has been formulated in Marx's work "Towards a Critique of the Political Economy," the dialectics of relations of production and forces of production are considered to be a fundamental force, which contributes to the configuration of the social system as a whole, or in Marxist terms, to each socio-economic formation (Marx 1978, 115). The effort to comprehend and evaluate this dialectic in the further economic analysis, particularly within Marxism, led to the separation between those that attribute the prime role to the forces of production (means of production, objects of production, working force) and those that attribute a bigger priority to the relations of production (property relations, class relations, etc.) and furthermore to the political and ideological conflict (Plamenatz 1963, 282–283; Blackledge and Hunt 1995, 160). This division prevailed for a long period in the Marxist camp not only in theory, but also on political, cultural and other levels.

At this point it is imperative that the importance of two points is emphasized. Firstly, as we already mentioned, Marx and Engels, on one hand, define relations of production as "forms of communication" (Marx and Engels 1978a, 67). On the other, (Marx 1978), the relations of production are seen as the base, above of which is erected all what with another term could be characterized as "communication forms" (law, policy, art etc.) and other social institutions. It is obvious that henceforth relations of production refer mainly to an economic-social category, the class relations (or property relations) and that the "forms of communication" have been removed from the base.

In order to comprehend this contradiction, one should question whether class/property relations are distinguished from the forms of communication, where class relations determine and shape forms of communication. a) How is the existence of relations of production possible without forms of communication. b) If we remove communication from "forms of communication," then what remains of them? The answer to the first question is that it is obvious that the class relations, as all social relations, are not conceivable without the communication aspect. According to George Gerbner, communication is "social interaction through messages" or symbolic constructions (Gerbner 1970, 72). Thus, the various class relations (also including their political form) are possible only via communication and the various forms and types of communication. Actually, class relations acquire substance and are transformed (to the particular historical form that they take in each society) via the forms of communication.

Based on our previous analysis, the answer to the second question, i.e. what remains from the "forms of communication" if we remove communication altogether, is: ideas. Consequently, at a second stage or moment, classic Marxism perceives the "superstructure" as a whole of ideas, as Marx himself wrote (Marx and Engels 1975, 68), that are shaped by the material base of society, in which the institutional mechanisms of the production of ideas are also included,.

This approach has been interpreted mainly in two ways. Firstly, the Marxist approach, especially the analysis of capitalism, was seen as a theoretically erroneous or one-sided approach. This stance has been especially popular within positivism, functionalism and Weberian sociology (Alexander 1987). The importance of the mode of production has been pointed out, but has been considered to be rather one-sided. In this case, the economy has been considered as an insufficient factor for further social analysis. Marx and Engels have also pointed out that the analysis of the societal organization must be completed by communication/culture or by what in Engels' words has been called "form" of the "content," which in its turn are the economic processes. This work, according Engels, had to be carried out by the next generation of Marxists (Marx and Engels 1978b, 469).

Secondly, the classic Marxist approach (mainly in Marx's "Capital") is characterized as a theoretical imprinting of a historical reality. Marx actually describes the way in which 19th century laissez faire capitalism operates (Russell 2006, 26–29), not capitalism in general or class societies in more general terms. In my opinion this assumption is also at the heart of the Williams' conclusion that the base–superstructure model is a bourgeois formula (Williams 1978, 75–82). Thus the analysis of further stages of capitalism should take into consideration the role of communication/culture.

So, no matter if one looks from inside or from outside at the initial Marxist position on the role of the mode of production or class relations in the organization of society, one can observe a convergence. It concerns the need to complete the role that is carried out by the "base" or more widely the mode of production, from the activities that take place in the superstructure. This conclusion, like similar developments in social theory, owes a lot to theoretical activity. However, the conclusions did not become only possible due to theory, they at the same time had to be applied in the ontological field (Horkheimer 1976, 213). Theories are social constructs and social constructions are never arbitrary, except in solipsism (Demertzis 2002, 144–175). Social constructions always organize through discourse a sum of events that are independent from individual subjects, not of the subject in general. Or they contain events that are objective as the natural or economic events (Demertzis 2002, 149–152).

The perception that the mature Marx described a specific socio-economic formation in a specific period, appears feasible at least for two reasons. Firstly, it corresponds to the more general course of his work from the abstract and general to the concrete and specific, and from the philosophical and general sociological analysis to the economic and political one. Secondly, the description of capitalism, capital, work, commodity etc. that Marx develops in "Capital," constitutes an analysis of an "ideotypical" capitalism. But it could historically be observed in the frame of liberal, laissez-faire capitalism, and particularly in Great Britain.

Any attempt to adopt this analysis in any other country or form of capitalism presupposes smaller or bigger modifications, as Engels himself underlines in his letter to Paul Ernst (Engels 1978a, 426–428). These "modifications" can be perceived either as an adjustment to different historical circumstances and/or as an adjustment to a different phase, as an adjustment to the "ideotype" of another phase in the development of capitalism.

3   The Genesis of Symbolic Capitalism

Seeing the ontological foundation for the characterization or the transformation of Marxist perceptions of base and superstructure as insufficient, one should turn attention to those facts that rendered it restrictive. The great transformation, according to the terminology set out by Polanyi (Polanyi 2001), is a change in the nature of capitalism that took place at the end of the 19th century. A result of this change was the appearance of monopolies or in other words organized capitalism (Lash and Urry 1987; Sennett 2008, 27) and the reduction of competitive, free market capitalist economy and the liberal state. But to look at this from another perspective, the rise of monopoly capitalism is connected to radical changes in the process of production, especially the social organization of work (Burawoy 1979), on the one hand and the rise a large public sector on the other (Hobsbawm 1978).

The significance of this change is immense for the study of communication from the Marxist perspective. Through this change, Baudrillard for example explains the development of media and the sovereignty of the mode of communication over the mode of production in an undisputed way (Baudrillard 1990, 112). Although Baudrillard correctly locates the point of historical transformation of capitalism, I believe however that he does not correctly interpret this change. Baudrillard locates this change in the market circulation of commodities and more specifically in the relationship between producer and consumer, between the commodity and its consumption. It is true that the circulation of commodities and financial capital can exercise influence over the production process, as Engels recognizes in his letter to Conrad Schmidt. But the "decisive moment" is production (Engels 1978b, 436).

The specificity of capitalism does not lie in the circulation or production of commodities (which existed before the capitalist mode of production), but in the production of surplus value and furthermore in generalized commodity production. "Capitalist production is not merely the production of commodities, it is essentially the production of surplus-value" (Marx 1979, 520). Circulation is the moment of realization of surplus value, not the moment of its creation. The most important condition for the production of surplus value is the relationship between capital and labour, where the labour force becomes itself a commodity (Jessop 2002, 12–13). The production of surplus value, and more precisely the rate of surplus value (s/v), is the historical form and essence of the capitalist relations of production. Thus, the phenomenon of monopoly as a relationship between producers and its changes are not explained or at least not located in the organization of production. From the Marxist point of view, any change in the evolution of capitalism is first and foremost a change in the form and method of the production of surplus value rather than the form of its realization (circulation of commodities), no matter how important this is for commodity production.

We can claim that the crisis of the 1870s was a crisis of the production system of surplus value in laissez faire capitalism, which according to representatives of the Regulation School (Aglieta 1979, Lipietz 1990) is characterized by extensive production of surplus value and economic development (of an individual company or national economy as a whole). The resolution of the crisis was achieved by turning to the intensive model of organized capitalism that included the appearance of monopolies. This constituted a different production system of surplus value that led to a different way of its realization.

In the extensive model (featuring laissez faire capitalism), both production and the increase in surplus value are ensured, in Marxist terms, mainly through increase of absolute surplus value production. Firstly, this takes place through wage reductions to the limits of survival combined with the extension of working hours and so on. The labour force here appears mainly as an unskilled and unwilling muscular force whose effective engagement in the production process is ensured through economic violence (lack of means of survival). Because of this function of capitalist enterprise, the intervention of politics, morality etc in the relations between capital and labour, apart from the economic means, is very difficult. This relation was present in the laissez faire capitalism of the 19th century, or the relationships between different parts of capital or between different enterprises. Secondly, and as a result of this, the extensive model (laissez faire capitalism), the absolute increase in surplus value and economic development are obtained by multiplying the business of a sole businessman through investment earnings (based on a secular or religious Protestant spirit) creating new production units.

Hence, laissez faire capitalism was a period of unbridled expansion of industrial capitalism that reformed the structure of the economy and fundamentally altered social relations, as well as the distribution and organization of population, in the manner that second wave societies were described by Alvin Toffler (Toffler 1982). Finally, in the extensive model, as a result of all aspects mentioned earlier, the leading role in increasing absolute surplus value, according to the terminology of Rueschmeyer, is played by the technical organization of labour (Rueschemeyer 1986), in other words the organization of machinery. The continuing revolution in technology results in the reduction of the necessary labour time and the increase of surplus labour time. To sum up, laissez faire capitalism is the macroscopic aspect of absolute surplus value production in capitalism.

In my view, within this form of the capitalist economy, social communication is to a paramount degree separated from work and vice versa, although it is subjected to the same rules as labour. The labour process is free of socially-organized communication – an end in itself, serving the needs and aspirations of its subjects. Moreover, socially organized communication is subjected to a great degree to the requirements of universal exchange in two ways. On the one hand, the social production and consumption of communication that is commercialized is characterized by the same procedures and relations between producers and businesses as well as the production of material commodities.

The producers of symbolic products have more or less the same relationship with their employer as a the factory worker (Pleios 1993, 49–50; Mosco 2009, 133). This model finds its theoretical expression in Marx's conception of the commodity. Marx considered as commodity any merchandise "whether addressed to the stomach or mind" (Marx 1979, 45), exactly because of the conditions and the means of its production, and because it is produced not to meet the needs of producers, but of consumers. On the other hand, the predominance of exchange relations is expressed through the predominance of natural language, and of written language and the press in social communication in particular.

Natural language as a semiotic system becomes the symbolic equivalent of value. It becomes the symbolic "currency" to redeem "on the show" any other representation. This is why print media become the predominant media and the content categories on the axis of information – literature become predominant (content categories) inside and outside print media (Pleios 1993, 51). In other words, in laissez faire capitalism, social communication is relatively separated from labour, but both fall under the same rules of production of surplus value on the one hand and commodity production on the other. This does not mean that all cultural production and communication are commercialized. On the contrary, the masses use largely forms and products of communication that are not commercialized. This statement is especially true for socially organized, i.e. commodified, cultural production.

However, there are limits beyond which the continuity of the extensive model and laissez faire capitalism is impossible. Classical Marxist political economy interprets the emergence of monopoly capitalism (organized capitalism) mainly as a result of the relations between different parts of capital, considering the relationship between capital and labour as stable. This means that monopoly is interpreted simply as a result of the integration of individual businesses targeting the largest company's monopoly profit. As mentioned earlier, the emergence of monopoly capitalism, as well as of liberal capitalism, should be thought of as part of production (at the micro-level) rather than as part of the market (the macro-level). More specifically, the emergence of monopolies is more related to the transformation of the organic composition of capital, the relationship between constant capital (dead labour) and living labour (the workers' labour) (Marx 1979, 627–664). But the increase of the organic composition of capital, due to the primary role of the technical organization of the labour, which Marx accepts in the long-term (Marx 1979, 627–664), is at the same time a process of the intensification of labour, if one has to face the declining rate of profit. In other words, the increase of the organic composition of capital is at the same time an increase of the productivity of the "total quantity of live and materialized labour production" (Richta 1976, 47). Thus, the emergence of monopoly capitalism (organized capitalism) must be associated with the increase of the relative surplus value and an increase in productivity, or otherwise the transition to a new, intensive model of development of the capitalist mode of production.

This is achieved through the transformation of the social, and especially the bureaucratic organization of labour in the production process rather than by changes in technology (Rueschmeyer, 1986; Sennett 2008, 28, Braverman 1974). "The way in which the enterprises were organized internally played the most important role" (Sennett 2008, 28). Therefore, it is no coincidence that the monopolistic organization of the economy (at the macro-level) is accompanied by forms of labour organization (at the micro-level), such as Taylorism, Fordism, "human relations", the Gantt system, Halsey, Rowan etc. which places emphasis on the social–organizational aspect of labour (Parker 2000; Pleios 1993, 54). In fact, the intensive model is the one that brings out this aspect of organization of labour as vital in the production process. On the contrary, the social organization of labour within the extensive model, does not constitute a problem that needs special attention. Within the extensive model the social organization of labour is a mere extension of technique – machines organize work and not vice versa.

Labour under monopoly capitalism is eventually organized into patterns that can very generally be described as "military." "The profits that markets put in jeopardy, bureaucracy sought to repair" (Sennett 2008, 28). This is especially true for models like Taylorism and Fordism. Sennett mentions that the application of a military pattern of organization to the industry, and further to the rest of society, was the form of labour organization that inspired Weber and that he kept in mind in all his work. In Sennett's words: "We owe the analysis of militarization of society [...] to Max Weber" (Sennett 2008, 28), who saw and analyzed it in his own country. Germany is regarded as the birthplace or, according to Lash and Urry, the "ideal type" (Lash and Urry 1987, 17–28) of such an industrial and social organization of capitalism. However, on the one hand, these patterns of (militarily) organized capitalism and society are characterized by a vertical and strict hierarchical organization requiring discipline, and on the other hand their effectiveness is based on the voluntary involvement of individuals.

These patterns are based on the assignment of certain tasks, which must be carried out with active participation (Sennett 2008, 30–39). They require acceptance by the workforce and its voluntary conformation to them. In such an organization of labour, the economic violence upon which liberal capitalism is based, is an insufficient incentive for the workforce to be efficient. On the contrary, if the process of production shall be effective, then the relationship between labour and capital has to be built and it was built on a consensus basis (Burawoy 1979, xii). In order to be effective in the new environment, the workforce needed to find a purpose, to adopt the purposes of the productive process as if they were its own and to seek their application and fulfillment. We could note that although Marx studied liberal capitalism, Weber looked into organized capitalism. However, they both equated capitalism in general with the form of capitalism they studied.

Therefore, to achieve the necessary level of control and voluntary participation of the workforce as an essential element of the intensive model, economic violence (hunger) and the exploitation of labour through absolute surplus value that have a divisive function do not suffice. It is necessary to integrate elements apart from the economy such as political and cultural ones to the economic culture and the production process. Such purposes could be initially established and set a political vision (such as democracy, nation, or later socialism etc) (Pleios 1996).

It is a fact that in the initial period of monopoly capitalism (when also the collective form of property conceals its private character), the intensive model was developed primarily as a reorganization between different forms of capital and businesses or, to be more accurate, between the state and monopolies. By the end of the First World War, this was indeed the case. Burawoy is right (Burawoy 1979, xi) on this point, but only regarding the initial period of organized capitalism, particularly in countries with less liberalism and a greater presence of a romantic spirit, in which the militarization of labour and of the whole of society was for different reasons easier to achieve, as e.g. in Germany, Austria, Italy, Russia, Greece etc. However, in countries influenced more by the liberal tradition, where personal gain is the existence and purpose of the state (Hobsbawm 2008, 51–52), or in countries where the intensive model exists, this development is not sustainable or feasible in the long term.

The problem of integrating extra-economic mechanisms into the production process, which ensure the voluntary participation and discipline of workers in the military organization of labour and make possible the production of relative surplus value (Jessop 2002, 56, 58), was solved by enlarged consumption (Pleios 2001, 207–209). Adorno and Horkheimer note that "significantly, the system of the culture industry comes from the more liberal industrial countries, and all its characteristic media, such as movies, radio, jazz, and magazines, flourish there" (Adorno and Horkheimer 2001, 79).

Enlarged consumption certainly served to offset the additional forces of labour spent in intensive production. But mostly enlarged (mass) consumption was enforcing productivity, not the other way round, as some scholars suggest (Jessop 2002, 7; Matsuyama 2002). There is no rational explanation why capitalists should increase salaries of their workers given their high productivity if at the same time the higher levels of workers' consumption couldn't increase their productivity. Productivity does not result only from "economies of scale" (Jessop 2002, 56). Increased productivity was a necessary condition for enlarged consumption only if enlarged consumption was a necessary condition for increased productivity. But from the capitalists' point of view, profits and not workers' way of life were (and still are) the purpose. Thus from the capitalists' point of view, enlarged consumption is justified only as a productive factor.

However, enlarged consumption could be a precondition of the intensive model to the degree to which: (a) extra (beyond a minimum existence) money is not saved in order to protect the business system from being accessed by new competitors, but it is spent on consumption and (b) when money is spent on commodities that can develop within the labour force the notions of voluntary participation and discipline. And this was (is) possible to the extent that the workforce is no longer a mass of workers excluded from privileges, but is upgraded and according to Arendt integrated in society or to some extent subjected to the same rights that the elite enjoy (Arendt 1991).

In other words, the problem was solved by the consumption of commodities – namely commodities that have a symbolic value (Baudrillard 1990; Arendt 1959, 72–83, 108–110) beyond their use value (which aims at the simple reproduction of labour power) as well as symbolic commodities (e.g. communication products). The form that this consumption took was individual.

The enlarged consumption of commodities – symbols and symbolic commodities – allowed the workforce to become subjects. Rosalind Williams in her work pointed out the connection between mass consumption and upper classes' life style (Williams 1991, 13). Thus the consumption of such commodities became means for the elaboration of common goals and meaning among the elites and the workforce. Or, as Marglin and Bhaduri have expressed it in macroeconomic terms: "If demand is high enough, the level of capacity utilization will in turn be high enough to provide for the needs of both workers and capitalists" (Marglin and Bhaduri 1990, 153). This way the workforce could share its interests with those of the elites. Thus, the main, not necessarily the more obvious, goal of the enlarged consumption was that the labour force accepted and served the historically shaped division of labour, not the diachronic division of the extra-economic power, as Baudrillard suggests (Baudrillard 2003).

In fact, the usefulness of enlarged consumption was not to form an effective workforce in terms of functionality of an unproblematic natural force, as assumed by human capital theory (Schultz 1961) or other analyses (Lash and Urry 1987, 67–68). It was, rather, to form an effective workforce with intentions and consciousness, in symbolic terms, which manifest themselves in terms of incentives, motivation, goals, etc. Such an operation is ensured at the point when consumption occurs within the context of consumerism as an ideology (Bocock 1997). In this perspective, consumerism is not so much the personal pursuit of the use value of commodities, but of their symbolic value, which represent socially acceptable virtues and ways of life (Pleios 2001, Chapter 3). In this sense, symbolic value differs from commodity fetishism because of its key productive function and usefulness.

On the political level, the problem was resolved with the implementation of Keynesian policies, or in other words by supplementing the system of mass production with arrangements that ensured mass consumption (Aglieta 1987; Lipietz 1990). Keynesianism is not only the origin of the explosion of the production of commodities – symbols, but also of the symbolic commodities of mass culture. However, this is not the main cause, but the result of the shift to intensive production, the production of surplus value, and the extended model of development. The economic cost of wide consumption is not an expense as it may seem, but an investment (the rate of labour force), without which intensive production and high business profit are impossible.

Thus, the result and precondition of intensive production is the consumption of commodities – symbols (and symbolic commodities) and vice versa. Enlarged (mass) consumption enforces productivity, not the opposite as Matsuyama suggests (Matsuyama 2002). Mass consumption aims to produce some "properties" of the labour force, and thus some factors that are necessary for mass production. In this sense enlarged consumption becomes a force of production. Its role is not limited to the sphere of circulation of symbolic commodities (directly) or/and commodity–symbols (indirectly). Besides, in many countries, the objects for enlarged consumption are being offered in natural, non-commodity form, including for example television, education or other media and cultural products (Allen 1992; Mosco 2009, 134).

This change is not only the cornerstone for the development of mass communication in general, but of visual communication as well. These visual media offer in a concrete manner the symbolic value of commodities and the notion of lifestyle that surrounds them. They offer the image of commodities as an essential precondition for the circulation of the commodity itself and also of the labourforce as a commodity. In other words, the circulation of the commodity's image becomes crucial for the circulation of the commodity itself (Adorno and Horkheimer 2001; Pleios 1993, Chapter 2; 2001, Chapter 3), not the opposite (Debord 1986). This shows the crucial role of culture in the capitalist mode of production and vice versa. But the enriched and costly circulation (and consumption) is possible to the extent that they can stimulate a higher productivity, which covers the cost of circulation (and consumption) and leads further to the rise of surplus value and economic growth. Thus the real scope and outcome of the enlarged consumption and circulation is the rise of surplus value (Pleios 2001, Chapter 3; 1996) and not its sharing.

However, in this way, mass communication is dynamically evolving as a mechanism that encourages and implements mass cultural consumption and provides the conditions for the production of (relative) surplus value and intensive production. In this sense, mass culture and moreover commercialized communication cease to belong to the realm of the superstructure. It becomes a "basic superstructure" in the same way that it constitutes a "superstructure base". Or, in other words "things become media and media becomes things" (Lash and Lury 2007, 4).

From this viewpoint, capitalism is changing significantly and is becoming a "symbolic capitalism." It is becoming a capitalism that produces and consumes commodities – symbols (and the actual labourforce is no longer a mere commodity and becomes a broader symbolic – cultural identity). Hence, in symbolic capitalism the symbolic-informational processes are embodied organically both in production (and the production of surplus value) and in the consumption of commodities as integral elements of the economic process (Webster 1995; Castells 1996, Chapter 4; Fuchs 2010b). In this way, communication is integrated again into labour but now with an instrumental logic and labour is integrated organically into communication, and into the process of the production of cultural products (cultural industries). But this integration is achieved in a way that connects these procedures organically as contributors to the system function as a whole. On the macro-level, the combination of "economic and extra-economic institutions and practices" becomes a key structural feature of symbolic capitalism (Jessop and Sum 2006, 1).

From this perspective, what Cultural Political Economy stresses (Jessop 1990), is rather a historical product of capitalism's evolution. In this process, symbolic capitalism appears in many national, cultural and other forms because communication and culture are not yet an epiphenomenon or simply a superstructure. On the contrary, they become a structural element of relations of production and of the mode of production. However, these different forms of symbolic capitalism do not constitute national or cultural exceptions compared to an "ideal" symbolic capitalism. They are rather specific forms of a more generalized phenomenon – symbolic capitalism. The relation between symbolic capitalism in general and the specific national or other symbolic capitalisms (e.g. Western European or American or Mediterranean capitalism) is the relation between the general and the specific. This problem is of great importance in theorizing symbolic capitalism, but its analysis lies far beyond the purposes of the present paper. Symbolic capitalism appears at the interception of two changes. First, the shift to or the establishment of relative surplus value within the relations of production (the intensive model of capitalist production) and second the introduction of enlarged consumption regulations that sustain the intensive model.

Furthermore, the diversity of symbolic capitalism depends mostly on three factors. Firstly, it depends on the type of welfare state that follows a specific form of enlarged consumption. Esping Andersen's study of welfare regimes concludes that there have been three (later four) types of welfare state: Liberal (e.g. USA), Corporatist-Statist (e.g. Germany), Social Democratic (e.g. Scandinavian countries) and Mediterranean (e.g. Greece) (Esping-Andersen 1990, 1999).

Following this typology, we could say that there have been four types of enlarged consumption.

(a)   A type of enlarged consumption based on limited state intervention on the one hand and individual distribution on the other. In that case, the means for enlarged consumption, a minimum social wage, are given mostly in the form of money to the working individual in order to buy education and healthcare services, mass media products etc (e.g. USA).

(b)   A type of enlarged consumption, based also on market relations on the one hand but on collective distribution on the other – families, professional groups etc (e.g. Germany). Within that model, local, religious, or other organizations provide non-commodity services (e.g. childcare services) to disadvantaged social groups.

(c)   A type of welfare state that is based upon state intervention and individualism. The means for enlarged consumption are given to the working individual not only in commodity form (wage), but also in non-commodity or natural form – direct access to education and health services, mass media products etc (e.g. Scandinavian countries).

(d)   A type of welfare state that is based also upon state intervention, but where the means for enlarged consumption, in commodity as well as in non-commodity form, are addressed to the family and professional or social groups etc (e.g. Greece).

Secondly, the variety of symbolic capitalism depends on the extent and form of traditional culture that prevails in society. More precisely, it depends on the functions of traditions in modern societies. Thompson (1995) supports the idea that traditions carry the potential for the following functions: interpretation, legitimation, normativity, and identity. According to Thompson, in modern societies only two of them, namely interpretation and identity functions, are still active. In my opinion, this is so in typical Western democracies. On the contrary, in authoritarian regimes tradition often had also less or more normative and legitimatory functions supported by state power.

This was the case in Greece for a long period of time. In this case, enlarged consumption is encapsulated in traditional, cultural nationalist or even religious practices and discourses (Tsoukalas 1983). In my opinion, the wider the presence of traditions (especially its normative and legitimatory functions) in the cultural system, the more extra-economic (e.g. political) scopes are being served by enlarged consumption. That may also mean a non-effective or non-rational interrelation between the intensive model on the one hand and the enlarged consumption on the other (Charalambis 1983). This results in a higher autonomy of enlarged consumption from the intensive model.

Thirdly, the variety of symbolic capitalism depends also on political culture and the political system in a given society. However, as I mentioned earlier, this needs more systematic elaboration.

4   The Two Eras of Symbolic Capitalism

Although we generally have not left behind us the era that initiated the crisis of 1870 and particularly the end of WWI, the period of symbolic capitalism does not have a homogeneous character. We can distinguish two distinct sub-periods. The first period is strongly connected to mass production, mass consumption and Fordism, and very generally it is the first/initial period of symbolic capitalism, which is organically linked to heavy industrial machinery on the hand and the hierarchical, one-dimensional old media on the other. The second period was initiated by the economic and cultural crisis of the 1960s–70s and the new phase of globalization that has been characterized by diversified production and consumption and is inextricably linked to information technologies and "new media" (Davis 1988, Castells 1991; Mosco 2009, 15).

4.1   The Initial, Symbolic (or Organized) Capitalism

The first era of symbolic capitalism, the one that from another perspective is the socio-economic core of a mature (vs. early) modernity, is actually a transition period between industrial capitalism of early modernity and post-industrial capitalism of late modernity. As mentioned earlier, this first era was shaped by mass production and mass consumption. More precisely, it was shaped by Fordism as a form of work organization and led to mass (intensive) production and enlarged consumption (monopoly regulation of labour relations) (Lipietz, 1990).

The model of mass production was not invented during by Fordism, but had already existed before, in early industrial capitalism (Chandler 1994, 1–14). In the words of Daniel Bell: "Almost all the major industries we still have – steel, electric power, telegraph, telephone, automobiles, aviation – were 19th century industries" (Bell 1999, 20). What Fordism did was that it directed the intensive pattern and extended it into any possible direction. The really new element was not mass production, but enlarged consumption (Baudrillard 1990, 112), characterized by commodities that were mass-produced. This development took place, as pointed out by representatives of the Frankfurt School, by transferring the model of massive industrial production to symbolic commodities (cultural industries) (Horkheimer and Adorno 1986). But, as we shall see below, the enlarged consumption of commodities – symbols or even more symbolic commodities – was the main factor of depletion of mature and any previous capitalism.

Enlarged consumption was a process of appropriation of all these symbolic values that were unthinkable without the mechanisms of promotion (e.g. advertising) and mass culture (Wernick 1991, Ewen 2001, Lash and Lury 2007). Through such mechanisms, the creation of an illusory social mobility within the labourforce and identification with the upper classes were enabled. In other words, the enlarged consumption became the basis of what Sennet described as "social capitalism" (Sennett 2008, 35–44). This fact resulted in achieving social cohesion, social peace, political stability (Breed 1958), as well as the planned systemic organization of society at the national level, which strengthened the nation state as a whole organization of society, and nationalism as ideology.

Consequently, the new development was really the industrial mass production of socially organized communication (Horkheimer and Adorno 1986). This was a key factor in intensive production. I don't think that Burawoy (1979) is right when he separates the consensus at the work place from the consensus achieved through media and enlarged consumption. In my opinion they are interconnected. The cultural industry includes the industrial mass production of many and different commodities or symbolic products, products that are organized by various symbolic systems. However, for reasons that I cannot elaborate here in details, for the most important reason for the emergence and reproduction of consumerism was the moving image (Pleios 2001, Chapter 4).

It should not be regarded as a coincidence that the period of the emergence of organized capitalism was not only the period of the flourishing of enlarged consumption and display devices, but also the period of the emergence and dominance of cinema and later of television in social communication. The moving image can be defined as a changing set of visual images (according to Arnheim the image represents an object to a higher degree of abstraction) (Arnheim 1969, 135–152) resulting in a specific performance of an abstract representation of symbolic importance.

In other words, this created at the level of communication and especially of text, what was for the simple worker organized capitalism at the level of production and especially at the level of enlarged consumption, i.e. it offered its prototype and meaning (Debord 1986; Ewen 1999; Pleios 2001, Chapter 3). In this sense not only television but also any iconistic medium can be a source of lifestyle patterns in consumer capitalism. Therefore, both cultural consumption in general and even more the consumption of moving images and enlarged consumption were interdependent with Fordist mass production (Benjamin 1968). If intensive production was the hallmark of organized capitalism, then the hallmark in public communication was the dominance of the moving image. Consumption commodities – symbols – constituted the core in the fields of society and culture.

I should note here that the moving image does not relate to the specific forms of audiovisual media such as cinema or TV, but is an attribute of many representational systems and particularly audiovisual ones. In fact, cinema, television, video and digital modern media (such as computers or the internet), are different and successive forms of the moving image that are in line with different forms of symbolic capitalism (Pleios 1993). Therefore, from a sociological and cultural point of view. they should not be compared only among themselves but mainly in relation to their respective socio-economic and cultural conditions in which they occur and which they serve and are served by them. In this sense, the enlarged consumption (of commodities – symbols)

and cultural industries, are indissolubly linked to the intensive, organized capitalism or in other words to the first period of symbolic capitalism. The enlarged
consumption and cultural industries allow for intensive production and its
dynamics, as well as profitability and financial development of countries and
businesses.

If one looks at this the other way round, the cost of enlarged consumption
and cultural industry (especially that of heavy cultural industry such as the
visual one) is covered by the high productivity model (Matsuyama 2002). This
relationship is certainly possible under the condition that it occurs in a strictly
national systemic organization. Looking into the matter from the Marxist perspective, we come to the conclusion that the "forms of communication" are no
longer part of the superstructure, but a condition that ensures the process of
production and the production of surplus value. They constitute a factor of
production. In other words, although capitalism is identical with the removal
of any extra-economic relations regarding the shaping of economic inequalities (Wood 1997), in its evolution, the extra-economic relations are organically
embedded in economic ones, especially in relations of production and the
production of surplus value.

But the question that is most interesting from the perspective of future
developments is the one about the boundaries of the system and the reasons
which rendered it historically obsolete. From the point that this issue is
approached, there are three conditions that make the system of intensive
organized capitalism viable: (a) mass consumption, which ensures mass production and therefore the functioning of the enlarged consumption as an
engine for intensive development, (b) the amortization of the costs of
enlarged consumption through the contribution of enlarged consumption
to increased productivity and surplus value, and therefore, the maintenance
of class stratification, (c) the national and systemic organization of society
based on this status.

These three conditions were shaken, which resulted in the beginning of the
degradation of organized intensive capitalism and the welfare state (Lash and
Urry 1987; Lipietz 1990). Differentiated consumer demand and flexible production became a key industrial tendency in the late 60s and onward (Jameson
1984, Harvey 1989, Castells 1991; Mosco 2009, 15). The rebellions of 1968 seem to
be uprisings against mass consumption and a turn to diversified, fragmented
and/or individualized consumption of commodities – symbols and symbolic
commodities (Perniola 1991, 30 40). Representatives of the Regulation School
showed that the enlarged consumption following an increasing trend could
further contribute to economic development and profitability, leading to an
inverse relationship, while the reduction of class differences that was caused

by a reduction in profitability led the ruling classes to react with cuts in welfare policies and the flow of capital abroad in search of cheaper inputs (Lipietz 1990; Vergopoulos 1999). Therefore, the national organization of capitalism changed due to the contemporary phase of globalization (Sassen 2009, 113–124).

Although these three factors are equally important, very often authors argue that one or two of them were catalytic in the overthrow of the system of mass production – enlarged (cultural) consumption with particular emphasis placed on globalization (Sassen 2009, Sennet, 2008). However, we must concentrate our attention to the core of the system on the micro-level. As mentioned earlier, this is the ability of consumption, through its symbolic functions, to contribute to the discipline of employees, organization and the logic of production, as well as to the increase of productivity and profitability. Therefore, the dismantling of the system should be sought in changes occurring on a symbolic-communicative level and its social and economic functions.

The enlarged consumption of commodity-symbols and of symbolic commodities can be put in a double sense, as Hall (1980) has shown for the second case, but above all it is a symbolic-communicative process, as the appropriation of symbolic value is more important in social terms. Production and the exchange and consumption of symbolic commodities in particular as an economic process cannot be explained without first understanding its symbolic-communicative dimension (Hall 1980). As a result, we must first explain the function of symbolic commodities as text in the frame of social conditions. This function was to provide an illusional individual social mobility, individual freedom from social constraints and individualization in general. Besides, especially in visual production as shown by Hall (Hall 1980), the basic mechanism of interpretation are the connotation and personal experiences and aspirations. Therefore, from this point onwards, mass consumption cannot satisfy the functions for which it was established. This fact is a straight questioning of its foundations, i.e. of mass production. On the other hand, the continuous expansion of the enlarged consumption, that is its nuclear element with the assistance of social demands, have contributed so that it cannot contribute to growth or cause a reduction in profitability and economic development (Lipietz 1990).

4.2   Deep Symbolic (or Disorganized) Capitalism

The crisis of organized, intensive (and symbolic) capitalism emerged as the imbalance between the efficiency of the production system on the one hand and the cost of enlarged consumption on the other. In other words, the enlarged consumption could contribute to an increased productivity (growth) of the economic system. While the cost of enlarged consumption remained stable, or (mainly) increased, the levels of productivity remained stable or increased.

This was expressed as a reduction in profits ("profit squeeze") (Marglin and Bhaduri 1990), which needed to be addressed in order to ensure the existence of class rule. As shown by the analyses of the representatives of the Regulation School, this crisis was actually a crisis of "under-productivity" or the decrease of the rate of productivity in the late '60s and '70s (Lipietz 1990; Cook 1990, 79–84). While the working class enjoyed the benefits of enlarged consumption, this did not lead to the purpose, for which it was established (to increase productivity and profitability of intensive production). It became a social and cultural process detached from its economic base in the given class structure.

This crisis was initially treated in two ways that, however, did not reach the root of the problem: (a) the flow of businesses abroad, where they could find cheaper labour (Elam 2000, 64–65) and/or (b) the reduction of enlarged consumption (Lipietz 1990; Pond 1989). Nevertheless, the radical treatment of the problem required the activation of the "interest" of employees so that their work could contribute to a productivity and profitability increase, as it was the case with the establishment of enlarged consumption. Thus, the idea was that the logic of symbolic capitalism should be maintained but the means by which its financial results are achieved should change. In other words, the production system should be reconstructed in the direction that the logic of consumption had changed (commodity-symbols and symbolic commodities) as well as social action had as a whole. Key elements of this change were the differentiation-individualization, active interaction of the public and the collapse of the one-way hierarchical action, the activation of the symbolic, the cultural capital of the public etc (Lash and Urry 1994).

The necessary changes in the production system that faced the crisis of "under-productivity" were completed by two simultaneous and interlinked transformations: firstly the technical organization of labour (Robins and Webster 1988; Toffler 1982; Webster 1995, Chapter 1) and secondly the social organization of labour (Lipietz 1994, Mouriki 1994). The introduction of digital technologies of automation, basically communication and information technologies (Richta 1976, Castells 1991; Mosco 2009, 15), has enabled the diversification of production in order to meet the diverse needs of consumption (Davis 2001). That had already been created through the "game" of communication in the field of enlarged consumption, which besides was the key factor for the maintenance and expansion of this consumption (Bauman 2005, 16–33; Pleios 2001, Chapter 3).

It should be underlined that beyond the sphere of production, the emergence of "new media" in the area of cultural consumption, such as the Internet, was the result not only of technological developments. It was mostly the result of the circumstance that these technological developments provided answers to the democratization demand and the individualization of the communication process. But that demand had already developed in the period of the "old media." "Old media" were long before the emergence of the «new media» the centre of theoretical, social and political criticism due to their centralized and one-dimensional nature (Baudrillard 1986, Manovich 2001).

This was perfectly logical as the logic of consumption of symbolic commodities and commodity-symbols evolved in the exact opposite direction from that of the "old media." The logic of cultural consumption had the characteristics of individual choice and the ability of participation, active personal involvement, negotiation of meaning. We should also note that the exact same logic of democratization and participation that is visible in cultural consumption (Jameson 1984), was also the case in the area of commodity–symbols' consumption (Brown 1992) and that democratization is an inherent and permanent process within enlarged consumption (McCracken 1988).

As far as the social organization of labour is concerned, the transformations made in order to attract "the interest" of workers were applied through the introduction of the so-called post-Fordist forms of work organization (Lipietz 1994, Mouriki 1994). In contrast to Fordism and its "single logic," post-Fordism does not consist of a single model of organization, but includes many different and complementary settings (Hirst and Zeitlin 1991). As Amin underlines: "The relationship between the ideal-type of dominant form of Fordism has also been questioned, with critics arguing that recognition of national diversity undermines the notion of a single, dominant Fordist logic" (Amin 1994, 11). Coriat also recognizes that the world wide spread of Fordism was the expansion of a single Fordist model – that of the American methods of mass production (Coriat 1997, 242). The multiple logic of post-Fordism makes perfect sense if one considers that the purpose is to cause the active participation of workers, characterized by different ways of thinking and living, not only on a global, but also on a national and local scale. On the macro-level it depends on "whether capital, labour, or the state has the most influence over the process of restructuring" (Lash and Baggueley 1988).

Despite their diversity, the post-Fordist settings are based on a new type of labour motivation, which can be described as "production initiative" as opposed to "production discipline," which is the case in the Fordist organization of labour (Pleios, 1996). The "production discipline" required the voluntarily discipline of employees concerning the logic and purpose of production, as well as the pace in order to satisfy the common interests of workers and employers, business and national economy, economy and state. Meeting the specific individual goals, lifestyles, etc. was a case of free time and enlarged consumption, which depended upon the efficiency of the production process.

On the contrary, "production initiative" combines the participation of the employees with a real interest in achieving personal goals, as if the success of the company, the overall process within the business, was a personal matter of the employee. "Production initiative" is characterized by "loyalty to the company" and a "more committed workforce" (Hickox and Moore 1992, 109). In this case, not only material economic objectives, but also the exercise o control and authority, the projection of particular views and taste, in a nutshell the complete manifestation of the personality of the individual, lies therein. Therefore, particular features of post-Fordism are to create a horizontal hierarchy, to transfer administrative responsibilities to the workforce, and also personal involvement, horizontal cooperation, participation, the effective use of educational, symbolic and cultural capital, the identification of the worker not only as producer, but also as a citizen and consumer (Lipietz 1997; Mouriki 1994; Sennett 2008).

The introduction of horizontal hierarchy, combined with other elements as well as the responsibility involved that is required due to the use of new technologies, lead to the false assumption of an elimination of class and other social differences in the production process. Thus, functions applied by enlarged consumption are now undertaken by the production process through a set of settings that are regarded as post-Fordist. This is the first, and in a macroperspective, perhaps the less obvious side of the change. The other one and more obvious change is constituted by the strengthening of the power and functions of the central units of a (worldwide) production system. Sennett remarks that "One of the consequences of the information revolution has thus been to replace modulation and interpretation of commands by a new kind of centralization" (Sennett 2008, 39). Sassen also points out that the functions of the central units of such a (global) system, especially in the area of finances and the new economy, are being strengthened (Sassen 2009, 99–100). Hence, these two sides of the new organization of labour taken together lead not to a military, but to a "gang" or "guerilla" like structure, as one can see for example in the advertising industry (Arvidsson 2007). It is similar to the military structure of organized capitalism but without any civic, political, ideological or other commitment, value system or restrictions, beyond effectivity and success. Sennett describes this new form of social organization of labour as "MP3 organization," and it differs from the pyramidal, hierarchical form of organized symbolic capitalism (Sennett 2008, 65–88). This form of labour can respond to the new technological organization (digital automation technologies) and to the needs of diverse, flexible and changing production and vice versa (Amin 1994, 14–15; Davis 2001).

Thus, a major difference of developed (deep) symbolic capitalism in comparison to both liberal and initial symbolic (or organized) capitalism is the simultaneous change in both the technological and social organization of labour. Unlike in the liberal capitalism of the 19th century when the technological organization of labour plays a key role, and the initial symbolic capitalism where the social organization of labour takes a decisive role in the deep symbolic (or disorganized) capitalism, both technology and social (re-)organization of labour now have the same importance. Technological change comes hand in hand with a new form of social organization of labour and vice versa based on the "production initiative." It is impossible to separate in technologies (of production) the technical aspects from communication aspects – social aspect and vice versa. It is a combination of technicality and communication forms. Thus, a key aspect of the work organization of labour, the organization of power relations in the production process, comes to overcome the inequality that results from property relations. That was covered symbolically by enlarged consumption, ensuring the discipline and active participation of the workforce, the objectives and rationale of intensive production.

The points that can be analyzed are numerous. Among them, two are of particular importance in our analysis. First of all, the changes made in the area of labour and the production process, at least concerning the structure and their rationale, from a temporal, spatial and social point of view derive from the field of enlarged consumption both of commodity-symbols and symbolic commodities, which were developed thanks to a variety of communication "games." In other words, it is rather post-Fordism that comes from postmodernism than the opposite, or at least in Gartman's view, postmodernism "dialectically influenced this economic change" (Gartman 1998, 119). Thus, it seems that changes in the mode of production are imported and incorporated into production to a great extent from the area of enlarged consumption. From a Marxist perspective, in the "new capitalism" not only the role of communication (and of the "superstructure" as a whole) stays intact, but it also becomes more vital as a factor of production, though in a new social form/structure. The change in communication forms serves as a guide and supplement for changes in production relations and the mode of production. Therefore, not only does it not get diminished, but it also becomes even more organic as far as the character of the new capitalism as symbolic capitalism is concerned.

Moreover, the fact that patterns of change in production come more or less from the area of (enlarged) consumption and socially organized mediated communication, implies that a part of the enlarged consumption has become superfluous. Its functions are undertaken by the changes in production and particularly in social organization of labour or, at least become more "rational" from an economic point of view (including the privatization and individual-ization of consumption) (Hamnet 1989). This does not only reduce the costs of consumption and therefore increases profitability in production, but also achieves a more solid consensus, an objective identification between workers and employers, and effective stability. This is valid especially at the micro-level, without needing to have long-term arrangements on the level of public poli-cies that the welfare state required (monopolistic regulation of labour) (Jessop 1994, Loader and Burrows 1994). Secondly, the (digital) technology used in the automation of production is structurally and functionally similar to that used in consumption (Sennett 2008; Barrett and Davidson 2008; Fuchs 2010b). This stands in contrast to what was happening in symbolic capitalism, where pro-duction technology differs significantly from the technology of enlarged con-sumer activity of symbolic products or commodity-symbols (Burawoy 1979). This has many side effects.

First and foremost, the ability to use technology and the culture of new technology acquired in the area of cultural consumption is a qualification needed to operate in the area of work (labour or education) and vice versa (Green, Reid and Bigum 1998, 22; Gualerzi 2010, 147). Secondly, among others, it has resulted in the relative decline of significance of formal qualifications compared to the merits (or the qualifications acquired at the workplace) of the labour market and the emergence of a new egalitarianism that eliminates the differences between different hierarchical levels of knowledge and qualifica-tions. As Thursfield points out: "technological innovations may, for example, deskill task but not the worker, although worker's skills may be devalued as a result of this process. In addition, although a worker may not possess formal qualifications, he or she may be high skilled in the task requirements of their particular occupation" (Thursfield 2003, 47). What formal education provides to the workforce in order to be effective in the post-Fordist work organization, is a working ethos and citizenship rather than a set of work skills and knowl-edge (Hickox and Moore 1992, 108–110). This means that the overall skills that are necessary at the workplace are a matter of socialization in a broad sense (Pleios, 2004). This is shown particularly in the "new media" and cultural con-sumption and public communication, especially on the Internet. As Poulet has shown regarding the interaction between press and the Internet, in the latter knowledge is equated with the opinion of amateurs on various issues and in general there is a widening egalitarianism, which overrides any established hierarchies of formal knowledge (Poulet 2009, 175–178). Successful is not the one who is good in one field, but the one that is becoming popular in the pub-lic. This also occurs in the production process, but through a set of complex interactions in a post-Fordist business (Sennett 2008; Terranova 2004, 20–27).

Thirdly, the use of new technologies in production, especially when coupled with strengthening functions of the central units of a system, eliminate the autonomy of individual sectors and their placement in a direct decision-making center, at the end of complex interactions (Sennet 2008; Sassen 2009). The same can be observed in the field of communication, which means that the MP3 structure becomes a more general structure of social action. Overcoming the independence of functional units, is something that characterizes texts as well, particularly in "new media." Differences of content categories tend to become assimilated to a great extent (Hill 2007). Almost all types of content fall within a new paradigm, that of "pleasant information" and not just information, as claimed by theories of the information society. "Information" is rather a quantitative-technical dimension of the content (Webster 1995). In qualitative terms, texts can coexist and can be shared because they have a common qualitative ground. They inform and at the same time they entertain. In other words, they are organized according to infotainment patterns (Thussu 2007) and this tends to eliminate the large differences between different types of content categories and the various texts (Pleios 2011, Chapter 2). The differences in the content categories are more quantitative and technical rather than textual.

Fourth, these processes in the sphere of production unfold mostly on a symbolic and functional level and less on an economic and structural–divisive one, as it was the case in initial symbolic capitalism. The differences in social class and economic level as well as the differences in the "order of discourse" (Fairclough 1995, 78) on the text level are realities that are significantly curtailed. Thus, the emergence of MP3 capitalism contributes to an even greater convergence and continuous dynamic permutation of production and consumption, work and communication, economy and culture (Toffler 1982; Fuchs 2010a). The difference is that Toffler focused on the functional aspect of the phenomenon rather than on the fact that it is based on social inequality and class relations that exist in the production process. The convergence and swapping of communication and production can take many forms.

Fuchs (2010a) indicates that the free work of the Internet user for entertainment purposes is utilized for product marketing, i.e. the entertainment of the user becomes work for profit. Despite the importance of other aspects of this convergence, its main dimension is surplus value production, i.e. (digital) communication enhances the productivity of labour force and thus reduces the time required for reproduction, not only in the field of the realization of surplus value, i.e. trade. Besides, "new media" and especially the Internet have been created according to the model of the telephone that in turn derived from business needs and reflects their organization and relationships (Garnham 2003).

However, from this approach, the distinction between the base and the superstructure disappears even further, as well as the distinction between work and communication, which allows focusing on the functional aspect of the phenomenon. Therefore, the use of "new media," which are at the same time means of production and means of communication, inevitably links the logic of labour to the logic of entertainment, the logic of production to the logic of consumption (Toffler 1982, Fuchs 2010a). A supporting role in this is played by the technical and institutional capacity of free and working time, leisure and work, workplace and leisure space. As a result, work is treated as a process of pursuing individual goals and personal pleasure and personal fulfillment process as a job, as an activity to produce useful causes for the subject. In my opinion this constitutes a typical distancing from the literal meaning of economic Marxism, but on the other hand it is a rapprochement of sociological and philosophical Marxism.

5   Conclusion

From the Marxist perspective, the analysis of social process acquires a practical importance to the degree to which it examines and participates in the process of social change, as it was claimed by Marx himself in the famous 11th Feuerbach thesis. Social science does not exist for its own sake (to explain the world), but for the change and progress of society. This way, this social analysis fulfills its social utility and functional existence in a society, in which there is a division of labour.

The question that arises is whether social change is a reality in deep symbolic capitalism. According to the analysis presented above, the development of relations of production within the capitalist mode of production, leads to revisions and even false democratization (at least partially) of the relations of production, power relations, and the management of the production process. Horizontal hierarchies, labour force participation, the transfer of administrative functions to the labour force etc. are signs of this change. Moreover, and most importantly, this change is organically associated with a certain form of communication, which is consistent with the so-called "information society" (Webster 1995; Castells 1996, Poster 1990). In deep symbolic capitalism, a core direction of change is towards power relations and production management and it is true that this side of deep symbolic capitalism has been neglected in the post-Fordist approach (Vallas 1999; Kennett 2003). Instead, in initial symbolic capitalism, the change was one of relations of consumption firstly and secondly of power relations. This reflects the strong relationship of initial symbolic capitalism with the past, with liberal capitalism. However, the change in the relations of production in deep symbolic capitalism appears as a continuation of changes in initial symbolic capitalism.

The social relations of power and management in the production process are perhaps the most primordial and long established relations of class and social inequality (Mann 1986), structured also (and mostly) symbolically and not only by economic means (Mouzelis 2008, 10). Perhaps that's why the changes in power relations seem to be more important in deep symbolic capitalism compared to initial symbolic capitalism. It is all about power relations and other forms of production relations are the means. It seems that the development of the capitalist mode of production and especially of its relations of production, due to their symbolization, leads to the point, where power relations become more or at least equally important compared to other forms of relations of production, despite the fact that this happens in order to hide the latter. Perhaps this circumstance fueled Baudrillard's postmodern criticism (as well as poststructuralism's approach), who recognized that relations of production (and consumption) serve power relations and not vice versa (Baudrillard 1990). From this perspective, we should consider postmodern social theory more as a distorted reflection of the reality of deep symbolic capitalism than as a set of diachronic truth claims.

Thus, it appears that relations of production (of deep symbolic capitalism) are associated organically with "forms of communication" of the information society. This change, as it happened earlier on with enlarged consumption, serves both the concealment of class inequality and capital accumulation/ the production of more surplus value. But what is most important is that the "forms of communication" are not considered as passive anymore when compared to relations of production.

In other words, communication in deep symbolic capitalism is becoming the guide of conservation or change of the mode of production and especially of its relations of production. Certainly something similar happened in the past with the democratization of consumption. However, this situation differs significantly in that this interaction is not regulated mostly at the macro- or midterm level, i.e. that of a whole national economy, but largely takes place at the micro-level of an enterprise or a local economy and, as a result, it is not necessary to keep up the regulations at the enterprise level with the regulations at the national level – in fact the national regulations are significantly cut down.

This conclusion leads us to a fundamental issue. The process of social change does no longer necessary depends mainly on the developments at the macro-level. In other words, changes in "relations of production" can be caused by appropriate changes in communication. It is not necessary to require regulations primarily at the level of a national society or transnational ones (or transnational formations). From the standpoint of classical Marxism, this has enormous significance. Firstly, social change (including change of class relations) can be achieved through the kind and forms of communication developed in deep symbolic capitalism and secondly it can be performed at the level of individual economic structures or businesses, changes that explain the historical basis of modern relativism. In other words, it is no longer essential to seize power in order for someone to be able to change the world, but as argued by John Holloway this can be done without seizing power (Holloway 2006, 340), changing the world from below, changing the world in parts. Holloway notes that today social relations can change the capitalist relations of production. The error of Holloway, in my opinion, is that he neglects the power of technology and especially the power of communication in social change.

Social change can partly be achieved in individual parts of the economic system, especially if one considers this system not as national or global, i.e. in the context of globalization. This does not mean that regulations at the macrolevel are not necessary. Social change at the workplace is impossible without its socio-political equivalent and vice versa. What links these two spheres is the tendency towards grassroots democracy. If deep symbolic capitalism and information technologies go hand in hand with horizontal hierarchies at the work place, then democratization in the economic sphere is impossible without grassroots democracy in the political sphere – and vice versa. In my opinion, the use of "new media," such as blogs, social media etc, in protests and symbolic politics is needed in order to achieve grassroots democracy, especially since "military" organized economies and hierarchical party democracies have failed. This could explain to some degree the "indignados" movements (all based on "new media") in very different countries, such as Egypt, Algeria, Spain, Greece, or the USA.

Greece has a failed, state-centered, economic system (Sakellaropoulos 1992; Kazakos 2001). At the same time, it has a failed (and corrupt) centralized party democracy (Lyrintzis, Nikolakopoulos and Sotiropoulos 1996). Thus, it can be explained, at least to some extent, why during the last two years (2010–2012), the "new media" have played a crucial role in the delegitimization of the political system as well as in the emergence of new grassroots political organizations and mobilizations. These movements would be unthinkable without the "new media" and new kinds of content (Lambrakou 2011). This movement in Greece has already been called "The Facebook May 1968." But the problem of social change remains unsolved until one can achieve grassroots regulations in the political sphere as well as in the relations of production.

Grassroots democracy in politics as well as in economy cannot be achieved only by use of "new media." In my opinion "new media" no matter where they are used, in politics or in the production process, are today still based on the "spectacle". Image/spectacle, though in a different manner, still play a key structural role in "new media" as well as in "old media" and enlarged consumption. However, in the process of social change, social scientists are no longer the generals, but the engineers of this change. In the age of information technologies, the functional and the revolutionary side of the social scientist converge to a new indivisible whole.

References

Adorno, Theodor and Horkheimer, Max. 1987. Sociology. Essays. Athens: Kritiki (in Greek).

Adorno, Theodor and Horkheimer, Max. 2001. The Culture Industry: Enlightenment as Mass Deception. In *Media and Cultural Studies*. Keyworks, edited by Meenakshi Durham and Douglas Kellner, 71–101. Oxford: Blackwell.

Aglietta Michael. 1979. A Theory of Capitalist Regulation: The US Experience. London: Verso.

Alexander, Jeffrey. 1987. Sociological Theory Since World War II. New York: Columbia University Press.

Allen, Robert. 1992. Audience-Oriented Criticism and Television. In *Channels of Discourse, Reassembled: Television and Contemporary Criticism*, edited by Robert Allen, 101–137. London: Routledge.

Althusser, Louis. 1990. *Positions*. Athens: Themelio (in Greek).

Amin, Ash. 1994. Post-Fordism. Models, Fantasies and Models of Transition. In *Post-Fordism: A Reader*, edited by Ash Amin, 1–39. Massachusetts: Blackwell.

Arendt, Hannah. 1959. *The Human Condition. A Study of the Central Dilemmas Facing Modern Man*. Garden City, New York. Anchor Books.

Arendt, Hannah. 1991. Society and Culture. In *The Media Culture,* edited by Kostas Livieratos and Takis Fragoulis, 121–126. Athens: Alexandria (in Greek).

Arvidsson, Adam. 2007. Creative Class or Administrative Class? *ephemera. theory & politics in organization* 7 (1): 8–23.

Barrett, Michael and Elizabeth Davidson. 2008. Exploring the Diversity of Service Worlds in the Service Economy. In *Information Technology in the Service Economy: Challenges and Possibilities for the 21st Century*, edited by Michael Barrett, Elizabeth Davidson, Catherine Middleton and Janice DeGross, 1–12. 2nd edition. New York: Springer.

Baudrillard, Jean. 1986. *Requiem for the Mass Media*. Athens: Eleftheros Typos (in Greek).

Baudrillard, Jean. 1990. *The Mirror of Production*. Athens: Alexandria (in Greek).

Baudrillard, Jean. 2003. *The Consumer Society. Myths and Structures*. London: Sage.

Bauman, Zygmunt. 2005. *Work, Consumerism and the Poor*. Berkshire: McGraw Hill.

Bell, Daniel. 1999. *The Coming of Post-Industrial Society. A Venture in Social Forecasting*. New York: Basic Books.

Benjamin, Walter. 1968. The Work of Art in the Age of Mechanical Reproduction. In *Illuminations*, edited by Walter Benjamin and Hannah Arendt, 219–253. New York: Harcourt, Brace and World.

Blackledge, David and Hunt Barry. 1995. Sociology of Education. Athens: Metechmio (in Greek).

Bocock, Robert. 1997. Consumption: Key Ideas. London: Routhledge.

Braverman, Harry. 1974. *Labor and Monopoly Capital: The Degradation of Work in the Twentieth Century*. New York: Monthly Review Press.

Breed, Warren. 1958. Mass Communication and Socio-Cultural Integration. *Social Forces* 37 (2): 109–116.

Brown, Doug. 1992. Doing Social Economics in a Postmodern World. *Review of Social Economy* 50 (4): 383–403.

Burawoy, Michael. 1979. *Manufacturing Consent. Changes in the Labour Process under Monopoly Capitalism*. Chicago: Chicago University Press.

Castells, Manuel. 1991. *The Informational City. Information Technology, Economic Restructuring and the Urban-Regional Process*. Oxford: Blackwell.

Castells, Manuel. 1996. *The Rise of the Networked Society*. Oxford, UK: Blackwell.

Chandler, James Jr. 1994. *Scale and Scope. The Dynamics of Industrial Capitalism*. Harvard: Harvard University Press.

Charalambis, Dimitris. 1983. *Clientelism and Populism*. Athens: Exandas (in Greek).

Cook, Phillip. 1990. *Back to the Future. Modernity, Postmodernity and Locality*. Winchester, MA: Unwin Hyman.

Coriat, Benjamin. 1997. Globalization. Variety and Mass Production. In *Contemporary Capitalism: The Embeddedness of Institutions*, edited by Roger Hollingsworth and Robert Boyer, 240–264. Madison, WI: University of Wisconsin.

Curran, James. 1979. Capitalism and Control of the Press, 1800–1975. In *Mass Communication and Society* edited by James Curran, Michael Gurevitch, and Janet Woollacott, 7–11. Beverly Hills: Sage.

Davis, Stanley. 2001. *Management: Managing the Future Now*. London: Simon and Schuster.

Debord, Guy. 1986. *The Society of Spectacle*. Athens: Eleftheros Typos (in Greek).

Demertzis, Nikos. 2002. *Political Communication. Risk, Publicity, Internet*. Athens: Papazisis (in Greek).

Elam, Mark. 2000. Puzzling out the Post-Fordist Debate: Technology, Markets and Institutions. In *Post-Fordism. A Reader*, edited by Ash Amin, 43–70. Oxford: Blackwell.

Engels, Friedrich. 1978a. Letter to Paul Ernst. In *Collected Works of Karl Marx and Engels Friedrich*, Vol. 10, 426–428. Sofia: Partizdat (In Bulgarian).

Engels, Friedrich. 1978b. Letter to Conrad Schmidt. In *Collected Works of Karl Marx and Engels Friedrich*, Vol. 10, 435–442. Sofia: Partizdat (In Bulgarian).

Ewen, Stuart. 1999. *All Consuming Images*. New York: Basic Books.

Esping-Andersen Gøsta (1990). *The Three Worlds of Welfare Capitalism*. Princeton: Princeton University Press.

Esping-Andersen Gøsta. (1999). *Social Foundations of Post-Industrial Economies*. New York: Oxford University Press.

Ewen, Stuart. 2001. *Captains of Consciousness. Advertising and the Social Roots of the Consumer Culture*. New York: Basic Books.

Enzensberger, Hans Magnus. 1981. *Toward a Theory of Mass Media*. Athens: Epikouros (in Greek).

Fairclough, Norman. 1995. *Media Discourse*. London: Edward Arnold.

Fuchs, Christian. 2010a. Grounding Critical Communication Studies: An Inquiry into The Communication Theory of Karl Marx. *Journal of Communication Inquiry* 34 (15): 15–41.

Fuchs, Christian. 2010b. Labor in Informational Capitalism and on the Internet. *The Information Society* 26 (3): 179–196.

Garnham, Nicholas. 1979. Contribution to A Political Economy Of Mass-Communication. *Media, Culture & Society* 1 (2): 123–146.

Garnham, Nicholas. 2003. *Emancipation, the Media and Modernity*. Athens: Kastaniotis (in Greek).

Gartman, David. 1998. Postmodernism; Or the Cultural Logic of Post-fordism? *The Sociological Quarterly* 39 (1): 119–137.

Gerbner George. 1970. Cultural Indicators: the Case of Violence in Television Drama. *The Annals of the American Academy of Political and Social Science*, 388: 69-81.

Golding, Peter and Graham Murdock. 2001. Culture, Communication and Political Economy. In *Mass Media and Society*, edited by James Curran and Michael Gurevitch, 25–52. Athens: Patakis (in Greek).

Green, Bill, Joe-Ann Reid, and Chris Bigum. 1998. Teaching the Nintendo Generation? Children, Computer Culture and Popular Technologies. In *Wired Up: Young People and the Electronic Media*, edited by Sue Howard, 19–41. London: UCL Press.

Gualerzi, Davide. 2010. *The Coming of Age of Information Technologies and the Path of Transformational Growth. A Long-Run Perspective in the Late 2000s Recession*. New York: Routledge.

Hall, Stuart. 1980. Encoding/Decoding. In *Culture, Media, Language*, edited by Stewart Hall, Dorothy Hobson, Andrew Lowe and Paul Willis, 507–517. London: Hutchinson, 1980.

Hamnet, Chris. 1989. Consumption and Class in Contemporary Britain. In *The Changing Social Structure*, edited by Chris Hamnet, Linda McDowell and Phillip Sarre, 199–213. London: Sage.

Harvey, David. 1989. *The Condition of Postmodernity. An Inquiry into the Origins of Cultural Change*, Cambridge: Blackwell.

Herman, Edward and Noam Chomsky. 2001. A Propaganda Model. In *Media and Cultural studies*. Keyworks, edited by Meenakshi Durham and Douglas Kellner, 180–217. Oxford: Blackwell.

Hickox, Mike and Moore, Robert.1992. *Education and post-Fordism: A New Correspondence? In Education for Economic Survival: From Fordism to Post-Fordisim*, edited by Phillip Brown and Hugh Laude, 95–116. London: Routledge.

Hill, Annette. 2007. *Restyling Factual TV*. London: Routledge.

Hirst, Paul and Jonathan Zeitlin. 1991. Flexible Specialization versus Post-Fordism: Theory, Evidence and Policy Implications. *Economy and Society* 20 (1): 1–156.

Hobsbawm, Eric. 1978. The Forward March of Labour Halted? *Marxism Today*, September: 279–286.

Hobsbawm, Eric. 2008. *The Age of Revolutions. 1789–1848*. Athens: Cultural Institute of National Bank (in Greek).

Holloway, John. 2006. *Change the World without Taking Power. The Meaning of Revolution Today*. Athens: Savalas (in Greek).

Horkheimer, Max and Theodor Adorno. 1986. *The Dialectics of Enlightenment*. Athens: Ypsilon/books (in Greek).

Horkheimer, Max. 1976. Traditional and Critical Theory. In *Critical Sociology: Selected Readings*, edited by Paul Connerton. Harmondsworth: Penguin.

Jameson, Fredric. 1984. Postmodernism or the Cultural Logic of Late Capitalism. *New Left Review* 146: 59–92.

Jessop, Bob. 1990. *State Theory. Putting Capitalist Economies in their Place*. Cambridge: Polity.

Jessop, Bob and Ngai-Ling Sum. 2006. *Beyond the Regulation Approach. Putting Capitalist Economies in their Place*. Cheltenham: Edward Elgar Publishing. J.

Jessop, Bob. 1994. The Transition to Post-Fordism and the Schumpeterian Workfare State. In *Towards a Post-Fordist Welfare State?*, edited by Brian Loader and Roger Burrows,13–17. London: Routledge.

Jessop, Bob. 2002. *The Future of the Capitalist State*. Cambridge: Polity Press.

Kazakos, Panos. 2001. *Between State and the Market. Economic Policy after War in Greece 1944–2000*. Athens: Patakis (in Greek).

Kennett, Patricia. 2003. Exclusion, Post-Fordism and the "New Europe". In *A New Europe? Economic Restructuring and Social Exclusion*, edited by Phillip Brown and Rosemary Crompton, 14–32. London: Routldege.

Lash, Scott and Paul Bagguley. 1988. Labour Relations in Disorganized Capitalism: A Five-Nation Comparison. *Environment and Planning D: Society and Space* 6 (3): 321–338.

Lambrakou, Zoi. 2011. New Social Movements in the Age of the Internet. The Case of Collective Action with the Use of New Media in Greece 2007–2011. Unpublished MA thesis. Athens: Department of Communication and Media Studies (in Greek).

Lash, Scott and Celia Lury. 2007. *Global Culture Industry. The Mediation of Things.* Malden MA: Polity.

Lash, Scott and John Urry. 1987. *The End of Organized Capitalism.* Madison, WI: The University of Wisconsin Press.

Lash, Scott and John Urry. 1994. *Economies of Signs and Space.* London: Sage.

Lipietz, Alain. 1990. *Mirages and Miracles.* Athens: Exandas (in Greek).

Lipietz, Alain. 1994, Post-Fordism and Democracy. In *Post-Fordism: a Reader,* edited by Ash Amin, 251–279. Massachusetts: Blackwell.

Lipietz, Alain. 1997. The Post-Fordist World: Labour Relations, International Hierarchy and Global Ecology. *Review of International Political Economy* 4 (1): 1–41.

Loader, Brian and Roger Burrows. 1994. Towards a Post-Fordist Welfare State? The Restructuring of Britain, Social Policy and the Future of Welfare. In *Towards a Post-Fordist welfare state?,* edited by Brian Loader and Roger Burrows, 1–13. London: Routledge.

Lyrintzis, Christos, Ilias Nikolakopoulos, and Dimitiris Sotiropoulos, 1996. Introduction. In Society *and Politics: Aspects of the Third Greek Republic 1974–1994,* edited by Christos Lyrintzis, Ilias Nikolakopoulos and Dimitiris Sotiropoulos, 19–42. Athens: Greek Society of Political Science and Themelio Publishing (in Greek).

Mann, Michael. 1986. *The Sources of Social Power: A History of Power from the Beginning to A.D. 1760. Vol. I.* Cambridge: Cambridge University Press.

Manovich, Lev. 2001. *The Language of New Media.* Cambridge, MA: MIT Press,

Marglin, Stephen and Bhaduri. Amit 1990. Profit Squeeze and Keynesian Theory. In *The Golden Age of Capitalism. Reinterpreting the Post-war Experience,* edited by Stephen Marglin and Huliet Schor, 153–186. Oxford: Chalderon Press.

Marx, Karl and Engels Friedrich. 1975. *For the Art.* Athens: Exandas (in Greek).

Marx, Karl and Engels Friedrich. 1978. *The German Ideology, Vol. 1.* Athens: Gutenberg (in Greek).

Marx, Karl and Engels Friedrich. 2001. The Ruling Class and the Ruling Ideas. In *Media and Cultural studies.* Keyworks, edited by Meenakshi Durham and Douglas Kellner, 39–42. Oxford: Blackwell.

Marx, Karl. 1978a. Towards a Critique of the Political Economy. In *Collected Works* of Karl Marx and Friedrich Engels, Vol. 7, 113–291. Sofia: Partizdat (In Bulgarian).

Marx, Karl. 1978b. Letter to Franz Mering. In *Collected Works of Karl Marx and Engels Friedrich,* Vol. 10, 477–472. Sofia: Partizdat (In Bulgarian).

Marx, Karl. 1979. *Capital.* Sofia: Partizdat (in Bulgarian).

Marx, Karl. 1983. *Pre-capitalist Economic Formations*. Athens: Kalvos (In Greek).

Matsuyama, Kiminori. 2002. The Rise of Mass Consumption Societies. *Journal of Political Economy* 110 (5): 1035–1070.

McCracken, Grant. 1988. *Culture and Consumption: New Approaches to the Symbolic Character of the Consumer Goods and Activities*. Bloomington, IN: Indiana University Press.

Mosco, Vincent. 2009. *The Political Economy of Communication*. London: Sage. 2nd ed.

Mouriki, Aliki. 1994. Politics of Reform and New Forms of Organization of the Labour. *Contemporary Issues*, vol. 54 (in Greek).

Mouzelis, Nicos. 2008. *Modern, Postmodern Social Theorizing. Bridging the Divide*. Cambridge: Cambridge University Press.

Parker, Martin. 2000. The Sociology of Organizations and the Organization of Sociology: Some Reflections on the Making of a Division of Labour. *The Sociological Review* 48 (1): 124–146.

Perniola, Mario. 1991. *The Society of Simulacra*. Athens: Alexandria (in Greek).

Plamenatz Petrov, John. 1963. *Man and Society*. London: Longman.

Pleios George. 2004. Labour and Meaning in Late Modernity: The Significance of Education and the Culture of Image. *Review of Social Research*, B2004(114): 61–87 (in Greek).

Pleios, George. 1993. *Moving Image and Artistic Communication*. Athens: Delphini (in Greek).

Pleios, George. 1996. The Crisis of Education in Mature Capitalism. *The Tribune of Social Sciences* 19: 143–185 (in Greek).

Pleios, George. 2001. *The Discourse of Image. Ideology and Politics*. Athens: Papazisis (in Greek).

Pleios, George. 2011. *The Society of Pleasant Information. Modernity and the News*. Athens: Kastaniotis (in Greek).

Polanyi, Karl. 2001. The Great Transformation. Boston: Beacon Press.

Pond, Chris. 1989. The Changing Distribution of Income, Wealth and Poverty. In *The Changing Social Structure*, edited by Chris Hamnet, Linda McDowell and Phillipe Sarre, 43–77. London: Sage.

Poster, Mark. 1990. *The Mode of Information: Poststructuralism and Social Context*. Chicago: Chicago University Press.

Poulet, Bernard. 2009. *The End of Newspapers and the Future of Information*. Athens: Polis (in Greek).

Richta, Radovan. 1976. *Civilization at Crossroads*. Athens: Rappas (in Greek).

Robins, Kevin and Frank Webster. 1988. Cybernetic Capitalism: Information, Technology, Everyday Life. In *The Political Economy of Information*, edited by Vincent Mosco and Janet Wasko, 44–75. Madison: University of Wisconsin.

Rueschemeyer, Dietrich. 1986. *Power and the Division of Labor*. Polity Press.

Russell, James. 2006. *Double Standard*. Lanham, MD: Rowman and Littlefield Publishers.

Sakellaropoulos, Theodoros. 1992. *State and Social Interests during the '80s*. Athens: Kritiki (in Greek).

Sassen, Saskia. 2009. *A Sociology of Globalization*. Athens: Metechmio (in Greek).

Schiller, Herbert. 1973. *The Mind Managers*. Boston: Beacon Press.

Schultz, Theodore. 1961. Investment in Human Capital. *The American Economic Review* 51 (1): 1–17.

Sennett, Richard. 2008. *The Culture of the New Capitalism*. Athens: Savalas (in Greek).

Terranova, Tiziana 2004. *Network Culture. Politics for the Information Age*. London: Pluto Press.

Thompson, John. 1995. *The Media and Modernity*. Cambridge: Polity Press.

Thursfield, Denise. 2003. *Post-Fordism and Skill: Theories and Perceptions*. Burlington: Ashgate.

Thussu, Daya Kissan. 2007. *News as Entertainment. The Rise of Global Infotainment*. London: Sage.

Toffler, Alvin. 1982. *The Third Wave*. Athens: Cactos (In Greek).

Tsoukalas, Konstantinos. 1983. Tradition and Modernity. Some General Issues. In *Hellenism and Greekness*, edited by Demetrios Tsatsos, 37–48. Athens: Estia.

Vallas, Steven.1999. Rethinking Post-Fordism: The Meaning of Workplace Flexibility. *Sociological Theory* 17 (1): 68–101.

Vergopoulos Kostas. 1999. *Globalization. The Great Mirage*. Athens: Nea Synora (in Greek).

Webster, Frank. 1995. *Theories of the Information Society*. London: Routledge.

Wernick, Andrew. 1991. *Promotional Culture: Advertising, Ideology and Symbolic Expression*. Thousand Oaks, CA: Sage.

Williams, Raymond. 1978. *Marxism and Literature*. Oxford: Oxford University Press.

Williams, Raymond. 2001. Base and Superstructure in Marxist Cultural Theory. In *Media and Cultural Studies*. Keyworks, edited by Meenakshi Durham and Douglas Kellner, 152–165. Oxford: Blackwell.

Williams, Rosalind. 1991. *Dream Worlds: Mass Consumption in Late Nineteenth-Century France*. Berkeley and Los Angeles, CA: University of California Press.

Wood, Ellen M. 1997. Modernity, Postmodernity or Capitalism?, *Review of International Political Economy* 4 (3): 539–560.

CHAPTER 6

Missing Marx: The Place of Marx in Current Communication Research and the Place of Communication in Marx's Work*

İrfan Erdogan

1   **Introduction: The Rationale and Subject of Study**

The control of thought and production, distribution and use of mental products has been one of the main concerns and praxis of the ruling forces throughout human history. As organized life has become complex with deepening inequalities, oppression and unjust distribution of power and wealth, the quantity and scope of the control of thought and behaviour has been expanded to every facet of life. In the 21st century, such control became a nightmarish issue of sustainability in such a way that the management of what, why and how to think and not to think, to feel and not to feel, to believe and not to believe, and to do or not to do was extended to every instance of the daily life of every individual at any age. From the first ancient empires to the demise of feudalism, the mental production, distribution and use were controlled by the theological and political power centres that owned not only the body and souls of the masses, but also the material riches. Then came the "freedom" associated with the capitalist mode of production: The absolute serf or semi-serf found himself/herself free from the yoke of owners/masters and outside and on the street with no means to produce his/her life; his/her freedom turned to be the freedom of owners from responsibilities of keeping a slave; his/her freedom became a new slavery called wage-slavery: He/she had no guarantee of food, clothing and shelter anymore. Those who were doing mental production in the interest of theological and political forces within and outside the church and castles were luckier because new and expanded opportunities, like steadily increasing number of schools and universities and mass media, were emerging outside the traditional centres of mental production. Two basic centres of knowledge production proliferated and gained prominence: (1) corporate research departments and

*   This chapter is a part of an ongoing study on the current orientations in mass communication theory and research. The Higher Education Council of Turkey funded the collection of data for the project. The author thanks Christian Fuchs for language-editing and Hakan Ugurlu for proofreading the chapter.

corporate research institutions, and (2) public and private universities. The political, economical and cultural forces gradually started feeling the necessity of complete control of knowledge production, dissemination and use. Capitalism had propagated and strongly stressed the freedom of thought and expression while waging war against feudalism. It turned into a limiter of freedom as soon as people demanded freedom, equality and justice under the capitalist system. Especially since the advent of neo-liberal policies, the control mechanisms were intensified all over the world by (1) the privatization of schools, (2) the marginalization of public education, (3) the revisions of curricula and educational policies, (4) turning university education into a vocational school level to cater the interests of the corporate world, (5) establishing programs like the Bologna Accord for regional or global standardization that serves specific interests, (6) directing research orientations away from critical inquiry for human development towards the development of institutional and corporate interests, (7) luring scholars towards functional orientations by providing relatively substantial financial rewards via institutional, regional, national, regional and international structures, (8) making some theoretical and methodological approaches dominant and others marginal through reward and punishment mechanisms and through monopoly control of the production, distribution and promotion of academic products, including the promotion and wide distribution of controlled alternatives. In any case, current dominant scholarly orientations in communication are driven by at least three main goals: (1) to climb up the academic ladder, (2) to sustain the prevailing system of personal interest actualisation in the university environment, (3) to get accepted, acknowledged and supported by the established networks of beneficial relations in the university, state institutions, local, regional, national and international foundations, mass media and corporations. The present dominant structure with its controlled-alternatives is a historical condition of dominance and struggle. It is the context of the intensifying political, economic and intellectual crises in the structures, structural relations and institutions of knowledge production. While positivist, empirical and fact-producing quantitative orientations are continuing to stand in the service of industrial interests, newly emerged approaches with the "post" prefix in their names are taking part in the justification, legitimization and mystification of the dominant production mode and relations by emphasizing utmost relativity and particularistic interpretative accounts of micro-units and by ignoring or refusing the unity of the regularities of social relations, their structure, and change and their historical character.

There are many functionalist studies supporting the relationship between universities and industrial structures, we can however see an increasing number of critical analyses on the same subject too (e.g. Schiller 1974; Gans

1975; Gorz 1980; Berube and Nelson 1995; Berube 1996; Martin 1998; Chouliaraki and Fairclough 1999; Cerwonka 2009; Domenech 2009; Gunaratne 2010; Erdogan 2014).

All these explanations indicate the existence of the control of mental production by means of numerous mechanisms that integrate private interests with the dominant interests. Furthermore, the control covers every sphere of life: It is actualized not only through the professional practices and professional ideologies, but also through the user choices that are influenced by the character of production, distribution and access. These historically structured mode of relations fall within Marx's theoretical explanation:

> The ideas of the ruling class are in every epoch the ruling ideas: i.e., the class which is the ruling material force of society is at the same time its ruling intellectual force. The class which has the means of material production at its disposal has control at the same time over the means of mental production, so that thereby, generally speaking, the ideas of those who lack the means of mental production are subject to it. The ruling ideas are nothing more than the ideal expressions of the dominant material relationships, the dominant material relationships grasped as ideas; hence of the relationships which make the one class the ruling one, therefore the ideas of its dominance.
> MARX AND ENGELS, 1969, 39

By using words like "generally speaking," "ruling" and "domination", Marx clearly excludes the one way causal relationship which eliminates the possibility of individual and class struggle via total control. If there was a one way determination and thus total control over minds and behaviour of people, not only the idea of struggle would be invalid but also revolutions and social change would be impossible. If the capitalist class was not interested in controlling the means and content of mental production, there would e.g. be no laws restricting the freedom of thought and expression, the journalists and intellectuals in Turkey would not be in jail waiting for trial more than 4 years, and intellectuals throughout the world would not be silent and apathetic in the face of such a "post-modern civil dictatorship"; the media would not be so acquiescent about oppressive measures and injustices all over the world; the large masses would not be quiet and accommodating; the journalists, intellectuals and academicians would not be talking about the existence of "participatory democracy" despite the obvious fact that they cannot have even a slight influence on the determination of their own salaries; and they would not align themselves with the ruling part of society. There would be no industries like advertising and public relations. Advertisers, agencies like CIA and foundations like Rockefeller and Ford would not spend billions of dollars for mind management.

Derived from the theoretical reasoning and statements above, it is expected that domination manifests itself in the nature of production, dissemination and use of mental products. In terms of journal articles, the formation and sustainability of domination includes heavy emphasis on certain theoretical orientations and issues, ample support of functional alternatives, and the elimination, marginalization or distortion of the real alternatives that Marx's approach poses. My study points out that the control of communication via the control of production and dissemination entails not a total control of the minds of people, but the existence of domination and struggle. All the ideas in a society are not and cannot be the ideas of the ruling class. Furthermore, every person carries dominant, conflicting or oppositional ideas to varying degrees. Not every bit of a dominant or oppositional idea can be right or wrong. The main point here is the nature of the connection of ideas to domination and struggle. It is argued that (1) the dominant theoretical and topic orientations of articles in the journals studied are functional for the capitalist mode of production, (2) Marx's theory and method and Marxist issues are mostly excluded from the communication field, (3) most alternatives are not alternatives to the interests of capitalism, but controlled and functional alternatives which are set against one another and especially against Marx and Marxism, and (4) Marx's thinking is represented in the form of false or forged assertions or downgraded by claiming that Marx did not say anything or said very little about communication.[1]

There are three basic aims of the article. The first one is to test the assumption that there are certain dominant theoretical and topic orientations in academic articles in Media and Communication Studies despite the quantitative multitude. The existence of such orientations only means that there is a dominant intersubjectivity feeding certain material and immaterial interests: Even if everybody says that the earth is flat, it does not make the earth flat, but such a claim works only as functional justification.

The second aim is to demonstrate that Marx and issues of the Marxist approach are mostly excluded from Media and Communication studies, and that Marx is invalidated fully or partially, evaluated negatively or criticized for various reasons if he is mentioned in an article. The exclusion or marginalization of Marx in the articles does not mean that Marx's theoretical approach is false or has no value or merit; rather, it means that Marx's approach has thus far been successfully ignored and dismissed with the help of false claims. Such

---

1 Fuchs (2010a) provides a unique answer to this baseless claim by analyzing Marx's writings on communication and systematically presenting them by focusing on the role of media production, circulation and consumption/reception in capitalism.

a marginalization and dismissal also indicates and proves the correctness of Marx's analysis of the general character of the ruling ideas. Therefore, the point is not that Marx is wrong, the point is rather that Marx and Marxist issues do not fit the structures of material and immaterial interests, relations and mindsets. They rather threaten the dominant practices. This reminds us of the motto of New York Times: "All the news that's fit to print".

The third aim is to show that the exclusion of Marx entails false justifications like claiming that Marx did not say anything about communication.

The structure of the article is as follow: The first part of the article examines (a) the statistical foundations of the studied topic, and (b) the presence of Marx and Marxism in the analysed articles published in communication journals that are cited in the Social Sciences Citation Index.

The second part of the article presents and discusses Marx's ideas on communication in order to demonstrate that Marx, contrary to prevailing assertions, said a lot about communication.

I used the phrase "missing Marx" in the title in order to indicate that (1) Marx is missing in articles in the "reputable" and the widely circulated journals and that (2) the communication field is missing (needs) Marx, because of (a) the value of his approach, (b) the prevailing domination of certain industry-oriented approaches that ignore or distort significant social and academic issues, (c) the increasing tendency of the usage of "supermarket books" by those who have limited mental comprehension capacities or are simply too lazy to spend time to read anything that forces him/her to think, and (d) the growing influence of popular gurus in communication schools. Unfortunately, *"academic fads come and go, the academy becomes complicit in such genuflection, and new gurus emerge and fade"* (Tomaselli and Shepperson 2010, 52), but their vestiges or bad copies remain. Being mystified by "body language" and "Neuro Linguistic Programming", and *"the unproblematic adoption of decontextualised ahistorical post-structuralist, post-disciplinary"* approaches are increasingly encroaching the communication field.[2]

---

2 In 1975, I had taken courses in communication, political science and research methods at Purdue University and the University of Pittsburgh since 1971. I had never heard of Marx's name in my communication classes and books. I had started searching and found the name of Dallas Smythe and I wrote to him telling him about the missing of Marx in communication courses in my schools and asked for his help in finding Marxist writings on communication. He called me and also gave me Herbert Schiller's name. It was the end of "missing Marx" for me, because Smythe and Schiller suggested to me readings that I had been looking for. Under the prevailing dominant sensitivities and interests, we all miss the "hearts and minds" like Marx, Che, Smythe, Schiller and all those who dedicate their life to the struggle for the freedom and dignity of all human beings.

2   Theoretical Basis of the Study

Decent and honourable scholars, like Herbert Schiller (1974 and 1992), Dallas
Smythe (1982), Ariel Dorfman (1983), Graham Murdock (Murdock and Golding
1977), Peter Golding (Murdock and Golding 1978), Nicholas Garnham, Yves de la
Haye (1980) and Armand Mattelart in the late 1960s and the following decades,
and Dan Schiller (2003 and 2007), Vincent Mosco (1996/2009 and 2008), Robert
McChesney (2008), Christian Fuchs (2010b and 2011b), Stuart Ewen, Lee Artz,
Nick Dyer-Witheford, Hanno Hardt (2000), Richard Maxwell (2001), Wasko,
Murdock and Sousa (2011) and the like in recent years, have shown that Marx/
Marxism is not dead and closely concerned with communication.

The production and distribution of Marx's writings and Marxist texts are also
part of the struggle for a better world. Regarding Marx's interest in communication,
Fetscher (1969) and Padover (1974) published a collection of Marx's writings on
the Freedom of the Press and Censorship. The International Mass Media
Research Centre's two books on Communication and Class Struggle (Mattelart
and Siegelaub, 1979), and a book about the Marx's writings on the means of
communication (Haye, 1980) are excellent pieces of work. It is not a coincidence that it is difficult to find these books in bookstores and libraries, but only
in the personal libraries of people like me.

The present study bases its theoretical framework solely on Marx, thus it
is not a classical Marxist, orthodox Marxist, neo-Marxist, autonomous
Marxist, post-Marxist or any kind of Marxist study. It tries to clarify the
dominant tradition and conscious marginalization of Marx and Marxist
oriented studies in the production of knowledge in the leading journals of
communication by employing an empirical design. It discusses Marx's
approach on communication by presenting his writings that are associated
with any aspect and/or type of communication. This presentation will also
show the importance of Marx and his approach in the communication
field, and will also demonstrate the invalidity, absurdity and ludicrousness
of the ideological and propagandist nature of contemporary claims like
the end of ideology-hypothesis, the meaninglessness of ideology, or that
Marx's analysis was based on economic reductionism, monolithic relations
between material conditions of production and mental conditions, the
primacy of superstructure or basis, etc.

Marx, as we will see in the following paragraphs, lucidly points out that
humans produce their own material and mental life, and they do so in a historical society organized by them. They produce their life conditions by reflecting their thoughts on material conditions and ideas, feelings, values and beliefs.
They sustain or change their material and/or immaterial conditions by acting

upon them. This theoretical reasoning brings along many conclusions. Some of the conclusions pertinent to the present study are:

(1)   The claims about Marxist reflectivity are false explanations, because we could never establish, develop and change life, make history and engage in the struggle for liberation if our thoughts were mere reflections of our material life. Marx talks about the dominant mode of production and relations and reminds us about the lasting existence of remnants of the old material and especially immaterial relations. One of the best examples is that the capitalists who rule the world today support the governments of theological political parties that come to power exploiting the religious and irrational beliefs of people. Marx argues: *"the individuals composing the ruling class [...] among other things rule also as thinkers, as producers of ideas, and regulate the production and distribution of the ideas of their age: thus their ideas are the ruling ideas of the epoch"* (Marx 1969, 39). *[We go astray] "if [...] we detach the ideas of the ruling class from the ruling class itself and attribute to them an independent existence, if we confine ourselves to saying that in a particular age these or those ideas were dominant, without paying attention to the conditions of production and the producers of these ideas, and if we thus ignore the individuals and the world conditions which are the source of these ideas"* (1969, 40; 1964, 79).

(2)   The ideas of economic determinism, reductionism or technological determinism are not immanent in Marx's works. For instance, a statement like "the traditional Marxist approach postulates a mechanical relation between economic structure and socio-cultural superstructure" (Grossberg, 1997, 22) is nonsense and a classic cold-war ideological propaganda for mind management geared toward unaware readers, students and academicians. It knowingly or unknowingly distorts the basic theoretical structure of Marxism. Marx commented that his work merely attempted to describe the path that Western capitalism developed from feudalism, and that one should not "transform his historical sketch of the development of Western European capitalism into historical-philosophical theory of universal development predetermined by fate for all nations, whatever their historic circumstances in which they find themselves may be. [...that view] does me at the same time too much honour and too much insult" (Padover 1979, 321). Engels provided a clear explanation for the same issue in a letter to Bloch in 1890:

According to the materialist conception of history, the ultimate determining element in history is the production and reproduction of real life. More than this neither Marx nor I have ever asserted. Hence if somebody twists this into saying that the economic element is the only determining one, he transforms that proposition into a meaningless, abstract, senseless phrase. The economic situation is the basis, but the various elements of the superstructure – political forms of the class struggle and its results, to wit: constitutions established by the victorious class after a successful battle, etc., juridical forms, and even the reflexes of all these actual struggles in the brains of the participants, political, juristic, philosophical theories, religious views and their further development into systems of dogmas – also exercise their influence upon the course of the historical struggles and in many cases preponderate in determining their form. There is an interaction of all these elements, in which, amid all the endless host of accidents (that is, of things and events whose inner interconnection is so remote or so impossible of proof that we can regard it as nonexistent, as negligible) the economic movement finally asserts itself as necessary. Otherwise the application of the theory to any period of history would be easier than the solution of a simple equation of the first degree.

MARX AND ENGELS 1962, 488

(3)   Technological determinism is an immanent element of the approaches of popularized stars like Daniel Bell, Marshall McLuhan and new popular gurus, who claim that the Internet brings about an "information and knowledge society" and "democratization". Contrary to the currently popular technological determinist idea establishing a causal connection between the Internet and the so-called information and knowledge society, a society becomes a knowledge society (a) only if the Internet provides "information and knowledge" which is functional to general interests and goes beyond controlling the interests, minds and behaviours of the millions via capturing and imprisoning them in front of a monitor and beyond marketing material and mental end-products of capitalist enterprises and institutions, and (b) only if people use the Internet to make sound decisions on meeting their daily rational needs. Democratization requires not only participation in public discussions, but also, most importantly, affecting the political and economical decision making processes. In short, as scholars like Herbert Schiller (1991), Dan Schiller (1993, 2000 and 2007), Christian Fuchs (2010a and 2011a), Vincent Mosco (1982 and 2004), Peter Golding (2000), Nicholas Garnham (2001) and Nick Dyer-Witheford (1999) vividly demonstrate, the Internet represents a new sphere and an extension of ongoing domination and struggle. In any case, the so-called information society, knowledge society or service society is still a capitalist society and the claim of "democratization" via the Internet is the acknowledgement that capitalist society is not a democratic society and was waiting for the Internet to rescue capitalism from such burden.

(4)   Marx neither ignores nor downgrades ideology in his explanations in *The German Ideology* and other writings and does not assign a determining or dependent position to it.

(5)   Claims like the ones that we have reached an "end of ideology" and "of grand narratives/theories" are ideological and function as tools for justifying various policies, including the "war against terror" ideology that helps to evade and ignore the ongoing terrorism in the workplace and of industrial policies. Ideology primarily means two things: (a) the structure of ideas/thoughts and (b) the study of ideas (just as sociology is the study of the "social"). "No ideology" or the "end of ideology" simply means "no idea", "no thought", "end of thinking", or "end of ideas". But no human being and organized human life could exist, if there were no idea/thinking/thought and structure(s) of ideas. "The end of ideology" (or the end of history or the claim of discontinuity that postmodernism is not a continuation of modernism) is the ideology of the global capitalism that institutes functional ignorance as knowledge. The justifications by establishing connections with grand theories, disintegration of the Soviet System, modernist era or any other things are simply forged factoids.

3   The Method of the Study

The study was designed as a combination of quantitative and qualitative research. The concept of method used here refers only to processes of data collection and analysis. The use of empirical data and statistical measures does not make a study a positivist-empirical research: A mainstream scholar designs a study based on a certain theoretical reasoning, collects and analyzes empirical data, and suggests that, for instance, it is necessary to establish water treatment plants to clean the polluted river. A Marxist scholar designs a study based on the Marxist theoretical framework, uses the same empirical process to collect data and even statistically analyze the data, and suggests that it is necessary to change the relations and processes of production in such a way that the river does not get polluted and we get clean water at any point of the river. We can prepare a survey questionnaire to analyse the attitudes, opinions and evaluations of workers in order to help a corporation's policies or in order to support whatever is right. Marx himself conducted critical empirical research when he e.g. prepared a survey questionnaire in 1880. It was distributed to 25,000 French workers to determine the working conditions and raise questions in the minds of workers about their working conditions and the issues presented in the questionnaire (Bodemann 1979; Babbie 2004, 243; Dei and Johal 2005).

3.1   Scope of the Study

The scope of the study covers articles about Marx in the communication journals cited in the Social Sciences Citation Index and Marx's ideas about communication.

Studying the nature of communication research orientations requires examination of published journal articles, books, master and doctoral theses, and institutional and industrial study reports. This task takes substantial time, money and intellectual workforce. This pressing fact required limiting the study to journal articles.

There are most probably more than a thousand journals carrying at least one article concerned with communication issues from time to time. However, the present study defines its study population as journals cited in the Social Sciences Citation Index that are accepted as "core journals", the "nerves of the discipline", "the barometer of the substantive focus of scholarship and research methods" most important to the communication field (Potter and Riddle 2007), and a measure of academic scholarship by universities throughout the world. There are also journals with critical and historical/dialectical materialist theoretical orientations, but we can hardly find such journals in the dominant control centres of the production and distribution channels. The ones that exist are most probably either functional-critical or quasi-critical ones or they represent controlled alternatives that are used for the legitimization of the prevailing dominant practices and the de-legitimization of real alternative sources and of products that are based on Marx's approach. Sure, there is a high possibility that we can find, as Herbert Schiller pointed out once (Schiller and Pool 1981) *"one pearl in ten truckloads of garbage"*, however, this only supports Marx's point and does not prove the existence of freedom of expression, equal opportunities and the like.

3.2   Determining Data and Information Sources

The first part of the study is designed to investigate the nature of the use of Marx. It requires an examination of published journal articles, books, master and doctoral theses, and institutional and industrial study reports. This task takes a lot of time, money and intellectual workforce. That is why the articles were selected by considering the fact that journal articles provide us with the most up-to-date knowledge about the subject in question.

There were over 800 journals in the Communication and Mass Media Complete Database Coverage List (EBSCO Publishing),[3] Proquest[4] and SSCI in

---

3 http://www.ebscohost.com/academic/communication-mass-media-complete; http://www.ebscohost.com/titleLists/ufh-coverage.htm.

4 http://www.proquest.com/en-US/catalogs/databases/detail/commabs-set-c.shtml.

2011. However, there were only 85 journals classified as communication journals in the Social Sciences Citation Index.[5] Six non-English and two journals were excluded from the study (Circulo De Linguistica Aplicada A La Comunicacion, Comunicacion Y Sociedad, Comunicar, Estudios Sobre El Mensaje, Javnost-The Public, Tijdschrift Voor Communicatiewetenschap, Journal of the SMPTE, and Text and Performance Quarterly), and, thus, total 77 journals were selected for the investigation.

The second part of the study focuses on examining the relevance of Marx in the communication field by challenging the claim that Marx said nothing or very little about communication or that his works have no significance for discussing communication. In order to demonstrate that Marx provided significant explanations, all the available writings of Marx were used to find and evaluate Marx's statements concerning communication.

3.3 Population, Sample, Data Collection and Analysis
The study population includes articles published between January 2007 and June 2011 in the 77 selected journals (Table 6.1).

TABLE 6.1   Journals included in the study

Asian Journal of Communication	Journal of Communication Disorders
Augmentative and alternative Communication	Journal of Computer-Mediated Communication
Communication Monographs	Journal of Health Communication
Communications Research	Journal of Media Economics
Communication Theory	Journal of Mass Media Ethics
Continuum	Journal of Language and Social Psychology
Crime Media Culture	Journal of PR Research
Critical arts	Journal of Social and Personal Relationships
Critical Studies in Media Communications	Journalism and Mass communication Quarterly
Cyberpsychology and Behavior	Journalism Studies
Cultural Studies	Language and Communication
Discourse Studies	Language and Intercultural Communication
Discourse and Communication	Language and Speech
Discourse and Society	Management Communication Quarterly

---

5 http://science.thomsonreuters.com/cgi-bin/jrnlst/jlresults.cgi?PC=J.

TABLE 6.1   *Journals included in the study* (cont.)

Ecquid Novi: African Journalism Studies	Mass Communication and Society
Environmental Communication	Media Culture and Society
European Journal of Communication	Media International Australia
European Journal of Cultural Studies	Media Psychology
Health Communication	Multilingua
Human Communication Research	Narrative Inquiry
IEEE Transactions on Professional Communication	New Media and Society
Information Communication and Society	Political Communication
Interasia Cultural Studies	Public Understanding of Science
Interaction Studies	Public Culture
International Journal of Advertising	PR Review
International Journal of Cultural Studies	PO Quarterly
International Journal of Language and Communication Disorders	Quarterly Journal of Speech
	Personal Relationships
International Journal of Conflict Management	Research on Language & Social Interaction
International Journal of Mobile Communication	Rhetoric Society Quarterly
International Journal of Press/Politics	Science Communication
International Journal of Public Opinion research	Screen
Journal of Advertising Research	Technical Communication
Journal of Advertising	Telecommunications Policy
Journal of African Media Studies	Text and Talk
Journal of Applied Communication Research	Theory Culture and Society
Journal of Broadcasting and Electronic Media	Television and New Media
Journal of Business and Technical Communication	Visual Communication
Journal of Communication	Written Communication

More than one method was used for the data collection:

(1)   In order to find out whether or not the articles used the Marx's name or Marxism in their main text, the whole population (10104 articles) was used in the data collection and analysis.

(2)   In order to analyze the nature of use of Marx, all the articles that mentioned Marx's name in their full text were filtered out (210 articles out of 10104).

(3)   In order to determine the general profile of the studied journals, the first article of the first issue of each year was selected in the study and, as a result, 385 articles from the 77 journals were coded and analyzed.

(4)   In order to analyse topics of studies, the first article of the each issue was selected, which amounted in 1386 articles.

Only the research articles were used for the study. Editorials, editors' reports/ comments, book reviews, articles labelled as "research in brief" or given similar designations and the like were excluded from the study.

Indicators of variables were tentatively assigned and new indicators were added in the process of data collection and data coding.

Basic orientations: Basic orientations included the publisher, basic types of communication (technologically mediated or not), study objectives, basic methodological structures and levels of study.

The use of Marx and Marxism: Identified were (1) the distributional share of the use of Marx and Marxism in all the journals that contain 10104 articles and (2) the nature of use of Marx and Marx's writings in the articles.

Theoretical orientations: The analysis included the determination and analysis of the distribution and nature of theoretical orientations of articles.

Issues studied: This analysis focused on the discussed issues.

The analysis was conducted with the help of quantitative and qualitative content analysis. The quantitative part dealt with the presentation and discussion of the distributional characteristics of data. Distributional characteristics were determined by frequency and dispersion analyses in order to test if Marx's statement holds true in the sense that the control of thoughts, beliefs and feelings are exercised through the nature of theoretical, issue and content orientations. The qualitative part was the logical evaluation of the quantitative and qualitative data collected from Marx's published materials.

4   Findings and Evaluations

4.1   *Basic Orientations*
4.1.1   Publishers
There were 25 publishers of the 77 journals. The leading ones are Routledge (Taylor & Francis) (29.9%) and Sage (28.6%). The rest follows far behind, ranging from 5.2% to 1.3%. This finding reflects the fact that Routledge and Sage dominate the international publishing business. Dominating the world's journal (and

book) publishing market, Routledge publishes over 2878 journals (http://www
.tandfonline.com). Sage is the world's 5th largest journal publisher and its publications include more than 645 journals spanning the Humanities, Social
Sciences, as well as Science, Technology, and Medicine. More than 280 Sage journals are published on behalf of 225 learned societies and institutions (http://
www.sagepub.com/journals.nav). The extent of the publishers' role in the ideological control of scientific production and dissemination in the communication
field requires investigation. One claim is that the worldwide circulations of, e.g.,
books like "Four Theories of the Press" in the early 1960s and recent "critical" or
"alternative" books are not produced primarily with ideological motives. The
basic idea is that publishers do not care about the ideological content. Their
main motive is material profit, and thus, they sell anything that helps them make
money. This is certainly true. However, the historical experiences indicate that
the ideological interest of the capitalist class (including feelings, religious beliefs
and war against the "enemy") becomes a ruling concern when the sustainment
of capitalism is at stake. Capitalists invest (and donate) a good deal of money for
the sustainable development of their local, national and global domination.

4.1.2   The Forms of Communication (Technologically Mediated or Not)
Over half of the 1386 studies (59.4%) are about technologically mediated communication, while 17.0% focus on technologically unmediated communication
(mostly self-communication and interpersonal communication). 23.6% deal
with no types of communication, but communication-related concepts, methods, theories, issues or processes. Traditional mass communication still occupies
half (49.9%) of the articles focused on technologically mediated communication (Table 6.2). Computer mediated communication follows far behind (13.6%).

4.1.3   Study Objectives
There are great varieties of objectives of the analysed articles. However, over half of
them (55.8%) do not state their objectives. Furthermore, 15.6% of the statements of
objectives are not objectives, but statements or restatements of methods. Hence,
the study shows that only 28.6% of all studies have a valid objective. Most objectives are effect and individual/receiver related. Very few "alternative" studies set as
an objective to question the industrial structure, whereas most of them come up
with objectives that focus on various identity issues (except class identity) and
stress the invalidity of class analysis and the euro-centrism of Marx's approach.

4.1.4   Methodological Structure
The findings show that 65.2% of the studies have mainstream orientations
(23.5% are administrative research and 15.5% are primarily academic, but serving

TABLE 6.2   *Distribution of technologically mediated communication*

Mediated communication	N	%
Mass communication in general	184	22.4
Newspapers/journalism	62	7.5
Radio	10	1.2
Television	82	10.0
Cinema/film	53	6.4
Magazines, journals	4	0.5
Books, novels	4	0.5
Music	6	0.7
Advertising and marketing communication	54	6.6
Public relations	21	2.6
Political communication via the media	7	0.9
Computer mediated communication	112	13.6
Mobile communication	22	2.7
Telecommunication	11	1.3
Human – robot communication	7	0.9
Others (technologically mediated): e.g., self, personal communication, interpersonal, group, organizational, technical, technology, professional communication	184	22.4
Total	823	100.0

industrial or institutional interests). There are studies that question the dominant structures and relations (e.g., media portrayal, identity, identity politics), and Marx and Marxist approaches. Such studies (postmodern, post-positivist, post-constructivist, post-colonialist, post-structuralist, liberal-pluralist and the like) occupy a little more than one fourth of all studies (27.5%). Studies that use a Marxist methodology (excluding post-Marxism) account for only 7.3%.

A wide variety of qualitative designs dominates the studies (61.0%), followed by positivist-empiricist quantitative designs (39.0%).

About three quarters (73.5%) of the quantitative studies are quasi-experimental single survey research. Quasi-experimental lab/clinic design occupies 25.9%. True experimental design amounts for only 0.6%. There is no true experimental design (lab or clinical) in mass communication research. Qualitative mass communication studies are mostly either parametric or non-parametric survey designs. There is a tendency toward developing measurement devices and validating them. However, this tendency is at a marginal level, since most studies still use Likert-type measures.

The quantitative studies are mostly at the exploratory descriptive assessment level (39.0%), followed by a causal/inferential design (32.2%), and a bivariate relational design (23.2%).

Almost all descriptive studies break a basic scientific rule: A study design at this level requires that there should be no or insufficient accumulation of knowledge in the state of the art of the research topic or a need to question the existing knowledge. Generally, the bivariate studies have serious methodological problems: they just compare variables and state relationships without a correlation design that requires relational hypotheses. Inferential/causal studies employ multivariate or factor analysis, but most of them have no hypotheses that require multivariate or factorial analysis.

All of these are indeed serious methodological problems, in addition to the fact that most studies are focused on the analysis of audiences/consumers for marketing purposes.

4.2   The Use of Marx and Marxism

As specified in the introduction, it is expected that use of Marx and Marxism in the analysed articles is at a marginal level and that the nature of use is negative. The findings below support such assumptions.

4.2.1   Using Marx's Name

Marx and Marxism occupy extremely marginal space in the journals. Of the 10104 articles published between 2007 and mid 2011 in communication journals, only 210 (2.1%) include the name of Marx and 450 (4.5%) contain Marx's name or the word "Marxism" at least once in the main text.

39 journals and 210 articles mention Marx's name in their main text. The great majority of these 210 articles uses Marx's name once (57.6%), twice (14.8%) and 3–5 times (14.8%). Although 2.1% of 10104 articles mention Marx, most of them are mere usages of his name as a part of their narration.

Theory, Culture and Society published over one fourth of the 210 articles (26.7%), followed by Cultural Studies (11.0%), Interasia Cultural Studies (6.7%), Rhetoric Society Quarterly (3.8%), Media, Culture and Society (3.3%), Communication Theory (3.3%), Continuum (3.3%), and Public Culture (2.9%) respectively.

There are just 15 articles that deal completely or mostly with Marx, of which 8 were published in Theory, Culture and Society, and 2 in Cultural Studies.

The chart below (Figure 6.1) clearly shows the highly skewed distribution based on 210 articles (2.1% of 10104) that use Marx's name.

The findings above and the highly skewed distribution shown in Figure 6.1 point out that the articles very rarely use or even mention Marx. However, the unexpected result is that Marx's name occupies a marginal place in the journals that feature mostly "critical articles". Table 6.3 shows that Marx appears at least

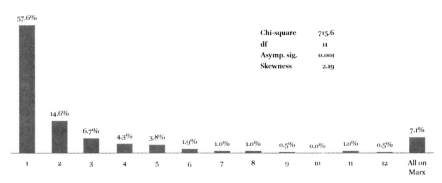

FIGURE 6.1   *Number of time Marx's name was used in the main text*

once in 56 (22.7%) of 247 articles in Theory, Culture & Society and the great majority (47 of 56) merely mentions Marx's name 1–3 times. This rate decreases to 13.5% in Cultural Studies, 10.0% in Rhetoric Society Quarterly, 9.7% in Interasia Cultural Studies, 4.6% in Critical Studies in Media Communication, and 3.3% in Media, Culture and Society.

4.2.2   Using Marx's Writings
Of 450 articles that mention Marx or Marxism at least once, 85.1% do not use any writing of Marx in their references, while 4.0% use *The Capital*, 1.5% *The German Ideology*, 1.1% *The Communist Manifesto*. Only seven articles use 2, three articles use 3, and two articles use more than 3 sources from Marx.

Such findings indicate the existence of an extremely low interest in reading Marx. It also shows that those who write something about Marx do not use Marx's own writings, but either secondary sources that support their stance or their own personal ideas of what Marx said, which implies the low and/or wrong knowledge communication scholars have of Marx's works.

While searching for sources, I also realized that there was a drastic drop in the use of Marx and Marxism since the beginning of the 1990s (especially since 1992) in these journals.

4.2.3   Nature of the Use of Marx's Name
The nature of the use of Marx's name differs widely, ranging from a very strong anti-Marxist position to a Marxist evaluation of a topic.

Over half (50.9%) of the 210 articles that use Marx's name, use it merely as part of an explanation with no evaluative or normative statement. Most of these articles mention Marx's name once or twice. The rest of the articles has various orientations toward Marx (Figure 6.2):

TABLE 6.3 *Distribution of the use of Marx's name in the main text of the articles*

Journals	Number of uses													Row total	Row%	N of articles analyzed	% use Marx
	1	2	3-5	6-12	a	b	c	d	e	f	g	h	i				
Asian J of Communication	2	1	0	0	0	0	0	0	0	0	0	0	0	3	1.4	104	2.9
Communication Monographs	1	0	0	0	0	0	0	0	0	0	0	0	0	1	0.5	104	1.0
Communication Theory	2	3	1	1	0	0	0	0	0	0	0	0	0	7	3.3	96	7.3
Continuum	3	3	1	0	0	0	0	0	0	0	0	0	0	7	3.3	247	2.8
Crime Media Culture	2	0	2	1	0	0	0	0	0	0	0	0	0	5	2.4	65	7.7
Critical arts	1	2	0	1	0	0	0	0	0	0	1	0	0	5	2.4	81	6.2
Critical Studies Media Communications	3	0	1	1	0	0	0	0	0	0	0	0	0	5	2.4	110	4.6
Cultural Studies	9	3	4	5	0	0	0	0	0	0	0	1	1	23	11.0	171	13.5
Discourse studies	1	0	0	0	0	0	0	0	0	0	0	0	0	1	0.5	150	0.7
Discourse and Society	3	0	1	0	0	0	0	0	0	0	0	0	0	4	1.9	124	3.2
Environmental Communication	0	1	0	0	0	0	0	0	0	0	0	0	0	1	0.5	80	1.3
European Journal of Communication	0	0	1	1	0	0	0	0	0	0	0	0	0	2	1.0	90	2.2
European Journal of Cultural Studies	5	0	0	0	0	0	0	0	0	0	0	0	0	5	2.4	114	4.4

TABLE 6.3   *Distribution of the use of Marx's name in the main text of the articles* (cont.)

Journals	Number of uses													Row total	Row%	N of articles analyzed	%use Marx
	1	2	3–5	6–12	a	b	c	d	e	f	g	h	i				
Transactions on Professional Communication	2	0	0	0	0	0	0	0	0	0	0	0	0	2	1.0	116	1.7
Information Communication & Society	6	0	0	0	0	0	0	0	0	0	0	0	0	6	2.9	195	3.1
Interasia Cultural Studies	9	1	2	1	1	0	0	0	0	0	0	0	0	14	6.7	144	9.7
International Journal of Conflict Management	2	0	0	0	0	0	0	0	0	0	0	0	0	2	1.0	88	2.3
International Journal of Press/Politics	1	0	0	0	0	0	0	0	0	0	0	0	0	1	0.5	110	0.9
International Journal of Public Opinion research	0	0	1	0	0	0	0	0	0	0	0	0	0	1	0.5	71	1.4
Journal of Communication	1	1	0	0	0	0	0	0	0	0	0	0	0	2	1.0	163	1.2
Journal of Computer-Mediated Communication	1	0	0	0	0	0	0	0	0	0	0	0	0	1	0.5	184	0.5

Journals	Number of uses													Row total	Row %	N of articles analyzed	% use Marx
	1	2	3–5	6–12	a	b	c	d	e	f	g	h	i				
J of Mass Media Ethics	2	0	0	0	0	0	0	0	0	0	0	0	0	2	1.0	82	2.4
Journalism Studies	4	1	1	0	0	0	0	0	0	0	0	0	0	6	2.9	219	2.7
Language & Intercultural Communication	1	0	0	0	1	0	0	0	0	0	0	0	0	2	1.0	88	2.3
Management Communication Quarterly	2	2	0	0	0	0	0	0	0	0	0	0	0	4	1.9	76	5.3
Mass Communication and Society	1	0	0	0	0	0	0	0	0	0	0	0	0	1	0.5	107	0.9
Media Culture & Society	4	1	1	0	0	0	1	0	0	0	0	0	0	7	3.3	210	3.3
New Media and Society	3	0	0	0	0	0	0	0	0	0	0	0	0	3	1.4	231	1.3
Public Culture	3	2	1	0	0	0	0	0	0	0	0	0	0	6	2.9	123	4.9
PR review	2	0	0	0	0	0	0	0	0	0	0	0	0	2	1.0	150	1.3
Quarterly J of Speech	1	0	1	0	0	0	1	0	0	0	0	0	0	3	1.4	85	3.5
Rhetoric Society Quarterly	5	1	2	0	0	0	0	0	0	0	0	0	0	8	3.8	80	10.0
Science Communication	1	0	0	0	0	0	0	0	0	0	0	0	0	1	0.5	92	1.1
Screen	2	0	0	0	0	0	0	0	0	0	0	0	0	2	1.0	74	2.7
Telecommunications Policy	2	0	0	0	0	0	0	0	0	0	0	0	0	2	1.0	258	0.8

TABLE 6.3   *Distribution of the use of Marx's name in the main text of the articles* (cont.)

Journals	Number of uses													Row total	Row %	N of articles analyzed	% use Marx
	1	2	3–5	6–12	a	b	c	d	e	f	g	h	i				
Theory Culture & Society	29	9	9	1	1	2	0	1	3	1	0	0	0	56	26.7	247	22.7
Television and New Media	2	0	1	0	0	0	0	0	0	0	0	0	0	3	1.4	100	3.7
Visual Communication	2	0	0	0	0	0	0	0	0	0	0	0	0	2	1.0	82	2.4
Written Communication	1	0	1	1	0	0	0	0	0	0	0	0	0	2	1.0	68	2.9
Total	121	31	31	12	3	2	2	1	3	1	1	1	1	210	100.0	4979	
%	57.6	14.8	14.8	5.7	1.4	1.0	1.0	0.5	1.4	0.5	0.5	0.5	0.5	100.0			

a   Provides a discussion using Marx's ideas
b   The whole article is dedicated to Marx/Marxism, Marxist view's, Marxist analysis or an evaluation of Marx or Marxism
c   Uses Marx to provide a Marxist analysis of class, exploitation, media and the like
d   The whole article uses a Marxist analysis of a topic
e   The whole article is dedicated to discuss the view of a person on Marx and Marxism
f   The whole article is about autonomous Marxism: the inadequacy of it or as alternative to classical Marxizm
g   The whole article uses Marx and Marxism throughout the article while discussing a marxist intellectual
h   The whole article uses Marx's ideas for the author's (Grossberg) revised theory of conjunctural analysis
i   The whole article is a decolonialist invalidation and accusation of Marx without presenting a reading of Marx

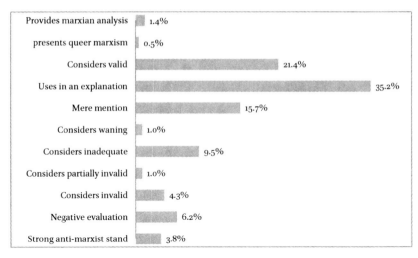

FIGURE 6.2   *Distribution of the evaluation of Marx in the analysed articles*

Negative evaluation (25.8%):

· 3.8% provide strong anti-Marx statements or negative evaluations (e.g., totalitarian, enemy of democracy, crude analysis; Eurocentric, utopian, pseudo-scientific).
· 10.5% provide a negative evaluation and consider Marx's ideas invalid (Marx's ideas about the base and superstructure; class; class conflict/struggle; ruling class and ruling ideas; the public sphere; theory of value; revolutionary change; the concept of labour; ideology; commodity fetishism; resistance).
· 1.0% consider Marx's ideas partially invalid.
· 10.5% consider Marx's thinking as waning and inadequate.

Positive stand/evaluation (23.3%)

· 21.4% use one or more concepts or theoretical approaches of Marx for explanation or analysis (for instance, men make history; aim is not only to understand, but to change society; the interplay of symbolic and material forces; creativity; humanism; labour; myth; ideology; slavery; technology; false consciousness; progress; proletariat; Asian modes of production; formal political equality; commodity, commodity production; fetishism; utopias; labour; class and exploitation; capitalist crisis; class struggle; press; freedom; historical materialism as basis of cultural studies; circulation and consumption; primitive accumulation).

· 1.4% provide some kind of Marxist analysis (the Internet, an issue, a historical explanation). These findings are very interesting because most of the
negative evaluations and invalidations do not have mainstream orientations as background.

4.3   Theoretical Orientations

The sample for the analysis of theoretical orientations of communication journals included 385 articles out of a total of 10104. The study found that the 385
articles used 150 theoretical approaches. This finding supports the routine com-
plaints of communication scholars that there are multitudes of theoretical
orientations in communications. It is true that there are many theoretical
approaches in communication, however, most of them, including sociology-
based, qualitative, structural-functionalist ones, are based on social psychology.

60.8% of all studies have study designs with no theoretical reasoning,
rationale or discussion at all (Table 6.4). Similarly, Potter, Cooper and Dupagne
(1993) found that 91.9% of their analysed articles had no theoretical
foundations. A study by Potter and Riddle (2007) found the same result for
57.1%. The result reported in Riffe and Freitag's study (1997) was also high:
72.4%. Kamhawi and Weaver (2003) found no theory in 69.5% of the articles in
their analysed sample.

Studies with theoretical structures that have a varying degree of proper
theoretical construction make up only 39.2%. Indeed, there is a very limited
number of studies that uses a theoretical framework for their study, provide
theoretical assumptions or extract research questions or hypotheses, and

TABLE 6.4   *Distribution of the existence of a theoretical structure*

Theoretical Content	N	%
Few theories/models are presented, but no theoretical framework is established for the study	7	1.8
No theory with theoretical reasoning/rationale/ discussion is presented at all	219	56.9
A ready theoretical approach was used, but no theoretical framework was established for the studying questions/hypotheses	8	2.1
A theoretical structure exists to a varying degree	151	39.2
Total	385	100.0

construct conclusions based on proper synthesis of their study findings, theoretical rationale and accumulated knowledge.

All these results show that there is a widespread tendency that researchers do not use a theoretical reasoning in their design and that Media and Communication Studies lack epistemological validity beyond providing information for control purposes.

Although the majority of the articles in this study does not have a specified theoretical framework, I found that 56% of all articles use mainstream approaches that are mostly based on social-psychology, followed by 9.8% the employ neo-liberal pluralism, 9.9% that are focused on various types of critical approaches, 8.6% that use post-structuralism. 4.7% are liberal-democrat in orientation,%3.9% constructionist, 2.6% post-modern, 2.6% have no-theoretical structure at all (they emphasize the functionality of a tool, procedure or application), 0.5% are post-colonial, 0.3% post-positivist, 0.8% neo-Marxist, and 0.5% critical political economy.

The problems of macro-level power relations, material and immaterial interests of organized power structures are not present in almost all theoretical approaches and study designs. Power and power relations are typically conceptualized (1) in terms of freedom of individual choices (by dominant approaches) or (2) in terms of "the death of the author" (the powerlessness of producing and disseminating industrial structures) in the face of an empowered individual audience that deconstructs and re-constructs everything according to his/her own free will, or (3) in terms of the popularized identity politics which are set against the focus on class identity, the mode and relations of production.

It seems like the term "Marxist political economy" is a cursed word: I did not see any article using the term. However, those approaches with a "post" prefix show interest in using the terms political economy and economic determinism interchangeably. They mostly advocate the end of political economy, class and ideology, and claim that all of these categories belong to the past. Political economy or critical political economy is used in a few articles.

4.4   *The Studied Topics*

The sample for the analysis of communication topics included 1386 articles of a total of 10104.

The topics that were identified in the analysis are presented under three categories: topics related to technologically mediated communication (823; 59.4%), technologically unmediated communication (236; 17.0%), and others that include anything that falls outside the first two groups (327; 23.6%).

The studies about the mediated communication have a rich variety, but 49.8% of all articles focus on mass communication related issues (Table 6.5).

TABLE 6.5   *Distribution of topics in technologically mediated communication*

Issues	N	%
Access	10	1.2
Accountability	2	0.2
Accuracy	1	0.1
Advertising, marketing	24	2.9
Attitude, perception and behaviour of media professionals	8	1.0
Audience reception, intertextuality, interpretation, evaluation, construction	6	0.7
Content: Media product analysis	31	3.8
Conversation (technologically mediated); managing impartiality	1	0.1
Culture, mediated multiculturalism; intercultural relations, cultural struggle	7	0.9
Development/history: media, communication education,	23	2.8
Discourse (technologically mediated)	17	2.1
Effect: Attitude, perception, behaviour, motivation, commitment, preferences, beliefs, participation, trust, emotions and personality of individuals	66	8.0
Effects in general	135	16.4
Effectiveness	11	1.3
Environment	3	0.4
Ethics	8	1.0
Media analysis	21	2.6
Identity and identity politics	14	1.7
Mediated interaction (parasocial and human-robot)	16	1.9
Internet, web, online games, use of social media	29	3.5
Language use	4	0.5
Policy, politics, law, regulation, control and freedom of communication, censorship	57	6.9
Media constructions/meaning	14	1.7
Media coverage/portrayal/framing, representation	77	9.4
Media education communication education	1	0.1
Media economics, industry, industrial relations	20	2.4
Method: model, measurement, data analysis	35	4.3
Production mode/relations (media, music industry)	2	0.2
Product design	2	0.2
Professional culture, values, practices, production	34	4.1

Issues	N	%
Research/study	15	1.8
Role/function of media	44	5.3
Space, audience viewing space	5	0.6
Surveillance	3	0.4
Source credibility	1	0.1
System/structure of media (mainstream)	5	0.6
Technology	9	1.1
Theory (includes theories in organizational communication, media, public relations, advertising and cultural studies)	47	5.7
Use of media (nature/character of use)	15	1.8
Total	823	100.0

The classical effect studies in mass communication still reign over others and have been extended to the new media (especially to computer-mediated communication). The concentration on effects and an expanding interests in media effects has been documented in many studies, like the one conducted by Shaw, Ham and Knott (2000), who provide a concise evaluation of the theories and the effect (and other) interests in communication studies and indicate that *"we live in a post-mass media age, but studies of the effects of mass media remain our strongest research tradition"* (p. 72).

The most common types of studies topics are effect related issues dealing with attitude, perception, behaviour, motivation, commitment, preferences, beliefs, participation, trust, emotions and personality of individuals and media (24.4%). Studies focusing on media content, portrayal and representation represent 14.9%. Only 3.5% of the studies focus on Internet-related issues (web, online games, use of social media).

Conversely, there is little interest in studying critical issues relating to industrial production, distribution and relations and working conditions and relations at the workplace. Mostly liberal-pluralists and those who use theories with a "post"-prefix are interested in media portrayal and representation beyond effect issues. Only 2.4% of 823 articles study one or more aspects of the industry (media economics, industry, industrial relations). However, only 3 of them use the Marxist approach (two critical political economy and one the neo-Marxist critical school). Such findings indicate that very few academicians are interested in studying issues related to the structure or nature of the communication industry.

Studies on technologically unmediated communication concern the rich variety of unmediated communication. However over one third of them (36.9%) deals with issues in interpersonal communication, technologically unmediated (conversation; word of mouth talk), interpersonal communication or technologically unmediated speech/oral communication. Organizational communication follows with 15.5%. Studies on various issues of self-communication occupy 10.2% (Table 6.6). None of these studies investigates issues related to

TABLE 6.6   *Distribution of issues in technologically unmediated communication*

Issues	N	%
Attitude, perception, behaviour, motivation, commitment, preferences, beliefs, participation, trust, emotions and personality of individuals	37	15.7
Conflict resolution/mediation, communicative strategy, risk reduction	3	1.3
Conversation, action, turn taking	3	1.3
Culture	2	0.8
Decision making	3	1.3
Discourse	5	2.1
Education	1	0.4
Effect	28	11.9
Effectiveness	8	3.4
Face management, relation maintenance, self-disclosure	7	3.0
Identity and identity politics	18	7.6
Individual's ability of thinking, memory, framing thoughts, expression, speaking, comprehension	7	3.0
Interaction: agency, conversation, listening, skills, natural occurrence	18	7.6
Intervention for children in the family environment	1	0.4
Language	7	3.0
Language learning	2	0.8
Language use	11	4.7
Method: model, measurement, data analysis	12	5.1
Narration: narrative, individual, life stories, refuge camps	10	4.2
Policy, politics, law, regulation, control and freedom of communication, censorship	1	0.4

Issues	N	%
Product (list, description)	1	0.4
Professionalism, professional practices	4	1.7
Racism, race talk	2	0.8
Reader's evaluation	1	0.4
Research/study	4	1.7
Rhetoric	3	1.3
Role of communication, talk, leadership	4	1.7
Situational and psychological factors of an individual's behaviour, speech	1	0.4
Speech	1	0.4
Surveillance	1	0.4
Technology (assistive, science, linguistic devices)	1	0.4
Theory	28	11.9
Vernacular science knowledge	1	0.4
Total	236	100.0

individual and/or interpersonal manifestations of the human condition in the economic, cultural and political organizations. They are mostly interested in (a) knowing psychological and behavioural/preferential characteristics of individuals, (b) the way individuals initiate and maintain personal relations, solve conflicts and end relations, and (c) ways and means for increasing employee's motivation, involvement and participation in their own exploitation at work.

Studies on other issues are concentrated on a multitude of issues (Table 6.7). Here too, the majority of issues are related to the effect, individuals' dispositions and behaviour. Engaging with a critical issue or conducting a critical analysis of an issue is at a minimum level.

Not only the present study but also almost all related studies found that there are vast varieties of issues, theoretical approaches and methods. According to Potter and Riddle (2007, 8), a wide range of effects and methods, and little overlap in research work "*could make it difficult for scholars to share definitions of key terms and a 'big picture' understanding of the overall field*". Potter's concern would be a valid one if the primary interest and concern of researchers were to understand the overall field.

TABLE 6.7   *Distribution of other issues*

Issues	N	%
Attitude, perception, behaviour, cognition, motivation, commitment, preferences, beliefs, opinions, participation, trust, emotions, affect and personality of individuals	32	9.8
Auditory systems	1	0.3
Collaboration and creativity, democracy, diversity	1	0.3
Conversion: religious	1	0.3
Culture, intercultural competence, transcultural literacy, art	12	3.7
Decision making	1	0.3
Development of a discipline	1	0.3
Discourse	1	0.3
Dispute resolution, organizations	9	2.8
Economics, human capital (drug testing on humans)	1	0.3
Effect	26	8.0
Effectiveness	5	1.5
Environment: protection	1	0.3
Ethics	2	0.6
Health: tanning and skin cancer	1	0.3
History, civil war; wine production	2	0.6
Identity and identity politics	19	5.8
Ideology, artefactual ideologies	2	0.6
Individual's adaptation to living environment	1	0.3
Individual's knowledge, memory, framing thoughts, expression	7	2.1
Individual's physical and mental health	1	0.3
Interaction: cooperation, cognitive processing, social relationship	19	5.8
Intervention for children in the family environment	1	0.3
Language learning, impairment	9	2.8
Language use, reading, learning	5	1.5
Language, type, semantics, history, development, structure, use	15	4.6
Leadership, multicultural	1	0.3
Method, learning, writing, training	7	2.1
Method: book design, explanation of a therapy	2	0.6
Method: model, measurement	22	6.7

Issues	N	%
Narration: transcultural narrative, trade, therapy	3	0.9
Nationalism, racialization, sexism, weapons promotion,	4	1.5
Organizational management, authority, cooperation, knowledge construction, change	4	1.5
Policy, politics, torture, participation, biopolitics, human rights, privacy	30	9.1
Pretend play: enacting hierarchical form of social organization	1	0.3
Public understanding of science	1	0.3
Research/study	14	4.3
Rhetoric: ethnicity, presidential	2	0.6
Simulation of nature: zoos	1	0.3
Space and time: global space, regionalization	3	0.9
Speech problems, symptoms, treatment, therapy, impairment, articulation	12	3.7
Surveillance, monitoring	1	0.3
Technology and technology use: imaging tools, devices, web applications	6	1.8
Theory (terrorism, colonialism, modernity, reality)	34	10.4
Violence: acid violence	1	0.3
Voting	1	0.3
Total	327	100.0

All the findings clearly indicate that dominant orientations of scholarly interest in communication research are based on the need of the industrial and institutional structure to know more about individuals and to assess media effects. The obvious implication of such orientations validates Marx's statement about the relationship between the ruling class and ideas in class societies. Under the prevailing scholarly interests and the factors that lead and feed the researchers/academicians, it becomes ridiculous, illogical and dysfunctional to ask questions like (a) why many scholars do not study the attitudes, perceptions, values, feelings, psychological health, racism, sexism, militarism and discourse of individuals belonging to the ruling class, (b) do not analyze the effect of their psychological disposition on the nature of production and distribution, the working conditions, minimum wage policies and miserable human and environmental conditions, and (c) do not suggest, at the end of the study, that the ruling class and their highly educated managerial cadres (not the people) should be educated, should go through sensitivity and empathy training, and should feel the feelings of being powerless, exploited, abused and misused.

The theories and study topics that have dominant communication studies in the last 60 years are still dominant. Some formerly marginal topics (especially hermeneutics, semiotics, constructivism and structuralism) are supplementary and fashionable alternatives now. They are the preferred theoretical approaches not because they have better explanatory power and epistemological and methodological validity, but because they are integrated into the global and glocal marketing and business interests, and because they are extremely functional for the mind and behaviour management, and thus, for the ruling interest of our times.

Most articles that refer to Marxism/Marx provide handy statements on the classical, economic determinist, reductionist, mechanistic or orthodox Marxisms, and make cliché judgments about Marxist reflectivity, historicism, Euro-centricism, fundamentalism, class bias, overdetermination, grand narrative and the like.

5   Marx's Place in Understanding Communication

A message, a word, talking, conversation, a communicative action or sending and receiving messages are not communication. We should not confuse communication with tools, means, expressions, representations, verbal and non-verbal actions or content of communication. Communication is one of the necessary conditions of biological and social existence of human beings: We could not produce and reproduce ourselves physically, psychologically, socially, economically or any other ways if we were unable to communicate. No communication means dead people, a dead society and a dead world. Nothing humanly is possible without communication. Communication, means of communication, language, symbols and the like do not exist individually; we do whatever we do in relation to each other and ourselves through the ways and means of material and mental production and social relations.

Marx takes a central place in understanding the importance, nature and the study of communication because he provided us with the most meaningful ways of knowing about anything related to communication. We can find the varying influence of his theoretical and methodological orientation in all alternative and liberal-democratic studies of communication. The most significant and enduring communication literature is based on approaches influenced by Marx's understanding of every aspect of human life. Marx is not part of the supportive mechanisms of dominant ways of reproducing the ruling interests, structures and relations. That is why it is the normalized part of the abnormal modes of reproduction of domination to ignore, exclude, chastise or downgrade Marx in Media and Communication Studies. Yet, Marx always finds his place in communication in the praxis of demystifying the mystified, the analysis of and struggle against the unjust and oppressive modes and relations of production, including intellectual and professional relations and practices in communications. Marx's humane interest, theory and method are starting points for or continuation of meaningful communication inquiry. However, we know that Marx also provided explanations concerning communication.

Findings in a specific organized time and organized place and/or organized relations can or cannot be valid in another time, place or relations, because of the changing conditions of theoretical reasoning/construction. Changes in conditions are not the necessary or sufficient condition for revisions or invalidation of a theory. A theory or a part of a theory looses its validity if the methodological structure of inquiry and/or the theoretical reasoning is unable to provide valid explanations for new, varying or changing conditions. Marx's theory is not a theory of maintenance, equilibrium, balance and justification of any organized mode and relations. It is a theory based on the study and explanation of the formation, maintenance and change. His theory and method should occupy a central place in understanding communication, because understanding communication requires understanding human and organized life beyond finding or forging justifications for it.

Marx's approach in communication mainly focuses on (1) the study of the nature of material production (material modes and relations) of communication (organization and practices of reproduction of structured-selves and communication products and thus reproduction of the human condition), (2) the study of immaterial production (immaterial modes and relations) of communication (production, dissemination and use of ideas, feelings, sensitivities, beliefs, information, knowledge, ignorance as knowledge), and (3) interrelations in and between the material and immaterial production of communication, but not in terms of reproducing the propagandist ignorance of the question of (a) what comes first (egg or chicken; base or superstructure), (b) overdetermination, (c) the death of the producer, and (d) the empowered individuals who deconstruct and reconstruct meanings according to their free will and wage struggle in front of the television and/or in the virtual world of cyberspace.

5.1   *Marx on Communication*

5.1.1   The Concept of Communication: What is Communication for Marx? We were educated in such a way that we have to know the definition, like the definition of communication. We cannot define communication with a single sentence. Communication (even an apple) cannot be correctly defined by a single or a few common properties. Furthermore, the answer to the question of what communication is does not come in five choices and one right answer. A scientific definition requires a kind of detailed explanation that includes properties/indicators of communication in general and a historically specific context so that we can learn what it is, and also provides exclusionary explanations so that we can learn what it is not. There are many definitions of communication, but none of them explains what communication is, because they are definitions focusing on the mechanics/processes of encoding and decoding, the observable interactions like sending and receiving messages, exchanging ideas, elements, functions, roles, goals or structures. Nobody communicates in order to send or receive a message or to create, construct, consume or deconstruct meanings. Communicative action, message, writing, saying something, reading a book or watching television do not constitute communication. Verbal expressions or any kind of mental or relational manifestations are also not "communication".

Marx does not define communication; however, we find very important explanations about communication in his writings. The following itemized presentation of Marx's understanding of communication invalidates (1) the claims that Marx did not deal with communication, (2) the assessment that Marx only talked about means of communication and (3) the evaluations that Marx reduced communication to "transportation".

I extracted phrases or sentences from Marx's writings and provided brief explanations:

·   *"Cheap and quick communications"* (Marx 1846): Existence of two indicators of two groups of the qualitative nature of communication.
·   *"Is the Iliad possible at all when the printing press and even printing machines exist? Is it not inevitable that with the emergence of the press bar the singing and the telling and the muse cease, that is the conditions necessary for epic poetry disappear?"* (Marx 1857b): historically accumulated and determined nature of communication and production of communication.
·   *"Conditions of Production and Communication; Political Forms and Forms of Cognition in Relation to the Conditions of Production and Communication"* (Marx 1857b): These are the titles in the main text. These titles indicate that

Marx is interested in conditions of communication, and the relationship of communication to political structures and cognition.

- *"The relations between productive power and the conditions of communication"* (Marx 1857b): This self-exploratory phrase indicates the importance of the conditions of communication in influencing the productive power.
- *"there are certain independent branches of industry in which the product of the productive process is not a new material product, is not a commodity. Among these only the communications industry, whether engaged in transportation proper, of goods and passengers, or in the mere transmission of communications, letters, telegrams, etc., is economically important"* (Marx 1885, Chapter 1, 17): Importance of the communication industry.
- "interfering with the British communications with Kurnaul and Meerut" (Marx 1857a): Control of communication.
- *"English line of communication between Agra and Delhi"* (Marx 1857a): Communication networks in the colonies.
- *"The Morning Chronicle, in its fourth edition, communicated a telegraphic despatch"* (Marx 1853): Communicating by sending a dispatch/content using the telegraph.
- *"The limited commerce and the scanty communication between the individual towns"* (Marx and Engels, 1969, 46): Quantitative nature of Communication and its outcome.
- *"The possibility of commercial communications transcending the immediate neighbourhood, a possibility, the realisation of which depended on the existing means of communication"* (Marx and Engels 1969, 47): Acknowledging the existence of various forms of communication, like commercial communications; implying that communication is done via means of communication; emphasizing the determining role of means of communication.
- *"Established means of communication"* (Marx and Engels 1969, 56): Role of established means of communication.
- *"Influence of the means of communication"* (Marx 1857b): influence/outcome of communication.
- "Louis Napoleon has communicated a similar message to his Senate and *Corps Législatif"*. (1854): Communicating a message.
- *"Centralisation of the means of communication and transport in the hands of the State"* (Marx 1848): Monopoly in communication; political economy of communication.
- "This market has given an immense development to commerce, to navigation, to communication by land" (Marx 1848): Development of communication and market influence on it.

- *"The bourgeoisie, by the rapid improvement of all instruments of production, by the immensely facilitated means of communication, draws all, even the most barbarian, nations into civilisation"* (Marx 1848): Role of development of the means of communication.
- *"This union is helped on by the improved means of communication that are created by modern industry"* (Marx 1848): Role of communication in society.
- *"An organised system of machines, to which motion is communicated by the transmitting mechanism from a central automaton"* (Marx 1867, Chapter 15, 3): Technology, organizational communication; machine-to-machine communication.
- *"The means of communication and transport were so utterly inadequate to the productive requirements of the manufacturing period"* (Marx 1867): Influence of the condition of communication in production.
- *"The means of communication and transport became gradually adapted to the modes of production of mechanical industry"* (Marx 1867): Political economy of communication; industrial relations, technological control.
- *"The improved means of transport and communication furnish the weapons for conquering foreign markets"* (Marx 1867): Role of communication in colonisation; international political economy of communication; war communication.
- *"The development of ocean navigation and of the means of communication generally, has swept away the technical basis on which season-work was really supported"* (Marx 1867): Role of communication in industrial development and relations, work force and trade.
- *"At a given stage of development of technology and of the means of communication, the discovery of new territories containing gold or silver plays an important role"* (Marx 1859a): Role of communication in development, colonization.
- *"It is clear that the progress of social production in general has, on the one hand, the effect of evening out differences arising from location as a cause of ground-rent, by creating local markets and improving locations by establishing communication and transportation facilities"* (Marx 1863–1883): Role of communication facilities; political economy of communication.
- *"Continental politicians, who imagine that in the London press they possess a thermometer for the temper of the English people, inevitably draw false conclusions at the present moment"* (Marx 1861a): In this article, Marx focuses on political communication; the relationship among media, politicians and people; the role of the press in war; close material relations between top

media professionals and ruling forces; the control of the press by politicians and corporate structures; the ownership of the press; interests that the London press upholds.

The short examples above also indicate that what Marx says in these short phrases is a lot more meaningful than, for instance, (a) millions of "effect analyses" that provide nothing more than distributional and relational information to serve the interests of marketing and/or political control and (b) some reception analyses that do talk about the nature of reception just like active audience theorists without using functionalist terminology and without analyzing receptors/individuals.

Marx said a lot more.

5.1.2   Location and Function/Role of Communication
          in Society and Social Development

Marx locates communication in every moment of the material and immaterial production of life. The explanations that Marx provides on ideas, the press, writing, means and roles of communication clearly indicate that communication for Marx is an essential factor for the existence of the societal production of life (that includes distribution, circulation and consumption). In addition to the ideas that are presented in the other sections of this chapter, the following explanation of Marx implies not only the relational aspect and role of communication, but also the necessity of communication in every sphere of social life:

"so soon as it (linen) comes into communication with another commodity, the coat. Only it betrays its thoughts in that language with which alone it is familiar, the language of commodities. In order to tell us that its own value is created by labour in its abstract character of human labour, it says that the coat, in so far as it is worth as much as the linen, and therefore is value, consists of the same labour as the linen. In order to inform us that its sublime reality as value is not the same as its buckram body, it says that value has the appearance of a coat, and consequently that so far as the linen is value, it and the coat are as like as two peas. We may here remark, that the language of commodities has, besides Hebrew, many other more or less correct dialects. [...] the equating of commodity B to commodity A, is commodity A's own mode of expressing its value." (Marx 1867, Chapter 1, 11) "The price [...] of commodities is, [...], a purely ideal or mental form. Although invisible, the value of iron, linen and corn has actual existence in these very articles: it is ideally made perceptible by their equality with gold, a relation that, so to say, exists only in their own heads. Their owner must, therefore, lend them his tongue, or hang a ticket on them, before their prices can be communicated to the outside world."

MARX 1867, Chapter 3, 1

Marx presents his ideas about the role of communication in writings ranging from the role of the press in society and the role of the means of communication in social change. His newspaper articles are good examples of political communication that are not reduced down to political campaigns, parliamentary processes and voter attitudes and preferences. He evaluated every important political event all over the world and wrote about the role of communication in the press, politics and public tendencies.

For Marx, technology is not a collection of tools, but technology means society at a certain level of development. Then, means of communication are integral parts of the maintenance and change, and, e.g., played a crucial role in the transition from the feudal mode of production to the capitalist mode, and also within the capitalist mode. Means of communication are employed and used in order to bolster the meaning, limits and potentialities of possible social relations and change.

Marx does not consider means of communication as a mere tool with a specific function: "*A house can serve for production as well as for consumption; likewise all vehicles, a ship and a wagon, for pleasure outings as well as a means of transport; a street as a means of communication for production proper, as well as for taking walks*" (*Marx 1859b*).

Marx provided explanations on communication and the relationship of the means of communication with factors that include every aspect of social production, distribution and consumption, maintenance and control of the social formation. His explanations are not limited within the circulation or as merely a certain technological means. Furthermore, it is a grave mistake to expect that Marx would locate communication at the centre of production of life and base his analyses on it or give primacy to the development of communication technology in society and social change.[6]

---

6   See Harold A. Innis for the powerful function of communication technology in maintenance and social change, Sut Jhally (1993) for evaluation of technological determinism, and Marshall McLuhan for effects of communication technology on the human sense organs and the transformation of the world to a global village.

5.1.2.1   *Development of the Means of Communication and Class Domination*
"All the progress of civilization, or in other words every increase in the
powers of social production, if you like, in the productive powers of
labour itself – such as results from science, inventions, division and combination of labour, improved means of communication, creation of the
world market, machinery etc. – enriches not the worker but rather capital;
hence it only magnifies again the power dominating over labour; increases
only the productive power of capital".
> MARX 1857C, 8

5.1.2.2   *Communication Facilities and the Magnitude of Productive Supply*
Stating that "*a definite quantity of potential productive capital must be available in some quantities for the purpose of entering by and by into the productive process*", Marx establishes causal relations that involve communication
facilities: "*the magnitude of this productive supply depends on the greater or
lesser difficulties of its renewal, the relative nearness of markets of supply, the
development of transportation and communication facilities*".
> MARX 1885, Chapter 13, 5

5.1.2.3   *Development of the Means of communication and the Cost of*
           Commodity Transportation
The capitalist mode of production reduces the costs of transportation of
the individual commodity by the development of the means of transportation and communication, as well as by concentration – increasing scale – of
transportation.
> MARX 1885, Chapter 6, 13

5.1.2.4   *Communication Facilities and the Speed/Time among Processes in*
           Order to Ensure the Continuity of Production
Marx explains this relationship by the example of coal supply: "*the rapid-
ity with which the product of one process may be transferred as means of
production to another process depends on the development of the transport
and communication facilities*".
> MARX 1885, Chapter 6, 8

5.1.2.5   *Developed means of Communication and the Density and the*
           Condition of the Division of Labour in Society
A relatively thinly populated country, with well-developed means of
communication, has a denser population than a more numerously
populated country, with badly-developed means of communication; and

in this sense the Northern States of the American Union, for instance, are more thickly populated than India. [...] In consequence of the great demand for cotton after 1861, the production of cotton, in some thickly populated districts of India, was extended at the expense of rice cultivation. In consequence there arose local famines, the defective means of communication not permitting the failure of rice in one district to be compensated by importation from another.

MARX 1867, Chapter 14, 9

5.1.2.6   *Development of the Means of Communication and Season-Work*
The development of ocean navigation and of the means of communication generally, has swept away the technical basis on which season-work was really supported.

MARX 1867, Chapter 15, 30

5.1.2.7   *Communication and Market Control*
The cheapness of the articles produced by machinery, and the improved means of transport and communication furnish the weapons for conquering foreign markets.

MARX 1867, Chapter 15, 22

5.1.2.8   *Communication and the Time of Commodity Circulation*
          and Change in Locations of Production
Marx explains the role of means of communication in the reduction of commodity circulation time, the growth of social wealth, social relations and change such as the deterioration of old and the rise of new centres of production:

whereas on the one hand the improvement of the means of transportation and communication brought about by the progress of capitalist production reduces the time of circulation of particular quantities of commodities, the same progress and the opportunities created by the development of transport and communication facilities make it imperative, conversely, to work for ever more remote markets, in a word – for the world-market. The mass of commodities in transit for distant places grows enormously, and with it therefore grows, both absolutely and relatively, that part of social capital that remains continually for long periods in the stage of commodity-capital, within the time of circulation. There is a simultaneous growth of that portion of social wealth which, instead of

serving as direct means of production, is invested in means of transportation and communication and in the fixed and circulating capital required
for their operation.

MARX 1885, Chapter 14, 2

the improvement of the means of communication and transportation
cuts down absolutely the wandering period of the commodities but does
not eliminate the relative difference in the time of circulation of different
commodity-capitals arising from their peregrinations, nor that of different portions of the same commodity-capital which migrate to different
markets. For instance the improved sailing vessels and steamships, which
shorten travelling, do so equally for near and distant ports. The relative
difference remains, although often diminished. But the relative difference may be shifted about by the development of the means of transportation and communication in a way that does not correspond to the
geographical distances. For instance a railway which leads from a place of
production to an inland centre of population may relatively or absolutely
lengthen the distance to a nearer inland point not connected by rail, as
compared to the one which geographically is more remote. In the same
way the same circumstances may alter the relative distance of places of
production from the larger markets, which explains the deterioration of
old and the rise of new centres of production because of changes in communication and transportation facilities. (To this must be added the circumstances that long hauls are relatively cheaper than short ones.)
Moreover with the development of transport facilities not only is the
velocity of movement in space accelerated and thereby the geographic
distance shortened in terms of time. Not only is there a development of
the mass of communication facilities so that for instance many vessels
sail simultaneously for the same port, or several trains travel simultaneously on different railways between the same two points, but freight vessels may clear on consecutive days of the same week from Liverpool for
New York, or goods trains may start at different hours of the same day
from Manchester to London.

MARX 1885, Chapter 14, 1

5.1.3   Production of Life: Material Production and the Production of Ideas
5.1.3.1   *The Production of Material Life*
The nature of and change in the material production of anything, including
material means of communication depends on the historical mode of production

at a certain time and place. The study of the production of communication primarily includes positioning and analyzing the organized activities within the local, national and international modes, relations and conditions of general production, and the investigation of the history and development of media industries and prevailing practices and conditions of production, distribution and consumption.

For instance, studying the praxis of media production and human conditions as end-products of dominant practices, Marx gives us a striking example in the English letter-press printing trade:

> There existed formerly a system, corresponding to that in the old manufactures and handicrafts, of advancing the apprentices from easy to more and more difficult work. They went through a course of teaching till they were finished printers. To be able to read and write was for every one of them a requirement of their trade. All this was changed by the printing machine. It employs two sorts of labourers, one grown up, renters, the other, boys mostly from 11 to 17 years of age whose sole business is either to spread the sheets of paper under the machine, or to take from it the printed sheets. They perform this weary task, in London especially, for 14, 15, and 16 hours at a stretch, during several days in the week, and frequently for 36 hours, with only 2 hours' rest for meals and sleep. A great part of them cannot read, and they are, as a rule, utter savages and very extraordinary creatures. [...] As soon as they get too old for such child's work, that is about 17 at the latest, they are discharged from the printing establishments.
>
> MARX 1867, Chapter 15, 31

Concerning the relationship between the revolution in the mode of production and the conditions of the means of communication, Marx points out the following connection:

> The revolution in the modes of production of industry and agriculture made necessary a revolution in the general conditions of the social process of production, i.e., in the means of communication and of transport. In a society whose pivot, to use an expression of Fourier, was agriculture on a small scale, with its subsidiary domestic industries, and the urban handicrafts, the means of communication and transport were so utterly inadequate to the productive requirements of the manufacturing period, with its extended division of social labour, its concentration of the

instruments of labour, and of the workmen, and its colonial markets, that
they became in fact revolutionized. In the same way the means of communication and transport handed down from the manufacturing period
soon became unbearable trammels on modern industry, with its feverish
haste of production, its enormous extent, its constant flinging of capital
and labour from one sphere of production into another, and its newly-
created connections with the markets of the whole world. Hence, apart
from the radical changes introduced in the construction of sailing vessels, the means of communication and transport became gradually
adapted to the modes of production of mechanical industry, by the creation of a system of river steamers, railways, ocean steamers, and telegraphs. But the huge masses of iron that had now to be forged, to be
welded, to be cut, to be bored, and to be shaped, demanded, on their part,
cyclopean machines, for the construction of which the methods of the
manufacturing period were utterly inadequate.

> MARX 1867, Chapter 15, 4

5.1.3.2   *The Production of Ideas*

According to Marx, the production (and distribution and use) of ideas should
be free from any repressive measures. Marx does not consider material production and the production of ideas as two independent spheres. For him, for
instance, newspaper production is a business that produces a material thing
called the newspaper and sells it; but at the same time, newspaper production
is a production of ideas on societal issues. For Marx, ideas are produced and
dependent on the conditions of life:

> Men are the producers of their conceptions, ideas, etc. – real, active men,
> as they are conditioned by a definite development of their productive
> forces and of the intercourse corresponding to these, up to its furthest
> forms. Consciousness can never be anything else than conscious exis-
> tence, and the existence of men is their actual life-process.

> MARX AND ENGELS 1969, 15

The following statement explains his most important theoretical and methodological uniqueness that distinguishes him from the idealist philosophy and its
new variants with the "post" prefix:

> Life is not determined by consciousness, but consciousness by life. In the
> first method of approach the starting-point is consciousness taken as the

living individual; in the second method, which conforms to real life, it is the real living individuals themselves, and consciousness is considered solely as their consciousness.

MARX AND ENGELS 1969, 15

5.2   *Marx on Mass Communication*

Marx wrote about every aspect of the press especially in his newspaper articles and personal letters. His interest in media continued until his death. The press was one of the substantial means of political struggle for him as well as the means of capitalist domination.

Marx can be considered a revolutionary political journalist who had the workers' emancipation in mind. Some of his articles in newspapers and letters to newspaper editors show his interest in mass communication and his understanding of communication, public opinion, public communication, press, freedom, freedom of the press, the nature of the relationship between newspapers and the governing power structure (censorship, professional participation in and justification of censorship, and struggle against censorship and participating journals).

His writings in the early 1840s are philosophical and journalistic pieces. They demonstrate Marx's interest in freedom of communication and the use of the press for promoting the ideas of freedom and struggle against censorship, injustice, political oppression, governmental and business corruption. He searched for truth, focused on the real conditions of the social, economic, and political environment and defended the work of journalists and the mission of the press against the pressures coming from the authorities. In his writings in the early 1840s, Marx defended freedom of thought and press and participated in the advancement of the bourgeois liberal revolution against the feudal structures and practices. However, he, after the second half of 1840s, considered press freedom as an emancipatory struggle of the working class and had no positive opinion about the law, press law and the bourgeois democratic parliamentary system. He was involved in the communist movement that struggled for democracy and freedom of the working class. For instance, the last issue of the *Neue Rheinische Zeitung* was printed entirely in red and contained an editorial notice, thanking the workers of Köln for their participation. The editorial ended with the slogan: "*emancipation of the working class*". His articles in 1843 were mostly on important current issues, attitudes of other newspapers and government restrictions and sanctions. In 1848 and 1849, he was highly critical of German papers. After moving to England in 1849, he started working as London correspondent of the *New York Daily Tribune* between 1852–1862. He wrote mostly on politics, war, international relations and government policies.

Marx considered the press as the mythmaking machine and his evaluation holds true more than ever for all the dominant media in the world today:

> Up till now it has been thought that the emergence of the Christian myths during the Roman Empire was possible only because printing had not yet been invented. Precisely the contrary. The daily press and the telegraph, which in a moment spreads its inventions over the whole earth, fabricate more myths in one day (and the bourgeois cattle believe and propagate them still further), than could have previously been produced in a century.
>
> MARX 1871

5.2.1   The Structure of the Media

Marx does not have any detailed analysis of the media structure, however his articles (e.g., Marx 1861a, 1861b) show how he approaches media ownership, politics and media practices: He goes beyond a simple explanation of ownership. He establishes multiple connections among material interests, the nature of media production and content, and explains the meaning and outcomes of these multiple relational links. He provides information about ownership, explicates the relationship between ownership and politics, relationship between top press professionals and politicians and business interests, connects them with professional practices geared toward propagating and buttressing private and political interests, and clarifies the public's place in it. Here are few instructive excerpts (all from Marx, 1861a):

> Continental politicians, who imagine that in the London press they possess a thermometer for the temper of the English people, inevitably draw false conclusions at the present moment. With the first news of the Trent case the English national pride flared up and the call for war with the United States resounded from almost all sections of society. [...] Hence, in the beginning, the peaceful and moderate tone of the London press in contrast to the warlike impatience of the people. So soon, however, as the Crown lawyers [...] had worked out a technical pretext for a quarrel with the United States, the relationship between the people and the press turned into its opposite. The war fever increased in the press in the same measure as the war fever abated in the people. [...]

But now, consider the London press! At its head stands The Times, whose leading editor, Bob Lowe, [...] is a subordinate member of the Cabinet, a kind of minister for education, and a mere creature of Palmerston. [...] A principal editor of Punch was accommodated by Palmerston with a seat on the Board of Health and an annual salary of a thousand pounds sterling. [...]

The Morning Post is in part Palmerston's private property. Another part of this singular institution is sold to the French Embassy. The rest belongs to the haute volée and supplies the most precise reports for court flunkeys and ladies' tailors. [...]

The Morning Advertiser is the joint property of the "licensed victuallers", that is, of the public houses, which, besides beer, may also sell spirits. It is, further, the organ of the English Pietists and ditto of the sporting characters, that is, of the people who make a business of horseracing, betting, boxing and the like. The editor of this paper, Mr. Grant, previously employed as a stenographer by the newspapers and quite uneducated in a literary sense, has had the honour to get invited to Palmerston's private soirees. [...] It must be added that the pious patrons of this liquor-journal stand under the ruling rod of the Earl of Shaftesbury and that Shaftesbury is Palmerston's son-in-law. Shaftesbury is the pope of the Low Churchmen, who blend the spiritus sanctus with the profane spirit of the honest Advertiser. [...]

The Morning Chronicle! [...] For well-nigh half a century the great organ of the Whig Party and the not unfortunate rival of The Times, its star paled after the Whig war. It went through metamorphoses of all sorts, turned itself into a penny paper and sought to live by "sensations", thus, for example, by taking the side of the poisoner, Palmer. It subsequently sold itself to the French Embassy, which, however, soon regretted throwing away its money. It then threw itself into anti-Bonapartism, but with no better success. Finally, it found the long missing buyer in Messrs. Yancey and Mann – the agents of the Southern Confederacy in London. [...]

The Daily Telegraph is the private property of a certain Levy. His paper is stigmatised by the English press itself as Palmerston's mob paper. [...] In the dignity and moderation dictated to it, it seemed so strange to itself that since then it has published half-a-dozen articles about this instance of moderation and dignity displayed by it. As soon, however, as the order to change its line reached it, the Telegraph has sought to compensate itself for the constraint put upon it by outbawling all its comrades in howling loudly for war. [...]

The Tory papers, The Morning Herald and The Evening Standard, both belonging to the same boutique, are governed by a double motive: on the one hand, hereditary hate for "the revolted English colonies'"; on the other band, a chronic ebb in their finances. They know that a war with America must shatter the present coalition Cabinet and pave the way for a Tory Cabinet. With the Tory Cabinet official subsidies for The Herald and The Standard would return. Accordingly, hungry wolves cannot howl louder for prey than these Tory papers for an American war with its ensuing shower of gold! [...]

Of the London daily press, The Daily News and The Morning Star are the only papers left that are worth mentioning; both work counter to the trumpeters of war. The Daily News is restricted in its movement by a connection with Lord John Russell; The Morning Star (the organ of Bright and Cobden) is diminished in its influence by its character as a "peace-at-any-price paper". [...] Most of the London weekly papers are mere echoes of the daily press, therefore overwhelmingly warlike. The Observer is in the ministry's pay. The Saturday Review strives for esprit and believes it has attained it by affecting a cynical elevation above "humanitarian" prejudices. To show "esprit", the corrupt lawyers, parsons and schoolmasters that write this paper have smirked their approbation of the slaveholders since the outbreak of the American Civil War. [...]

The Spectator, The Examiner and, particularly, MacMillan's Magazine must be mentioned as more or less respectable exceptions.

One sees: On the whole, the London press – with the exception of the cotton organs, the provincial papers form a commendable contrast – represents nothing but Palmerston and again Palmerston. Palmerston wants war; the English people don't want it. Imminent events will show who will win in this duel, Palmerston or the people. In any case, he is playing a more dangerous game than Louis Bonaparte at the beginning of 1859.

5.2.2   Freedom and the Media

The issue of freedom of human beings is the core concern of Marx in his theoretical orientation and all kinds of writings. His newspaper articles show his deep feelings for emancipation of individuals from every kind of oppression and slavery.

For Marx, *"freedom remains freedom whether it finds expression in printer's ink, in property, in the conscience, or in a political assembly"* (Marx 1842g). *"Freedom includes not only what my life is, but equally how I live, not only that I do what is free, but also that I do it freely. Otherwise what difference would there be between an architect and a beaver except that the beaver would be an architect with fur and the architect a beaver without fur?"* (Marx 1842f). *"Freedom is so much the essence of man that even its opponents implement it while combating its reality; they want to appropriate for, themselves as a most precious ornament what they have rejected as an ornament of human nature"* (Marx 1842e). Criticizing those who appropriate freedom for themselves and reject for others, Marx is very explicit:

> these gentlemen, because they want to regard freedom not as the natural gift of the universal sunlight of reason, but as the supernatural gift of a specially favourable constellation of the stars, because they regard freedom as merely an individual property of certain persons and social estates, are in consequence compelled to include universal reason and universal freedom among the bad ideas and phantoms of logically constructed systems. In order to save the special freedoms of privilege, they proscribe the universal freedom of human nature. Since, however, the bad brood of the nineteenth century, and the very consciousness of the modern knights that has been infected by this century, cannot comprehend what is in itself incomprehensible, because devoid of idea, namely, how internal, essential, universal determinations prove to be linked with certain human individuals by external, fortuitous, particular features, without being connected with the human essence, with reason in general, and therefore common to all individuals – because of this they necessarily have recourse to the miraculous and the mystical. Further, because the real position of these gentlemen in the modern state does not at all correspond to the notion they have of that position, because they live in a world beyond the real one, and because therefore imagination is their head and heart, being dissatisfied with their practical activity, they necessarily have recourse to theory, but to the theory of the other world, to religion, which in their hands, however, is given a polemical bitterness impregnated with political tendencies and becomes more or less consciously only a holy cloak for very secular, but at the same time fantastic desires.
>
> MARX 1842D

For Marx:

> "every restriction of freedom is a factual, irrefutable proof that at one time those who held power were convinced that freedom must be restricted, and this conviction then serves as a guiding principle for later views" (Marx 1842c). "Whenever one form of freedom is rejected, freedom in general is rejected and henceforth can have only a semblance of

existence, since the sphere in which absence of freedom is dominant becomes a matter of pure chance. Absence of freedom is the rule and freedom an exception, a fortuitous and arbitrary occurrence".

MARX 1842G

5.2.3   The Press: Censored and Free Press, Good and Bad Press

Marx's first interest was in the control of communication, mostly because of his journalistic endeavours starting in the early 1840s. He provided rich and striking discussions about freedom of the press and censorship in six articles written in May 1842. However, I also included other articles in the study.

Marx considers press as means of public communication and means of struggle for the truth and emancipation. According to him, *"the press is the most general way by which individuals can communicate their intellectual being. It knows no respect for persons but only respect for intelligence"* (Marx 1842g). He asks, *"do you want the ability for intellectual communication to be determined officially by special external signs?"* and explicates: *"what I cannot be for others, I am not and cannot be for myself. If I am not allowed to be a spiritual force for others, then I have no right to be a spiritual force for myself"*. He refuses to give *"certain individuals the privilege of being spiritual forces"* and expounds that *"just as everyone learns to read and write, so everyone must have the right to read and write"* (Marx 1842g).

He divides the press into two basic groups: those who go along with the authorities and free press (or people's press). Then, he compares their characteristics:

> free press is the ever-present, vigilant eye of the people's spirit, the embodiment of a people's trust in itself, the communication link that binds the individual to state and world, the embodied culture that transforms material struggles into spiritual ones while idealising their crude material form. It is the people's outspoken self-confession, whose redeeming power is well known. It is the spiritual mirror, in which a people discover itself, and insight is the first prerequisite of wisdom. It is the public spirit, which may be delivered to every cottage cheaper than coal gas. It is multifarious, ubiquitous, and omniscient. It is the ideal world, which emerges from the real world only to return to it as an enriched spirit, newly charged.
>
> MARX 1842F

The censored press remains bad even when it turns out good products, for these products are good only insofar as they represent the free press within the censored press, and insofar as it is not in their character to be products of the censored press. The free press remains good even when it produces bad products, for the latter are deviations from the essential nature of the free press. The essence of the free press is the characterful, rational, moral essence of freedom. The character of the censored press is the characterless monster of unfreedom; it is a civilised monster, a perfumed abortion.

MARX 1842E

Marx's following depiction of the censored press reminds us some of the basic tenets of the mainstream popular media today:

It is the censored press that has a demoralizing effect. Inseparable from it is the most powerful vice, hypocrisy, and from this, its basic vice, come all its other defects, which lack even the rudiments of virtue, and its vice of passivity, loathsome even from the aesthetic point of view. [...] the press lies continually and has to deny even any consciousness of lying, and must cast off all shame. [...] It is the malicious gloating which extracts tittle-tattle and personalities from the great life of the peoples, ignores historical reason and serves up to the public only the scandals of history; being quite incapable of judging the essence of a matter, it fastens on single aspects of a phenomenon and on individuals, and imperiously demands mystery so that every blot on public life will remain hidden. [...] For its part, therefore, the people sinks partly into political superstition, partly into political disbelief, or, completely turning away from political life, becomes a rabble of private individuals.

MARX 1842F

Marx does not accept the division of press as good press and bad press when the issue is censorship:

If one wants to speak of two kinds of press, the distinction between them must be drawn from the nature of the press itself, not from considerations lying outside it. The censored press or the free press, one of these two must be the good or the bad press. The debate turns precisely on whether the censored press or the free press is good or bad, i.e., whether it is in the nature of the press to have a free or unfree existence. To make the bad press a refutation of the free press is to maintain that the free press is bad and the censored press good, which is precisely what had to be proved. Base frames of mind, personal intrigues, infamies, occur alike in the censored and the free press. Therefore the generic difference between them is not that they produce individual products of this or that kind; flowers grow also in swamps. We are concerned here with the essence, the inner character, which distinguishes the censored from the free press. [...] A free press that is bad does not correspond to its essence. The censored press with its hypocrisy, its lack of character, its eunuch's language, its dog-like tail-wagging, merely realises the inner conditions of its essential nature.

MARX 1842E

5.2.4 Freedom of Press, Censorship and Struggle

There should be material existences of organized entities in specific relationships in order to talk about freedom, domination and struggle. Two such entities are the press and the organized body of censorship. Post-Napoleonic Germany had been promised a constitutionally established string of provincial parliaments. In 1823, Prussia formed eight parliaments (assemblies of the estates). They embraced the heads of princely families, representatives of the knightly estate, i.e., the nobility, of towns and rural communities. It was a parliamentary feudal system under the attack of the liberal bourgeoisie. Marx was part of the revolutionary struggle of the working class and also of the struggle of the bourgeoisie for the advancement of capitalism. Marx fought for freedom and dignity and against the official practices of press control and the manipulation of the truth. Marx identified press practices with the right of freedom of expression that governs the relations between the press and public and private authorities. Marx's articles were occasioned by the censorship instruction of the Prussian Government in December 1841 and the freedom of the press debates in the Rheinland province of Prussia, and they further include a discussion of "the censorship decree in the Provisional Federal Act on the Press" for the German states adopted on September 20, 1819.

Marx considers freedom of the press and censorship as historical fact. For him, the *"iterary period of strict censorship, is therefore clear historical proof that the censorship has undoubtedly influenced the development of the German spirit in a disastrous, irresponsible way"* (Marx 1842c).

The very first article addressing the freedom of the press, censorship and writers was titled *"Comments on the latest Prussian Censorship Instructions"* and was written between January 15 and February 10, 1842 and published in the *Anekdota zur neuesten deutschen Philosophie und Publicistik*, in 1843 (Marx 1842a; Marx 1842b).

Distinguishing himself from those who exclaim *"Beware of Greeks bearing gifts"* (beware of Trojan horse) even before the appearance of the new Prussian censorship decree, Marx explains that *censorship "is official criticism; its standards are critical standards, hence they least of all can be exempted from criticism, being on the same plane as the latter", and the censor "is accuser, defender and judge in a single person; control of the mind is entrusted to the censor"* (Marx 1842a). And he continues:

> Censorship is criticism as a monopoly of the government. But does not criticism lose its rational character if it is not open but secret, if it is not theoretical but practical, if it is not above parties but itself a party, if it operates not with the sharp knife of reason but with the blunt scissors of arbitrariness, if it only exercises criticism but will not submit to it, if it disavows itself during its realisation, and, finally, if it is so uncritical as to mistake an individual person for universal wisdom, peremptory orders for rational statements, ink spots for patches of sunlight, the crooked deletions of the censor for mathematical constructions, and crude force for decisive arguments?
>
> MARX 1842E

> *Addressing the nature of the decree, he reminds us that* "censorship is also to protect ruling forces from any kind of unwanted communication and criticism: The press is forbidden all control over officials as over such institutions that exist as a class of individuals" (Marx 1842a). *Marx declares that the censorship law is not a law:* "it is a police measure; but it is a bad police measure, for it does not achieve what it intends, and it does not intend what it achieves".
>
> MARX 1842F

In his articles, Marx also invalidates each rationale (such as human immaturity, good and bad press, and bad people with bad ideas) given by the speaker of the Assembly in order to justify the censorship. For instance, Marx argues:

> If the immaturity of the human race is the mystical ground for opposing freedom of the press, then the censorship at any rate is a highly reasonable means against the maturity of the human race. Man, individually and in the mass, is imperfect by nature. [...] The arguments of our speaker are imperfect, governments are imperfect, assemblies are imperfect, freedom of the press is imperfect, every sphere of human existence is imperfect. Hence if one of these spheres ought not to exist because of this imperfection, none of them has the right to exist, man in general has no right to exist. Amid all these imperfections, why should precisely the free press be perfect? Why does an imperfect provincial estate demand a perfect press? If then, by its very existence, everything human is imperfect,

ought we therefore to lump everything together, have the same respect
for everything, good and evil, truth and falsehood?

MARX 1842D

Invalidating the rationale, Marx continues:

in order really to justify censorship, the speaker would have had to
prove that censorship is part of the essence of freedom of the press;
instead he proves that freedom is not part of man's essence. He rejects
the whole genus in order to obtain one good species, for is not freedom
after all the generic essence of all spiritual existence, and therefore of
the press as well? In order to abolish the possibility of evil, he abolishes
the possibility of good and realises evil, for only that which is a realisation of freedom can be humanly good. We shall therefore continue to
regard the censored press as a bad press so long as it has not been
proved to us that censorship arises from the very essence of freedom of
the press.

MARX 1842D

Marx also emphasizes that the press freedom has a different character:
*"Freedom of the press has a justification quite different from that of censorship
because it is itself an embodiment of the idea, an embodiment of freedom, a positive good, whereas censorship is an embodiment of unfreedom, the polemic of a
world outlook of semblance against the world outlook of essence; it has a merely
negative nature"* (Marx 1842e).

Marx addresses the repressive conditions in Germany by indicating that
twenty two years (since the enactment of the censorship law at the end of 1819)
*"illegal actions have been committed by an authority which has in its charge the
highest interest of the citizens, their minds, by an authority which regulates, even
more than the Roman censors did, not only the behaviour of individual citizens,
but even the behaviour of the public mind"*. He provides an excellent discussion
on every futile approach to the problem (blaming the censors, individuals,
defects in the law or in institutions, nature of the law, newspaper correspondents and public) and concludes: *"resentment against the thing itself becomes
resentment against persons. It is believed that by a change of persons the thing
itself has been changed. [...] The real, radical cure for the censorship would be its
abolition; for the institution itself is a bad one, and institutions are more powerful
than people"* (Marx 1842a).

For Marx, *"only struggle can convince both the government and the people, as
well as the press itself, that the press has a real and necessary right to existence.*

Only struggle can show whether this right to existence is a concession or a necessity, an illusion or a truth" (Marx 1843a). *"Censorship does not abolish the struggle, it makes it one-sided, it converts an open struggle into a hidden one, it converts a struggle over principles into a struggle of principle without power against power without principle"* (Marx 1842a).

5.2.5   The Difference between Press Law and Censorship

Marx considers censorship law as a precautionary measure of the police against freedom. He compares it with press law in 1842:

> In the press law, freedom punishes. In the censorship law, freedom is punished. The censorship law is a law of suspicion against freedom. The press law is a vote of confidence which freedom gives itself. The press law punishes the abuse of freedom. The censorship law punishes freedom as an abuse. It treats freedom as a criminal, or is it not regarded in every sphere as a degrading punishment to be under police supervision? [...] The press law is a real law because it is the positive existence of freedom. It regards freedom as the normal state of the press, the press as the mode of existence of freedom, and hence only comes into conflict with a press offence as an exception that contravenes its own rules and therefore annuls itself. Freedom of the press asserts itself as a press law, against attacks on freedom of the press itself, i.e., against press offences. The press law declares freedom to be inherent in the nature of the criminal. Hence what he has done against freedom he has done against himself and this self-injury appears to him as a punishment in which he sees a recognition of his freedom. [...] Therefore the press law is the legal recognition of freedom of the press. It constitutes right, because it is the positive existence of freedom. It must therefore exist, even if it is never put into application.
>
> MARX 1842D

Marx's positive view of the law had changed within a few years. For instance, in 1848, he considered the Prussian Press Bill as "classic monuments of Napoleonic press despotism" (Padover 1974, 121). In 1849, he stated that the Prussian despotism was worse than the Napoleonic despotism:

> Prussian despotism, on the other hand, confronts me in the shape of an official with a superior, sacrosanct being. His official character is as integral part of his personality as consecration is of a Catholic priest. [...] To insult such a priest, even one who is not functioning, who is not present,

and who is back in private life, remains a profanation of religion, a
desecration.

Marx refuses the claims about the preventive nature of a law. According to
Marx, laws

> "cannot prevent a man's actions, for they are indeed the inner laws of life of
> his action itself, the conscious reflections of his life. Hence law withdraws
> into the background in the face of man's life as a life of freedom, and only
> when his actual behaviour has shown that he has ceased to obey the natural
> law of freedom does law in the form of state law compel him to be free, just
> as the laws of physics confront me as something alien only when my life has
> ceased to be the life of these laws, when it has been struck by illness. Hence
> a preventive law is a meaningless contradiction" (Marx 1842d). A preventive
> law, therefore, has within it no measure, no rational rule, for a rational rule
> can only result from the nature of a thing, in this instance of freedom.

MARX 1842E

5.2.6 Freedom of Press and Freedom of Trade

Human beings produce and reproduce their material and immaterial life. In
regard to the press, Marx clearly explains its role and nature of the relationship
between the material and immaterial production in the following sentence:
*"What makes the press the most powerful lever for promoting culture and the intel-
lectual education of the people is precisely the fact that it transforms the material
struggle into an ideological struggle, the struggle of flesh and blood into a struggle
of minds, the struggle of need, desire, empiricism into a struggle of theory, of reason, of form"* (Marx 1842i). This explanation demonstrates the connection and
distinction between the two, but also shows the simplicity and the invalidity of
the assertion that Marx/Marxism is an economic reductionist approach and
establishes wrong causal relationship between the base and superstructure.

Marx differentiates freedom of the press (journalists' right of free expression) from freedom of trade (right of business): *"If the press itself is regarded
merely as a trade, then, as a trade carried on by means of the brain, it deserves
greater freedom than a trade carried on by means of arms and legs. The emancipation of arms and legs only becomes humanly significant through the
emancipation of the brain, for it is well known that arms and legs become
human arms and legs only because of the head which they serve"* (Marx 1842g).

Marx does not accept the idea that freedom of the press is a part of freedom
of trade:

Freedom of trade, freedom of property, of conscience, of the press, of the courts, are all species of one and the same genus, of freedom without any specific name. But it is quite incorrect to forget the difference because of the unity and to go so far as to make a particular species the measure, the standard, the sphere of other species. This is an intolerance on the part of one species of freedom, which is only prepared to tolerate the existence of others if they renounce themselves and declare themselves to be its vassals. [...] Freedom of trade is precisely freedom of trade and no other freedom because within it the nature of the trade develops unhindered according to the inner rules of its life. [...] Every particular sphere of freedom is the freedom of a particular sphere, just as every particular mode of life is the mode of life of a particular nature. How wrong it would be to demand that the lion should adapt himself to the laws of life of the polyp!
MARX 1842G

To make freedom of the press a variety of freedom of trade is a defence that kills it before defending it, for do I not abolish the freedom of a particular character if I demand that it should be free in the manner of a different character? Your freedom is not my freedom, says the press to a trade. As you obey the laws of your sphere, so will I obey the laws of my sphere. To be free in your way is for me identical with being unfree, just as a cabinet-maker would hardly feel pleased if he demanded freedom for his craft and was given as equivalent the freedom of the philosopher.
MARX 1842G

Acknowledging that *"the press exists also as a trade, but then it is not the affair of writers, but of printers and booksellers"*, Marx pinpoints the crucial difference by stating that *"we are concerned here not with the freedom of trade of printers and booksellers, but with freedom of the press. [...] The primary freedom of the press lies in not being a trade"* (Marx 1842g).

5.2.7   Public Rights and Freedom
Marx defended the public's right and freedom while defending freedom of the press against the control by the ruling powers. For Marx,

The law against a frame of mind is not a law of the state promulgated for its citizens, but the law of one party against another party. The law which punishes tendency abolishes the equality of the citizens before the law. It is a law which divides, not one which unites, and all laws which divide are reactionary. It is not a law, but a privilege. One may do what another may not do, not because the latter lacks some objective quality, like a minor in regard to concluding contracts; no, because his good intentions and his frame of mind are under suspicion. The moral state assumes its members to have the frame of mind of the state, even if they act in opposition to an organ of the state, against the government. But in a society in which one organ imagines itself the sole, exclusive possessor of state reason and state morality, in a government which opposes the people in principle and hence regards its anti-state frame of mind as the general, normal frame of mind, the bad conscience of a faction invents laws against tendency, laws of revenge, laws against a frame of mind which has its seat only in the government members themselves. Laws against frame of mind are based on an unprincipled frame of mind on an immoral, material view of the state.

MARX 1842A

5.2.8   Writers, Professional Practices and Professional Ideologies

5.2.8.1   *On Writers*

Journalists (and academicians) in their professional practices have mainly one of two choices: The first one is to take the multiple risks and inconveniences and become an ardent follower of the truth. The second one is to run after a multitude of rewards, become a devoted follower and supporter of the status quo. In fact, an internal negotiation happens and the decision depends on mostly the degree of risk the journalist can take.

Marx was the first kind of journalist. For him, journalism is a tool for truth and of the struggle for emancipation. For Marx, *"truth is general, it does not belong to me alone, it belongs to all, it owns me, I do not own it. My property is the form, which is my spiritual individuality. [...] Truth includes not only the result but also the path to it. The investigation of truth must itself be true; true investigation is developed truth, the dispersed elements of which are brought together in the result"* (Marx 1842a). He despises any practice and law that prescribes the form, the spiritual individuality. Similarly, he also despises any professional practice that follows such a prescribed path.

The second type of journalist is not an honourable professional, even as much as the "dull bureaucrat" who censored Marx's articles. The journalist reproduces the same material and immaterial conditions, but he/she does it knowingly, consciously, premeditatedly and he/she mostly is aware of the fact that s/he is distorting, lying or fabricating factoids. However, he/she is not in the same material and mental condition as the dull bureaucrat or the servant-driver of Edward Bernays' Dum Jack (Ewen 1996). The dull bureaucrat named Lauenz Dolleschall would not let anyone *"making fun of divine things"*, thus would censor everything that looks suspicious to him and would say, as Marx quotes: *"Now it's a matter of my bread and butter. Now I strike out everything"* (cited Quotations are from Padover 1974: xviii). However, the journalist's decisions are not based on his/her irrational or illogical beliefs, but his/her well calculated interest: he/she would edit, thus censor everything that does not fit in his/her interest and interests of his/her employers.

In the defence speech during his trial in 1849, Marx described the duty of the press and journalists:

> I prefer to follow the great events of the world, to analyze the course of history, than to occupy myself with local bosses, with the police and prosecuting magistrates. However great these gentlemen may imagine themselves in their own fancy, they are *nothing*, absolutely *nothing*, in the gigantic battles of the present time. I consider we are making a real sacrifice when we decide to break a lance with *these* opponents. But, firstly, it is the duty of the press to come forward on behalf of the oppressed in its immediate neighbourhood. And furthermore, gentlemen, the edifice of servitude has its most specific support in the subordinate political and social powers which directly confront the private life of an individual, of a living person. It is not sufficient to fight against general relationships and the highest authorities. The press must decide to enter the lists against a *specific* police officer, a *specific* Public Prosecutor, a *specific* *Landrat*. [...] The first duty of the press now is *to undermine all the foundations of the existing political state of affairs*.
>
> MARX 1849B

The statement above indicates that Marx attributes an important role to the press and journalists in the struggle for freedom. For him, *"the press in general is a realisation of human freedom. Consequently, where a press there is freedom of the press"*. Then, for Marx the question of freedom of the press is not *"a question whether freedom of the press ought to exist, for it always exists. The question is whether freedom of the press is a privilege of particular individuals or whether it is a privilege of the human mind. The question is whether a right of one side ought to be a wrong for the other side. The question is whether freedom of the mind has more right than freedom against the mind"* (Marx 1842e).

His discussion and explanations on and defence of freedom of thought and communication and of the dignity of a writer are important lessons for certain media professionals (and academicians) who safely practice their daily money making business in shameless compliance with the interest of private and state powers, while other journalists (and academicians) are in jail more than five years without a proper trial for thinking and planning to overthrow the government in countries like Turkey, where a glocal civil dictatorship of global capitalism has been tested. Turkey has more journalists in prison than any other country in the world. More than 100 journalists are currently in prison. There are between 700 and 1,000 ongoing cases in Turkey that could result in more imprisonments and up to 3,000 years imprisonment (http://europe.ifj .org/en/articles?search=Turkey) Mustafa Balbay (a famous journalist and recently elected member of the parliament) and Prof. Dr. Mehmet Haberal (a worldwide famous medical doctor, president of Baskent University and recently elected member of the parliament) have been in jail for more than 3 years for planning a coup against the ruling government. Anyone who writes and says something about the situation is accused of "attempting to influence fair trial" and is put in jail (http://www.dha.com.tr/chp-leaders-immunity-in-danger-accused-of-attempting-to-influence-fair-trial-son-dakika-haberi_255874 .html). Current dominant professionalism in the media (and academia) is a despicable kind of professionalism that Marx criticizes in his articles.

Marx also sets the basic professional standard for media professionals by differentiating a writer/journalist from a businessperson:

> the writer, of course, must earn in order to be able to live and write, but he must by no means live and write to earn. [...] The writer does not at all look on his work as a means. It is an end in itself, it is so little a means for him himself and for others that, if need be, he sacrifices his existence to its existence. [...] The writer who degrades the press into being a material means deserves as punishment for this internal unfreedom the external unfreedom of censorship, or rather his very existence is his punishment.
>
> MAY 19, 1842G

Criticizing the division of authorised and unauthorised writers, Marx asks: *"for whom, then, is the division of writers into authorised and unauthorised intended?"* and he provides an answer and another question: *"Obviously not for the truly authorised, for they can make their influence felt without that. Is it therefore for the 'unauthorised' who want to protect themselves and impress others by means of an external privilege?"*. He adds:

> If the German looks back on his history, he will find one of the main reasons for his slow political development, as also for the wretched state of literature prior to Lessing, in the existence of "authorised writers." It was the unauthorised writers who created our literature. Gottsched and Lessing-there you have the choice between an "authorised"and "unauthorised"

writer! [...] Freedom of the press will certainly not be achieved by a crowd of official writers being recruited by you from your ranks. The authorised authors would be the official authors, the struggle between censorship and freedom of the press would be converted into a struggle between authorised and unauthorised writers.

MARX, 1842G

5.2.8.2   *On Professional Practices*

Marx has many statements in articles and letters to editors on the general and daily press practices (e.g.; Marx, 1842h; 1842i; 1842j; 1843a; 1843b; 1843c; 1848; 1849a; 1860; 1861a; 1861b). They can be grouped as follows:

· Writings about the government persecution of press by imposing a ban on newspapers: Marx questions the legitimacy of such persecutions and the nature of the condition of the press.
· Writings about the reactions of other newspapers and writers on government persecution of the press: Marx criticizes those who have unfair or unjust approaches.
· Remarks, replies, evaluations and criticism of the writings of the other journalists' about an issue, claim, assertion or criticism: Here we see statements ranging from agreement to strong polemics and accusations.
· Evaluation of strategic and/or stylistic exercises of the press.
· Evaluation of the press coverage on politics, relationship between press and politicians, press and people; attitudes of the press on war.
· Evaluation of the press in general.

Observing the attitude of the press towards the official use of repression and censorship measures, Marx heavily criticizes the German press (his assessment fits also e.g. Turkish media today):

The German daily press is certainly the flabbiest, sleepiest and most cowardly institution under the sun! The greatest infamies can be perpetrated before its very eyes, even directed against itself, and it will remain silent and conceal everything; if the facts had not become known by *accident,* one would never have learnt through the press what splendid March violets have been brought into being by divine grace in some places.

MARX 1849A

For Marx, the press should protect individuals, but not everybody: *"The press is obliged to reveal and denounce circumstances, but I am convinced that it should not denounce individuals, unless there is no other way of preventing a public evil or unless publicity already prevails throughout political life so that the German concept of denunciation no longer exists"* (Marx 1843d).

Marx positions the press in society and attributes a mediating role to press between the public and ruling forces. At the same time, he *considers the press as an indispensable means of voicing the needs and grievances of the people*:

> the rulers and the ruled alike are in need of a third element, which would be political without being official, hence not based on bureaucratic premises, an element which would be of a civil nature without being bound up with private interests and their pressing need. This supplementary element with the *head of a citizen of the state* and the *heart of a citizen* is the *free press.* In the realm of the press, rulers and ruled alike have an opportunity of criticising their principles and demands, and no longer in a relation of subordination, but on terms of equality as *citizens of the state;* no longer as *individuals,* but as *intellectual forces,* as exponents of reason. The "free press", being the product of public opinion, is also the creator of public opinion. It alone can make a particular interest a general one, it alone can make the *distressed state* of the Mosel region an object of general attention and general sympathy on the part of the Fatherland, it alone can mitigate the distress by dividing the feeling of it among all.
>
> MARX 1843E

For Marx, the language of the free press is the language of human conditions, not the determining factor of the human life and human relations. He emphasizes the use of language and its connection with the life conditions and bureaucratic report:

> The attitude of the press to the people's conditions of life is based on reason, but it is equally based on *feeling.* Hence it does not speak only in the clever language of judgment that soars above circumstances, but the passionate language of circumstances themselves, a language which cannot and should not be demanded of *official reports.* The free press, finally, brings the people's need in its real shape, not refracted through any bureaucratic medium, to the steps of the throne, to a power before which the difference between rulers and ruled vanishes and there remain only equally near and equally far removed *citizens of the state.*
>
> MARX 1843E

The nature of a writer and his/her professional practices indicate his/her professional ideology. The duty Marx assigns to the journalist and press, for instance, in his defence speech above, shows the professional worldview that he aligns himself with. On the other hand, Marx's criticisms about the writers and the press demonstrate the difference between the professional ideology of those who adhere to the dominant mode and relations and those who do not.

6   Conclusion

Theory in general is a systematic and consistent explanation of, e.g., organized human practices. Explanations should correspond to the explained, otherwise theory itself or theoretical explanation loses its validity and reliability. However, the validity and reliability can be forged by creating images on the correspondence of theory to practice and on the nature of the practices and/or explanations in such a way that the explanations, despite their irrelevant, inconsistent, inappropriate or incompatible nature, are made valid ones via extensive production, circulation and legitimization practices. Legitimization is done through at least two mechanisms: The first one is to establish domination through inter-subjectivity that is based on rationalized claims of objectivity and, furthermore, universality. The second one is the exercise of power that espouses such inter-subjectivity. Namely, such domination is gained and sustained through organized relations of power and personal interests in a society wherein production and reproduction of material life can be done through the praxis of human agents, who drive their consciousness from the organized material and immaterial life and at the same time, reflect their thinking/consciousness to their material and immaterial conditions. Hence, those who have the power and the means of control have advantages in deciding what, how and where to produce and distribute the material and immaterial products and services. The academic world and the nature of academic production become integral parts of this inter-subjective domination. The findings of the present study clearly indicate that the prevailing nature of academic journals' orientations in issue selection, problem formulation, study objectives, theoretical and methodological approaches carry particular expressions of domination. Most studies published in Media and Communication Studies-journals are various manifestations of mainstream approaches; all are interested in attitudes, interests, preferences and behaviours of individuals and advancing the functionality and interests of corporate and institutional structures. The remaining studies mainly serve as controlled or functional alternatives, with few exceptions. The prevailing dominance of variations of functionalism in communication studies has been discussed by various writers. For instance, Hardt (1997) points out the existence of a dominant functionalist perspective of communication research since the 1940s and a preoccupation with issue orientation based on the practical demands of a growing commercial invest-ment in the media industries. He also indicates that the ideological orienta-tions of U.S. Cultural Studies are determined by liberal-pluralist ideas and that they support commercial-industrial interests that guide the relationship between media and society.

Luring academics to participate and shaping of mental production and rela-tions through the numerous promotional ways and means by the power struc-tures are not new. There are many examples in the communication field: The psychological and cold war warriors (Lasswell, Shills, Lazarsfeld, Cantril, Dewitt, Gallop, Likert, Lerner, Berelson, Schramm, Pool and the like) received millions of dollars for involvement in ideological production and distribution by mili-tary and intelligence communities and foundations connected with them (e.g., FBI, CIA, Rockefeller, Ford and Carnegie Foundations, RAND Corporation). Such forms of participation by academicians are still a part of the practice of sustain-able domination. There are valuable studies concerning close relations among academicians, state structures and various foundations (e.g., Doob 1947; Schiller 1974 and 1992; Schiller 1982; Simpson 1994; Gary 1996; Glander 2000; Solovey 2001; Maxwell 2003; Pooley 2008; Summers 2008; Jonas 2010).

At present, psychological warfare activities and studies are extended to the entire civilian sphere of social life and include multitudes of legitimized and justified relations among multiple parties within a country and at interna-tional levels. Early studies with their funding allies helped to shape the forma-tion concept of communication and the direction of the communication field not only in the US, but also throughout the world. Recent studies continue to reproduce the ongoing warfare not only in the political arena, but also in the economic field in order to maintain sustainable development via mind-, interest- and behaviour-management.

One of the important implications of the present study is that participation in networks of profitable relations, the probability of getting financial benefits from various resources, getting formal recognition and success in university departments, finding a reputable place in ruling academic circles, getting pub-lished in leading scholarly journals, and getting funds from granting institu-tions, financing bodies and professional associations require an academic stance that (a) totally ignores the Marxist approach, (b) demonstrates an open anti-Marxist stand, (c) engages in trying to invalidate Marxist views by adopt-ing one of the secure and beneficial approaches based on culturalism, post-structuralism, post-modernism, post-positivism and the like, (e) provides mostly wrong and distorted explanations like claiming the demise of Marxism, the end of ideology, democratization, knowledge society, interdependence, decolonisation, identity, and a post-Marxist shift.

6.1   The Continuation of Theoretical Domination that Supports Ruling Power Structures

This study found that theories and methods used in Media and Communication Studies are mostly based on finding effects and developing the mechanisms of control of individual worldviews and behaviours. The dominant effect research has started with a simple model of persuasion and transmission that is characterized by direct and unmediated effects, typically based on persuasion and the audience modelling of observed behaviour. The interest in effects evolved to analytic constructs of audience motivation and disposition of active audience theories such as the elaboration likelihood model, attribution theory, cognitive consistency and selective exposure, and uses and gratifications theory. Adding the contextual context to the individual psychology and/or moving to macro explanations, theories like two-step- and multiple step-flow, diffusion theory, knowledge gaps and social network approaches brought about new research design techniques, especially on qualitative measures, interaction and historical data analysis. Moving to the macro level of design and analysis in the 1970s, the political, economic and institutional context of communication, theories like cultivation theory followed the liberal-democratic critical approach by emphasizing the cultivation of middle class ideology and cumulative effects of the media. For softening the media effects on the audience, theories like agenda setting and media dependency were emerged. Later, agenda melding, priming and framing theories were added to such approaches. In the neo-liberal atmosphere of the 1980s, theories like reception theory, liberal-pluralist cultural studies and identity theories emerged and proliferated alongside the dominant and evolving effects tradition. Concepts like reception, deconstruction, reconstruction and interpretation were put in circulation: The interpretative turn brought back the active and atomized individual. The present study found that such approaches do not receive much interest in most of the journals studied. Proliferation of and support for such approaches takes place in the peripheries of the ruling circles of current research practices. However, Klapper's summary of mass communication research in the 1960s and his suggestions seem still to be a leading guide for most studies in the communication field (Klapper 1960):

(a)   Mainstream orientations focus on various psychological dispositions of audience members;

(b)   Culturalists, social interactionists, liberal-pluralists and social psychologists have interests in the situated social context of message reception beyond socio-demographics;

(c)   Some post-structuralists focus on the structure of beliefs among audience members, not just the direction of beliefs as it was before;

(d)   Audience-reception analysts reintroduce the active audience thesis in a highly elaborate cover and participate in saving the industry from social responsibility.

Klapper's suggestions and the current pseudo-critical and functional alternative research orientations are important because they are all about "knowing people" in detail in order to control them.

Theoretical domination is maintained also through creating functional alternatives and promoting existing functional alternatives. Such maintenance and promotion is evident in academic relations and production. The present study found that the studies that try to totally or partially invalidate Marx or claim that Marxism is waning, inadequate, ethno-centric and insensitive to identities other than class identity are not mainstream or liberal-democrat oriented studies. Mainstream studies ignore and liberal-democrats generally appreciate Marx. The study findings indicate that Marx is not "contested, modified, and deformed, frequently distorted, overstated, and abused by enthusiastic practitioners and promoters" (Artz 2006, 6), but by various kinds of so-called "critical" or "alternative" approaches. The present study could not find any "enthusiastic promoter of Marx/Marxism" in articles, but found that "alternatives" are "alternative to Marx" and the most "critical" ones are in fact "criticism directed against Marx".

Another interesting, let's say "tactic," is that there has been a popular tendency since the late sixties that some writers (for instance, Foucault, Baudrillard, Laclau and Mouffe, and their followers) start with Marx and end with maintaining the invalidation, demise or inadequacy of Marx. This kind of tendency is very popular and fruitful because such mental products are the best mind management and control tools since they pretend to be the current and valid alternative voices (overtly or covertly directed against Marx).

6.2   Reproduction of Theoretical and Methodological Poverty

The present study also found that most of the studies, especially empirical and pseudo-empirical (survey) studies, seriously lack theoretical reasoning in design, hypothesis construction, and the presentation of conclusions. Similarly, some previous studies found low levels of theory use in Media and Communication Studies (Potter and Riddle 2007; Kamhawi and Weaver 2003).

Furthermore, the statements of study objectives are based on meeting the interests of industrial needs for knowing and controlling the audience/consumers and media/knowledge workers.

Such findings support the theoretical reasoning that such scholars only care about issues/problems related to personal and organized-private interests rather than establishing a sound theoretical rationale to explain the nature of any phenomena. Such an orientation further indicates that the academic world is mainly an integrated part of the capitalist industrial structure.

Most qualitative studies that claim that they are doing "discourse analysis" have inconsistent and conflicting theoretical narrations and provide no or no proper information about the way they perform the analysis. Providing many inconsistent theoretical statements and explanations and using highly restricted codes does not reduce or eliminate any uncertainty, rather increases it.

Most of the quantitative studies that use multivariate statistical analysis have no hypotheses that require multi-variate statistical testing. Namely, most hypotheses are hypotheses that are based on bivariate relations, hence require bivariate analysis. Furthermore, there are studies that provide only some questions, but do not extract any hypotheses, but do statistical analysis (including factor analysis or test causal relations without providing a causal hypothesis). All of this means that positivist-empirical research designs, data analysis and findings have serious validity problems.

6.3   The Marginalization, Downgrading or Keeping Out of Significant Alternatives, and the Promotion of Controlled and Functional Alternatives

Existence of domination means also the existence of the dominated, which makes domination and struggle for liberation continuous and dynamic. The struggle cannot be a monolithic one, rather it has multiple forms and levels that are interrelated not only with each other, but also with the various expressions of dominant practices. The present study found that there are articles with "critical and highly critical content", however very few can be considered a real/meaningful alternative that is based on, e.g., the idea that societal change means a change in the mode and the relations of production. Almost all of the "critical articles" are overtly or covertly, fully, mostly or generally anti-Marxian and are offsprings of, for instance, Durkheim, Heidegger, Husserl, Gadamer, Lacan, Deleuze, Guattari, Foucault, Baudrillard, Said, Habermas, Laclau and Mouffe.

"Criticizing" does not make a theoretical approach critical. "Marx beyond Marx" means a different methodological and theoretical musing if it is not based on Marx's approach. Theoretical approaches that base their main premises on, e.g., the change in the gender composition of parliament, ethnic composition of work force in wage-slavery or obtaining legal recognition of gay marriage are not "alternative orientations" or "critical orientations" because they want acknowledgement by and reintegration into the dominant structure that they criticize. The capitalist system does not become a humane system even if the parliament of capitalism is composed of 100% women, liberals, leftists or even communists. Then, the move away from class analysis to the current kinds of identity politics is an integral part of the global policy of diversion and "divide and rule". Moving away from the interest in social, economical and ideological/cultural studies and focusing instead on the individual expressions in daily life, away from human beings in organized relations to a constitutive function of textual or other discursive manifestations and the like does not constitute a socially responsible, "critical" and/or Marxian analysis. I consider them, in the final analysis, controlled and/or functional alternatives buttressing the current capitalist mode and relations.

The communication field was established by sociologists, social psychologists, and political scientists. It developed as a social science field. Communication stands at the intersection of every field in the social sciences (an all other sciences). However, it is not a stepchild or colony of scholars of any field who do research and write about communication without first having a sound knowledge about communication. I have been criticizing the situation in Turkey by declaring that the communication field is still colonized by those who do not read even the fundamental literature in communication, are mostly unsuccessful in their own fields and find secure place in the colony (the communication field). In recent years, the communication field has been colonized by the worst kind of outsiders, who are harmfully altering not only communication, but all fields of the social sciences. They come especially from literature, semiotics, and hermeneutics. The situation gets worse by the fact that an increasing number of scholars in communication, who have no background in literature, semiotics, or culture, join the band-wagon by doing cultural studies or discourse analysis. The new colonizers pull especially mass communication away from a field dealing with actual human relations in organized power structures and interest relations towards becoming a field of interpretations of the detached texts and meaningless discourses. Correspondingly, the findings of this study indicate that qualitative communication research is leaving the actual human relations and societal conditions aside and moves towards the analysis of the end products in such a way that the product, process or textual interaction (e.g., language, interpretation, deconstruction, or discourse) is made the "determining agent/factor."

6.4   *Producing the Material and Immaterial Riches and Poverty*[7]

The nature of domination and struggle in academic relations, as well as in journal- and article- publishing, depends on the historically determined conditions of the mode of production and production relations at a certain time and place. The development of a field and "exchange of scientific ideas" are deeply connected with establishing, sustaining/maintaining and expanding the dominance of intersubjectivities formed by various interest groups gathered around various ideologies/theories and research traditions that provide work security, status and financial enrichment. This dominance of the system of mutual interests involves the control of production and distribution of functional knowledge for the benefit of the system. In the 21st century, power relations and forms of competition within the scientific and research communities have been shaped in such a way that it reached to the point of "science and research in personal interests" which are realized through serving those who pay more in terms of money, fame and status.

There is a dominance of quantitative multitude, qualitative poverty and normalized abnormality in academic journals. Within this frame, the study findings provide support for the fact that there are at least three interrelated dominant immaterial productions (production of ideologies, thoughts, consciousness, beliefs, feelings, emotions, empathy, sensitivity and everything that is not material) in the current global economic and political marketplace.

The first one is the production of knowledge that is based on scientific research for the advancement of capitalist structures and relations. Such knowledge production is rarely done in universities, but mostly in controlled environments like in corporate R&D departments, private research firms and government institutions. Such knowledge is rarely produced for everybody and the market (not as a commodity); such knowledge is an undisclosed, secret and highly protected product. Such products can be marketed only when advanced knowledge is produced and control mechanisms are established. Such knowledge makes industrial production, advancement and control possible. We cannot see such knowledge in academic journals, unless it is found necessary to establish control and enhance market supremacy.[8] We have no access to them.

The second one is the kind of knowledge that is produced for mind and behaviour management. We can divide this knowledge production into a few sub categories:

---

7   See for valuable discussions on knowledge and production of knowledge: Marx 1971; Marx 1973; Marx & Engels 1969; Carchedi 2005; Fuchs, 2010a; Mosco & McKercher 2008; Mosco 2008; Schiller 1974 and 1987; Schiller 2007; Weiler 2006; Thompson 1997; Erdogan 2014.

8   See for various discussions: Blackburn 1973; Berube 1996; Allardt 1999; Gunarathe 2010; Fuchs 2010a; Tomaselli and Shepperson 2010; Bauer and Jensen 2011.

(1) **Knowledge about people:** Such knowledge: This kind of knowledge provides helpful information about people as consumers, customers and
voters for industrial and institutional decision and policymaking, implementation, auditing, monitoring and revisions. Marketing, advertising
and positivist-empirical communication studies work in this domain.

(2) **Knowledge for better work performance:** The purpose of this kind of
knowledge is to justify the existence of industrial structures and practices, work relations, wage policies and working conditions, and to
installs mind-sets and behavioural dispositions that make people work
harder and get gratifications from abstract thoughts, feelings, identifica-
tions at work. The exam and grading systems in schools prepare students
for readily accepting the structural inequalities in the industrial system.
Organizational communication studies that focus on communication
auditing, sensitivity training, empathy, effective communication, workers' attitudes, behaviour, work performance and relationships at work and
the like are designed for manipulation of workers so that there is better
performance without raising wages and improving working conditions.
Public relation activities within organizations carry the same purpose.

(3) **Knowledge for people:** This kind of knowledge is provided in order to
maintain a certain level and type of consciousness, feelings and sensitivities that justify the conditions of the prevailing mode and relations in life
and make people adjust to miserable conditions and ready for accepting
individual or mass killings enforced by the ruling forces (Jay Gould's
infamous statement saying that *"I can hire one half of the working class to
kill the other half"* has lost validity, because the ruling forces do not have
to hire them now since they are already hired and used). Some parts of
such knowledge (as in the production and use of emotions, religious and
superstitious values) are a continuation of successfully used strategies
of ruling forces throughout human history. Such ruling knowledge of
previous times are reshaped and reproduced in a country and distributed
globally in the same or glocalized forms and used by other dominant
classes in other countries. This is one of the essential parts of globalisation
of the capitalist mode. Content and significance of this knowledge are
not due to its universal validity, but due to the utmost functionality
for the ruling interests and practices. For instance, religious ideas and
sensitivities that made people refuse to watch television and consider
the use of radio and loudspeakers in mosques as a sin in the 1960s, were
reversed in 1970s. This is called the integration of the old functional Ideas,
structures and practices into the new interests and the ruling mode and
relations. This is true not only for the knowledge of people, but also for

knowledge for and by professionals throughout the world: Most articles in the 77 journals in this study were written by academicians from all over the world. Other parts of knowledge belong to the current mode of class domination. Whether it has trans-historical character or not, this kind of knowledge is used to sustain all probable kinds of domination over people. Furthermore, knowledge for people is functional for creating "conspicuous consumption" and consumer society, and for establishing a political atmosphere of certain interests, participation, enmity and readiness. This kind of knowledge's aim is to freeze people's intellect and interest at an early teenage level. Such "knowledge" (reproduction of ignorance as knowing) is provided by the mass media, cultural and political organizations and to a varying degree by formal education.

(4) **Knowledge for professionals and by professionals**: This is the kind of situationally conditioned knowledge that is produced in order to orient the attention, interest, research and educational concerns of scholars towards certain functional professional activities. The activities in daily organizational routines that are based on such knowledge reproduce organizational life. Most mental workers in the production of e.g. a television sitcom can have a false general knowledge about the nature of the product. However, such probability is rather low when it comes to newspaper editors, media professionals and scholars. A scholar is aware of the meaning of a theoretical and methodological choice he/she makes. It is a well calculated or predetermined preference. There is another character of the knowledge and knowledge production under discussion: the number of professional research findings and products that are actually used by the organizational decision makers are at a minimal level. However, most knowledge activities' goal is to keep academicians busy in certain orientations and relational domains. Products of such activities are useless piles of junks for industrial use and, at the same time, extremely useful for the industrial politics of mind and interest control. In this kind of production relations, most academicians are just like football fans: The masses are oriented toward watching or going to football games, the academicians are oriented toward doing research in certain dominant modes. The only difference between the academicians and the masses is that the masses get only psychological satisfaction, while academicians get extra benefits like money and status.

The third one is the production of knowledge on the conditions for knowledge production. We find at least two ruling strategic approaches here: Exclusion and distorted inclusion. One part of this kind of knowledge production has exclusionary character: As it was found in this study, it excludes Marx's (and Marxist) analysis of knowledge production and conditions of knowledge production. This exclusion is done through various mechanisms. The foremost one is the probable productive value or surplus creation probability of the production. For instance, the success of exclusion of an idea is achieved when individuals think that such idea (e.g. learning mass media theory) is useless or that supporting such an idea (e.g. talking about significance of marxist method in communication studies) is not rewarding. The inclusionary character includes various kinds of distortions, invalidations, downgrading, marginalization and inappropriateness.

The explanations about knowledge production above indicate that everyone in various positions in society as an individual and every organized entity participate in production (and dissemination and use) of knowledge. Individuals' knowledge and knowledge of organized entities and the behavioural manifestations are ideologically situated and show the nature of their positions in the class domination and struggle. In the present study, almost all communication scholars with very few exceptions position themselves to serve the interests of the capitalist class. This is most probably because they want to collect the material and immaterial rewards distributed by the same class and also stay away from multiple forms of punishment, which is applied on those who behave differently. They have no interest in the idea of knowledge created, distributed and used for the general interest. Moreover, they are not interested in influencing media practices, policies and taking any urgent social problem as an issue to investigate.

Such findings also provide support for Marx's conclusions on the nature of the distribution of wealth. The production of wealth is social since everybody participates in the process, but the distribution is private in such a way that a small number of people who own and control the means of production appropriate most of the wealth. The same problem exists in the production, distribution and use of knowledge: The distribution of wealth in terms of material gains and in terms of functional knowledge is highly controlled.

6.5   *Extending the Prevailing Structure of Interests and Relations to the New Media*

The present study found that most historically prevailing issues, problems, concerns, ideologies, methods and theories are also carried to and used in the new computer-mediated communication research. The similar mystifications and functional discussions we witnessed during the 1960s about television are reproduced about the Internet.

There are new issues and data collection techniques, because of the nature of new personal communication technologies like mobile phones and computer-mediated communication. However, they are only tools for the implementation of organized objectives, hence they do not change or abandon the prevailing ideological and material interests. Some new issues are renewed old-issues like the role and effects of the new media. There are also mystified new terms like social media, as if the other media are not social, not economical and not directorial and administrative. In fact, all new media are social, economical, industrial, administrative and directional. Technological multi-directionality does not make a communicative action democratic or symmetrical or two-way; a mobile phone is a multi-directional device a lot more than the Internet in terms of permitting a two or multi-sided flow. However, it is not the mobile phone or Internet that determines the nature of relations. The determining factor is the structured nature of power relations and interests. Two ways or multiple ways of a technological device cannot change the nature of power relations and the nature of communication. The mobile phone does not change the mode of relations between you and your boss, and does not alter the fact that your boss is your boss. Democratic relations and freedom of communication are impossible if any of the following determining factors are missing, banned or exercised by only one side. It does not matter if you use the Internet or the mobile phone or not, you are not free and your communication is not symmetrical or democratic if you cannot:

(1)   start or stop the communication
(2)   organize or influence the organization of time, place and conditions of interaction
(3)   fill, modify and change the content of communication as you wish
(4)   change or stop the nature of flow during the interaction (for instance, change the subject)
(5)   end the communication at any point
(6)   exert influence on the objective and outcome beyond being a mere participant

You can participate in every political discussion on the Internet; such participation does not make a political system a democratic system and such a use does not mean that the Internet is an agent of democratisation, since you cannot exert influence on the issues to be discussed, collective political decisions to be taken, implementations to be taken and the benefits to be divided/shared. The Internet is the most recent means of economical, political, mental, emotional and behavioural control; a newly added and improved popular opium of the people – especially of the young generation that is the most likely danger for the system. In essence, it is the new sphere of domination, control and struggle.

It is hard to find an Internet study that investigates the ways in which structure and use of Internet technologies worsens social inequities in terms of labour practices, distribution of wealth, and state surveillance activities, opens new ways of domination and struggle. However, there are many studies on the Internet's role in participatory democracy, bottom-up political forms (as if such forms were possible under the prevailing political structures). Many of them are eulogies to activist groups, the democratic underground, democratic and partisan public spheres. I must repeat that using communications media does not mean that we have reached or that we are at the level of participatory democracy. Participatory democracy or empowerment does not mean "use or consume" in a specific manner. Participating in consumption or use (including use for "writing, authorship") never means a democratic participation in daily life or empowerment as long as we are kept out of the power structure, as long as we are unable to influence the decision-making processes and ruling practices of the dominant forces. Did anybody change his/or her wage or working conditions through the Internet? I reiterate that the Internet is not a tool of emancipation, but a tool of dominance and struggle. We now have an additional medium controlled by economic and political interests. it is another contemporary field and means of struggle against dominance that has dramatically increased opportunities to observe us 24 hours.

7   Recommendations

Recommendations are useful only for those, who are in the habit of questioning himself/herself and anything and everything in life, and have no affect on those who align their own interest with those who pay the pipers, since they do not read articles like the present one. Those who read either are supporters, sympathizers or concerned by the Marxist approach. Some read just to know as much as possible. Some others read to collect information about the Marxist enemy. In any case, my recommendations based on the current study and accumulated knowledge are as follow:

Some studies have serious theoretical conceptual and methodological problems. Those who are not from the communication field, but conduct a study about communication, should first read the fundamental texts in communication studies beyond simple prescriptions of sender-message-channel-receiver-effect understandings and similar misconceptions. Those, who have a communication background, should either stay away from the popularized interest in cultural studies, discourse analysis, reception analysis, semiotics and the like or firstly gain necessary knowledge about, e.g., semiotics and methods in semiotics. Furthermore, it is part of academic decency not to do any evaluation and ignore the most basic textual context such as words like "in general", the sentence before or after a sentence. I also suggest that we should read the original sources if the issue is a person like Marx, who has been widely distorted.

Some studies have serious problems in choosing the socially significant issues, theory and method. This is mostly because of the prevailing nature of academia. I suggest it is time to start to question the dominant orientations and to study Marx's theoretical and methodological approach in search of significant ways for understanding the nature of communication in society and societal change. The functionalist theoretical approaches and their current versions and their explicit and implicit assumptions and outcomes for the organized human life and environment have been well documented and their resonance can still be felt in current communication scholarship. In light of this multifaceted dominance, a basic advantage of Marx's approach is that it provides a lot better theoretical and methodological means and ways of social inquiry. At the same time, it leads us to study socially significant issues with most meaningful manner by including all probable contextual determinants in understanding the nature of production, distribution and consumption of communication products, control, subversion, coercion, domination and struggle.

Marx's approach can enable a systematic study of communication across multiple levels of relationships/interaction and analyses, ranging from the individual to the global level. No approach has been valid enough to be able to facilitate the study of prevailing conditions, development and change. For instance, modernization/development studies based on equilibrium, structural functionalist or behaviourist approaches and their current versions do not only fall short in explanations, but also tend to create mystifications and factoids about media and communication related issues. Recent global crises also mean the crisis of prevailing dominant and neo-dominant approaches in sociology, political science, economics and communication. Hence, despite all the produced obstacles, Marx's approach remains the most viable approach to the study of any kind of communication, especially mass communication.

Although there are studies that have generated insightful theoretical, conceptual and practical explanations, there is still a growing need for better understanding of Marx and his contributions to the study of communication. Doing so, studying from time to time the nature of research orientations in Media and Communication Studies is an important and constructive academic initiative. Scholarly discussions on the status of the field, its historical development and its nature are a necessary outcome of such activity.

I believe that any initiative of Marxist scholars in the publishing and tenure environment is a meaningful and important contribution to Marxist Communication Studies and the communication field, given that even the use of the name of Marx can result and has historically often resulted in repression.

References

Artz, Lee, Steve Macek, S., and Dana Cloud. eds. 2006. *Marxism and Communication Studies: The Point is To Change* It. New York: Peter Lang.

Allardt, Erick. 1999. The Future of the Social Sciences in the 21st Century – A Comment. *Current Sociology* 47 (4): 13–17.

Babe, Robert. 2006. The Political Economy of Knowledge: Neglecting Political Economy in the Age of Fast Capitalism (as Before). Accessed February 4, 2012. http://www.uta .edu/huma/agger/fastcapitalism/2_1/babe.htm.

Babbie, Earl R. 2004. *The Practice of Social Research.* 10th ed. Belmont, CA: Wadsworth.

Bagdikian, Ben H. 1997. The Realities of Media Concentration and Control. *Television Quarterly* 29 (3): 22–28.

Bauer, Martin W., and Pablo Jensen. 2011. The Mobilization of Scientists for Public Engagement. *Public Understanding of Science.* 20 (1): 3–11.

Berube, Michael. 1996. Cultural Criticism and the Politics of Selling Out. Accessed January 28, 2012. http://www.altx.com/ebr/ebr2/2berube.htm.

Berube, Michael, and Cary Nelson.1995. *Higher Education under Fire: Politics, Economics, and the Crisis of the Humanities.* New York: Routledge.

Blackburn, Robin. 1973. *Ideology in Social Sciences.* New York: Pantheon.

Bodemann, Y. Michal. 1979. The Fulfilment of Fieldwork in Marxist Praxis. *Dialectical Anthropology* 4 (2): 155–161.

Boyer, Richard O., and Herbert M. Morais. 1965/1980. *Labor's Untold Story.* New York: UE.

Carchedi, Guglielmo. 2005. On the Production of Knowledge. In *The Capitalist State and Its Economy: Democracy in Socialism (Research in Political Economy, Volume 22)*, edited by Paul Zarembka, 267–304. Bingley: Emerald Group Publishing Limited.

Cerwonka, Allaine. 2009. Higher Education 'Reform', Hegemony, and Neo-Cold War Ideology. *Cultural Studies* 23 (5–6): 720–735.

Chouliaraki, Lilie, and Norman Fairclough. 1999. *Discourse in Late Modernity: Rethinking Critical Discourse Analysis.* Edinburgh: Edinburgh University Press.

Dei, George J.S., and Gurpreet S. Johal. 2005. *Critical Issues in Anti-Racist Research Methodologies.* New York: Peter Lang.

Dyer-Witheford, Nick. 1999. *Cyber-Marx: Cycles and Circuits of Struggle in High-Technology Capitalism.* Urbana, IL: University of Illinois Press.

Domenech, Antoni. 2009. University Autonomy, a Return to the Thirties. Accessed January 12, 2012. http://www.barcelonametropolis.cat/en/page.asp?id=23&ui=148#.

Doob, Leonard. 1947. Utilization of Social Scientists in the Overseas Branch of the Office of War Information. *American Political Science Review* 41 (4): 49–67.

Dorfman, Ariel. 1983. *The Empire's Old Clothes*. New York: Pantheon.

Erdogan, İrfan. 2014. Medya Teori ve Araştırmaları: Biliş ve davranış yönetimi amaçlı endüstri, devlet ve üniversite işbirliğinde, Medyanın Egemen ve Alternatif Açıklamaları (Media Theory and Research: Dominant and alternative explanation of media that aim at mind and behaviour management in cooperation with industry, state and university). Ankara: Erk.

Ewen, Stuart. 1996. *PR! A Social History of Spin*. New York: BasicBooks.

Fetscher, Iring, ed. 1969. *Karl Marx – Friedrich Engels. Pressefreiheit und Zensur.* Frankfurt: Europäische Verlagsanstalt.

Fuchs, Christian. 2010a. Class, Knowledge and New Media. *Media, Culture & Society* 32 (1): 141–150.

Fuchs, Christian. 2010b. Grounding Critical Communication Studies: An Inquiry into the Communication Theory of Karl Marx. *Journal of Communication Inquiry* 34 (1): 15–41.

Fuchs, Christian. 2011a. An Alternative View of Privacy on Facebook. Information 2: 140–165. Accessed February 7, 2012. http://fuchs.uti.at/489/.

Fuchs, Christian. 2011b. *Foundations of Critical Media and Information Studies*. New York: Routledge.

Gans, Herbert. 1975. Social Science for Social Policy. In *The Use and Abuse of Social Sciences*, edited by Irvin L. Horowitz, 3–23. New Brunswick, New Jersey: Transaction Books.

Garnham, Nicholas. 2001. The Information Society: Myth or Reality. Accessed January 12, 2012. http://www.er.uqam.ca/nobel/gricis/actes/bogues/Garnham.pdf.

Gary, Brett. 1996. Communication Research, the Rockefeller Foundation, and Mobilization for the War on Words. *Journal of Communication* 46 (3): 124–147.

Glander, Timothy R. 2000. *Origins of Mass Communications Research during the American Cold War: Educational Effects and Contemporary Implications*. Mahwah, NJ: Erlbaum.

Gorz, Andre. 1980. *On the Class Character of Science and Scientists*. In *Ideology of/in the Natural Sciences*, edited by Hillary Rose and Steven Rose, 59–71. Cambridge, MA: Scenkman Publishing.

Golding, Peter. 2000. Forthcoming Features: Information and Communications Technologies and the Sociology of the Future. *Sociology* 34 (1): 165–184.

Grossberg, Lawrence. 1997. *Bringing It All Back Home: Essays on Cultural Studies*. London: Duke University Press.

Gunaratne, Shelton. A. 2010. De-Westernizing Communication/Social Science Research: Opportunities and Limitations. *Media, Culture and Society* 32 (3): 473–500.

Hardt, Hanno. 1997. Beyond Cultural Studies – Recovering the 'Political' in Critical Communications Studies. *Journal of Communication Inquiry* 21 (2): 70–79.

Hardt, Hanno. 2000. Communication is Freedom: Karl Marx on Press Freedom and Censorship. *Javnost – The Public* 7 (4): 85–100.

Haye, Yves de la., ed. 1980. *Marx and Engels on the Means of Communication*. Paris: International General.

Jhally, Sut. 1993. Communications and the Materialist Conception of History: Marx, Innis and Technology. *Continuum: The Australian Journal of Media & Culture* 7 (1). Accessed December 2, 2011. http://wwwmcc.murdoch.edu.au/ReadingRoom/7.1/Jhally.html.

Jonas, Marie. 2010. A Short History of the Relationship between the American Psychological Association and the U.S. Military. hhttp://www.law.berkeley.edu/hist oryofAPAandMilitarypaper(final)11June10.pdf.

Kamhawi, Rasha, and David Weaver. 2003. Mass Communication Research Trends from 1980 to 1999. *Journalism & Mass Communication Quarterly* 80 (7): 7–27.

Klapper, Joseph. T. 1960. *The Effects of Mass Communication*. Glencoe, III: Free Press.

Martin, Brian. 1998. Tied Knowledge: Power in Higher Education. Accessed January 7, 2012. Http://www.bmartin.cc/pubs/98tk/tk02.html.

Marx, Karl. 1842a. Comments on the Latest Prussian Censorship Instruction. Accessed January 13, 2012. http://www.marxists.org/archive/marx/works/1842/02/10.htm.

Marx, Karl. 1842b. Prussian Censorship. Accessed December 10, 2011. Http://www .marxists.org/archive/marx/works/1842/free-press/ch01.htm.

Marx, Karl. 1842c. Opponents of a Free Press. Accessed December 10, 2011. http://www .marxists.org/archive/marx/works/1842/free-press/ch02.htm.

Marx, Karl. 1842d. On the Assembly of the Estates. Accessed December 10, 2011. http:// www.marxists.org/archive/marx/works/1842/free-press/ch03.htm.

Marx, Karl. 1842e. As a Privilege of Particular Individuals or a Privilege of the Human Mind?. (May 12) Accessed December 10, 2011. http://www.marxists.org/archive/ marx/works/1842/free-press/ch04.htm.

Marx, Karl. 1842f. Censorship. Accessed December 10, 2011. http://www.marxists.org/ archive/marx/works/1842/free-press/ch05.htm.

Marx, Karl. 1842g. Freedom in General. Accessed December 10, 2011. Http://www.marxists .org/archive/marx/works/1842/free-press/ch06.htm.

Marx, Karl. 1842h. Editorial Note: Communism and the Augsburg Allgemeine Zeitung. Accessed January 10, 2012. http://www.marxists.org/archive/marx/works/1842/10/22.htm.

Marx, Karl. 1842i. The Supplement to Nos. 335 and 336 of The Augsburg Allgemeine Zeitung on the Commissions of the Estates in Prussia. Accessed December 3, 2012 http://www.marxists.org/archive/marx/works/1842/12/10.htm.

Marx, Karl. 1842j. The Polemical Tactics of the Augsburg Newspaper. Accessed November 28, 2011. http://www.marxists.org/archive/marx/works/1842/11/29a.htm.

Marx, Karl. 1843a. The Ban on the Leipziger Allgemeine Zeitung. Http://www.marxists
.org/archive/marx/works/1842/12/31.htm.

Marx, Karl. 1843b. Polemical Articles against The Allgemeine Zeitung. Accessed
November 28, 2011. http://www.marxists.org/archive/marx/works/1843/01/03.htm.

Marx, Karl. 1843c. Stylistic Exercises of the Rhein- und Mosel-Zeitung. Accessed
November 28, 2011. http://www.marxists.org/archive/marx/works/1843/03/13.htm.

Marx, Karl. 1843d. Cabinet Order on the Daily Press. Accessed January 15, 2012. http://
www.marxists.org/archive/marx/works/1842/11/16a.htm.

Marx, Karl. 1843e. Justification of the Correspondent from the Mosel. Accessed January
12, 2012. http://www.marxists.org/archive/marx/works/1843/01/15.htm.

Marx, Karl. 1843f. Justification of the Correspondent from the Mosel. Accessed January
12, 2012. http://www.marxists.org/archive/marx/works/1843/01/15.htm

Marx, Karl. 1848. Articles by Marx and Engels in Neue Rheinische Zeitung. http://www
.marxists.org/archive/marx/works/subject/newspapers/neue-rheinische
-zeitung.htm.

Marx Karl. 1848b. Communist Manifesto. http://www.marxists.org/archive/marx/
works/1848/communist-manifesto/ch02.htm

Marx, Karl. 1849a. The Censorship. Accessed November 28, 2011. http://www.marxists
.org/archive/marx/works/1849/03/15b.htm.

Marx, Karl. 1849b. Speech by Karl Marx: The First Trial of the Neue Rheinische Zeitung. Accessed
November 28, 2011. http://www.marxists.org/archive/marx/works/1849/02/07.htm.

Marx, Karl. 1853. The War Question. *New-York Daily Tribune*, No. 3904. Accessed
October 21, 2009. http://csf.colorado.edu/mirrors/marxists.org/archive/marx/works/
nydt/531021.htm.

Marx, Karl. 1853b. Revolution in China and Europe. New York Daily Tribune 14 June.
Marxists Internet Archive, http://www.marxists.org/archive/marx/works/1853/06/14
.htm

Marx, Karl. 1853c. Revolution in China and Europe. New York Daily Tribune 14 June,
Marxists Internet Archive, http://www.marxists.org/archive/marx/works/1853/06/14
.htm

Marx, Karl. 1854. Declaration of War. – On the History of the Eastern Question. *New-
York Daily Tribune,* April 15. Accessed November 25, 2011. http://www.marxists.org/
archive/marx/works/1854/03/28.htm.

Marx, Karl. 1857a. Russian Trade with China. New York Daily Tribune 7 April, Marxists
Internet Archive, http://www.marxists.org/archive/marx/works/1857/04/07.htm.

Marx, Karl. 1857b. Introduction to a Contribution to the Critique of Political Economy,
Appendix I. Accessed November 23, 2011. http://www.marxists.org/archive/marx/
works/1859/critique-pol-economy/appx1.htm.

Marx, Karl. 1857c. The Revolt in India. *New-York Daily Tribune,* September 15. Accessed
Nevember 25, 2011. http://www.marxists.org/archive/marx/works/1857/09/15.htm

Marx, Karl. 1857c. The Grundrisse: Notebook III. The Chapter on Capital (Continuation). Accessed January 15, 2012. http://www.marxists.org/archive/marx/works/1857/grundrisse/ch06.htm.

Marx, Karl. 1859a. Critique of Political Economy. Accessed November 25, 2011. http://www.marxists.org/archive/marx/works/1859/critique-pol-economy/ch02_4.htm.

Marx, Karl. 1859b. Grundrisse: Threefold Character, or Mode, of Circulation. Accessed December 13, 2011. http://www.marxists.org/archive/marx/works/1857/grundrisse/ch13.htm#p678.

Marx, Karl. 1860. Letter to the Editor of the Free Press: Prosecution of the Augsburg Gazette. Accessed December 3, 2012 http://www.marxists.org/archive/marx/works/1860/02/04.htm.

Marx, Karl. 1861a. The Opinion of the Newspapers and the Opinion of the People. Accessed January 13, 2012. http://www.marxists.org/archive/marx/works/1861/12/31.htm.

Marx, Karl. 1861b. The North American Civil War (Collection of Articles). Accessed February 13, 2012. http://libcom.org/library/american-civil-war-karl-marx.

Marx, Karl. 1863–1883. Capital Volume III. Accessed November 25, 2011. http://www.marxists.org/archive/marx/works/1894-c3/ch39.htm.

Marx, Karl. 1964. *Selected Writings in Sociology and Social Philosophy.* (Translated by T.B. Bottomore). London: McGraw-Hill.

Marx, Karl. 1867. Capital Volume I. Accessed November 25, 2011. http://www.marxists.org/archive/marx/works/1867-c1/index.htm.

Marx, Karl. 1971. *The Economic and Philosophic Manuscripts of 1844.* N.Y: International Publishers.

Marx, Karl. 1871. Letter to Ludwig Kugelmann. Accessed January 12, 2012. http://solomon.tinyurl.alexanderstreet.com/cgi-bin/asp/philo/soth/getdoc.pl?S10022522-D000107

Marx, Karl. 1973. Grundrisse: *Foundations of the Critique of Political Economy.* London: Penguin.

Marx, Karl. 1975. *Contribution to the Critique of Hegel's Philosophy of Law.* Early Writings. London: Penguin.

Marx, Karl. 1976. *Capital.* Vol. I, Harmondsworth: Penguin Books.

Marx, Karl. 1977. *Preface to A Contribution to the Critique of Political Economy.* Moscow: Progress Publishers.

Marx, Karl. 1885. *Capital Volume II.* Accessed December 13, 2011. http://www.marxists.org/archive/marx/works/1885-c2/index.htm.

Marx, Karl, and Frederick Engels. 1846. *The German Ideology.* Accessed December 13, 2011. http://www.marxists.org/archive/marx/works/1845/german-ideology/ch01c.htm.

Marx, Karl, and Friedrich Engels. 1962. *Selected Works,* 2 vols. Moscow: Foreign Language Publishing House. http://www.marxists.org/archive/marx/works/1890/letters/90_09_21.htm.

Marx, Karl, and Frederick Engels. 1965. *Selected Correspondence (1955)*. 2nd ed. Moscow: Progress.

Marx, Karl, and Frederick Engels. 1969. *The German Ideology*. New York: International Publishers.

Mattelart, Armand, and Seth Siegelaub. eds. 1979. *Communication and Class Struggle: Capitalism, Imperialism*. Bagnolet: International Mass Media Research Center.

Maxwell, Richard. 2003. *Herbert Schiller*. Lanham, MD: Rowman and Littlefield Publishers.

Maxwell, Richard. 2001. *The Political Economy of Culture*. Minneapolis, MN: University of Minnesota Press.

McChesney, Robert W. 2008. *The Political Economy of the Media: Enduring Issues, Emerging Dilemmas*. New York: Monthly Review Press.

Mingers, John. 1996. A Comparison of Maturana's Autopoietic Social Theory and Giddens' Theory of Structuration. *Systems Research* 13 (4): 469–482.

Mosco, Vincent. 1982. *Pushbutton Fantasies*. Norwood, N.J.: Ablex Publishing.

Mosco, Vincent. 1996/2009. *The Political Economy of Communication: Rethinking and Renewal*. London: Sage.

Mosco, Vincent. 2004. *The Digital Sublime: Myth, Power, and Cyberspace*. Cambridge, MA: The MIT Press.

Mosco, Vincent, and Catherine McKercher. 2008. *The Laboring of Communication: Will Knowledge Workers of the World Unite?* New York: Lexington Books.

Mosco, Vincent. 2008. Knowledge Workers of the World! Unite? *Communication, Culture & Critique* 1 (1): 105–115.

Murdock, Graham and Peter Golding. 1977. Capitalism, Communication and Class Relations. In *Mass Communication and Society*, edited by James Curran, Michael Gurevitch and Janet Woollacoot, 12–43. London: Arnold.

Murdock, Graham, and Peter Golding. 1978. Theories of Communication and Theories of Society. *Communication Research* 5 (3): 339–356.

Padover, Saul K. ed. 1979. *The Letters of Karl Marx*. Englewood Cliffs, NJ: Prentice-Hall.

Padover, Saul K. ed. 1974. *On Freedom of the Press and Censorship*. New York: McGraw-Hill.

Philo, Greg, and David Miller. 2000. Cultural Compliance and Critical Media Studies. *Media, Culture and Society* 22 (6): 831–839. Accessed January 15, 2012. http://www.glasgowmediagroup.org/content/view/3/

Pooley, Jeferson. 2008. The New History of Mass Communication Research. In The History of Media and Communication Research: Contested Memories, edited by David Park and Jefferson Pooley, 43–69. New York: Peter Lang.

Potter, W. James, and Karyn Riddle. 2007. A Content Analysis of the Media Effects Literature. *Journalism and Mass Communication Quarterly* 84 (1): 90–104.

Potter, W. James, Roger Cooper, and Michel Dupagne. 1993. The Three Paradigms of Mass Media Research in Mainstream Journals. *Communication Theory* 3 (4): 317–335.

Riffe, Daniel, and Alan Freitag. 1997. A Content Analysis of Content Analyses: Twenty-Five Years of Journalism Quarterly. *Journalism & Mass Communication Quarterly* 74 (4): 873–882.

Schiller, Dan. 2003. End of the Telecom Revolution. Le Monde Diplomatique English Edition, August 2003. Accessed January 10, 2011. http://mondediplo.com/2003/08/08schiller.

Schiller, Dan. 2000. *Digital Capitalism.* Cambridge, MA: The MIT Press.

Schiller, Dan. 2007. *How to Think About Information.* Urbana, IL: University of Illinois Press.

Schiller, Dan. 1993. *Capitalism, information and Uneven Development.* In Communication Yearbook 16, edited by Stanley A. Deetz, 386–406. Newbury Park, CA: Sage.

Schiller, Dan. 1982. *Telematics and Government.* Norwood, NJ: Ablex Publishing.

Schiller, Herbert I. 1974. *Mind Managers.* Boston, MA: Beacon Press.

Schiller, Herbert I. 1987. *Culture Inc.: The Corporate Takeover of Public Expression.* New York: Oxford University Press.

Schiller, Herbert I. 1991. *Culture, Inc. The Corporate Takeover of Public Expression.* New York: Oxford University Press.

Schiller, Herbert I. 1992. *Mass Communications and American Empire.* Boulder, CO: Westview Press.

Schiller, Herbert I., and Ithiel de Sola Pool. 1981. Perspectives on Communications Research: An Exchange. *Journal of Communication* 31 (3): 15–23.

Shaw, Donald. L., Bradley J Ham, and Diana L Knott. 2000. Technological Change, Agenda Challenge and Social Melding: Mass Media Studies and the Four Ages of Place, Class, Mass and Space. *Journalism Studies* 1 (1): 57–79.

Simpson, Christopher. 1994. The Science of Coercion: Communication Research and Psychological Warfare 1945–1960. New York: Oxford University Press.

Smythe, Dallas W. 1982. *Dependency Road: Communications, Capitalism, Consciousness, and Canada.* Norwood, NJ: Ablex Publishing.

Solovey, Mark. 2001. Project Camelot and the 1960s Epistemological Revolution: Rethinking the Politics-Patronage-Social Science Nexus. *Social Studies of Science* 31 (2): 171–205.

Summers, Frank. 2008. Making Sense of the APA: A History of the Relationship between Psychology and the Military. *Psychoanalytic Dialogues* 18 (5): 614–637.

Therborn, Göran. 1976. *Science, Class and Society.* London: New Left Books.

Thompson, Herb. 1997. Ignorance and Ideological Hegemony: A Critique of Neoclassical Economics. *Journal of Interdisciplinary Economics* 8 (4): 291–305.

Tomaselli, Keyan G., and Arnold Shepperson. 2010. All the World's Brothel Metaphysics of the Text and Cultural Economy in the Information Age. *Critical Arts* 24 (1): 51–74.

Wasko, Janet, Graham Murdock and Helena Sousa, eds. 2011. *The Handbook of Political Economy of Communications*. Malden, MA: Wiley-Blackwell.

Weiler, Hans N. 2006. *Challenging the Orthodoxies of Knowledge: Epistemological, Structural and Political Implications for Higher Education*. In Guy Neave (ed.), Knowledge, Power and Dissent: Critical Perspectives on Higher Education and Research in Knowledge Society. Paris: UNESCO Publishing, *61–87*.

CHAPTER 7

Did Somebody Say Neoliberalism? On the Uses and Limitations of a Critical Concept in Media and Communication Studies

Christian Garland and Stephen Harper

The media and communication studies textbooks of the early 1980s constituted an ideological battleground for the struggle between liberal pluralism, on the one hand, and Marxism, on the other (see, for example, Gurevitch et al. 1982). Under the influence of European critical theory and British cultural studies, Marxist communication scholars talked of capitalism and class struggle, and accused pluralists of underestimating structures of domination (Hall 1982). With stronger roots in US sociological tradition, pluralist media critics advocated for democracy, chastising Marxists for their economic determinism or functionalism. While it is certainly possible to read the history of the relationship between Marxist and liberal pluralist approaches to media and cultural studies in terms of a series of rapprochements and overlaps (McLennan 1989), there can be little doubt that in recent decades, the pluralist perspective has all but vanquished its erstwhile ideological competitor.

Marxism has always, of course, been marginalised in media and communication studies. In the twentieth century, for example, McCarthyism in the US and the Radikalenerlass in Germany restricted the activities of Marxist communication scholars. Nevertheless, in the 1960s and 1970s, Marxism was a driving force in workers' struggles and a tangible presence in the academy. The critical marginalisation of Marxism became particularly apparent with the ebbing of class struggle in the 1980s and 1990s. In these decades, the disciplines of media and cultural studies, under the sway of a celebratory postmodernism, came to distinguish their pluralist wisdom from the supposedly "elitist" positions of the different Marxist traditions, continually emphasising the eclectic nature of their own standpoints and of the media cultures they critiqued. According to the pluralist paradigm, the newspaper reader, the television viewer, the radio listener are free to consume culture as active, empowered, resistant audiences in a marketplace of ideas underpinned and sustained by liberal democratic ideology. Following on from this there is the recognition that capitalism may have some shortcomings, but it is "the best we've got" and so must be made the best of: the capitalist system and its media institutions are seen to represent the best possible arrangement of things. The popularity of this perspective in the cultural studies milieu of the 1990s has reconfigured the ideological co-ordinates of cultural and media theory, so that for many critics today, the task of media and cultural criticism is no longer to critique capitalism, but to defend the principles of "democracy" and "pluralism" against unwelcome encroachments of the market – encroachments often understood as so many manifestations of "neoliberalism" or the "neoliberal agenda."

Indeed, the hegemony of pluralism in media and cultural studies has been accompanied by some telling terminological shifts. The word "capitalism," for instance, has all but vanished from the lexicon of the left – as sure a sign as any, as Slavoj Žižek (2007, 212) notes, of capitalism's ideological triumph. In the 1990s, as Boltanski and Chiapello (2005, ix) observe, "the term [capitalism] was simply struck from the vocabulary of politicians, trade unionists, writers and journalists – not to mention social scientists, who had consigned it to historical oblivion." Today, we would suggest, the term "neoliberalism" has largely replaced "capitalism" (and its more optimistic variant "late capitalism") in media and cultural studies discourse and the former word now appears in contexts where once we would have expected the latter. In an article on media ideologies, to take just one example, the prolific discourse analyst Teun van Dijk (2006, 121) discusses how media audiences recognise "racist, sexist or neoliberal" arguments. As such formulations suggest, the Marxism/pluralism dyad of yesteryear has largely given way to a new paradigm structured by the binary opposition between neoliberalism, on the one hand, and democracy (or, sometimes, in the Laclauian formulation, "radical democracy"), on the other. Today, it is neoliberalism, rather than capitalism as such, that preoccupies many academics working in the fields of media and cultural studies. As one leading media scholar, Natalie Fenton (2009, 56), puts it, "if media studies must do anything, then it must analyze and explain the cultural and political significance of [the] neoliberal market doctrine."

In itself, this enterprise is not necessarily misguided. In fact, as we argue below, much valuable work in media and cultural studies has proceeded on this basis. Yet even among critics who have embraced the term, neoliberalism is sometimes hazily defined and its conceptual intelligibility is often taken for granted (Mudge 2008). This chapter tries to clarify the relevance and utility of the concept of neoliberalism for critical scholarship in media and cultural studies, questioning whether the hegemonic acceptance of the term offers any genuine increase in critical purchase or explanatory power to critics of capitalist society and its media. In particular, it is argued that it has become something of an accepted practice in media and cultural studies to identify "neoliberalism" – rather than capitalism *per se* – as the ultimate target of critique. In Fenton's terms, neoliberalism is a "market doctrine" which has supplanted an earlier version of the same market in which the liberal democratic state imposed "checks and balances" on capitalist power and critiques of neoliberalism are often animated by a reformist concern to return to the former, social demo- cratic vision by "reclaim[ing] the state" (Wainwright 2003) from the forces of the market. The danger of such critiques, we argue, is that they may lead to a tep- idly agonised hankering after a long-gone "fairer," "more democratic" capital- ism and a call for the "renewal" of Keynesianism. In relation to the media and cultural industries, meanwhile, the attack on neoliberalism, while commend- able in itself, all too often entails a problematic defence of "public service" broadcasting as a bulwark against commercialisation.

This chapter seeks to contribute to a more radical critique of the function- ing of neoliberalism within critical discourse, challenging the assumptions frequently underlying the use of the term and its application to the media and cultural industries. Our own perspective on questions of media power is informed by Marx and Engels' well-known contention in *The German Ideology* that

> the ideas of the ruling class are in every epoch the ruling ideas, i.e. the class which is the ruling material force of society, is at the same time its ruling intellectual force. The class which has the means of material pro- duction at its disposal has control at the same time over the means of mental production, so that thereby, generally speaking, the ideas of those who lack the means of mental production are subject to it
>
> MARX AND ENGELS 1970/1845, 64.

For us, as for Marx and Engels, the mass media play a crucial role in helping to reproduce ideology and specifically the ideology which maintains capitalism to be an inevitable and immutable reality that is here to stay; for it is indeed "the ruling material force of society" (the value-form and profit motive) which "is at the same time its ruling intellectual force." The colossal influence wielded by the media's billionaire owners does indeed filter through all that they own and control, and directly or indirectly through majority and institutional shareholders these same representatives of the capitalist class acquire "the means of material production," thus gaining "control at the same time over the means of mental production." Moreover, in the epoch of reality television in which cameras are turned on atomised (non-)individuals by way of a spurious "democratic" populism, truly "the ideas of those who lack the means of mental production are subject to it," even in those rare instances where they acquire, fleetingly, celebrity status. But such subjection is not merely a consequence of neoliberalisation. As Marx and Engels' thesis indicates, the critical problem with the media and cultural industries is not simply that their character is determined by *market forces*, but that they represent the interests of a *ruling class*. Any properly Marxist media and cultural studies critique must therefore encompass both the so-called "free market" and the state that underwrites and coordinates that market in the interests of the capitalist class. Indeed, we hold that in the messy field of "actually existing" social reality, class and class struggle – and not some apologetic concept such as 'classism' – exist. Class struggle is, as Walter Benjamin was well aware, the "fight for the crude and material things without which no refined or spiritual things could exist." It is the material struggle between classes – that is, capital against labour and labour's struggle against the capital-labour relation itself, the value relation, and the wage relation – which defines the conditions of emancipation from them, and from abstract labour. To reduce all of this, we would argue, to a struggle against "the market" is to risk abandoning Marxism altogether.

Neoliberalism can be seen, in Andrew Glyn's (2007) phrase, "capitalism unleashed," a "political rationality" (Foucault 1988) entailing the de-socialization of economic activity and the espousal of, *inter alia*, coercive competition, state rationalization and factor mobility (or "globalization"). Above all, neoliberalism prioritises market forces over state intervention and dirigisme and the emergence of neoliberalism has been marked by a "motivated shift away from public-collective values to private-individualistic ones" (Barnett 2005, 7). The philosophical origins of neoliberalism lie, of course, in the free-market advocacy of economists such as Hayek and Friedman; but it was not until the late 1970s, as a result of a series of so-called "deregulatory" – or better, perhaps, "re-regulatory" – policies pursued by Western governments, that neoliberal ideology began to exercise material force. Over the following years, the state has retreated somewhat from social welfare provision and certain areas of economic organisation – through tenders to private third parties bidding for contracts to carry out the functions of the state, most recently observed in the proposal that policing be opened up to this process – resulting in a hyper-financialised, "globalised" economy and an increasingly privatised socio-political order that interpellates individuals as competitive and autonomous, monadic subjects (Harvey 2005). In the same period, media organisations have increasingly tended to defer to market imperatives and the ties that once bound them to the social groups that directed or controlled the state – such as political parties, the unions and the churches, have been loosened, especially in the US (McChesney 2001; Hallin and Mancini 2004; Hallin 2008).

As this broad-brush outline suggests, the concept of neoliberalism helps to illuminate many aspects of Western capitalism's struggle to suppress the working class over the last four decades. As an *ideology*, neoliberalism sees the market as a supreme good in itself; its accompanying rhetorical emphasis on "freedom" ultimately concerns the freedom to buy and sell and to acquire and maintain property. In effect, the essence of "freedom" becomes economic – the freedom to either work or starve and the freedom either to obey laws sanctioning this state of affairs or to face dire consequences. The neoliberal project might be described as a purer form of capitalism than Keynesianism; in effect: the imposition, as far as possible, of market imperatives at all times and in every area of life – the reign of the "cash nexus," in Marx's famous phrase. In contrast with the post-war Keynesian social compromise of full employment, a strong welfare safety net, public ownership of key industries, and state intervention to "pump prime" the economy when needed, neoliberalism prescribesprivatization, deregulation, structural unemployment, corporate tax breaks, and welfare "reform." In this sense, the neoliberal project was, and is, also a strategy aimed at restoring and maintaining *class power*, a response by capital to the seismic shocks generated by the worker and student revolts of the 1960s and 70s, no less than the ongoing economic crises of the latter decade (Harvey 2005).

Nevertheless, some qualifications are in order at this point. The extent to which the scope and remit of the capitalist state has been "rolled back" in recent years, for example, is debatable. John Dewey once remarked that "government is the shadow cast by big business over society" and the nation state remains pivotal in regulating capitalism. As Harvey (2005, 159–164) notes, the state has played a pivotal role in the upward redistribution of wealth in recent decades. In fact, without a state to coordinate the system of competition, market competitors would tear one another, and society, to pieces. The nation state thus functions as what Engels, in *Anti-Dühring* (1947/1878), called the "ideal collective body of all capitalists," regulating the chaos that arises as capitalist interests compete. Left-liberals and the more timid of the "anti-globalization" activists who advocate something similar to the "radical democracy" advocated by Laclau and Mouffe (1986) often complain that the role of the nation state is being usurped by transnational powers such as the International Monetary Fund and the World Bank. Yet these institutions were set up by American imperialism and have operated in its interest ever since. Indeed, given that supra-national bodies such as the OECD, WTO, G8 and G20, not to mention the EU, were all established by liberal democratic states, it is at best unconcincing to call for their reclamation from the market, or from the undue power of neoliberalism. As Ellen Meiksins Wood (2005, 138) puts it:

> many participants in movements of this kind are not so much anti-capitalist as anti-"globalization," or perhaps anti-neoliberal, or even just opposed to particularly malignant corporations. They assume that the

detrimental effects of the capitalist system can be eliminated by taming global corporations or by making them more "ethical," "responsible," and "socially conscious."

By the same token, it seems somewhat confused to express the concern that supra-state institutions that were *founded* by states committed to liberal democracy are "undemocratic" (see for example: Klein 1999; Monbiot 2001; Hertz 2002) for seeking to do the bidding of capital. What such critiques often overlook is the necessary inter-imbrication of the state and the market. Indeed, despite the global nature of the capitalist market, the nation state form remains indispensable for capitalism. As Saskia Sassen (2006) argues, the forces of "globalization," far from abolishing the nation state, operate within it – just as surely as the nation state exists within the global order. Thus, while elements of the nation state have been deterritorialized, the state retains its vital role in capitalist organization. "No other institution," as Wood (2005, 139) writes, "has even begun to replace the nation state as an administrative and coercive guarantor of social order, property relations, stability of contractual predictability, or any of the other basic conditions required by capital in its everyday life."

It could even be argued that capitalism's very survival over the last century has been premised upon an increasing fusion of state and market. As early as the end of the nineteenth century, Kautsky observed in *The Class Struggle* (1971/1892) that the state was being forced to take into its own hands an increasing number of functions, a trend that, as observers such as Bukharin and Trotsky noted, intensified in the early twentieth century. Indeed, at that time, in the face of revolutionary threat and the difficulties posed by the saturation of global markets, the relatively *laissez-faire* capitalism of the nineteenth century gave way to the statified planning regimes of Stalinism, fascism and New Deal-style social democracy. This interpretation is borne out by economic data from the early twentieth century: in both the UK and US, government spending as a proportion of Gross Domestic Product, while largely static throughout the nineteenth century, began to grow significantly in the 1920s, culminating, of course, in the post-war creation of the welfare state.

Critics of neoliberalism usually suggest that the swelling of the state in the post-war period began to be reversed in the Reagan-Thatcher years. Western capital's tendencies towards privatization and outsourcing, as well as the erosion of the welfare state since the 1980s, certainly bear this out. On the other hand, in recent years the US, UK, Irish and Icelandic states have responded to the economic crisis by bailing out failed banks with public money, reminding us that states intervene constantly and crucially in the operations of markets in order to maintain the conditions for capital accumulation. The military expenditures of supposedly neoliberal, Western states, meanwhile, are gargantuan and massive standing armies are used to conquer new markets overseas – an historically unprecedented situation. Such facts problematize any simplistic view of the last few decades as a period during which the state has been in retreat. In fact, from the perspective of the *longue durée*, the purview of the state can be seen to have significantly *increased* since the early twentieth century. It seems to us, then, that neoliberalism is a term that must be used with caution; it certainly should not be understood in terms of a simple weakening or diminution of the power of the liberal democratic state. At the very least, the foregoing observations oblige us to recognise neoliberalism as a "hegemonic *restructuring ethos*, as a dominant pattern of (incomplete and contradictory) regulatory transformation, and not as a fully coherent system or typological state form" (Peck et al 2010, 104; see also Ortner 2011). It might be added that the process of "neoliberalisation" has not been uniform, affecting some nations and geographical regions more profoundly than others (Hallin and Mancini 2004; Hallin 2008).

This is not to argue that neoliberalism is of no explanatory value to media critics and sociologists. Using the framework of neoliberalism, media sociologists have drawn attention to themes such as the celebritization of politics and the use of low-paid but flexible, or outsourced labour in the media industries (Deuze 2007). At the same time, textual and cultural critics have rightly highlighted some of the profoundly individualising aspects of late capitalist governmentality. In a series of books, Zygmunt Bauman (2000, 2007, 2011) has convincingly described and condemned the restless, "liquid" lifeworld of late capitalism, while Nick Couldry (2010), David Grazian (2010), John McMurria (2008) and Nick Stevenson (2010) have all commented astutely on the role of reality television in producing flexible, mobile and self-fashioning "entrepreneurial subjects" (du Gay 1996). In a similar vein, Janice Peck (2008) has skilfully outlined the ways in which the individualistic discourses of self-reliance emphasized in the self-help books and television talk shows of Oprah Winfrey serve to reinforce neoliberal orthodoxies. Such work is valuable in illustrating and critiquing the radical de-socialization of the media and cultural industries over the last two decades, prima facie evidence of which can be gleaned from a glance at the lifestyle and consumer programmes that dominate today's television schedules and whose ideal viewer appears to be a self-disciplining *homo economicus* concerned only with regulating her diet, climbing the property ladder and surgically enhancing her face.

But while the concept of neoliberalism facilitates valuable insights into the ongoing atomisation of contemporary institutions and subjectivities, it is not without its limitations as a tool of critical media analysis. For one thing, while

it is true that a good deal of contemporary media culture addresses its audiences as hyper-flexible, autonomous consumers, much of it is also more traditionally propagandistic, aimed at the creation of patriotic citizens of the
capitalist state. BBC political discussion programmes such as *Question Time*,
party political broadcasts and, indeed, political journalism in its entirety overwhelmingly reflect the material interests, and reinforce the symbolic power of
the capitalist state. So too does the BritishHelp for Heroes campaign, which –
whatever good offices it may facilitate – surely serves to instil nationalist and
militarist sentiment. This is to say nothing of the less obtrusive forms of "banal
nationalism" (Billig 1995) promoted in nationwide television magazine programmes and sports coverage. Although it may be unfashionable in contemporary media and cultural studies to describe the media in terms of state
propaganda, instilling a sense of loyalty to the capitalist nation remains a major
function of much of the media we consume, especially in so-called "public
service" broadcasting. Such poisonous additives of media propaganda and the
contextual fallacy used in the (very) selective presentation of information
retards and limits popular understanding of the world, and any critique from
emerging – as it is intended to do. Critiques of the media that focus only on
"neoliberal" agendas and ideologies risk failing to register this reality.

Indeed, besides the reactionary media institutions that serve as instruments
of right-wing propaganda, there exists in "developed" capitalist societies the
far more subtle – and thus far harder to critique – agenda-setting discourse of
the liberal media, which sets the terms of what is considered acceptable in
public debate, delimits the "sphere of legitimate controversy," in Daniel Hallin's
(1986) famous phrase. The public service media, in particular, diffuse and
reproduce what is considered acceptable discourse and thereby "manufacture
consent" and legitimacy for what will never – and must never – be called into
question. In the UK, where both of the authors are based, the news and current
affairs programming of BBC and Channel 4 television is sometimes considered
more "serious" than that of their commercial competitors. Yet it can be argued
that both Channel 4 and the BBC – long the bogus whipping boy of the hysteri-
cal tabloid press – are in reality at almost every turn faithful servants of vested
interests of private wealth and state power (Edwards and Cromwell 2005;
Garland 2011; Harper 2012). Historically, for example, the BBC has tended to
support the British government's foreign policy during both the Cold War
(Jenks 2006) and afterwards (Edwards and Cromwell 2005). Indeed, a Cardiff
University study into the BBC's reporting of the Iraq war showed that the BBC
was actually *less* critical of the invasion than its commercial competitors
(Lewis 2004). The point here is not that the quantity or quality of "serious"
news coverage broadcast by BBC and Channel 4 has diminished in recent

years; rather, it is that the "quality" news and current affairs programming on which both channels pride themselves constitutes the "acceptable discourse" of public debate, aimed at legitimizing liberal capitalism and preempting any critique of the system.

Our argument here is that too tight a focus on the undoubtedly malign influence of neoliberalism on politics or culture can cause us to neglect the equally, if not even more problematic machinations of both the state and the liberal media. Here we might consider, as an example, the left-liberal responses to the 2011 phone hacking "scandal" at Rupert Murdoch's *News of the World* newspaper, in which certain journalists were found to have hacked into the voicemail messages of a range of celebrities and ordinary members of the public. As is well-known, Murdoch's rise to power was facilitated by the "free market" media policies for which he noisily advocated and which he imposed on those who worked for him (McChesney 2001, 14). In fact, Murdoch was an early champion of neoliberal economic ideas and his friendships with politicians who shared what can be seen as his libertarian outlook, such as Margaret Thatcher and Ronald Reagan, were particularly important to his ascendancy (McKnight 2003). Whether explicitly or implicitly, many left-liberal scholars have identified Murdoch's commitment to neoliberalism as a fundamental element in the explanation not only of Murdoch's rise, but also of his fall from grace. One media scholar, for example, notes that the phone hacking scandal took place "in an era of untrammelled neoliberalism" (Savigny 2011). Indeed, identifying neoliberalism as the pernicious ideological background to the scandal, many media academics and activist organisations – such as the liberal campaign group Avaaz – have called for the reform of private media power (Freedman 2011).

Media commentators and victims of the phone hacking have rightly condemned the outrageous malpractice of the *News of the World* journalists. Yet in lambasting the embodiment of neoliberalism, Rupert Murdoch, in the wake of the scandal, left-liberal critics have tended to overlook the wider political context of the affair. By any standards, Murdoch is a powerful figure in the global media; but it should not be forgotten that Murdoch was brought down by a significantly more powerful coalition of forces, including anti-Murdoch factions within the British state and the non-Murdoch media, such as the BBC and *The Guardian*. Although the British state had known about phone hacking at the *News of the World* since at least 2007 (when two of the newspaper's journalists were jailed for related offenses), Murdoch's bid for full control of BSkyB must have raised concerns at the heart of the British establishment. It seems reasonable to suggest that the pro-US stance of the Murdoch media had become increasingly unpalatable to the British state, which may have felt it was time to bring News International under control and, however indirectly, to force Murdoch's hand in closing down his Sunday tabloid. In this context, the humbling of Rupert Murdoch and News International is best understood not as a modest victory for democratic accountability over the forces of global neo-liberalism, but as the entrammelling of a globally massive but nationally rather inconvenient private power bloc by the formidable forces of a dominant state faction and those elements within the media loyal to it. In class terms, the eruption of the scandal was the result of a well-timed intervention launched by one bourgeois faction against another. To understand Hackgate in this way is not to embrace a conspiracy theory, but to understand that the pragmatic co-operation of the various factions of the capitalist state is forever prone to breaking down, giving way to what Marx, in the third volume of *Capital* (1967/1894, 253), called a "fight among hostile brothers" whose outcome is "decided by power and craftiness."

Indeed, from a Marxist perspective, the exposure of phone hacking at the *News of the World*, together with the subsequent official inquiries into media ethics, demonstrates not so much the untrammelled influence of private media corporations, or the malignant effects of neoliberal ideology, as the power of the dominant factions of the nation state to act as an ideologically containing, regulatory force, reigning in or disciplining unruly elements. A class struggle perspective on the phone hacking affair would emphasize that the Leveson Inquiry into the affair and the voices calling for media "reform," far from constituting a counter-hegemonic force, represent a ruling class recuperation: media "reform," through the humbling of News International, was exactly what the dominant faction of the British ruling class sought. In this connection, it might be added that however heinous the crimes of the *News of the World* phone hackers may have been, it is unlikely that they can compare in their invasiveness to the everyday surveillance activities of the British state – a point politely disregarded in most discussions of the hacking scandal.

Our understandable eagerness to condemn the private media power repre-sented by the archetypically "neoliberal" Murdoch empire should not cause us to fall into the trap of uncritically supporting the regulatory reforms now being proposed by a state whose own apparatuses of surveillance may not bear close scrutiny. Nor should it cause us to overlook the thoroughly capitalist nature of the non-Murdoch media. *The News of the World* may have been the paradig-matic embodiment of confected, salacious scandal and the paper folded with an unconvincing claim that the newspaper's self-declared exceptionalism to the rules governing the "free press" was in defence of those same rules – the better to serve democracy and the best interests of that imaginary demo-graphic, "the public"; but as John Pilger (2011, 21) has written:

> Britain's system of elite monopoly control of the media rests not on News International alone, but on the *Mail* and the *Guardian* and the BBC, perhaps the most influential of all. All share a corporate monoculture that sets the agenda of the "news," defines acceptable politics by maintaining the fiction of distinctive parties, normalises unpopular wars and guards the limits of "free speech." This will be strengthened by the illusion that a "bad apple" has been "rooted out."

As Pilger's final sentence suggests, the attack on Murdoch by powerful elements of the state and the non-Murdoch media – whatever other effects it may have – has conservative ideological implications, reinforcing the myth that the liberal democratic media are, at least in the normal course of events, unconstrained by powerful interests.

The limitations of neoliberalism as a critical paradigm can also be apprehended through an analysis of the media coverage of the recent, and ongoing, global economic crisis. For many academic critics, the crisis represents a "crisis of neoliberalism" (Beder, 2009; Duménil and Lévy 2011) and of "free market" ideology, meaning "financialization" (Kotz 2008), privatization, deregulation, and an absence of state intervention in the economy. On the other hand, others, most notably the Marxist economist and neoliberalism sceptic Andrew Kliman (2010a, 2010b, 2012), argue that the crisis is rather a crisis of capitalism as a whole, whose fundamental cause is a falling rate of profit (see also Mattick 2011 and Fuchs 2011, 26–29). Kliman also argues (2012, 50–51) that while neoliberalism is useful in describing the dominant political and ideological landscape since the 1980s, "it is not a useful concept for explaining the trajectory of the economy over the last several decades." Here is not the place to engage in complicated debates over economic theory. Yet the doubts raised in Kliman's work at least give us leave to question the widespread populist *media* representation of the crisis as one of unregulated, free market capitalism. For many journalists, the crisis was caused by a short-sighted commitment to "neoliberal ideology," understood in terms of the excesses of a certain form of "extreme" capitalism and widely personified in the tabloid and even the liberal media by the stereotypical (and arguably anti-Semitic) figures of the "greedy banker" and the unscrupulous trader. As the liberal commentator David Marquand (2010, 27) put it in an article in *The Guardian*:

> For the last two years we have been living through the third great capitalist crisis of modern times; and it is not over yet. The neoliberal paradigm that has dominated policy-making throughout the developed world, not least in the institutions of global economic governance, has been turned

inside out. Markets, we have discovered (or rediscovered), do not always know better than governments. Private greed does not procure public benefits.

It has generally been argued, particularly by left-liberal journalists, that the best remedies for these ills are stronger financial regulation and the fostering of socio-economic "fairness" within the framework of a "responsible capitalism," as the *Guardian* journalist Polly Toynbee (2012, 27) has put it. Liberal journalists have thus tended to understand the economic crisis in populist and moralistic terms, complaining of the rampant greed of the laissez-faire financial sector – a discourse that has been very influential in framing the activities and objectives of the various Occupy movements that have sprung up across the world since 2011. Yet as one Marxist critic, the late Peter Gowan (2009), argues, the problem with such accounts is that

> while the New Wall Street System was *legitimated* by free-market, laissez-faire or neo-liberal outlooks, these do not seem to have been *operative* ideologies for its practitioners, whether in Wall Street or in Washington. Philip Augar's detailed study of the Wall Street investment banks, *The Greed Merchants* [...] argues that they have actually operated in large part as a conscious cartel – the opposite of a free market.

From this point of view, journalistic explanations of the economic crisis in terms of neoliberalism may have furnished some convenient media scapegoats, but they hardly provide an adequate or accurate account of the causes of, or possible solutions to, the economic recession. The "neoliberalism" theory has become a staple of mainstream media accounts of the crisis; yet the moralism and populism to which it often leads stand in sharp contrast to the materialist analyses of the recession offered by Marxist commentators such as Andrew Kliman (2012) and Paul Mattick (2011).

If neoliberalism is a problematic concept for media and cultural studies critics and practitioners, then so too is its slippery binary opposite, "democracy." In addition to calling for greater regulation of capitalism and capitalist media, critics of neoliberalism typically call for greater democracy in political life. But even where these appeals are not openly nationalist – as they seem to be in appeals to defend "our democracy" (e.g. Fenton 2011) – the tendency to posit democracy as the solution to the ills of neoliberalism is highly problematic for Marxists. For one thing, as Jodi Dean (2010) points out, liberal democracy, far from negating neoliberalism, constitutes its very conditions of possibility. To appeal to the liberal democratic state to reign in neoliberal excesses therefore seems contradictory. Something of the circularity of this position is observable in Michael Moore's documentary film *Capitalism: A Love Story* (2009). Moore's film movingly depicts the inhuman effects of capitalism upon working class people. However, the ending of the film is more problematic insofar as it seems to lay the blame for the horrors it details at the door of neoliberal, "financialized" and generally "out-of-control" capitalism. The film concludes with shots of Wall Street and Moore's calls for greater regulation of the banking sector; thus, having identified and excoriated many of the injustices of liberal democracy – and insisted upon the need to end the capitalist system – Moore proposes that the solution to the financial and institutional corruption he has identified is (and here Moore pauses, as if for thought) "democracy." In fact, Moore has elsewhere argued that his aim in making the film was to encourage his audience to become more "engaged in their democracy" (McGreal 2010, 32). Of course, the cause of the apparent contradiction here lies in Moore's use of two quite different definitions of "democracy": throughout the film, Moore rightly attacks democracy as a form of capitalist governance, while the more positive appeal to democracy at the film's end understands democracy in terms of grassroots, working class decision-making – a definition of democracy consistent with Marxist thought. Moore's argument, then, is not as contradictory as might at first appear. But the potential for slippage in the meaning of "democracy" suggests that, as with "neoliberalism," there is always a danger of backsliding in the direction of liberalism. As Jodi Dean (2009, 94) warns:

> the appeal to democracy remains unable to elaborate a convincing political alternative because it accepts the premise that we already know what is to be done – critique, discuss, include and revise. Left reliance on democracy thus eschews responsibility for current failures (*Look, democracy isn't perfect*) but also for envisioning another politics in the future.

For Marxists, indeed, to advocate democracy as the antidote to neoliberalism is not only to mistake the cause for the cure, but also to accept democracy as the goal of class struggle rather than, as Marx put it in "Critique of the Gotha Program" (1970/1875), "the last form of state of bourgeois society."

We would not presume to suggest that the foregoing brief reflections on the theoretical and analytical value of neoliberalism constitute anything like the last word on the matter. Nevertheless, we would argue that there is a need for those media critics and journalists who have recourse to the term "neoliberalism" to consider the ramifications of this usage. Neoliberalism does name verifiable shifts affecting certain areas of Western political and cultural life in recent decades, as noted in the best work on this subject, such as that of David

Harvey (2005). Yet the critique of neoliberalism too often functions as what Fredric Jameson (1981) calls a "strategy of containment" that precludes the structural critique of capitalism and its media institutions. Indeed, the political assumptions of many critics of *neoliberalism* are underpinned by the assumptions of *liberalism*, according to which a largely benign and neutral state needs to be reclaimed for democracy; anything more radical, after all, smacks of a tyrannising "grand narrative." The solutions suggested by the critics of neoliberalism are usually greater state intervention in the economy and the regulation of capitalism and the capitalist media. Yet, as Richard Wolff (2007) puts it, "leftists who see no further – who criticize neoliberal globalization and advocate a warmed-over welfare-state Keynesianism – have abandoned Marx's critical *anti-capitalist* project." A Marxist critique must move beyond the critique of "excessive," "financial," "de-regulated" or "neoliberal" capitalism to incorporate a critique of the value-form and the capital-labour relation. It must encompass both the commercial media and their more paternalistic – but no less capitalist – public service counterparts.

Moving beyond the critique of neoliberalism also entails discriminating between intra-class faction fights such as the *News of the World* scandal and identifying opportunities for working class self-assertion in the media. Indeed, the radical transformation of both the media and society requires the working class to struggle on its own class terrain; "the emancipation of the workers," as the famous phrase has it, "must be the work of the working class itself." To some extent, any radical transformation of the media will require the working class to organize itself and defeat capitalism. On the other hand, while we should be very wary of the often hyperbolic claims made for the liberatory potentials of the Internet and new media (Fuchs 2011; Morozov 2011; Curran et al. 2012), it is clear that new forms of networking and social media – insofar as they remain unbanned by the state and economically accessible to working class people – can promote working class consciousness and organisation against capital (Hands 2010; Fuchs 2011), creating a new media, as it were, in the shell of the old. Notably, the only commentary on Hackgate – to the authors' knowledge – that analysed the scandal in relation to its class character and to the tensions within global imperialism has appeared on the website of the Marxist group the International Communist Current (2011). Through this website and thousands like it, ordinary people are able to discuss how to confront and defeat not neoliberalism, but the capitalist system in its entirety.

For Marxists, neoliberalism was never a very adequate critical term, insofar as it has been understood as a regime of accumulation that is parasitical on, or extrinsic to the normal functioning of an otherwise unproblematic capitalism. Embedded in its usage, all too frequently, are the assumptions of liberal democracy, and those who employ the term are often horrified by their belated discovery that the state is, and always has been, hand in glove with capital. In any case, at the levels of policy and economics, the supposedly neoliberal epoch is in many ways over, as sovereign debt crises force capitalist states to adopt increasingly protectionist political strategies. Perhaps now, then, is the time to relinquish neoliberalism as an analytical category. Nor does the term seem to have much rhetorical value for radicals today. Mark Fisher (2009) points to the paradox that capitalism today, in the absence of visible alternatives, is widely understood as the only possible political system, thereby becoming paradoxically invisible. To replace capitalism, as a critical term, with neoliberalism, is to risk complicity with this "making invisible" of capitalism. Bertolt Brecht once quipped that "capitalism is a gentleman who doesn't like to be called by his name"; but if we wish to identify and overcome the socio-political ills of our time, it is imperative, as Jameson (1991, 418) recommends in a revival of the famous 1960s slogan, to "name the system" that causes them.

References

Barnett, Clive. 2005. The Consolations of "Neoliberalism". *Geoforum* 36 (1): 7–12.

Bauman, Zygmunt. 2000. *Liquid Modernity*. London: Polity.

Bauman, Zygmunt. 2007. *Liquid Times: Living in an Age of Uncertainty*. London: Polity.

Bauman, Zygmunt. 2011. *Culture in a Liquid, Modern World*. London: Polity.

Beder, Sharon. 2009. Neoliberalism and the Global Financial Crisis. *Social Alternatives* 8 (1): 17–21.

Billig, Michael. 1995. *Banal Nationalism*. London: Sage.

Boltanski, Luc and Ève Chiapello. 2005 *The New Spirit of Capitalism*. London: Verso.

Dean, Jodi. 2009. Democracy and Other Neoliberal Fantasies: Communicative Capitalism and Left Politics. Durham, NC: Duke University Press.

Couldry, Nick. 2010. *Why Voice Matters: Culture and Politics after Neoliberalism*. London: Sage.

Curran, James, Natalie Fenton and Des Freedman. 2012. *Misunderstanding the Internet*. London: Routledge.

Dean, Jodi. 2009. Democracy and Other Neoliberal Fantasies: Communicative Capitalism and Left Politics. Durham, NC: Duke University Press.

Dean, Jodi. 2010. Is Democracy Possible? Sure, This is what Democracy Looks Like. Accessed 14 March, 2012. http://jdeanicite.typepad.com/i_cite/2010/12/is-democracy-possible-sure-this-is-what-democracy-looks-like.html.

Deuze, Mark. 2007. *Media Work*. London: Polity.

Du Gay, Paul. 1996. *Consumption and Identity at Work.* London: Sage.

Duménil, Gérard and Dominique Lévy. 2011. *The Crisis of Neoliberalism.* Cambridge: Harvard University Press.

Edwards, David, and David Cromwell. 2005. *Guardians of Power: The Myth of the Liberal Media.* London: Pluto Press.

Engels, Friedrich. 1947/1878. *Anti-Dühring. Herr Eugen Dühring's Revolution in Science.* Moscow: Progress Publishers.

Fenton, Natalie. 2009. My Media Studies: Getting Political in a Global, Digital Age. *Television and New Media* 10 (1): 55–57.

Fenton, Natalie. 2011. Murdochgate and the News: We Need to Reframe Media and the Public Interest. *Our Kingdom.* http://www.opendemocracy.net/ourkingdom/natalie -fenton/murdochgate-and-news-we-need-to-reframe-media-and-public-interest.

Fisher, Mark. 2009. *Capitalist Realism.* Winchester: Zero Books.

Foucault, Michel. 1988. Politics and Reason. In *Politics, Philosophy, Culture: Interviews and Other Writings, 1977–84,* edited by Lawrence D. Kritzman, 57–85. New York: Routledge.

Freedman, Des. 2011. The BBC is Not Part of the Problem Raised at Hackgate. Accessed 14 March, 2012. http://www.opendemocracy.net/ourkingdom/des-freedman/ bbc-is-not-part-of-problem-raised-by-hackgate.

Fuchs, Christian. 2011. *Foundations of Critical Media and Information Studies.* Abingdon: Routledge.

Garland, Christian. 2011. Simulating Events as They Happen: Media Spectacle, Ideology, and Readymade Bogeymen. http://fu-berlin.academia.edu/ChristianGarland/ Papers/1143145/Simulating_events_as_they_happen_media_spectacle_ideology_ and_readymade_boogeymen.

Glyn, Andrew. 2007. *Capitalism Unleashed: Finance, Globalization and Welfare.* Oxford: Oxford University Press.

Gowan, Peter. 2009. Crisis in the Heartland. *New Left Review* 55. Accessed 14 March, 2012. http://www.newleftreview.org/A2759.

Grazian, David. 2010 Neoliberalism and the Realities of Reality Television. *Contexts* 9 (2): 68–71.

Gurevitch, Michael, Tony Bennett, James Curran, Janet Woollacott, eds. 1982. *Culture, Society and the Media.* London: Methuen.

Hall, Stuart. 1982. The Rediscovery of "Ideology": The Return of the Repressed in Media Studies. In *Culture, Society, and the Media,* edited by Michael Gurevitch et al., 56–90. London: Methuen.

Hallin, Daniel C. 1986. *The Uncensored War: The Media and Vietnam.* New York: Oxford University Press.

Hallin, Daniel C. and Paolo Mancini. 2004. *Comparing Media Systems: Three Models of Media and Politics.* Cambridge, MA: Cambridge University Press.

Hallin, Daniel C. 2008. Neoliberalism, Social Movements and Change in Media Systems in the Late Twentieth Century. In *The Media and Social Theory*, edited by David Hesmondhalgh and Jason Toynbee, 43–58. Abingdon: Routledge.

Hands, Joss. 2010. *@ Is For Activism*. London: Pluto.

Harper, Stephen. 2012. *Beyond the Left: The Communist Critique of the Media*. Winchester: Zero Books.

Harvey, David. 2005. *A Brief History of Neoliberalism*. Oxford: Oxford University Press.

Hertz, Noreena. 2002. *The Silent Takeover: Global Capitalism and the Death of Democracy*. London: Arrow.

International Communist Current. 2011. http://world.internationalism.org/.

Jameson, Fredric. 1981. The Political Unconscious. Ithaca, NJ: Cornell University Press.

Jameson, Fredric. 1991. *Postmodernism, or, the Cultural Logic of Late Capitalism*. Durham, NC: Duke University Press.

Jenks, John. 2006. *British Propaganda and the News Media in the Cold War*. Edinburgh: Edinburgh University Press.

Kautsky, Karl. 1892/1971. *The Class Struggle*. New York: W. W. Norton.

Klein, Naomi 1999. *No Logo*. Toronto: Knopf Canada.

Kliman, Andrew. 2010a. Master of Words: A Reply to Michel Husson on the Character of the Latest Economic Crisis. *Marxism 21*, 7 (2): 239–281.

Kliman, Andrew. 2010b. A Crisis of Capitalism (Not Neoliberalism, 'Financialised Capialism' or Low Wages). Accessed 14 March 2012. http://www.marxisthumanistinitiative.org/wp-content/uploads/2010/10/a-crisis-of-capitalism-rvsd-1027101.pdf.

Kliman, Andrew. 2012. *The Failure of Capitalist Production: Underlying Causes of the Great Recession*. London: Pluto.

Kotz, David M. 2008. *Neoliberalism and Financialization*. http://people.umass.edu/dmkotz/Neolib_and_Fin_08_03.pdf.

Laclau, Ernesto and Chantal Mouffe. 1986. *Hegemony and Socialist Strategy: Towards a Radical Democratic Politics*. London and New York: Verso.

Lewis, Justin. 2004. Television, Public Opinion and the War in Iraq: The Case of Britain. *International Journal of Public Opinion Research* 16 (3): 295–310.

Marquand, David. 2010. Green, Socialist, Republican: The New Politics Needs a Realignment of Mind: Tarted-up Neoliberalism Won't Cut It. The Great Question of Our Time Isn't the Deficit, but Halting the Capitalist Merry-Go-Round. *The Guardian*. May 26, 27.

Marx, Karl. 1967/1894. *Capital: Volume III*. Harmondsworth: Penguin.

Marx, Karl and Friedrich Engels. 1970/1845. *The German Ideology*. Ed. C J. Arthur. New York: International Publishers.

Marx, Karl. 1970/1875. *Critique of the Gotha Programme*. Moscow: Progress Publishers.

Mattick, Paul. 2011. *Business as Usual: The Economic Crisis and the Failure of Capitalism*. London: Reaktion.

McChesney, Robert. 2001. Global Media, Neoliberalism and Imperialism. *Monthly Review* 52 (10): 1–19.

McGreal, Chris. 2010. "Capitalism is Evil – You Have to Eliminate iI": After Guns and the Iraq War, Michael Moore is Now Taking on an Entire Political and Economic System in his Latest Documentary. So What Message Does the Man Who Once Planned to Become a Priest Have? *The Guardian*, January 30, 32.

McLennan, Gregor. 1989. *Marxism, Pluralism and Beyond: Classic Debates and New Departures.* London: Polity.

McMurria, John. 2008. Desperate Citizens and Good Samaritans: Neoliberalism and Makeover Reality TV. *Television and New Media.* 9 (4): 305–332.

McKnight, David. 2003. "A World Hungry for a New Philosophy": Rupert Murdoch and the Rise of Neo-Liberalism. *Journalism Studies* 4 (3): 347–358.

Monbiot, George. 2001. *Captive State: The Corporate Takeover of Britain.* London: Pan Books.

Morozov, Evgeny. 2011. *The Net Delusion: How Not To Liberate the World.* London: Allen Lane.

Mudge, Stephanie L. 2008. What is Neo-Liberalism? *Socio-Economic Review* 6 (4): 703–731.

Ortner, Sherry. 2011. On Neoliberalism. *Anthropology of This Century* 1. Accessed 14 March 2012. http://aotcpress.com/articles/neoliberalism/.

Peck, Janice. 2008. *The Age of Oprah: Cultural Icon for the Neoliberal Era.* Boulder, CO: Paradigm Publishers.

Peck, Jamie, Nik Theodore, and Neil Brenner. 2010. Postneoliberalism and its Malcontents. *Antipode* 41: 94–116.

Pilger, John. 2011. Amid the Murdoch Scandal, There's An Acrid Smell of Business As Usual. *New Statesman*, July 25, 21.

Sassen, Saskia. 2006. *Territory, Authority, Rights: From Medieval to Global Assemblages.* Princeton NJ: Princeton University Press.

Savigny, Heather. 2011. Media, Murdoch, Morals and Markets: Time for A New Kind of Politics? Accessed 14 March, 2012. http://dmt.uea.ac.uk/media/2011/07/13/media-murdoch-morals-and-markets-time-for-a-new-kind-of-politics/.

Stevenson, Nick. 2010. Education, Neoliberalism and Cultural Citizenship: Living in 'X Factor' Britain. *European Journal of Cultural Studies* 13 (3): 341–358.

Toynbee, Polly. 2012. Miliband Has Been Proven Right: Fairness Does Matter: How You Share Resources in Hard Times Counts More Than How You Share A Growing Cake. Even Cameron Has To Agree. *The Guardian*, January 10, 27.

Van Dijk, Teun A. 2006. Ideology and Discourse Analysis. *Journal of Political Ideologies* 11 (2): 115–140.

Wainwright, Hilary. 2003. *Reclaim the State: Experiments in Popular Democracy.* London: Verso.

Wolff, Richard D. 2007. Neoliberal Globalization is Not the Problem. *Monthly Review*. Accessed 14 March 2012. http://mrzine.monthlyreview.org/2007/wolff041207. html.

Wood, Ellen Meiksins. 2005. *Empire of Capital*. London: Verso.

Žižek, Slavoj. 2007. With Defenders Like These, Who Needs Enemies? In *The Truth of Zizek*, edited by Paul Bowman and Richard Stamp, 197–255. London: Continuum.

CHAPTER 8

The Coolness of Capitalism Today

Jim McGuigan

It's not just cheap labor

The iPhone is assembled in China by Foxconn, the largest electronics assembler in the world. US executives say they cannot function without companies like Foxconn. The Taiwanese company has a million workers, many willing to live in company dorms, work midnight shifts and spend 12 hours in a factory, six days a week. Chinese workers are cheaper than their American counterparts – but just as important, they are more flexible and plentiful, and thousands can be hired overnight.

CHARLES DUHIGG AND KEITH BRADSHAW 2012, 4

1   Introduction

In the study of communications and culture there are various different traditions of research. They may be incommensurate with one another or, alternatively, there may be grounds for synthesis between different schools of thought. Compatibility is especially difficult to achieve with regard to theorising and analysing the relation of political and economic factors to the determination of meaning. In the Marxist tradition, this has been a focal point of controversy and has resulted in schismatic lines of development. For researchers keen to avoid the kind of economic reductionism that once seemed to characterise Marxism, there has been a tendency to over-emphasise cultural autonomy and ideological determinacy in communications.

This chapter argues that the most satisfactory mode of cultural analysis in critical communication studies is multidimensional. That is, amongst other things, it takes account of the interaction between cultural-ideological and economic-political factors. However, critical multidimensionality does not so much present an alternative to economic reductionism of a Marxist kind today but instead it is obliged to challenge the ideological dominance of technological determinism. This is most notable and urgent with regard to the role of 'new media' and the significance of personalised and mobile communications in culture and society now.

2   Cultural Analysis and Political Economy

From the 1970s a split occurred between two traditions of Marxist-inspired communications research in Anglophone scholarship, in effect, between cultural analysis on the one hand and political economy on the other. The particular tradition of cultural analysis under consideration here, which had many precursors, became associated very largely at this time with the work of the Birmingham Centre for Contemporary Cultural Studies under the leadership of Stuart Hall. The tradition of political economy under consideration was associated most strongly with the work of Herbert Schiller and his associates in North America and, in Britain, with the work of Nicholas Garnham, Peter Golding and Graham Murdock; not so much with the Frankfurt School tradition of critical theory (see, for example, Murdock & Golding, 1973).[1] It is unnecessary to rehearse here the key themes in the work of these critical communications' scholars. However, it is necessary to indicate, albeit briefly, why the cultural studies' tradition became separated from the political economy of communications so sharply in the 1980s.

The separation had already been signaled as early as the 1950s by Raymond Williams, the most important founding figure of what came to be known as "British Cultural Studies" (Turner 2003). Commenting on the kind of Marxist writings on culture that had flourished to some extent in Britain during the 1930s, Williams (1963 [1958], 272–273) remarked in exasperation twenty years later, "To describe English life, thought, and imagination in the last three hundred years simply as 'bourgeois', to describe English culture now as 'dying' [as Christopher Caudwell had indeed done in the 1930s], is to surrender reality to a formula." Williams himself recognised that many Marxists were unhappy with such simplistic and windy rhetoric. Yet, even the more sophisticated Marxist ways of making sense of culture and society known to Williams at the time still left him perplexed as to the truth of the matter:

> Either the arts are passively dependent on social reality, a proposition
> that I take to be that of mechanical materialism, or a vulgar misinterpre-
> tation of Marx. Or the arts, as the creators of consciousness, determine
> social reality, the proposition which the Romantic poets sometimes

---

1   Interestingly, the Frankfurt School of critical theory that coined the term "culture industry" (Adorno and Horkheimer, 1979 [1944]) and inspired a great deal of critical communications research was more interested in the ideology critique of capitalist culture than the political economy of capitalism and, in this respect, had an affinity with 'the Birmingham School' of cultural studies, as Douglas Kellner (1997) has noted.

advanced. Or, finally, the arts, while ultimately dependent, with everything else, on the real economic structure, operate in part to reflect this
structure and its consequent reality, and in part, by affecting attitudes
towards reality, to help *or hinder* the constant business of changing it.
I find Marxist theories of culture confused because they seem to me, on
different occasions and in different writers, to make use of all these prop-
ositions as the need serves.

WILLIAMS 1963 [1958], 266–267

Not unusually, of course, the complaint here is not so much against Karl Marx
or Friedrich Engels (in fact, they are quoted favorably by Williams in 1958) as it
is against Marxists. Still, it did make Williams think at the time that he needed
to look beyond the Marxist tradition in order to develop his own theorising.
When he did eventually get around to naming his distinctive theoretical position as "cultural materialism" (Williams 1981), though, Williams certainly saw it
as broadly *Marxist* (see Williams 1977). Yet, by then – the 1980s – Williams was
no longer the leading light of 'British Cultural Studies'. Stuart Hall had become
the chief spokesperson for this newly popular field of study. Hall (1986 [1980])
asserted in his paper 'Cultural Studies – Two Paradigms' that "the names of
the game" in the field were "culturalism" and "structuralism"; and he gave short
shrift indeed to

> ...the attempt to return to the terms of a more classical 'political econ-
> omy' of culture. This position argues that the concentration on the cul-
> tural and ideological aspects have been wildly over-done. It would restore
> the older terms of 'base/superstructure', finding in the last-instance
> determination of the cultural-ideological by the economic, the hierarchy
> of determinations which both alternatives [culturalism and structural-
> ism] appear to lack. This position insists that economic processes and
> structures of cultural production are more significant than their cultural-
> ideological aspect: and that these are quite adequately caught in the
> more classical terminology of profit, exploitation, surplus-value and the
> analysis of culture as commodity. It retains a notion of ideology as "false
> consciousness."
>
> HALL 1986 [1980], 46–47

Hall may well have been right to complain about the undervaluing of the
determinacy of the cultural-ideological – that is, the problem of meaning,
which was too easily treated as "false consciousness" – by the political economy of communications perspective. Yet, it was extremely unfortunate to have

exiled terms like "profit","exploitation" and "surplus-value" from Marxist-inspired cultural analysis. Without an acknowledgement of them, cultural analysis would hardly be Marxist. It might well be something else. At that time, however, Hall probably did not intend to dispense entirely with Marxism if at all. Yet, he did, perhaps unwittingly, open the way for other exponents of "British Cultural Studies" effectively to do so.

For Hall, the question of ideology was crucial to the study of communications so how it was defined really mattered. His concept was focused upon signification, "ideological power: the power to signify events in a particular way" (Hall 1982, 69). In this respect, Hall was very much influenced by structural linguistics and how it could explain "the reality effect" of signification. He also drew upon the early Soviet linguist Volosinov's notion of the "class struggle in language" and the *multi-accentuality* of the sign, which was similar to Umberto Eco's emphasis on *polysemy*. Hall's (1997 [1974]) own *encoding/decoding* model of television discourse had already placed great stress on differential interpretations of meaning. Encoding/decoding had affinities with the uses and gratifications school of communications research, which also assumed an audience actively appropriating and making sense of media messages for its own purposes at the point of consumption. Inevitably, this way of thinking raised questions concerning just how active was the audience. For Hall and his closest followers, audience activity was motivated socially in relation to class, gender and ethnicity. For others, agency was played up much further, not only in media study but also in subcultural research. John Fiske (1989, 37), for instance, took this conception of the active audience/consumer in what was becoming an uncritical populist strand of Cultural Studies to an absurd extreme, at one point even comparing young people's pilfering of clothes in a shopping mall to the tactics of the Vietcong. At this absurd extreme, then, shopping had indeed become a revolutionary act. It was an absurdity that was gleefully derided by more economic-minded critics of communications and culture (see McGuigan 1992).

Stuart Hall himself never went to such lengths yet much of his work is quite evidently premised upon an avoidance of economic reductionism and, in consequence, there is a tendency to neglect economic factors and to exaggerate the role of ideology.[2] In this respect, he was drawn to the work of Louis

---

2   Hall himself never actually denied the importance of economic factors in his path-breaking work on law and order (Hall et al, 1978) and authoritarian populism/Thatcherism (Hall and Jacques 1983; Hall 1988), though political and ideological factors tended to be emphasised rather more in such work. The later "New Times" thesis (Hall and Jacques 1989) however, was obliged to take account of epochal transformation in political economy with the advent of

Althusser on ideology and Antonio Gramsci on hegemony. His dismissal of a caricatured concept of ideology as 'false consciousness', very much inspired by Althusserianism, begs a great many questions. It is reasonable to argue as Hall, Althusser and Gramsci have all done in their various ways that ideological power does not just reside in ideas but is inscribed in taken-for-granted practices and customary routines. Also, it is quite reasonable to assume that ideological assumptions are not wholly mistaken, that they have within them elements of truth or truthfulness. Otherwise, their appeal would be much weakened. However, it is not strictly necessary to dispense with the critical force of *a concept of ideology as distorted communications*, which is a rather more complex notion than "false consciousness." Although Hall – at least in his writings on ideology in the 1980s – retains the sense that ideology frames reality to serve the interests of the powerful (thereby, remaining largely in line with the dominant ideology thesis), he tends to evade proper consideration of a process of distortion when he actually critiques the claims of the powerful. Marx (1976 [1867], 163–164), however, did stress this aspect of distortion not only in denouncing dominant ideology but also when he described the process of commodity fetishism, which I take to be an ideological effect:

A commodity appears at first sight an extremely obvious, trivial thing. But its analysis brings out that it is a very strange thing, abounding in metaphysical subtleties and theological niceties. So far as it is a use-value, there is nothing mysterious about it, whether we consider it from the point of view that by its properties it satisfies human needs, or that it first takes on these properties as the product of human labour. It is absolutely clear that, by his activity, man changes the forms of the materials of nature in such a way as to make them useful to him. The form of wood, for instance, is altered if a table is made out of it. Nevertheless the table continues to be wood, an ordinary, sensuous thing. But as soon as it emerges as a commodity, it changes into a thing that transcends sensuousness. It

neoliberalism and in the light of historical setbacks for socialism. And, in an interview with Laurie Taylor, whilst admitting a certain disillusion and bafflement with contemporary politics, Hall insisted, "I am still a Marxist in terms of what Marx says about capital. Capital remains an incredibly revolutionary force. It has transformed our lives. We are now seeing yet another globalisation to create the world as a market for capital. This is about the seventh attempt. We've had all kinds of globalisations: imperial colonisation, Cold War American hegemony. Now Blair [still British PM at the time of the interview] aspires that capitalists should provide healthcare for my grandchild, that Barclays or Tesco should run my school. It's an astonishing aspiration. It only happens when capital becomes such a huge global force" (Hall & Taylor 2006, 16–17).

not only stands with its feet on the ground, but, in relation to all other commodities, it stands on its head, and evolves out of its wooden brain grotesque ideas, far more wonderful than if it were to begin dancing of its own free will.

For a cultural analyst now, that famous passage from Marx is especially pertinent when there is such a proliferation of heavily fetishised albeit useful communications gadgetry in everyday life that is not only at the hub of meaning in circulation but also of capital accumulation today, constituting a key nexus of ideology and economy.

So-called "post-Marxists" today are not only keen to avoid the taint of economic reductionism; they also prefer to risk sliding into relativism by adopting a conventionalist position in epistemology instead of pursuing a critical-realist interrogation of ideology whereby they might be required to distinguish between truth and falsehood. This is the case with J.B. Thompson (1990) who, nevertheless, provides an exceptionally useful heuristic typology of different modes of ideological representation (legitimation, dissimulation, unification, fragmentation and reification) each with its associated strategies of symbolic construction (such as displacement and euphemisation for dissimulation) that I have borrowed and applied in my own research on the Millennium Dome fiasco (McGuigan 2003).

3   Multidimensional Analysis

Since the 1980s, Cultural Studies has developed along several different trajectories to the extent that it is no longer possible to isolate a mainstream position with a discernible consensus around it except to note that it probably is no longer especially Marxist in any recognisable sense (see my account of the subsequent history in McGuigan, 2006 and updated in McGuigan, 2010a). It also ceased to be 'British Cultural Studies'. Following the election of Margaret Thatcher in 1979 and during the early phase of the neoliberal counter-revolution (that is, to Williams's (2011 [1961] "long revolution") that was underway in Britain from the 1980s, as an indication of the way things were going, a number of British exponents of Cultural Studies went to Australia, including John Fiske and Tony Bennett. Then, Bennett (1998) set about the construction of a Foucauldian and managerialist school of Cultural Policy Studies. Eventually, there was a North American takeover, especially signalled by the editorial control of the journal *Cultural Studies* moving to the USA under the command of Lawrence Grossberg. Fiske also moved to the USA. And, by the mid-2000s, it was possible to publish an anthology of work purporting to go beyond the American takeover to represent the thoroughgoing 'internationalisation' of Cultural Studies (Abbas and Erni 2005). Nevertheless, the Marxist dispute with the legacy of Hallian (Birmingham School) Cultural Studies continued, particularly with the alternative emergence of a multidimensional framework of analysis adopted by some scholars[3] that was curiously enough not so very different from Stuart Hall's and Richard Johnson's (1979) own earlier thinking about the shape of the field.

My own developed critique of "cultural populism" in Cultural Studies (McGuigan 1992, 1997, 2006, 2011) focuses upon two problematic issues: first, the ontological inadequacy of its one-dimensional methodology; second, its coalescence with neoliberal ideology. Cultural Studies from and inspired by the Birmingham School concentrated almost exclusively upon consumption by the end of the 1980s and left an extremely dubious legacy for education and research that spent much time and effort over subsequent years simply tracking and celebrating the pleasures of mass-popular consumption. Very little analytical work was done on production, either with regard to the labour process involved in making cultural products or in respect of the political economy of the media and cultural industries – that is, *capitalist* media and cultural industries. Moreover, textual analysis was qualified excessively by variants of reader-response theory and "ethnographic" audience research that was often of a slight and superficial character. Hall's "preferred reading" that was said to be encoded ideologically into media texts seemed to count for little in the face of freewheeling popular interpretation and creative use of cultural products by active audiences and consumers. Such methodology could not possibly account for the ontological complexity of culture in circulation. It could not explain how and why we get the communication and cultural products that we do. Only some kind of multidimensional analysis that takes account of both ideological *and* economic factors from production to consumption could do so satisfactorily (see, for example, Kellner 1997 on production, text and consumption).

Consumptionist Cultural Studies attributed an inordinate measure of agency to the consuming subject and, now with the advent of interactive, social-networking media, to the producerly consumer, reminiscent of Roland

---

3   A good example of a developed multidimensional analysis of communications and culture is
    Toby Miller and his co-authors' (2001, 2005) "global Hollywood" research, which grew out of
    a dissatisfaction with much film/screen studies and its exclusively textual orientation. An
    important concept derived from this work is the new international division of *cultural* labour
    (NICL).

Barthes's (1977 [1968]) "birth of the reader," a figure that was already there in the active audience. These hyperactive consumers, shoppers, readers, listeners, viewers, spectators, cybersurfers and, latterly, citizen journalists, bloggers and so on bear a striking resemblance to the sovereign consumer of neoclassical economics, the core ideological assumption of neoliberal, "free-market" capitalism. The customer as king or queen is the endlessly repeated mantra of neoliberalism, as though giant corporations were really beholden to the whims and wishes of ordinary people rather than the masters of the Universe. In order to dictate supply, it should be appreciated, the sovereign consumer must already be fully aware of what he or she wants and be able to imagine exactly what can be supplied as well. Ordinary people rarely if at all, to put it mildly, have access to such knowledge; nobody does. It is the producers who come up with the stuff and cultivate the tastes and habits of consumers. Yet, neoliberalism insists upon flattering our vanity as it picks our pockets. Even if the sovereign consumer was as all-knowledgeable as free-market "theory" presumes, only a very small number of such luminaries would actually be in possession of enough money in any case to buy whatever they want.

It is perfectly reasonable to reject the view of ordinary people that may have been held by some left-wing critics in the past as passive dopes overwhelmed by the lure of consumerism and the distortions of the media. It is also reasonable to doubt elitist assumptions concerning cultural value and have a more nuanced and discriminatory appreciation of mass-popular culture. These straw Marxists and their allegedly simplistic beliefs are easily dismissed as irrelevant. However, consumerist Cultural Studies and what I have called "cultural populism" simply inverted those assumptions and merely asserted the exact opposite virtually without qualification, thereby losing sight of the sheer power both economically and ideologically of capital.

Cool Capitalism

In the aftermath of the seemingly uninterrupted crisis of the past few years that erupted in 2007-8 there has been some fundamental questioning of the capitalist system and exploration of alternatives to it (such as Harvey 2010; McChesney and Foster 2010; Wright 2010). Yet there are still many serious critics of capitalism who treat its persistence as an unsurpassable given (for instance, Gamble, 2009). The legitimacy of capitalism as a civilisation remains strong, according to the 'realists' whose conventional wisdom spreads from Right to the Left across the political spectrum, even when its mode of production is faced with systemic collapse. This is, no doubt, at least partly attributable to the relatively parlous condition of the international Left, its confidence and indeed very existence shattered and nearly destroyed over the past thirty years. There are, however, promising signs of not just critical but practical rebirth in the rhizome laid down by the global justice movement from the turn of the Millennium, the advance of social democracy through the 2000s in South America, recent manifestations of the Occupy movement and growing labour unrest around the world.

Not so very long ago, the legitimacy of capitalism was constantly in doubt: its justification was called into question repeatedly. Critics pointed to the internal contradictions of capitalist political economy, recurrent crises of over-production, loss of conviction in dominant ideology, faulty apparatuses of ideological reproduction, cultural challenges to the hegemonic fashioning of "reality," outbreaks of class struggle and innumerable sites of political contestation, including feminist, gay and anti-racist campaigns. Now, radical political culture is much quieter if not exactly silent and the questioning of capitalism's legitimacy muttered only perhaps in jest. Why should such questioning appear to be unspeakable in contemporary discourse, if heard seriously at all in the public sphere, sounding nostalgic and distinctly *passé*? Is it really beyond our imaginative capacity to countenance an alternative? What imaginary prevents it?

The cardinal question that should concern us is not, however, only to do with explaining the diminution of criticism and opposition. Nor is it the big one, how does capitalism persist? But, rather, less ambitiously, how is capitalism justified? Admittedly, it would be mistaken to assume that capitalism's existence is accounted for by its ideological legitimisation alone. It is too deeply entrenched materially and institutionally – that is, systemically – to be propped up simply by ideas. Yet, Luc Boltanski and Eve Chiapello, (2005 [1999]) are right to argue that capitalism in its various phases has to be justified. There has to be some compelling justification and, indeed, sense of justice closely associated with it. Boltanski and Chiapello are also onto something when they suggest that the most efficient justification for a set of societal arrangements that contributes to its renewal and sustenance derives, paradoxically, from the appropriation of criticism. This insight may be counter-intuitive, though it is not difficult to note historical instances of the same, the stealing of the opposition's clothing, for instance, that was attributed to Disraeli in the nineteenth century. Just think of the role of socialism in the reconstruction and restoration of capitalism in the mid-twentieth century.

Boltanski and Chiapello distinguish between the *artistic critique* and the *social critique* of capitalism. These two forms of critique draw upon quite different sources of *indignation*. The social critique is indignant at the poverty and inequality associated with capitalism; and also challenges the opportunistic and egoistic values fostered by capitalism. These criticisms of capitalist civilisation have been heard much less since the 1970s. On the other hand, however, the artistic critique's indignation at disenchanting and inauthentic features of capitalism that are combined with a generalised sense of oppression has had greater resonance during the same period. Demands for autonomy, liberation, authenticity and singularity – values associated with May '68 and all that – have indeed been heard and, moreover, apparently integrated into the system. This "new spirit of capitalism" is very different from the asceticism of Max Weber's Protestant ethic that was supposed to have been the original value system of a rational and robust capitalism. The new spirit is characterised by the project-orientation of portfolio workers, which is a key feature of the managerial and networking mentality that is promoted by the voluminous literature coming out of business schools.

Capitalism may be an absurd system, as Boltanski and Chiapello argue, founded upon outrageous exploitation and manifestly destructive as well as creative, but few doubt its validity whatever the social and personal cost. How, then, is it justified so effectively? Ideological hegemony is not only obtained at the philosophical level (assuming that the free-market economics propounded by business schools, corporate expertise and mainstream news media deserve to be categorised as such) but also – and necessarily – in terms of cultivating popular consent. Adherence to capitalism does not result, most significantly, from reasoned agreement with the supposed truths of free-market economics and recognition of the deficiencies of socialist planning and command-management economics but much more importantly, instead, by misrecognition and imaginative construction at a mundane level, consonant with both the dull as well as the flashy routines of a capitalistic way of life.

The aim of the cool capitalism thesis that is outlined below, then, is to at least partly account for how latter-day, that is, neoliberal capitalism has constructed popular legitimacy of such a resilient kind that it goes beyond management ideology and propaganda into the texture and common sense of everyday life in spite of severe and recurrent economic crisis; and, indeed, worsening ecological conditions in the world today – all of which directly affects people's lives.

The basic definition of *cool capitalism is the incorporation of disaffection into capitalism itself.* It is, in Erving Goffman's (1971 [1959]) sense, a "front region" that is seductively tasteful in its appeal to populations at large, both the comparatively affluent and, indeed, the aspirant poor. There is, however, a "back region," rather like an industrialised kitchen with dirty secrets that do not meet health and safety standards. This back region is occasionally glimpsed and, in consequence, the fare on offer is called into question by troubled voices. Like in any good restaurant, the *maitre d'* must somehow cool out the customers who might otherwise take their custom elsewhere. Maybe it is "cool" to have a filthy kitchen and, in any event, you have to smash eggs in order to make an omelette; and sometimes they spill onto the floor where the rats hang out.

It is hardly necessary to point out how ubiquitously the word "cool" is used presently around the Earth; or, just as important, how widely embedded is the sensibility associated with that term whether the word is actually used or not. It is everywhere. Coolness is not some marginal or dissident trend. It is at the heart of mainstream culture insofar as we can speak of such a phenomenon at all.

In my book *Cool Capitalism* (McGuigan 2009), several examples of present-day coolness are given, particularly in commerce. The genealogy of the word and the discourses through which it has passed are also traced. "Cool" derives from West African *itutu*, the core meaning of which refers to composure in the heat of battle. Although it was closely associated with masculinity in origin, this may not have been exclusively so and, in any case, it is not exclusively so today. The American art historian, Robert Farris Thompson (1974, 1976 [1971]) has documented the aesthetics of *itutu* in the West and the South of Africa, its passage to the Americas with the slave trade and the formation of a cool culture of disaffection on the margins of US society. Generally speaking, coolness became a personal stance, mode of deportment and argot, associated with dignity under pressure in oppressive circumstances. It is a distinctive feature of 'Black Atlantic' culture (Gilroy, 1993) and it also became extremely prominent and attractive to others, including whites, especially through mid-twentieth century jazz culture.

Although coolness is difficult to pin down – and deliberately so – Pountain and Robins (2000) have, nevertheless, sought to identify three essential traits of the cool persona: *narcissism, ironic detachment* and *hedonism.* It is easy to call up plenty of sub-cultural examples over the years, either indirectly or directly related to black culture, from, say, Parisian existentialism to latter-day hip-hop culture. Very recently, an article in a philosophy magazine that was unusually on sale on the mass market celebrated coolness as a "fusion of submission and subversion." From this point of view, the cool person, albeit perpetually alienated, conducts a creative balancing act. The would-be philosopher in question obviously thinks coolness is still cool. Some black American commentators don't.

Social psychologists Richard Majors and Janet Mancini Billson (1993 [1992], xi) remarked several years ago in their empirical study of black masculinity in urban locales, "coolness may be a survival strategy that has cost the black male – and society – an enormous price." Whilst it represents black identity and pride in the ghetto such 'compulsive masculinity' in that context is also seriously damaging to both women and men, not to mention the druggy lifestyle, disorganised sociality and violent criminality – which is by no means confined to working-class black males in the USA.

Cool today is not only about black American culture; it is global and colourless. The sign floats free. And, key to the cool capitalism thesis, "cool" has traversed the political landscape, roughly speaking, from the Left to the Right. It is now more a sign of compliance than of resistance.

This argument is substantiated by Thomas Frank's (1997) research on "the conquest of cool" in which he claims that cool sensibility caught on in the American mainstream as long ago as the 1950s with the rise of rebels without a cause, rejecting the staid conformity fostered by post-Second World War organised capitalism in middle-class life *and business*. Nowadays, of course, nearly every management consultant you meet plays blues guitar. According to Frank, the counter culture caught on very rapidly in corporate America. Cool pose and the buzzword, "creativity" are now *de rigeur* in managerial ideology. And, as a couple of Swedish management theorists have pointed out, business today is "funky" (Ridderstrale and Nordstrom 2002 [2000]).

It is interesting that Frank confined his research on "cool" business and management discourse to the USA while Boltanski and Chiapello restricted their research to France. Yet, even French management texts are influenced by "Anglo-Saxon" neoliberal thought and, indeed, Gallic *cadres* read American management books. Cool capitalism is now a global phenomenon with albeit American roots, though by no means restricted to the USA. It is indisputably a feature of "Americanisation" but Americanisation, it has to be said, is only part of the story and too simple a way of understanding cool capitalism's presence in the world at large.

In their different ways, Boltanski and Chiapello's "new spirit of capitalism" and Frank's "conquest of cool" stress the role of managerial ideology in the organisational and cultural changes wrought by the neoliberal transformation of culture and society. Yet, the most evident site of "cool capitalism" in everyday life is consumer culture and the representation of "cool" commodities. This has been especially notable in the clothing industry addressed to the young with companies like The Gap and Nike drawing upon countercultural themes and symbolisation with their "rebel" gear. However, the coolest of all commodities today is the *all-purpose mobile communication device*, that is, on-line mobile phones and tablets, which is the subject of the next section. However, it should be emphasised that multidimensional analysis of culture in circulation involves textual analysis (see McGuigan 2008 and 2010a) and research into the labour process of production (see McGuigan 2010b and 2012) as well as the political economy and ideology of "cool" corporations.

4   The All-Purpose Mobile Communication Device

The all-purpose mobile communication device (apmcd) represents an ideal focus for critical communication studies today and constitutes a perfect test case for multidimensional analysis from a broadly Marxist perspective and, perhaps also, for the cool-capitalism thesis. The issues at stake are numerous and far-ranging.

In order to make sense of the significance of the apmcd in contemporary culture and society, it is necessary, first and foremost, to confront the old chestnut of technological determinism. The classical critique of technological determinism in communications was made by Raymond Williams (1974) in the 1970s and developed further by Brian Winston (1995 [1990], 1996) in the 1990s. It is unnecessary to rehearse those criticisms here (see my explication in McGuigan 2007). Suffice it to say that Williams stressed the importance of *intention* in technological innovation, that there always has to be a social motivation for investment, research and application in product development. In the original test case of television, Williams also linked technological development to the phenomenon of *mobile privatisation* that emerged historically with mass migration and urban industrialism. On-line mobile phones, laptops and tablets are exactly the kind of technological gadgetry that is functional to a yet more mobile and privatised way of life under conditions of late-modernity. They are extolled as such persistently in advertising and, more generally, in the technologically determinist propaganda that is a prominent feature of neoliberal political economy.

Still, however, technological-determinist explanation in relation to politics is a temptation even for the shrewdest of critics today. Take, for instance, the British journalist Paul Mason's (2012) account of the 2011 eruption of demo-cratic protest around the world, *Why It's Kicking Off Everywhere – The New Global Revolutions*. Recalling a debate he had with radical students in London, Mason (2012, 2) remarks, "is it the technology, the economics, the mass psy-chology or just the zeitgeist that's caused this global explosion of revolt? I inclined to a technological-determinist explanation." He enthuses about the social networking through Facebook and Twitter that contributed to mobilis-ing protesters in Tunisia and Egypt. "It's the network", blurts Mason, thereby also echoing Manuel Castells's (1996) largely technological-determinist take on the social impact of computer-mediated communications – emergence of "the network paradigm" – nearly twenty years ago. Yet within a page, Mason (2012, 3) was to somewhat contradict his own self-styled technological determinism:

> We're in the middle of a revolution caused by the near collapse of free-market capitalism combined with an upswing in technical innovation, a surge in desire for individual freedom and a change in human conscious-ness about what freedom means. An economic crisis is making the pow-erful look powerless, while the powerless are forced to adopt tactics that were once the preserve of niche protest groups.

Surely that passage suggests that the principal determination of democratic protest in 2011 was the economic crisis and, not unconnected to it, failed cor-rective policy measures, including the punishment meted out to ordinary people for the misdemeanours of finance capital. Other factors noted by Mason include "desire for individual freedom and a change in human con-sciousness" (which is actually a proposition about a cultural phenomenon rather than a technological phenomenon as such). Undoubtedly, digital and mobile technologies of communication and socially-embedded patterns of use among the young facilitated the mobilisation of bodies and the flow of messages from these communicative networks through the sluicegate of the international public sphere, thus appearing in amplified form in the publicity arena of "old media" like television. "New media" played their part, as did older media of, say, print or, further back, word-of-mouth in the past history of popu-lar protest and indeed revolutionary upsurge. There is no need, therefore, to fetishise "new media" as the sole cause of recent events since they surely are not. Peter Golding's (2000, 171) distinction between Technology One and Technology Two is helpful here in clarifying what is at stake analytically:

> Technology may be construed as the mechanisms by which human agency manipulates the material world. We can conceive of two forms of technological innovation. Technology One allows existing social action and process to occur more speedily, more efficiently, or conveniently (though equally possibly with negative consequences such as pollution or risk). Technology Two enables wholly new forms of activity previously impracticable or inconceivable. In essence many ICT s are more obvi-ously Technology One than Technology Two.

This rather measured distinction, which does not deny the importance of new media technologies but, at the same time, puts into serious doubt the usual hyperbolic claims concerning their capacity to "change the world." Clearly, digital communication systems, their multiple applications and the endless succession and upgrading of seductive gadgets make a difference but not in splendid causal isolation from various combinations with cultural, economic, ideological and political factors. Such gadgetry and the mythology surrounding it is a salient feature of cool capitalism. Take, for instance, the Apple Corporation and the late Steve Jobs. Such "cool" gadgets as the iPod, iPhone and iPad, useful as they undoubtedly are, nevertheless, exemplify the process of commodity fetishism and the obscuring of neoliberal capitalism's system of global exploitation.

The celebrification and, indeed, mystification of the entrepreneurial hero has been embodied perfectly in the figure of Jobs, who, from the point of view of critical communication studies, must be treated as a textual set of signs, that is, a media construct like any other celebrity figment of the mediated imagination (see Rojek 2001 on the social construction of celebrity). Kieran Healy (2011), for instance, has sketched "a sociology of Steve Jobs" by applying Max Weber's theory of charismatic authority to the Apple CEO. Jobs has also been the subject of considerable managerial fascination as a guide to business success (Gallo 2011) and biographical attention (Moritz, 2011 [2009]; Isaacson 2011), in fact, engendering a mini-publishing industry before and especially during the year of his death. His cool-dude persona and the smart gadgets that he presented to the public – though did not actually design himself – exemplify the incorporation of a certain kind of selectively constituted and apparently dissenting sensibility that is inherited from the 1960s' counter-culture whilst also making Apple the most profitable company in the world by the time of Jobs's death in October 2011.

In his sociology of Steve Jobs, Healy only mentions the manufacture of Apple products as an afterthought to his main concern with Jobs's "charisma." And, on the question of manufacture, Healy is quick to point out that Apple are not the only electronics firm that relies on a murky outsourcing and pernicious system of labour exploitation in "developing countries," most notably China. This is reminiscent of the problem with singling out Nike for special attention in the garment-industry campaign that became associated with Naomi Klein's (2000) *No Logo* at the turn of the Millennium in that they are not the only one. However, Nike and Apple are especially pertinent examples of the culture and political economy of transnational capitalism now since they have both cultivated a counter-cultural and rebel image that might at one time have been linked to anti-capitalism but is no longer so, thereby epitomising cool capitalism. Outsourcing the largely American corporations' digital electronics manufacture to low-pay economies where the policing of labour conditions and rights is relaxed to say the least, if existent at all, lagged behind garment manufacture but in recent years it has caught up dramatically.

In 2006, the Netherlands-based Centre for Research on Multinational Corporations (SOMO) reported on the structure of the mobile-phone industry, the network of firms along the supply chain all the way down to factories in Export Processing Zones (EPZ s) or Special Economic Zones (SEZ s) in places like Shenzen in Southern China (Wilde and de Haan 2006). Other research NGO s like China Labor Watch, based in New York, and Hong Kong's Students & Scholars Against Corporate Misbehaviour (SACOM) have produced ethnographic studies of the treatment of labour in Chinese factories. Reading their reports is reminiscent of Marx's use of the governmental 'blue books' on Victorian industry in the later part of *Capital* Volume One.

China Labor Watch (2011) studied ten electronics factories in Guangdong and Jiangsu provinces where they interviewed over four-hundred workers in late-2010. These factories supply products for Dell, Salcomp, IBM, Ericsson, Philips, Microsoft, Apple, Hewlett Packard and Nokia amongst others. They found that excessive hours of overtime were required, the minimum wages (usually $150-200 a month) paid did not actually cover living costs, work rates were highly intensive, tests excluded pregnant women from employment and typically formal labour contracts are either non-existent or their provisions not actually observed in practice.

It is vital to plumb the deep structures and processes of the industry, as such research aims to do, albeit rather more descriptively than critically, in order to grasp the moment of production in the circulation of communications technology and, in consequence, meaning. Usually, general publics around the world only learn of the most extreme abuses – particularly with regard to child labour – and instances of personal tragedy. A spate of suicides at the Taiwanese-owned Foxconn plants in China have been a particular focus of international attention in recent years, spurring SACOM (2011) to study where Foxconn manufactures iPods, iPhones and iPads in Shenzen, Chengdu and Chongqing. Apple was supposed to have demanded that Foxconn cleaned up its act but, as it turns out, to little or no avail, according to the Hong Kong researchers. The China Labor Watch (2011: 77) researchers from New York took a more sanguine view, arguing that, in response to criticism, "Foxconn had become the top performer in the electronics industry" in terms of wages, by paying new recruits $184.80 monthly, rising to the princely sum of $247.13 a month after six months on the job.

In March and April 2011 SACOM interviewed one-hundred and twenty workers in Shenzen, Chengdu and Chongqing, normally young people aged between 16 and 30, approached outside the factory gates. It was found that workers are

keen to do overtime because the basic wage is not enough but there is no guarantee that the overtime will actually be paid. SACOM gives an indication of the
schedule of a typical day for workers at the Chengdu plant where iPads are
made:

06.45 Wake up
07.15 Queue up for bus
07.45 Arrive at Foxconn (breakfast and punch card)
08.10 Work assembly
08.30 Work shift begins
11.20 Lunch
12.20 Work shift resumes
17.20 Dinner
18.20 Overtime shift begins
20.20 Work shift ends
21.00 Arrive at dormitory.
                      SACOM 2011, 12

Health and safety conditions are very poor at the factory in Chengdu, as they
are in other Foxconn facilities. Some quotations from workers in Chengdu give
a further sense of their lived experience:

> *"Though we produce for iPhone, I haven't got a chance to use iPhone. I
> believe it is fascinating and has lots of function. However, I don't think I can
> own one myself,"* a worker from Guanlan who joined Foxconn in February
> 2011 said.
>   *"I never dreamed that I will buy an iPad, it may cost me two months sal-
> ary. I cannot afford it. I come from a village to sell my labour at Foxconn, all
> I want is improve the living conditions of my family,"* a 24-year-old worker
> expressed.
>   *"Our salary is too low compare to the selling price of an iPad. We deserve
> more as we generate wealth for Apple every day,"* an assistant to frontline
> supervisor in Chengdu.
>   SACOM 2011, 19

Such empirical data brings home the dirty little secret of cool capitalism, a
secret that is not well concealed but nonetheless easily ignored. However,
breaking the silence, *The New York Times* (Duhigg and Barboza 2012, a, b) has
conducted a campaign of interrogation concerning Apple's operations in
China. The predominant theme of such journalism in the USA, however, has

been around the "fade" in "middle-class jobs" back home. "Middle class" is, of course, American for working class. The taken-for-granted assumption is that iPods, iPhones and iPads are manufactured in China rather than the USA because wages are much lower there. That is true but this may not be quite as significant as it appears at first sight. It has been calculated by academic economists that making iPhones in the USA would add only $65 dollars to the price since the price of labour is such a small part of the cost of making iPhones anyway, according to the *New York Times* journalists, Charles Duhigg and David Barboza (2012a, 6). It is also said, to further complicate matters, that the USA does not educate enough skilled engineering operatives at an appropriate sub-degree level. Yet more seriously, though, it may be that American workers are insufficiently docile for Apple's rapid capital-accumulation strategy. Duhigg and Barboza tell the story of how Steve Jobs complained about how easily the plastic screen scratched on the iPhone prototype just before launch in 2007. He demanded that it be replaced with glass screens within six weeks. When these replacement screens eventually arrived at the assembly plant in China around midnight:

> A foreman immediately roused 8,000 workers inside the company's dormitories, according to the executive. Each employee was given a biscuit and a cup of tea, guided to a workstation and within half an hour started a 12-hour shift fitting glass screens into beveled frames. Within 96 hours, the plant was producing over 10,000 iPhones a day.
>
> DUHIGG AND BARBOZA 2012A, 2

These extraordinary gadgets and their updates enhance the routine pleasures and everyday conveniences of the world's comparatively affluent but at a cost, the human cost of exploiting cheap labour and making life miserable for people who are prepared to work extremely hard under conditions that the world's affluent would not tolerate in order to overcome their relative poverty. A fully developed programme of Marxist analyses that explores various aspects of capitalism's cool culture, including information and communication technology as a complex social phenomenon and not just gadgetry, is vital here, tracing the economic-material and cultural-ideological nexus of communications today.[4] This is not to suggest that Marxism explains everything. However,

---

4 It would be unfortunate, however, if the kind of political economy of communications industry and technology in China that is researched by the likes Yu Hong (2008 & 2011) were not articulated in relation to cultural analysis of the lived experiences of the labour process referred to in this article and the ideological seduction of people around the world that is critiqued by the cool-capitalism thesis.

Marxism's great value remains – as was also the case one-hundred-and-fifty years ago – that it asks questions which the powerful would prefer not to be asked since the answers to such questions may demystify the world we live in and yet have so little control over.

References

Abbas, Ackbar and John Nguyet Erni, eds. 2005 *Internationalizing of Cultural Studies*. Malden MA: Blackwell.

Adorno, Theodor and Max Horkheimer. 1979 [1944]. *Dialectic of Enlightenment*. London: New Left Books.

Barthes, Roland. 1977 [1968]. The Death of the Author. In *Image, Music, Text*, edited by Stephen Heath, 142–148. London: Fontana,

Bennett, Tony. 1998. *Culture – A Reformer's Art*. London: Sage.

Boltanski, Luc and Chiapello Ève. 2005 [1999]. *The New Spirit of Capitalism*. London: Verso.

Castells, Manuel. 1996. *The Rise of the Network Society*. Malden, MA: Blackwell.

China Labor Watch. 2011. *Tragedies of Globalization – The Truth Behind Electronic Sweatshops*. New York: China Labor Watch.

Duhigg, Charles and Keith Bradshaw. 2012. Where the iPhone Work Went. *The New York Times* Articles selected in association with *The Observer*, 29 January, pp1,4.

Duhigg, Charles and David Barboza, 2012a. How the US Lost Out on iPhone Work. *The New York Times*, 21 January.

Duhigg, Charles and David Barboza, 2012b. In China, Human Costs are Built Into an iPad. *The New York Times*, 26 January.

Fiske, John. 1989. *Understanding Popular Culture*. London: Unwyn Hyman.

Frank, Thomas. 1997. *The Conquest of Cool – Business Culture, Counterculture, and the Rise of Hip Consumerism*, Chicago, IL: University of Chicago Press.

Gallo, Carmine. 2011. *The Innovative Secrets of Steve Jobs – Insanely Different Principles for Breakthrough Success*. New York: McGraw Hill.

Gamble, Andrew. 2009. *The Spectre at the Feast – Capitalist Crisis and the Politics of Recession*. London: Palgrave Macmillan.

Gilroy, Paul. 1993. *The Black Atlantic and Double Consciousness*. London: Verso.

Goffman, Erving. 1971 [1959]. *The Presentation of Self in Everyday Life*. Harmondsworth: Penguin.

Golding, Peter, 2000, Forthcoming Features – Information and Communication Technologies and the Sociology of the Future, *Sociology* 34.1, 165–184.

Hall, Stuart, 1997 [1974]. The Television Discourse – Encoding and Decoding. In *Studying Culture – An Introductory Reader*, edited by Ann Gray and Jim McGuigan, 28–34. 2nd edition London: Arnold.

Hall, Stuart, 1982, The Rediscovery of 'Ideology' – Return of the Repressed in Media Studies, Gurevitch, Michael, Tony Bennett, James Curran & Janet Woollacott, eds., *Culture, Society and the Media*, London: Methuen, 56–90.

Hall, Stuart. 1988. *The Hard Road to Renewal and the Crisis of the Left*. London: Verso.

Hall, Stuart. 1986 [1980]. Cultural Studies – Two Paradigms. In *Media, Culture & Society – A Critical Reader*, edited by Richard Collins, James Curran, Nicholas Garnham, Paddy Scannell, Philip Schlesinger and Colin Sparks, 33–48. London: Sage.

Hall, Stuart, Chas Criticher, Tony Jefferson, John Clarke and Brian Roberts. 1978. *Policing the Crisis – Mugging, the State, and Law and Order*. London: Macmillan.

Hall, Stuart and Martin Jacques, eds. 1983. *The Politics of Thatcherism*. London: Lawrence & Wishart.

Hall, Stuart and Martin Jacques, eds. 1989. *New Times – The Changing Face of Thatcherism in the 1990s*. London: Lawrence & Wishart.

Hall, Stuart and Laurie Taylor, 2006, Culture's Revenge, *New Humanist*, March/April, 14–17.

Harvey, David. 2010. *The Enigma of Capital – And the Crises of Capitalism*. London: Profile.

Healy, Kieran. 2011. A Sociology of Steve Jobs. http://kieranhealy.org/blog/archives/2011/10/10/a-sociology-of-steve-jobs/ downloaded 19-01-12.

Hong, Yu. 2008. Distinctive Characteristics of China's Path of ICT Development – A Critical Analysis of Chinese Developmental Strategies in Light of the East Asian Model. *International Journal of Communication* 2: 456–471.

Hong, Yu, 2011. *Labor, Class Formation, and China's Informationized Policy of Economic Development*. Langham, MD: Lexington.

Isaacson, Walter, 2011, *Steve Jobs*, London: Little, Brown.

Johnson, Richard. 1979. Histories of Culture/Theories of Ideology – Notes on an Impasse. In *Ideology and Cultural Production*, edited by Michèle Barrett, Philip Corrigan, Annette Kuhn and Janet Wolff, 49–77. London: Croom Helm.

Kellner, Doulas. 1997. Critical Theory and Cultural Studies. In *Cultural Methodologies*, edited by Jim McGuigan, 12–41. London: Sage.

Klein, Naomi. 2000. *No Logo – Taking Aim at the Brand Bullies*. London: HarperCollins.

Majors, Richard and Janet Mancini Billson. 1993 [1992]. *Cool Pose – The Dilemmas of Black Manhood in America*. New York: Touchstone.

Marx, Karl. 1976 [1867]. *Capital* Volume 1, tr. Ben Fowkes, Harmondsworth: Penguin.

Mason, Paul. 2012. *Why It's Kicking Off Everywhere – The New Global Revolutions*. London: Verso.

McChesney, Robert and John Bellamy Foster. 2010. Capitalism, the Absurd System – A View from the United States. *Monthly Review Press* 62 (2): 1–12.

McGuigan, Jim. 1992. *Cultural Populism*. London: Routledge.

McGuigan, Jim. 1997. Cultural Populism Revisited. In *Cultural Studies in Question*, edited by Marjorie Ferguson and Peter Golding, 138–154. London: Sage.

McGuigan, Jim. 2003. The Social Construction of a Cultural Disaster – New Labour's Millennium Experience. *Cultural Studies* 17 (5): 669–690.

McGuigan, Jim. 2006. The Politics of Cultural Studies and Cool Capitalism. *Cultural Politics* 2 (2): 137–258.

McGuigan, Jim. 2007. Technological Determinism and Mobile Privatisation. In *New Media Worlds – Challenges for Convergence*, edited by Virginia Nightingale and Tim Dwyer, 103–117. Sydney: Oxford University Press.

McGuigan, Jim. 2008. Apprentices to Cool Capitalism. *Social Semiotics* 18 (3): 309–319.

McGuigan, Jim. 2009. *Cool Capitalism*, London: Pluto.

McGuigan, Jim. 2010a. *Cultural Analysis*, London: Sage.

McGuigan, Jim. 2010b. Creative Labour, Cultural Work and Individualisation, *International Journal of Cultural Policy* 16 (3): 323–333.

McGuigan, Jim, 2011, From Cultural Populism to Cool Capitalism. *Art and the Public Sphere* 1 (1): 7–18.

McGuigan, Jim. 2012.Cool Capitalism at Work, In *The Cultural Career of Coolness*, edited by Ulla Haselstein, Irmela Hijiya Kirschnereit, Catrin Gersdorf and Elena Giannoulis. Lanham, MA: Lexington Books.

Miller, Toby, Nitin Govil, John McMurria and Richard Maxwell. 2001. *Global Hollywood*, London: British Film Institute.

Miller, Toby, Nitin Govil, John McMurria, Richard Mazwell and Ting Wang. 2005. *Global Hollywood 2*. London: British Film Institute.

Moritz, Michael. 2011 [2009]. *Return to the Little Kingdom – Steve Jobs, The Creation of Apple, And How it Changed the World*. London: Duckworth.

Murdock, Graham and Peter Golding. 1974. For a Political Economy of Mass Communications. In *The Socialist Register 1973*, edited by Ralph, Miliband and John, Saville, 205–244. London: Merlin'.

Pountain, Dick and David Robins. 2000. *Cool Rules – Anatomy of an Attitude*. London: Reaktion.

Ridderstrale, Jonas and Kjell Nordstrom. 2002 [2000]. *Funky Business – Talent Makes Capital Dance*. London: Pearson.

Rojek, Chris. 2001. *Celebrity*, London: Reaktion.

Students & Scholars Against Corporate Misbehaviour (SACOM). 2011. *Foxconn and Apple Fail to Fulfil Promises – Predicaments of Workers after the Suicides*. Hong Kong: SACOM.

Thompson, John B. 1990. *Ideology and Modern Culture – Critical Social Theory in the Era of Mass Communication*. Cambridge, MA: Polity Press.

Thompson, Robert Farris. 1974. *African Art in Motion*. Berkeley & Los Angeles, CA: University of California Press.

Thompson, Robert Farris, 1976 [1971]. *Black Gods and Kings*. Bloomington, IN: Indiana University Press.

Turner, Graeme. 2003. *British Cultural Studies – An Introduction*. London: Routledge.

Wilde, Joseph and Esther de Haan. 2006. *The High Cost of Calling – Critical Issues in the Mobile Phone Industry*, Amsterdam: Centre for Research on Multinational Corporations (SOMO).

Williams, Raymond, 1963 [1958], *Culture and Society 1780-1950*. Harmondsworth: Penguin.

Williams, Raymond. 1974. *Television – Technology and Cultural Form*. London: Fontana.

Williams, Raymond. 1977. *Marxism and Literature*. Oxford: Oxford University Press.

Williams, Raymond. 1981. Marxism, Structuralism and Literary Analysis. *New Left Review* 129: 51–66.

Williams, Raymond. 2011 [1961]. *The Long Revolution*. Cardigan: Parthian.

Winston, Brian. 1995[1990]. How are Media Born and Developed? In *Questioning the Media – A Critical Introduction*, ed. John Downing, Ali Mohammadi and Annabelle Sreberny-Mohammadi. 54–74. London: Sage.

Winston, Brian, 1996, *Technologies of Seeing – Photography, Cinematography and Television*. London: British Film Institute.

Wright, Erik Olin, 2010, *Envisioning Real Utopias*, London: Verso.

CHAPTER 9

Critical Political Economy of Communication and the Problem of Method

Brice Nixon

1   Introduction

The critical political economy of communication, culture, media, and information has been defined, examined, and re-examined by a number of eminent political economists over the course of at least four decades. That collective self-reflectivity I take to be a necessary and productive quality of critical theorizing. What does not seem to have been addressed, however – at least not sufficiently – is the critical *method* by which political economy is a critical theory. By method, I mean a particular use of human reason to produce knowledge of human existence. Critical theory relies on a critical method, and a critical method for Marx is a historical materialist dialectical method. In fact, that method is the foundation of Marx's critical poltical economy. Thus, Marx is an essential source for considering the nature of that method, in addition to being an essential source for the theory and concepts of political economy. In this chapter, I attempt to outline an engagement with the dialectical method that I suggest is necessary for a critical political economy of communication, and I attempt to demonstrate the productive potential of such an engagement by connecting it to the "blindspot" debate about the place of communication in Marxist theory initiated by Smythe (1977). The political economy of communication can be a critical theory of how audience activities of consuming culture and making meaning are made a source of value if it is further developed by the Marxist dialectical method.

There is a now decades-long division of the field of critical media and communication studies into political economy and cultural studies (Gandy 1995). However, as Peck (2006) has argued, we shouldn't be bored with the "political economy vs. cultural studies" debate because the assumed division at the heart of the debate is a problem for a critical understanding of communication, culture, and media. The treatment of culture, and particularly the subjective signifying activities of consumers of culture (or, audiences), as a separate realm from the economy with which political economy is concerned makes it impossible to adequately understand the processes through which signification is capitalized, while the political economy *of communication* should be fundamentally concerned with those processes. Peck (2006, 94) argues that non-dialectical thinking is the reason culture and the economy are treated as "distinct areas of human existence" by both political economy and cultural studies rather than as terms for aspects of the social world and social practice. Smythe (1977) created an opening for the political economy of communication to see how audience activities are actually key to understanding communication industries with his theory of the audience commodity. While I argue the audience commodity does not accurately explain the role of audiences in the capitalization of communication – the treatment of communication processes as processes of capital circulation and accumulation – Smythe's concept of audience *labour* provides a productive but as yet unexplored path forward. A dialectical method of theorizing is the means by which the concept of audience labour can provide a foundation for more adequately understanding communication as capital because it is the means by which signification is understood an aspect of the same "whole and connected social material process" (Williams 1977, 140, quoted in Peck 2006, 104) in which capital circulates.

Marx and a number of Western Marxists developed a historical and materialist dialectical method. By *historical materialist dialectical* method, I mean the use of human reason to produce knowledge of human existence by seeing it as a historical *process* within a material *reality*, thereby enabling an understanding of human social being as interrelated and contradictory as it actually is. Such reason is dialectical in that it is "knowledge and comprehension of man by man" (Sartre 2004, 823) in which knowledge and the known, the subject and the object, are dialectically related. Dialectical reason, then, contrasts most clearly with analytical reason, by which knowledge is produced by separating reality into distinct parts. Such reason cannot grasp the whole of human existence because it sees fundamental separations as existing in reality (e.g., "culture" and "economy," "society" and "nature," "mental" and "material"), or, even more fundamentally, asserts an unbridgeable separation of subjective knowledge and objective existence (e.g., Kant 2009). While, as Hegel (1977, 11) said of the knowledge produced by dialectical reason, "the True is the whole." For Marx, human existence is both individual and social, differentiated and unified, so any real knowledge of it must be able to see it in that dialectical sense. A dialectical method as employed by Marx (1990, 103) is "critical and revolutionary" because it is a means to produce consciousness of the social reality of which every individual is a part but which, as a social reality, is thereby a *social* product. The dialectical method of reasoning is the means by which Marx produced his own critical thought. It is that dialectical method that is the critical foundation of Marx's critical theory, thus I define "critical theory" specifically as theory produced by means of a historical materialist dialectical method, which I also refer to here as a critical or Marxist dialectical method.

I do not claim that there is only a subjective, epistemological dialectic – that there is only a dialectical *method* – and not an objective, ontological dialectic. The method of knowing existence and existence itself cannot be separated in that way if knowledge is to reflect reality ("[T]he dialectic is both a method *and* a movement in the object" (Sartre 2004, 20)). The question I raise in this chapter is the nature of the method of the critical political economy of communication, an issue within media and cultural studies, not philosophy, thus I do not deal with the dialectic itself. My answer to the question of method is the Marxist dialectical method. Because that critical dialectical method is the critical foundation of Marx's work, it is necessary for political economists who wish to be similarly *critical* to be self-conscious of their *method* of theorizing as much as they are self-conscious of their political-economic theory and its concepts so that those concepts, and even the theory itself, do not become static but instead remain perpetually critical. This chapter is intended to contribute to a consideration of the critical dialectical method of theorizing as it is relevant to the critical political economy of communication.

My goal in this chapter is to make the issue of method a central concern of critical political economy and to demonstrate some of the potential of the historical materialist dialectical method in relation to understanding the processes by which communication is treated as capital. First, I discuss the critical political economy of communication as it has been defined by those who have had a significant role in its development in the late-20th and early-21st centuries. Method in the sense that I define it above does not seem to have played a significant role in defining the critical nature of that political-economic theory, although I note two scholars who have dealt with the critical dialectical method of theorizing culture and communication: Dan Schiller and Christian Fuchs. Second, I examine the role of dialectical method in the work of Marx. I argue Marx's historical and materialist dialectical *method* is at least as important for the critical political economy of communication as the specifics of his political-economic theory. Third, I consider the development of the historical materialist dialectical method in the 20th century by Western Marxists who did not attempt to use it as a method of political-economic theorizing but instead as a method of theorizing culture and consciousness. I argue their use of dialectical reasoning to critically understand culture and consciousness is a crucial link between Marx's political economy and the critical political economy of communication. Finally, I connect the Marxist dialectical method to the critical political economy of communication by considering how it enables insights into the capitalization of communication, and particularly signification.

2   Critical Political Economy of Communication:
      The Problem of Method

Beginning in the 1970s, a number of scholars contributed to the conscious development of a political economy focused on communication, culture, media, and information. In addition to distinguishing their "political economy" from the dominant neo-classical "economics," those scholars generally defined their approach as "critical." A brief intellectual history of those definitions over more than four decades makes clear the unifying characteristics of that critical political economy. I group them all under the label critical political economy of "communication," although others consider the more appropriate overarching label to be "culture," "media," or "information." While the continuous efforts to clarify, define, and critique the precise nature of the critical political economy of communication is one of its most productive features – enabling it to follow actual historical change – its *method* does not seem to have received the same attention. Schiller (1996) and Fuchs (2011b) are two exceptions. I argue for an engagement with method that is as continuous and widespread as consideration of the theoretical categories and concepts has been.

When "method" has been specifically discussed, it has tended to be *techniques* of analytical reasoning rather than method in the more fundamental sense of self-conscious critique and declaration of the way in which the human capacity to reason is used to produce "knowledge." In the tradition of Enlightenment thinking, that is what Marx meant by "method," whether discussing his method or that of other political economists or philosophers, and it seems to be equally important for critical political economists of culture to deal with the question of method. Importantly, Marx (1990, 102–103) identified his method with the dialectical method of Hegel, which he claims to have modified to make it "critical and revolutionary." By "method," then, I am referring to what can be considered questions of "philosophy," but I do not argue that all critical political economists of culture must also be philosophers; rather, it is simply necessary to engage with the work of those who have considered what specifically makes for a "critical" method. Discussions of dialectical method by Marx and Western Marxists are a necessary methodological foundation for a critical political economy of communication. I do not find much evidence of such methodological consideration in the definitions of the critical political economy of communication, and I claim that has had and continues to have important implications for the theory itself. In particular, the signifying activities of consumers of culture have yet to be systematically incorporated as a fundamental aspect of the capitalization of communication.

There have been numerous definitions of the critical political economy of communication offered over the last four decades. Murdock and Golding (1973, 205) define the "political economy of mass communications" as an understanding of the "basic features" that "underpin and shape the economic context and political consequences of mass communications." They argue it is necessary to see mass media organizations as "first and foremost" profit-based businesses producing commodities. Media businesses are just like every other capitalist business. But, they are also quite distinct from other industries because of the nature of the commodities they produce: Their products are also ideas objectified into "cultural" products (e.g., television shows, news stories, music). That dual nature of cultural products – they are both "commodities" and "ideas" – is a theme present in all definitions of critical political economy of communication. For Murdock and Golding, the most important task of a political-economic theory is to clarify concretely and specifically how "ideology" is produced (207) by articulating "the general and systematic constraints" generated by media industries' production of culture as a commodity (223). The culture produced is limited by its commodity nature, which creates a general "ideological" effect of reinforcing the status quo (226–227). The political economy of "media" is an analysis of the way capitalist power relations are legitimated (232). While Murdock and Golding outline basic theoretical aspects and the recent history that makes such a theory necessary, the issue of method is not addressed.

Garnham's (2006/1986) statement remains an essential foundation of a critical political economy of communication. However, it is primarily a discussion of specific *theoretical* issues, with the dialectical method itself only implicit, although strongly so. Because he stops short of such direct methodological consideration, Garnham fails to completely reject vulgar materialism. While Garnham insightfully critiques exactly the aspects of Marxist theory that must be addressed by a critical political economy of communication (base/superstructure, the means of mental production, ideology, the production of culture), he does not fully resolve the issues he highlights. He relies on a partially reified concept of "the economic" and his political economy of communication is thus also partially reified: Culture can be understood by understanding its historically specific "economic" production. Signification is completely eliminated from consideration. "The economic," is then an "evasion" (Williams 1977, 93; Garnham 2006/1986, 207). Ultimately, Garnham's position is insightful but contradictory, which is what makes his essay a necessary and useful starting point for a critical political economy of communication.

In critiquing Garnham on those grounds, it might seem as though I am questioning the entire premise of a political economy of communication, but my goal is just the opposite: By arguing that political-economic theory can nei-ther exclude human activity related to "meaning-making," "consciousness," "ideology," or "subjectivity," nor consider it something that is understood once "class" and "capital accumulation" are critically theorized (Garnham 2006/1986, 203), I am attempting to expand the terrain of political economy. It seems that the production of culture, as an objective signifying process, has been incorpo-rated in a way that avoids a reductionist "reflection" theory – and that is pre-cisely one contribution of the critical political economy of *communication* to critical political economy in general – but the subjective signifying process, as an aspect of the production of consciousness, remains mostly outside politi-cal economy even though consciousness was the first thing Marx (1978d) attempted to show was materially produced.

In one example of the contradictions of the essay, Garnham (2006/1986, 206) actually articulates that precise issue: "[W]e could say that the purpose of a political economy of culture is to elucidate what Marx and Engels meant in *The German Ideology* by 'control of the means of mental production.'" But Garnham's critique of Williams reveals a refusal to fully deal with the implica-tions for critical political economy of "control of the means of mental produc-tion": It must also be a critical political economy of *signification*, dealing directly with the problem of "ideology" by means of its own critical method. Again, Garnham is clear in his assertion of the need to see cultural production as the production of commodities and ideas, but the full significance of that production of ideas, which Murdock and Golding (1973, 206) also highlight as the aspect of real importance in cultural production, is left unaddressed: Consumers of culture also actively *produce* ideas.

While Williams (1977; 1980a; 1980b) pushes for the elimination of all reified methods of theorizing social production by incorporating what he saw as the last significant barrier – culture as *material* production – Garnham (2006/1986, 207) pushes back by way of historical specificity and a distinction between "the economic" and "the material." He mistakenly finds Williams to be ignoring the specificity of capitalist production and counters with a reified "economic per-spective," while missing the significance of Williams' critique of the *method* of theorizing. Williams (1977; 1980a; 1980b) demonstrates that, if the concepts and categories of political economy are to remain critical, and if Marxist theory is to remain a critical theory of the social production of human life itself (Marx 1978a, 4), the concepts and method of Marx's theorizing must also be used to theorize the production of culture. In contrast to that, Garnham (2006/1986, 208) makes what is perhaps his most problematic claim: the distinction between "social form" and "cultural form," between which there is "an essential divide." He concludes with the claim that culture and consciousness are not material until "they are translated into social forms." The production of consciousness, and its relationship to culture, is thereby banished from the political economy of communication.

Smythe provides the means to reclaim for the critical political economy of communication the space abandoned by Garnham, although Smythe also fails to fully overcome the problems he identifies. Smythe (1977) focuses attention precisely on the production of consciousness by means of the critical dialectical method of Marx. He does not stop at consideration of production by the culture industries but also theorizes audiences as producers rather than consumers. For Smythe, "control of the means of mental production" is in the hands of the "consciousness industry." Members of the audience are forced to work for advertisers, who buy audience labour-power from media companies. Importantly, however, by Smythe's method of theorizing individuals are seen to labour in the production of their own consciousness (and the whole process is seen as social). Smythe does not fully develop his insight, but he provides the basis for a further development. He directly addresses the necessity of a dialectical method: "[T]he way to a Marxist theory of how ideology is produced by monopoly capitalism is to use an historical, materialist, dialectical method always seeking the reality of class struggle" (Smythe 1978, 126).

The primary theoretical aspects outlined in the late 1970s have remained the foundation of the critical political economy of communication. Jhally (1989, 66) describes it is a theory of "the economic context of…mass-mediated culture," or what are called "the cultural industries." Like Murdock and Golding, Garnham, and Smythe, Jhally emphasizes the importance of the dual nature of cultural production as commodity production – it produces both commodities for exchange on the market and objects with cultural meaning – and the necessity for the critical political economy of communication to account for both. Jhally insightfully claims the Frankfurt School (particularly in "The Culture Industry" (Horkheimer and Adorno 2002)) is one half of a critical political economy of communication, alongside those more typically identified as political economists (e.g., the scholars discussed in this section). However, Jhally's (1989, 80) claim that the exchange-value of cultural commodities dominates the use-value is indicative of the need to further expand the theoretical scope by reconsidering the method of theorizing: While the claim seems to be a simple statement of fact about commodities in a capitalist society, it enables political economists to ignore the use-value, or "meaning," of cultural commodities. The production of culture is thus only partially grasped, since "meaning" is central to the process, and audience signification is again pushed aside as something that can only be understood by other means of theorizing.

More recent definitions of the primary aspects of the critical political economy of communication also echo the earlier definitions (e.g., Garnham 2011; Meehan, Mosco, and Wasko 1993; Mosco 2009; Wasko, Murdock, and Sousa 2011). Meehan, Mosco, and Wasko's (1993, 113) discussion of "method" is telling: It makes no reference to the dialectical method of reasoning while claiming use of what it describes as the "*analytical*" methods of sociology, history, and political economy, including Marx. It is clear the significance and specifics of Marx's dialectical method have been missed. Meehan, Mosco, and Wasko are indeed correct that "a reassessment of method" is necessary (115). In a wide-ranging survey of the specifics of the critical political economy of communication, Mosco (2009) fills in the details of how scholars have theorized communication, culture, media, and information by the general approach first outlined in the 1970s. However, his relatively brief discussion of the "philosophical foundation" of the theory does not address the dialectical method, and his description of the "critical" epistemology of the theory is telling: Critical is understood in relation to other, presumably uncritical, theories that also have different values (10), rather than the method of reasoning that Marx considers the critical foundation of his political economy. Wasko, Murdock, and Sousa (2011, 1–2) define the "critical" aspect of critical political economy similarly – that is, by virtue of the content of the theory rather than the method of theorization. Garnham (2011, 42) has recently criticized the field for remaining "stuck with a set of problems and terms of analysis that history has simply passed by," "a tired and narrow orthodoxy." While that critique points directly to problems of method, Garnham instead limits his critique to the concepts and contents of the theory itself.

Calabrese (2004, 2) agrees with the defining characteristics of a critical political economy of communication outlined by the authors already noted, but he also urges precisely the theoretical development toward which this chapter is intended to contribute: a deeper engagement with "*the production and circulation of meaning*" (ibid., 9). He also specifically cites the dialectical method of theorizing as the key to that development (ibid., 9–10). In one sense, then, this chapter is a contribution further "toward a political economy of culture," a contribution in which the dialectical method is the primary focus.

Two scholars in the field of critical political economy of communication who have dealt with the question of method are Fuchs (2011b) and Schiller (1996). As their considerations of method seem to be exceptions within the field, I highlight them as a necessary starting point for the development of the theory. Fuchs (2011b, 97) defines a "critical" theory of communication and media similarly to the critical political economists discussed above: "the analysis of media, communication and culture in the context of domination,

asymmetrical power relations, exploitation, oppression and control."
Importantly, he also specifically insists that "dialectical philosophy" is essential
for critical theory in general (ibid., 3–71) and critical media and information
studies as an aspect of critical theory (ibid., 112–121). In developing the latter
point, Fuchs concentrates on media as technology of communication and thus
specifically elaborates on how the critical dialectical method is a means to produce a "complex technology assessment" (ibid., 112) and to see the dialectical
relationship between media and society. My focus is on meaning, so I want to
expand on his discussion by demonstrating the method is useful beyond the
avoidance of technological determinism (either optimistic or pessimistic).

Schiller (1996) emphasizes Williams' discussions of the critical method of
theorizing culture and communication as essential to what he considers a necessary development of a "unified conceptual framework" for theorizing communication. Schiller calls for a framework unified around the concept of
"labour" so that human communication can be understood as an active human
process but one that is not separate from other aspects of human social existence. He argues against what he considers to be the theoretical reification of
"intellectual labour" as something distinct from "manual labour." While the
"dialectical method" is not Schiller's explicit focus, he clearly promotes that
critical method of theorizing.

3   Marx's Dialectical Method: Historical, Materialist, Critical, Revolutionary

Lukács (1971) argues that method is the essence of Marxism. To be "Marxist,"
then, is to follow Marx's method rather than to take what he wrote about a
capitalist system of production as a definitive, absolute statement. Political
economy, then, must be produced by that dialectical method if it is to be similarly critical and revolutionary. The Western Marxists who have explicitly
engaged with the dialectical method, however, have not been those working in
the area of political economy; they have been those Marxists who went back to
the question of method as a way to figure out how to be Marxist without being
economistic. The critical political economy of communication that later developed in relation to Western Marxism re-emphasized the importance of the
categories of Marxist political economy for understanding communication
and culture but seems to have done so by reiterating Marx's political economy
without also engaging with the method that produced it.

Marx (1990, 103) considers his critique of political economy "critical
and revolutionary" by virtue of his dialectical method. It is a critical and

revolutionary method because it is not a means to producing thinking that celebrates existing society but is rather a means to produce consciousness of society as a product of human action that is thus historical rather than eternal, and that is thus transformable. The dialectical method, and the theory produced by it, is critical and revolutionary in terms of the consciousness it is a means to produce. For Marx and Marxists, such critical knowledge of society is a necessary means for the social production of a society of freedom and equality. Marx's dialectical method is the foundation of his critique of classical political economy, through which he simultaneously produces his own critical, revolutionary political economy. It enables him to produce knowledge of capitalist society by seeing that society as the product of a social *process* of production, and to see the nature of that process itself. "Society" is a product, and Marx's critical political economy is a means by which the producers can become conscious of their production; Marx's dialectical method is the means by which he produces that critical political economy:

> In its rational form, [the dialectic] is a scandal and an abomination to the bourgeoisie and its doctrinaire spokesmen, because it includes in its positive understanding of what exists a simultaneous recognition of its negation, its inevitable destruction; because it regards every historically developed form as being in a fluid state, in motion, and therefore grasps the transient aspect as well; and because it does not let itself be impressed by anything, being in its very essence critical and revolutionary.
>
> MARX 1990, 103

In a number of his works, Marx critiques the method – the use of reason – of others. It is possible to define Marx's critical, revolutionary dialectical method without seeing it as a specific method for political economy but instead as a means of using human reason in a particular way that can produce knowledge of the world as it is. In Volume I of *Capital*, Marx (1990) describes what he considers to be the difference between his "materialist" dialectical method and that of Hegel:

> My dialectical method is, in its foundations, not only different from the Hegelian, but exactly opposite to it. For Hegel, the process of thinking, which he even transforms into an independent subject, under the name of "the Idea," is the creator of the real world, and the real world is only the external appearance of the idea. With me the reverse is true: the ideal is nothing but the material world reflected in the mind of man, and translated into forms of thought. (102)

Marx thereby attempts to establish the materialist basis of his dialectical method: An understanding of the "material" world *of* humans is the means by which to understand human social existence. The "material" world is, for Marx, the product of human activity but the relationship is dialectical: "circumstances make men just as much as men make circumstances" (Marx, 1978d, 165). Marx (1978b) says a *"true materialism"* that is a *"real science"* is one in which the basic principle is "the social relationship 'of man to man,'" (108). Marx (1978c) also says a critical, revolutionary materialism conceives reality as *"human sensuous activity, practice"* (143). That materialist method is a dialectical method that sees humans as the ones "who change circumstances," although they are then also "products of circumstances" (144). Human "essence," the essence of human existence, is not an individual quality; it is social: It is "the ensemble of the social relations" (145). "Social life is essentially *practical*"; understanding "human practice" in the material world is the method by which to understand social life (145).

Marx (1978b), critiques the method of classical political economy as being, essentially, uncritical and counter-revolutionary in part because it is ahistorical. It is a method of producing a consciousness of society that does not see it as fundamentally human-produced and, therefore, does not see it as something that can be changed, certainly not something that should be changed. The consciousness produced is one in which existing society – the essence of it, at least – is understood as natural and eternal. Through that consciousness, human activity *reproduces* existing society. By virtue of that method of reasoning, political economy inherently sides with the interests of capitalists. That is evident in the categories of classical political economy, which Marx (1973, 104) claims are "fixed, immutable, eternal categories" that are supposed to represent eternal relations of production. Thus, classical political economists produce an understanding of bourgeois institutions as natural institutions. "In this they resemble the theologians, who likewise establish two kinds of religion. Every religion which is not theirs is an invention of men, while their own is an emanation from God" (120–121). For political economists, present-day relations "are themselves natural laws independent of the influence of time. They are eternal laws that must always govern society. *Thus there has been history, but there is no longer any*" (121, emphasis added). In contrast, Marx (1973, 106, emphasis added) says, "[a]ll that exists, all that lives on land and under water, exists and lives only by some kind of *movement*. Thus the movement of history produces social relations." Economic categories are ideas produced by humans; they are *"historical and transitory products"* (110).

In *The German Ideology*, Marx (1978d) defines the fundamental premises of his method: actual human history, meaning human material social being, or human life, as it is comprehensible to humans. Thus the first premise is "the existence of living human individuals" (149):

> The premises from which we begin are not arbitrary ones, not dogmas, but *real premises* from which abstraction can only be made in the imagination. They are the real individuals, their activity and the material conditions under which they live, both those they find already existing and those produced by their activity (149).

Marx re-emphasizes the premises of his method a number of times (154, 155), so it should be clear that the human social process of production that *is* human life is the foundation of his means of using human reason to understand what is in fact a social totality. It is precisely because that totality is in fact a constantly moving social *process* of human material activity that Marx asserts it is possible for humans to have knowledge of it.

While Marx's (1978a) statements about "structure" and "superstructure" in the Preface to *A Contribution to the Critique of Political Economy* can and have been interpreted as his declaration of the greater importance of the economic "base," they can be understood differently if they are placed in the context of what, in the crucial paragraph, he *twice* says is the thing in which he is most interested: humans producing their own lives.

> In the social production of their life, men enter into definite relations that are indispensable and independent of their will, relations of production which correspond to a definite state of development of their material productive forces. The sum total of these relations of production constitutes the economic structure of society, the real foundation, on which rises a legal and political superstructure and to which correspond definite forms of social consciousness. The mode of production of material life conditions the social, political and intellectual life process in general. It is not the consciousness of men that determines their being, but, on the contrary, their social being that determines their consciousness (4).

I will restrict my comments on that dense statement to a few key points. The "social production" of human life is the crucial concept to grasp in order to see the critical and revolutionary extent of Marx's method. It is not an economic determinism. It is a means to know real human social life. To say social being determines social consciousness is not to say that "the economy" determines everything else; "the economy" is an abstraction that is not inherently critical, while Marx uses "the economic structure of society" as a critical concept to describe something concrete: the social and material conditions in which human existence is produced. That perspective on the "social production" of human life should make clear why, for Marx, political economy was a useful means of producing his own consciousness of that social production: Political economy is the theory of material production. Developing that theory with a critical, revolutionary method – a historical materialist dialectical method – makes it a critical, revolutionary theory, and one that is knowledge of *all* human production, or all human life, not just "economic" production.

4   Western Marxism: Developing a Critical, Revolutionary,
         Dialectical Method

Marx's historical materialist dialectical method was further developed by a number of Western Marxists in reaction to the "Marxism" of the Soviet Union, in which the dialectic became a law of nature rather than a human capacity to reason. A re-emphasis on the dialectical method was a means to make Marxist theory critical rather than reified. The Western Marxists I consider – Lukács, Marcuse, Horkheimer, Lefebvre, Sartre, and Williams – did not attempt to produce a method for political economy but instead contributed to the on-going production of a critical theory of society to demonstrate that the Marxist method is not an economistic or reductionist means of dealing with the aspects of human life that have (problematically) been considered part of the "superstructure" that "reflects" or is "determined" by the material "base." Lukács, Marcuse, Horkheimer, Lefebvre, and Williams all reiterate the historical materialism of Marx's dialectical method; Sartre develops that method itself. A Marxist political economy of communication must necessarily deal with that problem within Marxism, therefore it must deal explicitly with questions of method.

    Lukács (1971) outlines the basic critical method of theorizing in the Marxist sense. Important to such a critical theory is a "process of abstraction" (6), but that does not mean the theory is divorced from real human history. On the contrary, the method of critical theory is to abstract *from* history. There is, thus, a dialectical relationship between theory and history within the method. In the case of a critical theory, actual history is the specific source for abstraction. By that method, critical theory moves beyond the "real existence" of facts to their "inner core" (8). At the heart of a dialectical method of theorizing is "the simultaneous recognition and transcendence of immediate appearances" (8). By seeing "the isolated facts of social life as aspects of the historical process" and integrating them "in a totality," critical theory becomes a way to turn "knowledge of the facts" into "knowledge of *reality*" (8). Theory, as "knowledge of the whole" (Lukács 1971, 10; an indication of the importance of Hegel (1977, 11) for the Marxist dialectical method), is a "dialectical conception of totality" that makes it possible "to understand reality as a social process" (13). It is consciousness *of* existence, a necessary aspect of a conscious existence that is capable of producing a different reality. By that critical and revolutionary method, critical theory is also a theory of social change:

> Only when the core of existence stands revealed as a social process can existence be seen as the product, albeit the hitherto unconscious product, of human activity. This activity will be seen in its turn as the element crucial for the transformation of existence (19).

Marcuse (1976) defines the Marxist dialectical method similarly, as the means to reveal existence as a social process so that it can be consciously transformed. By virtue of the method used, the theory produced is "a practical one; praxis does not only come at the end but is already present in the beginning of the theory" (Marcuse 1973, 5). It is a critical, revolutionary theory because it is knowledge that informs real action. Because being is dialectical, it "can only be grasped dialectically" (Marcuse 1976, 16). Humans can understand themselves and the world they create – the social process in its totality – as historical and dialectical because that social totality *is* historical and dialectical. That social process is human history itself, and it is that material social process for which the method is a means of producing consciousness. "Only because and insofar as the real is historical, it is dialectical; the real can and must be understood through the dialectical method" (19).

What Horkheimer (1972) labels "critical theory" is produced by that same historical materialist dialectical method. It is the method of theorizing that Horkheimer attempts to show differentiates a "critical" theory from a "traditional" theory. In fact, Horkheimer's definitive essay might be more aptly titled, "Traditional and Critical *Method.*" A Marxist theory is a critical theory produced by means of a critical method. A critical dialectical method demands critical *theorizing*, not static theory. The traditional method of theorizing, on the other hand, produces a theory that is *uncritical* consciousness of the reality of social being. For traditional theory the basic requirement is "harmony": "all the parts should intermesh thoroughly and without friction" and there should be no contradictions (190). In the traditional method, theory and history are separated. "There is always, on the one hand, the conceptually formulated knowledge and, on the other, the facts to be subsumed under it," and that method of subsumption is called "theoretical explanation" (193). Traditional theory is a theory of the status quo. The reproduction of existing society necessitates uncritical consciousness. Critical theory is inherently a theory of social change: It sees society as a material social process of production by means of its historical materialist dialectical method. It is consciousness that is critical and revolutionary because it can envision "the rational state of society," "a future society as a community of free men" (216–217).

Lefebvre also reiterates the critical and revolutionary aspect of the historical materialist dialectical method. Against the method of "dogmatic," simplified, and "economistic" Stalinist Marxism, Lefebvre (2009) defines a "dialectical" form of materialism that is produced by a critical, revolutionary method. Lefebvre's *Dialectical Materialism* is a critique of Stalinist "dialectical materialism" as a philosophy of Nature, with "the laws of the dialectic" as "the laws of Nature" (1–3). Lefebvre's dialectical materialism can be defined negatively as "opposed to those doctrines which limit human existence, either from without or within, by subordinating it to some external existence or else by reducing it to a one-sided element or partial experience seen as being privileged and definitive" (98). In particular, Lefebvre wants to reinstate "alienation" as a foundational concept, in opposition to the method of dogmatic Marxism that rejects or de-emphasizes it (4). For Lefebvre, the *historical materialist* dialectical method is a means to produce critical, revolutionary consciousness of "the dialectical movements within the human and social reality" (5).

> Dialectical materialism's aim is nothing less than the rational expression of the Praxis, of the actual content of life – and, correlatively, the transformation of the present Praxis into a social practice that is conscious, coherent and free. Its theoretical aim and its practical aim – knowledge and creative action – cannot be separated.
>
> LEFEBVRE, 2009, 100

Like Lefebvre, Sartre attempts to counter a "Marxism" that is produced by non-dialectical reason. Sartre's *Search for a Method* and *Critique of Dialectical Reason* develop the Marxist dialectical method itself. For Sartre (1968), philosophy is method (5); it is "a method of investigation and explication" (5) to produce consciousness. Soviet "Marxism" separates theory and practice into "pure, fixed knowledge" and "empiricism without principles" (22). "[I]t has ceased to live with history" (29). What Sartre (2004, 27) calls "external," "transcendental," or "universal" dialectical materialism is a method of seeing human history as simply an aspect of natural history. For Sartre, that method provides no foundation for the possibility of the truth of human knowledge since the movement of history is in nature, outside of human influence. Instead, Sartre insists, the dialectical method must be historical materialism, in which to live and to know are the same (thinking is "a particular form of human activity") but being is irreducible to thought (25, 33). "Knowledge" is itself historical (Sartre 1968, 4), thus, it is socially and materially produced; it is a process of "knowing" (4). The method of "knowing" must also be historical and material: It must be critically dialectical. For Sartre, that is a historical materialist dialectical method that is a "regressive-progressive and analytic-synthetic method" (148), a "heuristic" method that "teaches us something new because it is at once both regressive and progressive" (133). The product is critical, revolutionary consciousness, which makes the method "a social and political weapon" (5).

Although Williams also reiterates Marx's historical materialist dialectical method, he also brings the theoretical discussion back to communication and culture. As with the other Western Marxists discussed in this section, Williams attempts to demonstrate that Marxism is not a theory of mechanical materialism or economic determinism or reductionism. In *Marxism and Literature*, Williams (1977) insists on understanding communication, culture, and consciousness as materially and socially produced. Underlying the dialectical method for Williams is what he describes as an indissoluble, continuous, material social process. That indissoluble process is the unity of different individual human activities, and all such human activities are material. Williams draws on what is a similarly fundamental concept for Marx (1978b; 1978c; 1978d): human material social activity, or labour.

Williams (1977) specifically questions the usefulness of the concept of "ideology." He recognizes its use by Marx as an effort to push for a dialectical method by critiquing attempts to separate and prioritize "consciousness" or "ideas." Williams argues that Marx sees consciousness "from the beginning as part of the human material social process, and its products in 'ideas' are then as much part of this process as material products themselves" (59–60). The human material social process is an "indissoluble process" that includes consciousness and thought (61). Williams says the concept of "ideology" might be insufficient for the redefinition of the products and processes of social signification that is necessary to reinvigorate Marxist cultural theory (71), and the use of the concept within critical political economy in a way that displaces the subjective signifying process suggests he is correct.

As Williams makes clear, the problem for a critical dialectical method is precisely how to distinguish aspects of what is actually a whole, continuous social process in order to gain knowledge of that process. The Western Marxists considered here have produced complementary answers to that question. Williams makes his own significant contribution in a way that is directly useful for a critical, revolutionary political economy of communication: The method must be to understand *all* human activity as material production. Williams (1977) critiques the non-dialectical Marxism that divides the whole social process into material production and mental labour/consciousness/thought/culture, a method that he says results in a position that seems "too materialist," or materialist in a vulgar sense, but is actually not materialist enough (90–92). That form of materialism fails "to understand the material character of the production of a cultural order" (93). To overcome that failure, Williams says, it is necessary "to look at our actual productive activities without assuming in advance that only some of them are material" (94). It is in the precise spirit of that statement that a critical political economy of communication that accounts for signification can be developed by means of a dialectical method.

One development within Western Marxism that represents a major alternative to the historical materialist dialectical method I explore and advocate in this chapter is the Italian or autonomist tradition of Marxism. Specifically, the autonomist concept of "immaterial labour" (e.g., Lazzarato 1996) is a theoretical challenge to what I claim is the necessary development of a critical political economy of communication that accounts for subjective signification processes. In one sense, the autonomist method of theorizing immaterial labour is a direct challenge to Williams' "cultural materialism," which I cite as particularly useful for the critical political economy of communication. The autonomist method appears to be neither fully dialectical nor fully materialist, since its foundation is that "immaterial" activity is *now* a basic aspect of human life because of technological change (Terranova 2009). Culture and consciousness are essentially distinct from "material" processes and, thus, cannot be understood by the historical materialist dialectical method. A "non-economic critique of political economy" is now necessary because value "is increasingly becoming social and subjective" (Terranova 2009). The autonomist social factory thesis is that social relations produce economic value (Terranova 2009). While I agree with the need to develop a theory of the subjective and the cultural – I push critical political economy toward subjective signification – the autonomist method that makes culture and consciousness only *now* theoretical objects is problematic. The historical materialist dialectical method provides a means to see the production of both culture and consciousness as productive human activities prior to the development of computer technologies. The concept of immaterial labour appears to be a product of exactly the reification of "intellectual" labour that Schiller (1996) critiques. Terranova (2000) is right to see "cultural" and "affective" activities as labour, and she argues for labour as the fundamental category (e.g., 40). She is also correct that we are all "knowledge workers" (42): Culture and consciousness are basic aspects of all human life. But in seeing such activities as *immaterial* labour, she relies on a method that prevents the totality of the social process that is human life from being understood as such. Work processes have not *now, abruptly* "shifted from the factory to society" (33); Work processes within a capitalist society have always entailed labour outside the strict confines of the factory and every other "workplace." That is particularly true in relation to the production of consciousness and the productive, signifying activities of consumers of culture.

5   Toward a Critical Political Economy of Capitalizing on Cultural
       Consumption and Signification: The Dialectical
       Method as Solution

A critical political economy that can explain communication as capital in theoretical terms must be concerned with the specificities of the way in which communication processes are turned into processes of capital circulation and accumulation. Following Marx's method of beginning from the premises of "real individuals, their activity and the material conditions under which they live" (Marx, 1978d, 149), we can then take up Williams' (1980a, 47) argument for theorizing the consumption of cultural objects as "an activity and a practice" of "active perception and interpretation." Analysis then entails discovering "the nature of a practice and then its conditions" (47). A historical materialist dialectical method of inquiry for the abstract, theoretical analysis that enables the construction of a political economy (Marx 1990, 90, 102) is a means of determining the conditions of practices of cultural consumption.

That method also entails an analysis of the dialectical relationship between the "singularity" of consumption and the "generality" of production (Marx 1993, 89; Harvey 2012) in capitalizing on communication. Although cultural consumption and subjective signification are singular processes for any individual, they are also general processes in that they are part of the "whole and connected social material process" (Williams 1977, 140) of human life. The most essential aspect of the capitalization of communication is the transformation of singular, subjective processes of cultural consumption and signification into processes subsumed under the general production of social life under conditions that enable the appropriation of value and accumulation of capital by one class. In theorizing that process of capitalization, I conceptualize the subjective processes of cultural consumption and signification as "audience labour" (Nixon, 2014). Capitalizing on communication requires the exploitation of audience labour. That exploitation is achieved by controlling the conditions of audience practices of consumption. The "particularity" of distribution

(Marx 1993, 89) is then also an important aspect of the method. Because audience labour is a singularity in which the product, subjective meaning, is not alienable from the signifying producer, audience labour-power cannot be commodified. Smythe's audience commodity thesis does not hold. But controlling the conditions of audience labour does enable the extraction of value through relations of distribution: rent and interest. The equivalent of a rent payment can be extracted directly from cultural consumers in exchange for access to (but not ownership of) the object of their consumption. The equivalent of an interest payment can be extracted from advertisers in exchange for borrowing partial control over the object of cultural consumption (Harvey 2006, 68–74, 255–260, 330–372, 266–270; Nixon, 2014).

That political economy also provides a means to gain insights into the real historical processes by which communication has been capitalized by controlling the conditions of cultural consumption. I consider that a history, not a political economy, although such historical work has long comprised a considerable amount of the scholarship characterized as "political economy" (e.g., McChesney 1993; 2004; Schiller 1999; 2007; Schiller 1989; 1992). None of that historical work has addressed the role of audience activities as exploited audience labour. Williams' (1980b) call for a "history of 'communicative production'" is a useful (and seemingly unexplored) starting point for this historical analysis. It seems we can identify a capitalist mode of *communicative* production with a long history that continues in relation to digital communicative production. The history of communication as capital has been a history of controlling the conditions of cultural consumption and signification – a history of audience labour exploitation. This is a history of "the culture industry" (Horkheimer and Adorno 2002). I will briefly consider this history by way of three examples of capitalizing on communication through the exploitation of audience labour.

The apparent origins of capitalizing on communication by controlling the conditions of cultural consumption are found in the creation of copyright. In Britain, there had long been a separation of cultural consumers from the means of consumption under the monopoly of the state licensing system in the 16th and 17th centuries (Bettig 1996, 17–22; Feather 2006, 26–27; Starr 2004, 28). The limitation on production created a limitation on consumption. During that time, the Stationers Company had a monopoly power to capitalize on that situation because its exclusively granted right to own a printing press (Blagden 1960, 21) gave it a monopoly power to extract rent payments in exchange for access to the meaning objectified and materialized in books. The conditions of capitalization were liberalized with the passage of the Statute of Anne in 1710 – the first "modern" copyright law. That parliamentary act created the legal conditions for transforming a monopoly system into a potentially competitive market, since the right to own culture became the right of anyone who could produce it, or, importantly, any publisher who could acquire that ownership right from the actual producer (i.e., author) (Bettig 1996, 23). The book publishing industry developed specifically under that liberalized power to control the conditions of cultural consumption and exploit the audience labour of reading by extracting payment from readers in exchange for access but not ownership, since copyright ensures that ownership remains with the copyright holder.

The commercialization of news in the U.S. in the 19th century is another example of the development of an industry that capitalizes on communication specifically through its ability to exploit audience labour. The newspaper industry's increasing reliance on advertising revenue (Baldasty 1992) was based on its control over the conditions of news consumption. Even without a copyright in news, newspaper capitalists controlled the conditions of news consumption by virtue of the materiality of that process: news could only be consumed in an objectified, material form, i.e., in print. That gave newspaper capitalists the power to extract payment in exchange for access to news and, thereby, directly exploit the audience labour of reading news. The commercialization of news was a significant further development of the capitalist mode of communicative production, as it was the creation of a second means of using control over the conditions of cultural consumption to extract value. Newspaper capitalists lent part of their control over the conditions of consumption to advertisers, by lending them part of the space in a newspaper, in exchange for what amounts to an interest payment. Newspaper capitalists maintained control and de facto ownership of the space in their newspapers, and at the end of the advertising process they owned that valuable space plus surplus-value in the form of interest. Since the payment is extracted from advertisers but based on control over audience activities, I refer to this as an indirect exploitation of audience labour. Advertisers, meanwhile, were specifically interested in the control over the conditions of the productive, signifying aspect of audience labour that they gained by borrowing space in a newspaper, because it was the only way they could affect the singular process of subjective meaning-making in the hope that the product of that process would be demand – or, a "consumer consciousness" (Smythe 1977, 1, 6).

Capitalizing on communication by controlling the conditions of cultural consumption and directly or indirectly exploiting audience labour is also a dominant aspect of communication as capital in the digital era. The recent work on digital labour (e.g., Andrejevic 2002; 2011; Fuchs 2010; 2011a) has not accounted for the digital labour of audiences and the exploitation of that labour, which is as fundamental to the capital accumulation strategies of "platform" industries as it is to "content" industries. Google capitalizes on communication through its control over the conditions of cultural consumption, such as the consumption of Web search results or videos on YouTube. It primarily does so by indirectly exploiting digital audience labour to generate advertising revenue. Google lends to advertisers part of the space next to search results or YouTube videos in return for a payment akin to interest. Advertisers gain power to affect the signifying activities of consumers of search results or videos by transforming part of the object of their consumption into an advertisement.

References

Andrejevic, Mark. 2002. The Work of Being Watched: Interactive Media and the Exploitation of Self-Disclosure. *Critical Studies in Media Communication* 19 (2): 230–248.

Andrejevic, Mark. 2011. Surveillance and Alienation in the Online Economy. Surveillance & Society 8 (3): 278–287.

Baldasty, Gerald J. 1992. *The Commercialization of News in the Nineteenth Century*. Madison, WI: The University of Wisconsin Press.

Bettig, Ronald V. 1996. *Copyrighting Culture: The Political Economy of Intellectual Property*. Boulder, CO: Westview Press.

Blagden, Cyprian. 1960. *The Stationers' Company: A History, 1404–1959*. Cambridge, MA: Harvard University Press.

Calabrese, Andrew. 2004. Toward a Political Economy of Culture. In *Toward a Political Economy of Culture: Capitalism and Communication in the Twenty-First Century*, edited by Andrew Calabrese and Colin Sparks, 1–12. Lanham: Rowman & Littlefield.

Feather, John. 2006. *A History of British Publishing* (2nd Ed). London, UK: Routledge.

Fuchs, Christian. 2010. Labor in Informational Capitalism and on the Internet. *The Information Society* 26 (3): 179–196.

Fuchs, Christian. 2011a. "Web 2.0, Prosumption, and Surveillance." *Surveillance & Society* 8 (3): 288–309.

Fuchs, Christian. 2011b. *Foundations of Critical Media and Information Studies*. London: Routledge.

Gandy, Oscar H., ed. 1995. "Colloquy." *Critical Studies in Mass Communication* 12 (1): 60–100.

Garnham, Nicholas. 2006/1986. Contribution to a Political Economy of Mass-Communication. In *Media and Cultural Studies: KeyWorks*, edited by Meenakshi Gigi Durham and Douglas M. Kellner, 201–229. Malden: Blackwell Publishing Ltd.

Garnham, Nicholas. 2011. The Political Economy of Communication Revisited. In *The Handbook of Political Economy of Communications*, edited by Janet Wasko, Graham Murdock, and Helena Sousa, 41–61. West Sussex: Blackwell Publishing Ltd.

Harvey, David. 2006. *The Limits to Capital*. London: Verso.

Harvey, David. 2012. History Versus Theory: A Commentary on Marx's Method in *Capital*. *Historical Materialism* 20 (2): 3–38.

Hegel, G.F.W. 1977. *Phenomenology of Spirit*. Translated by A. V. Miller. Oxford: Oxford University Press.

Horkheimer, Max. 1972. Traditional and Critical Theory. In *Critical Theory: Selected Essays*, 188–243. New York: Herder and Herder.

Horkheimer, Max and Theodor W. Adorno. 2002. The Culture Industry: Enlightenment as Mass Deception. In *Dialectic of Enlightenment: Philosophical Fragments*. Edited by Gunzelin Schmid Noerr. Translated by Edmund Jephcott. Stanford: Stanford University Press.

Jhally, Sut. 1989. The Political Economy of Culture. In *Cultural Politics in Contemporary America*, edited by Ian H. Augus and Sut Jhally, 65–81. New York: Routledge.

Kant, Immanuel. 2009. *Critique of Pure Reason*. Translated and Edited by Paul Guyer and Allen W. Wood. Cambridge: Cambridge University Press.

Lazzarato, Maurizio. 1996. Immaterial Labor. *In Radical Though in Italy: A Potential Politics*, edited by Paolo Virno and Michael Hardt, 133–147. Minneapolis: University of Minnesota Press.

Lefebvre, Henri. 2009. *Dialectical Materialism*. Translated by John Sturrock. Minneapolis: University of Minnesota Press.

Lukács, Georg. 1971. *History and Class Consciousness: Studies in Marxist Dialectics*. Translated by Rodney Livingstone. Cambridge: The MIT Press.

Marcuse, Herbert. 1973. The Foundation of Historical Materialism. In *Studies in Critical Philosophy*, 1–48. Translated by Joris de Bres. Boston: Beacon.

Marcuse, Herbert. 1976. On the Problem of the Dialectic. *Telos* 27: 12–39.

Marx, Karl. 1973. *The Poverty of Philosophy*. New York: International Publishers.

Marx, Karl. 1978a. Marx on the History of His Opinions. In *The Marx-Engels Reader* (2nd Ed), edited by Robert C. Tucker, 3–6. New York: W. W. Norton & Company, Inc.

Marx, Karl. 1978b. Economic and Philosophic Manuscripts of 1844. In *The Marx-Engels Reader* (2nd Ed), edited by Robert C. Tucker, 66–125. New York: W. W. Norton & Company, Inc.

Marx, Karl. 1978c. Theses on Feuerbach. In *The Marx-Engels Reader* (2nd Ed), edited by Robert C. Tucker, 143–145. New York: W. W. Norton & Company, Inc.

Marx, Karl. 1978d. The German Ideology: Part I. In *The Marx-Engels Reader* (2nd Ed), edited by Robert C. Tucker, 146–200. New York: W. W. Norton & Company, Inc.

Marx, K. 1990. *Capital: A Critique of Political Economy: Volume I*. London: Penguin.

Marx, Karl. 1993. Introduction. In *Grundrisse: Foundations of the Critique of Political Economy (Rough Draft)*, 81–111. Translated by Martin Nicolaus. London: Penguin.

McChesney, Robert W. 1993. *Telecommunications, Mass Media, and Democracy: The Battle for the Control of U.S. Broadcasting, 1928–1935*. New York: Oxford University Press.

McChesney, Robert W. 2004. *The Problem of the Media: U.S. Communication Politics in the Twenty-First Century*. New York: Monthly Review Press.

Meehan, Eileen R., Vincent Mosco, and Janet Wasko. 1993. Rethinking Political Economy: Change and Continuity. *Journal of Communication* 43 (4): 105–116.

Mosco, Vincent. 2009. *The Political Economy of Communication* (2nd Ed). Los Angeles: Sage.

Murdock, Graham and Peter Golding. 1973. For a Political Economy of Mass Communications. *Socialist Register* 10: 205–234. Accessed October 7, 2011. http://socialistregister.com/index.php/srv/article/view/5355/2256.

Nixon, Brice. 2014. Toward a Political Economy of 'Audience Labour' in the Digital Era. *tripleC: Communication, Capitalism & Critique* 12 (2): 713–734.

Peck, Janice. 2006. Why We Shouldn't Be Bored with the Political Economy Versus Cultural Studies Debate. *Cultural Critique* 64: 92–126.

Sartre, Jean-Paul. 1968. *Search for a Method*. Translated by Hazel E. Barnes. New York: Vintage Books.

Sartre, Jean-Paul. 2004. *Critique of Dialectical Reason: Volume I: Theory of Practical Ensembles*. Edited by Jonathan Reé. Translated by Alan Sheridan-Smith. London: Verso.

Schiller, Dan. 1996. *Theorizing Communication: A History*. New York: Oxford University Press.

Schiller, Dan. 1999. *Digital Capitalism: Networking the Global Market System*. Cambridge: The MIT Press.

Schiller, Dan. 2007. *How to Think About Information*. Urbana: University of Illinois Press.

Schiller, Herbert. 1989. *Culture, Inc.: The Corporate Takeover of Public Expression*. New York: Oxford University Press.

Schiller, Herbert. 1992. *Mass Communications and American Empire* (2nd Ed). Boulder: Westview Press.

Smythe, Dallas. 1977. Communications: Blindspot of Western Marxism. *Canadian Journal of Political and Social Theory* 1 (3): 1–27.

Smythe, Dallas. 1978. Rejoinder to Graham Murdock. *Canadian Journal of Political and Social Theory* 2 (2): 120–127.

Starr, Paul. 2004. *The Creation of the Media: Political Origins of Modern Communications*. New York, NY: Basic Books.

Terranova, Tiziana. 2000. Free Labor: Producing Culture for the Digital Economy. *Social Text* 63: 33–58.

Terranova, Tiziana. 2009. The Internet as Playground and Factory: Prelude Part III (speech). Accessed March 29, 2012. http://vimeo.com/6882379.

Wasko, Janet, Graham Murdock, and Helena Sousa. 2011. Introduction: The Political Economy of Communications: Core Concerns and Issues. In *The Handbook of Political Economy of Communications*, edited by Janet Wasko, Graham Murdock, and Helena Sousa, 1–10. West Sussex: Blackwell Publishing Ltd.

Williams, Raymond. 1977. *Marxism and Literature*. Oxford: Oxford University Press.

Williams, Raymond. 1980a. Base and Superstructure in Marxist Cultural Theory. In *Problems in Materialism and Culture*, 31–49. London: Verso.

Williams, Raymond. 1980b. Means of Communication as Means of Production. In *Problems in Materialism and Culture*, 50–63. London: Verso.

CHAPTER 10

"Feminism" as Ideology: Sarah Palin's Anti-feminist Feminism and Ideology Critique*

Michelle Rodino-Colocino

Introduction

This book explores the relevance of Karl Marx's works for Critical Media and Communication Studies, in general, and of Marxist concepts for investigating and intervening in struggles involving the production of knowledge and media content, in particular. The volume also attends to the significance of Marx during dangerous "end times" marked by climate crisis (Žižek 2010) and global capital that has grown "more concentrated and predatory than ever" (Eagleton 2011, 7). Capitalism appears to be in crisis, although given past economic and ecological disasters since Marx's day, it would be more accurate to describe such status as ongoing rather than novel in the twenty-first century. However, as Eagleton argues, the sharpening of capital's concentration, in addition to its adaptability and ruthlessness over the past three centuries, make Marxism all the more relevant for its trenchant critique of capitalism. Thus, for Marxists it is the worst of times (material reality is most fraught and life at risk) and therefore, the best of times for doing Marxist-informed critique.

We could say the same for feminism. In the wake of "post-feminism," the "sensibility" in news and entertainment media that recognizes the success of political struggle against sexist oppression only to dismiss it as passé, feminist media scholars find much to study in the endurance and ruthlessness of patriarchy (Gill 2007, McRobbie 2004, Vavrus 2002). Feminist analysis and political struggle, like that informed by Marxism is also precarious work (one hopes), as Eagleton (2011) points out.[1] Marxists hope to witness, if not bring about, an end to their object of study (capitalism), just as the teleology of feminism is

---

* I would like to thank editors Christian Fuchs and Vincent Mosco for their insightful comments on earlier drafts of this chapter. Thanks also to Dunja Antunovic for her excellent research assistance for this project.

[1] It is worth noting, however, that Eagleton's mention of feminists appears with little explanation, and thus, reads as a non sequitur in a book otherwise about Marx and Marxism: "If there are still Marxists or feminists around in twenty years' time, it will be a sorry project" (Eagleton 2011, 2).

patriarchy's downfall.[2] After all, more than two-thirds of the world's poor, illiterate, and refugees are female; women do the bulk of unpaid work at home and in the workforce, and poor and Third World women undertake the "caring work" (nannying, elder care, cleaning, and sex work) that make First World lifestyles possible (Ehrenreich and Hochschild, 2002). In the US, the most industrialized country with the highest income inequality, feminism appears under attack by the prospects of "postfeminist" media and culture and by right-wing female politicians who call themselves "feminist." Thus, in addition to bringing Marxism back, it is time to revive the project of a marxist-feminist partnership, but not necessarily a "marriage," a metaphor that suggests unequal power relations, as Lisa McLauglin (2002) points out and as Heidi Hartmann's (2010) seminal (and recently republished) essay makes clear.

The following analysis contributes to the revival of a healthy feminist Marxism and Marxist feminism by exploring the "feminism" of Sarah Palin. Palin declared herself a "feminist" in 2010 and, using a folksy, populist rhetorical style, articulated anti-feminist arguments and policy. At first glance, Palin's feminism may appear as trivial campaign discourse designed to appeal to right-wing women during the midterm elections. But Palin's brand of feminism shows the "crafty," "resourceful" nature of anti-feminism (and ultimately, of patriarchy) that Eagleton (2011, 8) locates in today's capitalism. As an anti-feminist discourse that revises history to claim authenticity, and therefore, legitimacy against a feminism that is allegedly outdated and wrongheaded, Palin's feminism complements postfeminism's contention that liberal and radical feminism is "so done" (Douglas 2010). Conservative Palinite feminism, in contrast, is part of a larger move of the right-wing anti-choice movement to reclaim feminism as theirs. During the US midterm elections of 2010, at least two prominent Senatorial candidates embraced feminism or were cast as feminists by the anti-choice political action committee, the SBA List (Susan B. Anthony List), which generates revised histories of first-wave feminism to support anti-choice candidates.

In addition to contributing to a fruitful partnership between feminism and Marxism generally, I also want to underscore something quite specific about Sarah Palin's "feminism" that is relevant to the work of critical media and communication scholars: Palinite feminism works ideologically in Marx's sense of the word. I stated as much in a recent analysis of political campaign discourse (Rodino-Colocino 2012), where I observed that Marx's conceptualization of ideology captures Palin's brand of feminism because it turns the meaning of feminist politics on its head and benefits elites who possess tremendous

---

2   For Armand Mattelart (1978), critical communication scholars should create conditions that put capitalism into crisis.

political-economic power. This observation is worth developing for several reasons.

First, studies that have applied Marxist ideology critique in communication and media studies have been fruitful. Nicholas Garnham (2000) argues, for example, that theories of the "information society," especially Manuel Castell's careful analysis of it, work "as an ideology" in ways that Marx and Engels describe, "to elicit uncritical assent to whatever dubious proposition is being put forward beneath its protective umbrella" (Garnham 2000, 140). Theories of the "information society," specifically, view "networks" (and primarily, the internet), rather than capitalism as primary organizer and driving force, and consequently, place undue and misplaced emphasis on technologies as resources that need to be "accessed" in order to boost productivity and individual wealth.[3] "Information society" theories, furthermore, exert political and economic power, and like ideology, have material effects. In the U.S., as elsewhere around the world, government agencies and private corporations have funded initiatives to move "information have-nots" to the "right" side of the "digital divide" (Sterne 2000, U.S. Department of Commerce 1995). Without addressing systemic problems, like structural unemployment, however, such efforts help reproduce "that monstrosity, an industrial reserve army," that as Marx explained, was "kept in misery in order to be always at the disposal of capital" (Marx 1867, 314).

Dana Cloud's (1998) *Control and Consolation in American Culture and Politics – Rhetoric of Therapy* draws on Marx and Engels' conceptualization of ideology to critique "therapeutic discourse" that serves as a source of consolation in the face of downsizing, outsourcing, and falling wages. Psychotherapy, since its popularization at the turn of the twentieth century, redirects workers' discontent, revolutionary thought, sentiment, and action inward, to self-improvement, personal responsibility, and adaptation. Such discourse blames individual workers and privatizes a key material, political-economic problem of capitalism: the drive to cut labour costs and boost profits for business owners. By substituting consolation for political and economic compensation, especially in the case of Gloria Steinem's feminist-therapeutic turn, "therapeutic discourse" consequently, "has become a commonplace diversion from political engagement in contemporary American society" (p. xi). Such "diversion" reinforces capitalism and other oppressive systems including patriarchy and white supremacy. Cloud's and Garnham's studies contribute to scholarship in communication and media studies that engage in analysis of Marx's primary texts on ideology (Cloud 2001, Fuchs 2009, 2010; Hall 1985, 1986; Larrain 1982),

---

3   Information and network technologies may also tap additional surplus value by dividing, deskilling, and speed up work, and, of course, are also products of such labor, sold as commodities.

consider the place of ideology critique in communication and media studies (Dorfman and Mattelart 1991; Garnham 1983; Golding and Murdock 1997; Goldman 1992; Kellner 1989, 1995; Mosco 1994; Murdock 1997; Smythe 1997), and more specifically, that argue that Marxist communication studies have focused too closely on ideology critique, to the exclusion of other moments in commodity production (Garnham 1979; Smythe 1997), comment on the Frankfurt School's ideology critique (Aune 1994, Schatz 2004), and expand on and apply Marx's conceptualization of ideology (Herman and Chomsky 1988; Ewen 1976; Mattelart 1991; Wernick 1991; White 1992; Williamson 1978).[4]

As fruitful as these studies are, however, misinterpretations of Marx's ideology have dampened its application in Critical Media and Communication Studies. Thus, a second reason to closely engage with Marx's and Engels' primary texts on ideology is to correct and revitalize Marxist ideology critique in the field. Stuart Hall's (1986) explanation of ideology, for example, misreads Marx and Engels' *The German Ideology* (which constitutes just one location in Marx's oeuvre that develops the concept) as arguing for "fixed correspondences" between class position and the ability to produce ideology. Hall mistakes Marx and Engel's brief discussion of "ruling ideas" for a conceptualization of ideology (Hall 1986, 31; also see Hall 1985, 97; and Larrain 1991). On the basis of this misreading, Hall calls for a conceptualization of ideology that allows for "no necessary correspondences" (1985, 94) and, more generally, for a "Marxism without guarantees" (Hall 1986) as the title of this seminal essay suggests.[5] Following this, Hall's reading of ideology informed work in critical media and communication studies (Grossberg 1986; Lewis 1992; Makus 1990). Thus, the concept of ideology needs to be polished and publicized as a tool for critical communication and media studies.

Finally, conducting a close analysis of Marx's "ideology" may suggest that rather than bring such a conceptualization "back," readers may determine that such critique has never quite left. Some scholars have engaged in Marx's ideology critique without recognizing it as such. As Christian Fuchs argues is the case with Dwayne Winseck's analysis of record industry rhetoric, "you are more into ideology critique than you think you are" (Fuchs and Winseck 2011, 262). I suspect that my own research would show that I was similarly "more into ideology critique" than I may have acknowledged. Thus, I hope the following chapter will inspire others to overtly embrace ideology critique of media and culture as Marx theorized and practiced.

---

4 Key Frankfurt School works the conduct ideology critique analyzed by critical media and communication scholars include Adorno (1997), Adorno and Horkheimer (1994) and Marcuse (1972).
5 Colin Sparks (1989) explains Hall's debt to Ernesto Laclau's *Politics and Ideology in Marxist Theory* (pp. 85–86).

Marx practiced ideology critique in two ways: intellectually and politically. What I mean by this is that Marx engaged in ideology critique of media, as his philosophical and journalistic writings show. Marx also meant to press criticism into action through practice ("praxis"). As Saul Padover's (1974) translation of Marx's essays on freedom of the press and censorship demonstrate, Marx's investigative journalism on poverty and the Prussian press' censorship of his analyses moved him more radically to the left, from a liberal democrat to a communist (Rothman 1975). For Marx, ideology critique and political activism were deeply interconnected. When Marx famously said, "Philosophers have only *interpreted* the world, in various ways; the point, however, is to *change* it" (Marx 1983, 158, emphasis in original), he meant to argue for the importance of the interrelationship between critique and political action. As Steve Macek (2006) explains, this aphorism highlights the importance of understanding capitalism, as means to inform political activism, which can also, in turn, inform critique of capitalism. Such insight, put into practice, guards against retreating into idealism thorough ideology critique, which Garnham (1983) cautiones against.

Because Marx's ideology critique promises intellectually and politically fruitful interventions, it is time to revive both the concept and method in Critical Media and Communication Studies. Or, borrowing from the Occupy Wall Street movement, it is time to "occupy ideology." Such occupation requires that we read Marx's (and Marx and Engels') writings that use the term "ideology" in addition to those that do not. A philosopher, historian, and journalist, Marx was a prolific writer. Thus, synthesizing Marx's oeuvre is not easily given to summary in one essay. Nevertheless, the following essay analyzes key texts from Marx's writings to explore his theorization of ideology. The point of this chapter is threefold: to describe the main tenets of Marx's theory of ideology by critically engaging in the work of Marx and Engels, to flesh out the claim that Palinite "feminism" works ideologically as Marx and Engels describe, and, consequently, to demonstrate that ideology critique is important intellectual work for feminist Marxist scholars. As I suggest in the conclusion, this is work that should inform scholars' political activism.

2   Marx's Conception of Ideology[6]

2.1   *"Ideology" in Marx's Early Writings*
Central to Marx's conceptualization of ideology is the notion of ***distortion***. But it is a specific kind of distortion that serves a particular function. In the early

---

6   See italicized, bolded items in Table 10.1, p. 298.

stages of his intellectual development (through 1844), Marx developed the idea of *inversion* that formed the foundation for his theory of ideology.[7] In *Critique of Hegel's Doctrine of the State* (written in 1843; Marx 1992), Marx borrows from Feuerbach to critique Hegel's theory of the state for taking for its subject an "abstract person" rather than foregrounding "the realization of the real, empirical person" (Marx 1992, 98). Hegel's conceptualization of the state, consequently, "does not proceed [as it should] from the real person to the state, but from the state to the real person" (ibid., 98). As Jorge Larrain (1991) argues, Marx faults Hegel with inverting reality on this point – in conceptualizing the state as an abstraction from which real people (as real subjects) emerge, rather than the other way around. What Marx calls "human activity" (i.e., human history, humans' making history), then, "necessarily appears as the activity and product of something other than itself" (Marx 1992, 98). Representing human activity and real human existence as products of an abstract "Idea," then, leads Hegel to "convert the subjective into the objective and the objective into the subjective with the inevitable result that an *empirical person* is *uncritically* enthroned as the real truth of the Idea" (ibid., 98f). This inversion, Marx argues, stem's from the philosopher's purpose: "For as Hegel's task is not to discover the truth of empirical existence but to discover the empirical existence of the truth...In this way Hegel is able to create the impression of *mystical profundity*" (ibid., 99). Thus, even in this early passage (and throughout the work), we see a budding historical materialism, an argument for "real," "empirical existence" that determines history, from the ground up, as it were, rather than proceeding from the Idea (the abstract) on down.

Hegel errs again, in Marx's view, by also inverting the relationship between civil society and the bourgeois state. According to Marx's reading of Hegel, the bourgeois state is left to overcome its own contradictions (that stem from the clash of private interests that it serves) and determine civil society (Larrain 1991; Marx 1992). In regards to conceptualizing the relationship between the bourgeois state and civil society, Marx argues,

> Hegel's chief error is that he regards *contradiction in the phenomenal world as unity in its essence, in the Idea.* There is however [sic] a profounder reality involved, namely an *essential contradiction*, e.g., in this case the contradiction in the legislature is itself only the self-contradiction of the political state, and hence of civil society.
>
> MARX 1992, 158

---

7   The following interpretation of Marx's theorization of ideology, developing through three stages of Marx's writings, is indebted to Jorge Larrain's (1991, 1996) analyses.

For Hegel, an abstract idea determined reality, and such a position inverted reality. Another key point here is that because the bourgeois state really is an abstraction, Hegel's inversions sprang from reality not misunderstanding; they were not "mere illusions" or falsehoods (Larrain 1991, 12). To underscore this, Larrain draws readers to Marx's observation that "Hegel should not be blamed for describing the essence of the modern state as it is, but for identifying what is with the *essence of the state*" (Marx 1992, 126–127, emphasis in original). Marx continues, "That the rational is real is *contradicted* by *the irrational reality* which at every point shows itself to be the opposite of what it asserts, and to assert the opposite of what it is" (ibid., 127). Thus, Hegel's inversion covers up the contradictions of the bourgeois state that serves private interests but is beholden to rival influences. Such a cover up also lends legitimacy to the state by precluding critique of its essence.

Marx (1992) further explains how inversion works in *A Contribution to Hegel's Philosophy of Right* (written from 1843–1844), which builds on Feuerbach's critique of religion. Here Marx argues that if in religion, the powers of man appears in an inverse relationship to those of God, it not only reflects reality but also points to deficiencies for which religion serves as compensation. Larrain (1991) points to Marx's argument (borrowing from and then exceeding Feuerbach's) that "Man makes religion, religion does not make man" (Marx 1992, 13; see also Marx 1992, 244). Reading further around this quote, we see that Marx moves immediately from this Feuerbachian formulation to arguing, "Religion is indeed the self-consciousness and self-esteem of man who has either not yet won through to himself or has already lost himself again." This points to the **compensatory function** ideology serves. From here, Marx cautions readers, "But *man* is no abstract being squatting outside the world. Man is *the world of man,* state, and society. This state and this society produce religion, which is an inverted consciousness of the world, because they are an inverted world." The inversions that constitute religion are, in other words, real not imagined; religion reflects the inverted world in which "man, the state, and society" coexist.

Adding, "Religion is the general theory of this world…its universal basis of *consolation* and *justification*," Marx highlights ideology's function as symptomatic of and compensation for an unjust world. Although he quips that religion is "the opium of the people," Marx emphasizes, "*Religious* suffering is at one and the same time the *expression* of real suffering and a protest against real suffering. Religion is the sigh of the oppressed creature, the heart of a heartless world and the soul of soulless conditions" (ibid., 244). Religion springs from real suffering, wrought by real contradictions, as Hegel's notion of the state sprang from real inversions that masked actual contradictions.

Thus, "the struggle against religion is therefore indirectly the struggle against that world whose spiritual aroma is religion" (ibid., 244). Addressing religious suffering, moreover, requires action in the real world, real action by real people, not mere philosophizing. Extinguishing the illusions people have about their spiritual relationship to the world under Christianity, for example, requires that people change lived conditions. Putting it poetically, "The abolition of religion as the *illusory* happiness of the people is the demand for their *real* happiness. To call on them to give up their illusions about their condition is to *call on them to give up a condition that requires illusions*" (ibid., 244). For Marx, contra Feuerbach, the truth (alone) will not set people free, but action in the real world, informed by the truth, holds such potential.

2.2 Historical Materialist "Ideology"

Thus, in these early writings Marx previews a theory of ideology that constitutes his historical materialism: humans make ideas and history, and therefore, intervention in the material world brings about changes in that world. Additionally, the material world is, under capitalism, fraught with contradictions that cause suffering and beg remedy through intervention into these contradictions. Although Marxist scholars typically point to *The German Ideology* (written from 1845–1846) as offering a "first formulation of the materialist conception of history" (Larrain 1991, 16), or even to the "outline" of historical materialism "jotted down" in his "Theses on Feuerbach" (1845; Kumar 2006, 79), Marx's earlier criticism of religion (1843–1844) proves a significant starting point for Marx's critique of the real, sensuous world. As Marx puts it in *A Contribution to Hegel's Philosophy of Right*, "The criticism of religion is therefore in *embryo* the *criticism of that vale of tears* of which religion is the *halo*" (Marx 1992, 244). As Larrain (1991) points out, theory, in this text, serves a central and material purpose in history-making and in the proletariat's revolution. Marx contends that "the proletariat finds its *intellectual* weapons in philosophy" which can lead to "emancipation [that] will transform the *Germans* into *men* [sic]" (Marx 1992, 256). The point of criticism, even at this early stage in Marx's intellectual development, is liberation in the material world as this metaphor makes clear: "Criticism has plucked the imaginary flowers on the chain not in order that man shall continue to bear that chain without fantasy or consolation but so that he shall throw off the chain and pluck the living flower" (ibid., 244).

On this last point and in *The German Ideology* (1996), Marx and Engels criticize the Young Hegelians for positing ideas as "the real chains of men," to which they would "have to fight only against these illusions of consciousness" (Marx and Engels 1996, 41).[8] The source of oppression, is therefore, not a product of consciousness, but products of the real, material world. Thus, *action* is required for liberation. But by critiquing mere ideas, the Young Hegelians support the status quo and thus, "are the staunchest conservatives." For by "only fighting against '*phrases*'...to these phrases [the Young Hegelians] are only opposing other phrases" (ibid., 41). No matter how "'world-shattering'" their statements, then, "they are in no way combating the real existing world when they are merely combating the phrases of this world" (ibid., 41). As a result, such intellectual work amounts to "only further embellishments of [the] claim to have furnished...discoveries of universal importance" (ibid., 41). Dana Cloud (2001) alludes to the importance of this passage to underscore the significance of materialist rhetorical critique to "explain the connections between phrases on the one hand and economic interests and systems of oppression and exploitation on the other" (Cloud 2001, 7). Thus, when Marx said, "Philosophers have only *interpreted* the world, in various ways; the point, however, is to *change* it" (Marx 1983, 158), he was elaborating on this argument and calling for action in the material world.[9] In this way, Marx was developing his theory and method of historical materialism that approached history as contingent, human-made.

The German Ideology is also noteworthy for contributing to Marx's historical materialism generally and for its conceptualization of ideology as a "camera obscura" specifically. In an oft-cited passage that introduces the concept, Marx and Engels (1996) discuss the relationship of human beings to material reality, the mode of production (called "productive forces"), relations of production (called "the intercourse"), and ideas:

> The production of ideas, of conceptions, of consciousness, is at first directly interwoven with the material activity and the material intercourse of men [sic], the language of real life...Men [sic] are the producers of their conceptions, ideas, etc. – real, active men [sic], as they are conditioned by a definite development of their productive forces and of the intercourse correspond to these... (p. 47).

Ideas, in other words, are manufactured by people (who engage in "mental production," 47) but are constrained by material conditions. As Marx and Engels later explain, material reality under capitalism can be a tricky thing; it

---

8   The Young Hegelians were leftist Prussian intellectuals who followed and responded to Hegel. Marx became a young Young Hegelian while studying philosophy at the University of Berlin in the late 1830s.

9   Emphasis in original.

produces and is produced by contradictions that turn reality upside down. "If in all ideology men and their circumstances appear upside-down as in a camera obscura," Marx and Engels argue, "this phenomenon arises just as much from their historical life-process as the *inversion* of objects on the retina does from their physical life-process" (Marx and Engels 1996, 47). Thus, like the bourgeois state Hegel describes, ideology inverts reality because reality is indeed inverted. This is a key ingredient of ideology that makes it an especially useful tool for analyzing Palin's feminism and other cultural artifacts that represent an inverted world (Larrain 1996).

It is also worth noting that Marx and Engels (1996) do not argue that ideology springs exclusively from members of the ruling class, as Stuart Hall (borrowing from Laclau) suggests is the case. Although Marx and Engels claim that "The ideas of the ruling class are in every epoch the ruling ideas, i.e., the class which is the ruling *material* force of society, is at the same time its ruling *intellectual* force" (Marx and Engels 1996, 64), they mean to elaborate on the argument that material reality determines ideas, not the other way around. Additionally, here Marx and Engels refer to "ideas," not "ideology," a key distinction that seems forgotten by arguments like Hall's that interpret Marx's notion of ideology as claiming ruling class origins. That this is not the case should be clear enough by reading a bit further down, where Marx and Engels describe how the division of labour

> manifests itself also in the ruling class as the division of mental and material labour, so that inside this class one part appears as the thinkers of the class (its active, conceptive ideologists, who make the perfecting of the **illusion of the class about itself** their chief source of livelihood), while the others' attitude to these ideas and illusions is more passive and receptive, because they are in reality the active members of this class and have less time to make up illusions and ideas about themselves...
>
> MARX AND ENGELS 1996, 65; *emphasis added*

Thus, ideology may be produced by members of the ruling class who are its **"conceptive ideologists,"** including politicians like Sarah Palin. Ideological content, furthermore, may emanate from any individual or cultural organ attached to any class or class fraction, as Marx and Engels do not specify a "necessary correspondence" between ideological production and class, as Hall (1985, 1986) argues. Additionally, this passage suggests that ideologists who are *members of the ruling class create illusions about themselves.* Marx and Engels do not elaborate on what "illusions about themselves" means in practice. Thus, a number of questions arise: do ruling class conceptive ideologists "perfect illusions" about the role of capitalists, as a class in society? Do conceptive ideologists of the ruling class "perfect illusions" about the forms their power should take, and specifically, in regards to the extent of their control over working conditions, pay, civil rights, and public debate (and our media system)? It is important to keep these elements of ideology in mind when analyzing Palin's feminism, as it appears to speak to elites and nonelites, but it may also *convey illusions that capitalist patriarchs and their representative hold about themselves as a class, illusions that reinforce the synergistic relationship between capitalism and patriarchy*.

2.3   *"Ideology" in Marx's Mature Writings*

In later works, from *Grundrisse* (written from 1857–1861, published in 1939) through *Capital* (vol. I, 1867; vol. II, 1885, vol. III, 1894), Marx distinguishes between appearances or "phenomenal forms" on the one hand and real relations or "the essence" on the other (Larrain 1991, 31). Under capitalism, these two spheres are contradictory, and yet, constitute material reality. Thus, Marx refines and makes more complex earlier arguments that ideas must be understood as springing from and thus reflecting material reality: **under capitalism, material practices are real and yet can work ideologically**. The **wage**, for example is a real, phenomenal form that compensates workers for their labor, but the wage hides the fact that workers are not paid for all of their labor-time. The wage mystifies "the essence" of profit-making in the capitalist mode of production, the production of surplus value. As Marx explains in *Capital vol. I*, surplus value is the ratio of "surplus labor" to "necessary labor." Surplus labour is the time a worker works for the capitalist beyond the time it takes for her to produce the equivalent of her wage through necessary labor. The more surplus labor, the more surplus value she produces for the capitalist. Surplus value may be increased by extending or intensifying the workday, thereby expanding "absolute surplus value," or by shortening the amount of time it takes for workers to produce their subsistence, thus expanding "relative surplus value." Relative surplus value increases as an effect of reducing the amount workers need to produce to cover living expenses or as an effect of devaluing labour power (Marx 1867). None of this is revealed in the wages workers receive or in the prices of commodities. In the chapter in *Capital* on wages, Marx (1867) explains,

> On the surface of bourgeois society the wage of the labourer appears as the price of labour, a certain quantity of money that is paid for a certain quantity of labour. Thus people speak of the value of labour and call its expression in money its necessary or natural price.

...In the expression – value of labour, the idea of value is not only completely obliterated, but actually reversed. It is an expression as imaginary
as the value of the earth. These imaginary expressions, arise, however,
from the relations of production themselves. They are categories for the
phenomenal forms of essential relations. That in their appearance things
often represent themselves in inverted form is pretty well known in every
science except Political Economy.

Let us next see how value (and price) of labour-power, present themselves in this transformed condition as wages.

...As the value of labour is only an irrational expression for the value of
labour-power, it follows, of course, that the value of labour must always
be less than the value it produces, for the capitalist always makes labour-
power work longer than is necessary for the reproduction of its own value...
[A] part only of the working day...labour-is paid for, [but it] appears as
the value or price of the whole working day of 12 hours, which thus
includes...unpaid [labour]. The wage form thus extinguishes every trace
of the division of the working day into necessary labour and surplus
labour, into paid and unpaid labour. All labour appears as paid labour.

MARX 1867, 373–375

**The wage's great ideological triumph, then, is to obscure the fact that work-
ers are not paid for all of their work**. The notion "wage" rests on a theory of
value (the classical political economists' theory of value) that makes an essential inversion regarding "value" as something natural that can be expressed
simply by a "price." As Marx argues, "value" has no inherent value and, under
capitalist production, is produced by the additional, unpaid labour of workers
that wages-for-hours-worked hide. Thus, Marx argues,

...[T]he money-relation conceals the unrequited labour of the wage labourer.
Hence, we may understand the decisive importance of the transformation
of value and price of labour-power into the form of wages, or into the value
and price of labour itself. This phenomenal form, which makes the actual
relation invisible, and, indeed, shows the direct opposite of that relation,
forms the basis of all the juridical notions of both labourer and capitalist,
of all the mystifications of the capitalistic mode of production, of all its
illusions as to liberty, of all the apologetic shifts of the vulgar economists.

MARX 1867, 375

Throughout *Capital, vol. 1*, Marx notes how capitalist production works through
these phenomenal levels of appearance that appear natural, are "real," and yet

hide their inner workings, which bear contradictions. Thus, Marx discusses how "productive power," which workers sell to capitalists, "appears as a power with which capital is endowed by Nature a productive power that is immanent in capital" (1867, 228).

Earlier in his analysis, Marx discusses the transformation and circulation of money as involving these "two antithetical phases" wherein money is transformed into a commodity, and another, "the sale," through which the commodity is transformed again into money. "'M-C-M'," Marx concludes, emphasizing the level of phenomenal appearance that is also constitutive of material reality, "is therefore in reality the general formula of capital as it appears prima facie within the sphere of circulation" (ibid., 106). Appearances, puzzles, and mystifications work alongside material reality throughout *Capital,* that sets as one of its tasks as to "solve the riddle presented by money" (ibid., 33).

A useful explanation of ideology under capitalism also appears in *Capital vol. III* (edited by Engels). Without using the word, "ideology," the following discussion of **"competition"** walks readers through the dynamic process of ideology as it works in capitalism through material (in production) and discursive (via conceptions) means that involve **inversions** that are real (i.e., they are phenomenal), that hide (or mystify) yet positively signify, and that **enable capitalism to work (i.e., benefit the ruling class)**:

> What **competition** does not show, however, is the determination of value, which dominates the movement of production; and the values that lie beneath the prices of production and that determine them in the last instance. Competition, on the other hand, shows: (1) the average profits... (2) the rise and fall of prices of production caused by changes in the level of wages... (3) the fluctuations of market-prices... All these **phenomena seem to contradict the determination of value by labour-time** as much as the nature of surplus value consisting of unpaid surplus-labour. Thus **everything appears reversed in competition.** The final pattern of economic relations as seen on the surface, in their real existence and consequently in the conceptions by which the bearers and agents of these relations seek to understand them, is very much different from, and indeed quite the reverse of, their inner but concealed essential pattern and the conception corresponding to it.
>
> MARX 1894, 146, *emphasis added*

Perhaps what Marx calls the **"Fetishism of commodities,"** widely known as **commodity fetishism**, best encapsulates his theory of ideology, illustrating a mature historical materialism that critiques real phenomenal forms that obscure deeper (and also real) relations. Without using "ideology," Marx illustrates how commodities work ideologically to **conceal** the labour that produced them (and the "dead labor" they thus constitute); they appear as things that have exchange value and thus, appear as relations between things instead of relations between people (i.e., relations among the many workers from whom capitalists extract surplus value in the process of producing the things that become commodities). The opposite, as Marx shows throughout *Capital*, is true. Commodities are real, they are phenomenal forms, but they hide deeper relations between people that constitute relations of capitalist production, specifically, the exploitation of labor. Treating commodities as having values expressed in the money form (i.e., bearing prices) mystifies the process of producing value and lends a veneer of equality, since prices suggest the trade of equivalent values. Profit appears to emanate from simply making more money than commodities cost, as a simple subtraction of cost-price from selling price, instead of emanating from worker's production of surplus value, which can be calculated by the ratio of surplus to necessary labor. Viewing commodities as things traded for money, again, **turns upside down** the social and contradictory relations between classes. "A commodity" Marx (1867) argues,

> is therefore a mysterious thing, simply because in it the social character of men's labour appears to them as an objective character stamped upon the product of that labour; because the relation of the producers to the sum total of their own labour is presented to them as a social relation, existing not between themselves, but between the products of their labour.
>
> MARX 1867, 46–47

Fetishizing, or treating commodities as things, then, **benefits the ruling class** of capitalists by **lending an air of fairness and thus legitimacy** to relations of production. Marx compares **"Fetishism of commodities"** to a form of capitalistic worship and in this way, harks back to his early critique of religion,

> In order, therefore, to find an analogy, we must have recourse to the mist-enveloped regions of the religious world. In that world the productions of the human brain appear as independent beings endowed with life, and entering into relation both with one another and the human race. So it is in the world of commodities with the products of men's hands. This I call the **Fetishism** which attaches itself to the products of labour, so soon as they are produced as commodities, and which is therefore inseparable from the production of commodities.
>
> MARX 1867, 47

TABLE 10.1   *Elements of Marx's theory of ideology*

Distorts an inverted world. Represents capitalist relations of production as inverted, which they are in reality. Thus, there is nothing "false" about ideology.

Examples include wages and commodity fetishism.

Conceals political-economic contradictions.

Offers justification for capitalism.

Promises compensation and consolation for oppression under capitalism.

Serves the interests of the ruling class.

Conveys illusions members of ruling class have about themselves.

Ideology critique informs activism against capitalist exploitation and capitalism in general; such activism may inform ideology critique.

Bourgeois political economists, as Marx calls them, thus, have served as **conceptive ideologists** for capitalists who benefit from mystifying exploitative relations of production, and in this way, erect an economic religion of sorts. Synthesizing elements of ideology from the three phases of Marx's intellectual development, commodity fetishism explains how material practice and language together **distort, invert, conceal, justify, compensate, and serve the interests of the ruling class.** If ideology turns reality upside down, additionally, this appearance points to real inversions, real contradictions that need righting so that people can "pluck the living flower" and enjoy the sweetness of real liberation.

Additionally, Marx and Engels argued that ideology does not spring exclusively from the ruling class, but that which is generated by ruling class members and their associates may point to illusions they hold about themselves. Finally, for Marx and Engels, conducting ideology critique promises to inform **practices (i.e., actions and activism)** necessary to end oppression wrought by capitalism. As I discuss below, Sarah Palin's brand of feminism exemplifies Marx's theory of ideology summarised in Table 10.1. Its critique underscores the need for feminist activism aimed at eradicating the oppressive, synergistic systems of capitalism and patriarchy.

3   Palin's "Feminism" as Marx's Ideology[10]

In a May 14, 2010 speech at a fundraising breakfast for the pro-life political action committee, Susan B. Anthony List (SBA List), Sarah Palin embraced

---

10   See italicized, bolded items in Table 10.2, p. 306.

"feminism." Palin praised the group for "returning the women's movement back to its original roots," which spring from the goals of the "earliest leaders of the women's rights movements, [who] were pro-life...[w]omen like your namesake...and Elizabeth Cady Stanton" who demanded women's suffrage and an end to abortion that Stanton and her feminist peers often called "infanticide." In her book *America by Heart*, released in November 2010, Palin elaborates on her connection to Stanton and Anthony, praising "our foremothers in the women's movement [who] fought hard to gain the acceptance of women's talents and capabilities as equal to men's" (Palin 2010a, 140). Stanton and Anthony's embrace of the "laws of nature" and laws that "nature's God entitle them" earned Palin's praise. Palin interprets these words, part of the Declaration of Sentiments written in 1848 following the Seneca Falls convention for women's rights, as proof that "original feminists" "didn't believe that men were oppressors, women were victims, and unborn children merely 'personal choices'" (ibid., 141). "They believed," Palin continues, "that we were children of God, and, as such, we were all – men, women, our littlest sisters in the womb, everyone – entitled to love and respect" (ibid., 141). According to Palin, abortion is unnatural, ungodly, inhumane, and anti-feminist.

Examining how Palin's appropriation of SBA List feminism works ideologically requires that we ground our discussion in an understanding of feminism. Although it is beyond the bounds of this chapter to give a full historical account of feminist political movements and debates around feminism's definition, it is helpful to share some details. First, regarding the "first wave" feminists with whom Palin claims to "feel a connection," it is important to understand that nineteenth-century feminists like Susan B. Anthony and Elizabeth Cady Stanton agitated for women's right to vote because, among other goals, they wanted to stop marital rape. One way of thwarting women's service as "slaves to men's lust" in marriage, as Stanton put in commentary in *The Revolution* in 1868, was to extend suffrage to women as well as rights to education (Beisel and Kay 2004, 512). These goals served each other: stopping marital rape served as a rhetorical exigency that demanded remedy by politically empowering women (by extending suffrage). Stanton and Anthony deemed abortion "infanticide" but did so to highlight the brutal results of men's sexual abuse of women that, in turn, demanded women's political empowerment. Second, they represented one faction within the nineteenth century women's movement in the US, and a radical and controversial one at that, which viewed abortion as the "natural consequence" of husband's raping their wives (Beisel and Kay 2004, 513). Like other suffragists of the day, Anthony and Stanton also drew on racist, nativist discourse and racist financiers to organize for women's suffrage.

Our understanding of how Palinite feminism works ideologically also calls for a definition of feminism that can include various moments in its history, a definition that gets at its roots as a political movement. As bell hooks (1984) argues, engaging in intellectual and political feminist work requires consensus about feminism's meaning. Hooks' description of feminism as "a movement to end sexist oppression," enables intersectional analyses that take race, ethnicity, sexual orientation, ability, and class into account. Rather than hinge on "equality," which begs unproductive (and counterproductive) questions like "equal with whom?," feminism understood as seeking to "end sexist oppression" emphasizes the constructive goal of the movement. The purpose of hooks' "feminism," furthermore, "is not to benefit solely any specific group of women, any particular race or class of women. It does not privilege women over men" (hooks 1984, 26). Additionally, this notion of feminism can be pressed into the radical transformation of society because it challenges systems of domination, namely patriarchy, but it may also contribute to anti-capitalist revolution. Thus, for hooks, "feminism is neither a lifestyle nor a ready-made identity or role one can step into" (ibid., 26). Feminism is best rendered through verbs not adjectives.

Palin's brand of feminism appears as a movement that supports an identity and a proliferation of adjectives. Additionally, looking at the historical record, Palinite feminism works against the goals of first-wave "original feminists," from whom it claims to descend. Palin's vice presidential candidacy in 2008 glimpse the feminism she would embrace during the 2010 midterm elections. "Dissident feminist" Camille Paglia noted several days after the Republican's nominating convention that Palin "represented an explosion of a brand new style of muscular American feminism" (Paglia 2008, para. 10). Next in her much maligned 2008 interview with Katie Couric, Palin answered affirmatively when asked if she considered herself a feminist (Gallagher, 2010).

Sarah Palin's SBA-List speech in May 2010, furthermore, describes her brand of feminism as one that harks back to the ("muscular") pioneering spirit of American frontierswomen that stands in sharp relief to the feminized, inauthentic feminists of the East Coast. Just over halfway through her 34-minute speech, Palin thanked the organization "for being home to a new conservative feminist movement" that has begotten "an emerging conservative feminist identity," Palin bemoaned that for "[f]ar too long when people heard the word "feminist" they thought of the faculty lounge at some East Coast woman's college [sic], right?" In contrast to what she imagines to be passive academic feminism, Palin's springs from the hardy Western frontier,

I'd like to remind people of another feminist tradition, kind of a western feminism, it's influenced by the pioneering spirit of our foremothers who went in wagon trains across the wilderness and they settled in home-steads. And these were tough, independent pioneering mothers whose work was as valuable as any man's on the frontier. And it's no surprise that our western states that gave women the vote, the right to vote way before their East coast sisters in a more genteel city, perhaps, got it right. These women, they had dirt under their fingernails, and they could shoot a gun, and push a plow and raise a family all at the same time...These women, our frontier foremothers...loved this country, and they made sacrifices to carve out a living and a family life out of the wilderness. They went where no women had gone before. I kind of feel a connection to that tough, gun-totin' pioneer feminism of women like Annie Oakley and them.

PALIN 2010B

Palin, thus, assumed a "tough mother" voice and strong "mother tongue" (Foust 2004; Jetter, Orleck and Taylor 1997; Parry-Giles and Parry-Giles 1996; Rodino 2005, Triece 2012) to conjure images of "tough, gun-totin' pioneer feminism" Palin associates with icons like Annie Oakley. The adjective-heavy language that describes "western," "pioneering," "frontier," "tough," "gun-totin'" feminism contrasts with descriptors for the "East coast," "genteel" feminism that Palin opposes (Palin mispronounced the "g" in "genteel" by giving it a French-sounding "zh" like the "g" in "mirage"). In this way, Palin's is a form of identity feminism that promises **compensation** (i.e., being considered an "authentic feminist") and works against the political goals of ending women's oppression by posing feminism as a static lifestyle and title (brand?) to embrace rather than as a movement that requires activism (i.e., actions and verbs). As hooks explains, even when such lifestyles appear quite radical, for example, in visions of a "counter-culture" that consist of a "woman-centered-world wherein par-ticipants have little contact with men" (hooks 1984, 26), such formations involve "diverting energy from feminist movement that aims to change soci-ety" (ibid., 26). Additionally, in as much as Palin **congratulates** the SBA List for fostering "a new conservative feminist movement" she does so for its produc-tion of an "emerging conservative identity" that harks back to an earlier one shared by women with dirty hands that sowed fields and raised children in the Wild West.

Although they did such undainty work, US frontierswomen were not neces-sarily suffragists. This was true for Annie Oakley, whom Palin singles out for representing "pioneer feminism" that won voting rights (or at least enjoyed them) before their East coast sisters. Despite her career as show-woman sharp-shooter who entertained audiences for four decades and who symbolized the modern, liberated woman, Oakley opposed extending suffrage to women. Pointing to negative outcomes of opening suffrage to all women, Oakley was known for saying, "If only the good women voted" (Kasper 1992, 213). "Little Sure Shot," furthermore, refused to support the suffrage movement because it was unladylike. Additionally, divisions that formed between the radical National Women's Suffrage Association (founded by Susan B. Anthony and Elizabeth Cady Stanton) that barred men and the American Woman Suffrage Association (founded by Julia Ward Howe and Lucy Stone) that welcomed them threatened to alienate audiences and, consequently, hurt Oakley's show business (Riley 2002). Added to the misinterpretation of Anthony's and Stanton's reasons for calling abortion "infanticide" and the lack of appreciation for their radical stance (not to mention their radical newspaper *The Revolution*), Palin's embrace of Oakley for representing early feminism and American women's voting rights turns history on its head, as Marx's "ideology" does. Additionally, the **inversion** represented here exists in reality: in the end Palin supports the confluence of capitalist and patriarchal – not feminist – interests.

Perhaps more counterproductive to the feminist movement – and indeed, more dangerous to women than her inversion of history – is that Palin's poli-cies stand to oppress women. In *America by Heart*, Palin discusses how her brand of feminism opposes those of "the left-wing," who, during her 2008 vice presidential run, "didn't know what to make of an Alaskan chick out on the campaign trail talking about the Second Amendment, kids (the more the mer-rier!), and America's urgent need for greater security through energy inde-pendence" (Palin 2010a, 137). Although this seems in some ways, like a casual "throw away" line, (and one that echoes nearly verbatim an aside in her SBA-List speech), it alludes to policy positions that include loosening restrictions on gun ownership and opening the Arctic National Wildlife Refuge. These are; positions that most women oppose (Public Takes Conservative 2009; Saad 2009; Walsh 2008). Palin also opposes material support of poor households through state subsidy and instead supports the Earned Income Tax Credit that reduces tax burdens on low-income households, a position that threatens US single-mother headed households, 42% of which survive below the poverty line (Single Mother Poverty 2011).[11] Thus, Palin's brand of feminism serves to **justify** policies that, rather than end women's oppression, **marginalize wom-en's political voice and erode their financial wellbeing.**

---

11   See also: http://www.issues2000.org/Sarah_Palin.htm.

Most anti-feminist of Palin's policy positions, however, is her stance on abortion. Even in cases of rape and incest Palin opposes abortion (Goldman 2008).[12] Although she alludes to God and her Christian religious philosophy in defense of the right of women to enjoy equality with men, Palin articulates her position on abortion as exemplifying "new," true feminism:

> Together the pro-woman, pro-life sisterhood is telling the young women of America that they are capable of handling an unintended pregnancy and still pursue a career and an education. Strangely, many feminists seem to want to tell these young women that they're *not* capable, that you *can't* give your child life and still pursue your dreams. The message is: 'Women, you are not strong enough or smart enough to do both. You are not capable'.
>
> The *new* feminism is telling women they are capable and strong. And if keeping a child isn't possible, adoption is a beautiful choice. It's about empowering women to make *real choices*, not forcing them to accept false ones. It's about compassion and letting these scared young women know that there [is help] for them to raise their children in those less-than-ideal circumstances.
>
> PALIN 2010A, 153, *emphasis in original*

After this explanation, Palin shares her own experiences with "less-than-ideal circumstances": learning of her son Trig's Down's syndrome during her pregnancy and the momentary temptation to consider abortion. "God will never give me something I can't handle," Palin told herself. "Less-than-ideal" circumstances also include teen pregnancies like her teenaged daughter Bristol experienced. According to Palin, despite her youth and unwed status, Bristol's decision to bear the child was "[n]ot an easy road, but the right road" (Palin 2010a, 155). Palin omits discussion of rape and incest, however. In doing so, Palin lets the phraseology "less-than-ideal" circumstances euphmenize bearing children as a result of such tragedies. Restricting abortion in cases of rape and incest, of course, limits women's choices, and therefore, disempowers women. Palinite feminism **promises compensation and consolation** for supporting policy positions that would further oppress women.

This stance also **turns upside down** Anthony's and Stanton's arguments for women's suffrage, particularly men's sexual abuse of women, which, as a

---

12   Palin supports abortion only when pregnancy endangers the mother's life.

"natural consequence," drove women to abort babies. Recall that the goal of Anthony's and Stanton's feminism was not to criminalize abortion, but to high-light the consequences of men's sexual abuse of women to mobilize support for women's voting rights. When Palin argues that Anthony and Stanton advocated for unborn children and women because the rights of both were connected, she also neglects the primacy of women's sexual exploitation in Anthony's and Stanton's feminism,

> Founders of the American women's movement such as Susan B. Anthony and Elizabeth Cady Stanton did not believe abortion was good for women. Quite the contrary, they saw the rights of the unborn child as fundamen-tally linked to the rights of women.
> PALIN 2010A, 156

Palin's version of SBA-List feminism **distorts** suffragists' use of abortion as a rhetorical exigency meant to highlight women's sexual oppression not to sup-port legal restrictions on abortion. Anthony and Stanton intended for women to have more not less control over their bodies and hoped to secure such con-trol by expanding women's political power.

Palin also sidesteps the racism, classism, and covert and overt links to eugenics that underlay Anthony's, Stanton's, and other American suffragists' opposition to abortion. The historical record shows that Anthony and Stanton concurred with postbellum physicians' stated goal of preserving white middle class women's fer-tility in the face of immigration and loosened restrictions on citizenship. And, although Stanton and Anthony did not lobby for the criminalization of abortion for white women, they articulated fears of falling Anglo-Saxon power when they likened abortion to infanticide. As Stanton argued in *The Revolution* in 1868:

> The murder of children, either before or after birth, has become so fright-fully prevalent that physicians...have declared that were it not for immi-gration the white population of the United States would actually fall off!
> BEISEL AND KAY 2004, 512

Stanton's position represents the "positive eugenics" of the late nineteenth and early twentieth century that encouraged wealthy white women to procreate and discouraged poor, racial minority and newly immigrated women to seek birth control and abortion. Palin singles out Planned Parenthood founder Margaret Sanger as the "[o]ne great exception to the culture of life promoted by early feminists" (Palin 2010a, 157), but neglects other first wave feminist "excep-tions" like Charlotte Perkins Gilman and Victoria Woodhull, who advocated prevention of the "unfit" from bearing children and even supported government control of women's fertility (Carpenter 2010; Perry 2005). Woodhull, who cautioned against breeding "imbeciles," furthermore, held a position quite contrary to Palin's championing of "life" in "less-than-ideal circumstances," a position that informed Palin's "decision" to bear her youngest child. Thus, in some ways, first wave feminists' advocacy of birth control for undesireables runs counter to both Palin's version of feminism and to the very premise of feminism as a movement to free women from sexist oppression. **Palin's feminism distorts an already inverted feminism**, just as capitalist ideology distorts an already inverted economy.

The racism mobilized in eugenicist arguments against abortion for whites ("positive eugenics") and for abortion for poor southern European and Asian women ("negative eugenics") also traded on the "wages of whiteness" (Roediger 2007), the notion that whiteness, more specifically, Northern Europeanness, conferred cultural authority that compensated for various forms of political-economic power. Historians David Roedgier (2007) and Alexander Saxton (1971) have demonstrated that to unite white workers even socialist labour organizers drew on fears that Chinese workers would steal whites' jobs. When considered together with her regressive stance on immigration, including support of Arizona's "papers please" law (SB 1070) that required individuals who "look" like immigrants to carry immigration documents (Condon 2010; Palin 2010a), Sarah Palin's feminism **updates wages of whiteness for today's conservative women**.

Serving an additional ideological function, Palinite feminism also **serves the interests of the ruling class** by supporting patriarchal capitalism. By opposing direct subsidies to poor families and supporting restrictions on abortion, Palin's "feminist" discourse supports the availability of poor American women as sources of cheap labour desperate to work any job. In this way, Palin's policies and rhetoric serve to maintain the "reserve army of labor" Marx has described as essential to the production of surplus value (Marx 1847, 1867), and thus to the very reproduction of capitalism. Such policies also support patriarchy. Unable to find sustenance through state support, poor women would remain eager to work, or, perhaps marry a man, since men out earn women and two-thirds of American adults living in poverty are women. At least twice as likely to live in poor households than white women, Latinas and African American women may feel even more pressure to work than whites in the US (Kendall 2010). By opposing choice, Palin's "feminism" also promotes patriarchy by denying women reproductive rights that men enjoy without question (as one recently proposed bill underscores, Gumbrect 2012), and may make women even more vulnerable economically. Thus, Palinite

TABLE 10.2   *Comparison of Marx's theory of ideology with palinite "feminism" as ideology*

Elements of Marx's theory of ideology	Palinite feminism as Marx's theory of ideology
Distorts an inverted world. Represents capitalist relations of production as inverted, which they are in reality. Thus, there is nothing "false" about ideology. Examples include wages, competition, and commodity fetishism.	Palinite feminism (PF) distorts first wave feminism by turning its critique of abortion upside down; PF also obscures the inversion of first wave feminist eugenicists who embraced birth control of those deemed "unfit" racially, economically, and mentally. PF distorts Annie Oakley's position on women's voting rights: Oakley opposed extending suffrage to all women.
Conceals political-economic contradictions.	PF conceals contradictions between feminism as a movement against sexist oppression and capitalism that draws on patriarchal relations for survival.
Offers justification for capitalism.	PF offers a justification for sexist oppression of women (i.e., denying women reproductive rights on the basis of its alleged link to "authentic feminism"); offers justification for policies unpopular with women and that stand to erode women's financial wellbeing.
Serves the interests of the ruling class.	PF supports policies that maintain the "reserve army of labor" that capitalism and patriarchy need to survive (i.e., women willing to work for lower wages, in lower-waged fields then men and additionally, make marriage more and divorce less economically attractive for women). Palin's campaign and the campaigns of her "mama grizzlies" were heavily funded by capitalist patriarchs.
Ruling class' "conceptive ideologists" produce ideology that conveys illusions members of ruling class have about themselves.	PF points to illusions that "conceptive ideologists" Palin and her supporters (SBA-List organizers and wealthy patrons like the Koch brothers) have about their role in women's political history; PF is not a grassroots philosophy.
Ideology critique informs activism against capitalism and activism against capitalist exploitation, which may inform ideology critique.	Critique of Palinite feminism can inform feminist activism aimed at ending sexist oppression, which may inform critique of "feminism" as ideology

feminism underwrites policies that support what Marx (1867) called the "dull compulsion of the economic," that under capitalism, "completes the subjection of the labourer to the capitalist." Since Palin's policies and rhetoric subjectify women workers (including unemployed and underemployed women), her "feminism" reinforces sexist oppression.

Finally, **Palin's feminism supports candidates funded by capitalist patriarch brothers Charles and David Koch**, owners and executives of the energy exploration and consumer product conglomerate Koch Industries. The fourth and fifth richest people in the world (Kroll and Dolan, 2011), the Kochs developed synergistic relationships with Palin and 2010's neoconservative Senatorial and Congressional candidates who oppose choiced. In 2010 the brothers contributed $128,000 to the speaker's bureau employed by Sarah Palin and $1.9 million to the Tea Party Express that supported neoconservative, anti-choice "mama grizzly" candidates Angle, Bachmann and O'Donnell in 2010 (Good 2010, Loder and Evans 2011, Mayer 2010, Vogel 2010). Thus, despite rallying behind women with "dirt under their fingernails," Palin's "feminism" represents the policy objectives of wealthy patriarchs. Palinite feminism, then, offers insights into the **illusions capitalist-patriarchs have about themselves as a class** and, more specifically, illustrates the work of **Sarah Palin as a "conceptive ideologist"** for capitalists, patriarchs, and the synergies between them. See Table 10.2 for a summary of how Palin's "feminism" fucntions like Marx's ideology.

4 Conclusion

I have argued in this chapter that Sarah Palin's brand of feminism works as ideology in the ways that Marx and Engels defined the concept. Palinite feminism justifies women's domination under capitalism and patriarchy by inverting a reality already inverted by these systems of domination. It offers to conceal and compensate for such domination and serves interests of the ruling class (wealthy capitalist patriarchs) over and above women, women of color, and political economic non-elites (including men). Palin's anti-feminist "feminism" refines illusions that capitalist patriarchs, their representatives, and allies craft about themselves. The "feminism" that Palin represents, after all, is not an "authentic," "original" one, but rather, a rendition distorted (and inverted) by patriarchy. Nor is Palin's feminism evidence of an ever encroaching "postfeminism." Borrowing from Susan Douglas' (2010) comical interpretation of postfeminism, I suggest that Palinite feminism is "good, old-fashioned sexism that reinforces good, old fashioned, grade-A patriarchy" (10). At least one poll suggests that Palin's patriarchal "feminism" resonates more with men than with women (Stan 2010). And it works through Palin's folksy, Alaskan brogue and trademark wink.

Understanding how ideology works can help critical media and communication scholars craft more effective critiques and aim actions at the wellspring of anti-feminist ideology – material reality – so that we do not, as Marx and Engels cautioned in *The German Ideology*, fight "phrases with phrases" (Marx and Engels 1996, 41). Thus, questions this analysis raise include: how can Marxist feminist communication and media scholars intervene in the production of capitalist-patriarchal ideology to frustrate efforts to enact policies under its banner? How can we use such knowledge to bring about reform and radical change that emancipate women and workers?

One insight from this analysis is that ideologues seem to want to rewrite history in ways that sanitize it, that imagine the history of the women's movement as not necessarily racist or concerned with the reproductive capacity of middle class white women. Perhaps an important intellectual project for Marxist feminist scholars is to revive and publicize this history through public scholarship (intellectual work shared with a nonacademic audience) in addition to academic publications and course offerings. The same should be done for the very history of the confluence of capitalism and patriarchy, as suggested by Heidi Hartmann's (2010) description of contradictions inherent in the longstanding capitalist-patriarchy partnership. The family wage, an offspring and enabler of this union, has been decimated over the past several decades, yet patriarchal ideology seems to be working overtime to reclaim the wages of white masculinity. What other texts, images, and discourses work in this way? Critical media and communication scholars are well positioned to analyze such dynamics.

Such critique, furthermore, should highlight the social, cultural, and political economic aspects of this history that are ripe for change and perhaps only threatened by a coming together of people oppressed in multiple ways: by race, ethnicity, immigrant status, class, gender, sexuality, and ability. In some ways, the Occupy Wall Street movement engaged in such work and borrowed from feminist consciousness-raising to do so (Rogers 2011). How else can intellectual and political work inform each other? How can critical scholars of communication and media use ideology critique to inform political action? As Marx's aphorism that the "point is to change it" suggests, such critique would also become more trenchant as scholars become activists and embrace activism in scholarship (Cloud 2011; Macek 2006; Rodino-Colocino 2012). Perhaps there are "intellectual weapons" to be found in philosophy, as Marx (1992, 258) suggested in his early writings. In the end, I am calling on scholars to take action not simply to overturn ideology to reveal "the truth." Borrowing from Marx's critique of religion, I am calling on critical scholars of media and communication to take action to overturn *"a condition that requires illusions"* (Marx 1992, 244).

References

Aune, James Arnt. 1994. *Rhetoric & Marxism*. Boulder: Westview Press.

Beisel, Nicola and Tamara Kay. 2004. Abortion, Race, and Gender in Nineteenth-Century America. *American Sociological Review* 69: 498–518.

Carpenter, Cari, ed. 2010. *Selected Writings of Victoria Woodhull: Suffrage, Free Love, and Eugenics*. Lincoln: University of Nebraska.

Cloud, Dana. 2011. The Only Conceivable Thing to Do: Reflections of Academics and Activism. In *Activism and Rhetoric: Theories and Contexts for Political Engagement*, edited by Seth Kahn & JongHwa Lee, 11–24. New York: Routledge.

Cloud, Dana. 2001. The Affirmative Masquerade. *American Communication Journal* 4 (3): 1–12.

Cloud, Dana. 1998. *Control and Consolation in American Culture and Politics*. Thousand Oaks: Sage.

Condon, Stephanie. 2010. Palin: Obama Doesn't Have the 'Cojones' for Immigration Reform. *CBS News*, August 2. Accessed April 8, 2012. http://www.cbsnews.com/8301 -503544_162-20012319-503544.html.

Dorfman, Ariel and Mattelart, Armand. 1991. *How to Read Donald Duck: Imperialist Ideology in the Disney Comic*, translated by David Kunzle. New York: International General.

Douglas, Susan. J. 2010. *The Rise of Enlightened Sexism: How Pop Culture Took us from Girl Power to Girls Gone Wild*. New York: St. Martin's Griffin.

Eagleton, Terry. 2011. *Why Marx was Right*. London: Yale University Press.

Ehrenreich, Barbara and Arlie Russell Hochschild. 2002. Introduction. In *Global Woman: Nannies, Maids, and Sex Workers in the New Economy*, edited by Barbara Ehrenreich and Arlie Russell Hochschild, 1–13. New York: Henry Hold and Company, LLC.

Ewen, Stuart. 1976. *Captains of Consciousness: Advertising and the Social Roots of the Consumer Culture*. New York: McGraw Hill.

Foust, Christina R. 2004. A Return to Feminine Public Virtue: Judge Judy and the Myth of the Tough Mother. *Women's Studies in Communication* 27 (3): 269–293.

Fuchs, Christian. 2010. Grounding Critical Communication Studies: An Inquiry Into the Communication Theory of Karl Marx. *Journal Of Communication Inquiry* 34 (1): 15–41.

Fuchs, Christian. 2009. Some Theoretical Foundations of Critical Media Studies: Reflections on Karl Marx and the Media. *International Journal Of Communication* 3: 369–402.

Fuchs, Christian, and Dwayne Winseck. 2011. Critical Media and Communication Studies Today. A Conversation. *TripleC (Cognition, Communication, Co-Operation): Open Access Journal For A Global Sustainable Information Society* 9 (2): 247–271.

Gallagher, Maggie. 2010. Sarah Palin's Girl Power. *Real Clear Politics*, May 5. Accessed March 17, 2012 http://www.realclearpolitics.com/articles/2010/05/20/sarah_palins_girl_power_105650.html.

Garnham, Nicholas. 2000. Information Society as Theory or Ideology: A Critical Perspective on Technology. Education and Employment in the Information Age. *Information, Communication & Society* 3 (2): 139–152.

Garnham, Nicholas. 1983. Toward a Theory of Cultural Materialism. *Journal of Communication* 33 (3): 314–329.

Garnham, Nicholas. 1979. Contributions to a Political Economy of Mass-Communication. *Media, Culture & Society* 1 (2): 123–146.

Gill, Rosalind. 2007. Postfeminist Media Culture: Elements of a Sensibility. *European Journal of Cultural Studies* 10 (2): 147–166.

Golding, Peter, and Graham Murdoch. 1997. Ideology and the Mass Media: The Question of Determination. In *The Political Economy of the Media Volume I*, edited by Peter Golding and Graham Murdock, 476–506. Brookfield: Edward Elgar Publishing Company.

Goldman, Robert. *Reading Ads Socially*. 1992. New York: Routledge.

Goldman, Russell. 2008. Sarah Palin Explains Abortion Stance, Explains 'bridge to nowhere' Support. *ABC News*, September 12. Accessed April 6, 2012. http://abcnews.go.com/Politics/Vote2008/sarah-palin-defends-abortion-stance-explains-bridge-support/story?id=5787748#.T3dNCxxSupw.

Good, Chris. 2010. Sharron Angle Gets a Tea Party Bump. *The Atlantic*, May 14. Accessed April 12, 2012. http://www.theatlantic.com/politics/archive/2010/05/sharron-angle-gets-a-tea-party-bump/56741/.

Grossberg, Larry. 1986. History, Politics and Postmodernism: Stuart Hall and Cultural Studies. *Journal of Communication Inquiry*, 10 (2): 61–77.

Gumbrecht, Jamie. 2012. Georgia Democrats Propose Limits on Vasectomies for Men. *CNN, February 21*. Accessed April 6, 2012 http://news.blogs.cnn.com/2012/02/21/georgia-democrats-to-propose-limitations-on-vasectomies-for-men/.

Hall, Stuart. 1985. Signification, Representation, Ideology: Althusser and the Post-Structuralist Debates. *Critical Studies in Mass Communication* 2 (2): 91–115.

Hall, Stuart. 1986. The Problem of Ideology: Marxism without Guarantees. *Journal of Communication Inquiry* 10 (2): 28–44.

Hartmann, Heidi. 2010. The Unhappy Marriage of Marxism and Feminism: Towards a More Progressive Union. In *Marx Today: Selected Works and Recent Debates*, edited by John F. Sitton, 201–228. New York: Palgrave MacMillan.

Herman, Edward. S., and Noam Chomsky. 1988. *Manufacturing Consent: The Political Economy of the Mass Media* New York: Pantheon Books hooks, bell. 1984. *Feminist Theory from Margin to Center*. Boston: South End Press.

Jetter, Alexis, Annelise, Orleck, and Diana, Taylor. 1997. *The Politics of Mother-hood: Activist Voices from Left to Right*. Hanover, NH: University Press of New England.

Kasper, Shirl. 1992. *Annie Oakley*. Norman: University of Oklahoma Press.

Kellner, Douglas. 1989. *Critical Theory, Marxism, and Modernity*. Baltimore: John Hopkins University Press.

Kellner, Douglas. 1995. *Media Culture. Cultural Studies, Identity, and Politics Between the Modern and the Postmodern*. New York: Routledge.

Kendell, Diana. 2010. *Sociology in Our Times: The Essentials*. Belmont: Wadsworth, Cengage Learning.

Kroll, Luisa and Kerry A. Dolan. 2011. World's Billionaires 2011: A Record Year in Numbers, Money and Impact. *Forbes,* March 9. Accessed April 6, 2012. http://www .forbes.com/2011/03/08/world-billionaires-2011-intro.html.

Kumar, Deepa. 2006. Media, Culture, and Society: The Relevance of Marx's Dialectical Method. In *Marxism and Communication Studies: The Point is to Change it*, edited by Lee Artz, Steve Macek and Dana Cloud, 71–86. New York: Peter Lang.

Laclau, Ernesto. 1977. *Politics and Ideology in Marxist Theory*. London: Verso.

Larrain, Jorge. 1996. Stuart Hall and the Marxist Concept of Ideology. In *Stuart Hall: Critical Dialogues in Cultural Studies*, edited by David Morley and Kuan-Hsing Chen, 47–70. New York: Routledge.

Larrain, Jorge. 1991. *Marxism and Ideology*. Vermont: Gregg Revivals.

Larrain, Jorge. 1982. On the Character of Ideology Marx and the Present Debate in Britain. *Theory, Culture & Society* 1 (1): 5-22.

Lewis, Charles. 1992. Making Sense of Common Sense: A Framework for Tracking Hegemony. *Critical Studies In Mass Communication* 9 (3): 277–292.

Loder, Asjylyn and David Evans. 2011. Koch Brothers Flout Law Getting Richer with Secret Iran Sales. *Bloomberg*, October 3. Accessed April 12, 2012. http://www.bloomberg.com/ news/2011-10-02/koch-brothers-flout-law-getting-richer-with-secret-iran-sales.html/.

Macek, Steve. 2006. From the Weapon of Criticism to Criticism by Weapon: Critical Communication Scholarship, Marxism, and Political Activism. In *Marxism and Communication Studies: The Point is to Change it*, edited by Lee Artz, Steve Macek and Dana Cloud, 217–242. New York: Peter Lang.

Makus, Anne. 1990. Stuart Hall's Theory of Ideology: A Frame for Rhetorical Criticism. *Western Journal Of Speech Communication* 4 (4): 495–514.

Marx, Karl. 1847. *Wages*. Accessed April 8, 2012. http://www.marxists.org/archive/ marx/works/1847/12/31.htm.

Marx, Karl. 1894. *Capital Vol. III*, edited by Frederick Engels. Accessed April 8, 2012. http://www.marxists.org/archive/marx/works/1894-c3/index.htm.

Marx, Karl. 1867. *Capital: A Critique of Political Economy,* Vol. I. Accessed April 8, 2012. http://www.marxists.org/archive/marx/works/1867-c1/.

Marx, Karl. 1992. *Early Writings*. Translated by Rodney Livingstone and Gregor Benton. New York: Penguin.

Marx, Karl. 1983. Theses on Feuerbach. In *The Portable Karl Marx*, edited by Eugene Kamenka, 155–158. New York: Penguin.

Marx, Karl and Engels, Frederick Engels. 1996. *The German Ideology*, edited by C.J. Arthur. New York: International Publishers.

Mattelart, Armand. 1978. The Nature of Communications Practice in a Dependent Society. *Latin American Perspectives*, 5: 13–34.

Mattelart, Armand. 1991. *Advertising International: The Privatisation of Public Space*. New York: Routledge.

Mayer, Jane. 2010. Covert Operations: The Billionaire Brothers Who are Waging a War against Obama. *The New Yorker*, August 30. Accessed April 8, 2012. http://www.newyorker.com/reporting/2010/08/30/100830fa_fact_mayer.

McLaughlin, Lisa. 2002. Something Old, Something New: Lingering Moments in the Unhappy Marriage of Marxism and Feminism. In *Sex & Money: Feminism and Political Economy in the Media*, edited by Eileen R. Meehan and Ellen Riordan, 30-46. Minneapolis: University of Minnesota Press.

McRobbie, Angela. 2004. Post-Feminism and Popular Culture. *Feminist Media Studies* 4(3): 255–264.

Mosco, Vincent. 1994. *The Political Economy of Communication: Rethinking and Renewal*. Thousand Oaks: Sage.

Murdock, Graham. 1997. Blindspots about Western Marxism: A Reply to Dallas Smythe. In *The Political Economy of the Media Volume I*, edited by Peter Golding and Graham Murdock, 465–475. Brookfield: Edward Elgar Publishing Company.

Padover, Saul, K., ed. 1974. *Karl Marx: On Freedom of the Press and Censorship*. New York: McGraw-Hill.

Paglia, Camille. 2008. Fresh Blood for the Vampire. *Salon*, September 10. Accessed March 17, 2012. http://www.salon.com/2008/09/10/palin_10/.

Palin, Sarah. 2010a. *America by Heart: Reflections on Family, Faith, and Flag*. New York: Harper Collins.

Palin, Sarah. 2010b. Sarah Palin Remarks on Pro-Life Agenda. *C-Span Video Library*. Accessed April 8, 2012. http://www.c-spanvideo.org/program/LifeAg.

Perry, Michael. 2005. *Lady Eugenist: Feminist Eugenics in the Speeches and Writings of Victoria Woodhull*. Seattle: Inkling Books.

Parry-Giles, Shawn, J. and Trevor, Parry-Giles. 1996. Gendered Politics and Presidential Image Construction: A Reassessment of the 'Feminine Style'. *Communication Monographs* 63: 337–353.

Public Takes Conservative Turn on Gun Control, Abortion. 2009. Pew Research Center. Accessed March 31, 2012. http://www.people-press.org/2009/04/30/public-takes-conservative-turn-on-gun-control-abortion/.

Riley, Glenda. 2002. *The Life and Legacy of Annie Oakley.* Norman: University of Oklahoma Press.

Rodino, Michelle. 2005. War Mothering. *Feminist Media Studies* 5 (3): 380–385.

Rodino-Colocino, Michelle. 2012. "Man Up," Woman Down: "Mama Grizzlies," "Feminism," and Tree House Politics. *Women and Language, 35*(1), 79–95.

Rodino-Colocino, Michelle. 2012. Participant Activism: Exploring a Methodology for Scholar-Activists Through Lessons Learned as a Precarious Labor Organizer. Communication, Culture & Critique, 5(4): 541–562.

Roediger, David. 2007. *Wages of Whiteness: Race and the Making of the American Working Class.* New York: Verso.

Rogers, Stephanie. 2011. What Occupy Wall Street Owes to Feminist Consciousness-Raising. *Ms. Magazine Blog,* December 13. Accessed April 8, 2012. http://msmagazine.com/blog/blog/2011/12/13/what-occupy-wall-street-owes-to-feminist-consciousness-raising/.

Rothman, Stanley. 1975. Marx the Journalist. *Columbia Journalism Review* July/August: 57–58.

Saad, Lydia. 2009. Before Recent Shootings, Gun-Control Support was Fading. Gallup. Accessed March 31, 2012. http://www.gallup.com/poll/117361/recent-shootings-gun-control-support-fading.aspx.

Saxton, Alexander. 1971. *The Indispensible Enemy: Labor and the Anti-Chinese Movement in California.* Berkeley: University of California Press.

Schatz, Thomas. 2004. *Hollywood: Critical Concepts in Media and Cultural Studies.* New York: Routledge.

Single Mother Poverty in the United States in 2010. 2011. *Legal Momentum,* September 15, The Women's Legal Defense and Education Fund. Accessed April 30, 2012. http://www.ncdsv.org/images/LM_SingleMotherPovertyInTheUS-2010_9-15-2011.pdf.

Smythe, Dallas. 1997. Communications: Blindspot of Western Marxism. In *The Political Economy of the Media Volume I,* edited by Peter Golding and Graham Murdock, 438–464. Brookfield: Edward Elgar Publishing Company.

Sparks, Colin. 1989. Experience, Ideology, and Articulation: Stuart Hall and the Development of Culture. *Journal Of Communication Inquiry* 13 (2): 79–87.

Stan, Adele, M. 2010. Sarah Palin's Brand of 'Feminism' More Popular with Men than with Women. *AlterNet.* Accessed April 8, 2012. http://www.alternet.org/news/148976/sarah_palin%27s_brand_of_%22feminism%22_more_popular_with_men_than_women/.

Sterne, Jonathan. 2000. The Computer Race Goes to Class: How Computers in Schools Helped Shape the Racial Topography of the Internet. In *Race in Cyberspace,* edited by Beth Kolko, Lisa Nakamura and Gil B. Rodman, 191–212. New York: Routledge.

Triece, Mary. 2012. Credible Workers and Deserving Mothers: Crafting the "Mother Tongue" in Welfare Rights Activism, 1967–1972. *Communication Studies* 63 (1): 1–17.

U.S. Department of Commerce, National Telecommunication and Information Administration. 1995. Falling Through the Net: A Survey of the "Have-Nots" in Rural and Urban America. Accessed April 19, 2012. http://www.ntia.doc.gov/ntiahome/fallingthru.html.

Vavrus, Mary. 2002. *Postfeminist News: Political Women in Media Culture*. Albany: State University of New York Press.

Vogel, Kenneth P. 2010. Face of the Tea Party is Female. *Politico*, March 26. Accessed April 8, 2012. http://www.politico.com/news/stories/0310/35094.html.

Walsh, Bryan. 2008. Palin on the Environment: Far Right. *Time*, September 1. Accessed April 6, 2012. http://www.time.com/time/politics/article/0,8599,1837868,00.html.

Wernick, Andrew. 1991. *Promotional Culture: Advertising, Ideology and Symbolic Expression*. Thousand Oaks: Sage.

White, Mimi. 1992. Ideological Analysis and Television. In *Channels of Discourse, Reassembled* (2nd edition), edited by Robert C. Allen, 161–202.

Williamson, Judith. 1978. *Decoding Advertisements: Ideology and Meaning in Advertising*. New York: Marion Boyars.

Žižek, Slavoj. 2010. *Living in the End Times*. London: Verso.

CHAPTER 11

Propaganda as Production*

Gerald Sussman

1   Introduction

"The more production comes to rest on exchange value, hence on exchange, the more important do the physical conditions of exchange – the means of communication and transport – become for the costs of circulation. *Capital by its nature drives beyond every spatial barrier. Thus the creation of the physical conditions of exchange – of the means of communication and transport – the annihilation of space by time – becomes an extraordinary necessity for it*" – Karl Marx (1973, italics added).

"We Are All Workers" – Levi's ad

As a living praxis, one of the critical tasks of Marxism is the application of its incisive logic toward interpreting the current conditions of the labour process and the modern production of surplus value. I argue that in the informational mode of development, ideology and propaganda have become all the more central to corporate capitalism, which indeed relies *on systemic propaganda as an infrastructure* in its relentless domination of time and space, including the digital array of digital media. The new media are centrally important in reproducing the ideological preconditions underpinning state legitimacy at home and abroad and, a fatal contradiction, in deepening the abstraction, alienation, and dehumanization of labor, ultimately destroying the very basis of its legitimacy. The accumulation, coercion, and cultural functions of the various instruments of mainstream media in support of the capitalist mode of production – within what has become a neoliberal *promotional economy* – have intensified and yet are increasingly transparent, making its false ideology (the grand narrative behind its propaganda) considerably more vulnerable to challenge and disruption. If anything, the internationalization and automation of production enabled through digital technology has only magnified the Marxian approach to understanding the radical changes in capital accumulation and worklife (Dyer-Witheford 1999, 5–6).

---

* The author wishes to thank Sy Adler and Evguenia Davidova for their critiques of an earlier draft of this chapter.

In this chapter, I look at formal Marxist interpretations of *ideology* from four principal sources of that discussion, Marx & Engels, Lukács, Gramsci, and Althusser, and apply their thinking to present day revisionist marxian analyses of labour to build on the critical intersection of the two. I argue that the neo-liberal economic system, with particular focus on the United States, from one based on manufacturing employment (now down to below 10 percent from 16.5 percent in 1987 and an even starker decline in its share of GDP: 11 percent in 2010 from 25 percent in the early 1980s) to one built on services, including financial and information services, has transformed the political and ideological culture. In this context, promotion and ideology-based propaganda[1] have risen to central *factors of production* – while directly influencing the casualization, informalization, and precarity of labor.

This chapter draws in part on the work of the Italian Autonomistas and their "social factory" thesis in which distinctions between formal and informal labour and producer and consumer continue to break down.[2] To this I add the importance and *organic role* of systemic propaganda in reducing the status of citizens to individuated consumers and of citizenship to spectatorship. I start with core ideas regarding base and superstructure to set up the Marxian framework and proceed to a general discussion of the uses of propaganda in the contemporary production process, the neoliberal economic context, ideology and class consciousness, and the relationship of ideology and propaganda to the informalization of labour in the social factory.

2   Propaganda and Ideology as Base and Superstructure

In his Preface to *A Contribution to a Critique of Political Economy* (1859), Marx distinguished the realm of the social relations of production (the base) from

---

1   The general distinction I make between promotion and propaganda is that promotional activities are individuated acts on behalf of specific products and policies, whereas propaganda (which incorporates promotion) is undertaken for the broader purpose of constructing ideological hegemony over the whole society. On the distinction between ideology and propaganda, the former is a world view (a way of making sense), while the latter is a set of discursive and symbolic practices derived from a particular form of ideological sense-making.

2   There is an intensive debate about whether the Autonomistas are indeed marxists. That debate is beyond the scope of this chapter. I wish only to infer that what constitutes labour has changed with the intensification of capitalist relations of production within the digital informational mode of development and the extension of production from the factory to the social factory.

that of the ideological (legitimating) institutions (the superstructure) that help to maintain the political order:

> In studying such transformations [leading to revolution] it is always nec-
> essary to distinguish between the material transformation of the eco-
> nomic conditions of production, which can be determined with the
> precision of natural science, and the legal, political, religious, artistic or
> philosophic – in short, ideological forms in which men become conscious
> of this conflict and fight it out.

That men (sic) would fight it out makes clear that what Marx had in mind about ideology is that while it is dominated by the institutions of capital, it is nonetheless contested terrain over which conflict continuously resurfaces, and not simply a predictable sphere predetermined by virtue of the control of the productive forces.

However, capital is never complacent about the risks associated with ideol-ogy. In its relentless and ever-expanding drive toward totalizing power over people and non-human resources and over time and space, late capitalism has mapped out consciousness as its final frontier. This involves a deeper order of production and continuous reproduction of ideology and public persuasion necessitated by the service character of the digital economy and aimed at cul-tivating passivity, the promotion of desire, and the construction of neoliberal materialist identities. What do I mean by *propaganda*? To begin with, propa-ganda refers to organized doctrinal texts communicated throughout the voice, print, audio/visual, and symbolic media in the service of state and corporate interests (and of aspiring power interests). *Systemic propaganda* means the penetration of promotional activities into almost every sphere of public life: the conduct of domestic politics and foreign affairs, the selling of public policy, the marketing of goods, services, and public and private institutions, the profu-sion of household and personal consumption within the "culture-ideology of consumerism" (Sklair 2001), with social psychological inducements to self-commodification (adoption of the insignia, habits, and discursive practices of the commodity culture) and an informalized "prosumer" labour force. It is also found in the wholesale infomercialization of news and mass media and spec-tacularization of public culture, joined by intensified subterranean and sub-liminal advertising, the commercialization of public space and public events, and in the promotion of self-promotion (via websites, Facebook, blogs, Twitter, etc.). The range and depth of promotion throughout the cultural and political life of the United States and other countries has led to what a group of critical scholars have termed a "propaganda society" (see Sussman 2011). By *promotion* I mean a lower-level regular employment of advertising, marketing, direct marketing, public relations (PR), and other direct selling initiatives on behalf of the more prosaic objectives of both elites and non-elites and performed by those trained as active promotional and self-promotional agents.

On the question of *ideology*, I first turn to Marx & Engels. In *The German Ideology*, they start with the universal structure of the commodity, which is the material embodiment of the social relations of production reified within capitalist ideology as a relationship not among workers but among things. The reification takes the form of what Marx (1967) referred to as the "commodity fetish," the objectification of the commodity dwelling on the outward appeal of a thing without reference to the intrinsic exploitative conditions of labour and unpaid "externalities" that brought such a thing into existence and the circuit of exchange. Representations of an independent character of commodities, orphaned from their direct producers, are thus made to appear natural. The "superstructure" is a realm of consciousness-molding (ideology), a range of activities produced by institutions (e.g., formal education, church, media, courts, corporate self-promotion, government agencies) acting as the legitimating, sometimes oppositional, agents acting for/against the capitalist "base" (sphere of production) to regulate compliance with (or resistance to) the hegemonic designs and values of the ruling class.

Where does the Marxist concept of ideology fit into an explanation of contemporary societal conditions? Marx and Engels clearly understood the power of ideology to indoctrinate the working class and to redirect their attention from the system of exploitation:

> Morality, religion, metaphysics, all the rest of ideology and their corresponding forms of consciousness, thus no longer retain the semblance of independence. They have no history, no development; but men, developing their material production and their material intercourse, alter, along with this their real existence, their thinking and the products of their thinking...generally speaking, the ideas of those who lack the means of mental production are subject to it. The ruling ideas are nothing more than the ideal expression of the dominant material relationships, the dominant material relationships grasped as ideas.
>
> MARX AND ENGELS 1845

For Marx & Engels (1845), "language is practical consciousness," and we can interpret "language" to cover a broad swath of communication(s), including advertising and marketing, in the reproduction of hegemonic ideology and the materialist realm from which it springs. In the material universe that Marx inhabited, his emphasis was understandably placed on the central importance of communications as an infrastructure of capitalist production inasmuch as communications was confined to servicing the production and circulation of basic necessities of nineteenth century life. The hegemonic power (cf Gramsci 1971) of ideological state apparatuses (cf Althusser) in his era was at an early phase of the emerging consciousness industries (cf Enzensberger). Marx died before the takeoff of the modern advertising agency and the onset of mass marketing that eventually established consumerism as a dominant way of life and as one that supervised a more efficient circuit of production-consumption. The velocity of circulation in the late nineteenth century could not compare to the contemporary speed with which capital, especially finance and other immaterial forms of capital (advertising, fashion, cultural activities, software, data files, works of art, photography, and the like), are moved around the world.[3] "Brand value" is an *immaterial* form of value creation – the socialization of capital – in which consumers identify with the (fetishized) lifestyle ideas associated with the commodity (Arvidsson 2005). As Hardt and Negri (2000, 24) observed about the new form of material order: "Biopower...refers to a situation in which what is directly at stake in power is the production and reproduction of life itself," or what Foucault called "disciplines of the body" (Foucault, 1990).

Marx generally regarded ideology as a construct of dominant repressive regimes, writing in *The German Ideology* (1845) the familiar epigraph, "The ideas of the ruling class are in every epoch the ruling ideas...," expressing the interests and dominant material relationships of the state, whereas his intellectual progeny have tended to view ideology as a necessary function of *any* state, capitalist, theocratic, or socialist. Indeed, within the Soviet Union, the uses of agitation and propaganda (agitprop) were regarded as means to educate the masses about socialism and to animate and activate them in the pursuit of social rectification. Marx, however, saw ideology primarily as the means by which the interests and dominant material relationships of the capitalist state and a mythical understanding of capital are naturalized in public consciousness, a theme further critically elucidated by Antonio Gramsci.

Marx thus associated "ideology" with the *false consciousness* spread by the ruling class, a superstructural project intended to enjoin the obedience of the working class (the function of legitimation). For that reason, Marx devoted little attention to ideology as an *alternative* form of consciousness that could prepare workers to embrace socialism, though he did describe the moment in the class struggle when the proletariat turn from a class "in itself" (*an sich*) to a class "for itself" (*für sich*) (Marx 1971). For Gramsci, the domination of classes

---

3   By 2010, the volume of daily currency trading worldwide reached $4 trillion (Watts 2010).

(hegemony)[4] in capitalist societies operates more by consent than by coercion. The task of working class liberation, he argued, rests with educated radicals, the organic intellectuals (members of the working class who articulate a practical understanding of repression and struggle through active counter-ideology) capable of seeing through the miasma of bourgeois propaganda.

Althusser as well regarded ideology in dialectical terms and treated it as a formative aspect of class identity, though he attributed its power more in structural terms (*infra*). For Althusser, ideology establishes ways of thinking and acting. As he noted:

> the reproduction of labour power requires not only a reproduction of its skills, but also, at the same time, a reproduction of its submission to the rules of the established order, i.e. a reproduction of submission to the ruling ideology for the workers, and a reproduction of the ability to manipulate the ruling ideology correctly for the agents of exploitation and repression, so that they, too, will provide for the domination of the ruling class "in words."
> ALTHUSSER 1994, 104

Althusser argued that under capitalism it is principally the education system that reproduces the culture of compliance; in an earlier era, the Middle Ages, it was the Church. These days the dominant (mainstream) media perhaps exercise even greater hegemony over the minds of working people than do formal educational institutions, a point made by the Frankfurt School theorists, particularly Herbert Marcuse (1964), who regarded media-driven consumerism as a totalitarian ideology for pacifying the working class. As a practice, propaganda relies on ideological understandings to effect its intended results.

In the workplace, ideology operates at each stage of production. Workers must be prepared to lend their power to the production process. They must also internalize the discipline in the workplace needed for its smooth operation. Ideology next assumes a critical function in the circulation of commodities (the role of advertising, marketing, branding, and other promotional activities are critical here). And finally ideology is central to the conversion of commodities at the point of sale where they are transformed into money for sellers and into consumption for buyers (Kjøsen 2010). In the production of digital commodities, the points of production and consumption are nearly coterminous, annihilating

---

4   The hegemonic culture is one in which the values of the bourgeoisie become the "common sense'" values of the whole society; where the working class identifies its own interests with that of the bourgeoisie and thereby desists from resistance or rebellion.

space by time and permitting capital to rapidly increase the velocity of circulation and the entire circuit of production-consumption.

Raymond Williams (1973), however, argued that ideology should not be con-
strued as merely instrumentalist or reductionist:

> For if ideology were merely some abstract imposed notion, if our social
> and political and cultural ideas and assumptions and habits were merely
> the result of specific manipulation, of a kind of overt training which
> might be simply ended or withdrawn, then the society would be very
> much easier to move and to change than in practice it has ever been or is.

Rather, ideology is constructed through interplay between base and superstructure, between culture, including its residues of earlier cultural epochs, and
the reflexive practices of cultural, social, and political economic institutions.
Capitalist ideological reproduction is achieved not through the repression of
dissent as much as its *appropriation* within limited and commodified confines
of protest, stripped of spontaneous or revolutionary impulses. Capital takes no
prisoners in its assault on all manifestations of cultural resistance.[5] In one of the
more explicit consumerist efforts to wipe out memories of revolutionary
thought, Macy's logo, a five-pointed red star, 60 years ago would have brought its
executives before the House Un-American Activities Committee. Saks Fifth
Avenue uses designs that are stylized in the form of Constructivist state-run
department store ads in the 1920s Soviet Union (Wilson 2009). The Bank of
Montreal repurposed Bob Dylan's countercultural anthem, "The Times They Are
A-Changin'," to sell banking services. Ads for Fortune 500 company Levi Strauss,
produced by the Wieden & Kennedy PR firm, sell jeans with such slogans as: "We
Are All Workers," "Made Strong for the New Work," and "Everybody's Work is
Equally Important." It wasn't a quote from Marx, when an ad called "2011 Jeep
Grand Cherokee Manifesto Commercial" (Brian 2010) ran with the slogan,
"Things We Make, Make Us," but it sounds as if it were.

---

5 Among the many examples of such appropriation of dissent are: the fashion of "convict"
   pants; clothing bearing names like Ideology, Propaganda, and Revolution; Das Kapital and
   Che Guevara t-shirts; "The Body Shop" capitalizing on the ideology of the environmental
   movement; Mercedes Benz car ads ripping off the eponymous song title lyrics of Janis Joplin;
   corporate polluters greenwashing themselves (to which culture jammers like Adbusters
   retaliate); the PR industry's "astroturfing" and "guerrilla marketing"; corporate tycoons
   assuming the pose of global philanthropists; Apple Computer marketing its identity as
   rebellious, even while it brutally exploits its workers in China to the point of inciting active
   rebellion (Harris 2012).

Capitalism repeatedly draws on rebels and revolutionaries for its self-aggrandizing inspirations, a tribute of sorts to the irrepressible character of radical leaders and working people. But it repackages and commodifies radical movements without any reference to the original sources or contexts. Truly radical ideas and representations are never patented, but once stolen by capital they are converted to property. Perhaps even sections of the *Communist Manifesto* may one day be copyrighted, with infringement suits directed at anyone who dares to publicly recite its passages – similar to Time Warner's ownership of the ubiquitous happy birthday song.

In the digital informational era, the promotional aspects of production take on a higher valorizing importance inasmuch as the manufacturing base has been relocated en masse to low wage (third world) industrial zones comprising the new international division of labor. This leaves Western economies the task of selling and consuming the commodities produced offshore. In the United States, where shopping is regarded as the most important personal activity outside of work and sleep, circulation has become the most critical aspect of wealth creation – the circulation of that which is affectively produced in the first place (in effect the circulation of circulation). Immaterial promotion is thus key to the maintenance of the capitalist mode of production, the overarching ideological sphere, and the unending waging of class warfare and pursuit of cultural hegemony over workers, wherever they may cluster.

3   Propaganda and the Mode of Production

Where does contemporary commercial ideology fit into Marx's superstructure thesis? In the 19th century, communications came into its own as a means of supporting industrialization, urbanization, and mediatization of the leading industrial cities and states. Marx was among the most prescient observers of the power of communications to speed up the process of commodity production and circulation and in the spreading profanity of a rogue capitalist system and ideology that, as he and Engels put it, "batters down all Chinese walls" (Marx and Engels 1848). For the most part, however, Marx looked at communications, most especially the telegraph, as an instrument serving the production sphere – in contrast to the dominant ideology, then and now, that construes technological history within traditional hagiographic renderings of Morse, Bell, Edison, and others and as a genealogy of their "inventions" (see Sussman 1997, especially Chapters 3 and 4). With the advancement of communications in commerce[6]

---

6   Telegraphy was also crucial in the development of financial markets and in consolidating the power of Wall Street over national capital.

(the facilitating role of telegraphy in newspapers, newspapers in radio, radio in television, and the like), later marxists such as Gramsci and Lukács took a deeper interest in and appreciation of the ideological functions of communications.

Since the Second World War, the capitalist state increasingly has exercised ideological control over the accumulation, coercion, and legitimation processes with the aid of advanced technology and the sweeping presence of (*pace* Althusser) Repressive State Apparatuses and the less blunt instruments of Ideological State Apparatuses. State legitimacy rests in part on its capacity to represent and internalize in the consciousness of its citizens its *raison d'etre* and its policies and manner of administration as natural, just, and in the best interests of the populace. Ideology is stored propaganda (and vice versa), employed toward specific state and commercial objectives and ratified through the general beliefs, values, assumptions, and received ideas that propagate its cultural power. In the sphere of material culture, propaganda is central to the production of commodities, in the manufacture of desire (without use value there is no exchange value), and in the broader ideology of consumption as a way of life (*consumo, ergo sum*).

As Mike Wayne suggests, to update Marx we need not only to consider formal marxist categories of analysis but to review them in light of a changed world that takes into consideration the "increasing importance of culture, communication, the exchange of ideas, feedback systems, data analysis and so forth, in the production process" (2003, 45). In a *promotional economy*, the forces of production are dedicated to circulating domestically- or foreign-made products and requires a system of surveillance and information processing to fuel its steady stream of propaganda. It also involves a systematic violation of norms of privacy of millions of people on whose lives it relies for its behavioral data harvesting and valorization – constituting in effect an "identity labor" force. This panoptic power in turn rests on a heightened fetishizing of commodity culture that induces workers and consumers (and intermediary "prosumers" – see *infra*) to submit not just their knowledge but their personal profiles to the labour process and commodity value formation.

In his widely cited discussion of audience as labor, Dallas Smythe (1977, 1981) anticipated a future in which sections of capital would deepen the range of its efforts toward the commodification of consciousness and a closer reliance on the value-producing consumer (*prosumer*). Smythe focused on advertising and the "work" of audiences, which he understood to be a demographic, in the watching of ads. Thus the audience, acting as a "labour force," a deviation from the orthodox Marxist view of surplus value creation (what he saw as a "blindspot" in its communication research), is itself treated as a commodity. But what he did not live long enough to witness were the advanced scientific methods by which advertisers watch the watchers. His most important insight

was that promotion breaks down the separation between producers and consumers, between work and leisure, and between use value and exchange value.
Advertisers pay for audiences' TV and print media watching (or radio listening)
time to sell them not only specific commodities but also the habituation to
consumption, and they are happy to pay for audiences' attention, particularly
those audiences with the propensity to consume their products.[7]

Corporate ideology reifies and universalizes false consciousness by conceal-
ing the exploitative nature of the commodity, as if it were something beyond
the labour and labour conditions embedded in its materialization – and
through identification with possession of those commodities (I am what
I own). In this way the object becomes the subject, and the subject becomes
the object. Indeed, capitalism could not operate without attending to the
molding of what Lukács called a "unified structure of consciousness" amongst
the workforce – as producers (engaged in exchange value), as consumers
(engaged in use value), and as administrators and self-administrators of the
system of production. "Bureaucracy implies the adjustment of one's way of life,
mode of work and hence of consciousness to the general socioeconomic premises of the capitalist economy" (Lukács 1971).

The propaganda and promotional functions of the state, particularly when
the success of the economy depends on the sales effort, have never been more
critical to its survival. Apostles of neoliberal doctrine, particularly in the United
States, seek to bring the remainder of nature and independent social life into
the circuit of production and consumption through a deepened international
division of labor, segregating the manual from mental and creative from
robotic aspects of work. As U.S. manufacturing industries and agriculture have
been shrinking, services have come to represent 80 percent of GDP, with
"knowledge intensive services" representing 22 percent of GDP and the largest
single segment of the U.S. workforce in 2012 (National Science Foundation,
2014). The promotional industries, including advertising, marketing, public
relations, branding, and sales management, are crucial to the circulative
aspects of production in the U.S. economy, which, with only 4 percent of the
world population consumes a quarter of global energy output and a third of
the world's paper and plastic; the average American as of 2000 consumed 53
times more than the average Chinese person (Tilford 2000) though that ratio is
certainly changing with China's rapidly developing consumer economy.

---

7   To this far-sighted analysis, Jhally and Livant (1986) offered the more nuanced explanation of
    the co-production of "watching time" by networks that purchase the "watching power" of
    audiences and sell it to advertisers.

Both the growth and concentration of the U.S. promotional economy is astounding. Just 100 advertisers (of nearly 40,000 firms) represent 41 percent of the country's total advertising expenditures (Wood 2008). Advertising alone was an estimated 2.6 percent of GDP in 2007 or $153.7 billion (TNS Media Intelligence 2007), while worldwide spending on advertising reached close to $500 billion in 2008 (Mullaney 2009). And although advertising momentarily slowed during the start of the recession, 2008–2009, PR has continued to expand. Total U.S. spending on communications in 2008 was estimated at $923.91 billion, a 5.4 percent growth over the previous year (IT Facts 2008). This staggering figure is close to Australia's entire GDP and larger than all but 13 (out of 200) other countries. The infrastructure for propaganda and promotion has never been more permeative.

The promotional culture reaches into all phases of political, economic and social life. The expression "public space" is fast losing its meaning, as one is confronted by a visual spectrum in American cities that are filled with advertising and commercial logos. High school stadiums bear the imprint of commercial advertising, while soft drink companies compete for school "pouring rights." Trams and bus stops are branded with corporate identities as are professional sports stadia and even theater tickets. Probably as many people watch the Super Bowl for its 30-second ads, each of which in 2014 cost on average $4 million, as those interested in the game itself.[8] Personal websites, blogs, Twitter, and Facebook accounts and e-book readers come with conspicuous commercial advertising. With the help of a compliant Supreme Court, which in 2010 ruled in favor of permitting nearly unlimited spending by "super PAC s" (*Citizens United v. Federal Election Commission*), American federal elections are expected to cost over $8 billion in 2012. Most of this spending will end up as 30-second TV political spots, for which political media consultants will collect a 15 percent commission. (For a longer discussion of corporate branding, see Sussman 2011.)

4   **Neoliberalism, Ideology, and the Informalization of Living Labor**

Traditional propaganda normally was employed in the service of *specific* policy or project outcomes of the state; *systemic propaganda* derives from a

---

8   The amount of actual ball-in-play time for an average 185-minute televised National Football League game comes to just 11 minutes; the rest is advertising (a third), replays, huddling, and just shots of players standing around. (Biderman 2010). This calculation of TV advertising time doesn't include the visual space covered by corporate logos adorning player uniforms and stadium billboards, fences, green screens, and merchandise.

generalized and globally integrated strategy of development rooted in neoliberal political economy and supportive technological infrastructure. One can date the transition to systemic propaganda to the beginning of "deindustrialization,"[9] deregulation, and flexible accumulation, starting in the 1970s. Aided by digital communications technology, boundaries, economic and moral, public and private, that long stood intact to that point began to crumble like the Berlin Wall. With the shift from fordism to a more flexible mode of production, capital is able to capture "larger pools of social and cultural knowledge" (Terranova 2000, 38), which it transforms into commodities and private wealth. Despite the severe crisis of the 1970s, capitalism was anything but finished and was not about to yield to a crisis of confidence, a legitimation crisis – what Jimmy Carter sermonized at the time as a national "malaise." The neoliberal project acquired a political leadership with Reagan and Thatcher that reinvigorated capitalist expansionism. Althusser (1994) argued, however, that the capitalist state does not depend for its vitality on innovations in the technological sphere or on particular individuals but does require a recharging of its ideological channels: "To my knowledge, *no class can hold State power over a long period without at the same time exercising its hegemony over and in the State Ideological Apparatuses*" (*italics in original, 112*).

Indeed, with its grounding more firmly embedded in services than manufacturing and with greater emphasis on individuated consumption, neoliberalism is marked by increased investments in cultural production and in the proliferation of signs (Goldman 1992) that permeate every sphere of society. The selling of commodities, material and immaterial, is now intrinsic to the corporate capitalist state's mode of economic, political, and cultural (re)production, such that the consumerist life becomes the norm of a corporatist state society, making propagandists of those engaged in this collective effort to convert citizenship to spectatorship. The promotional (capitalist) economy is the most predatory of all forms of industrial economies, as it is designed to colonize not only the bodies of its workers, as in the manufacturing system, but also their consciousness, identity, behavior, and personality – as well as the leadership of the state. Well over half of the members of the u.s. Congress become lobbyists, lawyers, or executives of corporations once they formally

---

9   The term "deindustrialization" is somewhat contentious, depending on whether one views economy in national or global terms. If the latter, one can argue from a world systems perspective that manufacturing although spatially decentered remains centralized in terms of control, and that the overseas transnational corporate workforce is constituted as part of a common labour formation with the design, R&D, promotional, and sales workers that are employed in the core countries.

leave their government posts, normalizing business practice as an extension of government service.[10]

In the promotional economy, the consciousness of the workforce is "atomized" for the segmented tasks of commodity production, through which workers become alienated from any sense of their independent productive capacities and further marginalized as remote appendages to mechanical production. The logic of such development and the resources employed for its implementation, including digital technology and objectified labor, are spread out over time and space. The relatively stable conditions of work that once existed vanish from mainstream public discussion, and the life of uncertainty, instability, and precarity becomes the general social norm. That is to say, within a specific mode of development,[11] all life is organized under a regime and discipline of understanding (ideology) and a division of labour assigned to the main tasks of that regime.

The transition from a fordist regime to what Harvey (2007) calls one of "flexible accumulation" necessitated a deeper level of worker discipline that could expand capitalist control over the spatially dispersed and disaggregated workplace. Time-motion methods of managing workers in the manufactory offered lessons for tertiary sector jobs, such that standardized, routinized, regimented, repetitive tasks could be instituted in service employment, in effect creating not a post-industrial as much as a *hyperindustrial* society (Sussman 2011, 11–12). Workers' subjectivity, seized and surveilled as serviceable in the production-consumption circuit, becomes the veritable *property* of capital. Informal identity labour is integrated with formal labor, with the predominant form of work rooted in informational services and the promotional industries.

Fordist (routinized) labor, meanwhile, is effectively expanded through the collapsing and convergence of job descriptions or expectations in which promotional performance is appended to jobs that in the past did not include them, such as the scripted speech of chain-store cashiers ("Did you find everything you were looking for?"), customer relations employees, technical support and other call-center operators, and wait staff who in their transactions with

---

10   According to the Center for Responsive Politics (2012), of those members of the 111th Congress (2009–2011), 52 percent went to become lobbyists or clients of lobbyists; an additional 5.2 percent worked for political action committees and 22.1 percent of the rest became executives of private organizations.

11   Manuel Castells (1996) uses the term of "mode of development" to refer to the digital media of production and exchange. He regards the digital informational mode of development as akin to the centralizing force of electricity in the making of the industrial world a century earlier.

consumers suggest additional purchasing options ("Would you like a drink with that order?" and the like). Similarly, TV sportscasters and radio talk show hosts are now expected to plug products on-air. Promotional behavior under the new work requirements is intended to increase exchange value, thus enabling an intensification of exploitation (the surplus value appropriated and valorized under such ultra-commodified "labour power").

In the neoliberal promotional economy, with the infrastructural support of digital technology, capital has undergone a major restructuring, driven by both organizational and technological opportunities and necessities – and characterized by deregulation, privatization, deterritorialization, cutbacks in government social spending, technological and institutional convergences, union-busting, erosion of the public sphere, manufacturing and service sector outsourcing, and a deepening of consumerist ideology. When not long ago, one could still imagine the separation of the workplace and home life, work and leisure, public and private space, producer and consumer, formal and informal labor, today with corporate capital at the forefront of social and political changes, these and other such dichotomies are converged and subsumed under a corporate aegis. Before entering and after departing the formal workplace, workers routinely submit their identity data, through covert surveillance and institutionalized identity theft, but often through "voluntary" means as well, for the production and marketing of goods and services. In these surplus value-generating activities, "prosumers" are employed consciously or unconsciously as free informal labor,[12] undertaking such labour using their own equipment and software (computers, programs, and internet connections). The intensification of labour extraction in a system in which informational aspects of production have become increasingly available and necessary has led to a changing form and composition of labour in material and immaterial goods production.[13]

---

12   One form of crowdsourcing is local television stations' use of their websites, blogs, Facebook, Twitter, YouTube, and special apps for soliciting news tips, photos, video, and feedback from prosumer audiences, in some cases on an exclusive (quasi-contractual) basis. Certain high-end cameras are marketed as "prosumer" quality.

13   The formal workplace is not by any means the sole locus of value creation. There is in fact a presumption of free labour that now prevails in many spheres of daily life: self-checkout at shopping centers, submission to various kinds of polling and consumer surveys, consumer data profiling created through "cookies" and credit card surveillance, registration for the use of websites, the use of ATM machines instead of tellers, and many other, often inconspicuous, acts that convert consumer behaviors and information into factors of production, further mystifying (fetishizing) the nature of the commodity.

Creative industries also regularly announce, usually online, the outsourcing of problem-solving activities to amateurs or specialists willing to participate without standard pay, perhaps in hopes of a prize or status of some sort, in finding solutions that profit the company – a system of free or very modestly compensated labour the industry calls "crowdsourcing."[14] Inasmuch as such work contributes to the creation of exchange value, people at large and outside the formal workplace have come to constitute a major source of informal labour (in the crowdsourcing example via the liberal use of their knowledge for software production). As one study noted, "the co-creation economy is about experimenting with new possibilities for value creation that are based on the expropriation of free cultural, technological, social, and affective labor of the consumer masses" (Zwick, Bonsu and Darmody 2008, 166). The principal form of labour involved in commercial crowdsourcing or surveillance is pro-motional in character, reinforcing the appeal and ideological aspects of the consumerist economy. Businesses want to know how to better design, market, and brand their products and look to audiences for that knowledge.

Such new forms of labor, compelled by speedup in a promotional economy, one in which the space between production and circulation is potentially reduced to zero (Kjøsen 2010, 83), generates a greater reliance on mental over physical labor. This "immaterial labor," writes Tiziana Terranova, a critic from the Autonomista persuasion, "involves a series of activities that are not nor-mally recognized as 'work' – in other words, the kinds of activities involved in defining and fixing cultural and artistic standards, fashions, tastes, consumer norms, and, more strategically, public opinion" (Terranova 2000, 41), but which are nonetheless part of the "process of valorization" (Lazzarato 1996, 132–133). That is to say, consumers help to produce the value of a commodity, even if only within a narrow range of resources that such labour is able or willing to invest in a given commodity creation.[15]

---

14   The willingness of workers to supply their free intellectual labour to a private entrepre-neur represents the power of reification of commodities disassociated from their social relations of production. Informal labour that contributes aesthetic, social, or affective appeal to commodities or that helps establish their marketable potential is in most instances *free labor*, not wage labor, sometimes offered voluntarily, more often captured by stealth. It demonstrates what Hardt and Negri (2000) have argued about the intensifi-cation of capital's internalized direction, though, I would contend, this does not mean that capital has abandoned its spatially aggrandizing ambitions.

15   The Autonomistas, including Terranova, Lazzarato, Tronti, and others, are sometimes placed between orthodox marxists and anarchists, though they embrace notions of class in ways that anarchists do not. The principal difference between orthodox and autono-mist marxism on the question of class is that the latter takes a broader view of what and

The traditional categorical boundaries between production and consumption have thus begun to wither. In a parallel manner, the distinction between traditional media products and advertising has also begun to disappear in the age of mega-media, the "infomercial," product placement, news plugola (the marketing of parent or affiliated network assets as part of the news agenda; see Higgins and Sussman 2007), and numerous other forms of commercial crossover that shift the construction of commodities from direct and formal to more indirect and informal sources of production. As one critical technology scholar comments, "the direct exploitation of labour is becoming less important as a source of profit and the private exploitation of social knowledge is becoming more important" (Tessa Morris-Suzuki, cited in Arvidsson 2007, 11). Surveillance is also normalized at the level of popular media culture. The journalist Chris Hedges notes how "'Big Brother' and 'Survivor' glamorize the intrusiveness of the surveillance state" to draft voyeuristic impulses of audiences in the project of self-commodification (Hedges 2009, 39).

In the selling economy, increased importance is given to the circulation of commodities, which makes both its promotion and the larger culture of consumerism (ideology) central to the creation of surplus value. There is a separate sphere of activity, which can be called the production of consumption, involving the various promotional activities (advertising, marketing, public relations, sales management, branding, and the like), which are industries in and of themselves. The mobilization of people as prosumers in the promotional economy leads to what Mario Tronti (see Cleaver 1992) identified as the "social factory" – the production of all by all, a deeper level productive and ideological penetration integrating the social relations of production and consumption, "where the whole society becomes an articulation of production." Within the social factory, where capital focuses more of its attention on cultural production, the consumer imagines her/himself to have a communitarian identity through access to the commodity. Raymond Williams (1973), concerned with the prevailing ideology of capitalism, urged that "we should look not for the components of a product but for the conditions of a practice... the point of departure, in practical and theoretical work, within an active and self-renewing Marxist cultural tradition."

Hyperindustrialization of work routines is typical in retail sales, telemarketing, automobile service, clerical jobs, and other low-wage, non-professional

---

who constitutes a class formation. In the context of a state where factory labour has greatly diminished in scale and where work is increasingly embedded in immaterial forms of production, it would appear appropriate to reconsider class constituency, although the concept of the social relations of production is as valid as ever.

occupations, often organized with precise automated pavlovian signaling systems (e.g., buzzers and flashing lights in fast food restaurant kitchens, predictive dialing technology at call centers) that pace the routinized output of workers. Though there is now a more geographical dispersion of manual and mental labor, the conveyor belt method of production looks very much the same for the millions of workers tied to checkout counters, call centers, and fast food assembly lines, as it does in the manufactory setting. Even medical clinic physicians are regimented by the clock and pressured to treat patients as proceed units with taylorist regularity.

With new forms of immaterial capital and an informalized labour pool, there are no speed limits to the circulation of immaterial commodities. The reproduced value of commodities in digital format is potentially immense as there are no added production costs associated with each retransmission, hence superexploitation of those who produce but do not own the prototype. Capital in fact must withhold the release of digital commodities in order to prepare for its circulation (advertising, marketing, etc.) (Kjøsen 2010, 83). Once released, however, it is relatively easy for others to reproduce and recirculate items on a shareware basis. File sharing is commonly treated as "copyright infringement" from the capitalist standpoint, but could just as easily be regarded as a social redistribution of compensation in kind for the lost appropriation of surplus value in commodity production – A better social distribution of compensation, would be broader, more beneficial social benefits, such as single payer national healthcare, free higher education, livable minimum wages, and the guarantee of decent housing for all.

5   **"All the King's Horses and All the King's Men Couldn't Put Humpty Together Again": The Coming Collapse of State Legitimacy?**

Under neoliberalism and the digital communications system, the consumer has become far more integrated not only as an end user of production (consumption) but as a *factor* of production – the *prosumer* labour force. In the promotional economy in which surveillance and communications in general are now vital aspects in perfecting the circuit of production, from the sweatshops in China to the internetshops in America to final consumption, there are no longer well-defined boundaries to what constitutes labour (those who create exchange value). Far from undermining the Marxist theory of value and the related precepts of exploitation and alienation, the idea of promotional labour places Marxism at the center of understanding the new global economy. The biggest change in the past 35 years or so is the rise of the promotional economy in which the central economic (and cultural, political, and ideological) activity is selling, whether it be tangible commodities, largely produced offshore, or public policies.

With the system of production so entwined in the system of consumption, the ensemble of the "social factory," the present assignment of ownership of production knowledge to the capitalist class is fundamentally disputable. The form of value creation in the promotional economy makes conspicuous the fact that commodity production derives from socially constructed knowledge (Virno 2001) – what Marx (1973) called the "general intellect." Capital relies on the general intellect to increase productivity and sustain its rate of profit. In the social factory, the scope of the general intellect on which capital can directly draw is vastly enlarged through the means of digital contact, surveillance, knowledge expropriation, and the promotion of desire. But, as Negri (2006), Žižek (2009), and others have argued, capitalism has *privatized* the general intellect, the result of which is an "increase of surplus labor time [that] *prevents* more and more people from enjoying the free time of creative learning and experimentation that would lead the general intellect to flourish" (Smith n.d., 5; italics in original).

The increasing use of informalized labour in the form of surveys, polling, crowdsourcing, focus groups, web use, media subscription, credit card surveillance, cookies, "cool-hunting," and myriad other ways of employing identity labour of consumers as value producers (prosumerism) makes virtually everyone a bonafide shareholder in the production of goods and services. That is, the capitalist system has converted the society as a whole into a production "factory" and into what has become a system of socially organized consumption (Lazzarato 1996), with labour functions extended throughout the matrix of personal, social, and work life. The system of patents, trademarks, and copyrights, always an ideological and legal as much as a property instrument for the control of production and regulation of society by the capitalist class, has become an anachronistic residue of a market practice that has no relationship to how production is actually constituted.

In a production system conceived as a reification of the "general intellect," the appropriate form of ownership would be collective. Of course the name given to a system in which ownership is assigned to the whole society is socialism. Is socialism possible? In the promotional economy, it is all the more transparent that the working class as a whole[16] produces the wealth of nations, ergo

---

16   Hardt and Negri (2000) choose to refer to the class of non-capitalists as the "multitude," a
      rather vague description of the "99 percent'". Even if Marx's term "petty bourgeoisie"
      (those with capitalist administrative functions, such as lawyers, accountants, corporate

there has never been a more compelling justification for workers to claim political power on that basis. The creative designs of communications to manage capitalist society can also be employed and are being employed to undermine it (Wikileaks exposés, the Edward Snowden leaks, growing distrust of the mainstream media, media "piracy" and hacking, anti-advertising movements, growing uses of alternative media, Occupy social networking, and other on-the-ground and mediated forms of resistance). There are clear signs of rupture in US domestic ruling ideology, but physical, economic, political, and social conditions likely will have to further deteriorate before a counter-ideology, based on collectivist thinking can take shape and produce propaganda and massive public protest in line with radically different notions of social progress, teleology, and the role of the individual in society.

What forms of opposition and resistance are presently feasible, and how can they rejuvenate a sense of class struggle? In a digital informational environment, mental labour is indeed difficult to keep proprietary, and there appears to be an unrelenting grassroots effort to maintain the principal information sharing and social networking system, the Internet, as a system of free exchange. No democratic state worthy of the name can exist without a vibrant communication system that provides citizens with the means to make informed and rational political and personal and collective choices. There cannot be a complete negation of all that has evolved under capitalism, but there can be a reappropriation of the promotional means of production toward the cultivation of a harmonious work life, with far less emphasis on consumption and far more value placed on planetary coexistence with all peoples and all life forms. It is important for social activists to fight for an open Internet system and at the same time for recovery of the airwaves. The Occupy Movement needs to include local and network TV channels as targets for occupation, because they still represent the principal sources of "news," information, propaganda, and ideology for most Americans. Their constant stream of misinformation, ideological distortion, and destructive consumerism and imperialist jingoism has been lethal to the prospects of a more democratic society.

An active and enlightened source of free exchange on the web, based on principles of inclusiveness and social justice, can contribute to a wakening and reawakening of the spirit of the commons and to deep challenges by the working class as a whole (the social factory) to state institutional repression and the

---

scientists and engineers, and others) is out of fashion, his concept of class stratification is more substantial than the undifferentiated notion of "multitude." However, both Hardt and Negri and Marx use terminology, whether multitude or proletariat, that tend to wash over cultural and practical distinctions based on race, ethnicity, and gender.

fatuousness of its class-centered rationalizations of power. This level *and con-sciousness* of collective agency in turn can form the alternative of cooperative labour and the radical deconstruction of and reflexivity of refusal toward corporatism and the erosion of its hegemonic ideology and and anti-social propaganda, the formation of socialist political institutions, and the gradual elimination of the many forms of exploitation and alienation and class reproduction itself. When the conditions are right, and with the aid of digital media, albeit originally designed for other promotional purposes, a *tsunami* of revolt, like that witnessed in the "Arab Spring," will spread across the shores of the United States and its corporate capitalist world system allies, cancelling the grand imperialist theft of worker knowledge and creativity and substituting collectivization for privatization in the common interest of citizenship and human survival.

References

Althusser, Louis 1994. Ideology and Ideological State Apparatuses (Notes Toward an Investigation). In *Mapping Ideology*, edited by Slavoj Žižek, 100–140. London: Verso.

Arvidsson, Adam 2005. Brands: A Critical Perspective. *Journal of Consumer Culture* 5 (2): 235–258.

Arvidsson Adam 2007. Creative Class or Administrative Class: On Advertising and the 'Underground'. Ephemera 7 (1): 8–23.

Biderman, David. 2010. 11 Minutes of Action. *Wall Street Journal*, January 15. Online edition.

Brian. 2010. In Want of Things We Can Touch. Anidea website. Accessed February 3, 2012. http://anidea.com/strategy/in-want-of-things-we-can-touch/.

Castells, Manuel. 1996. *The Rise of the Network Society: The Information Age: Economy, Society and Culture*. Cambridge, MA: Blackwell.

Center for Responsive Politics. 2012. Revolving Door: Former Members of the 111th Congress. Open Secrets.Org website. Accessed March 1, 2012. http://www .opensecrets.org/revolving/departing.php?cong=111.

Cleaver, Harry. 1992. The Inversion of Class Perspective in Marxian Theory: From Valorisation to Self-Valorisation. In *Essays on Open Marxism: Theory and Practice*, Vol. 2, edited by Werner Bonefeld, Richard Gunn and Kosmos Psychopedis, 106–144. London: Pluto Press.

Dyer-Witheford, Nick 1999. *Cyber-Marx: Cycles and Circuits of Struggle in High-Technology Capitalism*. Urbana, IL: University of Illinois Press.

Foucault, Michel. 1990, *The History of Sexuality. Vol. 1. An Introduction*. Trans. Robert Hurley. New York: Vintage.

Goldman, Robert. 1992. *Reading Ads Socially*. New York: Routledge.

Gramsci, Antonio 1971, *Selections from the Prison Notebooks*. New York: International Publishers.

Hardt, Michael and Antonio Negri. 2000. *Empire*. Cambridge, MA: Harvard University Press.

Harris, Paul. 2012. Apple Hit by Boycott Call over Worker Abuses in China. *The Observer*, January 28. Online edition.

Harvey, David. 2007. *A Brief History of Neoliberalism*. New York: Oxford University Press.

Hedges, Chris. 2009. *Empire of Illusion: The End of Literacy and the Triumph of Spectacle*. New York: Nation Books.

Higgins, Carey L. and Gerald Sussman. 2007. Plugola: News for Profit, Entertainment, and Network Consolidation. In *Urban Communication: Production, Text, Context*, edited by Timothy A. Gibson and Mark Lowes, 141–162. Lanham, MD: Rowman & Littlefield.

IT Facts. 2008. Telecom Spending to Reach $923.91 Bln in 2008. Accessed February 29, 2012. http://www.itfacts.biz/telecom-spending-to-reach-92391-bln-in-2008/11091.

Jhally, Sut and Bill Livant. 1986. Watching as Working: The Valorization of Audience Consciousness. *Journal of Communication* 36 (3):124–143.

Kjøsen, Atle Mikkola. 2010. An Accident of Value: A Marxist-Virilian Analysis of Digital Piracy. Master's thesis, University of Western Ontario. Accessed January 14, 2012. http://uwo.academia.edu/kjosen/Papers/387636/An_Accident_of_Value_A_Marxist-Virilian_Analysis_of_Digital_Piracy.

Lazzarato, Maurizio. 1996. Immaterial Labor. In *Radical Thought in Italy: A Potential Politics*, edited by Paolo Virno and Michael Hardt, 132–146. Minneapolis: University of Minnesota Press.

Lukács, Georg. 1971. *History and Class Consciousness: Studies in Marxist Dialectics*. Cambridge, MA: MIT Press.

Marcuse, Herbert. 1964. *One-Dimensional Man: Studies in the Ideology of Advanced Industrial Society*. Boston: Beacon Press.

Marx, Karl. 1859. Preface: *A Contribution to a Critique of Political Economy*. Accessed December 18, 2011. http://www.marxists.org/archive/marx/works/1859/critique-pol-economy/preface.htm.

Marx, Karl. 1967. *Capital. Vol. 1*. New York: International Publishers.

Marx, Karl. 1971. *The Poverty of Philosophy*. Moscow: Progress Publishers.

Marx, Karl. 1973, *The Grundrisse*. Trans. M. Nicolaus. New York: Penguin. Accessed December 12, 2011. http://www.marxists.org/archive/marx/works/1857/grundrisse/ch10.htm.

Marx, Karl and Friedrich Engels. 1845. *The German Ideology*. Accessed December 14, 2011. http://www.marxists.org/archive/marx/works/1845/german-ideology/ch01b.htm.

Marx, Karl and Friedrich Engels. 1848. *Manifesto of the Communist Party*. Accessed December 13, 2011http://www.marxists.org/archive/marx/works/1848/communist-manifesto/ch01.htm.

Mullaney, Tim 2009. Global Ad Spending to Fall in 2009, Forecasters Say. Bloomberg News. Accessed January 13, 2012. http://www.bloomberg.com/apps/news?pid=news archive&sid=aZ2ysUouRIYo&refer=home.

National Science Foundation. 2014. U.S. Knowledge-Intensive Services Industries Employ 18 Million and Pay High Wages. Accessed October 20, 2014. http://www.nsf.gov/statistics/2015/nsf15300/?org=NSF.

Negri, Antonio. 2006. *Goodbye Mr. Socialism: In Conversation with Raf Valvola Scelsi*. New York: Seven Stories Press.

Sklair, Leslie. 2001. *The Transnational Capitalist Class*. Malden, MA: Blackwell.

Smith, Tony (n.d.). The 'General Intellect' in the *Grundrisse* and Beyond. Accessed March 23, 2012. http://www.public.iastate.edu/~tonys/10%20The%20General%20Intellect.pdf.

Smythe, Dallas W. 1977. Communications: Blindspot of Western Marxism. *Canadian Journal of Political and Social Theory* 1 (3): 1–27.

Smythe, Dallas W. 1981. On the Audience Commodity and Its Work. In *Dependency Road: Communications, Capitalism, Consciousness, and Canada*, 22–51. Norwood, NJ: Ablex.

Sussman, Gerald. 1997. *Communications, Technology, and Politics in the Information Age*. Thousand Oaks, CA: Sage.

Sussman, Gerald. 2011. Introduction: The Propaganda Society. In *PropagandaThe Society: Promotional Culture and Politics in Global Context*, edited by Gerald Sussman, 1–21. New York: Peter Lang.

Terranova, Tiziana. 2000. Free Labor: Producing Culture for the Digital Economy. *Social Text* 18 (2): 33–58.

Tilford, Dave. 2000. Why Consumption Matters. Sierra Club. Accessed February 12, 2012. http://www.sierraclub.org/sustainable_consumption/tilford.asp.

Virno, Paolo. 2001. General Intellect. Trans. Arianna Bove. Accessed January 18, 2012. http://www.generation-online.org/p/fpvirno10.htm.

Watts, William L. 2010. Daily Foreign-Exchange Turnover Hits $4 Trillion. *Market Watch*.AccessedJanuary22,2012.http://www.marketwatch.com/story/daily-currency-trading-turnover-hits-4-trillion-2010-09-01.

Williams, Raymond. 1973. Base and Superstructure in Marxist Cultural Theory. Accessed December 15, 2011. http://www.rlwclarke.net/courses/LITS3303/2008-2009/04CWilliamsBaseandSuperstructureinMarxistCulturalTheory.pdf.

Wilson, Eric. 2009. Consumers of the World Unite. *New York Times*. Online edition, January 7.

Wood, Deborah J. 2008. *Hanon McKendry Buys into Alternative Media Firm for Online Advertising Growth*. Accessed January 22, 2012. http://www.rapidgrowthmedia.com/devnews/mndscpe1002.aspx.

Žižek, Slavoj. 2009. *First as Tragedy, Then as Farce*. London: Verso.

Zwick, Detlev, Samuel K. Bonsu and Aron Darmody. 2008. Putting Consumers to Work: "Co-Creation" and New Marketing Govern-Mentality. *Journal of Consumer Culture* 8 (2): 163–196.

CHAPTER 12

Updating Marx's Concept of Alternatives*

Peter Ludes

1   Introduction

Since the first phases of industrialization and democratization in the 19th century, many scholars have contributed eminently to interpreting these economic and political upheavals. Prominently among them were, e.g., Karl Marx and Norbert Elias – among the contemporary ones Jürgen Habermas and Ulrich Beck. Which insights can be gained via explicitly constructed synopses of and dialogues between a few of their highlighted perspectives? Which new insights will be gained via and in terms of such an intergenerational dialogue, concerning driving forces and/or impeding forces? Such an endeavour leads well beyond one theory tradition alone, even if it is as important as the various strands of Marxian analyses and theories, of Marxist organizations and activities.

Yet, from the outset a strong Western bias must be acknowledged, both in terms of the historical phases of industrialization, urbanization, bureaucratization, education, or democratization taken into account as well as the social scientific theories used to interpret and change social conditions. "How different would the history of sociology or anthropology have been if Max Weber (say) had come from India, Emile Durkheim from Cuba or Norbert Elias from Martinique?" (Burke and Pallares-Burke 2008, 17)

No theory by one author alone can claim to have developed a globally pertinent theory of alternatives. Yet (Marx 1973: Grundrisse, 77, put into parentheses), "if we did not find concealed in society as it is the material conditions of production and the corresponding relations of exchange prerequisite for a classless society, then all attempts to explode it would be quixotic." (Marx 1973, Grundrisse English ed., 159) Therefore, this chapter will (1) situate Marx's concept of an alternative classless society in a network of later attempts at

---

* My research into the sociology of alternatives, since the seventies of the past century, gained from discussions with Daniel Bell, Harvard, and Norbert Elias, Bielefeld and Amsterdam. Since 2009, I discussed the more encompassing project sketched in section 1 in the context of the research centre Humanities, Modernity, Globalization in the School of Humanities and Social Sciences of Jacobs University Bremen. Kind thanks also to two reviewers of tripleC.

understanding long-term developments and detecting alternatives; (2) specify Marx's concept of an alternative classless society with a selection of highly pertinent quotations, referenced both in the original German and in English, which calls for a complementary update in terms of more recent studies, e.g., by Norbert Elias, Jürgen Habermas, and Eric Hobsbawm; and (3) discuss some chances and limits of alternatives at the beginning of the 21st century in terms of global risk challenges and human rights.

2   Intergenerational Dialogues

From Elias's classic theory of long-term social processes, to be sketched below, including those of more realistic sociological means of orientation and communication, two major components are basic to my inquiry: (1) Individual authors and their works are not the most important or decisive units of analysis, but intergenerational figurations, which combine to new types of insights. (2) Not only the concepts of individual authors and of short-term orientations are at stake, but the very notions of a scholarly "work," to be transformed in terms of a "collective authorship or mind." This will lead from a traditional history of ideas to an equal footing of authors from quite different epochs and thereby a collective enlightenment scope, taking into account long-term ambiguities as well as dis-/continuities, shifts or break ups, i.e. tilting phenomena.

This diagnosis requires a concrete research project to enlarge the scope of theory-formation beyond traditional texts and efforts for global knowledge beyond Western biases (Featherstone and Venn 2006; Jin 2007). In order to re-allocate the status of widely acknowledged eminent theoreticians – whose special importance for international social theory formation cannot be deepened here – this chapter focuses only on Marx's concept of alternatives, yet in a more encompassing project on the works by the following eleven theoreticians (1) Karl Marx; (2) Friedrich Nietzsche; (3) Max Weber; (4) Georg Simmel; (5) Sigmund Freud; (6) Karl Mannheim; (7) Norbert Elias; (8) Alfred Schütz (and Thomas Luckmann); (9) Jürgen Habermas; (10) Niklas Luhmann; and (11) Ulrich Beck.

As recently examined by Danowksi and Park (2009, 351), "[i]t would be of interest to map the network structure among public intellectuals, based on their co-appearance in the same discussion threads. However, when the study was pilot tested, sufficient co-occurrence of public intellectuals in the same discussion threads was not found to warrant such an analysis." Their findings show "on the internet, dead public intellectuals have a social afterlife, a sociomorphic quality that continues in cyberspace. This is a cultural domain in which discursive formations involving public intellectuals continue to evolve. The findings relate to the existing body of research concerning evaluations of online discussion" (Danowski and Park 2009, 352). They conclude: "It would be fruitful to [...] use more traditional methods of content analysis. While thread-edness is a message content-based construct, it is only an indirect measure of content. It is more clearly a measure of the persistence of discussion associated with a public intellectual and related ideas, not the composition of the threads. Their semantic composition would be a valuable component of a broader attention to public intellectuals and the internet" (Danowski and Park 2009, 353).

Intergenerational Dialogues will advance in this direction, exemplifying the transformation of the humanities and social sciences in terms of online sources, discourses, and publications. The concept of "dialogues" implies that no hierarchy is presumed or aimed at, but a focus on those theory elements, which combine to innovative synopses, less dependent on their historical or ideological roots. This procedure suspends traditional concepts of biologically and culturally shaped generations, as advanced, e.g., by Karl Mannheim. It deviates from more traditional histories of ideas arguing for the priority of certain thinkers, e.g., Fuchs' (2009) excellent article on Marx and the media.

Therefore, the selected works will not be interpreted as distinct outcomes of generation-specific conditions and insights, but as combining to a joint process of intergenerational knowledge creation and reflection, beyond biological time spans – which, nevertheless are taken into account for preliminary interpretations and the selection of variations of concepts of, e.g., societal alternatives.

A very simple and therefore transparent synopsis of the time horizon of the more encompassing research is sketched in Figure 12.1 below.

If we select only two major concepts for each individual work, e.g., for Karl Marx "classless society" and "alternatives" (as core elements of semantic fields), the number of all possible links between such 22 concepts amounts to 231. This network of concepts is visualized in Figures 12.2 and 12.3, below:

These figures visualize the increasing interconnectedness of this intergenerational dialogue, leading individual works into the background and the network of concepts into the foreground. Thereafter, similar synopses of online publications will lead to even larger data sets and more complicated visualizations.

Already in 1929, Karl Mannheim developed a dynamic synthesis of diverse perspectives beyond class and political group barriers, challenged by his contemporary Antonio Gramsci. This intellectual challenge becomes more demanding, namely to investigate well beyond traditional national perspectives and to see and show synopses beyond current orientations and now living

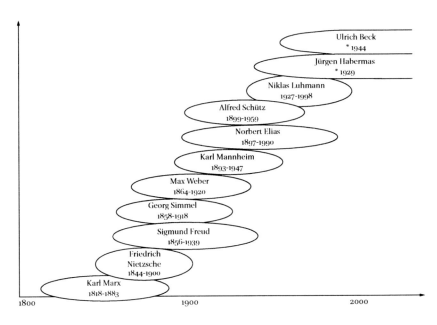

FIGURE 12.1   *A synopsis of eleven selected public intellectuals from Marx to Beck*

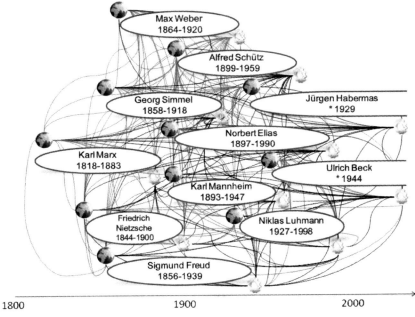

FIGURE 12.2   *A synopsis of collected writings by eleven selected public intellectuals from Marx to Beck with 231 links for 22 variations of concepts of two selected concepts, emphasis on the authors*

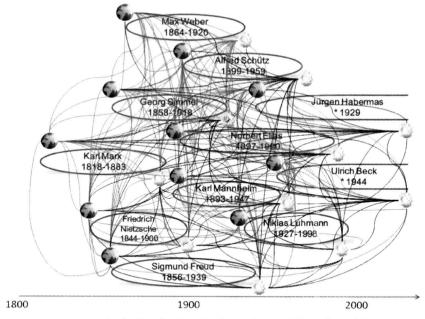

FIGURE 12.3 *A synopsis of collected writings by eleven selected public intellectuals from Marx to*
Beck with 231 links for 22 variations of concepts of two selected concepts, emphasis
on the intergenerational network of knowledge creation

generations. Mannheim's assistant Elias inquired in his "Habilitationsschrift"
from 1933 on the Court Society into a major phase prior to industrial capitalism
as an important example for the historic development of state institutions,
behaviour standards and personality traits. Elias's later (1939, in English 2000)
interpretations of books on manners as observers and standards of human
behaviour and personality structures in the context of increasing
interdependencies between various social strata and functional realms as well
as the monopolization of physical force and taxation by state institutions laid
the basis for his outline of a theory of the civilizing process in the West. State
formation, behaviour standards and personality structures were seen together.
His insights, however, also allow for a better understanding of multiple
civilizing processes in historically differentiated cultural zones. (Cp. with
explicit references to Elias Ben-Rafael and Sternberg 2001.)

According to Elias's theory of long-term unplanned civilizing processes,
networks of interdependencies are multi-dimensional and multi-functional,
and only very partially known or intelligible to the actors or authors – which
points beyond any attempt at discovering universal principles of socio-
economic developments and revolutionary progress. They are so numerous

(cp. Elias's chapter 3 on Game models and his calculation of the complexity of social relationships in Elias 1978, 101, Table 1) that it is impossible for any individual actor or author to oversee millions of connections already in small-scale networks. It is even less probable that individuals can calculate advantages and disadvantages, costs and benefits of individual actions within such networks or even parts of figurations beyond their own lifetimes. Elias (1939, cp. Ludes 1989) mainly argued that unplanned long-term social processes predominate any kind of short-term individual constraints and options as well as affective ties and deep-seated levels of anxieties. Such unintended consequences of social actions, strategies, interdependencies of knowledge, and risky unawareness have become a major concern of Ulrich Beck's (1992, 2008a and 2008b) theory-formation on reflexive modernization.

In contrast, Habermas focused on (communicative) *actions* rather than on the means of production, class relationships, civilizing processes, or a risk society, relying on the Weberian tradition of action theory and rationalization processes. Habermas (1981, vol. 1, 439 and 446) focuses on interactions, which can be verbalized. In his theory of communicative action, "total experiences" as a prerequisite for "existential truths" (cp., e.g., Wolff 1976) come closest to dramaturgical actions, fundamentally expressive, calling for existential truth or authenticity in a subjective world. But for any type of discourse, its participants must mutually accept and listen to each other, be trustworthy and act trustfully. In historic terms, sacred traditions offer limitations, which have been only partially transformed and replaced in secularizing phases of social development. Most prominently, in his "Theory of Communicative Action," Habermas (1981, vol. 2, 585) postulated three distinct social realms, namely science, ethics, and arts, whose communication across realms had to be taken into account. Both the distinction and the complementarities condition and frame any discourse on diagnoses and even more so on strategies for actions. In more recent writings, Habermas (1999, 2011) emphasized the "inclusion of the other." Similar to Kurt H. Wolff's emphasis on the historic rupture of the possibility of human self-destruction as a challenge for historically new understandings of all kinds of social relations, Habermas (2001, 125) focused also on the dangers of gene-technology and especially cloning as transforming human autonomy.

Therefore, a globalizing discourse theory does not only require existential truths as prerequisites, but also intergenerational ties, i.e. an alternative social institution, which requires questioning current self-understandings of autonomous individuals, parties, or classes and time horizons limited to individual life-spans. Some attempts at using original Marxian insights from the 19th century for the beginning of the 21st century, from analyses of the early phases of industrialization without any bourgeois and/or proletarian democratization, especially the right to vote or some state and public control of decision-making in companies fall behind Marx's achievements of analyzing socio-economic developments with a multiplicity of perspectives. Only thereby his critiques of the German ideology or of the political economy of the early and mid-19th century could be developed for new types of "alternatives." Therefore, this chapter aims at updating Marx's concept of an alternative, classless society in terms of a few social scientific studies from the past decades. Since this update – which implies fundamental upheavals for historically new conditions – begins with Marx's original sketches, a few especially pertinent quotations will be offered; in this context, it appears as obvious that this should be done in English, although concepts always carry on some original language connotations, which often get lost even in excellent translations. As Bielsa (2011, 205) states, "the global dominance of English is expressed [...] in [...] domesticating translation [...] which disrupts the cultural codes of the translating language."

I draw attention only to two "words" in Marx's writings: "bedingen", which may be translated as "to condition" or "to determine", originally is similar to "provide with things" or "provide with material", which does not necessarily refer to a "material basis". "Notwendigkeit", as another example, implies the necessity to turn over misery, "Not-Wendigkeit," not necessarily socio-economic determinism (Fleischer 1972, 74 and 142). "British and American sociology have neglected the important role translation plays in the discipline, both in mediating the international circulation of theory and in key methodological aspects of social research, a lack of interest that can in part be explained as a product of current global inequalities and the dominant position of the Anglo-American academy in the world." (Bielsa 2011, 212)

3   How Did Marx Specify an Alternative, Classless Society?

Reviewing all writings of the Collected Works of Marx in German (MEW) led to a reconstruction of major prerequisites, impediments and characteristics of an alternative, classless society already more than three decades ago (Ludes 1979 and 1980). Mainly in writings not intended for publication including the "Economic-Philosophical Manuscripts," the "Grundrisse" and letters, Marx repeatedly asserted that the conscious control of economic and social processes is desirable and realizable. He also stressed the possibility and desirability of fundamental transformations of human character-formations like a general need for surplus labour, work discipline, solidarity with one's own as well as future generations; moreover, a decline or even abolition of traditional institutions like property, the family, money and finally the state at least in its repressive functions.

Marx (see table 1 in Ludes 1979, 130) named about 210–215 times specific prerequisites, 50–55 times impediments for a classless society, and warned that material wealth might lead to golden chains fettering workers within capitalism.

He sketched characteristics of a classless society in about 150 passages.

"The German Ideology" (MEW 3, 424) for example considered the division of labour together with private property as limits of productivity: "We have already shown above that the abolition of a state of affairs in which relations become independent of individuals, in which individuality is subservient to chance and the personal relations of individuals are subordinated to general class relations, etc. – that the abolition of this state of affairs is determined in the final analysis by the abolition of division of labour. We have also shown that the abolition of division of labour is determined by the development of intercourse and productive forces to such a degree of universality that private property and division of labour become fetters on them. We have further shown that private property can be abolished only on condition of an all-round development of individuals, precisely because the existing form of intercourse and the existing productive forces are all-embracing and only individuals that are developing in an all-round fashion can appropriate them, i.e., can turn them into free manifestations of their lives. We have shown that at the present time individuals must abolish private property, because the productive forces and forms of intercourse have developed so far that, under the domination of private property, they have become destructive forces, and because the contradiction between the classes has reached its extreme limit. Finally, we have shown that the abolition of private property and of the division of labour is itself the association of individuals on the basis created by modern productive forces and world intercourse" http://www.marxists.org/archive/marx/works/1845/german-ideology/cho30.htm (accessed March 30, 2012).

Yet, in Volume 1 of "Capital" (MEW 23, 512), Marx postulated the suspension of the old division of labour. http://www.marxists.org/archive/marx/works/1867-c1/ch15.htm#S1 (accessed March 30, 2012). In an earlier version of the sixth chapter of the first volume of Capital, Marx foresaw the ambivalence of scientific progress, which increases human control over nature, but also over workers (Resultate, 80f): "The application of the forces of nature and science [...] are [...] things which confront the individual workers as *alien, objective,* and *present in advance*" http://www.marxists.org/archive/marx/works/1864/economic/cho2b.htm (accessed March 30, 2012).

In his speech at the anniversary of the "People's Paper," Marx argued in 1856:

> At the same pace that mankind masters nature, man seems to become enslaved to other men or to his own infamy. Even the pure light of science

seems unable to shine but on the dark background of ignorance. All our invention and progress seem to result in endowing material forces with intellectual life, and in stultifying human life into a material force. This antagonism between modern industry and science on the one hand, modern misery and dissolution on the other hand; this antagonism between the productive powers and the social relations of our epoch is a fact, palpable, overwhelming, and not to be controverted. [...] The English workingmen are the firstborn sons of modern industry. They will then, certainly, not be the last in aiding the social revolution produced by that industry, a revolution, which means the emancipation of their own class all over the world, which is as universal as capital-rule and wages-slavery http://www.marxists.org/archive/marx/works/1856/04/14.htm (accessed March 30, 2012).

About two years before his death, Marx wrote to Domela Nieuwenhuis in 1881:

The thing to be done at any definite given moment of the future, the thing immediately to be done, depends of course entirely (sic!) on the given historical conditions in which one has to act. But this question is in the clouds and therefore is really the statement of a phantom problem to which the only answer can be – the *criticism of the question* itself. No equation can be solved unless the elements of its solution are involved in its terms. [...] Perhaps you will point to the Paris Commune; but apart from the fact that this was merely the rising of a town under exceptional conditions, the majority of the Commune was in no sense socialist, nor could it be. [...] It is my conviction that the critical juncture for a new International Workingmen's Association has not yet arrived and for this reason I regard all workers' congresses, particularly socialist congresses, in so far as they are not related to the immediate given conditions in this or that particular nation, as not merely useless but harmful. They will always fade away in innumerable stale generalised banalities http://www.marxists.org/archive/marx/works/1881/letters/81_02_22.htm (accessed March 30, 2012).

Even more fundamental are the following prerequisites, which were not yet met by the beginning of the 21st century and thereby reduce the applicability of Marx's (and Engels's) early "Manifesto":

National differences and antagonism between peoples are daily more and more vanishing, owing to the development of the bourgeoisie, to freedom of commerce, to the world market, to uniformity in the mode of production and in the conditions of life corresponding thereto. The supremacy of the proletariat will cause them to vanish still faster. United action, of the leading civilised countries at least, is one of the first conditions for the emancipation of the proletariat. In proportion as the exploitation of one individual by another will also be put an end to, the exploitation of one nation by another will also be put an end to. In proportion as the antagonism between classes within the nation vanishes, the hostility of one nation to another will come to an end http://www .marxists.org/archive/marx/works/1848/communist-manifesto/ch02.htm (accessed March 30, 2012)

In the "Grundrisse," Marx elaborated some of his earlier thoughts. Thus:

> When the limited bourgeois form is stripped away, what is wealth other than the universality of individual needs, capacities, pleasures, productive forces etc., created through universal exchange? The full development of human mastery over the forces of nature, those of so-called nature as well as of humanity's own nature? The absolute working-out of his creative potentialities, with no presupposition other than the previous historic development, which makes this totality of development, i.e. the development of all human powers as such the end in itself, not as measured on a *predetermined* yardstick? Where he does not reproduce himself in one specificity, but produces his totality? Strives not to remain something he has become, but is in the absolute movement of becoming?.
>
> MARX 1973, *Grundrisse English ed., 488* = Marx 1974, *Grundrisse German ed., 387.*
> *See also ibid., 440*

Marx's discussion of labour as "real freedom" is also worth to be quoted extensively. Marx says in the "Grundrisse":

> Certainly, labour obtains its measure from the outside, through the aim to be attained and the obstacles to be overcome in attaining it. But [...] that this overcoming of obstacles is in itself a liberating activity – and that, further the external aims become stripped of the semblance of merely external natural urgencies, and become posited as aims which the individual himself posits – hence as self-realization, objectification of the subject, hence real freedom, whose action is, precisely, labour [...]. Labour becomes attractive work, the individual's self-realization, which in no way means that it becomes mere fun.
>
> MARX 1973, Grundrisse English ed., 611 = Marx 1974, Grundrisse German ed., 505

This passage, the whole context of which Marx put into brackets, points beyond a strict separation between the realm of necessity during labour time and the realm of freedom during leisure time. It shows that one must differentiate between general characteristics of labour, common in all types of society, in this case the characteristics that one works in order to arrive at aims which have been posited and that one has to overcome obstacles in attaining them, and characteristics specifying class societies, in this case that the aims of the labour process have been posited by those who own and/or control the productive means and appropriate the surplus labour of those who neither own nor control the productive means but work with them in order to survive or to live adequately according to the respective historical and cultural standards.

Marx never combined his various insights to a theory of prerequisites, impediments, phases and characteristics of an alternative classless society. Yet based on a synopsis of his writings, the following impediments can be systematized: Capitalism is quite flexible and grants only what is absolutely necessary to prolong its existence, classes are divided into sub-classes, petty bourgeois proprietors defend the capitalist system. The organizations of repression, namely the army and the police forces, improve their operations over time. Veiling techniques in the mass media as well as the exploitation of scientifically enhanced control repress pre-revolutionary sentiments and activities.

Rather than class conflicts, national wars dominated the 20th century. "Workers of all Countries Unite!" was a call for action, not a diagnosis. Class solidarity is undermined by actions against minorities. Economic-social developments become less transparent; capitalists do not only wear character masks, but can also become invisible beyond most democratizing control. There is more to loose than chains – and in an age of means of mass destruction, not only a world can be won, it can also be lost. Short-term survival needs or granted privileges delay mid- and long-term goals – the more active workers left their home countries since the 19th century for more promising new worlds. The longer capitalism exists, the more it may appear as a historical necessity, deeply engrained in all major institutions. Therefore mainly a networking of alternatives already realized at smaller scales will contribute to revolutionary upheavals that can be successful in long terms also for generations after the revolution, i.e. an overthrow of economic, cultural and political exploitation and repression.

In general, Marx's procedure of specifying alternatives was a projection of rational planning within companies to a national and even world economy and of highly motivated, politically active and responsible workers to all citizens of a classless society. Do the socio-economic processes since the mid-19th century not require more up to date concepts of alternatives? Which characteristics are made obsolete according to more recent theories of de-/civilizing processes, emancipative discourses, and system-specific rationalities?

A few of the historical limits of Marx's concept of alternatives can be sketched via a more general specification of a sociology of alternatives taking into account the pertinent theories of Elias (esp. 1939 and 1984), Habermas (mainly 1962, 1981, 2006 and 2007), and Luhmann (1995, 1996, 1997 and 2010; cp. Ludes 1989 and 2011), e.g., development patterns of state formations and failing states, de-/civilizing behaviour standards, focusing on means of violent destruction and of self-/constraints (rather than on the means and relations of production), discourses, system-specific rationalities and functionally equivalent alternatives. All these impediments to and transformations of the prerequisites for a classless society require new diagnoses and actions.

In general, alternatives are usually understood as desirable (historically necessary, "notwendige," which already for Marx meant: revolting against misery), consistent, and realizable social actions, processes, or structures fundamentally different from the predominant ones: As Marx emphasized particularly in the "Grundrisse" (quoted above): if there were no concrete models of alternative social relations in present societies, any attempt at overthrowing them would be utopian. In Marx's early metaphor from "A Contribution to the Critique of Hegel's Philosophy of Right" (http://www.marxists.org/archive/marx/works/1843/critique-hpr/intro.htm [accessed March 30, 2012]): "these petrified relations must be forced to dance by singing their own tune to them!"

Somewhat similar to Marx's diagnosis of a monopolization of the productive means and potentialities of economic wealth, Elias postulated a more general mechanism of the monopolization of various means of control as a major integrator of ever increasing interdependencies, going hand in hand with:

· An increase of population size, communication, the division of labour, the use of money and urbanization,
· An increase of taxes and the domination by centres of power,
· The decrease of power and income of the aristocracy, its loss of the monopoly of the effective use of weapons, enhancing the dependence on others,
· A development of new war technologies,
· The purchase of soldiers, and
· A monopolization of the state's exercise of physical force financed by taxes.

According to Elias' theories of civilizing processes and of the developments of more realistic means of orientation, sociological diagnoses should not limit themselves by highlighting either the means and relations of production (like Marx) or disenchantment, bureaucratization, and rationalization (like Max

Weber). These realms should not be separated for they remain highly interdependent and shaped by the density of populations or the degree and type of the monopolization of physical force. *Long-term intergenerational interdependencies point beyond alternatives within any living generation's reach.* Since the experiences, anxieties, projects, constraints, and self-control of billions of past humans have led contemporary generations to the present conditions, these chains cannot be exploded or unfettered nor would this be desirable for they have become deeply engrained patterns of humans and institutions. The chains of generations are stronger than the fetters of capitalism. Or, in Marx's (Marx and Engels, Selected Works 1, 398) words in "The Eighteenth Brumaire of Louis Bonaparte": "The tradition of all the dead generations weighs like a nightmare on the brain of the living."

In contrast to Marx's philosophical speculations about transformations of human nature, which he considered as basic for a classless society as the socialization of the means of production, especially in the Paris manuscripts and the "Grundrisse," Elias interpreted books on good manners over centuries as indicators of actual changes of the behaviour and personality structures of the secular upper strata in the West in the context of state formations and state failures. In Elias's (1977/2009, 9, 13, 16f) words:

> Complementary processes of functional differentiation, social integration, and civilization are strands of this complex long-term development. [...] One encounters simultaneously a deepening mood of doubt regarding the worth of such progress. People accept its advantages and fear its dangers. [...] The same holds for the shifts and fluctuations that are taking place in the power differentials between state societies. [...] Therefore, it is to the unplanned contradiction between the continual advance of scientifically acquired means of orientation in the sphere of non-human nature and of the corresponding chances for the exercise of control [...] and the relative backwardness in the development of the human world [...] that we must attribute a large measure of the growing strength of the voices and doubt in the value of all progress [...] One remains, correspondingly, incapable of developing more adequate means of orientation towards and of controlling such progress.

Elias (1977/2009, 27f) continues: "One may think, for example, of the false planning that would be involved if, without systematic sociological investigation of its development potential [...] one imposed the pure economic models of relatively capital-rich industrial societies on to a capital-poor society with a predominantly illiterate peasant population." Alternative intergenerational

long-term goals (cp. Elias 1984) can become means of orientation and communication only if they take into account chances and limits of (de-) civilizing
processes and of the developments of more realistic means of orientation and
communication as well as demographics and the length, density, and intensity
of intergenerational figurations.

4   Chances and Limits for Alternatives at the Beginning of the 21st Century?

The Google founders and their employees who have grown up with the Internet
have "considered its principles to be as natural as the laws of gravity. [...] But
Page had a real vision: just as Google's hardware could be spread around the
world in hundreds of thousands of server racks, Google's brainpower would be
similarly dispersed, revolutionizing the spread of information while speaking
the local language" (Levy 2011, 5 and 271). New types of information mining and
knowledge networking have undermined the 19th and 20th century prioritiza-
tions on land, natural resources, labour power and capitalist organization as
main or even only sources of (surplus) value. Fuchs (2012, 6) argues: "Google
would loose its antagonistic character if it were expropriated and transformed
into a public, non-profit, non-commercial organization that serves the common good".

From the perspectives of the 20th and early 21st century social sciences, Marx
focused on the economic class struggles, hardly on political developments. An
exception is the work "The Eighteenth Brumaire of Louis Bonaparte," which
gave us insights into the role of the "Lumpenproletariat" and the corruption of
politics. Only an especially pertinent statement on peasants may be quoted
here, for it shows Marx's awareness of blatant differences between the peasants and industrial workers, still highly important, e.g., in contemporary China
and India: "The small-holding peasants form a vast mass [...] much as potatoes
in a sack of potatoes. [...] In so far as there is merely a local interconnection
among these small-holding peasants [...] they do not form a class" (Marx and
Engels, 1969, 398). Yet, this inability of communication provides us also with an
example of the relevance of information technologies and devices for a new
"working-class network society" (Qiu 2009).

Concerning political developments, Otto von Bismarck (1815–1898), for
example, was the major political figure in Germany during (and beyond)
Marx's lifetime and chancellor from 1871 to 1890. Analyzing his autobiography
"Erinnerung und Gedanke" and his (partially dubious) talks with various con-
temporaries as well as a major biography of Bismarck by Gall (1983) showed

how different the historic challenges, conflicts, and victories are. Experiences with and attitudes towards physical violence and the role of the state far surpass considerations of economic developments. This applies also to the first social democratic chancellor of the Federal Republic of Germany (1969–1974), Willy Brandt's autobiographical writings and a biography on him (see Ludes 1989, book 2).

Marx and Engels recognized the failure of the 1848 bourgeois revolutions and even acknowledged "Bismarck's 'historically progressive' achievement of German unity, they did not fully work out its implications" (Hobsbawm 2011, 71). This is in line with Hobsbawm's (2011, 86) diagnosis that "ahistorical voluntarism" is less adequate and successful than political decisions in the "framework of historical change, which did not depend on political decision," Rosa (2005, 477f) concludes in a similar manner, yet in terms of basic institutional upheavals, that the political project of modernity – due to the de-synchronization of socio-economic development and political steering – may have reached its end, giving way to a short-term muddling through. A recent account of "Confidence Men" (Suskind 2011) offers a few examples of how "the Audacity of Hope" (Obama 2006, cp. accounts of the first female chancellor of Germany in Langguth 2010, esp. 371f) is cut off by the influences that Wall Street and Washington have had on the US President.

Therborn (2010, 13) emphasized the significant "concentration of capital, just as Marx predicted" in the US from 1905 to 1999 as well as the development of "new terrain": "Habermas abandoned the systemic contradictions analyzed by Marxist theory, replacing it first with a distinction between different kinds of action and knowledge interests, and later with a conflict between the social system and the 'life-world'" (Therborn 2010, 79, see also 123 for possible long-term future alternatives).

Kurt H. Wolff (see the discussion of an existential turn in sociology in Ludes 2007) emphasized that the human potential of self-destruction became ever more obvious since the atomic bombs on Hiroshima and Nagasaki in 1945. This threat to human survival reframed and undermined all previous social diagnoses. Since the end of the Cold War, military budgets decreased in many democratic and richer countries, partially due to the higher technological efficiency of ever more advanced systems of mass destruction. State budget shares were balanced somewhat and for limited phases in order to finance welfare measures and repair costs in capitalist crises.

Marx's and later sociological theories "have assumed that the basic institutional formations that developed in European modernity [...] will 'naturally' be taken over, with possible local variations, in all [...] modernizing societies [...] But the reality that emerged proved to be radically different. Developments

[...] did not bear out the assumption of 'convergence' of modern societies. They actually indicated that the various modern autonomous institutional arenas – the economic, the political, the educational or the family are defined and regulated and combine in different ways in different societies and in different periods of their development" (Eisenstadt 2010, 2). According to Eisenstadt (2010, 12), various trajectories and interpretations of modernities and modernizations decouple from Westernization.

The detection of alternatives is therefore characterized by the co-ordination of often highly distinct life worlds, patterns and rhythms of change and corresponding common sense or social scientific theories. There is no standard continuum of measure-units, as they have existed for generations for time, space, or economic values. It must rather be developed for any realistic long-term alternative. Only via the mutual feed back of concepts of alternatives in all their major dimensions of desirability, consistency, and the potentials for the realization of "desirable" actions, processes or structures, can fundamental transformations be prepared. Obviously, such attempts will be fettered time and time again by privileges that defend and enhance class struggles from above (which Warren Buffet considered as successful in the US) and by veiling alternatives.

Therefore, a critique of the political, cultural and mediated networked synchronization of alternatives requires the following long-term efforts (see Ludes 1989, book 2 and Ludes 2011, ch. 1):

· Since there is no physical or biological model for the perception of alternatives, intergenerational networks of alternative social models must be ascertained and enhanced.
· Since the discrepancies of systems and life worlds (to use Habermas's theory of communicative action) do neither allow for near-natural standardizations nor for discourse-based agreements or contracts, other modes of co-ordination will come into the focus of analyses and synopses, characterized by cognition, communication and cooperation.
· Yet these modes of interaction are continuously threatened by violent conflicts or even wars. One needs to develop means of communication and orientation, which enable societal alternatives, that are not only grounded in class analyses, but in networking long-term goals.
· This implies the re-synchronization of functionally distinct realms in the minds of people across generations. Thereby ever more realistic concepts of alternatives emerge, which could again shape the mentalities, especially the projects of actions and institutions as well as master narratives of ever more groups of people taking into account their mutual interdependencies over longer periods of trajectories.

- Such clarifications will allow for some standardization of alternatives, for limited areas, realms, times and issues.
- Only if such standards appear as more or less obvious, not only in cognitive but also affective terms, will they function as acceptable thresholds of otherwise timeless discourses.

This diagnostic challenge calls for an intergenerational dialogue of theory-formation, in which the means of orientation and communication, of control and self-control, of reproduction and destruction inter-depend with those of production. The variety of culture-specific, transcultural and even globalizing alternative actions, processes, and structures and of criteria for their specification and agreement is so wide that no conscious consensus can be reached. Such models of orientation and communication clearly point beyond individual, short-term perceptions and must allow continuous feedback from the intended and unintended consequences of interactions and "inter-passivities" for various classes, groupings and time horizons. Thereby common standards emerge, which contribute to new behaviour patterns and mentalities. Consciously communicated alternatives always are embedded in less conscious horizons and frameworks (cp., e.g., Honneth 2011, 540–567).

Habermas (2011, 33–38) proposes human rights as a regulatory institution, which Ludes (2011, chapter 8) puts into the context of traditional print, broadcast and web media, symbolically generalized media of communication of money, power, truth or love, and the long-term means of orientation, space, time, and alternatives. Since the historically new global crisis of financial capitalism with its repercussions of economic fragilities and state bankruptcies, Habermas (2011, 100–129) sees a re-shuttling of "political alternatives," which would have been deemed unrealistic before. He calls for the right for unbiased political communication, especially concerning communication about the weapons of mass destruction employed by the global financial markets. The continuous interventions of state regulations in the crisis made transparent that capitalism cannot reproduce itself autonomously from the state, but rather drives the state to collect taxes that are used for resolving capitalism's state of emergency.

Yet: "The evolution of humankind is a contingent, open-ended process, driven primarily through five fields of forces of the mode of livelihood, of demographic ecology, of distributions of recognition, rank and respect, of cultures of learning, communication and values, and of politics" (Therborn 2011, 84). Only self-critical re-conceptualizations of traditional concepts can serve as driving forces for radical transformations of informational capitalism, which, however, tends to monopolize rankings of valuable information and knowledge (cp., e.g., Halavais 2009). Therefore, the appropriation of ICT s in the service of alternative commons has become a major means of revolting against the oligopoly of the means of production and destruction via new means of cognition, communication and cooperation (cp. Fuchs 2011a, Section 5). "Given that alternatives frequently do not want to build their organizations on commodities and advertising because they think this will corrupt their political goals, they are frequently facing problems like lack of resources, precarious self-exploitative labour, lack of attention/visibility, etc." (Fuchs 2011b).

Yet, in addition to these and the impediments to Marx's trajectories towards an alternative, classless society sketched above, we must see clearly that the very base of Marx's diagnosis has become obsolete: More than two thirds of the world were almost completely outside of Marx's research (despite a few reflections in newspaper articles on India), namely almost all of Asia, Africa, Latin America. In globalizing socio-economic, military, terrorist, ecological, communication processes in the 21st century, these previously excluded regions and populations will shape also the rules of globalizing capitalism.

A recent "Citizen's Guide to Capitalism and the Environment" (Magdoff and Foster 2011, all following quotations will refer to this book) may exemplify the projection of analyses from one country, i.e., the United States, to a global theory. A rhetorical device is the unqualified use of "we," e.g.: "We are constantly being told" (7), "we have an economic system" (12), "our economic system [...] we must look" (30), "We must also recognize" (38) and so on till the call for collective actors, which are even more vague that previous conceptions of a class in and for itself, e.g., "people organizing and fighting" (131), "society decides" (135), or "We the people" (151). Similarly, the political economical analyses, mainly based on developments in the United States and exclusively on publications in English, not taking into account any of the above theories from, e.g., Elias, Habermas, Hobsbawm, or Therborn, reify "the economic system" (12, 30), the "present system" (36), "capitalism" (7, 56, 101), "the capitalist system" (59), "the system" (83–85), "the democratic system" (91), "the current system," "the logic of the system" (93), "system," "the system," "the capitalist economic system" (96f) "capitalist society" (111) or "society" (66, sometimes referring to the US alone, sometimes to the whole world without clear distinctions). Based on these generalizations, even more universal "realistic alternatives" are proposed, "Creating an entirely different system [...] a truly revolutionary form of change – the transition to a new system altogether": The simplifying "planning" proposed becomes evident in the metaphor of "what the house is to be like [...]. Similarly, once society decides that it is critical to fulfil the basic needs of people, then – after some general agreement is reached as to what these needs are – a system that plans production and distribution is required in order effectively to achieve those ends" (135). Compared to this "Guide," Marx's original concept of a classless society may appear as more concrete and aware of historic circumstances – and Habermas's theory of communicative action and discourses as even more realistic.

Magdoff and Foster's analysis is based on the ecological catastrophes due to a (US, global) capitalism inevitably based on economic growth and endless profit seeking, yet it neglects, e.g., "liberal market and more cooperative varieties of capitalism" (Lane and Wood 2009). The very short reference to Beck (111) avoids Beck and others' publications on reflexive modernization, unintended consequences, and methodological nationalism. Therefore, also in the light of this "Guide," the intergenerational dialogue proposed in this chapter offers alternative theory strands to be taken into account.

Worldwide, mixed economies and regulations dominate. Or are there state societies, in which various public institutions do not exert some degree of control over capitalist enterprises? So-called communist societies failed and the globally important "communist" People's Republic of China never met the prerequisites for and characteristics of a classless society, which were sketched above. (See Mennell 2003, de Swaan 2003 and Mao's calls for violence as summarized in Chang and Halliday 2005, especially chapters 45–51).

As Vogel (2011, 706f) argues: "The transition from a predominantly rural to a predominantly urban society and the spread of a common national culture are among the most fundamental changes that have occurred in Chinese society since the country's unification in 221 B.C. [...] When China began opening in the 1980s, there were virtually no rules in place for food and drugs, product and workplace safety, working conditions, minimum wages, or construction codes. [...] The situation in China under Deng was reminiscent of the rapacious capitalism of nineteenth-century Europe and the United States, when there were no anti-trust laws and no laws to protect workers. [...] In some ways the situation in China during the Deng era was also similar to the nineteenth-century American West before there were local laws and courts."

Concerning global challenges, I will only quote at length Beck's elaboration of his risk society theory in 2008 (b):

> the fundamental principles of modernity, including the free market principle and the nation-state order itself, become subject to the change, the existence of alternatives, and contingency. You might even say, the historical power of global risk is beyond all the 'saviours' brought forth by history: not the proletariat, not the excluded, not the Enlightenment, not the global public, not the migrants of global society – if anyone or anything at all, it is the perceived risks facing humanity, which can be neither

denied nor externalized, that are capable of awakening the energies, the consensus, the legitimation necessary for creating a global community of fate, one that will demolish the walls of nation-state borders and egotisms – at least for a global moment in time and beyond democracy. [...] However, global risk public spheres have a completely different structure from the 'public sphere' explored by Jürgen Habermas. Habermas's public sphere presupposes that all concerned have equal chances to participate and that they share a commitment to the principles of rational discourse. The threat public sphere is as little a matter of commitment as it is of rationality. The images of catastrophes do not produce cool heads. False alarms, misunderstandings, condemnations are part of the story. Threat publics are impure, they distort, they are selective and stir up emotions, anger and hate. They make possible more, and at the same time less, than the public sphere described by Habermas. [...] World risk is *the* unwanted, unintended obligatory medium of communication in a world of irreconcilable differences in which everyone is turning on their own axis. Hence the public perception of risk forces people to communicate who otherwise do not want to have anything to do with one another. It imposes obligations and costs on those who resist them, often even with the law on their side. In other words, large-scale risks cut through the self-sufficiency of cultures, languages, religions and systems as much as through the national and international agenda of politics; they overturn their priorities and create contexts for action between camps, parties and quarrelling nations that know nothing about each other and reject and oppose one another. That is what 'enforced cosmopolitanization' means: global risks activate and connect actors across borders, who otherwise do not want to have anything to do with one another. [...] It is evident, that the taken-for-granted nation-state frame of reference – what I call 'methodological nationalism' – prevents the social sciences from understanding and analyzing the dynamics and ambivalences, opportunities and ironies of world risk society.

Correspondingly, global catastrophes and trends refer more to fatal discontinuities than the falling profit rate, e.g., influenza pandemics, transformational wars, terrorist attacks, global warming, changing water and nitrogen cycles, loss of biodiversity, antibiotic resistance. For example, poor "water quality is a much more common problem. In 2005 more than 1 billion people in low-income countries had no access to clean drinking water, and some 2.5 billion lived without water sanitation [...] About half of all beds in the world's hospitals were occupied by patients with water-borne diseases. [...] Contaminated water and poor sanitation kill about 4,000 children every day [...] Deaths among adults raise this to at least 1.7 million fatalities per year. Add other waterborne diseases, and the total surpasses 5 million. In contrast, automobile accidents claim about 1.2 million lives per year [...] roughly equal to the combined total of all homicides and suicides, and armed conflicts kill about 300,000 people per year" (Smil 2008, 199).

Both Habermas (2011) and Hessel (2011) argue for building more on the Human Rights declaration of the United Nations, which can be interpreted as a substantial globalizing progress compared to Marx and Engels's "Communist Manifesto" and its partially similar concrete proposals. The United Nations and UNESCO have evolved as institutions, which despite all their deficiencies when compared to utopian socialism lead us beyond previous nation-centered analyses; they lead us also beyond a bias on industrialized economies.

This diagnosis combines two exemplary and complementary forces calling for alternatives, namely "the perceived risks facing humanity" (Beck 2008b) and the enhancement of human rights: as global challenges requiring global institutions. Suggestions for solutions to such global challenges therefore need various approaches, not a monopolistic political economic diagnosis; some such complementary strategies have been prepared by the UNESCO's Human Development Reports since 1990. They integrate perspectives from and on all unequally developed regions, strata, and genders and take into account problems usually out of the sight of previous social theoreticians.

As Marx and Engels postulated in the "Communist Manifesto": "United action, of the leading civilised countries at least, is one of the first conditions for the emancipation of the proletariat" (quoted in Section 2). In 2011, the Human Development Report stressed: "Yet there are alternatives to inequality and unsustainability. Growth driven by fossil fuel consumption is not a prerequisite for a better life in broader human development terms. Investments that improve equity – in access, for example, to renewable energy, water and sanitation, and reproductive healthcare – could advance both sustainability and human development. Stronger accountability and democratic processes, in part through support for an active civil society and media, can also improve outcomes. Successful approaches rely on community management, inclusive institutions that pay particular attention to disadvantaged groups, and cross-cutting approaches that coordinate budgets and mechanisms across government agencies and development partners. [...] Disadvantaged people are a central focus of human development. This includes people in the future who will suffer the most severe consequences of the risks arising from our activities today" (UNESCO Human Development Report 2011, ii and 1).

Therefore, only the application of the methods of Marx's original generalization of alternative models to more encompassing social developments as well as a critique of political economy can act as foundation for the creation of an update of Marx's concept of alternatives for the 21st century. It must be combined with more globalizing prerequisites and impediments for realms not determined by the modes of production and beyond short-term political goals. Re-combining social scientific long term diagnoses with emancipative actions against the exploitation of the majorities of societies and humankind is a challenge worth to become more dominant in a sociology of alternatives.

References

Beck, Ulrich. 1992. *World Risk Society*. Cambridge: Polity.

Beck, Ulrich. 2008a. *Weltrisikogesellschaft*. Frankfurt am Main: Suhrkamp.

Beck, Ulrich. 2008b. *Risk Society's 'Cosmopolitan Moment'*. Lecture at Harvard University, November 12th, 2008.

Ben-Rafael, Eliezer and Yitzak Sternberg, eds. 2001. *Identity, Culture and Globalization*. Leiden: Brill.

Burke, Peter and Maria L.G. Pallares-Burke. 2008. *Gilberto Freyre: Social Theory in the Tropics*. Oxford: Peter Lang.

Bielsa, Esperanza. 2011. Some Remarks on the Sociology of Translation: A Reflection on the Global Production and Circulation of Sociological Works. *European Journal of Social Theory* 14 (2): 199–251.

Chang, Jung and John Halliday. 2005. *Mao: The Unknown Story*. London: Jonathan Cape.

Danowksi, James A. and David W. Park. 2009. Networks of the Dead or Alive in Cyberspace. *New Media & Society* 11 (3): 337–356.

De Swaan, Abram. 2003. Dyscivilization, Mass Extermination and the State. In *Sage Masters of Modern Social Thought. Norbert Elias*, edited by Eric Dunning and Stephen Mennell, Volume II, 119 – 136. London, Thousand Oaks, and New Delhi: Sage.

Eisenstadt, Shmuel. 2002. *Multiple Modernities*. New Brunswick and London: Transaction.

Eisenstadt, Shmuel. 2010. *Modernity and Modernization. Sociopedia.isa*: 1–15.

Elias, Norbert. 1939/2000. *Über den Prozess der Zivilisation. Soziogenetische und psychogenetische Untersuchungen. Erster Band: Wandlungen des Verhaltens in den weltlichen Oberschichten des Abendlandes. Zweiter Band: Wandlungen der Gesellschaft. Entwurf zu einer Theorie der Zivilisation*. Frankfurt am Main: Suhrkamp, 4th edition (1st edition Basle 1939). *The Civilizing Process* (English: translated by Jephcott, E.) Oxford, Malden, Mass.: Blackwell Publishing, 2000.

Elias, Norbert. 1978. *Was ist Soziologie?* Munich: Juventa.

Elias, Norbert. 1984. Knowledge and Power: An Interview by Peter Ludes. In *Society and Knowledge: Contemporary Perspectives in the Sociology of Knowledge and Science,* edited by Nico Stehr and Volker Meja, 203–241. New Jersey: Transaction.

Elias, Norbert. 1977/2009. Towards a Theory of Social Processes. In *Norbert Elias Collected Works, Volume 16: Essays III. On Sociology and the Humanities,* edited by Richard Kilminster and Stephen Mennell, 9–39. Dublin: University College Dublin Press.

Featherstone, Mike and Couze Venn. 2006. Problematizing Global Knowledge and the New Encyclopaedia Project. An Introduction. *Theory, Culture & Society* 23 (2–3): 1–20.

Fleischer, Helmut. 1972. *Marxismus und Geschichte.* Frankfurt am Main: Suhrkamp.

Fuchs, Christian. 2009. Some Theoretical Foundations of Critical Media Studies: Reflections on Karl Marx and the Media. *International Journal of Communication* 3: 369–402.

Fuchs, Christian. 2011a. *Internet Prosumption in Contemporary Capitalism.* Presentation at the European Sociological Association Conference on "Social Relations in Turbulent Times." September 8th. Geneva, Switzerland.

Fuchs, Christian. 2011b. *Mail to the Author.* October 11th, 2011.

Fuchs, Christian. 2012. Google Capitalism. *tripleC* 10 (1): 42–48.

Gall, Lothar. 1983. *Bismarck. Der weiße Revolutionär.* Frankfurt, Berlin, and Vienna: Ullstein.

Habermas, Jürgen. 1962/1990. *Strukturwandel der Öffentlichkeit: Untersuchungen zu einer Kategorie der bürgerlichen Gesellschaft.* Neuwied/Berlin: Luchterhand. (Frankfurt am Main: Suhrkamp, 1990).

Habermas, Jürgen. 1981. *Theorie des kommunikativen Handelns. 2 Volumes.* Frankfurt am Main: Suhrkamp.

Habermas, Jürgen. 1999. *Die Einbeziehung des Anderen.* Frankfurt am Main: Suhrkamp.

Habermas, Jürgen. 2001. *Die Zukunft der menschlichen Natur.* Frankfurt am Main: Suhrkamp.

Habermas, Jürgen. 2006. Political Communication in Media Society: Does Democracy Still Enjoy an Epistemic Dimension? The Impact of Normative Theory on Empirical Research. *Communication Theory* 16 (4): 411–426.

Habermas, Jürgen. 2007. Keine Demokratie kann sich das leisten. *Süddeutsche Zeitung,* May 16th.

Habermas, Jürgen. 2011. *Zur Verfassung Europas. Ein Essay.* Berlin: Suhrkamp.

Halavais, Alexander. 2009. *Search Engine Society.* Cambridge, Malden: Polity Press.

Hessel, Stéphane. 2011. *Engagez-vous!* La Tour-d'Aigues: Éditions de l'Aube.

Hobsbawm, Eric. 2011. *How to Change the World. Marx and Marxism 1840–2011.* London: Little, Brown.

Honneth, Axel. 2011. *Das Recht der Freiheit. Grundriss einer demokratischen Sittlichkeit.* Berlin: Suhrkamp.

Jin, Huimin. 2007. Redefining Global Knowledge. *Theory, Culture & Society* 24 (7–8): 276–280.

Lane, Christel and Geoffrey Wood. 2009. Capitalist Diversity and Diversity within Capitalism. *Economy and Society* 38 (4): 531–551.

Langguth, Gerd. 2010. *Angela Merkel.* Munich: dtv.

Levy, Steven. 2011. *In the Plex. How Google thinks, works, and shapes our Lives.* New York, London, Toronto, and Sydney: Simon & Schuster.

Ludes, Peter. 1979. *Der Begriff der klassenlosen Gesellschaft bei Marx.* Frankfurt and New York: Campus.

Ludes, Peter. 1980. Marx's Notion of a Classless Society. *International Journal of Contemporary Sociology* 17: 1–54.

Ludes, Peter. 1989. *Drei moderne soziologische Theorien. Zur Entwicklung des Orientierungsmittels Alternativen.* Göttingen: Schwartz.

Ludes, Peter. 2007. Existential Truths as Prerequisites for a Globalizing Discourse Theory. In *The Sociology of Radical Commitment: Kurt H. Wolff's Existential Turn*, edited by Gary Backhaus and George Psathas, 115–136. Lanham etc.: Lexington Books.

Ludes, Peter. 2011. *Elemente internationaler Medienwissenschaften: Eine Einführung in innovative Konzepte.* Wiesbaden: VS Verlag für Sozialwissenschaften.

Luhmann, Niklas. 1995. *Gesellschaftsstruktur und Semantik: Studien zur Wissenssoziologie der modernen Gesellschaft, Volume 4.* Frankfurt am Main: Suhrkamp.

Luhmann, Niklas. 1996. *Die Realität der Massenmedien.* Opladen: VS Verlag für Sozialwissenschaften.

Luhmann, Niklas. 1997. *Die Gesellschaft der Gesellschaft.* Frankfurt am Main: Suhrkamp.

Luhmann, Niklas. 2010. *Die Politik der Gesellschaft.* Berlin: Suhrkamp.

Magdoff, Fred and John Ballamy Foster. 2011. *What Every Environmentalist Needs to Know about Capitalism. A Citizen's Guide to Capitalism and the Environment.* New York: Monthly Review Press.

Mannheim, Karl. 1929. *Ideologie und Utopie.* Bonn: Friedrich Cohen.

Marx, Karl and Friedrich Engels. *MEW.* 1956–1968. *Volume 1–19, 23–35 and Supplementary Volume I.* Berlin: Dietz.

Marx, Karl. 1969. *Resultate des unmittelbaren Produktionsprozesses. Das Kapital. I. Buch. Der Produktionsprozess des Kapitals. VI. Kapitel.* Archiv sozialistischer Literatur 17. Frankfurt am Main: Verlag Neue Kritik.

Marx, Karl and Frederick Engels. 1969. *Selected Works in three Volumes. Volume 1.* Moscow: Progress Publishers.

Marx, Karl. 1973. *Grundrisse. Foundations of the Critique of Political Economy (Rough Draft).* Translated with a Foreword by Martin Nicolaus. London: Penguin Books in association with New Left Review.

Marx, Karl. 1974. *Grundrisse der Kritik der politischen Ökonomie (Rohentwurf)*, *1857–1858, Appendix 1850–1859*. Berlin: Dietz.

Mennell, Stephen. 2003. Asia and Europe: Comparing Civilizing Processes. In *Sage Masters of Modern Social Thought. Norbert Elias,* edited by Eric Dunning and Stephen Mennell, *Volume II*: 101–117. London, Thousand Oaks, and New Delhi: Sage.

Obama, Barack. 2006. *The Audacity of Hope*. New York: Three Rivers Press.

Qiu, Jack L. 2009. *Working-Class Network Society: Communication Technology and the Information Have-Less in Urban China*. Cambridge, MA: MIT Press.

Rosa, Hartmut. 2005. *Beschleunigung. Die Veränderung der Zeitstrukturen in der Moderne*. Frankfurt am Main: Suhrkamp.

Smil, Vaclav. 2008. *Global Catastrophes and Trends. The Next 50 Years*. Cambridge, MA and London: MIT Press.

Suskind, Ron. 2011. *Confidence Men. Wall Street, Washington, and the Education of a President*. New York: Harper Collins.

Therborn, Göran. 2010. *From Marxism to Post-Marxism?* London and New York: Verso.

Therborn, Göran. 2011. *The World: A Beginner's Guide*. Cambridge: Polity Press.

UNESCO. 2011. *Human Development Report. 2011. Sustainability and Equity: A Better Future for All*. Accessed April 1, 2012. http://hdr.undp.org/en/reports/global/hdr2011/download/.

Vogel, Ezra F. 2011. *Deng Xiaoping and the Transformation of China*. Cambridge, MA, and London: Harvard University Press.

Wolff, Kurt H. 1976. *Surrender and Catch. Experience and Inquiry Today = Boston Studies in the Philosophy of Science Volume LI*. Dordrecht and Boston: Reidel.

CHAPTER 13

Conceptualising and Subverting the Capitalist Academic Publishing Model

Wilhelm Peekhaus

1 Introduction

> "The means of effective communication are being expropriated from the intellectual worker."
>
> MILLS 1951, 152

The situation Mills bemoaned some six decades ago has proceeded apace, reaching a level today that borders on complete expropriation. Similar to most sectors in the communications and media industries, academic journal publishing has experienced a significant wave of consolidation over the last couple of decades. The consequent result is a market dominated by a handful of oligopolistic mega-publishers that wield an inordinate amount of power, as made manifest most prominently in skyrocketing journal subscription costs and a drastic lockdown of content through strict application of copyright and licencing restrictions. While these effects have been widely discussed, particularly among library and information studies and communication and media studies scholars and practitioners, less work has thus far been conducted in trying to account theoretically for these industry developments and their impacts. Even less prevalent in the existing literature is any systematic attempt to interrogate these issues from a critical political economic approach that considers capital's compulsion to alienate the actual producers from their product, which represents an appropriation of the free labour that underwrites the academic publishing system (notable exceptions include Merrett (2006) and Striphas (2010)).

In an effort to respond to some of these lacunae, this chapter seeks to interrogate and situate theoretically from a Marxist political economic perspective various aspects and tensions that inhere in the contemporary academic journal publishing environment. I propose to examine both the expanding capitalist control of the academic publishing industry and some of the efforts being made by those seeking to counter the negative effects of such capitalist control. In order to engage with these issues, the material presented in this chapter is informed by the following three questions. First, what are the structural characteristics of the academic publishing industry and how do they impact the scholarly communication system? Second, what efforts have been made by various actors to respond to the crises in the dominant capitalist model of academic publishing? Third, what novel, and potentially more radical, strategies might be offered to actively subvert capital's control of academic publishing?

I suggest that we can conceptualise the responses to these questions by returning to Marx's concepts of 'primitive accumulation' and 'alienation'. Drawing mainly on Volume I of *Capital*, my goal will be to demonstrate that primitive accumulation, understood as a continuing historical process necessary for capital accumulation, offers an apropos theoretical lens through which to contemplate contemporary erosions of the knowledge commons that result from various enclosing strategies employed by corporate academic journal publishers. As a theoretical complement, I will further suggest that some of the elements of alienation Marx articulated in respect of capitalist-controlled production processes capture the contemporary estrangement experienced by the actual producers of academic publications. The exegetical account of alienation offered here will draw primarily on Marx's discussion in the *Economic and philosophical manuscripts*. Aside from demonstrating the continued relevance of the concepts of primitive accumulation and alienation, part of my purpose will be to advance the case that, despite a relatively privileged position vis-à-vis other workers (albeit one increasingly under attack), academic cognitive labourers are caught up within and subject to some of the constraining and exploitative practices of capitalist accumulation processes.

In developing my arguments, the chapter will first provide an overview of the commercial academic journal publishing industry, including some of the consolidation trends experienced over the last couple of decades, as well as its major structural characteristics and their effects on the dissemination of scholarly research. Having established this empirical context, the following section will articulate Marx's concepts of primitive accumulation and alienation. The attempt here will be to make conceptual sense of the way that these broader structural characteristics of the academic publishing industry function as mechanisms of enclosure of the knowledge commons and alienation of the actual producers in support of capitalist accumulation imperatives. The focus will then shift to a discussion of the open-access movement as an active, remedial response to the enclosing and alienating effects inherent in the capitalist-controlled academic publishing industry. As the discussion here will demonstrate, open-access publishing is not inherently anti-capitalist. For that reason, we need to distinguish between traditional open access and the more explicitly anti-capitalist attempts to guarantee open access, in what we might term a commons-based open-access regime that more accurately reflects the actual nature of peer and commons-based scholarly knowledge production and dissemination. In the penultimate section, and in response to question three, I will suggest some basic strategies as well as a possible alternative model for academic publishing that, building on open-access projects, would radically subvert capitalist control.

2   A Survey of the Commercial Academic Publishing Industry and its Impact on the Scholarly Communication System

Before considering an alternative model to the control exercised by for-profit corporations on the scholarly communication system, we first need to establish the broad contours of this system. As is relatively well known, Henry Oldenburg, the first Joint Secretary of the then newly founded Royal Society of London, published in 1665 the world's first scholarly journal, *Philosophical Transactions*. Oldenburg established the journal to fulfil four functions that continue today as part of the scholarly communication process: registration, which ensures the article is connected to the author as well as the intellectual property right holder; certification of the quality of the research through peer review; dissemination of the research; and archiving to ensure historical preservation and future availability of research. The scholarly publishing system remained confined largely to learned societies for roughly the following three centuries, until commercial publishers began to recognise and exploit the profit potential of academic literature. This more contemporary commercialisation of academic journal publishing has been traced to the 1946 launch of *Biochimica et Biophysica Acta* by Robert Maxwell, who built and plundered a major publishing empire in the United Kingdom that began with academic publishing (Campbell 2012). This transformation in academic publishing was fuelled by both an exponential increase in the production of scientific and technical information after World War II and the post-war economic boom in the 1950s and 1960s, during which governments in many developed countries began injecting substantial funds into post-secondary education and research. Some of this funding would be employed to create and sustain a growing market for scholarly literature based on the profit motive that is now worth billions of dollars annually.

Indeed, as Ware and Mabe (2009) pointed out several years ago, and confirmed by the latest available data, the scholarly publishing industry has enjoyed steady annual growth in numbers of both journals and articles. According to the most recent data collected by the consulting firm Outsell, revenues in 2011 for the science-publishing industry amounted to US$9.4 billion.[1] Based on 1.8 million English-language articles published annually in 27,000 journals, this figure translates into gross revenue of slightly more than US$5,200 per article (as cited in Van Noorden 2013b).

Similar to other information and communication sectors, the academic publishing industry has experienced significant levels of consolidation over the past two decades. According to Munroe (2007), by 2004 a mere 12 European and North American publishing companies dominated western academic publishing, which generated total annual revenues of US$65 billion. The increasing consolidation in academic publishing documented by Munroe (2007) has continued since her initial study, with the field now dominated by ten major corporations. The top three publishers of scientific journals (Elsevier, Springer, and Wiley-Blackwell) account for approximately 42 percent of all articles published. While there are over 2,000 academic journal publishers and, according to Campbell (2012), scholarly societies own and control approximately half of all peer-reviewed journals, no other publisher beyond the big three accounts for more than a three percent share of the journal market (McGuigan and Russell 2008). In part, this concentrated degree of control has been made possible because these large commercial publishers have been very successful in acquiring many of the most prestigious and high-circulation journals across almost all academic disciplines. Indeed, in the 1980s, a number of scholarly and professional societies began selling their journals to commercial publishers in an effort to avoid the cost and logistical burdens involved in publication and distribution processes. These sales also helped generate additional revenues to subsidise society activities and membership fees (McGuigan and Russell 2008; Kranich 2004).

2.1 Selective Merger & Acquisition Activity within the Academic Publishing Industry

Although more selective than exhaustive, the following examples of major mergers and acquisitions over the last decade establish the scale of the largest players in the academic publishing industry. The magnitude of these deals offers an important indicator of the lucrative nature of journal publishing,

---

1 Information about the current make-up of the academic publishing industry, including aggregate revenue figures, is surprisingly difficult to locate. Most authors tend to draw on data collected by two private consulting firms, Outsell and Simba Information. However, the price tag of the report compiled by Outsell is $1,850. The price of Simba's report, $3,250, is even more prohibitive. Multiple efforts by the author to secure a copy of either report through interlibrary loan failed.

which is underwritten largely by the free labour of (mostly) academics. Thanks to aggressive merger and acquisition activities that actually date to the 1970s, Reed Elsevier is now one of the world's largest publishers of science, technology, and medicine (STM) journals. This Anglo-Dutch conglomerate, whose stock is quoted on the London, Amsterdam, and New York stock exchanges, also specialises in the subject areas of law, education, and business. According to Reed Elsevier, in addition to a catalogue of over 2,500 journals available through *ScienceDirect*, the world's largest database of scientific and medical research, the company publishes almost 20,000 new clinical reference works and health sciences and science and technology book titles annually. The company is also active in the business information segment of publishing, offering over 100 business magazines across a wide range of sectors. Reed Elsevier similarly owns LexisNexis, an online legal and news portal that contains over 4 billion searchable documents available from several thousand databases compiled from over 35,000 legal, business, and news sources.[2]

In early 2003, Candover and Cinven, a London-based venture capital firm that specialises in large buyouts and buyins, acquired controlling interests in Kluwer Academic Publishers from the Dutch company Wolters Kluwer for €600 million. Later that same year, Candover and Cinven bought BertelsmannSpringer from Bertelsmann Media Worldwide for €1.1 billion (in 1999, Bertelsmann had acquired 85 percent of Springer Verlag, including its scientific journals). Candover and Cinven subsequently merged these two publishing businesses into Springer, at the time the second largest STM publisher in the world, with annual publications in 2004 of almost 1,350 journals and 5,000 books, and revenues of €880 million. According to the company's website, it now possesses the world's largest collection of STM books, journals, protocols, and reference works (2,741 journals). In 2006, John Wiley paid

---

2 In 2013, Elsevier acquired Mendeley, a cloud-based research management and social collaboration platform for an estimated £45 million (Mance 2013). Mendeley's desktop and cloud-based tools allow researchers to manage and annotate documents, create citations and bibliographies, and collaborate on research projects. Critics of the acquisition were quick to question whether Mendeley, under Elsevier control, would be given the latitude to fulfil its original mission of providing a truly open platform. Although Mendeley claims on its blog (Q&A section – http://blog.mendeley.com/press-release/qa-team-mendeley-joins-elsevier/) that it will remain provider-neutral and not favour Elsevier in terms of the content delivered by its search and recommendation engine, skeptics pointed out that smaller acquired companies seldom have the capacity to alter the corporate culture of the parent company. Since Elsevier maintains all the power, remaining true to the principles of openness and transparency will depend upon the whim of a parent company that is driven solely by the goal of wringing maximum value from user-generated content.

£572 million to acquire Blackwell Publishing, which, at the time, published around 600 books a year and over 800 journals, many of which are from professional and scholarly societies (Munroe 2007). Together, these two companies produce over 1,400 peer-reviewed journals across a wide range of academic disciplines, including the social sciences, humanities, and STM.

According to economist Mark McCabe (2002), who was employed in the late 1990s in the United States Justice Department's Antitrust Division, merger and acquisition activity within the academic publishing industry played a role in subsequent journal price increases of biomedical titles between 1988 and 2001. Other researchers have similarly determined that prices charged by commercial publishers average between four and six times those levied by non-profit publishers, when considered on a per-page basis (Bergstrom and Bergstrom 2004). Such inflated prices no doubt explain the staggering profit levels that the major academic publishing companies have been able to book. In 2006, Reed Elsevier earned an operating profit of almost 31 percent on its STM publications. Wiley carved out an operating profit of over 45 percent on its journals in these same disciplines, while Blackwell, which is involved more in social science publishing, generated a profit of 28 percent. Taylor and Francis's academic and scientific division brought the company an operating profit of over 26 percent, while the Thomson Corporation realised a 24 percent operating profit from its health and science publishing activities (Pirie 2009). According to analysts at Bernstein Research, which upgraded its stock outlook for Reed Elsevier in September 2014 to market-perform from underperform in 2011, open access has done little to challenge the market strength of the leading subscription publishers. Instead, these analysts suggest that open-access funding models may actually be contributing to the profits of STM journal publishers. This assessment has certainly been borne out in the case of Elsevier, which has been steadily increasing its operating profit margins over the last few years for its STM journals: 36 percent (£724 million) in 2010, 37 percent (£768 million) in 2011, 38 percent (£780 million) in 2012, and 39 percent (£826 million) in 2013. These same analysts predict further consolidation of the industry, which would favour the larger players such as Elsevier (Aspesi and Luong 2014).

2.2   *Structural Characteristics of the Academic Publishing Industry*

In addition to an increasingly consolidated industry, there are structural characteristics specific to the market for journal articles of which capital is able to avail itself in asserting its grip on academic publishing. One particularly potent mechanism of control is the almost universal practice among commercial journal publishers to make publication of scholarly articles contingent upon the author agreeing to transfer the intellectual property rights in a work to the publisher. This ability to demand ownership rights in the work of academic labourers has been partly facilitated by a relatively conservative system of tenure and promotion that reinforces the *status quo* of corporate-controlled journal venues.

The nature of academic scholarship has also contributed to the power of capital. Unlike typical goods, competing journals and journal articles, although often complementary because of overlapping subject areas, are rarely substitutes for one another. This lack of fungibility augments substantially the monopoly power of publishers, particularly those that control the top-ranked journals in their respective fields. This is because academic library collection development policies are driven by the underlying objective to maintain and expand research holdings, which motivates collection development librarians to subscribe to as many of the key journals of record as is fiscally possible. Indeed, because of pressure from faculty to ensure easy access to key disciplinary journals, demand is relatively price-inelastic and differences in quality across journals are not typically reflected in price differentials. Similarly, librarians are often loath to replace an existing journal with a new one, despite possible price advantages, until they are certain of its quality, as judged by the broader research community. And because those journals with the highest reputations in a discipline typically attract the best papers, it can be a long and arduous process for new journals to establish a sufficiently rigorous reputation. Cognisant of this captured market situation, publishers have an incentive to engage in profit maximising behaviour, such as levying price increases far in excess of inflation and bundling practices (Bergman 2006; McCartan 2010).

2.3   *Supply Side Pressures*

On the supply side, a dominant sales strategy adopted by the major academic publishers in response to these structural conditions was the introduction of bundling practices, through which publishers sell access to an aggregated collection of anywhere from dozens to hundreds of electronic journals rather than individual titles. Such practices force librarians to subscribe to journals that they might not otherwise want as part of their collection in order to obtain those they do require. Referred to in the trade as 'The Big Deal', these typically multi-year contracts, although sometimes providing price caps over the life of the deal, have been critiqued by some for their almost Byzantine pricing structures that prohibit libraries from cancelling even a single title in the collection during the period under contract (Bergman 2006). Given their all or nothing nature, these deals also erode librarian control over the content and scope of a library's collection. More fundamentally problematic, libraries are actually only renting access to these electronic journals, with no guarantee that back issues will continue to be available should the library terminate the contract. Given the archival function of libraries, many librarians and academics would find it unacceptable to lose access to past scholarly works. This fact, not lost on publishers when setting prices for bundled offerings, further undermines a library's bargaining power when negotiating new contracts. These bundles also represent significant portions of a library's annual acquisitions budget, so when cuts in the collection have to be made it is often the stand-alone journals from smaller publishers that are cancelled. Aside from reducing access for the community served by the academic library, bundling practices therefore also intensify the tendencies towards concentration and monopoly power of the commercial publishing oligarchs.

2.4   Serials Crisis

Industry consolidation, working in tandem with the captured demand side of the market, gave rise to what is commonly referred to as a 'serials crisis', which is shorthand for a double-pronged dilemma faced by academic libraries beginning in the 1990s: skyrocketing journal prices coupled with static or declining library budgets. For example, the average serial unit cost more than tripled between 1986 and 2003, increasing from US$89.77 to US$283.08 (Greco et al. 2006). This increase far outpaced the 68 percent rate of inflation during this same period. In terms of overall serials expenditures, libraries had increased their average serials budgets by just over 260 percent from almost US$1.5 million in 1986 to slightly more than US$5.3 million in 2003. In comparison, monograph expenditures actually declined about two percent when adjusted for inflation – US$1.1 million in 1986 to US$1.85 million in 2003 (Greco et al. 2006). Perhaps more revealing of the true extent of the serials crisis is the significantly increased expenditure on library materials as a proportion of overall academic library budgets. In 1986, materials (journals and books) represented just over 32 percent of an average library budget for an Association of Research Libraries (U.S.) member. By 1995, the proportion had risen to just under 36 percent, and by 2000 and 2003 the proportion reached 39 percent and 43 percent, respectively (Greco et al. 2006). Caught between the Scylla of higher prices and the Charybdis of reduced funding, librarians responded with strategies that typically included cancelling some subscriptions, not subscribing to new journals, and reducing the number of books purchased in order to shore up the amount of funds available for journals. Unfortunately, the impact on monograph acquisitions has been felt in both absolute and relative terms; because the number of monographs has also been rising, libraries are now acquiring an even smaller proportion of available titles.

Even in the most recent years following the global economic meltdown of 2008, serials prices rose at rates between four and five percent, well above the negative rate of inflation in 2009 and the 1.6 percent level of inflation in 2010 (Bosch, Henderson, and Klusendorf 2011). According to EBSCO (2011), between 2007 and 2011 journal prices increased by almost 30 percent for U.S.-based titles and almost 34 percent for non-U.S. titles.[3] Serials prices increased by another six percent in both 2012 and 2013. This compares to a consumer price inflation rate of 1.7 percent in 2012, meaning that journal prices continue to escalate at rates that far outstrip both library budgets, which remain flat, and broader levels of price inflation in society. Average journal price increases for 2014 are forecasted to remain between six and seven percent (Bosch and Henderson 2013).

In contradistinction to some industry proponents, researchers have provided empirical evidence to defeat claims that seek to equate price with quality of a journal. Finding no correlation between high costs and high quality among high-impact economics journals, Greco et al. (2006) determined that the highest quality journals, based on ISI[4] citation indices, were published by non-profit publishers who charged substantially lower subscription fees than commercial publishers. Overall, Greco and his colleagues ascertained that subscription fees, price per page, and price per ISI citation were consistently lower for non-profit publishers than for commercial academic publishers. Although these authors point out that they did not complete similar analyses for journals in the social sciences and humanities, their preliminary analysis supports the hypothesis that comparable patterns exist in the majority of periodicals in these fields (Greco et al. 2006).

2.5   Deconstructing the Added-Value Myth

In an attempt to justify the high rents they extract when selling access to the knowledge created by academic labourers, publishers typically invoke claims about adding value to the broader knowledge ecology. Such assertions completely sidestep the reality that unpaid academic labour provides the content, peer review, and editorial work[5] being appropriated by journal publishers. These types of claims also occlude the additional time and money burdens

---

3   The higher price of non-U.S. journals might be explained, in part, by the weakness in the U.S. dollar since 2008.

4   ISI is now known as Thomson Reuters Web of Knowledge.

5   Although a few publishers pay editors a small stipend, it is typically well below the true value of the person's labour.

typically downloaded onto authors should their manuscript contain colour material, or require copyright release for images and other copyrighted material they might want to incorporate into their work. And even this value-added work is appropriated by publishers who coerce authors into surrendering their intellectual property rights as a precondition for publication. That having been said, it is true that authors receive the value-added services of typesetting, marketing, and, in some cases, copyediting. Academics also realise indirect benefits such as tenure, promotion, and scholarly recognition. And as users, academics benefit from and are becoming increasingly accustomed to a variety of electronic services such as full-text search capabilities, issue and table of contents alerts, citation tracking and export, etc.

Yet, according to a Deutsche Bank analyst, no commercial academic publisher adds a magnitude of value to the publishing process that would warrant the profit margins the major oligarchs are earning:

> In justifying the margins earned, the publishers, REL [Reed Elsevier] included, point to the highly skilled nature of the staff they employ (to pre-vet submitted papers prior to the peer review process), the support they provide to the peer review panels, including modest stipends, the complex typesetting, printing and distribution activities, including Web publishing and hosting. REL employs around 7,000 people in its Science business as a whole. REL also argues that the high margins reflect economies of scale and the very high levels of efficiency with which they operate.
>
> *We believe the publisher adds relatively little value to the publishing process.* We are not attempting to dismiss what 7,000 people at REL do for a living. We are simply observing that if the process really were as complex, costly and value-added as the publishers protest that it is, 40% margins wouldn't be available.
>
> AS CITED IN MCGUIGAN AND RUSSELL 2008, *para. 18; emphasis added*

When even investment analysts cast doubt on the veracity of the claims advanced by commercial publishers about the purported value they add to the publishing process, clearly something is amiss. Indeed, as Clarke (2007) points out in his analysis of alternative approaches to scholarly publishing, the main value added by publishers – journal branding and active marketing, aggressive customer management, and content protection – are mainly of interest and accrue to owners and shareholders, not the scholars actually producing and using the work. Economists Conley and Wooders (2009, 82) are similarly critical of industry contentions about purported value added, arguing that by far the greatest part of spending by commercial publishers is related to advertising for subscriptions, fulfilling subscriptions, and policing access to content, as well as managing all this, paying taxes, employing lawyers and accountants, and so on. None of this activity is closely related to facilitating scholarly communication.

Industry consolidation, coerced assignment of copyright, bundling, and increasingly prohibitive pricing practices as employed by the Elseviers and Springers of the world to wring maximum surplus value out of scholarly research and communication processes indicate the extent to which academic publishing is increasingly subsumed within the capitalist mode of production. In order to make conceptual sense of this situation, the following section of the chapter seeks to demonstrate that Marx's concepts of primitive accumulation and alienation provide an apposite theoretical lens through which to understand and analyse the structure and practices of the contemporary academic journal publishing environment.

3   Conceptualising Capitalist Control through the Lenses of Primitive Accumulation and Alienation

Marx provides his deepest discussion of primitive accumulation in Volume I of *Capital*, where he develops a critique of the 'so-called primitive accumulation' articulated by classical political economists. At its most basic, primitive accumulation can be understood as providing the origin of the separation between producers and the means of production; a separation that is responsible for the alienated character of labour and thus for defining the opposition inherent in capitalist social relations. As articulated most fully in the *Economic and philosophical manuscripts*, the alienation of labour under capitalist social relations manifests itself in four ways, two of which are most germane to the present work.[6] The first consequence of the estrangement of practical human activity – of labour – is a resulting alienated relationship between the worker and the product of labour, which, because of private property and the capital-labour relation, appears as something alien – as a power independent of the

---

6   In elaborating his third characteristic of capitalist alienation, Marx contemplates the effects of alienation on the person's relationship to other people when engaging in productive activity, itself a fundamentally social activity. The fourth type of alienation that Marx develops in the *Economic and philosophical manuscripts* is the notion of alienation from species-being – alienation from a person's being as a member of the human species.

actual producer. Because the product of the worker's labour is an alien object that belongs to the capitalist paying her wage, the more that she toils under capitalist social relations the more powerful becomes the alien, objective world she brings into being against herself. Although this basic idea inheres in the production of academic journal articles, it does require a slight adaptation. Publishers own the means of dissemination not production, as is the typical Marxist understanding of the alienation inherent in capitalist social relations premised on wage labour. Although an argument could be made that capitalist control of journal content – a necessary factor of production in subsequent research – represents partial capitalist control of the means of production. In any event, the perhaps stronger argument is that this type of control facilitates an even more insidious form of exploitation and alienation since the capitalist provides neither a wage nor the means of production (in the strictest sense), yet accumulates the benefit of the product of intellectual labour. At perhaps an even more fundamental level, an argument could be advanced that, from Marx's dialectical perspective, alienation reaches farther back than the estrangement among direct producers from the means of production and the resulting products of social labour to include the alienation inherent in the disconnect between the driving motivation of capital, the profit motive, and the fulfilment of socially-produced human needs (Burkett 1999; Mandel 1968).

A second and related aspect of the alienation of labour encompasses the relationship of the worker to the act of production within the labour process. Under the control of capitalist production processes, not only is the product of labour objectified in an alien object that holds power over the actual producer, but the corresponding form of productive activity renders the worker's own labour as something alien and opposed to him, reflecting an estrangement from himself and from his own activity. Rather than offering satisfaction in and of itself, alienated labour is external to the worker, something sold to and thus belonging to someone else. Through its alienability, the relationship of the worker to his activity becomes an example of what Marx refers to as 'self-estrangement':

> ...estrangement manifests itself not only in the result, but also in the *act of production*, within the *activity of production* itself. ... So if the product of labour is alienation, production itself must be active alienation, the alienation of activity, the activity of alienation. The estrangement of the object of labour merely summarizes the estrangement, the alienation in the activity of labour itself.MARX 1975, 326; emphasis in original

Under the dominance of capitalist social relations, we witness the social separation of the conditions of production from the control of the direct producers in service of capitalist valorisation. As the empirical evidence presented in the previous section illustrates, this dual form of alienation inheres in the scholarly communication process that is dominated by commercial publishers, who have been quite successful in wresting the outputs of scholarly research from the control of direct producers in service of capitalist accumulation imperatives.

Primitive accumulation thus represents an historically specific and class-differentiated relationship of control over the necessary means of social production. Most contemporary scholars engaging in a re-invigoration of primitive accumulation[7] as a theory for comprehending contemporary capitalist development tend to agree on three additional basic points about this concept. First, primitive accumulation should be understood as a continuous process that remains vital for capitalist accumulation. As Marx informs us,

> the capital-relation presupposes a complete separation between the workers and the ownership of the conditions for the realization of their labour. As soon as capitalist production stands on its own feet, it not only maintains this separation, but reproduces it on a constantly expanding scale.
>
> MARX 1992, 874

That is, the separation between producers and the means of production, a central category of Marx's critique of political economy, is the constitutive presupposition of accumulation and thus common to both primitive accumulation and accumulation in general – capital presupposes this separation. In Marx's own words,

> the manner in which the capitalist mode of production *expands* (takes possession of a greater segment of the social area) and subjects to itself spheres of production as yet not subject to it...entirely reproduces the *manner* in which it arises altogether.
>
> MARX 1994, 327; *emphasis in original*

---

7 Depending upon the theorist to whom one refers, the nominal term employed to reflect the phenomenon of primitive accumulation differs. Glassman (2006) discusses 'primitive accumulation', 'accumulation by dispossession', and 'accumulation by extra-economic means', though he seems to favour the original term coined by Marx. McCarthy (2004) speaks of accumulation by 'extra-economic means'. Bonefeld (2001, 2002) and De Angelis (2001, 2007) remain true to Marx, employing the term 'primitive accumulation'. Harvey (2003, 2006) prefers to substitute the updated predicate 'accumulation by dispossession' for what he believes is the dated 'primitive accumulation'.

The *Grundrisse* similarly weighs in on the issue: "Once this separation is given, the production process can only produce it anew, reproduce it, and reproduce it on an expanded scale" (Marx 1993, 462). As Marx again points out in Volume III of *Capital*,[8] accumulation is really nothing more than primitive accumulation "raised to the second power" (Marx 1967, 246). In Part III of his *Theories of surplus value*,[9] Marx is even more explicit about the continuous nature of primitive accumulation, contending that accumulation "reproduces the separation and the independent existence of material wealth as against labour on an ever increasing scale" (Marx 1972, 315). For this reason, accumulation "merely presents as a *continuous process* what in *primitive accumulation* appears as a distinct historical process" (ibid., 272; emphasis in original). We thus note that Marx's discussion of primitive accumulation contains a basic ontological connection between primitive accumulation and expanded reproduction, such that accumulation in general represents a form of intensified primitive accumulation (Bonefeld 2001, 2002; De Angelis 2001, 2007; Mandel 1975).

While there is a temporal element that distinguishes primitive accumulation from accumulation proper – indeed, the *ex novo* separation between producers and the means of production represents an *a priori* historical event – the critical distinction between the two is grounded less in temporality and more in the conditions and exigencies that comprise the separation. As Marx (1993, 459; emphasis removed) tells us in the *Grundrisse*, "once developed historically, capital itself creates the conditions of its existence (not as conditions for its arising, but as results of its being)." That is, once produced, capital must reproduce the separation between producers and the means of production (and, indeed, expand this reproduced separation). In order to normalise capitalist social relations, increasingly larger swaths of the population must be brought into the fold of capitalist commodity production through

> the silent compulsion of economic relations [that] sets the seal on the domination of the capitalist over the worker. Direct extra-economic force is still of course used, but only in exceptional cases. In the ordinary run of things, the worker can be left to the 'natural laws of production', i.e. it is possible to rely on his dependence on capital, which springs from the

---

8   Volume III of *Capital*, subtitled *The complete process of capitalist production*, was compiled by Engels based on notes left by Marx. It was originally published in 1894, eleven years after Marx's death.

9   Marx worked on the three volumes of *Theories of surplus value* in the 1860s. Considered by some to be the fourth volume of *Capital*, this work was published posthumously by Karl Kautsky.

conditions of production themselves, and is guaranteed in perpetuity by them.

MARX 1992, 899

Once we recognise that primitive accumulation satisfies a precondition for the expansion of capital accumulation, the temporal element assumes a secular form that encompasses not only the period in which the capitalist mode of production emerges, but also the reproduction and expansion of the capitalist mode of production. The upshot of this process is that capitalist production entails both the production of surplus value and the reproduction of social relations of production in an inverted form – social production alienated through private property and the commodity form (Bonefeld 1992; De Angelis 2007).

The second point about primitive accumulation is that it manifests in a variety of forms, including the privatisation of once public goods, which has the ultimate effect of re-organising class relations in favour of capital. As presented above, what might be considered the public-good character of academic research and its dissemination has been transformed through extensive enclosing practices into a relatively new source of capital accumulation.

The third feature of primitive accumulation speaks to its spatial ambition. Despite a general ethnocentrism present in Marx's work (an ethnocentrism that Marx readily admits), he discusses both the historical and the global elements of the processes of primitive accumulation, through which a privileged minority relentlessly pillaged the means of production from the people of pre-capitalist civilisations around the world:

> The discovery of gold and silver in America, the extirpation, enslavement and entombment in mines of the indigenous population of that continent, the beginnings of the conquest and plunder of India, and the conversion of Africa into a preserve for the commercial hunting of blackskins, are all things which characterize the dawn of the era of capitalist production. These idyllic proceedings are the chief moments of primitive accumulation.
>
> MARX 1992, 915

Ensuring an expanded reproduction of capital depends upon enveloping new spheres of production and peoples within the web of capitalist social relations of (re)production. Having historically extended the territorial reach of capitalist social relations through colonialist expansion and the imposition of private property rights across the globe, primitive accumulation in the twenty-first century has become both more extensive and intensive, affecting an enormously broad range of spatio-social activity.

In practice, primitive accumulation motivates efforts by capital to enclose more and more areas of our social existence that can be mined for extraction of surplus value. Enclosures thus all share the basic universal character of separating people from access to any social wealth that falls outside the purview of competitive markets and money as capital. That is, in line with the elaboration above about the basic element of the theory of primitive accumulation, enclosures provide a mechanism for realising the *ex novo* separation between producer and the means of production (De Angelis 2007; Harvey 2003, 2006).

3.1   *Capitalist Academic Publishing as an Alienating Instance of Primitive Accumulation*

As we saw above, capital has availed itself of a number of strategies to subvert toward its own accumulation imperatives the knowledge produced in common by members of the academy. Ever larger swaths of the social knowledge produced by academic labourers are being enclosed by capital, which represents intensified efforts to privatise research output paid for largely by the public purse and thus rightly belonging within the public domain. Recognising new opportunities for accumulation associated with the burgeoning volume of journals and research articles discussed above, capital began exerting a stranglehold over this industry and the processes of scholarly communication in what can be interpreted as yet another area of social existence now brought under capitalist control, thus reinforcing the idea that primitive accumulation remains a continuous social process. By appropriating the free labour that sustains the production, peer review, and editing of scholarly communication and then locking the resulting content behind intellectual property rights, licencing agreements, and technological protection mechanisms, capital has developed a very lucrative model in service of its own accumulation imperatives.

The result of these processes is an increasing individuation and alienation of scholarly producers that dispossesses them of their material capacity to consciously control their product and potentially their labour processes. While there might not be a formal separation of academic producers from the most basic means of production, research production, or perhaps more precisely its dissemination and use, nonetheless are subsumed increasingly within the capitalist mode of production. This increasing enclosure of scholarly communication and academic publishing within the capitalist market nexus that is informed by property rights, alienability, and capital accumulation represents a contemporary instance of primitive accumulation and alienated productive activity.

Moreover, efforts by capital to bring academic publishing profitably within its control involve the same spatial ambitions outlined previously in respect of primitive accumulation. Although clearly more intense in the global North, scholars in the global South are also increasingly confronted by such efforts, particularly as more and more feel compelled to publish in western academic journals. Moreover, these examples demonstrate how contemporary processes of primitive accumulation and the consequent expanding capitalist control of social production processes are exacerbating the alienation Marx elaborated to include new strata of producers beyond the orthodox Marxist emphasis on the industrial proletariat and waged labour.

However, the imposition of an *ex novo* separation represents a social process that, in practice, is susceptible to contestation by oppositional social forces seeking to recover those social spaces appropriated by capital and to re-invigorate them as spaces of commons. Capital is thus compelled to wage a two-front war in its battles for enclosure: invading and enclosing new realms of social existence that can be subverted in service of capital's accumulation priorities in the face of resistance, and defending those enclosed areas governed by accumulation and commodification imperatives against *ex novo* guerrilla movements struggling to liberate enclosures from capitalist control. The point to take from this discussion is that not only does separation occur *ex novo*, but that *ex novo* opposition can also form in response to capitalist enclosure (De Angelis 2007). Enclosures, and the responses they engender, thus represent strategic problems for capital. They pose limits that must be overcome if capital is to be successful in colonising new areas of social existence or in sustaining those areas already enclosed from attacks by alternative social forces seeking to de-commodify such spheres and transform them into commons. We note, therefore, that limits to capital are both endogenous and exogenous. In the former, capital itself identifies and defines a limit that it must overcome, and in the latter, that limit is defined for capital by the oppositional social forces that strive to liberate an already enclosed space. But regardless of how limits are identified, it is critical to recognise that counter-enclosures (read commons) represent alternatives that seek to circumscribe accumulation imperatives either by resisting enclosure strategies or by liberating enclosed areas of social life. Commons therefore tend to emerge out of struggles against their negation. "Therefore, around the issue of enclosures and their opposite – commons – we have a foundational entry point of a radical discourse on alternatives" (De Angelis 2007, 139). As the following section demonstrates, a number of struggles have been waged against capitalist enclosure of academic journal publishing.

4   Open-Access Responses to Crises in the Capitalist Model
     of Academic Publishing

In response to several of the trends in the academic publishing industry that
have clearly disadvantaged both authors and libraries – that is, the producers
and the predominant purchasers of scholarly output – a sustained movement
has emerged over the last decade and a half that advocates for and develops open-access models for academic research. For example, the Santa Fe
Convention in 1999 gave birth to the Open Archives Initiative, which was
tasked originally with developing a 'low-barrier interoperability framework'
that would facilitate access to e-print archives.[10] Soon thereafter, in December
2001, the Open Society Institute convened a conference in Budapest to interrogate issues around open access to scholarly research. This conference, which
laid the foundation for the subsequent Budapest Open Access Initiative
(BOAI), was one of the defining moments of the then nascent open-access
movement. Indeed, the BOAI was the first internationally-focused, formal
statement to articulate a commitment to open access, which is defined as
follows:

> By 'open access'..., we mean its [scholarly literature] free availability on
> the public internet, permitting any users to read, download, copy, distrib-
> ute, print, search, or link to the full texts of these articles, crawl them for
> indexing, pass them as data to software, or use them for any other lawful
> purpose, without financial, legal, or technical barriers other than those
> inseparable from gaining access to the internet itself. The only constraint
> on reproduction and distribution, and the only role for copyright in this
> domain, should be to give authors control over the integrity of their work
> and the right to be properly acknowledged and cited.
>   N.A. 2002, *para. 3*

Informed by the underlying premise that scholarly research should be freely
accessible online, the BOAI suggests two complementary strategies to achieve
and sustain such access. The first suggestion is self-archiving. Recognising that
many scholars might lack the technical capacity to deposit their research in
open electronic archives, the BOAI includes language about the need for tools

---

10   Although this remains a fundamental mission of the Open Archives Initiative, it has since
      broadened the scope of its work to include development of a technological framework
      and standards not restricted by type of content or economic mechanisms surrounding
      that content.

and assistance. Some thought was similarly given to users. By conforming to the standards being developed at the time by the Open Archives Initiative, the drafters of the BOAI envisioned optimal capture and seamless aggregation by search engines of all the emerging electronic repositories. Such standards would alleviate the need for users to know what and where all the separate archives are in order to access content. The second strategy relies on expanding the number of open-access journals, both *de novo* journals and those that elect to transition to open access. Given the underlying emphasis on free access that informs the BOAI, these open-access journals are encouraged to employ copyright in ways that ensure permanent open access. Moreover, and at an even more fundamental level of change, the BOAI suggests that open-access journals should avoid price barriers to access by eliminating subscription or user fees. Instead, open-access journal producers are exhorted to seek out and develop alternative funding sources, including government and foundation grants, author charges, or any other mechanism appropriate to the disciplinary and national context in which the journal is located. Indeed, flexibility, experimentation, and adaptation to local conditions are key elements expressed in the BOAI for ensuring rapid uptake and sustained longevity of the open-access movement.

Within a couple of years, additional international statements in support of open access emerged across a range of disciplines. For example, the Bethesda Statement on Open Access Publishing was drafted in April 2003 by a group of scientists and representatives from universities and medical institutions, funding agencies, libraries, and publishers. Specific to biomedical research, this statement affirms a commitment to open-access publishing and deposit of all published work and supplemental materials in electronic repositories that ensure open access, unrestricted distribution, interoperability, and long-term archiving (e.g., for biomedical research PubMed Central). At a meeting in October 2003 in Berlin, a very similar statement was adopted for sciences and humanities research (Berlin Declaration on Open Access to Knowledge in the Sciences and Humanities).

The two models suggested by the BOAI have subsequently emerged as the chief mechanisms for delivering open access to scholarly literature. According to Carroll (2011), a member of the Creative Commons[11] Board since 2001, full

---

11   As outlined on its website, the Creative Commons project provides infrastructure that
      consists of a set of copyright licences and tools designed to create a balance inside the
      traditional "all rights reserved" setting that copyright law creates. These tools provide cre-
      ators a simple, standardised way to keep their copyright while permitting certain uses of
      their work – a "some rights reserved" approach to copyright. The ultimate goal is to create,

open access to content requires easy online accessibility, gratis availability, and unrestricted re-usage rights, save attribution for the original creator. To the degree that either of the latter two characteristics is satisfied, scholars and practitioners distinguish between 'Gratis' and 'Libre' open access. The former eliminates only price barriers while the latter removes at least some permission barriers. Irrespective of whether works are offered Gratis or Libre, there are two accepted models for delivering open access to scholarly works: 'Gold' and 'Green'. The primary distinction between Gold and Green open access is based on venue or delivery vehicle (i.e., journal or repository) rather than price or user rights, which delineates Gratis from Libre. Gold open access refers to peer-reviewed publication in an open-access journal, whereas Green open access involves deposit of the work in an electronic institutional or subject repository.

Depending upon the particular repository, it might provide access to pre-prints,[12] post-prints,[13] or both. For example, one of the earliest subject repositories was ArXiv, which Paul Ginsberg developed in 1991 to archive physics pre-prints. Since its inception, ArXiv has expanded its subject area coverage and now provides open access to over 700,000 e-prints in physics, mathematics, computer science, quantitative biology, quantitative finance, and statistics. PubMed Central, another electronic repository, houses full-text articles from biomedicine and the life sciences. Developed and maintained by the United States National Library of Medicine, this online archive of biomedical journal articles experienced significant growth when the National Institutes of Health (NIH) mandated, as of 7 April 2008, that all researchers who receive NIH funding deposit into PubMed Central complete electronic copies of their peer-reviewed articles within 12 months of publication.[14] As of late 2014, PubMed

---

maintain, and expand a vast digital commons, a pool of content that can be copied, distributed, edited, remixed, and built upon, all within the boundaries of copyright law (http://creativecommons.org/about).

12   Pre-prints are drafts of articles before they have undergone peer review and thus have not yet been published in a journal.

13   A post-print is a draft that has undergone peer review. These versions may not always be identical to the published article, depending on whether the author retains copyright and, if not, whether the publisher allows such deposit. However, more and more commercial publishers are permitting Green open access, although often only after a publisher-specified embargo period has lapsed. Project SHERPA/RoMEO tracks publishers' open access policies at the following URL: http://www.sherpa.ac.uk/romeo/statistics.php ?la=en&flDnum=|&mode=simple.

14   With compliance rates at around only 75 percent in 2012, the NIH issued a notice (NOT-OD-12-160) in November of that year indicating that the agency would, in the

Central contained 3.2 million items, including articles, editorials and letters. The Wellcome Trust, Britain's largest non-government funding body and one of the world's largest science funding bodies, has had an open-access policy in place since October 2006. That policy stipulates that electronic copies of any peer-reviewed journal articles developed on the basis of research funded by the Trust must be deposited into PubMed Central or any other PMC International sites (e.g., Europe PMC) within six months maximum of the

---

following year, begin delaying processing of non-competing continuation grant awards if publications arising from that award were not in compliance with the NIH public access policy. The award would not be processed until recipients had demonstrated compliance. A subsequent notice (NOT-OD-13-042) issued in February 2013 established that the new compliance policy would apply to all non-competing continuation grant awards with a start date of 1 July 2013 or beyond. The stricter enforcement of the open-access policy appears to be bearing fruit. In May 2013, NIH-funded authors approved more than 10,000 peer-reviewed articles for inclusion in PubMed Central, which represents an almost 100 percent increase from the average monthly deposit rate of 5,100 articles in 2011–12 (Van Noorden 2013a). In a memorandum from 22 February 2013, the Director of the White House Office of Science and Technology Policy directed all federal agencies that expend over $100 million annually for research and development to develop plans to support open access to and re-use of research results, including both publications and digital data, funded by the federal government. Each affected agency was given six months from the date of the memorandum to submit a draft open-access plan to the Office of Science and Technology Policy. As a guideline only, and one that can be altered by petitioning the relevant agency, the policy suggests a maximum embargo period of 12 months for open access to the final, peer-reviewed publication. Full access to a publication's metadata is to be made available at the time of publication (Holdren 2013). This White House memorandum came a week after the introduction in the United States Congress of a bill entitled 'Fair Access to Science and Technology Research of 2013' (introduced in the Senate as bill S.350 and in the House of Representatives as bill H.R.708), which would require all federal agencies with annual extramural research expenditures of over $100 million to ensure that electronic copies of the final, peer-reviewed articles that stem from the funding are made freely available online to the public within a maximum of six months from publication in a journal. Similar to the White House memorandum, this bill stresses the importance of being able to reuse the peer-reviewed literature, including through such techniques as computational analysis, in order to advance science and improve the lives and welfare of Americans and others around the world. After reading in each respective chamber, the Senate version of the bill was referred to the Committee on Homeland Security and Governmental Affairs and the House version was referred to the House Committee on Oversight and Government Reform, where both remain. The chances of this bill being passed into law remain unclear. Indeed, similar versions of this bill were previously introduced into Congress in 2006, 2009/2010, and 2012.

journal publisher's official date of publication.[15] In addition to these well-known examples, a search in late 2014 of the Registry of Open Access Repositories returned over 3,800 entries for international institutional and cross-institutional repositories.[16]

Beyond the mounting success of the Green model that relies on repositories, recent research provides additional evidence that open-access journal publishing has matured into a sustainable form of scholarly publication (Laakso et al. 2011). In fact, a quick search of the Directory of Open Access Journals revealed over 10,000 registered journals as of late 2014. Perhaps more importantly, many of the early open-access journals remain active and the average number of articles per journal and year has almost doubled between 1993 and 2009. Similarly, relative to growth rates in the overall volume of peer-reviewed research articles, the number of articles in open-access journals has expanded at a much higher rate. In part, this has occurred because in recent years several high-impact and high-volume journals have transitioned to open access (Laakso et al. 2011). Although annual growth rates of the number of articles appearing in open-access journals has declined during the period from 2005 to 2009, which Laakso and his colleagues (2011) refer to as the consolidation years of open-access publishing, they are still averaging around 20 percent annually.

---

15   Wellcome Trust announced in April 2012 that it would begin sanctioning researchers who fail to comply with this policy. Effective 1 April 2013, articles that receive funding from the Trust to cover article-processing charges must also be licensed using the Creative Commons Attribution licence (CC-BY). This change was implemented to ensure the widest possible re-use of scholarly works (e.g., for text- and data-mining purposes or creating a translation). This stipulation may not sit well with those researchers for whom the creation of derivative works, particularly by corporate entities, would be anathema. The policy was expanded in October 2013 to include scholarly monographs and book chapters authored and co-authored by new Trust grant-holders that arise as part of their grant-funded research. The expanded policy will apply to all existing grant-holders beginning in October 2014 (Wellcome Trust n.d.).

16   The Registry of Open Access Repositories, which is part of the EPrints.org network, is hosted at the University of Southampton and is funded by the JISC. Historically, the acronym stood for 'Joint Information Systems Committee' but the work of this organisation has evolved and expanded over time. The stated goal of this registry "is to promote the development of open access by providing timely information about the growth and status of repositories throughout the world. Open access to research maximises research access and thereby also research impact, making research more productive and effective" (n.a. 2012b). The other leading list of open repositories around the world is the Directory of Open Access Repositories (OpenDOAR).

As might also be expected given such monumental growth, open-access infrastructure and technical applications have advanced considerably. In particular, Open Journal Systems, a journal management and publishing system developed by the Public Knowledge Project, has become a widely used software platform by over 5,800 open-access journals.[17] And, no doubt in response to the various open-access statements articulated above, the use of licensing agreements appropriate to the goal of facilitating unrestricted access to the scholarly literature has increased quite substantially.

Finally, and again reflective of the increasing institutional support for open-access research as articulated in the Bethesda and Berlin declarations, many more funding agencies and institutions now permit the inclusion of open-access fees in research budgets (Laakso et al. 2011). Such institutional support is particularly important because the Gold model of open-access journal publication eschews user fees. Although Gold open-access journals employ a wide variety of financing models, the most typical model relies on levying article-processing charges for accepted articles to be published. Although some journals will waive fees if they represent an insurmountable barrier to publication for the author. A number of journals that have been successful in attracting some form of institutional support waive publication fees altogether (Laakso et al. 2011).

It is also important to note the positive benefits of open-access publishing for the broader knowledge ecology. For example, a study from the United Kingdom, which modelled the economic implications of alternative scholarly publishing systems, draws the conclusion that expanded open-access publishing would likely provide significant long-term net benefits along the entire scholarly communication cycle and to the broader economy. Although lower during a transitional period, the authors of the report suggest that the net benefits would likely be positive for both open-access publishing and self-archiving alternatives

---

17   Open Journal Systems (OJS) is part of a broader suite of software developed and maintained by the Public Knowledge Project, which includes Open Conference Systems, Open Harvester Systems, and Open Monograph Press. OJS covers every stage of the refereed publishing process, from submissions through to online publication and indexing. OJS is open source software available gratis to any journal that wants to pursue an open-access publication model. As of 2014, the system has had 19 upgrade releases and is available in 30 languages. The Public Knowledge Project is an effort funded by the Canadian federal government to expand and improve access to research. The other partners involved in the project include the Canadian Centre for Studies in Publishing at Simon Fraser University, the University of British Columbia, and Stanford University.

(i.e., the Gold route) and for concurrent subscription-based publishing and self-archiving (i.e., the Green route) (Houghton et al. 2009).[18]

4.1   Capitalist Co-optation of Open-Access Publishing

Further, albeit disconcerting, evidence of the growing sustainability of open-access publishing comes from a number of commercial publishers, who have begun to offer open-access options to authors. For example, Springer has implemented a program called Springer Open Choice, which permits authors to make their journal article in an otherwise subscription-based journal freely available to anyone, at any time, in exchange for payment of an open-access publication fee of US$3,000/€2,200 plus tax. Since 2006, Taylor & Francis Group has offered a similar program called iOpenAccess. Renamed in 2012 to Taylor & Francis Open Select, authors must pay US$2,950/£1,788/€2,150 to permit open access to their article. The Sage Choice program provides authors this

---

18   The United Kingdom government announced on 16 July 2012 that it was accepting the recommendations articulated in the report issued a month prior by the Working Group on Expanding Access to Published Research Findings (dubbed the Finch Report, after committee chairperson Janet Finch). Research Councils UK (RCUK), the collaborative body comprised of the seven United Kingdom research councils responsible for funding research in higher education, similarly announced a consequent policy shift beyond its traditional Green open-access mandate to also support Gold open access effective 1 April 2013. The working group, which had been tasked by the House of Commons Business, Innovation and Skills (BIS) Committee with developing recommendations for effective and sustainable models for expanding access to published research findings, enumerated ten recommendations in its report. The most relevant recommendation for purposes of this chapter is the clear support for the Gold model of open access funded through article-processing charges. Almost immediately upon its publication, critics of the report charged that mandated Gold open access would not only restrict researchers' freedom to choose appropriate journals venues but it would also be unnecessarily expensive since United Kingdom institutions of higher education would have to continue paying subscription fees for traditional toll journals (at least until a significant transition to open-access journals had been achieved) while assuming the additional costs of paying for article-processing charges (Harnad 2012). RCUK backtracked somewhat and revised its policy to permit Green open access, while still indicating its preference for immediate open access (i.e., Gold open-access models). RCUK will assist researchers in covering article-processing charges by providing block grants to institutions that receive substantial RCUK funding. If the Green route to open access is chosen, the policy stipulates maximum embargo periods of six months for articles in science, technology, engineering, and mathematics disciplines and 12 months for articles in the arts, humanities, or social sciences. With the exception of biomedical research (the Medical Research Council has had a policy in place since 2006), these embargo periods may be doubled during the five-year transition period.

option at a cost of US$3,000/£1,600 in the science, technology and medical fields and US$1,500/£800 in the humanities and social sciences. These hybrid models that remain subscription based but offer the opportunity for individual authors to pay a fee to make their articles freely available electronically are particularly lucrative for publishers, who are essentially paid twice for the same article. This double dipping, as it has come to be known colloquially, is particularly threatening to the long-term financial sustainability of the scholarly communication system.

Commercial publishers have also adopted Gold open-access models. In 2012, Taylor & Francis launched Taylor & Francis Open, which is a suite of peer-reviewed, rapid publication, fully open-access journals across a range of subject areas. Article-processing charges for this program vary by journal. In February 2011, Wiley-Blackwell launched Wiley Open Access, a new publishing program that currently publishes over 30 open-access science and medical journals. Publication fees vary by journal and range between US$800 and US$3,000. The perhaps most stunning example to date of corporate recognition of the accumulation potential of open-access publishing came in 2008, when Springer purchased BioMed Central for a reported US$35 million. BioMed Central was launched in 2000 as an early for-profit, open-access publisher that charged authors a fee of US$500 to have accepted articles published. Springer subsequently quadrupled this article-processing charge to US$1,940 an article, although there was some variation among the journals published by BioMed Central (certain journals had processing fees over US$2,500). As of July 2014, there appears to be more variation in pricing across BioMed Central journals, with a few charging lower fees of US$1,735 and most charging between US$1,960 and US$2,650.

The fact that there is such a range of article-processing charges indicates that they are less a reflection of actual production costs and instead based more on a calculus of what the market will bear. Similar to the captured demand side of the market that offers publishers the opportunity to grossly inflate journals prices, at the production level a similar logic applies given that authors, or at least well-funded authors, will likely remit high fees to publish in high impact journals. This might be partly offset if there are enough substitute journals but that remains unclear. Gold open-access models may thus inaugurate a new form of the serials crisis, in which the fiscal burden is displaced from libraries onto faculty as expensive subscriptions are replaced with costly article-processing charges.

But it is not just the major publishers who have begun to exploit the open-access model of publishing for purposes of capital accumulation. For example, Bentham Science Publishers, which is headquartered in the United Arab

Emirates and has offices in Oak Park, Illinois and Bussum, the Netherlands, claims to publish over 230 open-access journals in the disciplines of science, technology, medicine, and social sciences. This for-profit company's business model is based on charging authors flat rate article-processing charges of US$800 for research articles, US$900 for review articles, US$600 for mini-review articles, US$600 for letters, and US$450 for book reviews (Poynder 2008b).[19] Bentham has been the subject of criticism among a number of academics for aggressive email marketing practices deployed to solicit editorial board members and article submissions. Some have characterised the company's practices as spamming since the email solicitations have often been very poorly targeted. For example, academics in a particular discipline were invited to contribute papers in a completely unrelated discipline or even join editorial boards of journals publishing in areas clearly beyond the subject matter specialty and even discipline of the person asked. And according to some academics, repeated requests to be removed from the company's marketing database went unanswered (Poynder 2008a).

Although such marketing *faux pas* may be shrugged off as unprofessional efforts to expand the scope of content it publishes, the company was involved in a more egregious example of the dangers of letting the profit motive inform academic publishing. After having received numerous emails asking him to contribute his research to one of Bentham's journals, Phil Davis decided that he would test the rigour of the company's peer-review system. He used SCIgen, a software programme that generates grammatically correct, yet "context-free" (i.e., nonsensical) essays in computer science, to construct a bogus research paper entitled "Deconstructing Access Points" that he submitted in January 2009 to Bentham's *The Open Information Science Journal* (TOISCIJ).[20] Davis listed the two fictitious co-authors as David Phillips and Andrew Kent. Although complete with figures, tables, and references, the article's professional surface appearance was quickly betrayed upon a cursory reading. For example: "In this section, we discuss existing research into red-black trees, vacuum tubes, and courseware [10]. On a similar note, recent work by Takahashi suggests a methodology for providing robust modalities, but does not offer an

---

19   The actual ownership of the company remains shrouded in secrecy. Despite repeated requests for this information by Richard Poynder, Bentham's Editorial Director, Matthew Honan, would only state that the company is "owned by a number of individuals, and the legal part of the business is based in the United Arab Emirates" but that he could not disclose the names of these people (Poynder 2008b, 14).
20   According to the Bentham website, this journal has been discontinued (http://benthamopen.com/toisj/MSandI.htm).

implementation [9]." The fabricated institutional affiliation – The Center for Research in Applied Phrenology based in Ithaca, New York (a name that yields the acronym CRAP) – similarly failed to set off alarm bells at the journal.[21] Within about four months, 'first author Phillips' (aka Phil Davis) received an acceptance letter from Ms Sana Mokarram, the Assistant Manager of Publication, in which she requested that the US$800 article fee be sent to the company's post office box in the SAIF Zone, a tax-free complex in the United Arab Emirates. According to Davis, the acceptance letter, despite claims to the contrary, offered no evidence that the article actually went through peer review (Davis 2009b; Shepherd 2009). To be fair, it should be noted that Davis also submitted the article to another of Bentham's journals and in that case it was rejected by the editor based on reviewer comments (Davis 2009a). Although certainly not definitive, the case of Bentham does hint at the ways that the dissemination of academic research, even under the banner of open access, can be subsumed within the logic of capital in ways that portend potentially disastrous results for the broader knowledge ecology.

4.2   Systemic Weaknesses of Current Commercial Open-Access Models

Open-access models have performed admirably well in expanding the amount of valuable knowledge produced in the academy that now flows freely into the public domain. And while I am very sympathetic to these models of knowledge dissemination, they remain plagued by certain weaknesses. The first problem inheres in Green open access, which cannot exist without the actual production of journals (electronic or print) that fulfil the functions of the scholarly communication system by providing the article of record, assigning the appropriate credit to authors, and providing the professionally produced version to those with access (i.e., access to subscription-based content). Put another way, the packaging and distribution/dissemination of the content has to be paid for in some way. The solution I propose in the next section of the chapter responds to this weakness in a way that avoids the concerns inherent in Gold open-access models.

A second problem is specific to Gold open access, which eschews subscription fees. While the thinking behind this principle is both understandable and commendable, it requires that a journal secure some source of external funding or levy author charges. The first strategy can be problematic since funding sources are very seldom guaranteed long term, thus placing the longevity of the journal in question. And author charges could represent unacceptable hurdles to publishing for those academics who possess negligible or even

---

21   Phrenology is a pseudoscience based on the belief that the shape of the skull indicates certain mental faculties and character traits.

non-existent research budgets. Given the emphasis within the neo-liberal university on commodifiable research and the consequent redistribution of university budgets and research grants, I suspect that many people in the social sciences and, especially, the humanities might experience precisely such difficulties. And as also discussed previously, article-processing charges are even higher in those open-access journals controlled by commercial publishers. Since decisions about tenure and promotion rely so heavily on peer-reviewed output, underfunded academics might thus be compelled to publish in conventional journals, thereby further reinforcing the *status quo* of commercial publishing.

Indeed, based on economic modelling employing the 'platform market' model, a number of authors contend that Gold open-access models may not be the appropriate solution to ensuring the widest possible availability of scholarly research since article-processing charges may introduce their own market distortions in the form of reduced article submissions from authors without the resources needed to pay these fees (McCabe, Snyder, and Fagin 2013). McCabe and his colleagues (2013) therefore suggest that it may not be authors who would be most adversely affected by such a situation but rather high-demand readers who would have appreciated the articles that did not appear because of the high article-processing charges. This underscores the need to consider new and possibly more radical strategies that respond to the weaknesses in the contemporary scholarly communication system.

One potential solution might be for universities to establish and fund publishing programs, perhaps administered by university libraries, that academics could draw on to cover author charges. However, the current fiscally-challenged environment of higher education does not bode well for the chances of such a solution materialising, particularly since during any transition period libraries would also need to continue paying for high-priced, capitalist-controlled journals. And in developing countries this would presumably be even less of an option, thus threatening to further marginalise non-western knowledge and scholars. Moreover, as mentioned previously, if funding agencies and universities begin to apportion more funds to cover publication fees, corporate publishers will maintain their control and their rent-seeking behaviour as they shift their revenue models from a subscription base to author fees.

This leads to the third and more systemic problem of current open-access models, particularly the Gold route. While they might challenge on the fringes, for the most part they not only leave in place the dominant capitalist model that is proving so disastrous, but they also add additional costs to the overall system of knowledge production and dissemination.

What the examples in this and the previous section of the chapter clearly demonstrate is that open access *per se* is not inherently anti-capitalist. Indeed, these corporate strategies represent a direct response by capital to subvert the open-access model in service of its own accumulation imperatives. In fact, content delivery through the online open-access model contributes to commercial publishers' profits by reducing many of the traditional costs associated with physically publishing a paper journal (materials, printing, inventory management, and distribution costs) and consequently lowering marginal costs of electronic production to almost zero. Given the historical ability of capital to often successfully decompose class struggle and re-appropriate for its own ends the creativity produced in common by autonomous workers, the increasing adoption of open-access models by commercial publishers is a worrisome trend that demands a counter-response by academics. As perhaps the first part of that response, we need to sharpen the distinction between open access that can be harnessed to serve capital, and explicitly anti-capitalist open access, in what we might term a commons-based open-access regime that more accurately reflects the actual nature of peer- and commons-based scholarly knowledge production.

5   Building on and Radicalising Open Access

As part of the first salvo against the dominant, capitalist-controlled academic publishing industry, all academics, but especially tenured faculty, need to be reminded of their role in the broader knowledge ecology and the constraining effects that the current capitalist model of journal publishing exercises on this ecology. At the risk of stating the obvious, this is critical since academics benefit from their work being widely disseminated and used (and hopefully cited), not from royalty streams. Put more directly, there is a disconnect between the factors motivating the typical academic writer and the profit maximising behaviour of commercial publishers. Unfortunately, the conservative value and reward system of the academy, with peer review at its core, continues to frustrate efforts to subvert the current scholarly communication/publishing system. In their extended study of the state of academic journal publishing, Greco et al. (2006) ascertained that prestige of publication venue and high readership in the particular discipline, as well as peer review rather than the ownership status of the journal publisher (i.e., commercial or non-profit) remain the dominant motivating criteria among a sizable majority of scholars when making their decisions as to where to publish their research. Indeed, more recent surveys from both the United Kingdom and the United States indicate that aside from low levels of awareness of the opportunities for publishing in open-access journals, most academics feel hamstrung by "the existing reward systems of tenure/promotion (and even grant making) which favor traditional publishing forms and venues" (Cullen and Chawner 2011, 462). Such institutional and cultural inertia poses an immense challenge if younger students and academics, despite being more adept and comfortable with new technologies, are socialised into the current system in a way fails to challenge, let alone, subvert the *status quo*.

Open-access proponents, and particularly those seeking to abolish capital's parasitic appropriation of academic publishing, therefore need to engage in more radical, awareness-raising activities that shake academics out of their complacency to the *status quo* of journal publishing. Part of that effort includes convincing academic librarians to engage in more sustained efforts to educate faculty members about the exorbitant costs libraries incur when subscribing to commercial journals. Of their own accord, faculty members seldom concern themselves with, let alone inquire about, the high price of journal subscriptions.

5.1   *Citation Advantages of Open Access*

In response to such challenges, scholars need to be made aware of the emerging evidence about the utility of open access for research recognition. A number of bibliometric studies reveal that, although there is variation across disciplines, research published in open-access journals tends to enjoy a citation advantage over metered content of between 25 and 250 percent (Gargouri et al. 2010; Antelman 2004; Eysenbach 2006; Hajjem, Harnad, and Gingras 2005; Norris, Oppenheim, and Rowland 2008; Donovan and Watson 2011). And in response to charges (charges typically emanating from proponents of the current journal publishing system) about possible author self-selection bias, Gargouri et al. (2010) have determined that the citation advantage that accrues from making research open access is not due to a quality bias on the part of authors, but instead is attributable to a quality advantage through which users, unencumbered by access constraints, are able to more easily select what to employ and cite. Put another way, the open-access advantage is not a quality bias but rather a quality advantage because it maximises accessibility and consequently citability (Gargouri et al. 2010; see also Hajjem, Harnad, and Gingras 2005).

5.2   *Mandating Green Open Access*

At an institutional level, and as open-access champion Steven Harnad has long been advocating, universities need to mandate self-archiving policies so that academics begin engaging in this method of scholarly dissemination on a regular basis. By eventually normalising such practice, academics and universities would satisfy more fully the dissemination function of the scholarly communication system. A number of universities in the United States, including Harvard, MIT, Princeton, and the University of California system, have embarked on precisely this path and established open-access policies that grant the university a non-exclusive, irrevocable licence to distribute a faculty member's scholarly articles on a non-profit basis (see the Coalition of Open Access Policy Institutions (COAPI) website – http://www.sparc.arl.org/COAPI). Typically, the individual universities then establish an institutional repository to house the articles. Any faculty member can usually apply to the university for a waiver of the licence requirement if the publisher refuses to permit open-access archiving. Moreover, not all policies require immediate deposit. The waiver option and lack of an immediate deposit requirement have been critiqued by some within the open-access movement for introducing a degree of indeterminacy that could potentially undermine open-access archiving. On the user side, open-access repositories could increase their up-take by enhancing metadata standards and quality, as well as search functions. To this end, institutional archives should consider adopting the standards developed by the Open Archives Initiative, as well as best practices from other established repositories.

5.3   Breaking the Impact of the Journal Impact Factor

As another element in the effort to supplant capitalist control of the scholarly communication system, and in direct response to the increasing corpus of evidence that outlines the benefits of open access, we must similarly begin to task tenure and promotion committees with developing new models of assessment that reduce the extant reliance on citation metrics and publication in marquee journals, which inhibit faculty, particularly untenured members, from publishing their work in open-access journals. A group of editors and publishers of scholarly journals meeting on 16 December 2012 during the Annual Meeting of The American Society for Cell Biology in San Francisco took up precisely this issue and developed a set of recommendations that have become known as the San Francisco Declaration on Research Assessment. The declaration consists of 15 different recommendations aimed at funding agencies, institutions, publishers, organisations that supply metrics, and researchers (although 18 recommendations are enumerated, three are similar across these targeted stakeholder groups). The following three themes run across all of the recommendations: eliminate the use of journal-based metrics, such as Journal Impact Factors, when making funding, appointment, and promotion decisions; assess research on its own merits rather than on the basis of the journal in which the research is published; and make full use of the opportunities afforded by electronic publishing (e.g., relax unnecessary word limits in articles and explore new impact measures of research impact, including qualitative indicators). The declaration similarly calls for an open and transparent process for computing all metrics. The number of parties that have signed the declaration has risen from originally 155 individuals and 82 organisations to over 12,000 individuals and 547 organisations by late 2014 (n.a., n.d.).

Given the potent gatekeeping function of citation indices, many of which are owned by Thomson Reuters, brief consideration of their role in the capital-ist-controlled journal publishing industry is warranted. The extensive control that commercial publishers exercise over the major citation indices could be leveraged to exclude open-access journals not published by the major corpo-rate players. Although Thomson Reuters claims on its website for Web of Science (an index of 12,000 international journals in the sciences, social sci-ences, arts, and humanities) that it indexes open-access journals, the actual number of such journals is not publicised. In addition to unilateral power to decide which journals to include in its indices, Thomson Reuters exerts a sig-nificant influence on journal publishing through its annual calculations of journal impact factors. The company calculates a journal's impact factor by dividing that year's number of citations to all the articles published in the par-ticular journal by the number of articles considered 'citable' by Thomson Reuters in the immediately preceding previous two years. Yet, accountable only to its shareholders rather than the actual authors and readers of scholarly research, Thomson Reuters refuses to divulge the criteria it employs to deter-mine what counts as a 'citable' article. In their terse assessment of the compa-ny's method of calculating journal impact factors, the editors of *PLoS Medicine* "...conclude that science is currently rated by a process that is itself unscien-tific, subjective, and secretive" (*PLoS Medicine* Editors 2006, para. 8).

Beyond this complete lack of transparency, journal impact factors are sus-ceptible to a number of additional critiques. For example, the distribution of citations provides no causal evidence about the quality of a particular journal. Similarly, limiting the calculation to two years after publication biases the sta-tistic, particularly for those disciplines in which uptake of new work takes lon-ger. Perhaps more troubling, the calculation fails to properly distinguish between and weight things such as article type (original research articles ver-sus editorials, reviews, and letters), multiple authorship, self-citation, and lan-guage. This shortcoming lends itself to impact factor manipulation if a journal publishes a few highly cited pieces of research and/or many review articles, which often garner more citations than novel research articles. This might also explain the frustrating, and seemingly increasing, practice among some jour-nal editors to 'suggest' to prospective authors that they cite other articles from the journal. With regard to tenure and promotion decisions, these weaknesses are exacerbated and can become truly detrimental for academics if journal impact factors are made to serve as proxies and the sole assessment metric for research quality. Indeed, because the impact factor is based on citations to all articles in a journal for a given year, it is incapable of rendering any evaluation about the quality of a specific author or article published in the journal (*PLoS Medicine* Editors 2006).

Their control by capital, coupled with their systemic political, linguistic, and geographic biases, renders current citation indices and their attendant system of journal impact factors largely antithetical to efforts to recuperate academic publishing from capital. Fortunately, competition is emerging in the form of programs and applications for alternative metrics to measure scholarly impact.[22] Although these tools remain very much at a nascent stage in which their effectiveness, validity, potential value and flaws, and their relationship to established measures requires deeper interrogation, it is promising that such tools are being developed. Despite the fact that indexing services require significant capital outlay that can be cost-prohibitive for smaller publishers, not to mention scholarly societies that may only publish a handful of titles, more open-access versions of scholarly indexing are becoming available, such as PubMed (contains more than 21 million citations to biomedical literature) and Citeseer[x], which aid users in locating scholarly articles and in some cases tracking citations (Striphas 2010).[23] Since both of these resources have been supported by federal grants in the United States, a project to develop an open source and transparent direct alternative to Thomson Reuters would presumably attract government funding. Indeed, given the push to increase access to scholarly research in both the United States and the United Kingdom,[24] perhaps a collaborative project would be possible. In terms of actual oversight and maintenance, I suggest that national academic library associations would be suitable candidates. Here I also think that international collaboration would be warranted in order to respond to some of the weaknesses in the current system that tends to under-represent and undervalue scholarship along North/South trajectories. Through a combination of cultural change and technological development, there exists the potential to break capital's stranglehold on

---

22   Altmetrics.com links to a number of alternative tools for measuring scholarly impact: http://altmetrics.org/tools/.

23   Google Scholar is also increasingly popular but reliance on it is not a viable option given its corporate ownership. The same is now true for Mendeley given its acquisition by Elsevier.

24   *Supra*, notes 14 and 18.

this important gatekeeping function in academia and the journal publishing industry.

5.4 *Efforts to Subvert the Status Quo*

The boycott of Elsevier, which gained substantial support, is a good example of precisely the type of actions needed to re-appropriate academic journal publishing from capital. This protest grew organically out of the blog posting in mid-January 2012 by Cambridge University mathematician Timothy Gowers, in which he wrote that he would no longer publish papers in any of Elsevier's journals or serve as a referee or editor for them. By mid-April of the same year, almost 10,000 researchers from around the world had pledged to support the boycott of Elsevier. The online statement of protest, which was organized by Tyler Neylon, raises three key objections to the business practices of Elsevier. First, individual journal prices are much too high. Second, because of these high prices libraries are compelled to avail themselves of publisher-developed bundles when ordering serials. As noted previously, very often these bundles include journals that are superfluous to a particular library's collection. Finally, Elsevier supported the proposed *Research Works Act* in the United States, a bill introduced in the House of Representatives in December 2011 that would have reversed and banned federal policies that require researchers who receive federal funding to deposit their research papers in open-access repositories within one year of publication.

Elsevier's defence for its support of this proposed legislation, as outlined in an open letter on its website, demonstrates the unbridled hubris of commercial publishers:

> Why then do we support this legislation? We are against unwarranted and potentially harmful government laws that could undermine the sustainability of the peer-review publishing system. The RWA's purpose is simply to ensure that the US government cannot enshrine in law how journal articles or accepted manuscripts are disseminated without involving publishers. We oppose in principle the notion that governments should be able to dictate the terms by which *products of private sector investments are distributed*, especially if they are to be distributed for free. And private sector means not just commercial publishers like Elsevier, but also not-for-profit and society publishers.
>
> N.A. 2012A, *para. 5; emphasis added*

The laughable claim about undermining peer review relies on a failure to appreciate the true locus of effort that permits the peer-review system to function:

voluntary labour of academics. Similarly, the indignation registered against a government-compelled distribution of "private sector investments" obfuscates the free labour provided by academics that comprises the bulk of the content Elsevier sells.[25] One wonders just how much private investment a company is making when it earns a profit margin of 39 percent on revenues of over £2.1 billion in 2013 (Aspesi and Luong 2014).

In 2000–01, a similar petition directed against publishers who refused to permit deposit of articles in electronic repositories attracted the support of almost 34,000 scholars. Although it is unclear how many people actually remained true to the pledge, the more important development was the creation of Public Library of Science by some of the people who spearheaded the campaign. Originally developed as an electronic repository in 2000, Public Library of Science founders, Harold Varmus, Patrick Brown, and Michael Eisen, expanded quickly into Gold open access and began publishing open-access journals in 2003, when they launched *PLoS Biology*. As a non-profit publisher, Public Library of Science currently produces seven peer-reviewed, open-access journals in the field of biomedicine.

5.5   *Toward a More Radical Transformation of Academic Publishing*
Taking a cue from such projects, we need to more publicly proclaim, including among large numbers of academics, the highly exploitative division of labour that inheres in commercial academic publishing. As mentioned previously, academics provide the majority of labour that sustains the production of scholarly knowledge, including the actual research and writing, peer review, and editing. It is time for academics to re-appropriate from capital the products and processes of their collective labour in order to revitalise the knowledge commons in ways that serve the public good rather than capitalist accumulation imperatives. I therefore believe that we need to become even more radical in our solutions to the capitalist enclosure of our knowledge ecology. And although this might require significant amounts of persuasion among some of our more conservative colleagues, I want to suggest that logistically such a re-appropriation would be less difficult.

There already exists a basic publishing infrastructure in the form of non-profit university presses, which should be able to substitute easily for commercial publishers in ways that would not require the assignment of copyright by

---

25   In the face of substantial pressure, Elsevier formally withdrew its support for this bill on
      27 February 2012. However, in its statement the company made it clear that it will continue to oppose legislated efforts to extend open-access mandates. On the same day, the
      sponsors of the bill announced that they would no longer try to move it through Congress.

authors or the imposition of onerous pricing and licensing contracts on library customers. Indeed, university presses have substantial historical experience in facilitating the dissemination of scholarly research across multiple product lines (trade books, scholarly monographs, textbooks, and journals). And as pointed out previously, there exist freely available, technologically sophisticated digital publishing platforms (e.g., Open Journal Systems) of which university presses could avail themselves. I therefore contend that university presses are best positioned to fulfil the key aspects of the scholarly communication system in ways that would promote access while also remedying the fiscal instability of the current corporate-dominated model.

I realise that this proposal will fall flat among those open-access advocates for whom user fees are anathema. Nonetheless, I think this suggestion recommends itself for several reasons. First, this proposed solution provides the imprimatur of a university press, which would ensure the registration and validation functions of a journal while avoiding the problems associated with predatory (scam) open-access publishers. Second, without the profit motive and bloated marketing and legal budgets, university presses should be able to produce and distribute academic journals at prices much lower than is currently the case. Indeed, by employing open source journal management platforms, university presses could eliminate many of the traditional costs associated with physically publishing a paper journal (materials, printing, inventory management, and distribution costs) and similarly lower their marginal costs of electronic production to almost zero. In fact, I would further suggest that the cost differentials would be so large as to permit university presses to charge libraries much more affordable prices for journals, while still retaining some level of revenue that could be employed to cross-subsidise monograph publishing and provide better author services such as copyediting, particularly for those authors whose native language is not English. Moreover, because this solution fits the current funding model of serials acquisition, it would require very little change within the university or the library to implement. Although some type of national, and possibly international, co-ordination, perhaps in the form of library and publisher consortia, might be required to facilitate the logistics of developing pricing models that would ensure equitable access across institutions of higher education. Here too I think that national academic library associations could play an immediate and effective role. Given the massive cost savings, libraries might face a challenge in trying to convince university administrators that the cost savings obtained in serials budgets remain within the library system to shore up other areas that have long been neglected because of the serials crisis. Finally, this proposal aligns with the Green open-access model since it would permit academics to deposit their scholarly research in an institutional or subject repository after a rela-tively short embargo period (e.g., six months). Again, I recognise that Gold open-access proponents who advocate for immediate access to scholarly liter-ature will find this proposal wanting. While I agree, in principle, that broader segments of society have a right to access research produced by academics employed by publicly-funded institutions of higher education, I question whether there is a need for immediate access. I would assert that, with the pos-sible exception of medical research, a 6- or 12-month embargo would not rep-resent a major hindrance to ultimate access by the broader public.

Since many journal titles are actually owned by commercial publishers, my proposed solution would almost certainly require the creation of new journals. Again, I think any difficulty here would result mainly from conservative torpor within the academy since it really is the quality and reputation of the journal editor and the editorial board that contributes to the success of a particular journal in attracting scholarly contributions. The task is therefore to convince significant numbers of editorial boards to stop providing their free labour to capitalist publishers, who then sell back that work to libraries at inflated prices. I am in no way underestimating the power of inertia within the academy and hence the scope of this challenge. But, there are a number of precedents for editorial boards deciding to resign en-masse and successfully launch compet-ing journals. For example, the entire editorial board of the *Journal of Library Administration* resigned in March 2013 in protest over what board members maintained were overly restrictive copyright demands by the publisher, Taylor & Francis, which the journal's editor feared were inhibiting authors from publishing in the journal. Taylor & Francis eventually agreed to relax some of the copyright restrictions but only for those authors willing and able to pay a US$2,995 article-processing charge.[26] For further examples of success-ful campaigns by editorial boards to rid themselves of commercial control, see *Journal declarations of independence* at the following URL: http://oad.simmons .edu/oadwiki/Journal_declarations_of_independence.

---

26   Taylor & Francis provoked further controversy and the threat of a mass resignation of the editorial board of the journal *Prometheus: Critical Studies in Innovation* when it delayed for eight months the publication of an article critical of the profits earned by commercial publishers of academic journal articles. Taylor & Francis backed down and permitted publication of the article in May 2014 but not without first adding a disclaimer to all the articles in the issue warning that "the accuracy of the content should not be relied upon" (Jump 2014, para. 9). This is a very apropos illustration of the fundamental disconnect between the goals of commercial publishers and the values that inform the scholarly communication system.

Given the general tenor in broader society, in which increasingly larger numbers of people are disaffected by our current socio-economic conditions, we may be at a critical juncture point. By this I mean that people appear much more critically attuned to the exploitative practices of capital. We need to seize on this disaffection and make more people aware, both within and outside of the academy, of the deleterious effects capitalist control has on the knowledge ecology. Only by revealing and openly challenging such exploitative relations of production will we recover and restore our labour products and processes in service of a vibrant and sustainable knowledge commons. Commercial publishers have had their gilded age. Now it is time for them to go the way of the dinosaur.

6   Conclusion

As elaborated above, Marx critiques capital as an alienating social form because it privatises the product of another's labour as property, thus rendering it susceptible to the exigencies of atomised market exchange from which an inequitable distribution of the wealth generated by social production obtains. The object of labour increasingly appears as alien property to the actual producers as the means of their existence and of their activity is concentrated progressively in the hands of capital. Corporate control of academic publishing through strategies and practices such as industry consolidation and forced assignment of copyright represents a new modality of capitalist primitive accumulation that strives to appropriate and enclose the knowledge commons that otherwise would emerge from the unrestricted flow of academic research. "Capital has from the start sought to enclose the commons. From colonization to slavery, from the work day to the home, from activity to the deepest thoughts and feelings, the history of capital is its extension into the human commons" (Neill, Caffentzis, and Machete n.d., Section v, para. 46).

The evidence presented in respect of the capitalist academic publishing industry is similarly testament to the expanding range of actors caught up in practices of primitive accumulation and capitalist control of social production processes. Despite a still relatively privileged position vis-à-vis other workers, it is precisely through such capitalist-controlled processes that cognitive workers in the academy are being robbed of control over their works, and scholarly research production and communication practices more broadly, as academic journal publishing becomes increasingly integrated into capitalist relations of production and exchange.

Capital's expanding exploitation of social labour brings with it a corresponding substitution of value accumulation imperatives for use value as the driving motivation for production, leading to a situation in which the social conditions that provide the basis for social production come to confront labour as the power of capital:

> The forms of socially developed labour...appear as *forms of the development of capital*, and therefore the productive powers of labour built up on these forms of social labour – consequently also science and the forces of nature – appear as *productive powers of capital*. In fact, the unity of labour in co-operation, the combination of labour through the division of labour, the use for productive purposes in machine industry of the forces of nature and science alongside the products of labour – all this confronts the individual labourers themselves as something *extraneous* and *objective*, as a mere form of existence of the means of labour that are independent of them and control them....And in fact all these applications of science, natural forces and products of labour on a large scale...appear only as *means for exploitation* of labour, as means of appropriating surplus-labour, and hence confront labour as *powers* belonging to capital.
>
> MARX 1963, 390–392; emphasis in original

The prescience and sagacity of Marx's thought to our contemporary situation cannot be emphasised strongly enough when considering the material presented in this chapter, particularly in respect of the way capital has and continues to successfully appropriate the massive amounts of 'free' labour that sustain the content production and evaluation of the academic journal publishing industry. Put another way, capitalist control of academic publishing expedites the private expropriation of much of the value that is produced in common through the cooperative relationships inherent in scholarly production. Under the dominance of capitalist social relations, we thus witness a further instance of the social separation of the conditions of production from the control of the direct producers in service of capitalist valorisation.

Yet there is hope. The success of the open-access movement and models has demonstrated that there are viable alternatives to the capitalist control of academic publishing. However, as argued above, the dominant open-access regime suffers from inherent neutrality in respect of economic model that renders it susceptible to capitalist appropriation and exploitation. The author-pay model does nothing to destruct the commodity logic of academic publishing but instead merely transfers the revenue source from users/readers to the actual producers (authors), which introduces yet another level of exploitation of the producers. Thus, while sympathetic to the goals and objectives of (Gold) open access, I believe that the more formidable imbalance in the scholarly publishing system is the presence and substantial control exercised by for-profit publishers. I have therefore suggested that we need to become more radical in our thinking and our actions in order to wrest control of academic publishing from the current capitalist oligarchs. The requisite technological, logistical, and financial capacities exist for scholarly journal publishing to be reclaimed by members of the academy through their non-profit university presses. What remains to be effected is an awakening among producers and users of the scholarly communication system to the need to avail themselves of these capacities in order to exert autonomous self-control over this system that remains so vital to the educational mission of both faculty and academic librarians.

Indeed, given the contemporary importance of information and knowledge to capitalist accumulation imperatives, the struggle against the enclosure of scholarly research represents a potentially critical element in the broader efforts to subvert capital. As Pirie (2009, 54) forcefully asserts,

> [i]t would challenge the dominant fetishized understanding of informational systems that uncritically accepts the commodification of information. The undermining of corporate control in this sector must be understood as a dangerous threat to the stability of the regime as a whole.

If nothing else, my hope is that this chapter engenders further discussion, elaboration, and eventual implementation of strategies that return complete and common ownership of the products and processes of academic knowledge creation to the actual producers and users.

References

Antelman, Kristin. 2004. Do Open-access Articles Have Greater Research Impact? *College and Research Libraries* 65 (5): 372–382.

Aspesi, Claudio, and Helen Luong. 2014. Reed Elsevier: Goodbye to Berlin – the Fading Threat of Open Access (Upgrade to Market-Perform). New York: Sanford C. Bernstein & Co., LLC.

Bergman, Sherrie S. 2006. The Scholarly Communication Movement: Highlights and Recent Developments. *Collection Building* 25 (4): 108–128.

Bergstrom, Theodore C. and Carl T. Bergstrom. 2004. Can 'Author Pays' Journals Compete with 'Reader Pays'? *Nature Web Focus*. Accessed 3 December 2011. http://www.nature.com/nature/focus/accessdebate/22.html.

Bonefeld, Werner. 1992. Social Constitution and the Form of the Capitalist State. In *Open Marxism*, edited by Werner Bonefeld, Richard Gunn and Kosmas Psychopedis, 93–132. London, GB: Pluto Press.

Bonefeld, Werner. 2001. The Permanence of Primitive Accumulation: Commodity Fetishism and Social Constitution. *The Commoner* 2 (September): 1–15.

Bonefeld, Werner. 2002. History and Social Constitution: Primitive Accumulation is not Primitive. *The Commoner* March 2002. Accessed 8 December 2007. http://www .commoner.org.uk/debbonefeld01.pdf.

Bosch, Stephen, and Kittie Henderson. 2013. The Winds of Change: Periodicals Price Survey 2013. *Library Journal* 138 (8). Accessed 18 May 2013. http://lj.libraryjournal .com/2013/04/publishing/the-winds-of-change-periodicals-price-survey-2013/.

Bosch, Stephen, Kittie Henderson, and Heather Klusendorf. 2011. Periodicals Price Survey 2011: Under Pressure, Times Are Changing. *Library Journal* 138 (8): 30–35.

Burkett, Paul. 1999. *Marx and Nature: A Red and Green Perspective*. New York: St. Martin's Press.

Campbell, Robert. 2012. Introduction: Overview of Academic and Professional Publishing. In *Academic and Professional Publishing*, edited by Robert Campbell, Ed Pentz and Ian Borthwick, 1–14. Oxford: Chandos.

Carroll, Michael W. 2011. Why Full Open Access Matters. *PLoS Biology* 9 (11): e1001210. Accessed 7 January 2012. http://www.plosbiology.org/article/info:doi%2F10.1371% 2Fjournal.pbio.1001210.

Clarke, Roger. 2007. The Cost Profiles of Alternative Approaches to Journal Publishing. *First Monday* 12 (12). Accessed 10 January 2012. http://firstmonday.org/htbin/ cgiwrap/bin/ojs/index.php/fm/article/view/2048/1906.

Conley, John P. and Myrna Wooders. 2009. But What Have You Done for Me Lately? Commercial Publishing, Scholarly Communication, and Open-Access. *Economic Analysis & Policy* 39 (1): 71–87.

Cullen, Rowena and Brenda Chawner. 2011. Institutional Repositories, Open Access, and Scholarly Communication: A Study of Conflicting Paradigms. *The Journal of Academic Librarianship* 37 (6): 460–470.

Davis, Phil. 2009a. Adventure in Open Access Publishing. The Scholarly Kitchen (12 March). Accessed 4 April 2012. http://scholarlykitchen.sspnet.org/2009/03/12/ bentham-publishers/.

Davis, Phil. 2009b. Open Access Publisher Accepts Nonsense Manuscript for Dollars. The Scholarly Kitchen (10 June). Accessed 4 April 2012. http://scholarlykitchen. sspnet.org/2009/06/10/nonsense-for-dollars/.

De Angelis, Massimo. 2001. Marx and Primitive Accumulation: The Continuous Character of Capital's "Enclosures". *The Commoner* 2 (September): 1–22.

De Angelis, Massimo. 2007. *The Beginning of History: Value Struggles and Global Capital*. London: Pluto.

Donovan, James M. and Carol A. Watson. 2011. Citation Advantage of Open Access Legal Scholarship. Athens: University of Georgia School of Law.

EBSCO. 2011. Five Year Journal Price Increase History (2007–2011). Ipswich, MA: EBSCO.

Eysenbach, Gunther. 2006. Citation Advantage of Open Access Articles. *PLoS Biology* 4 (5): e157. Accessed 10 November 2012. http://dx.doi.org/10.1371%2Fjournal.pbio.0040157.

Gargouri, Yassine, Chawki Hajjem, Vincent Larivière, Yves Gingras, Les Carr, Tim Brody, and Stevan Harnad. 2010. Self-selected or Mandated, Open Access Increases Citation Impact for Higher Quality Research. *PLoS ONE* 5 (10): e13636. Accessed 4 November 2011. http://www.plosone.org/article/info:doi/10.1371/journal.pone.0013636.

Glassman, Jim. 2006. Primitive Accumulation, Accumulation by Dispossession, Accumulation by 'Extra-economic' Means. *Progress in Human Geography* 30 (5): 608–625.

Greco, Albert N., Robert M. Wharton, Hooman Estelami, and Robert F. Jones. 2006. The State of Scholarly Journal Publishing: 1981–2000. *Journal of Scholarly Publishing* 37 (3): 155–214.

Hajjem, Chawki, Stevan Harnad, and Yves Gingras. 2005. Ten-year Cross-disciplinary Comparison of the Growth of Open Access and How it Increases Research Citation Impact. *IEEE Data Engineering Bulletin* 28 (4): 39–46.

Harnad, Stevan. 2012. Why the UK Should Not Heed the Finch Report. In *The Impact of Social Sciences Blog*. London: London School of Economics Public Policy Group. Accessed 15 July 2012. http://blogs.lse.ac.uk/impactofsocialsciences/2012/07/04/why-the-uk-should-not-heed-the-finch-report/.

Harvey, David. 2003. *The New Imperialism*. Oxford: Oxford University Press.

Harvey, David. 2006. *Spaces of Global Capitalism*. New York: Verso.

Holdren, John P. 2013. Increasing Access to the Results of Federally Funded Scientific Research. Washington, D.C.: Office of Science and Technology Policy.

Houghton, John, Bruce Rasmussen, Peter Sheehan, Charles Oppenheim, Anne Morris, Claire Creaser, Helen Greenwood, Mark Summers, and Adrian Gourlay. 2009. Economic Implications of Alternative Scholarly Publishing Models: Exploring the Costs and Benefits. London: JISC.

Jump, Paul. 2014. Resignations Threat over Taylor & Francis 'Censorship'. *Times Higher Education*. Accessed 23 June 2014. http://www.timeshighereducation.co.uk/news/resignations-threat-over-taylor-and-francis-censorship/2013752.article.

Kranich, Nancy. 2004. The Information Commons: A Public Policy Report. New York, NY: Brennan Center for Justice.

Laakso, Mikael, Patrik Welling, Helena Bukvova, Linus Nyman, Bo-Christer Björk, and Turid Hedlund. 2011. The Development of Open Access Journal Publishing from 1993 to 2009. *PLoS ONE* 6 (6): e20961. Accessed 18 January 2012. http://dx.doi.org/10.1371%2Fjournal.pone.0020961.

Mance, Henry. 2013. Reed Elsevier to Pay £45m for Social Network. *Financial Times*, 9 April. Accessed 1 November 2014. http://www.ft.com/cms/s/0/cac07b12-a076-11e2-88b6-00144feabdc0.html#axzz3KcYCmEOs.

Mandel, Ernest. 1968. *Marxist Economic Theory*. New York: Monthly Review Press.

Mandel, Ernest. 1975. *Late Capitalism*. Translated by J. De Bres. London, GB: NLB.

Marx, Karl. 1963. *Theories of Surplus Value: Part I*. Moscow: Progress Publishers.

Marx, Karl. 1967. *Capital: A Critique of Political Economy: The Process of Capitalist Production as a Whole*. Edited by F. Engels. Vol. III. New York: International Publishers. Original edition, 1894.

Marx, Karl. 1972. *Theories of Surplus Value: Part III*. Translated by J. Cohen. London: Lawrence & Wishart.

Marx, Karl. 1975. Economic and Philosophical Manuscripts (1844). In *Early Writings*. New York: Vintage Books.

Marx, Karl. 1992. *Capital: A Critique of Political Economy*. Translated by B. Fowkes. Vol. I. London: Penguin Books.

Marx, Karl. 1993. *Grundrisse: Foundations of the Critique of Political Economy*. Translated by M. Nicolaus. London: Penguin Books.

Marx, Karl. 1994. Economic Manuscript of 1861–63 (Conclusion). In *Karl Marx, Frederick Engels: Collected Works*. New York: International Publishers.

McCabe, Mark J. 2002. Journal Pricing and Mergers: A Portfolio Approach. *The American Economic Review* 92 (1): 259–269.

McCabe, Mark J., Christopher M. Snyder, and Anna Fagin. 2013. Open Access Versus Traditional Journal Pricing: Using a Simple "Platform Market" Model to Understand Which Will Win (and Which Should). *The Journal of Academic Librarianship* 39 (1): 11–19.

McCartan, Patrick. 2010. Journals and the Production of Knowledge: A Publishing Perspective. *British Journal of Political Science* 40 (2): 237–248.

McCarthy, James. 2004. Privatizing Conditions of Production: Trade Agreements as Neoliberal Environmental Governance. *Geoforum* 35 (3): 327–341.

McGuigan, Glenn S., and Robert D. Russell. 2008. The Business of Academic Publishing: A Strategic Analysis of the Academic Journal Publishing Industry and its Impact on the Future of Scholarly Publishing. *Electronic Journal of Academic and Special Librarianship* 9 (3). Accessed 18 December 2011. http://southernlibrarianship.icaap .org/content/v09n03/mcguigan_g01.html.

Merrett, Christopher. 2006. The Expropriation of Intellectual Capital and the Political Economy of International Academic Publishing. *Critical Arts: A South–North Journal of Cultural & Media Studies* 20 (1): 96–111.

Mills, C. Wright 1951. *White Collar: The American Middle Classes*. New York: Oxford University Press.

Munroe, Mary H. 2007. The Academic Publishing Industry: A Story of Merger and Acquisition. Report prepared for the Association of Research Libraries & The Information Access Alliance. Accessed 2 December 2011. http://www.ulib.niu.edu/ publishers/.

n.a. 2002. *Budapest Open Access Initiative*. Accessed 12 November 2011. http://www .budapestopenaccessinitiative.org/read.

n.a. 2012a. *A Message to the Research Community: Elsevier, Access, and the Research Works Act.* Accessed 6 February 2012. http://www.elsevier.com/wps/find/intro.cws_home/elsevierstatement.

n.a. 2012b. *Registry of Open Access Repositories.* Accessed 15 February 2012. http://roar.eprints.org/.

n.a. n.d. *The San Francisco Declaration on Research Assessment.* American Society for Cell Biology. Accessed 15 November 2014. http://am.ascb.org/dora/.

Neill, Monty, George Caffentzis, and Johnny Machete. n.d. *Toward the New Commons: Working Class Strategies and the Zapatistas.* Accessed 13 December 2011. http://www.oocities.org/CapitolHill/3843/monty5.html.

Norris, Michael, Charles Oppenheim, and Fytton Rowland. 2008. The Citation Advantage of Open-Access Articles. *The Journal of the American Society for Information Science and Technology* 59 (12): 1963–1972.

Pirie, Iain. 2009. The Political Economy of Academic Publishing. *Historical Materialism* 17 (3): 31–60.

PLoS Medicine Editors. 2006. The Impact Factor Game. *PLoS Medicine* 3 (6), http://www.plosmedicine.org/article/info:doi/10.1371/journal.pmed.0030291.

Poynder, Richard. 2008a. The Open Access Interviews: Matthew Honan. In *Open and Shut?* Accessed 10 February 2012. http://poynder.blogspot.com/2008/04/open-access-interviews-matthew-honan.html.

Poynder, Richard. 2008b. The Open Access Interviews: Richard Poynder Talks to Matthew Honan, editorial director, Bentham Science Publishers. Accessed 10 February 2012. http://www.richardpoynder.co.uk/Honan.pdf.

Shepherd, Jessica. 2009. Editor Quits After Journal Accepts Bogus Science Article. *The Guardian* June 18, http://www.guardian.co.uk/education/2009/jun/18/science-editor-resigns-hoax-article.

Striphas, Ted. 2010. Acknowledged Goods: Cultural Studies and the Politics of Academic Journal Publishing. *Communication and Critical/Cultural Studies* 7 (1): 3–25.

Van Noorden, Richard. 2013a. NIH Sees Surge in Open-Access Manuscripts. In *Nature News Blog*: Nature News Group. Accessed 2 July 2013. http://blogs.nature.com/news/2013/07/nih-sees-surge-in-open-access-manuscripts.html.

Van Noorden, Richard. 2013b. The True Cost of Science Publishing: Cheap Open-Access Journals Raise Questions About the Value Publishers Add for Their Money. *Nature* 495 (28 March): 426–429.

Ware, Mark and Michael Mabe. 2009. The STM Report: An Overview of Scientific and Scholarly Journal Publishing. Oxford: International Association of Scientific, Technical and Medical Publishers.

Wellcome Trust. n.d. Open Access Policy: Position Statement in Support of Open and Unrestricted Access to Published Research. London: Wellcome Trust. Accessed 13 July 2013. http://www.wellcome.ac.uk/About-us/Policy/Policy-and-position-statements/WTD002766.htm.

CHAPTER 14

Marx, Free Speech and the Indian Media*

Padmaja Shaw

1 Introduction

All of 172 years after Karl Marx began his career as a journalist in Europe with a brilliant defence of free speech in 1842, in 2014 a fresh debate has arisen on free speech as it is understood and practiced all over the world. While the people fighting repressive regimes are struggling to win basic freedoms of life, liberty, association and speech, the people in liberal democracies are demonstrating on the streets their sense of outrage at globalised capitalism taking away those very freedoms of life, liberty, association and speech.

Analysts have likened the current global crisis of capitalism to the conditions prevailing across Europe at the time of the revolutions of 1848. The 20th century consensus about bourgeois-democracy being the most stable formation is being challenged.

Throughout history, the relationship between democratic struggles and the goals of establishing working-class control over production have remained problematic and sometimes have been lost sight of. While it is the thesis of Marxian analysis that the problem lies in the capitalist mode of production and its unbridled quest for profits, which tries to prevent the inevitable emergence of the working-class as a dominant force, the 20th century saw the unprecedented use of media as instruments for promoting the interests of global capital.

Media industries have played a major role in building and sustaining the prevailing social consensus around the notion of bourgeois-democratic stability. The gradual corporatisation of media has made it an integral part of the circuit of capitalist production, and a major player in creating and sustaining capitalist societies. Given this, can we expect the corporate media industry to protect the rights of the people? Are the 'free' media institutions in democratic societies providing space for working-class struggles? Is it possible for a journalist working for a media corporation to question the basic premises of bourgeois democracy?

* I would like to express my gratitude to Prof. G. Haragopal, human rights activist and retired professor of Political Science, University of Hyderabad, for his comments on this chapter.

It is necessary to revisit Karl Marx's works to understand his conception of free speech both for the ideological framework he had developed as well as for the remarkable and radical role he played as a journalist all his adult life. Marx, for a good part of the 19th century (1842 to 1865), has written extensively as a journalist on every important issue, including the revolutionary awakening that gripped much of Europe and elsewhere. During these years he edited *Rheinische Zeitung*, *Neue Rheinische Zeitung,* contributed to a variety of papers both in German and in English, which included *The People's Press, Die Presse, Neue Oder Zeitung,* and several other papers including around 487 (singly 350, by Engels 125, jointly with Engels 12) articles for *The New York Daily Tribune* as its Europe correspondent. Though, while he was writing for *The New York Daily Tribune,* since the English language translation of the Communist Manifesto was still not available, Marx was not known widely as the author of the revolutionary document in the English-speaking world (Ledbetter 2007). Marx's column in *The New York Daily Tribune* was welcomed because of its concern with people's issues that matched founder Horace Greeley's stated objective for starting the *Tribune* as a sensible counter to the frivolous penny press of his time (Emery and Emery 1954, 124).

Three major aspects that Karl Marx deals with in his journalistic writings have a deep contemporary resonance in countries like India: freedom of speech and censorship, the press as a part of free trade, and the role of media in bourgeois democracies. This chapter will present Marx's major arguments on all the three issues and will then examine the role of Left parties and intellectuals in creating and expanding spaces for exercising the constitutionally guaranteed right to free speech in India.

2   Free Speech and Censorship

In the 1840s, despotic monarchs ruled much of Europe. Journalists and writers were constantly subjected to stringent censorship, as most of the countries had no traditions of free speech or a Bill of Rights that guaranteed any rights (Padover 1974, xi). In 1841, the Prussian cabinet issued a censorship decree that expanded the scope of the existing censorship edict, to suppress anything that was critical of the "fundamental principles of religion and offensive to morality and good will."

Karl Marx, a young Hegelian at 24, burst on to the political scene of Germany with his incisive analysis of freedom of speech and censorship. In a series of articles published in *Rheinische Zeitung* between May 5 and 19, Marx posed an impassioned challenge to the pronouncements of the elected representatives of the Sixth Rhineland Landtag on censorship:

The censorship law...is not a law, it is a police measure; but it is a *bad police measure*, for it does not achieve what it intends, and it does not intend what it achieves. ... The censorship makes every forbidden work, whether good or bad, into an extraordinary document, whereas freedom of the press deprives every written work of an externally imposing effect.

PADOVER 1974, XIII

Marx's opposition to censorship was not driven by any desire for an unregulated press. He argued for press laws that would be administered by independent judiciary:

"...censorship...makes arbitrariness into a law. ... Just as a press law is different from a censorship law, so the *judge's* attitude to the press *differs* from the *attitude of the censor.*

... The independent judge belongs neither to me nor to the government. The dependent censor is himself a government organ... The judge has a *definite* press offence put before him; confronting the censor is the spirit of the press. The judge judges my act according to a definite law; the censor not only punishes the crime, he *makes* it... The censorship does not accuse me of violating an existing law. It condemns my opinion because it is not the opinion of the censor and his superiors. My openly performed act, which is willing to submit itself to the world and its judgment, to the state and its law, has sentence passed on it by a hidden, purely negative power, which cannot give itself the form of law, which shuns the light of day, and which is not bound by any general principles."

"*A censorship law is an impossibility* because it seeks to punish not offences but opinions, because it cannot be anything but a *formula for the censor,* because no state has the courage to put in general legal terms what it can carry out in practice through the agency of the censor. For that reason, too, the operation of the censorship is entrusted not to the courts but to the police." (Italics in original)

MARX 1842A

Describing true censorship as criticism that is the very essence of the freedom of the press, Marx argued that censorship is criticism as government monopoly, but that the government wants to apply it in secrecy and does not itself want to suffer any criticism (Marx 1842b). Drawing a further distinction between press law and censorship he wrote:

In a press law, freedom punishes. In a censorship law, freedom is punished. The censorship law is a law of suspicion against freedom. The press

law is a vote of confidence which the press gives itself. The press law punishes the misuse of freedom. The censorship law punishes freedom as
misuse. ... Thus press law, far from being a repressive measure against
freedom of the press, is merely a means to discourage repetition of violation through a penalty. ... Laws are not repressive measures against freedom, any more than the law of gravity is a repressive measure against
movement. ... Rather, laws are positive, clear, universal norms, in which
freedom has won an impersonal, theoretical existence independent of
the caprice of any individual. ... Press law is the legal recognition of
freedom.

MARX 1842C

About freedom of the press, he wrote:

The free press is the ubiquitous vigilant eye of a people's soul, the embodiment of a people's faith in itself, the eloquent link that connects the individual with the state and the world, the embodied culture that transforms
material struggles into intellectual struggles and idealises their crude
material form. It is a people's frank confession to itself... It is the spiritual
mirror in which a people can see itself, and self-examination is the first
condition of wisdom.

MARX 1842D

For Marx, the press is the "most general way for individuals to communicate
their intellectual being. It knows no reputation of a person, but only the reputation of intelligence" (Marx, 1842e). Marx believed that a revolutionary movement must participate in public life and educate the proletariat and that it is
necessary to protect free speech, as newspapers are the primary instruments of
public communication (Hardt 2000).

Writing on widespread distress in the Mosel province, Marx explained the
need for a free press:

To solve difficulties, the administration and the administered need a
third element, which is political without being bureaucratic, an element
that does not derive from bureaucratic presuppositions, that is, civic
without being directly entangled in private interests and their needs. This
complementary element, composed of a political head and a civic heart,
is a *free press* (italics in original). ... The "free press," as it is the product of
public opinion, also produces public opinion, and it alone has the power
to make a special interest into a general interest. ... It alone has the power

to alleviate the misery, if for no other reason than that it distributes the
feeling of misery among all.

MARX, 1843

By October 1842, Marx became the editor of *Rheinische Zeitung*, his genius
widely recognised. As editor of the paper, with regular contributions from
Engels and other young Hegelians, Marx led a crusade for a unified Germany
and championed working-class issues. A significant aspect of Marx's early
practice of journalism was his relentless effort to fight all attacks on free
speech, whether from state decrees or from lead articles in rival papers of
the time like *Kölnische Zeitung*, which wielded significant influence among the
conservative Christian readership of the province. Marx would use his incisive
logic and biting wit to expose the hypocrisy of the rival newspapers, which
supported various forms of repression of the Prussian state.

However, the two papers Marx edited between 1842 and 1849, *Rheinische
Zeitung* and *Neue Rheinische Zeitung*, were hounded by the governments of the
time and finally shut down. After the closure of *Rheinische Zeitung*, Marx left
Germany, but returned in 1848 after the revolutionary changes to start *Neue
Rheinische Zeitung*. In a point-by-point refutation of the Prussian Press Bill
introduced by post-revolutionary Prussia, Marx exposed how the new bill was
in glaring contradiction to press freedom:

> From the day this law goes into effect, the officials can commit any despo-
> tism, any tyranny, any illegality, with impunity; they can coolly flog or
> order to be flogged, arrest and hold without a hearing; the only control,
> the press, has been made ineffective... Indeed, what remains of freedom
> of the press if that which *deserves* public contempt can no longer be held
> up to public contempt?
>
> MARX 1848

In a typical example of his sharp wit, he adds: "He (Herr Hansemann) should
also declare it punishable to expose the officials to public ridicule besides
penalising their exposure to public contempt. This omission might otherwise
be painfully regretted."

Well before moving to Britain, Marx would mercilessly expose the deliber-
ate attempts at anti-working-class propaganda by some of the German newspapers. Marx demolished the 'curious things' *Neue Berliner Zeitung* reported
on the leaders of the Chartist movement in England, (Marx 1848). In the prevailing context of authoritarianism and censorship, Marx also exposed the
rights violations perpetrated by officials.

In 1849, Marx was compelled to leave Germany. He lived the rest of his life in London. He reported for *The New York Daily Tribune* as Europe correspondent from August 1851 to February 1862. The *New York Daily Tribune* grew rapidly and became the largest circulated English daily selling 300,000 copies. Marx was a leading and widely read economic journalist of his time. (Musto 2008, 163).

3   On Free Trade and Free Press

Individuals and investors espousing various ideological streams of the time owned the 19th century press in Europe and elsewhere. The issue of the status of free press and whether it can be subsumed under the general notion of "freedom of the trades" was debated in the legislatures of the time. Marx subjected the idea to detailed analysis. He argued: "freedom of the trades is only freedom of the trades and no other freedom, for in it the nature of the trade forms itself unhindered according to its own inherent rules; freedom of the courts is freedom of the courts, if the courts promote the inherent rules of the law, and not those of another sphere, such as religion. Every definite sphere of freedom is the freedom of a definite sphere..." (Marx 1842f). He said, to defend the freedom of a sphere, it has to be conceived in its essential character, not in its external relationships. "...*is the press* free which degrades itself to the level of a trade? The writer, of course, must earn in order to be able to live and write, but he must by no means live and write to earn. ... *The primary freedom of the press lies in not being a trade.* The writer who degrades the press into being a material means deserves as punishment for this internal unfreedom the external unfreedom of censorship, or rather his very existence is his punishment." (Marx 1842g; italics in original).

Marx, however, acknowledged that the press is also a trade, but it is not the business of the writer, but those of the printers and book dealers. Through a clear definition of the freedom of the press, Marx has charted a road map for using the spaces provided by liberal democracy for expanding the freedoms of the individual. Prof Haragopal[1] says that rights define limits of freedom. In the bourgeois conception, the individual is seen as egoistic and confrontational and therefore there is a need to define the limits of freedom. When society is seen as a collective, such a limiting definition is not required. Human

---

1   Personal interview, 16 March, 2012. G. Haragopal, a political scientist, eminent human rights
     activist, has retired as professor of Political Science from the University of Hyderabad.

rights activists believe that individual freedom has to be reconciled with the collective freedoms and the two are not necessarily antagonistic.

Marx's analysis of press freedom and the status of the press as a trade have special significance to the politics of the Left in bourgeois democratic countries like India, where the Left has continued to play a constant if not significant role in the polity. Before discussing the Left's role in expanding democratic freedoms through the press, a brief overview of the status of Left politics in India is necessary.

4   The Left in India

By the time India attained independence from British rule in 1947, there was a prominent left-of-centre political strand in the anti-colonial struggle. The 1917 Russian revolution influenced and inspired sections of the anti-colonial struggle (Nair 2009) in addition to the movement that was beginning to take shape by the 1920s under Mohandas Karamchand Gandhi. Within the Indian National Congress (the major political party of the time) itself, there were power centres of various ideological hues: bourgeois democratic thinking represented by Gandhi himself and Fabian socialism, represented by Jawaharlal Nehru, the first Prime Minister of independent India. Outside this circle, there were revolutionary groups all over the country that were challenging British rule with armed insurgencies of various intensities.

As elsewhere in the world with the Left, the need to work with the bourgeois-democratic form to achieve socialist goals was the challenge in India as well (Nair 2009). In the anti-colonial struggle in India, some Marxist groups provided intellectual and ideological basis and worked with the Gandhian/mainstream bourgeois mobilisation, but radical revolutionary groups operating outside this sphere of influence carried out armed insurgencies in various parts of the country (Rajimwale 2009a).

India had 565 princely states (monarchies) before Independence. The Hyderabad state, considered the world's richest kingdom at that time was ruled by the Nizams. The Nizams' administration was done through the intermediary network of *jagirdars* (local elites who collected taxes) and *deshmukhs* (high-caste elites). The region had feudal and semi-feudal land relations. The peasantry was subject to oppressive labour practices through debt-bondage and coercion. The extreme conditions of exploitation of the peasantry gave rise to radical politics that resulted in the armed uprising by the peasantry against the rule of the Nizam (Vakulabharanam 2006). At the cusp of national independence in 1947–48, an uprising, called the *Telangana Armed Peasant*

Struggle,[2] under the leadership of the Left took control of over 3,000 villages and began to implement radical reforms: redistribution of land to the poor, providing schooling and healthcare. (Pucchalapally 1973a).

However, the armed struggle was brutally suppressed by the newly independent Indian state using the Indian army, calling it "police action" (Pucchalapally 1973b). The police action was used to restore the redistributed land to the feudal lords, while promising land reforms to appease the people (Pucchalapally 1973c). The Communist parties were banned in 1948 and several of the leaders went under-ground. The armed struggles in Telangana, and elsewhere in Kerala and in Tripura, have been inspiring episodes in the history of the Indian communist movement but the following phase gave rise to several debates.

First, when democratic elections were held in Andhra Pradesh, many of the communist leaders of the peasant movement got elected to the legislature with large majorities. In one of the southern states, Kerala, the first Marxist government in India came to power in 1957 through the electoral process (Rajimwale 2009b). Two decades later in eastern India, the Communist Party of India (Marxist) was elected to power in West Bengal in 1977 and was re-elected to power thereafter for 34 years in succession till 2011. The argument, therefore, of the possibility of the Left attaining political power through democratic elections has remained significant, at least in some parts of India, while the constraints placed by the bourgeois-democratic framework on elected Left governments is still a matter of debate.

Second, strengthened by the electoral experience, Marxist groups that believed in using the bourgeois-democratic route to achieve socialist objectives questioned the feasibility of taking on the might of a well-armed state through an armed struggle. The mainstream Marxist parties that had joined electoral politics consider the armed struggle adventurism. Earlier, in 1964, this led to a formal split between the communist parties that espoused the revolutionary path and those that preferred democratic methods of achieving socialist goals. The revolutionary armed groups have splintered into several smaller groups since but have expanded their reach and presence significantly.

In 1967, another armed peasant insurgency from the Naxalbari area of West Bengal brought back radical Left politics (Marxist-Leninists espousing Maoist strategies of political mobilization) into the political discourse in India. This

---

2   A detailed analysis of the armed struggle is available at: http://www.scribd.com/doc/15379761/
Telangana-Peoples-Armed-Struggle-19461951-Part-One-Historical-Setting. P Sundarayya, an
active participant/ideologue of the armed struggle, was Central Secretary of the Communist
Party of India, later became General Secretary of the Communist Party of India (Marxist).

continues in various forms and levels of intensity in large parts of central India called the "red corridor," where some of the groups control the political and economic life in these areas. Some reports suggest that the Maoist influence has spread from an estimated 56 of India's 626 districts in 2001 to more than 200 districts by 2010 (The Economist[3] 2010). These groups are also implementing radical-Left reforms such as redistribution of land, collectivisation, literacy and healthcare for the people, in order to establish prototype communities. However, the state has been using special armed forces and special laws to contain and repress these groups over the last 60 years with steady loss of life on both sides.

In contrast, the communist parties that participate in the electoral politics have found that there has been a steady erosion of their political base among the proletariat as all the other political parties (including the extreme Right) have their own trade unions and student wings. The process of the "jobless economic growth" of the Indian economy since Independence, the breaking up of the industrial enclaves of textile, jute and other manufacturing activities that provided ideological coherence to trade unionism, the policies that brought about economic liberalisation since 1991, further contributed to the erosion of the proletarian base. The more insidious process of co-opting the vocabulary and mobilisation techniques of the communist parties by the centrist and even the radical-Right groups as a rhetorical device in electoral politics has added to the confusion about Left identity in popular perception.

Other than the formally identifiable groups of the Left, there are a large number of Marxist intellectuals, journalists, academicians, lawyers, judges, civil liberties activists and even bureaucrats, who like to characterise themselves as the 'independent Left'. This is necessitated because in the Left movement(s) in India, groups have identified themselves with the Russian communists, with Maoism, Leninism, Trotskyism, Stalinism and so on. The independent Left provides a vibrant ongoing critique and direction to the Left movement in general, without espousing any later interpretations of Marxism.

The 'parliamentary Left' that comprises a set of Left parties, which run Left coalitions in some states and work together in parliament, face criticism from the 'independent Left'. The 'independent Left' groups say that these parties lack internal democracy and are moulded on the discredited legacies of Stalinism. The 'independent Left' groups feel that the electoral loss and decline of Left parties need not necessarily mean the decline of the Left in India. They feel that "the Left outside the parliament, the left as a culture of democracy

---

3   The news item describes the nature of conflict accompanied by a detailed map of areas under Maoist influence.

and resistance, a network of movements and organisations, and a new more vigorous set of campaigns will *continue to flourish"* (Menon 2011).

The Left groups that are engaged in the armed insurgencies have despised mainstream democratic struggles as irrelevant to the achievement of socialist goals. They question how an elected government can bring about radical transformation when it is compelled to work within the rigid framework of bourgeois democracy – with bureaucracy, judiciary and legislative processes that are designed to deny the rights of the working class.

5   Journalism and The Left

The presence of the Left in journalism in India is as complex a tapestry as the larger canvas of the Left political sphere. Its presence can be understood as the project of keeping the working-class struggles in public discourse as a counter to the manufactured consensus around bourgeois-democratic stability. The nature of Left interventions in the media, and understanding which kind of intervention helps in expanding the democratic values inherent in the Marxist praxis will provide lessons for the future.

There are three sources for the Left-of-centre input in journalism in India: 1. The periodical publications by Marxist parties; independent Left-of-centre entities; recently, websites and party-run TV news channels, 2. "Left-leaning" intellectuals writing in mainstream newspapers and magazines, 3. Journalists working for national and regional media organisations.

"Left-leaning" is used here to broadly signify those who research and write about agrarian and industrial class struggles, political-economy critiques of state policy, the capitalist development paradigm and large-scale displacement of communities, the critique of caste and religious identity politics, human and civil rights issues, globalisation and its consequences, the critique of capitalism and its impact on lives of common people, etc. However, the writers identified below may not define themselves as "Left leaning" or Marxist.

The journalists certainly would not like to be labelled as Left or Marxist, as social concern without an ideological tag is their primary source of credibility. But there are several journalists who have distinguished themselves by reporting on important political and economic developments from a Left perspective.

5.1   *Publications by Marxist Parties, Independent Left-of-Centre Entities*
5.1.1   Marxist Party Periodicals
The Marxist parties bring out printed publications – newspapers, magazines, and journals – as an integral part of their activities. Both the mainstream

communist parties (Communist Party of India [CPI] and Communist Party of India Marxist [CPI(M)]) publish daily newspapers in English and in Indian languages in addition to periodicals meant for women's groups, students, industrial and agricultural workers.

The orientation of the publications is primarily to explain the 'party line' and to spread information on mobilisation programmes. The parties are rigidly structured and hierarchy-bound, without much possibility of open debate on ideological issues. Therefore, it is rare to see party-run newspapers rigorously debating ideological issues. They concentrate on strategic positions the party will take in response to specific issues of the day. Because they are seen as tools for propaganda, none of them are widely circulated though they are quoted from in mainstream media when the party line is in debate. Both the main-stream media and the state agencies monitor these publications to keep track of the 'party line'. The Marxist parties also maintain websites with historical and contemporary information. In 2011, the CPIM launched a TV news channel in Kerala. Later, also in West Bengal and in Andhra Pradesh.

Most of the splinter groups of the radical Left maintain an active publica-tions programme of booklets and pamphlets. The publications are intended primarily to inform the cadre but also to send a message to the outside world about their ideological position.

5.1.2   Independent Left Publications
Weekly publications like the *Mainstream*, started in 1962 by the veteran Marxist and journalist Nikhil Chakravartty, represent the independent-Left publica-tions that are open to shades of Left-of-centre opinion (Goyal 1998).

Economic and Political Weekly (earlier known as Economic Weekly) that has been published since 1949 (Economic and Political Weekly website 2012), is a unique publication that has been a platform for consistent and vibrant independent-Left scholarship. Academicians, journalists, human rights activ-ists and others write both analytical commentaries on contemporary issues and well-researched academic articles on social, cultural, political and eco-nomic matters that affect the working class.

Mainstream and *Economic and Political Weekly*, both are published in English and have circulation among intellectuals and academicians. Neither of the publications has a popular base, but both have been economically viable mainly supported by subscription revenues and some non-commercial adver-tising. The founders of both the magazines have passed away but the new edi-tors are carrying forward the traditions and the spirit of the publications.

In the new media era, Kafila is a collective blog by 'independent Left' intel-lectuals that began in October 2006 (Kafila website 2012). It has provided an independent platform for debate on contemporary issues. There are several other such publications/websites/blogs with similar spheres of circulation such as *Frontier* (Frontier website 2012) published from Kolkata and *CounterCurrents* (CounterCurrents website 2012) that have been sites for voicing dissent and providing alternatives to the mainstream perspectives on issues.

5.2   *Left-Leaning Intellectuals Writing for Mainstream Newspapers and Magazines*

There are a number of scholars and academicians who have been writing from a Left perspective on politics and economics in India, sometimes through regular columns for newspapers and magazines. *The Hindu* and *Frontline*, both from a major publishing house from Southern India, Kasturi and Sons, has provided a platform over the years for Left-leaning academicians and journalists. *The Hindu* is a 134-year-old newspaper based in the south Indian state of Tamil Nadu. It publishes out of 13 cities and has a circulation of 4.06 million (The Hindu Website 2012). It has a formidable reputation for integrity and professionalism.

Frontline is a news magazine from the same publishing house and carries a substantial number of in-depth analytical articles on a wide variety of topics. N Ram, who was the editor-in-chief of the group and edited both *The Hindu* and *Frontline* for several years, who had made no secret of his allegiance to the Communist Party of India (Marxist), has provided space for Left-leaning writers like Praful Bidwai, C P Chandrashekhar, Jayati Ghosh, Aijaz Ahmed, and Vijay Prashad. The magazine gives regular space to issues related to the working class, workers in the unorganised sector, and issues of tribal peoples (Frontline magazine 2012).

Others like Ashok Mitra, Utsa Patnaik and Prabhat Patnaik also have a significant presence in mainstream media. The columns written by some of the scholars are syndicated and publish in several newspapers and magazines. The widely circulated national newspapers and magazines have been providing spaces occasionally for multi-perspective debate, Left of centre views being an important part of it.

5.3   *Journalists Working for National and Regional Media Organisations*

There are two categories of journalists, who have been active in the media: 1. Journalists working for the mainstream English media that occupy a large mind-space among the urban elite; 2. Journalists who work for the language press with very large circulations among a particular language group.

5.3.1   Mainstream English Language Media

The total circulation of newspapers in India is 329 million copies. There are 82,222 registered newspapers in India (RNI website 2012). In both magazine and newspaper journalism, there have been several journalists in India, who have consistently addressed people's issues and used the news columns for building critical awareness about important issues in politics and economy of the nation.

Prominent among them is Vinod Mehta, till recently the editor-in-chief of the *Outlook* group, who describes himself as "Left-liberal" (Mehta 2012a). During his distinguished career as a journalist, Mehta has broken major stories on anti-people policies of the state and cases of corruption, abuse of power and mis-governance. The stories have had national impact. The stories on industrial action by unions and special economic zones that were carried by *Outlook* also give a more rounded perspective, giving space for the workers' point of view. The magazine *Outlook* also gave extensive space to the radical Left opinion of Arundhati Roy, the Booker prize-winning author and activist. In an interview with Bhatt, Mehta said: "I am a Left Liberal, so *Outlook* is a Left Liberal magazine... I make sure...the inequality of our people is reported. The government cannot say that market forces are going to determine anything and everything. We have a broad vision of what India should be like and we try, and I emphasise this word, we try in our publication to promote that idea" (Mehta 2012b).

Palagummi Sainath has been reporting on the agrarian crisis, the impact of globalisation on the agrarian sector, the widespread rural distress leading to the suicides of thousands of farmers and handloom weavers. P Sainath is the Rural Affairs Editor of The Hindu. He has published a best-selling book, *Everyone Loves a Good Draught*, a compilation of a series of his reports on rural distress from various parts of rural India. Sainath was working with the largest circulated multi-edition newspaper, *The Times of India*, when he toured the rural areas in the country on a *Times* fellowship and published 84 op-ed reports (Thakurta 2012, 504).

Sainath says that the media in India are politically free, but are imprisoned by the profit motive of their proprietors. He says that in the worst of newspapers one might still find spaces where they talk of poverty and agrarian distress, but for that people have to die in sufficiently large number to merit the news space (Palagummi 2008a). He says that almost anything that is worthwhile in journalism is born out of dissent. No establishment journalist has ever been considered great (Palagummi 2008b).

Paranjoy Guha Thakurta, who has worked with newspapers such as *The Telegraph* and news magazines like *India Today*, is also a television commentator. Thakurta published major investigative stories on corporations and filed court cases to challenge the state and its relationship with the corporations. The 2G spectrum allocation controversy is the latest of such investigations, which is still unravelling in Indian courts.

Thakurta[4] (2012) says that communism has never been a pejorative in Indian politics as is the case elsewhere. Mainstream newspapers owned by big corporate entities like *The Times of India* or *The Telegraph* of Kolkata give space to Left columnists and journalists even as the newspapers take a recognisable anti-Left stand editorially.

Other than the journalists quoted here, there are many others who have been reporting on working class issues as well as environment, gender, trade unions, agrarian crisis and foreign affairs, shaping public opinion on policy issues.

5.3.2   Language or Vernacular Journalism

The Indian language or vernacular press has grown rapidly with improving literacy in the country. The largest circulated newspaper in the country is *Dainik Jagran*, a Hindi-language newspaper with a circulation of 16.4 million copies. Other major language papers are *Dainik Bhaskar* (Hindi), *Eenadu* (Telugu), *Malayala Manorama* (Malayalam). In fact, *The Times of India* is the only English-language paper that figures among the top-ten papers in India. Since India is geographically divided based on the predominant language spoken in each region, the newspaper circulation is usually understood to cater to both the geographical area and the linguistic groups.

Apart from the staff reporters on the payroll, the language newspapers depend heavily on the informal networks of stringers who provide wide access to the far corners of each state. In Andhra Pradesh state, there are close to 9,000 stringers working for the newspapers.

Both the major Left parties, CPI and CPI(M) run their own daily newspapers in addition to other publications. The radical Left revolutionary groups, in addition to the party publications for their internal circulation, have also developed access to the stringers of mainstream newspapers initially. Later, the party cadre themselves began working as stringers and rural reporters with newspapers.

A study (Kasanagottu 1996, 202) says: "The cadres/supporters, sympathisers of Left-wing groups infiltrate the newspaper organisations. Former activists today occupy higher positions in the newspaper offices. ... The cadres also infiltrate the grassroots rural stringer network. These stringers are the major contributors of Naxal[5] news in the columns of newspapers."

Kasanagottu states that newspaper managements also wittingly or unwittingly recruit people associated with various Naxalite groups for two reasons.

---

4   Personal interview, 17 Jan.

5   'Naxal' refers to the Marxist-Leninist-Maoist radical Left groups (sometimes also called Maoists) who are waging an armed insurgency against the Indian state. The movement began in a place called Naxalbari in West Bengal in 1967.

Firstly, the Left-wing sympathisers/activists have literary flair that can be exploited by newspapers. Secondly, the journalists' contacts with Naxalites make sensational stories possible, which would otherwise be difficult to get.

A study by Stevenson (2000, 228)) says that some journalists have joined the Naxalites and some Naxalites have joined the ranks of journalists. Naxalites join a mainstream profession like journalism generally for reasons of personal safety. In Godavarikhani, a Staff Reporter of *Vishalandhra* (vernacular paper run by the Communist Party of India) joined the Jana Rakshana Samithi (roughly meaning, People's Protection Association). Later, he left the movement and started a Telugu weekly. However, he was killed in an "encounter"[6] with the police.

Stevenson adds: "On the other hand, there are a sizeable number of stringers and contributors (no staff reporters) in each district who were earlier with the Naxalite movement and have surrendered. This only indicates how the press provides a cover for such activists and the power the press wields in society." He says, the Left cadres believe that the law enforcement personnel are generally careful with journalists as their harassment can lead to negative publicity.

This has been a major source of conflict between the state and media in the state's battle against Left-wing insurgencies. In states where the insurgency has been long-term and low intensity for decades, many journalists have lost their lives on suspicion of being Maoist informers. As many of the groups have been banned for several decades now, the journalists have been sources of information for the general public on the one hand and targets for state reprisals on the other. There are also instances when the revolutionary groups suspect their journalist conduits of being informants of the police and subject them to repression. The journalists working at the lowest rung of journalism, representing a wide range of ideological perspectives, are faced with pressures from both the security establishment of the state and the Left groups (Lankesh 2010). Nevertheless, they open up spaces for Left opinion in mainstream language journalism.

6   Free Speech and Commercial Media In India

The press in India has been working within the bourgeois liberal tradition. But within the intellectual and structural constraints of that system, there have been spaces for Left thought to articulate its position. If sometimes it is the

---

6   An 'encounter' is a euphemism for field executions by the security forces of the state. This has been a routine strategy of the state to 'deal' with Left-wing extremist groups and their sympathisers in civil society.

ideology of the owners, sometimes it is the editor who makes these spaces available.

A more interesting phenomenon is the spaces created by the competitive market forces. According to Paranjoy Guha Thakurta,[7] when he offered a major investigative story to a news magazine, the story was turned down as the magazine just came out of a battle with the business group that was the subject of the news story. Thakurta offered the story to a widely circulated business daily from a powerful media house, which immediately picked up the story. Apart from the competitive edge, many journalists believe, it is easier for a major newspaper/media house to confront the power of the state and the corporations than for a smaller newspaper. The very diversity of the media industry makes space for dissent and debate possible, for whatever reason.

Another senior journalist, Mahesh Vijapurkar,[8] who worked with major newspapers like the *Indian Express* and *The Hindu* since the mid-1970s said that in his career the editors never discouraged publication of a story because of a threat to their commercial interests. They merely ensured that public interest was served by the stories and that information was verified adequately before it was published. This was also reiterated by Paranjoy Guha Thakurta,[9] who said that both the corporate media houses and the editors of newspapers he has worked with gave considerable freedom to the journalists, as long as the information put out is sufficiently vetted and verified.

Interestingly, there are different perceptions among the journalists interviewed on the sources of threat to free speech in India. Sevanti Ninan[10] says that journalists treat corporate issues with caution, sometimes because of the advertising clout of the corporations, but often also because the journalists have internalised the neo-liberal ideology. She also feels that the journalists may not see any of this as a free speech issue.

Mahesh Vijapurkar says the threat to free speech in India comes mostly from the internal dynamics of the media industry. According to him, top leadership of television networks instructing their reporters to hype up news stories on lean news days and to give opinion with news, poses a greater threat to credibility of news media. He also believes that the state or the politicians do not pose much threat to free speech because the privately owned media provide a powerful platform for them, despite the occasional transgressions.

---

7   Personal interview, 20 January 2012.
8   17 February 2012. Telephone interview. Mahesh Vijapurkar has worked for *The Hindu* for over 30 years and worked with DNA as fault-finder.
9   Personal interview, 20 January 2012.
10   Email interview, 5 February 2012. Sevanti Ninan is a senior journalist, columnist and editor of a media watch website *The Hoot*.

In a similar vein, Vinod Mehta says: "Corruption is at the top, unfortunately, at the editor's level. It is at that level the agenda of a paper is decided. They have been compromised, have taken favours, have other interests and they are the people who have betrayed the profession."

A common factor among some of the senior journalists like Mehta, Thakurta and Sainath, who have built their reputation by writing on political and economic issues taking an anti-imperialist, anti-globalisation stand, is also their faith in democracy and the role of journalism in enlarging opportunities for dissent and debate. Their contribution to keeping the Left debate alive is as significant as the role of independent Left journals like *Mainstream* and *Economic and Political Weekly,* as their publications are also more accessible to the general reader. The advertising agenda of their publications does not seem to impinge on their functioning as independent journalists, perhaps because there is a strong constituency for Left opinion among readers.

It must be recognised, even if some journalists have bent to the commercial or political influences, that the profession still has space for independent journalism.

The journalists working at the suburban and district levels have also kept up the news flow from remote locations about both the activities of the state and the Left-wing groups. However, they often bear the brunt of intolerance of dissent from the radical groups and repression by the state. In the heartland of Indian democracy in the red corridor areas, affected states have promulgated draconian Newspeak laws like the Public Security Acts that allow arbitrary arrests of not only the activists of banned Left political outfits but also a complete blackout of information. Journalists are not allowed to enter some of these areas where paramilitary Special Forces are in control. Public intellectuals[11] who raise human rights questions are arrested or have to face the threat of anachronistic sedition laws.

The commercial media are compelled to pay heed to public perceptions, if only to survive in the marketplace. In the mainstream media, it is this that facilitates reportage of state repression in the red corridor and arrests and assassinations of human rights activists in conflict areas. To that extent, the mainstream media play an adversarial role. This is not to say that all reportage is unbiased and fair. The framing of the issues, the state machinery, politicians, bureaucracy, and the corporations using the media for "spin" is another debate. However, in a free speech environment, the truth surfaces on one platform or

---

11   Dr Binayak Sen, a paediatrician working among the tribal communities was under arrest for several years and is given bail by the Supreme Court recently. Arundhati Roy, the author-activist was threatened with arrest for her views on Kashmir, under sedition laws.

another and reaches the public, even when the news filters[12] are constantly at work.

Though the mainstream commercial media provide spaces for the dissenting voices, the commercial content drowns out these voices, leading to a significant debate in recent times on the need to rein in commercial interests in the media, the role and desirability of press laws to preserve democratic values. There was a vociferous debate on mainstream media about the Indian state's attempt to censor intermediaries providing online services like Google, Facebook and Twitter. But a similar debate was not raised by either the "parliamentary Left" or by the mainstream media about the blanket censorship and blackout of information in the red corridor areas and other "insurgency areas" of North-Eastern India or Kashmir.

The newspapers and publications of the Left parties are moulded on the agit-prop mode and are clearly perceived as tools of propaganda both by the general reader and the parties themselves. The parliamentary Left has deep ideological disagreement with the radical Left groups waging a prolonged armed struggle against the state. But this has also stopped the parliamentary Left from vigorously opposing the censorship and draconian laws that are being used by the bourgeois state. In the long-term, this can severely shrink the democratic spaces that are already eroding rapidly. The parliamentary Left parties have been unable to encourage rigorous theoretical debate on issues because of what Prabhat Patnaik (2011) in his incisive analysis calls "empericisation." He explains:

> What distinguishes a communist party is not that it does not 'soil its hands' with mundane, everyday politics, ...but that its process of engagement even at this level is imbricated by its project of transcending capitalism, informed by a consciousness of what Lukacs[13] (1924) had called 'the actuality of the revolution'. ...If this theory linking the 'here and now' to the overall project of transcendence is absent from the praxis engaged in 'here and now', then we have a process of empericisation of the movement. ... Such empericisation in the context of our polity gives rise to at least three kinds of tendencies: first, it gives rise to the range of 'sins' attributed to the party by its opponents...such as careerism, 'satrapism',

---

12   Noam Chomsky enumerates five filters in his discussion of the Propaganda Model in "Manufacturing Consent": Ownership of the medium, funding sources, sources, flak, anti-communist ideology.

13   Lukacs, Georg (1924): *Lenin: A Study of the Unity of His Thought*, re-published by New Left Books, London, 1970.

bureaucratism, and bossism at the local level. Secondly, it gives rise to a tendency to 'adjust' to given situations to prevent losses, instead of carrying it forward as a part of revolutionary praxis. This in turn entails a process of alienation of the party from the 'basic classes' that it is supposed to struggle for, viz, the workers, peasants, agricultural labourers, and the rural poor. The 'party interests' are seen in isolation from, and as being distinct from, the interests of the basic classes, and for the defence of the 'party interests' immediate, 'here and now' measures are thought of and resorted to, which may well diverge from the interests of the basic classes. Third, empericisation leads to a shrinking of the distance between the communist party and the other political formations.

In a contemplative piece about K. Damodaran, one of the founders of the communist party of Kerala, his son K.P. Sasi (2012) gives insights into the working of the communist parties in India at various stages of recent history. It reveals the lack of democratic functioning, ideological helplessness battled by even the senior leadership in the Left parties. Part of the problem also arises because of the failure of the Left governed states in achieving visible transformation towards greater democratic freedoms or significantly better governance or material conditions.

Both the critiques reveal that there has been a gap between the ideological position of Marx and the practice of Marxism in India. Both these critiques show the need for the Left parties of all shades to negotiate with and expand the scope of bourgeois freedoms, much like Marx, and to create conditions for transcending capitalism and imperialism.

If within the political parties of bourgeois democracies there is no scope for free speech and democratic debate, it would not carry conviction to assert rights against the state and capital when those agencies choose to limit them. It is important to identify basic guiding principles and to institutionalise them, to adopt and strengthen positive features of liberal democracy in the transition to socialism and its transformed social content.

Freedom of the press is an essential part of the philosophical tradition of Marxism and has been an important instrument in Marxist praxis. According to Draper (1974a, 101–124): "For Marx, the fight for democratic forms of government – democratization in the state – was a leading edge of the socialist effort; not its be-all and end-all but an integral part of it all."

Draper (1974b, 118) also discusses what Marx refers to as the "Democratic Swindle." According to Draper, "Marx (in a letter to Engels on 14 September 1864) calls the United States "the model country of the democratic swindle" not because it was less democratic than others but for precisely the opposite reason. The fact that the US had developed the formal structure of the constitutional republic in the most democratic forms meant that its bourgeoisie likewise had to develop to its highest point the art of keeping the expression of popular opinion within channels satisfactory to its class interests... Marx and Engels analysed bourgeois-democratic politics as an exercise in convincing a maximum of the people that they were participating in state power, by means of a minimum of concessions to democratic forms." In India too, the formal structures of democracy have been in place for long but the bourgeoisie and capital have successfully "swindled" democracy in practice.

Therefore, the debate around bourgeois democracy versus socialist democracy is also significant for free speech. According to Sudipta Kaviraj:

> Democracy in principle (or as a whole) is not bourgeois – either in the sense of being conferred by the bourgeoisie on their people, or in being won by the struggles of the bourgeoisie. The general form of democracy today is a result won by proletarian and radical struggles to widen the narrow circle of political rights under liberal capitalism. It would be a great pity if democracy is not historically separable from the capitalist social form. In any case, the Marxian criticism of bourgeois democracy is not that capitalism realises democracy and that it is bad. Rather that what is bad about capitalism is that it does not realise democracy. As long as unequal classes exist, democracy must remain formal. This implies that when classes disappear, (under socialism) or nearly disappear, can the formal apparatuses of democracy enjoy real conditions of success.
>
> KAVIRAJ 1989, 50–58

An important aspect of Marx's discussion of democracy was his views on bureaucracy. Marx understood that a bureaucracy could "own" a state as its private property and that when it did, it would make a fetish out of internal hierarchy and external secrecy. The democratic right to change policy, and own the state becomes possible when the citizens and workers, without risking anything can command those who carry out technical and administrative functions. If not, the bureaucracy tends to own the state as its private property (Harrington). In other words, the bureaucracy acts as an instrument of this "democratic swindle."

Marx's argument about free speech and censorship early in his career as a journalist was in opposition to the draconian Prussian laws of censorship that were being used as instruments to retard democratisation. But when he founded the *Neue Rheinische Zeitung* with the support of liberals of Cologne who later became legislators and began to compromise their ideological positions for remaining in power, Marx was both brutal and relentless in his criticism. But his paper was shut down because of the censorship edicts of the time that he was challenging.

In India, the constitutionally guaranteed right to free speech, the diversity of voices in media provides spaces for challenging not just the prevailing bourgeois consensus but also the ideological compromises of the Left primarily because all political parties market their policies in "public interest."

On the other hand, material reality of people has made radical politics inevitable in some parts of India, and sections of mainstream media misrepresent this reality, much as what Marx describes as the role of the British press in war-mongering during American Civil War, while the people were opposed to it (Marx, 1861). Marx also describes the nature of ownership and political pressures on the media, while recognising the honourable exceptions like *The Spectator, The Examiner* and *MacMillan's Magazine* in this article.

In Indian media industries, the widening economic interests of the owners, their growing control over the political establishment and the emergence of oligopolies has been a looming threat to free speech. This manifests in its worst forms in the resource-rich areas like the red corridor where contradictions between the rights of the indigenous people and the corporate attempts to capture natural resources are played out. The battle to control information flows inevitably draws media persons into its vortex, even as major media houses (such as Dainik Bhaskar group) are owned by the corporate entities that are active in the area. And it is the synergies between the national and regional media that have brought such issues into public discourse (Vishnu 2013). A coalition of forces that includes civil society groups, constitutional institutions like the Supreme Court and sections of media, is involved in the long-drawn battle for protection of human rights.

In the later part of his life, Marx was living and working in Britain where censorship was not as problematic as it was in Germany of 1840s. During this phase, Marx was finding ways of using the freedoms available under bourgeois democracy to expand freedoms of the working classes. Marx, while engrossed in writing some of his classic works during this phase, used the newspaper columns to interpret the unfolding historical events from a class perspective. Whether as editor, correspondent or as opinion writer, it was fairly common to see Marx openly criticise newspapers by name, by specific pieces or stand taken by a newspaper on issues. Marx would subject them to logical, detailed criticism in an effort to provide the reading public with an alternate explanation. It is rare in Indian journalism to see criticism of rival papers, either ideologically or to challenge unethical practices.[14]

---

14   In case of the "paid news" scandal that engulfed big media in India during the last parliamentary elections, several regional and national journalists wrote about and publicly

SHAW

In the Indian context, though diversity of media industry aided by an independent judiciary and enabling legislations like the Right to Information Act has made exposing abuse of political, bureaucratic and corporate power possible, the interventions of the media tend to evoke different responses from the state depending on the perceived power of media to influence large segments of public opinion. When English language media with a large urban educated audience challenge the state, the state is compelled to respect the constitutional rights of the media to freedom of expression. In case of local media houses working in the hinterlands, the state cracks down heavily. Any transgressions by the regional language media (as in insurgency areas of the red corridor) are severely punished or suppressed by a slew of legislations that enable the state to suspend fundamental rights guaranteed by the Constitution of India. Many journalists have been shot dead in 'encounters'.[15] In fact, over the years, this dual strategy has been adopted routinely by Indian state, giving India an image of a vibrant democracy, while great abuses of human rights also occur in large pockets of the country. It is also reflected in the perceptions of the senior journalists from national media who feel that the state is not as much of threat to free speech as the internal problems of the industry and the journalists' lack of integrity.

The parliamentary Left have not played a visible role in challenging these tendencies of the bourgeois state. The independent Left along with the journalists and Left intellectuals working with the mainstream media are better placed to take up the challenge, because of their perceived independence and integrity. The parliamentary Left faces more difficulties as the parties had opportunities to hold office through democratic elections and have been unable to unambiguously demonstrate the benefits that an elected Marxist government can yield, either through policies or through day-to-day issues of bureaucratic management.

According to Harrington, Marx defined socialism in the most profound sense of the word as the "truth of" bourgeois democracy, as democracy stripped of the structural limitations imposed on it by capitalist class society. The exposure

---

denounced (a fairly rare occurrence) the practice of newspapers giving favourable hardnews coverage to rival political candidates after accepting huge unaccounted-for payments. Press Council of India instituted a committee (with Paranjoy Guha Thakurta and Srinivas Reddy) to enquire into the affair. The report names several major newspapers indulging in this practice.

15   For instance, journalist Hemachandra Pandey was killed in an encounter on the intervening night of 1–2 July 2011. Retrieved on 23 March 2014 from http://timesofindia.indiatimes .com/city/hyderabad/Azad-encounter-case-HRF-submits-affidavit-to-CBI/articleshow/8807175.cms.

of journalists at the ground level to the might of the state often make it possible for the mainstream media to exert pressure for asserting rights and policy change. The mainstream media in India have been a powerful presence in the political space of Left politics, both as its critics and as its champions. The looming threat today is the consolidation of ownership, which till now has been diverse.

It is for the political entities of all hues that place themselves Left-of-centre, to recognise this truth and to work for the deepening and strengthening of democracy in India. The press is the most potent instrument for deepening democratic values and the wider and deeper engagement of the Left in the critical segments of the media that are widely read, heard and seen is essential to this process.

7   Conclusion

Transcending the structural limitations of bourgeois democracy is the task before the Left. Indian polity accepts a set of democratic ground rules and independent agencies like the civil society groups and the judiciary have been playing an important role in challenging both executive and corporate power to an extent. Sections of media have been a potent instrument and ally of both judiciary and the civil society groups.

Revisiting the free speech debate in the context of Marx's analysis makes it clear that it is necessary to ensure that independent constitutional authorities like the judiciary and coalitions of progressive public opinion are strengthened. Strong press laws are required to rein-in the undemocratic exercise of power by corporate media, and to protect and expand the spaces for exercising the constitutionally guaranteed right to free speech. In this process of expanding democratic freedoms, the greater battle is also to challenge corporate and state censorship in all its forms. The Indian experience indicates that independent journalism that highlights the interests of the marginalised classes, despite the challenges it faces, can play a significant and historical role in the politics of democratisation and liberation.

References

CounterCurrents website. 2012. http://www.countercurrents.org/aboutus.htm.

Draper, Hal. 1974. Marx on Democratic Forms of Government. In *The Socialist Register.* Accessed December 9, 2011. http://www.marxists.org/archive/draper/1974/xx/democracy.html.

Economic and Political Weekly website. 2012. http://beta.epw.in/about_us/.

Emery, Michael, and Edwin Emery.1954. The Press and America. NY: Prentice-Hall.

Frontier website. 2012. http://sites.google.com/site/frontierweekly/aboutfrontier.

Frontline magazine. 2012. Accessed January 25, 2012. http://www.frontlineonnet.com/.

Goyal, D.R. 1998. Remembering Nikhil Chakravartty. *Economic and Political Weekly.* XXXIII(29). July 18. 1911.

Hardt, Hanno. 2000. Communication is Freedom: Karl Marx on Press Freedom and Censorship. *Javnost – The Public* 7(4): 85–100. Accessed November 26, 2011.http://javnost-thepublic.org/article/pdf/2000/4/6/.

Kafila website. 2012. http://kafila.org/about/.

Kaviraj, Sudipta. 1989. Perestroika: Reflections on the Theory of Power. *Social Scientist* 17 (194–195). July-August, 50–58.

Kohir, Stevenson. 2000. *Press and Insurgency – A Case Study of Naxalite Insurgency in Andhra Pradesh*, Unpublished Ph.D Thesis, Department of Communication and Journalism, Mangalore University.

Lankesh, Gauri. 2010. Operation Media Gagging: The Karnataka Police has 'threatened' a reporter for interviewing Maoists. *Tehelka* 10 May. VII (19). Accessed November 26, 2011. http://www.tehelka.com/story_main44.asp?filename=Ne150510proscons.asp.

Ledbetter, James. 2007. *Karl Marx: Dispatches for the New York Tribune*. Edited by James Ledbetter, xix. NY: Penguin.

Lukacs, Georg. 1924. *Lenin: A Study of the Unity of His Thought*. London: New Left Books. Re-published 1970. As quoted in Patnaik 2011.

Marx, Karl. 1842a. On Freedom of the Press: Censorship. *Rheinische Zeitung*, 135, Supplement, May 15. Accessed December 10, 2011. http://www.marxists.org/archive/marx/works/1842/free-press/ch05.htm.

Marx, Karl. 1842b. Debates on Freedom of the Press and Publication. In *Karl Marx On Freedom Of The Press & Censorship*, edited and translated by Saul Padover, 27. NY: McGraw-Hill.

Marx, Karl. 1842c. Debates on Freedom of the Press and Publication. In *Karl Marx On Freedom Of The Press & Censorship*, edited and translated by Saul Padover, 29. NY: McGraw-Hill.

Marx, Karl. 1842d. On Freedom of the Press: Censorship. *Rheinische Zeitung*, 135, Supplement, May 15. Accessed December 10, 2011. http://www.marxists.org/archive/marx/works/1842/free-press/ch05.htm.

Marx, Karl. 1842e. As a Privilege of Particular Individuals or a Privilege of the Human Mind? *Rheinische Zeitung*, May 12. Accessed December 10, 2011. http://www.marxists.org/archive/marx/works/1842/free-press/ch04.htm.

Marx, Karl. 1842f. Debates on Freedom of the Press and Publication. In *Karl Marx On Freedom Of The Press & Censorship*, edited and translated by Saul Padover, 39. NY: McGraw-Hill.

Marx, Karl. 1842g. Debates on Freedom of the Press and Publication. In *Karl Marx On Freedom Of The Press & Censorship*, edited and translated by Saul Padover, 40-41. NY: McGraw-Hill.

Marx, Karl. 1848a. The *Neue Berliner Zeitung* on the Chartists. *Neue Rheinische Zeitung*, June 24. Accessed December 10 2011. http://www.marxists.org/archive/marx/works/1848/06/24b.htm.

Marx, Karl. 1848b.ThePrussianPressBill. *Neue Rheinische Zeitung*, July 19. Accessed December 12, 2011. http://www.marxists.org/archive/marx/works/1848/07/20a.htm.

Marx, Karl. 1843. The Mosel Region and the Cabinet Order of December 24, 1841. In *Karl Marx On Freedom Of The Press & Censorship*, edited and translated by Saul Padover, 77. NY: McGraw-Hill.

Marx, Karl. 1861. The Newspapers and the Opinion Of The People. *Die Presse*, 25 December. Accessed March 25, 2012. http://www.marxists.org/archive/marx/works/1861/12/31.htm.

Mehta, Vinod. 2012a. Interview with Sheela Bhatt. Accessed January 26, 2012. http://www.rediff.com/news/slide-show/slide-show-1-corruption-unfortunately-is-at-the-editor-level/20120130.htm.

Mehta, Vinod. 2012b. Interview with Sheela Bhatt. Accessed January 26, 2012. http://www.rediff.com/news/slide-show/slide-show-1-corruption-unfortunately-is-at-the-editor-level/20120130.htm.

Menon, Nivedita. 2011. 'End of the Left' in India? Statement by Leftists after Recent Election Results. 24 May. *KAFILA*. Accessed January 25, 2012. http://kafila.org/2011/05/24/end-of-the-left-in-india-statement-after-recent-election-results/.

Musto, Marcello. 2008. *Karl Marx's Grundrisse: Foundations of the Critique of Political Economy 150 Years late.* Oxon, UK: Routledge.

Nageshwar, K. 1996. *The Socio-political Foundations of the Press.* Unpublished PhD Thesis, Department of Political Science, Osmania University.

Nair, Somasekharan K. G. 2009. Indian Communists versus Marxism-Leninism. *Mainstream.* XLVII(34) 8 Aug. Accessed February 2, 2012. http://www.mainstream-weekly.net/article1558.html.

Padover, Saul. K 1974a. *Karl Marx On Freedom Of The Press & Censorship.* Edited and translated by Saul Padover, xi. NY: McGraw-Hill.

Padover, Saul. K. 1974b. *Karl Marx On Freedom Of The Press & Censorship.* Edited and translated by Saul Padover, xiii. NY: McGraw-Hill.

Palagummi, Sainath. 2008a. Interview with NewsClickin. 22 June. Accessed January 25, 2012. http://www.youtube.com/watch?feature=endscreen&NR=1&v=bu9W53Skr28.

Palagummi, Sainath. 2008b. Interview with NewsClickin. 22 June. January 25, 2012. http://www.youtube.com/watch?v=QewCqpgBiuw&feature=related.

Patnaik, Prabhat. 2011. The Left in Decline. *Economic and Political Weekly.* 16 July. XLVI (29). Accessed on February 5, 2012. http://www.epw.in/system/files/pdf/2011_46/29/The_Left_in_Decline.pdf.

Pucchalapally, Sundarayya. 1973a. *Telangana People's Armed Struggle, Part 2.* 27–35. Accessed on February 5, 2012. http://www.scribd.com/doc/15380676/Telangana-Peoples-Armed-Struggle-19461951-Part-Two-First-Phase-and-Its-Lessons.

Pucchalapally, Sundarayya. 1973b. *Telangana People's Armed Struggle, Part 2.* 42. Accessed February 5, 2012. http://www.scribd.com/doc/15380676/Telangana-Peoples-Armed-Struggle-19461951-Part-Two-First-Phase-and-Its-Lessons.

Pucchalapally, Sundarayya. 1973c. *Telangana People's Armed Struggle, Part 2.* 35–36. Accessed February 5, 2012. http://www.scribd.com/doc/15380676/Telangana-Peoples-Armed-Struggle-19461951-Part-Two-First-Phase-and-Its-Lessons.

Rajimwale, Anil. 2009a. Ajoy Ghosh: The Creative Marxist. *Mainstream.* XLVIII (1) 26 Dec. Accessed February 2, 2012. http://www.mainstreamweekly.net/article1843.html.

Rajimwale, Anil. 2009b. Ajoy Ghosh: The Creative Marxist. *Mainstream.* XLVIII (1) 26 Dec. Accessed February 2, 2012. http://www.mainstreamweekly.net/article1843.html.

RNI website. 2012. Accessed January 25, 2012. https://rni.nic.in/.

Sasi, K.P. (2012). K Damodaran: An Unfinished Chapter. *Countercurrents.org.* 17 March. Accessed January 25, 2012. http://www.countercurrents.org/sasi170312.htm.

Thakurta, Paranjoy Guha. 2012. *Media Ethics.* N. Delhi: Oxford.

The Economist.2010. Maoist Insurgents in India: More Bloody and Defiant. 22 July. Accessed January 25, 2012.http://www.economist.com/node/16650478.

The Hindu Website. 2012. Accessed January 25, 2012. http://www.thehindu.com/navigation/?type=static&page=aboutus.

Vakulabharanam, Ramakrishna. 2006.Towards Becoming Andhra Pradesh. In *Fifty Years of Andhra Pradesh: 1956–2006*edited by R.S. Rao, V.H. Rao and N. Venugopal, 44–46. Hyderabad: Centre for Documentation, Research and Communication.

Vishnu, G. 2013. The Iron Lady of Jharkhand. *Tehelka.* Accessed February 5, 2014. http://www.tehelka.com/the-iron-lady-of-jharkhand.

CHAPTER 15

The Ideology of Media Policy in Argentina*

Pablo Castagno

1 Introduction

By examining Argentina, my purpose is to explore how state and political cadres endeavour to contain the social tensions spanning from states' essential contradiction as institutions that claim to represent the general and national interests of citizens while reproducing the transnational class domination in which global capitalism is based.[1] Specifically, I argue the media constitutes a key field of state ideological regulation and political struggle. By ideology, I mean the goal of dominant political groups and classes to disseminate their own ideas throughout a society such that these ideas become dominant (Marx and Engels 1998/1846), cohering social formation in a process of cultural and political leadership (Gramsci 2000, 200–210) and absorbing or articulating in this way the discourses of other groups and classes in order to nullify their potential antagonism (Laclau 1978, 187–189). Further, I understand those symbolic practices as having an objective role in hiding the real nature of society, shaped by antagonisms (Marx 1990/1867, 163–177; Horkheimer 1989/1932, 55). I use regulation here to connote the institutionalisation of ideologies throughout the state in the form of legal instruments, state policies, discursive practices, and so on.

Conceptualising ideological regulation in this way, I engage with views maintaining that Karl Marx's work and subsequent interpretations of Marxist thought facilitate analysis of the media as an unfixed object integrated into the general political-economic process through which structural contradictions in capitalism are played out, reproduced, contested or transformed (Murdock and Golding 1973; Garnham 1979; Wayne 2003; Artz, Macek and Cloud 2006; McChesney 2007; Mosco 2010; Fuchs 2011). These works' shared critical theoretical and methodological approach situates the study of the media within the totality of the social relationships constituting a given historical moment. In concrete terms, my task is to investigate how political cadres respond to

* I would like to thank Lisel Hintz for her thoughtful comments on this chapter.
1 Following Manuel Castells' work, by global capitalism I mean an economy whose core components have the potential to work as a unit in real time and on a planetary scale (2000, 105).

corporations' pressures to increase profits, aim to legitimate the state apparatus, and cope with the democratic demands of citizens and workers in the context of capitalist crises and political turmoil.[2] Following Marx, I understand
capital crises to be phases of rupture in the realisation of profits through the
exchange of commodities (Marx 1978c, 443–465). These crises include different
episodes, such as the 2007–2008 financial crash, and are characterised by
attempts from the dominant class to ensure capitalist profits.

At the empirical level, Argentina constitutes an interesting and relevant
political field of analysis due to its profound capitalist slump in 2001–2002, its
previous crises, and its periodic shifts in state ideology. I argue that the contemporary history of media transformation in Argentina has three political
epicentres: the implementation of new media legislation (Law 22,285, 1980)
by the military junta dictatorship (1976–1983),[3] the modifications that the
democratic and neoliberal government of Carlos Menem (1989–1999) introduced to that legislation, and the approval of a law on media democratisation
by Cristina Fernández de Kirchner's government (2007-present) in 2009. In
terms of political orientation, the current government represents a continuation of Néstor Kirchner's period (2003–2007). Néstor Kirchner was the president elected following the devastating financial collapse of the neoliberal
project in 2001–2002. This slump pushed forty percent of the total population
into unemployment and sub-employment and half of the total population
under the line of poverty (Oficina de la CEPAL 2010; Lozano 2005, 4),[4] deeply
eroding state legitimacy. Both Menem and Kirchner belonged to the Partido
Peronista, a formerly national-populist party that emerged in the 1940s. Yet
while Menem implemented thorough neoliberal reforms targeted at assuring
the state's link to global capitalism (Castagno, 2014a), so-called *kirchnerismo*
has constituted a complex case of state continuity and change.[5] In other
words, I believe that Argentina's media policy constitutes a challenging case
to analyse how media policy shapes ideologies of state reproduction in contradictory ways.

---

2   Following Nicos Poulantzas, I understand that political cadres constitute a social category,
    not a class (1969, 72). Their function is to reproduce the state, which is also essential for the
    dominant economic class and capitalism as a whole.
3   The Executive Power was in charge of three chief commanders from the army, the navy, and
    the air force.
4   Sub-employment refers to workers that work less than 35 hours per week although they wish
    to work more hours.
5   By *kirchnerismo* I mean the political forces centred on the governments of Kirchner and
    Fernández de Kirchner.

Exploring these periods of contemporary history, my central question is how media policy is related to the various state projects aimed at resolving the capitalist collapses and responding to the political contestation by workers and citizens in the mid-1970s, late 1980s, and 2001–2002.[6] Drawing from Marxist theory on political-economic crises and Marxist method, my historical approach to this research question seeks to explain the contradictory relationships among the state, capital accumulation, the media, and citizens. My general objective is to identify and explain the ideological variations in media policy across the various political regimes and governments, and my specific objective is to analyse Cristina Fernández de Kirchner's reform of class and ideological relationships within the audiovisual media system. For this research, my qualitative investigation examines media legislation on broadcasting and audiovisual communication services as part of the state's various political economy projects. I define media legislation as a field of power in which citizens, social movements, political cadres, and the capitalist media struggle to establish state parameters according to which media resources are distributed and public communication delimited.[7] This field simultaneously contains, reflects, and constitutes the social totality in which it is immersed. My principal argument is that *kirchnerismo* has perpetuated a bourgeois state project of capitalist transnationalisation, initially enforced by the military dictatorships between 1955 and 1983 and later pushed forward by Menem's government (Portantiero 1974, 1977; Castagno 2010; 2014) but that, as the project's current iteration, *kirchnerismo* has relied on state national-populist forms of media-ideological regulation different from the previous nationalist-authoritarian and neoliberal ideological regulations. Focusing on media policy, I seek to critically highlight the rift between social reality and state claims by examining the limits of Fernández de Kirchner's democratic reform.

1.1   *Situating the Media: Capitalist Crises and State Transformations*
Marx's work is crucial for thinking realistically about the state and the capitalist system. Distinct from other perspectives in the social sciences and political economy, Marx's historical-materialist method analyses the contradictions and class conflicts that constitute the historical process under capitalism. Marx demonstrates that modern history is shaped by fundamental antagonisms

---

6 My distinction between workers and citizens is analytical. I explicitly observe that not all citizens resisting state oppression struggle to realise a project of working-class solidarity.

7 I thus analyse thematic issues such as state regulation of media ownership, administration of broadcast licences, capital accumulation in the media sector, regulation of information and communication technologies (ICT), and democratisation of the media.

between capital and wage labour, and between the socio-economic dynamics and the political life of societies. For Marx, apprehending and representing concrete reality is part of the revolutionary practice of building an equal and free society (Lukács 2000/1923, 3). His research method is grounded in critical theoretical approaches, and is aimed both at grasping the distance between social reality and current social values and dialectically overcoming the distinction between social research and practical-critical activity (Marx 1998/1845, 572–574).

Marx observes that capitalism is characterised by cycles of capital accumulation and crises. As noted above, by crises he means phases of interruption in the process of reproduction of capital (Marx 1978, 446). He demonstrates that this reproduction is based on firms' exploitation of wage labour for the production of commodities (exchange value) to be exchanged in the market for sums of money: capitalism pays the labour class only the socially necessary amount of money for its reproduction and obtains its force for the production of surplus-value, which takes a commodity-form. According to Marx, capital is the accumulation of exchange value and requires the constant circulation of capital and commodities (1978/1867, 302–336). For any enterprise to obtain profits, capital accumulation is necessary to guarantee an expansion of the workforce, employ more technology in production, increase the relative exploitation of labour per unit of time, and produce more and cheaper commodities to compete on the market. Marx explains that, consequently, capitalism needs to balance capital investment and the means of consumption, or consumer commodities (Marx 1992/1885). He highlights that crises occur due to the propensity of the capitalist system "to exploit the maximum amount of labor without any consideration for the actual limits of the market or the needs backed by the ability to pay; and this is carried out through the continuous expansion of reproduction and accumulation, and therefore constant conversion of revenue into capital" (Marx 1978, 465). He also notes that the bourgeoisie – the dominant economic class – endeavours to resolve crises through the "enforced destruction of a mass of productive forces," "the conquest of new markets," and "the more thorough exploitation of old ones" (Marx and Engels 1978/1848, 478).

By applying this theoretical perspective we can discern two central turning points in contemporary global capitalism. The first is located during the early 1970s. As David Harvey and other authors demonstrate, it was in this period that the cycle of capital accumulation spanning from the end of World War II encountered serious difficulties in the United States and elsewhere (Harvey 1991, 140–147). Political cadres and the transnational bourgeoisie responded to that crisis in capitalist profitability by dismantling mechanisms of state economic interventionism and establishing a neoliberal agenda (Smith 1997; Duménil and Lévy 2004; Harman 2009). Since then we have seen how state cadres privatised state-owned companies, eliminated labour rights, contributed to the displacement of commodity production to cheaper regions, liberalised international trade, eliminated rules restricting the concentration and centralisation of capital, protected the independence of finance capital from the state, attempted to resolve the crisis in industrial profitability by intensifying the production of financial commodities – for instance, through the privatisation of state pension systems – and expanded the commodification of culture by stimulating the production of new media, tourist, leisure, and sports commodities.[8] Today it is evident that this neoliberal project has run up against obstacles and a global capitalist crisis is emerging (Harman 2009; McNally 2011). This is revealed in the slump of Gross Domestic Product (GDP) in the European Union and the United States in the period 2008–2009, and in the parlous rates of GDP growth during the last five years, especially within the European Union (The World Bank 2014). Indeed, before the emergence of the current crisis in the North, the neoliberal project had already collapsed in many Southern states. As a result, critical authors assert about the persistence of a global crisis (McNally 2011).

My contention is that media research needs to be situated in that historical process. To put it in Gramscian terms, we need to investigate how contradictions in the economic structure have repercussions on political, ideological, and cultural formations (Gramsci 2000, 427). At the same time, we must examine how political and cultural practices transform the economic structure – i.e. the manner by which dialectically active cultural, political, and economic processes constitute and transform one another. For example, inspired by Marx's study of the processes of revolution and counter-revolution altering the state and private property (1978/1852), Antonio Gramsci employs the category of organic crisis for explaining the periods of disturbance in commodity exchange and state formation. For Gramsci, one of the principal signs of an organic crisis is when the dominant economic class observes that the current forms of political representation do not ensure effective class domination, because the subaltern classes resist this political formation (2000, 217–221). In these historical situations, the subaltern classes move to a state of political activity by refusing the ruling class's hegemony, the rule of the ruling class is sustained only by coercion, and a "crisis of the state as a whole" emerges (Gramsci 2000, 218).

---

8   In Marxist terms commodification refers to the transformation of use-values into exchange products (Mosco 2010, 127).

In that light, I contend that the media is one of the state spheres in which political groups and classes establish new ideological articulations, alliances, and hegemonies to cope with an organic crisis. In Gramsci's terms, hegemony refers to the political, cultural, and moral directives consented to by citizens and workers (2000, 194). The importance of this function of the media increases concurrently as the organic crisis erodes the contracts among institutional actors (governments, trade unions, business associations) and the relationship of citizens to political parties. Further, since the media is a cardinal medium smoothing the general process of commodification and capital accumulation (Mosco 2010, 130; Fuchs 2009; 2011, 135–160), the media sphere is an essential space in which the dominant economic class can intensify commodity exchange after any capitalist collapse. In brief, considering the media from a Marxist standpoint I examine the class and political struggles to reproduce capital accumulation and state legitimacy, or to create alternative media, political, and economic systems. This kind of investigation is essential for a dialectic view of the state as an unstable formation that needs to reproduce the domination of both the transnational bourgeoisie and of listening citizens. In other words, the analysis of media policy allows for the application of two Marxist views to the state (Held 1991, 144): the state as the "committee for managing the common affairs of the whole bourgeoisie" (Marx and Engels 1978/1848, 475) and the state as an institution that has some relative autonomy despite its reproduction of dominant bourgeois interests (Marx 1978a; Poulantzas 1969). While Marxist studies have tended to stress the capitalist reproductive role of the media as an institution of ideological control (Althusser 2001/1970, 95), it is also important to grasp the state's imbalance between reproduction and hegemony.

2   Ideological Instability in Argentine Media Policy

Cristina Fernández de Kirchner's media reform represents part of the progressive political debate around the collapse of the neoliberal project in 2001–2002, when the state defaulted on its government bonds and sharply devalued its currency after three years of economic recession. This discussion centres on the nature of the state established by the neoliberal government of Carlos Menem (1989–1999) and the military dictatorship (1976–1983). *Kirchnerismo* proponents' argument is that the military junta introduced the neoliberal shift and Menem deepened it. This is a convincing interpretation with which political cadres can appeal to the citizenry because the dictatorship implemented a structural capitalist adjustment plan that repressed workers and citizens.

The military junta aimed to eliminate the dissent of critical citizens toward the state and to forcibly subjugate workers through state terrorism and economic policies. The regime kidnapped, tortured, murdered, and "disappeared" thousands of workers, students, and political activists (CONADEP 2003, 296);[9] reduced wages; liberalised foreign trade for corporations to import technology, boost so-called labour productivity, and increase exports; and interwove the economy with Northern finance capital – raising state debts and absorbing corporations' debts.[10]

Yet what is missed in the narrative of *kirchnerismo* is that the state had been pursuing its policy of subduing labour and assuring the state's link to Northern capitalism since the armed forces' *coup d'état* against the democratic government of Juan Domingo Perón in 1955, who had implemented a project of national capitalism (Portantiero 1974; 1977; Brennan and Rougier 2009; Castagno 2010).[11] Following a cycle of dictatorships (1955–1958, 1966–1973), the military junta intensified both state coercion and the economy's interdependence with Northern capitalism. This assault came after a period in which workers were seriously challenging the hegemony of the state and capital through labour organisation on the shop floor, in new trade unions, and through general strikes and political mobilisation (Werner and Aguirre 2009, 167–260). This organic crisis in state authority coincided with a deepening of the economic recession and a hyperinflationary crisis in 1975,[12] along with the

---

9   National Commission on the Disappearance of People. The democratic government of
    Raúl Alfonsín established CONADEP.

10 For non-Marxist approaches that consider these facts see, for example, Calcagno (1988)
    and Rapoport (2003). The official state narrative today tends basically to highlight the
    military junta's disappearance of citizens and the military junta's corruption in indebting
    the state. In other words, it does not situate those crimes within the capitalist conditions
    of the state.

11 For instance, while by 1957, 64 of the principal 100 corporations were national companies
    and the rest multinational corporations, by 1971, 72 of the principal 100 corporations were
    multinational firms and the rest national firms, usually linked to the latter (Sourrouille
    1985, 51). As Juan Carlos Portantiero critically puts it, "Two basic alternatives were open
    [in the mid 1950s]. One was to force the course of development directed until then by
    Peronism toward a model of development based on a solid alliance between the state and
    national capital. The other was to create conditions for a new stage of capitalist develop-
    ment by means of the implementation of a politics that, emphasizing dependence, would
    be able to guarantee the control of the economy to the most concentrated sectors"
    (Portantiero 1974, 102). For non-Marxists views on capitalist trans-nationalisation during
    the 1960s see Juan Vital Sourrouille (1985) and Guillermo O'Donnell (1988).

12 By 1975 the symptoms of the capitalist crisis were evident in Argentina: annual inflation
    climbed to 182.8 percent, the GDP and investments stagnated, fiscal deficit skyrocketed to

pressures from advanced capitalist countries – what I term Northern capitalism –
to displace capital to new geographical zones (Harvey 1991, 185).

I posit that adopting a longer historical perspective reveals that what varies
in the interlocking of the Argentine state with Northern capitalism are the
regulatory frameworks, coercive mechanisms, and ideological forms through
which the state and political cadres demand the compliance of citizens to the
state and capital. Continuity in the state strategy of capitalist transnationalisation is seen in its promotion of foreign investments, its consolidation of the
export-led dimension of the economy, its facilities for multinational corporations to export capital, and its periodic adjustments to discipline so-called
labour productivity according to global standards. The various regulatory and
ideological tactics are observed clearly in the establishment of either dictatorial or democratic regimes and in the political cadres' appropriation of centre-
left or popular-democratic – *Peronista* – ideologies. Thus, in terms of ideological
tactics, the dictatorships implanted repressive nationalism to counter the
demands of workers, trade unions, the Partido Peronista, and national-leftist
parties. They accused resistant Peronist workers, national-leftist sectors of the
Partido Peronista, and armed national-leftist groups of demagogy, corruption,
and international terrorism under the influence of international socialism.
The military junta's Law 22,285 on broadcasting (1980), synthesising the so-
called national security doctrine, is a case in point.

For example, the military junta set the regulation of broadcasting under the
control of the Executive Power (the chief commanders of the junta). It also
established that representatives from the army, the navy, the air force, the
Secretary of Public Information, and the State Secretary of Communication,
along with two representatives of the private media associations, must administer the institution regulating the media (Comité Federal de Radiodifusión,
COMFER).[13] Moreover, the Law 22,285 demanded that media content had to be
in accordance with the institutions of the "Republic," the national tradition,
and the moral norms of Christianity. The law required broadcasters to "disseminate information and collaborate [with the Executive] to satisfy the needs
of national security."[14] State and commercial broadcasters were requested to
avoid content that would diminish patriotism and to eliminate content that
would exalt ways of life or ideologies contradictory to the social, moral, and
political norms of the country (art. 5 and decree 286/81). This ideological coercion

---

16 percent, foreign debt rose, foreign trade deteriorated, and trade unions finally rejected
a drastic currency devaluation and wage freeze in 1975 (Rapoport 2003, 694–695).

13   Federal Broadcasting Committee.
14   Art. 7.

included a ban on not-for-profit media.[15] The *de facto* legislation on broadcasting was thus a condensation of nationalist authoritarianism, the state apparatus, and commercial media's interests. However, the dictatorship's achievement of its desire for capitalist growth through repressive nationalism was contradictory because, for example, its mechanisms of ideological coercion partially limited the broadcasting of media contents.

State authoritarianism supported capitalism by suppressing labour and cultural dissent, but at the same time set barriers to capital circulation and accumulation. For instance, besides the overtly nationalist constraints, the media legislation restricted the production of media commodities by establishing moral limits on the broadcasting of content. It required broadcasters to abstain from delivering "sordid, corrupting or repulsive news" and depicting "obscene gestures," "sexual perversions," "the triumph of evil," or "public commotion."[16] Law 22,285 demanded media companies to broadcast mainly national content, established Spanish as the only media language, requested the COMFER to authorise the information circulated by FM radios, and forbade the formation of private broadcasting networks.[17] It also prohibited the dissemination of media ratings or the broadcasting of game shows and the use of telephone calls in broadcasting content.[18] These regulations restricted capital accumulation not because corporations could not commodify nationalist or moral products, but because they limited the range of use-values that corporations could commodify.

Such legislation also limited capital accumulation by restraining capital centralisation, concentration, and commercialisation.[19] It stipulated that commercial broadcasters could not own press companies, administer public services, or manage more than four broadcasting licences.[20] It also impeded broadcasters from becoming subsidiaries of foreign corporations; and from selling licences, and commercialising shares for the first five years in operation.[21] On

---

15   Art. 45.

16   Law 22,285 (art. 18) and decree 286/81 (Art. 1). On the dictatorship's repression of cultural life see also Guillermo O'Donnell (1984).

17   Arts. 15, 19, 58 and 68. Decree 286/81. Forty percent of the total content broadcast had to be national content.

18   Arts. 24 and 25.

19   In Marxist terms, concentration refers to the accumulation of capital *vis-à-vis* the labour process (capital concentrates all the means of production in many firms), and centralisation refers to the command and ownership of different economic sectors or sub-sectors by a corporation (Shaikh 1991, 76–77).

20   Art. 43.

21   Arts. 45 and 46.

commercialisation – that is, on the establishment of relationships between audiences and advertisers (Mosco 2010, 132) – Law 22,285 forbade advertising during programmes, restricted advertising production to national firms, and prohibited advertisements offensive to "the integrity of the family and Christian morality."[22] In short, while the military junta aimed to resolve the organic crisis of the 1970s and consolidate transnational capitalism, at least in the media market it restrained capital accumulation via the form of moral coercion and cultural control it assumed. In this sense, it is illustrative that the dictatorship controlled the state-owned television channels, privatising the television channels Canal 9 and Canal 2 just before leaving power in hands of the democratic government of Raúl Alfonsín.[23]

After the impasse of Alfonsín's government – in which neither the dominant economic class nor workers could resolve the long-lasting economic stagnation – the democratic government of Carlos Menem (1989–1999) removed the dictatorship's restrictions on the media market. Menem promised workers that he would end the crisis and increase social equality, yet he established wide-ranging neoliberal reforms to favour capital. In the media field, his government eliminated former moral constraints and authorised companies to broadcast content in other languages, advertisements during programmes, game shows, telephone calls integral to shows,[24] and brands' catalogues.[25] The new legislation first permitted the state-owned television channel to broadcast advertising and then increased advertising time,[26] while also authorising broadcasters to deliver ratings statistics – a procedure communicating the idea that within society specific audiences exist for advertisers to entice.[27] Those regulatory changes increased the commodification and commercialisation of media content, allowing the emergence of programmes previously unimaginable: talk shows, discussions of political scandals, crime reporting, cheap humour programmes with hosts promoting a battery of brands, a myriad of game shows, and porn on cable television. In short, Menem's media policy rendered evident what Marx highlights: capitalism is indifferent to the actual content of the commodity. In Marx's words, "Could commodities themselves

---

22   Art. 23.

23   The dictatorship returned those television channels to their original owners. In 1974 Perón's government had put those television channels under state control.

24   The most successful show of the 1990s (*Hola Susana*) broadcast game shows in which the audience had to call the show to participate.

25   Decrees 1062/98, 1005/99, and 1065/99.

26   Decrees 1652/96 and 1005/99.

27   Decree 1062/98. The constitution of audiences is fundamental for the process of commodification. As Dallas Smythe observes (1977), the capitalist media needs to produce audiences for advertisers. For a critical review see Vicent Mosco (2010, 136–138).

speak, they would say: Our use-value may be a thing that interests men. It is not part of us as objects. What, however, does belong to us as objects, is our value. Our natural intercourse as commodities proves it. In the eyes of each other we are nothing but exchange-values" (1978/1867, 328).

Menem's government also nourished capitalism by altering rules on media ownership. It privatised the state-owned television channels Canal 13 and Canal 11, authorised press and telephone companies to own television channels and cable networks,[28] increased from four to twenty four the number of licences that media corporations could administer,[29] removed time limits on selling media corporations' shares,[30] allowed the formation of broadcasting networks, and removed restrictions on the transference of licences.[31] In addition, Menem's legislation on foreign investments pampered the movement of capital in and out of the media market. The Law 21,382 (1993) and 53 new treaties on foreign investments – which have pre-eminence over national laws[32] – established the state's equal treatment of foreign and national capital as well as authorised international investors to repatriate profits and capital without barriers. Menem's neoliberal policy thus facilitated media centralisation and concentration, and on a transnational basis no less. For example, the press company Grupo Clarín became the largest multimedia group;[33] in particular, its company Cablevisión bought cable television networks throughout the country, administering about 260 cable television licences.[34] At the same time, new global capital flowed into the market. For instance, Telefónica International –

---

28 Law 23,696/89 (art. 65). The Law 26,053/99 (Art. 1) forbade public service companies to administer broadcasting licences, but this restriction was removed through legislation authorising foreign firms the same rights that their countries give to Argentine capital. See afterwards.

29 Law 23,696/89 (art. 65).

30 Decree 1062/98.

31 Decree 1771/91 and 1005/99.

32 National Constitution (art. 75).

33 According to press information from La Nación on December 20, 2011 (http://www.lanacion .com.ar/1434200-grupo-clarin-y-vila-manzano-dos-de-los-mayores-multimedios-del-pais, accessed on February 15, 2012), by 2011 Grupo Clarín controlled the 47 percent of the total cable television market, nine television channels (owned and represented), five cable television channels, the second most listened-to radio (Radio Mitre) and numerous radio licences, the most widely read newspaper (Clarín) and other ten newspapers and magazines, 37 percent of the shares of the firm controlling paper commercialisation for newspapers, and shares in top audiovisual companies. See also Grupo Clarín's website (http:// www.grupoclarin.com/areas_y_empresas/clarin, accessed on February 15, 2012).

34 See, for instance, the report of newspaper Perfil on April 5, 2009: "En guerra con Clarín, el gobierno decidió frenar la fusión de cables," (http://www.diarioperfil.com.ar/edimp/0353/ articulo.php?art=13669&ed=0353, accessed on January 15, 2012).

a company that emerged out of the privatisation process in Spain – acquired Canal 11 and went on to administer nine other television licences, Liberty Media Corporation bought a quarter of the shares of Cablevisión and Goldman Sachs purchased eighteen percent of the shares of Grupo Clarín (CEPAL 2002, 97).

Thus we see that Menem's media policy was integrated into his neoliberal state machinery. This policy implemented new pro-capitalist labour legislation, liberalised trade, privatised all state-owned companies, swapped the foreign debt incurred by the former regime for global government bonds, partially privatised the state pension system, promoted transnational capital investments, and enforced a monetary regime based on the automatic convertibility of Argentine pesos into dollars at a parity exchange level (Castagno 2014a).[35] In sum, according to the Menem administration the market would deliver all the material and symbolic goods that the government believed the state could no longer distribute, but in effect neoliberalism dramatically increased social inequality. The media outlets circulated messages tempting consumers to join the so-called First World: Miami's shopping malls or European sports events, for example (Castagno 2014b). Yet, as cultural critic Beatriz Sarlo described in the early 1990s, with Menem in power Argentina lived "in the cultural climate of what is considered 'postmodernity' in the frame of a nation fractured and impoverished. Twenty hours of daily television, on fifty channels, and the public school without any symbolic or material resources" (Sarlo 1994, 7). This systemic social inequality rose throughout the 1990s and became politically unsustainable for the state. By the late 1990s unemployment reached 18 percent and poverty 30 percent (Lozano 2005, 4). In this context of inequality, the media blamed corrupt politicians for Argentina's neoliberal economic woes in moral terms (Castagno 2010). To explain this issue using Roland Barthes' analysis of media myths (1972/1957), the media communicated a partial critique on individual cases of corruption. But this rhetoric distracted citizens from paying attention on the larger mechanisms of consent by purchase through which the political cadres implemented the state reform.

Nevertheless, Argentina's problems intensified in early 1999, when Brazil – a major Argentine trade partner – devalued its currency. Under these conditions, Argentines elected the centre-right coalition ALIANZA,[36] which promised to

---

35   Menem's government established an ad-hoc "Euro:" as the Euro replaced former national currencies in the European Union, in Argentina the dollar (i.e., the currency that works as universal monetary equivalent in Marxist terms) became a state tool with which to discipline the economy, pressuring labour to adapt to the competitive strength of the dollar in the global economy (Castagno 2014a).

36   Alianza para la Educación, la Salud y el Empleo (Coalition for Education, Health and Employment) formed by the traditional party UCR and the centre-left coalition FREPASO.

prosecute political corruption, a practice intimately linked to the privatisation of state-owned companies (Verbitsky 1991). Despite this promise, the ensuing government only strove to preserve the neoliberal macroeconomic framework, increasing working-class austerity and honouring government bonds' payments.[37] This assault provoked a reversal in citizens' expectations. In turn, workers and citizens resisted the rounds of neoliberal austerity. For example, the two confederations of trade unions carried out eight general strikes, the social movement of unemployed workers gained momentum (Svampa and Pereyra 2003), and in key districts blank votes won the parliamentary elections of 2001.[38] In late 2001 citizens in major cities filled public squares, forcing President Fernando de la Rúa to resign. Citizens rejected the President and the main political parties under the motto: "They Must All Go!" (Solanas 2004; Pousadela 2008). Yet, despite those demonstrations, the traditional political parties remained, electing a new president through a parliamentary pact. In the name of the nation, President Eduardo Duhalde turned the slump into a capitalist exit: his government sharply devalued the currency and lowered wages,[39] cleared big corporations' banking debts at the expense of citizens' saving accounts, and repressed the protest of unemployed workers (Castagno 2010, 317–338). This moment of crisis in state authority ended with the election of President Néstor Kirchner in 2003.

3   The 'Post-Neoliberal' State and the Media

"[T]he question of the state also involves what one might call its 'transformative' possibility."

    JOHN BEVERLEY, *Latinamericanism After 9/11 (2011, 115)*

---

37   ALIANZA approved a labour law that removed collective bargaining; reduced state workers' wages; aimed to privatise trade unions' health funds; and swapped junk government bonds, passing them to national and global pensioners (Castagno 2010, 287–289).

38   In the cities of Santa Fe and Buenos Aires, blank ballot papers and spoiled ballot papers won the election. In Buenos Aires province, blank ballot papers and spoiled ballot papers came in second. In Córdoba, they placed third. Argentina has a presidential system of government with an Executive Branch, a bicameral legislature formed by the Senate and the Chamber of Deputies (Congreso Nacional), and a Judicial Branch. I use the term parliament to refer to that bicameral legislature.

39   Currency devaluation meant that even four years after the crisis, average wages were eleven percent below their level in 2001 (Graña and Kennedy 2008, 65). Devaluation changes the relative prices in the economy. Wages (set in the national currency) deteriorate in relation to commodities exported abroad (set in dollars).

Despite its proponents' explicit disavowal of neoliberal policies and their professed national-popular political orientation, *kirchnerismo* has sustained the long state-capitalist project of embedding the economy in global capitalism and enforcing an unequal class structure. Firstly, in commodity production, currency devaluation and the hike in global commodity prices (agricultural goods, energy, mining) combined to intensify the export-led dimension of the Argentine economy and conquer new markets: between 2003 and 2010 annual exports rose from US$29.9 billion to a peak of US$84 billion,[40] increased by the export of cars to Brazil, soy to Asia, and mining products to the global market. Northern capital controls this backbone of capitalist reproduction (Chudnovsky and López 2001, 96).[41] Secondly, the governments of Néstor Kirchner and Cristina Fernández de Kirchner reduced the public foreign debt as percentage of GDP (41.5 percent by 2013) and nationalised the private pension system. Yet the debt burden is evident if we take into account that the Central Bank is indebted to the local banking system, there are outstanding legal demands from global creditors to the state, both the Central Bank and the new state pension fund have a vast amount of government bonds in their portfolios,[42] and significant interest payments and capital payments to global creditors are due during the next four years.[43] In other words, *kirchnerismo* has to a great degree passed the debt burden along to pensioners, while it refuses to grant pensioners the 82 percent of the current wage corresponding to their former labour activities. Thirdly, *kirchnerismo* re-established collective bargaining, but the percentage of workers outside the formal labour market (and thus collective bargaining) remains, at its

40   Balanza comercial argentina, Instituto Nacional de Estadística y Censos (INDEC): http://www.indec.mecon.ar/ (accessed November 15, 2014).

41   As result of the neoliberal reform of the 1990s, multinational corporations went on to control about 99 percent of total automobile exports, 99 percent of total mining exports and 62.4 percent of total agricultural exports—vegetal oils and grains (Chudnovsky and López 2001, 96).

42   By 2001 the private pension system had about 76 percent of workers' pension funds in government bonds, which the state then defaulted on and finally swapped for discounted bonds in 2005 (Castagno 2010, 159–176). A decade later, the state pension fund has 57.8 percent of its funds invested in government bonds (ANSES 2011). More than thirty-five percent of those bonds are invested in pesos, while the unofficial inflation rate is three times the official one. This means that future pensions are being devalued. Indeed, the government did not use the nationalised private pension fund (the new state pension fund) to raise the pensions of workers that had contributed to the private pension system, and so in practice appropriated those funds.

43   The official information actually recognises the debt problem when it states that it does not compute the debt items I mentioned. See, for example, Oficina Nacional de Crédito Público 2012. For a critical press account on the public debt see Giuliano 2014.

lowest estimate, 34 percent of the total working population.[44] This is an important factor in explaining why the percentage of wages in GDP has tended to remain stagnant since the 1970s (Graña and Kennedy 2008, 4), when the capitalist assault intensified. Next, *kirchnerismo* claims to have reduced household poverty to 3.7 percent of the total households, but this figure is based on outdated statistics that establish the monthly sum an average family of four needs to live at 1,783 pesos (US$210) (CBT, Canasta Básica Total).[45] In short, the fact that *kirchnerismo* keeps reproducing an unequal transnational class structure is revealed in Argentina's export of approximately 105 billion dollars to Northern financial centres between 2007 and 2012 (Damill and Frenkel 2009, 22; Cano 2011; CIFRA 2013, 17), all in the context of a global slump.

Nevertheless, *kirchnerismo* has also contributed popular-democratic reforms to the pre-existing state formation. For example, it persuaded the Supreme Court to annul Menem's government decree that had pardoned former commanders for their crimes, implemented a minimum subsistence payment for children of unemployed families, established a more democratic mechanism to elect the judges of the Supreme Court, legalised same-sex marriage, and partially democratised the media. These policies answered citizens and workers' demands to a degree, especially between 2003 and 2011. As an activist from the community radio station *La Posta* phrased it during parliamentary discussions of the media reforms, "We believe that the challenges that democracies face in this conjuncture, and in our country since the crisis of 2001–2002, has to do with answering the demands of large social sectors to participate in the administration, control and implementation of public policies" (FARCO 2009, 42).[46] My task in this chapter is to evaluate the extent to which Cristina Fernández de Kirchner's media reform (Law 26,522) has grasped and addressed these popular-democratic demands to participate in the implementation and development of public policies.

At first glance these media reforms seem to have significantly addressed popular demand for participation. The new law (and the other progressive

---

44   Report from the Instituto Nacional de Estadística y Censos (National Institute of Statistics and Census, INDEC) on June, 2011 (http://www.argentina.ar/_es/economia-y-negocios/C8227-el-trabajo-en-negro-cayo-al-341-por-ciento.php, accessed on January 15, 2012).

45   CBT measures the poverty line. It only includes food, clothes, education, transport, and other services. In contrast, according to Observatorio de la Deuda Social Argentina (2014), 17.8 percent of the households and 27.5 percent of the persons from the total households and the total population live under the poverty line.

46   FARCO is the Argentine Forum of Community Radios; it represents about 80 community radio stations and promotes social solidarity, democracy, public transparency, diversity, and pluralism.

public policies of *kirchnerismo*) enjoyed substantial consent from media activists, not-for-profit media organisations, community media, human rights organisations, trade unions, and academics (Baranchuk and Usé 2011; Busso and Jaimes 2011). These civil society actors developed the progressive guidelines of Coalición para una Radiodifusión Democrática (Coalition for Democratic Broadcasting), which united those various sectors and pressured the government to change media legislation.[47] The coalition was a social movement consonant with international movements of media activists that struggle to define the media as an institution of public interest, establish communications as a human right, and democratise the media (International Commission 1980; Hackett and Zhao 2005). Regardless of whether this perspective may in fact be compatible with the capitalist system, its advocacy helps to change political perceptions, establish legal instruments for democratic emancipation, and destabilise the realm of commercial media. That is, the struggle to build a new public sphere seems important for what Gramsci refers as a long "war of position" for cultural and political emancipation (2000, 225–228). As Vicent Mosco argues, one way to employ the concept of the public sphere effectively is to define it "as a set of social processes that carry out democracy, namely advancing equality and the fullest possible participation in the complete range of economic, political, social, and cultural decision-making" (2010, 152). I argue that the results obtained by the Coalición must be read in this tactical manner: the media reforms opened new horizons for democratic and socialist emancipation. In this sense, by observing the new field of struggle, my approach differs from other critical Marxist perspectives that believe the new law is *just* an "expression of inter-bourgeois rivalry" to appropriate new media spaces (Henkel and Morcillo 2013, 36).

Thus, the advancement of the Law on Audiovisual Communication Services specifies its definition of audiovisual services as activities of public interest through which the human right to communicate is expressed.[48] Indeed, the law stipulates the state must protect the right to information, participation,

---

47   The Coalition reunited more than three hundred organisations from civil society (e.g., community media, trade unions, human rights organisations, public universities).

48   The law overstates its scope. It claims to be about the development of information society but it fundamentally applies to broadcasting, cable television and satellite television; since it defines that audiovisual communication services are based on a programming timetable (Art. 4). It neither regulates the Internet nor telecommunications, though in one occasion it refers to broadcasting to "mobile receivers" (Art. 4). Similarly, it does not give specifications on digital television platforms (Televisión Digital Abierta, Open Digital Television), as I explain next. The law is also overcharged with notes detailing Northern legislations.

and freedom of speech. It stresses that the goal of audiovisual services is the promotion of diversity, universal access, and participation. Based on this voluntaristic perspective, the law nevertheless guarantees the right of not-for-profit media to enter the media sphere. Specifically, it requires that the state distribute broadcasting, cable television, and digital platforms' licences on equal terms among state media providers, commercial media providers, and not-for-profit media providers; the latter are civil society institutions (foundations, civic associations, churches, trade unions, social movements' organisations, and community media) that provide media services to their communities. Further, the law automatically authorises public universities, the Catholic Church, and indigenous communities to administer audiovisual licences.

However, five years after the reform, the democratic record of the new policy seems to have greatly favoured the commercial and state sectors. For example, by 2013 AFSCA (Autoridad Federal de Servicios de Comunicación Audiovisual), the public institution in charge of regulating the media system, had granted approximately 94 percent of 550 private media's radio licences to the commercial sector.[49] At the same time, by 2014 AFSCA had only "recognised" 200 community radio stations. Similarly, it authorised 38 radio stations for indigenous communities, but only six are operating at the present. At the same time, AFSCA reserved 1132 radio frequencies for local governments and 36 TV stations to provincial governments. It also authorised a total of 59 radio and TV stations to local and provincial governments, 44 radio stations to the Catholic Church, and a total of 252 radio and TV stations to educational institutions (AFSCA 2014a). Therefore, the new policy appears to be consolidating commercial and state media providers (including the Catholic Church, as part of the state apparatus). This is why in November 2014, not-for-profit media organisations such as the Red Nacional de Medios Alternativos (RNMA),[50] which identifies with working-class' needs and perspectives, reunited with AFSCA authorities to demand the complete implementation of the law. They demand that AFSCA move forward in authorising radio and television licences to community media providers, and specifically claim that five years after Law 26,522, AFSCA has still not elaborated the technical plan required by the law to divide the public airwaves among the different media sectors.[51] In this regard, one central issue of dispute between the RNMA and AFSCA is that the law does

49   Based on press information from Krakowiak (2013).
50   National Network of Alternative Media.
51   Diálogo por el Reconocimiento, Red Nacional de Medios Alternativos [Dialogue for Recognition], http://www.rnma.org.ar/noticias/18-nacionales/2211-dialogo-por-el-reconocimiento (accessed on November 13 2014).

not recognise community, alternative, and popular media fields as another specific sector to receive licences.

The obstacles to media democratisation are perhaps clearer if we take into account the digital television platform – Televisión Digital Abierta (TDA) – established by the state in 2010 to complement satellite and cable private television systems. In late 2014, about 39 per cent of the channels operating in the TDA digital platform belong to the national state and the provinces, 39 per cent of television channels are commercial media, and 12 per cent of television channels are in the hands of public universities.[52] In addition, a large (and pro-government) trade union (UOCRA, Unión Obrera de la Construcción) has one television channel in the system, the semi-autonomous Instituto Nacional de Cines y Artes Audiovisuales (INCAA, National Institute of Film and Audiovisual Arts) has one television channel, and the two other television channels belong to other states. These results contradict the spirit of the law to divide the audiovisual spectrum in equal terms among state, commercial, and non-for-profit media. No community media participates in system. Moreover, in my view the procedures to create the TDA system are obscure or at least state-centred. Though Cristina Fernández de Kirchner's government established the Sistema Argentino de Televisión Digital Terrestre (SATVD-T) by decree on August 2009 (Decree 1148/2009), the law on audiovisual communication services, approved two months later by the Parliament, did not refer to it.[53] The federal government's Ministerio de Planificación Federal, Inversión Pública y Servicios is in charge of implementing the TDT/TDA system through the Consejo Asesor del Sistema Argentino de Televisión Digital Terrestre (Advisory Board of the Argentine Earth Digital Television System), which is integrated with other Ministries as well (Decree 1148/2009).[54] In terms of civic participation, the decree simply states that the Consejo Asesor may invite representatives from the private media, universities, social organisations, labour unions and so on to an ad-hoc consulting forum (art. 3). Furthermore, by 2014 the AFSCA had twice cancelled

---

52   A task for future research is to observe how public universities' media relate to the processes of state and capital reproduction.

53   Law 26,522 simply states that current regulations, universal access and participation must be respected when digital platforms are established (art. 93). Moreover, the regulation of the law's art. 93 (Decree 1225/2010) refers to the Decree 1148/2009.

54   Ministry of Federal Planning, Public Investment and Services. The TDA platform includes a system of Televisión Digital Terrestre (earth digital TV) and a system of Televisión Digital Satelital (satellite digital TV). The state organ in charge of implementing the overall system is the Consejo Asesor, which it is "within the orbit" of the Ministry of Federal Planning and integrated by the other Ministries of the federal government (Decree 1148/2009, Art. 2; Res. 1785/2009).

its bidding process for granting licences in the TDA digital platform. Not-for-profit media organisations also asserted they could not afford the price of the bidding specifications to participate in the selection process and the monthly sum required by the state to operate audiovisual services in the newly digital platform (Faro TV et al. 2011). They claimed that the new media policy has in reality "enlarged the state but not the communities" (CoorDeCAAP 2011).[55]

At the regulatory level, everything the ruling state cadres does is thus in name of the public interest. Nevertheless, in reality the media institutions ruling cadres establish are not effectively public. For instance, Law 26,522 conflates public and state institutions, which are controlled by the federal government. In particular, despite including the participation of parliamentary political sectors and representatives from trade unions, public universities, indigenous communities, and human rights organisations in debates over proposed legislative reform and in the new regulatory institutions, it is still the case that the Executive Power is in charge of implementing the law through AFSCA.[56] The Executive Power and the dominant national political party nominate a large proportion of the representatives of AFSCA: three out of seven, without considering their probable influence in nominating two additional representatives through the votes of the representatives of the provincial governors. In Argentina the political party that wins the national presidential election normally wins most of the provincial elections and has majority in the parliament – see Table 15.1.[57] Similarly, the law does not establish any mechanism through which the administration of state media may become independent from the state – and more importantly, the federal government;[58] the state company Radio y Televisión Argentina Sociedad del Estado (RTA S.E.) manages all the state's media and is mostly controlled by the Executive Power and the dominant national political party.[59]

---

55   Coordinadora en Defensa de la Comunicación Comunitaria, Alternativa y Popular (Organisation in Defense of Community, Alternative and Popular Communication). CoorDeCCAP united about 60 not-for-profit media organisations and was established by RNMA (see above).

56   Art. 7.

57   Thus, the press frequently reports that on controversial issues only the two representatives from other political parties have voted differently from the rest of AFSCA's members.

58   In contrast, the Coalición por una Radiodifusión Democrática stated in its proposal that state media must be public (2011, 157).

59   The institutional mechanism to nominate RTA S.E. directors is similar to the case of AFSCA (Arts. 119, 132).

TABLE 15.1   *Regulatory institutions (arts. 12–16, 19, 32)*

> AFSCA is the state body in charge of applying the legislation, elaborating technical norms and controlling monopolistic practices.
> The Executive Power nominates two officials to AFSCA; a parliamentary commission nominates three officials belonging to the three largest political sectors in the parliament; the Consejo Federal de Comunicación Audiovisual (CFCA, Federal Council on Audiovisual Communication Services) nominates two officials (one has to belong to a public university that offers a communication degree).
> CFCA is constituted by the representatives of the provincial governments (23) and the government of Buenos Aires city; three representatives of the private media associations; three representatives of the associations of non-for-profit media producers; one representative of the state media; one representative of the broadcasting stations of public universities; three representatives of the trade unions within the media sector; one representative of human rights organizations; and one representative of all the indigenous ethnic groups.
> CFCA advises and proposes policies to AFSCA.
> The Executive Power can directly authorise (previous selection process) broadcasting licences in cities with more than 500,000 inhabitants.
> The Defense of the Public office receives denounces from citizens.

Another crux of discussion is the regulation of licences. As mentioned above, the new legislation basically limits previous neoliberal reforms by dividing in equal terms the broadcasting spectrum and audiovisual space for distributing licences among the commercial media, the state, and not-for-profit media. It also reduces from 24 to 10 the number of licences a single broadcaster can hold, forbids audiovisual providers to transfer licences, establishes 24 as the number of licences a cable television company can administer, and impedes cable television companies from owning broadcasting television channels (Table 15.2). Moreover, the law mandates that cable television and satellite television companies deliver Latin American, state, provincial, and local channels.[60]

Kirchnerismo thus claims the new law severely restricts media monopolies and increases diversity. Yet the peril is that the repetitive official discourse against media concentration would become akin to beating a dead horse. To put it differently, from a Marxist standpoint it is necessary to highlight that

---

60   For instance, after Law 26,522, cable television companies had to deliver the Venezuelan television channel Telesur, the state movie channel IncaaTV (Argentine films), and the state channel for children Paka Paka. All this expanded media diversity.

TABLE 15.2   *Administration of licences (Arts. 2, 25, 29, 37, 38, 41, 45, 89)*

> ➤ The audiovisual space is divided among state, commercial and not-for-profit audiovisual providers in equal terms (thirty-three percent of every audiovisual space for each sector of providers).
> ➤ Licences cannot be transferred.
> ➤ The provider of audiovisual services by satellite (one licence for the whole territory) cannot hold any other audiovisual licence. One provider of audiovisual services cannot administer more than ten broadcasting licences. One provider of paid audiovisual services utilising cable networks cannot administer more than twenty-four licences.
> ➤ Any provider of audiovisual services cannot reach more than thirty-five percent of the national audience.
> ➤ In every locality one audiovisual provider cannot administer more than one AM radio, two FM radios, and one television or cable television licence.
> ➤ Cable television companies cannot deliver more than one cable television signal of their own.
> ➤ All national public universities will receive one radio and one television licence.
> ➤ All state institutions and the Catholic Church have the right to receive licences.
> ➤ Every indigenous ethnic group has the right to one radio and one television licence in each locality it is based.
> ➤ All local governments have the right to one FM radio licence. Each province and Buenos Aires city has the right to one AM radio licence, one FM radio licence and one television licence.

---

media concentration and centralisation is a result of capitalist competition and of the tendency of the rate of profit to fall. Marx explains that as firms introduce more technology in production to produce more and cheaper commodities to compete on the market,[61] less human labour is exploited per commodity and mass of commodities, so in relative terms profits tend to fall. In Marx's account surplus-value and profits are a direct result of the exploitation of human labour.[62] In turn, to counteract this tendency, firms need to optimise the use of constant capital (fixed capital, technology), intensify the exploitation

---

61   As I noted above, this increases the concentration and centralisation of capital.
62   The rate of surplus-value refers to the proportion of unpaid labour that workers transfer to the capitalist class over the necessary labour time that workers spend reproducing their needs, and is paid as wages — variable capital (Marx 1990/1867, 320–329). The rate of profit is the relationship of surplus-value to total capital (variable and constant capital) over a cycle of capital reproduction (Marx 1991, 132–140).

of labour, and create new associations of production (Marx 1991/1894, 317–375). Briefly, while for bourgeois economics 'pure' competition is the antithesis of concentration, Marx demonstrates how the concentration and centralisation of capital are dialectically related to market competition among firms (Shaikh 1991, 76; Fuchs 2009, 381).

Thus, if media regulations are not carefully established they cannot restrict "concentration," due to the need of media companies to accumulate capital. In this regard, the law is confusing: it is filled with references to the elimination of monopolies, but also stipulates that AFSCA needs to promote competition and investment.[63] Lawmakers did not consider the contradiction between media competition and concentration because they did not have any intention of altering the capitalist foundations of the media: the regulation of concentration is simply part of a discursive and institutional project of adding popular-democratic accretions to the existing system. In effect, the new law maintains 24 licences for cable television providers, authorises satellite television companies (currently the American multinational Direct TV) to provide services to the whole national space with only one licence, forbids telephone companies to enter the media market but authorises cable television companies (e.g., Telecentro) to provide telephone services,[64] keeps authorising cross-ownership between press and media companies, and fundamentally allows any capitalist undertaking that the law on foreign investments and the treaties on international investments signed by Argentina authorises – even when the same Law 26,522 explicitly prohibits the foreign ownership of media companies in Argentina.[65] As noted above, in Argentina international treaties have supremacy over national laws. For example, the multinational company PRISA cited those international treaties in rejecting current regulations (AFSCA 2014a).

In addition, the latest project of Fernández de Kirchner's government removed one important constraint of Law 26,522 on capital accumulation (art. 25, section d), which forbade public service companies to provide audiovisual services. In December 2014, the Parliament approved Law 27,078 to regulate information and communications technology (ICT). This law allows ICT

---

63   Art. 12.

64   The original project of *kirchnerismo* authorised telephone companies to enter the cable television market. It is unclear whether the government deleted this article in order to attract positive votes from centre-left deputies to the project or due to power issues involving the main telephone company Telefónica International, which currently controls about the 90 percent of the Argentine telephone market.

65   Foreign capital cannot control more than thirty percent of the shares of any audiovisual company (Art. 29), but this limitation is removed in case of international treaties on investments.

companies to supply audiovisual services, and authorises audiovisual companies to provide ICT services (Art. 9). The law also permits ICT providers to transfer licences (Art. 13). Though this typical regulation on media convergence favours capital centralisation, supporters of the project keep repeating the state mantra on competition. Leftist working-class forces are thus right to claim that the so-called "Digital Argentina Law" benefits transnational telecommunication companies such as Telefónica and large media groups (Solano 2014, 6). In fact, the government sent the new project to Parliament just after licensing 3G and 4G mobile telecommunication frequencies to large companies (Movistar/Telefónica, Claro, Telecom Personal, Arlink), some of them transnational corporations. In my view, these regulations clearly reveal the ultimate capitalist goal of Fernández de Kirchner's government to forge private conglomerates in the large communication sector.

In that sense, even the so-called anti-monopoly regulation on cable television licences mentioned above is interesting to consider closely. Law 26,522 authorises 24 licences for cable television companies in different localities, but it does not define what those localities are.[66] This signifies that cable television companies could exert political pressure to define those localities in their advantage. In this sense, a press declaration from the, by then, Chief Executive Officer (CEO) of the former second-largest cable television company, Grupo Uno – on the number of cable television licences managed by his company by 2012 is particularly revealing (De Santis 2012). Refuting the view that the company was administering more licences than those authorised by the law, the CEO maintained that the issue was resolved with new administrative regulations. These regulations agglomerated all the licences corresponding to localities situated in the greater metropolitan area of Mendoza city, where Grupo Uno rules the cable television market. Furthermore, in 2014, AFSCA approved Grupo Uno's plan to divide itself among various firms currently controlled by Grupo Uno's former owners or creditors (AFSCA 2014a). Briefly, these different firms administer the substantial core of the licences Grupo Uno managed before as a whole.

The new law, then, has left judicial and administrative paths open for corporations. This is also seen in Article 161, which gives companies one year to adapt to the new legislation and make disinvestments if necessary. Between 2009 and 2013, Grupo Clarín rejected this stipulation through legal recourse, which has stopped the implementation of the law. Finally, the Supreme Court stated in late 2013 that Law 26,522 is constitutional and thus AFSCA required Grupo

---

66   "The regulatory authority will determine the territorial and demographic limits of the
      licences" (Art. 45, section c).

Clarín to obey it. In turn, the firm presented a plan to divide itself in six groups. Nevertheless, AFSCA alleged that behind the apparent division there was an underlying structure of business connections among principal owners and shareholders. Consequently, by late 2014 Clarín's case remains unresolved. The issue itself became the principal area of ideological contention between *kirchnerismo* and the "concentrated corporations," and between a central corporation and the power bloc *kirchnerismo* established. In my view, beyond this specific rivalry, the case reveals how difficult it is for the capitalist state to limit the market process of capital centralisation with legal prohibitions that corporations neutralise with different legal, though I believe not democratic, means or through the circulation of capital itself.[67] In this sense, even when a corporation would be forced to sell some of its units, other media corporations would buy them. Thus, in reality the scenario is that media centralisation is influenced by the desires of the Executive Power and the judiciary to favour certain media conglomerates at expense of others. For example, prior to Law 26,522, Kirchner's government authorised Grupo Clarín to acquire the cable television company Multicanal and reach 47 percent of cable television consumers (Laboratorio de Industrias Culturales 2011). Further, as I analyse in the next section, along with its partial democratisation of the media, the spirit of *kirchnerismo* would be to build state-commercial media associations.

4   Populism Revisited

> "Only when relationships have so far developed and conflicts of interest have reached such an intensity that even the average eye can penetrate beyond appearances to what is really going on, does a conscious ideological apparatus in the full sense usually make its appearance."
>
> MAX HORKHEIMER, *Notes on Science and the Crisis* (1989/1932, 55)

For a Marxist approach, it is important to consider the theoretical implications we can draw from the case of *kirchnerismo* and its media policy. My argument is that the governments of Néstor Kirchner (2003–2007) and Cristina Fernández de Kirchner (2007-to the present) contributed popular-democratic accretions to the existing state formation by articulating demands for human rights, media democratisation, collective bargaining, and social security. This entailed a partial populist mobilisation of citizens. As Ernesto Laclau argues, populism

---

67   It is interesting to note that AFSCA approved 35 out of 40 projects from media companies to adapt to the new regulations.

is a mode of political construction characterised by the articulation and mobilisation of popular demands against the institutional formation that is not answering them. These particular demands are heterogeneous but they share mutual dissatisfaction with the institutional status quo (Laclau 2009, 97–103). Populism thus tends to spring up in periods of state crisis. According to Laclau, "the people" of populism appears when a *plebs* (the masses, the underprivileged) claims to be the whole community (*populus*), establishing a frontier in the political field against the supposed enemies of the people. The *populus* thus emerges as a political subject collectivising or "hegemonising" heterogeneous popular demands in a relation of equivalence (2009, 150–151). Crucially, the *populus* is not a pre-existing social group but the result of an act of nomination, for which a leader who condenses popular demands and popular affects, and mobilises the *populus* against the previous institutional status quo is essential (Laclau 2009, 128–130). For instance, in Argentina Néstor Kirchner became a leader that represented popular opposition to neoliberalism and to the residual elements of the dictatorial period. Yet, as Laclau maintains, populism as a form of political construction can appear in different political movements (2009, 29). In his early work it was thus important for Laclau to observe how populist constructions are ideologically dependent on the class projects of hegemonic political groups (Laclau 1978, 223).[68] In other words, populism, as mode of political construction, may be linked to different class ideologies. In my view, Laclau's late work on populism tends to deemphasise this class articulation, but I contend consideration of the latter is crucial in developing a theory of populism from a Marxist perspective.

In this light, I argue it is important to observe how *kirchnerismo* articulated its populist logic with its class project, which as I considered previously as consisting in reproducing capitalist transnationalisation. In other words, *kirchnerismo* needs to resolve the contradiction between its populist construction and its capitalist reproductive role. Its proponents may seek this resolution by rhetorically exaggerating its break with the status quo. For example, *kirchnerismo* defended its media legislation by saying it eliminated the media law of the dictatorship and Grupo Clarín's monopoly. However, sooner rather than later mending structural cracks with rhetoric proved impossible. *Kirchnerismo* has therefore needed to find an institutional-ideological arrangement to accommodate its populist discourse within its capitalist aims. In the media sphere, such an economic arrangement has consisted in the promotion of national media content. This constitutes the political project of *kirchnerismo*: that is, its

---

68   For instance, Perón linked his populism to the pre-existing project of national capitalism.

way to ideologically and materially adapt citizens' demands to its fundamental class project. For instance, Law 26,522 promotes state-commercial conglomerates: its Article 153 on public policies specifically established that the Executive Power "must adopt policies destined to promote the formation and development of national audiovisual conglomerates in all the formats and media platforms, facilitating the dialogue, cooperation and business organisation among economic actors, public institutions, private institutions, and academic institutions, in benefit of competitiveness."[69] The law also obligates audiovisual providers to broadcast a minimum level of Argentine national content, with the objective of both strengthening the national media industry and increasing jobs in the audiovisual field (Table 15.3).

As Chris Harman observed on the contradictions between the state bureaucracy and capital, the state bureaucracy "cannot ignore the needs of national capital accumulation without risking its own longer term future" (2009, 113). In Harman's view, the ruling cadres of the state bureaucracy become "political capitalists" when they seek "to promote the development of the sibling capitals operating within an individual state" (2009, 115). In Argentina, the promotion of the national media industry permits *kirchnerismo* to ideologically adapt its populist discourse to the existing capitalist goals of the state.[70] It also allows *kirchnerismo* to establish a certain national basis of capital (and thus social) reproduction within a regime of capital accumulation that is fully integrated into global capitalism and dominated by Northern transnational corporations. Of course, this arrangement is progressive in the sense that it is a cultural force counteracting, or at least parallel to, the expansion of the North American and European commercial media.[71] It may also diversify media content and increase participation in the media system. At the same time, however, it integrates content from state media producers, not-for-profit media, and small commercial producers into the capitalist media industry. In this way, the project

---

69   This desire to reconcile media diversity and businesses is certainly not just seen in Argentina. Even UNESCO's declaration on cultural diversity is ambiguous (2002). It establishes that cultural goods — as vectors of identity, values and meaning — must not be treated as mere commodities or consumer goods (Art. 8). In other words, cultural goods are still partially seen as commodities.

70   It goes without saying that this national content is different from the nationalist-repressive culture industry of the military junta. For example, new state television channels Encuentro or IncaaTV broadcast documentaries on social protests or films that question the existing society.

71   On the global expansion of the American and European media industry see, for instance, Herbert I. Schiller (1992/1969), Armand Mattelart and Seth Siegelaub (1979), and Lee Artz and Yahya R. Kamalipour (2003).

TABLE 15.3   *Audiovisual contents (arts. 65, 67)*

> Radios must broadcast thirty percent of national music and seventy percent of national content out of the total music and content broadcast. Half of the national music broadcast has to be from Argentine musicians who own the rights to commercialise their music.
> Sixty percent of the total programmes broadcast by television channels must be produced in Argentina. In the largest cities, so-called independent producers (i.e., with no ownership links to the channel) must produce thirty percent of the total programmes of television channels.
> Television channels and radios must produce and broadcast thirty percent and fifty percent respectively of their total programming.
> Cable television and satellite television must deliver the channels of their area belonging to the state, the public universities, the provinces and Buenos Aires city.
> The principal television channels (reaching more than twenty percent of the population) are required to broadcast eight new national films or three produced television films per year.

---

of a national culture industry helps to reproduce capitalism by adding use-values to the commercial media – a procedure that is common in contemporary culture (Crawford 1992, 15). Furthermore, the development of the national culture industry is not necessarily contradictory to global capital, as is seen when transnational corporations participate in the national media system or when the state television channels themselves mediate the events of the global culture industry. As a consequence, and in contrast, it would be desirable for a practical socialist agenda to take advantage of the promotion of national content in order to press the state to implement truly public cable television channels or public digital platforms in which those cultural productions could be further developed democratically. A case in point is the state online platforms and audiovisual catalogues BACUA (Banco Audiovisual de Contenidos Universales Argentino) and CDA (Contenidos Digitales Abiertos), implemented by the Advisory Board mentioned above.[72] The Consejo Asesor has also granted funds through public tenders to so-called independent media productions.[73] However, according to its website, BACUA media content is apparently available to state and commercial television channels in the TDA

---

72   Audiovisual Bank of Universal Argentine Contents, and Open Digital Contents.
73   The Consejo Interuniversitario Nacional (CIN) also participates in the commitee to select grantees. CIN represents all the public universities in the country.

system for free.[74] BACUA thus ultimately transforms more use-values into commodities. Moreover, researchers Cristian Henkel and Julián Morcillo also observed that state tenders for media producers actually increase job insecurity in the media field because they establish temporary contracts and outsource media production (2013, 57–65). On the whole, the state remains the larger outsourcer of employment in Argentina.

Furthermore, there is another problem in those state arrangements seeking to regulate the contradictions between the state and capital, and between citizens' demands and the state. The menace of *kirchnerismo* is that, *pace* its populism, it would paradoxically be implementing what Marx observes as Bonapartist, authoritarian exits to the structural antagonism between private property and working-class demands.[75] In Marx's account, "Bonapartism" appears as an authoritarian regime aimed at saving both the state and private property from socialist revolution, for which the state undermines bourgeois rights. While that kind of political regime is not analogous with *kirchnerismo* – in 2011, for instance, Cristina Fernández de Kirchner was re-elected with 54 percent of the votes – it is worth noting that some human rights organisations currently denounce coercive deviations in the national government aimed at controlling social protests.[76] Nevertheless, I do want to employ the term Bonapartism in a comparable way when considering the establishment of complex and confusing state ad-hoc arrangements that, despite altering private property contracts, allow the state to continue reproducing both state hegemony and capitalist development. This kind of Bonapartist *fuite en avant* consists in creating what I term grey zones of capitalist activity and state authority. Though they are not illegal, these grey zones are exempt from the democratic control of citizens.[77]

---

74   See http://www.tda.gob.ar/tda/141/16150/bacua.html, Accessed November 23, 2014.
75   In *The Eighteenth Brumaire of Louis Bonaparte* (1978/1852), Marx analysed the rise to power of Louis Napoleón Bonaparte in France during 1848 and 1852. Marx observed that Bonaparte accumulated power in the Executive at expense of civil society and the political representatives of the bourgeoisie yet protected the material interests of the bourgeoisie in confusedly implementing capitalist development. See David Held (1991, 147–150).
76   The most controversial issue is the government's newly approved legislation on terrorism. According to the Coordinadora Contra la Represión Policial e Institucional (CORREPI, Organisation Against Police and Institutional Repression) the state could use the new legislation to repress social protests and labour strikes (CORREPI 2011).
77   I develop this idea from Javier Auyero's concept of gray zone (2007), inspired in Primo Levi's work. Auyero explained the social relationships linking political cadres, political brokers, police forces, and food rioters in Argentina. He clarified the clandestine connections between routine politics, collective violence and everyday life.

A case in point in the media field is the television programme *Fútbol Para Todos* (Football for Everybody); football is the most popular sport in Argentina and a marker of national identity. In 2009 Cristina Fernández de Kirchner's government suddenly agreed with the Association of Football Clubs (AFA) to broadcast the football league's matches in exchange for a significant sum, paid for by taxpayers and apparently distributed to football clubs. AFA broke its contract with TyC/Cablevisión and televised football events were put under state administration. As a result, the state television channel (TV Pública) now broadcasts free football events to citizens, while previously TyC/Cablevisión only delivered them to its subscribers. *Fútbol Para Todos* has thus been an important populist-democratic move for *kirchnerismo*, which claims to have recovered the goals that the private media had "kidnapped" – a pun on the military junta's crimes. And yet, behind the screen of the state television channel, a media company, which competes to accumulate capital to enter the global media market, produces *Fútbol Para Todos*, according to press information.[78] Another case in point is the firm AR-SAT (Empresa Argentina de Soluciones Satelitales S.A.), created by the federal government to establish the digital television system (TDA/TDT), provide telecommunication and satellite-based services, and develop a fiber-optic network to link the entire territory and the state administration (Law 26,092/2006). This is an impressive and satisfactory achievement. If we look at the legal status of the firm, however, we find that is an anonymous society controlled by the Ministerio de Planificación (Ministry of Planning) as principal shareholder (Law 26,092/2006, Decree 634/2010) and administered by the Autoridad Federal de Tecnologías de la Información y las Comunicaciones (Federal Authority on Information Technology and Communications, Law 27,078), but there is no press information on the rest of the shares.

Thus, in examining all the aspects of the recent media policy, I believe that the frontier between state and private capital is therefore obscure or, at the very least, needs more clarification. This kind of opaque business-state association is visible in other problematic areas – for instance, in the government's manipulation of official statistics on inflation, which benefits some financial retributions on government bonds at the expense of others; in the government's support of

---

78   Of course, this production is nevertheless legal. See, for example, the press report of El Cronista on January 13, 2012: "La productora preferida de la familia Kirchner desembarcó en Europa" (http://www.cronista.com/contenidos/2012/01/13/noticia_0037.html, accessed on February 1, 2012), and the press report of La Nación, "El gobierno adjudicó a La Corte un millonario contrato por el fútbol" on April 24, 2014 (http://www.lanacion.com .ar/1684674-el-gobierno-adjudico-a-la-corte-un-millonario-contrato-por-el-futbol, accessed on November 3, 2014).

Northern mining companies extracting natural resources through open-mining pits that are resisted by communities and ecological movements (Svampa and Antonelli 2009); and in the government's agreement with Northern oil companies, which includes so-called "confidential clauses" (Roveri 2014), to extract gas and oil from the soil by employing the controversial method of hydraulic fracturing (*fracking*). Other grey areas include the facilities that corporations have utilised to export capital between 2003 and 2012, the subsidies that the state grants to inefficient railway companies, the government's use of state pension funds to finance capital and the state treasury, and the government's directing state advertising toward media groups apparently sharing an affinity with the official political line.[79] In short, the ideological, ambivalent mechanism of contemporary Bonapartism consists in establishing moderate legal regulations to contain citizens' demands for democratisation in some areas, while at the same time eroding other legal regulations to benefit the state bureaucracy and the trans-national capitalist class.

5   Conclusion

As Alex Callinicos observes in his reading of Lenin and Daniel Bensaïd (Lenin 1965; Bensaïd 2004), for Marxism it is crucial to consider the specificity of the political field as a play of transfigured powers through which the totality of social antagonisms, contradictions, and struggles are translated into new languages, displaced, or condensed (Callinicos 2012). Marx refers to this political practice when, questioning state power, he mocks the self-deceiving costumes with which politicians wish to conceal from their own view the limitations of the content of their practices (1978/1852, 598). Argentina is not an exemption: from time to time state actors change, and the drama varies according to the political repertoires the state seems cyclically to repeat in distinct ways – nationalist authoritarianism, economic liberalism, and different forms of populist discourse. My argument is that those ideological forms, or modes of

---

79   On the government's manipulation of state statistics see the declaration from the group of public university economists Plan Fénix on the right to information (Plan Fénix 2012). On the increase of subsidies to railway companies see Mario Damill and Roberto Frenkel (2009, 64). On the apparently unequal distribution of governmental advertising among media groups see, for instance, the following information from newspaper Perfil on September 5, 2010: "Pauta oficial: aumenta la brecha entre medios oficialistas y críticos" (http://www.diarioperfil.com.ar/edimp/0501/articulo.php?art=24047&ed=0501, accessed on January 15, 2012).

political construction, are destined to conceal the central structural contradiction of the state as an institution that must represent the general and national interests of citizens while reproducing a transnational capitalist process that – centred on the global North – increases misery in Argentina and therefore the resistance of citizens and workers to the state and capital. This is rendered all the more evident in the periods that Gramsci terms organic crises, as in the 1970s and partially in the early 2000s. In this sense, *kirchnerismo* has been successful up until now in countering the crisis in state hegemony that erupted in 2001–2002. This dialectic approach to the state is complementary to Marxist works that consider the subjective connections of political cadres to the dominant economic class (Miliband 1969), or, more importantly, the structural role of the state in organising capitalist reproduction (Poulantzas 1969; 1973) – a perspective I also employed.

Further, considering the state ideological forms mentioned above, I argue the media sphere is a basal field through which the state aims to cloak its central contradiction. This field is an arena of political struggle, except when dictatorial regimes completely substitute coercion for hegemony. That is, I emphasise that political regimes and governments in Argentina have attempted to repress, conceal, integrate, or displace in different ways the social antagonisms connected to the capitalist crises and political convulsions of the 1970s and the late 1990s. As I demonstrated, the nationalist-authoritarian media regulations established by the military junta, the neoliberal administration of the media by Menem's government, and the idiosyncratic project of populist discourse, partial democratic reforms, national promotion with some degree of state economic intervention, and transnational capitalist reproduction of *kirchnerismo* are regulatory and ideologically distinct. The ideology of media policy in the capitalist state consists in its denial or regulation of the antagonisms between workers and capital, and citizens and the state. Yet every ideology is a historical form with different impacts on the social classes that introduce distinct material conditions for political action. In my view, we need to assess these conditions dialectically to avoid establishing mechanistic relationships between class domination, political life and media transformations. This approach entails observing how every state ideological form relates to previous contradictions and is contradictory in particular ways: the dictatorship restrained capital forces in the media while repressing dissent to favour capitalist interests, and Menem's government opened the way to mass dissatisfaction when its market allures of wealth were not translated into the daily-life of workers. Similarly, *kirchnerismo* could see its own regulations evaporate if the popular-democratic demands it partially addressed surpass the letter of its media reform, its manoeuvres to accommodate workers to transnational capital, and its dubious, grey zones of capitalist interests and state authority.

References

AFSCA. 2014a. *5 Años de Políticas en Comunicación Audiovisual*. Buenos Aires: Autoridad Federal de Servicios de Comunicación Audiovisual. Accessed November 23, 2014. http://www.afsca.gob.ar/Varios/pdf/5-anios-de-politicas-comunicacionales-agosto_2014.pdf.

AFSCA. 2014b. *Ley de Servicios de Comuncación Audiovisual. Propuestas Presentadas Formalmente*. Buenos Aires: Autoridad Federal de Servicios de Comunicación Audiovisual. Accessed November 23, 2014. http://www.afsca.gob.ar/wp-content/uploads/2012/12/Adecuaciones_presentadas.pdf.

Althusser, Louis. 2001/1970. Ideology and Ideological State Apparatus: Notes for an Investigation. In *Lenin and Philosophy and Other Essays*, edited by Louis Althusser, 85–126. New York: Monthly Review Press.

ANSES. 2011. *Fondo de Garantía de Sustentabilidad del Sistema Integrado Previsional Argentino, Informe Mensual Octubre*. Buenos Aires: ANSES. Accessed February 10, 2012. http://www.anses.gob.ar/FGS/politicastransparencia/archivos/informes/Boletin_FGS_11_2011.pdf.

Artz, Lee and Yahya R. Kamalipour, eds. 2003. *The Globalization of Corporate Media Hegemony*. Albany: State University of New York Press.

Artz, Lee, Macek, Steve, and Dana L. Cloud, eds. 2006. *Marxism and Communication Studies: The Point is to Change It*. New York: Peter Lang.

Auyero, Javier. 2007. *Routine Politics and Violence in Argentina: The Gray Zone of State Power*. Cambridge: Cambridge University Press.

Baranchuk, Mariana, and Javier Rodríguez Usé, eds. 2011. *Ley 26.522: Hacia un Nuevo Paradigma en Comunicación Audiovisual*. Buenos Aires: AFSCA and Universidad Nacional de Lomas de Zamora.

Barthes, Roland. 1972/1957. *Mythologies*. New York: Hill and Wang.

Bensaïd, Daniel. 2004. *Une Lente Impatience*. Paris: Stock.

Beverley, John. 2011. *Latinamericanism After 9/11*. Durham: Duke University Press.

Brennan, James P., and Marcelo Rougier. 2009. *The Politics of National Capitalism: Peronism and the Argentine Bourgeoisie, 1946–1976*. University Park: University of Pennsylvania Press.

Busso, Néstor, and Diego Jaimes, eds. 2011. *La Cocina de la Ley: El Proceso de Incidencia en la Elaboración de la Ley de Servicios de Comunicación Audiovisual en Argentina*. Buenos Aires: FARCO.

Calcagno, Alfredo Eric. 1988. *La Perversa Deuda*. Buenos Aires: Legasa.

Callinicos, Alex. 2012. The Crisis Wears On. *International Socialism: A Quarterly Journal of Socialist Theory* (133). Accessed February 1, 2012. http://www.isj.org.uk/index .php4?id=773&issue=133.

Cano, Fernando. 2011. Dudas Argentinas. *El País*, October 30. Accessed February 27, 2012. http://elpais.com/diario/2011/10/30/negocio/1319979149_850215.html.

Castagno, Pablo. 2010. *"The State Crisis in Argentina: Global Fantasies and National Containment."* PhD diss., George Mason University.

Castagno, Pablo. 2014a. Symbolic Economies: Money, Neoliberal Law and National Politics in Argentina. *Cultural Studies and/of the Law.* A Special Issue of the *Cultural Studies* Journal, 28 (5–6), edited by Jaafar Aksikas and Sean Johnson Andrews, 809–843. London: Routledge.

Castagno, Pablo. 2014b. Primer Mundo. In *Diccionario del Léxico Corriente de la Política Argentina. Palabras en Democracia (1983–2013),* edited by Andreína Adelstein and Gabriel Vommaro, 299–302. Los Polvorines: Universidad Nacional de General Sarmiento.

Castells, Manuel. 2000. *The Rise of the Network Society.* Oxford: Blackwell.

CEPAL. 2002. *La Inversión Extranjera en América Latina y el Caribe.* Santiago de Chile: Naciones Unidas.

Chudnovsky, Daniel, and Andrés López. 2001. *La Transnacionalización de la Economía Argentina.* Buenos Aires: EUDEBA/CENIT.

CIFRA. 2013. *Informe de Coyuntura Nª 12.* Buenos Aires: Centro de Investigación y Formación de la República Argentina-Central de Trabajadores de la Argentina.

Coalición por una Radiodifusión Democrática. 2011. 21 Puntos Básicos por el Derecho a la Comunicación. *In La Cocina de la Ley: El Proceso de Incidencia en la Elaboración de la Ley de Servicios de Comunicación Audiovisual en Argentina,* edited by Néstor Busso and Diego Jaimes, 155–161. Buenos Aires: FARCO.

CONADEP. 2003. *Nunca Más: Informe de la Comisión Nacional sobre la Desaparición de Personas.* Buenos Aires: CONADEP.

COORDECAAP. 2011. Comunicado de Prensa ¿Qué Está Concursando AFSCA? Buenos Aires: CoorDeCAAP. Accessed January 15, 2012. http://argentina.indymedia.org/ news/2011/11/799065.php.

CORREPI. 2011. Comunicado de Prensa: Leyes Antiterroristas. Buenos Aires: CORREPI. Accessed January 15, 2012. http://correpi.lahaine.org/?p=1103.

Crawford, Margaret. 1992. The World in a Shopping Mall. In *Variations on a Theme Park: The New American City and the End of Public Space,* edited by Michael Sorkin, 3–30. New York: Hill and Wang.

Damill, Mario and Roberto Frenkel. 2009. Las Políticas Macroeconómicas en la Evolución Reciente de la Economía Argentina. *Seminarios de Economía N° 112.* Banco Central de la República Argentina. Accessed February 28, 2012. http://www .bcra.gov.ar/pdfs/investigaciones/PaperFrenkel_Damill.pdf.

De Santis, Juan Pablo. 2012. Daniel Vila: Los Medios Mensajeros de la Ideología Tienen Una Pauta Importante. *La Nación*, February 2. Accessed February 7, 2012. http://www.lanacion.com.ar/1444898-daniel-vila-queremos-un-desguace-de-cablevision-y-multicanal.

Duménil, Gérard, and Dominique Lévy. 2004. *Capital Resurgent: Roots of the Neoliberal Revolution*. Cambridge: Harvard University Press.

FARCO. 2009. *Nueva Ley de Medios Audiovisuales: Desafíos Para los Medios Comunitarios y Populares*. Buenos Aires: FARCO.

Faro TV et al. 2011. Carta a AFSCA: Televisión Digital ¿Para quién es la democratización? Accessed February 10, 2012. http://argentina.indymedia.org/news/2011/07/788002.php.

Fuchs, Christian. 2009. Some Theoretical Foundations of Critical Media Studies: Karl Marx and the Media. *International Journal of Communication* 3: 369–402.

Fuchs, Christian. 2011. *Foundations of Critical Media and Information Studies*. New York: Routledge.

Garnham, Nicholas. 1979. Contribution to a Political Economy of Mass Communication. *Media, Culture & Society* 1 (2): 122–146.

Giuliano, Héctor. 2014. Deuda Pública y Presupuesto 2015. *ACTA: La Agencia de Noticias de la CTA*. Accessed November 15, 2014. http://www.agenciacta.org/spip.php?article13426.

Gramsci, Antonio. 2000. *The Antonio Gramsci Reader: Selected Writings 1916–1935*. New York: New York University Press.

Graña, Juan M., and Damián Kennedy. 2008. Salario Real, Costo Laboral y Productividad, Argentina 1947–2006. *Documentos de Trabajo 12*. Buenos Aires: Centro de Estudios sobre Población, Empleo y Desarrollo. Accessed January 10, 2012. http://www.econ.uba.ar/www/institutos/economia/Ceped/publicaciones/dts/DT%2012%20-%20Grana%20Kennedy.pdf.

Hackett, Robert A. and Yuezhi Zhao, eds. 2005. *Democratizing Global Media: One World, Many Struggles*. Lanham: Rowman and Littlefield.

Harman, Chris. 2009. *Zombie Capitalism: Global Crisis and the Relevance of Marx*. London: Bookmarks Publications.

Harvey, David. 1991. *The Condition of Postmodernity: An Inquiry into the Origins of Cultural Change*. Oxford: Blackwell.

Held, David. 1991. *Modelos de Democracia*. Madrid: Alianza Editorial.

International Commission for the Study of Communication Problems. 1980. *Many Voices, One World: Towards a New More Just and More Efficient World Information and Communication Order*. London: Kogan Page.

Henkel, Cristian, and Julián Morcillo. 2013. *La Palabra Liberada: Una Crítica Marxista a la Ley de Medios*. Buenos Aires: Eudeba.

Horkheimer, Max. 1989/1932. Notes on Science and the Crisis. In *Critical Theory and Society: A Reader,* edited by Stephen E. Bronner and Douglas M. Kellner, 52–57. New York: Routledge.

Krakowiak, Fernando. 2013. Con Luz Verde Para Transmitir. *Página/12*, June 2. Accessed November 15, 2014. http://www.pagina12.com.ar/diario/elpais/1-221367-2013-06-02 .html.

Laboratorio de Industrias Culturales. 2011. *Una Aproximación a las Industrias Culturales.* Buenos Aires: Secretaría de Cultura. Accessed January 15, 2012. http://lic.cultura.gov .ar./investigaciones/industrias/index.php.

Laclau, Ernesto. 1978. *Política e Ideología en la Teoría Marxista: Capitalismo, Fascismo, Populismo.* Madrid: Siglo XXI Editores. English version: Laclau, Ernesto. 1977/2012. *Politics and Ideology in Marxist Theory: Capitalism, Fascism, Populism.* London: Verso.

Laclau, Ernesto. 2009. *La Razón Populista.* Buenos Aires: Fondo de Cultura Económica. English version: Laclau, Ernesto. 2005. *On Populist Reason.* London: Verso.

Lenin, Vladimir I. 1965. *Collected Works, Volume 32.* Moscow: Foreign Languages Publishing House.

Lozano, Claudio. 2005. Los Problemas de la Distribución del Ingreso y el Crecimiento en la Argentina Actual. Buenos Aires: Instituto de Estudios y Formación de la Central de Trabajadores Argentinos.

Lukács, Georg. 2000/1923. *History and Class Consciousness: Studies in Marxist Dialectics.* Cambridge: The MIT Press.

Marx, Karl. 1978a. The Eighteenth Brumaire of Louis Bonaparte. In *The Marx-Engels Reader*, edited by Robert C. Tucker, 594–617. New York: W. W. Norton & Company.

Marx, Karl. 1978b. Capital, Volume One. In *The Marx-Engels Reader*, edited by Robert C. Tucker, 294–438. New York: W. W. Norton & Company.

Marx, Karl. 1978c. Crisis Theory. In *The Marx-Engels Reader*, edited by Robert C. Tucker, 443–465. New York: W. W. Norton & Company.

Marx, Karl. 1990/1867. *Capital: A Critique of Political Economy: Volume I.* London: Penguin Books.

Marx, Karl. 1991/1894. *Capital Volume III.* London: Penguin Books.

Marx, Karl. 1992/1885. *Capital Volume II.* London: Penguin Books.

Marx, Karl. 1998/1845. Theses on Feuerbach. In *GermanThe Ideology*, edited by Karl Marx and Friedrich Engels, 572–574. Amherst: Prometheus.

Marx, Karl, and Friedrich Engels. 1978/1848. Manifesto of the Communist Party. In *The Marx-Engels Reader*, edited by Robert C. Tucker, 469–500. New York: W. W. Norton & Company.

Marx, Karl, and Friedrich Engels. 1998/1846. *The German Ideology.* Amherst: Prometheus.

Mattelart, Armand and Seth Siegelaub, eds. 1979. *Communication and Class Struggle. Vol. 1: Capitalism, Imperialism.* New York: International General.

McChesney, Robert W. 2007. *Communication Revolution: Critical Junctures and the Future of Media.* New York: The New Press.

McNally, David. 2011. *Global Slump: The Economics and Politics of Crisis and Resistance.* Oakland: PM Press.

Miliband, Ralph. 1969. *The State in Capitalist Society.* New York: Basic Books.

Mosco, Vincent. 2010. *The Political Economy of Communication.* London: Sage Publications.

Murdock, Graham and Peter Golding. 1973. For a Political Economy of Mass Communications. *The Socialist Register* 10: 205–234.

Observatorio de la Deuda Social Argentina. 2014. Comunicado de Prensa: Estimaciones de Tasas de Indigencia y Pobreza (2010–2013). Totales Urbanos. Informe Final/ Abril 2014. Buenos Aires: Pontificia Universidad Católica Argentina.

O'Donnell, Guillermo. 1984. Democracia en la Argentina Micro y Macro. In *Proceso, Crisis y Transición Democrática*, edited by Oscar Oszlack, 13–30. Buenos Aires: Centro Editor de América Latina.

O'Donnell, Guillermo. 1988. *Bureaucratic Authoritarianism: Argentina, 1966–1973, in Comparative Perspective.* Berkeley: University of California Press.

Oficina de la CEPAL en Buenos Aires. 2010. *Evolución de la Desocupación en Algunas Áreas Urbanas.* Buenos Aires: CEPAL. Accessed January 21, 2012. http://www.cepal .org/cgi-bin/getprod.asp?xml=/argentina/noticias/paginas/9/9839/P9839 .xml&xsl=/argentina/tpl/p18f.xsl&base=/argentina/tpl/top-bottom.xsl.

Oficina Nacional de Crédito Público. 2012. *Deuda del Estado Argentino. Datos al 30-6-2012.* Buenos Aires: Ministerio de Economía. Accessed November 15, 2014. http:// www.mecon.gov.ar/wpcontent/uploads/2012/11/informe_deuda_publica_30-06-12-nuevo.pdf.

Plan Fénix. 2012. Derecho a la Información. *Página/12*, February 14. Accessed February 14, 2012. http://www.pagina12.com.ar/diario/economia/2-187536-2012-02-14.html.

Portantiero, Juan Carlos. 1974. Dominant Classes and Political Crisis in Argentina Today. *Latin American Perspectives* 1 (3): 93–120.

Portantiero, Juan Carlos. 1977. Economía y Política en la Crisis Argentina: 1958–1973. *Revista Mexicana de Sociología* 39 (2): 531–565.

Poulantzas, Nicos. 1969. The Problem of the Capitalist State. *New Left Review* (58): 67–78.

Poulantzas, Nicos. 1973. *Political Power and Social Classes.* London: New Left Books.

Pousadela, Inés M. 2008. Participation Vs. Representation? The Experience of the Neighborhood Assemblies of Buenos Aires. In *Democratic Innovation in the South: Participation and Representation in Asia, Africa and Latin America,* edited by Ciska Raventós, 71–122. Buenos Aires: Consejo Latinoamericano de Ciencias Sociales.

Rapoport, Mario. 2003. *Historia Económica, Política, y Social de Argentina.* Buenos Aires: Ediciones Macchi.

Roveri, Nicolás. 2014. Los Acuerdos "Confidenciales" de YPF Chevron. *Prensa Obrera,* N° 1340.

Sarlo, Beatriz. 1994. *Escenas de la Vida Postmoderna: Intelectuales, Arte, y Videocultura en la Argentina*. Buenos Aires: Ariel.

Schiller, Herbert I. 1992/1969. *Mass Communication and American Empire*. Boston: Beacon Press.

Shaikh, Anwar. 1991. Centralization and Concentration of Capital. In *A Dictionary of Marxist Thought*, edited by Tom Bottomore. 76–77. Oxford: Blackwell Publishing.

Smith, Paul. 1997. *Millennial Dreams: Contemporary Culture and Capital in the North*. London: Verso.

Smythe, Dallas W. 1977. Communications: Blindspot of Western Marxism. *Canadian Journal of Political and Social Theory* 1 (3): 1–27.

Solanas, Fernando. 2004. *Memoria del Saqueo*. Directed by Fernando Solanas. Buenos Aires: Cinesur S.A., ADR Productions, Thelma Film AG.

Solano, Gabriel. 2014. Gobiernan para Telefónica y Telecom. *Prensa Obrera*, N° 1339.

Sourrouille, Juan Vital et al. 1985. *Transnacionalización y Política Económica en la Argentina*. Buenos Aires: CET.

Svampa, Maristella, and Mirta A. Antonelli, eds. 2009. *Minería Transnacional, Narrativas del Desarrollo y Resistencias Sociales*. Buenos Aires: Biblos.

Svampa, Maristella, and Sebastián Pereyra. 2003. *Entre la Ruta y el Barrio: La Experiencia de las Organizaciones Piqueteras*. Buenos Aires: Editorial Biblos.

The World Bank. 2014. Data. Accessed November 13, 2014. http://data.worldbank.org/indicator/NY.GDP.MKTP.KD.ZG.

UNESCO. 2002. *Declaration Universelle de L'unesco sur la Diversite Culturelle*. Paris: UNESCO.

Verbitsky, Héctor. 1991. *Robo Para la Corona: Los Frutos Prohibidos del Árbol de la Corrupción*. Buenos Aires: Planeta.

Wayne, Mike. 2003. *Marxism and Media Studies: Key Concepts and Contemporary Trends*. London: Pluto Press.

Werner, Ruth, and Facundo Aguirre. 2009. Insurgencia Obrera en la Argentina 1969–1976: Clasismo, Coordinadoras Interfabriles y Estrategias de la Izquierda. Buenos Aires: Ediciones IPS.

CHAPTER 16

"Means of Communication as Means of Production" Revisited*

William Henning James Hebblewhite

1   Introduction

In this Chapter I attempt to analyze and critique the assertion made by Raymond Williamsthat means of communication can be understood as a means of production. I seek to do this in the context of a critical enquiry of Williams' paper *Means of Communication as a Means of Production* (2005[1978]). It will be my thesis that Williams work opens up new possibilities in *new communications* theory. However I contend that despite opening up these possibilities, Williams' own theory is unable to develop these possibilities to their ultimate conclusion and we must turn towards Althusser's structural Marxism to assist in such development. The essay itself will be structured in three main sections. In the first section I'll outline Marx's definition of the means of production and how he viewed the means of communication as a form of the relations of production. I will also discuss Marx's base-superstructure and what defining the means of communication as the relations of production does for this understanding of society. In the second section I'll outline Raymond Williams' argument for identifying the means of communication as a means of production, drawing on the workprovided by Williams over his career, I'll argue that while Williams offers an interesting proposition, his argument is based on a definition of terms like 'production', which reduce their capability to express what the explicit means of production are. I'll argue that while Williams' wants to insist that production is beyond that of just 'commodity production', the use of communications now is one in which the information provided by the means of communication is treated like a commodity. In the last section, I want to examine how elements of Althusser's philosophy can produce the theoretical intervention necessary to examine the the internet as a means of communication identified as 'means of production'

* The author would like to acknowledge the help of Lachlan Doughney who inspired the idea for this chapter and to Aaron Harrison and Brook Novak who were not only supportive while researching and completing drafts of this chapter, but offered excellent feedback throughout its process.

which produces 'information as a commodity'. The aim of this chapter is two-fold. To develop a foundation for the continued analysis of the means of communication such as the Internet, in the vein of Marxist theory and, to attempt to overcome the criticisms of structuralism that are contained in Raymond Williams' work.

2   Karl Marx and the Means of Production

The *Preface* to *a Contribution to the Critique of Political Economy* (Marx 1994) has often played the role of the rosetta stone in helping interpret much of Marx's work. In this rather short text it is one passage that has garnered the most attention:

> In the social production of their existence, men inevitably enter into definite relations, which are independent of their will, namely relations of production appropriate to a give stage in the development of their material forces of production. The totality of these relations of production constitutes the economic structure of society, the real foundation, on which arises a legal and political superstructure to which correspond definite forms of social consciousness. The mode of production of material life conditions the general process of social, political and intellectual life. It is not the consciousness of men that determines their existence, but their social existence that determines their consciousness. At a certain stage of development, the material productive forces of society come into conflict with the existing relations of production or – this merely expresses the same thing in legal terms – with the property relations within the framework of which they have operated hitherto. From forms of development of the productive forces these relations turn into their fetters. Then begins an era of social revolution. The changes in the economic foundation lead sooner or later to the transformation of the whole immense superstructure. In studying such transformations it is always necessary to distinguish between the material transformation of the economic conditions of production, which can be determined with the precision of natural science, and the legal, political, religious, artistic or philosophic – in short, ideological forms in which men become conscious of this conflict and fight it out. Just as one does not judge an individual by what he thinks about himself, so one cannot judge such a period of transformation by its consciousness, but, on the contrary, this consciousness must be explained from the contradictions of material life, from the

conflict existing between the social forces of production and the relations of production. No social formation is ever destroyed before all the
productive forces for which it is sufficient have been developed, and new
superior relations of production never replace older ones before the
material conditions for their existence have matured within the framework of old society. Mankind thus inevitably sets itself only such tasks as
it is able to solve, since close examination will always show that the problem itself arises only when the material conditions for its solution are
already present or at least in the course of formation.

MARX 1994, 211

The passage itself is rich with information that can help guide our understanding of the *means of production*. Beginning with the idea that "the totality of relations of production constitute the economic structure of society...on which
arises a legal and political superstructure" (Marx 1990, 211),which outlines the
hotly contested idea of the base-superstructure thesis, to the idea that "at a certain stage of development; the material productive forces of society come into
conflict with the existing relations of production" (ibid.). The passage in the
Preface provides an excellent entry point by which to formulate an understanding of the *means of production*. It is these two important segments from the passage of the preface that concern us in this chapter. If Raymond Williams' proposal
that the means of communication are a means of production then this would
necessitate a rethinking of society's structure, or would it? In order to understand the problem, we need to first be able to understand the elements that are
used in constructing the problem. The main elements, as we see in the title of
Williams essay, are: 1.) The *means of communication* and 2.) the *means of production*. It may bemay argued that the title of the essay *Means of Communication as
a Means of Production* identifies the means of production as a larger category
than the means of communication, that the means of communication become
just a subcategory of the means of production. Seem in this way it is then necessary, that if we are to identify the means of communication as a means of production, to come to an understanding of what the means of production are.

In Marx's work, the means of production refers to two elements of production, instruments of labour and raw materialis, that when entering into a labour
process becomes a unified productive force. According to the account of *historical materialism* that is outlined in the passage above that these elements, the
instruments of labour and the raw materials are then an aspect, in their development, of the conflict that arises between the productive forces and the relative
production. As such they play a role in defining the social structure... For Marx
"an instrument of labour, is a thing, or a complex of things, which the worker

interposes between himself and the object of his labour and which serves as a conductor, directing his activity onto that object" (Marx 1990, 285). While there is debate surrounding the actual means of production and what can and cannot be understood by them, G.A. Cohen (2000) argues that such things as strength, skills, knowledge, and intelligence are not an aspect of either raw materials or instruments of labour but that they are in effect a means of the labour process. The ambiguity of terms such as *means of production* and *instruments of labour* allow for discrepancies in how one describes such elements of the productive process. It seems then that what an instrument of labour is, according to such a definition, is an instrument such as a hammer, or even a factory, anything which focuses activity on an object of labour. Despite the broadness of such a concept, it become even broader when we take into account Marx's assertion that "we may include among the instruments of labour...all the objective conditions necessary for carrying on the labour process" (Marx 1990, 286).

We can, I believe, infer then that included in the instruments of labour are the raw materials and objects of labour. We must also be careful about the conflation of the raw materials with the objects of labour. While all raw materials are objects of labour, it cannot be said that all objects of labour are raw materials. In Marx's sense raw materials are only to be understood as raw materials if they have already passed through the labour process (Marx 1990). It is then possible to assert that a plank of wood is a raw material, while a tree standing in the forest is a natural resource. The difference between them is that the plank of wood has been worked on already by instruments of labour to turn it into such a product. According to what I've said above, the instruments of labour can be understood as the totality of the means of production. This is because for Marx any form, which provides the objective conditions for carrying out labour, is an instrument of labour. Seeing as such that the object of labour is needed for labour to take place, we can infer then that an object of labour is an instrument of labour, which is worked on by other instruments of labour to produce a product for consumption. We may perhaps say then that, the means of production are nothing more then the instruments of labour. Considering that the productive forces are the unity between the labour process and the means of production, it is the attribution of 'work' to the instruments of labour that unifies them as productive forces.

3   Marx and the Means of Communication as a Means of Production

How does this pertain to our discussion that the means of communication are a means of production? If we are to interpret the *means of production* as an *instrument of labour* which is a necessary condition of the labour process, then we must provide evidence that the *means of communication* are an *instrument of labour* and that the *means of communication as a means of production* provide a necessary condition for the labour process.

In *Capital* Vol 1, in the section entitled *Machinery and Large Scale Production*, Marx discusses the relation of the means of production and the means of Communication. He writes briefly that "the revolution in the modes of production of industry and agriculture made necessary a revolution in the general conditions of the social processes of production," these "social processes of production" are what Marx calls the "means of communication" and the "means of transportation" (Marx 1990, 506). When Marx was writing, these forms of *social processes of production* could be seen actualized in the telegraph and railroad systems. However, Marx does not often speak of the "means of communication" apart from the times he speaks of the means of transportation. In fact it is difficult, at least in the work of *Capital,* to evaluate any discernible differences between what Marx calls the means of communication and the means of transportation. This is given strength by comments that Marx makes in Vol. 11 of *Capital* in asserting the non-commodificatory aspects of the communication industry "for moving commodities and people and the transmission of mere information" (Marx 1992 134). If we follow Marx, can we not then ascertain, from the Preface to *The Contribution of a Critique of Political Economy* that the means of communication are a form of relations of production for Marx? By the relations of production we may understand the totality of the social relationships that promote production and reproduction of the means of life. We see this in the *Preface* where Marx writes that "in the social production of their existence, men inevitably enter into definite relations, which are independent of their will, namely relations of production appropriate to a given stage in the development of their material forces of production"(Marx 1994, 211).

In the sense that we attribute the means of communication as relations of production we refer to the social relations of production, thus understood as the socio-economic relations that constitute the social structure of society. What we see here is the necessary foundations between the material productive forces (instruments of labour + labour) and the social relations of production (the means of communication and transportation). It is easy to recognize the means of communication as relations of production in exactly the way Marx has set it out. What we see in Vol 2. of *Capital* is another type of distancing, in which the communications industry is signaled out as an important branch of industry, along with the transport industry, "in which the product of the production process is not a new objective product" (Marx 1992 134). For Marx, both the transport industry and the communications industry do not produce new products, but only "displace people and things" (Marx 1992 135). It is well documented in *Capital,* as shown above, that for Marx the means of communication were closer in structure and process to the means of transportation then they were to the means of production, and even developed in the same way when revolutionized (Marx 1990, 506). What is remarkable and in need of further discussion is that in the revolution of the means of transportation and the means of communication they become fetters upon the large-industry manufacturers (which we may understand as productive forces). According to Marx, at a stage in the development of the material forces of production the social relations of production block (or fetter) any further development. At this stage, social revolution takes place which revolutionizes the relations of production allowing for further development of the productive forces. Of course if Marx argues that the means of communication are a relation of production, then at some stage we must confront a contradiction between what Marx says about the means of communication and what Raymond Williams says. In the next sections I will look at Raymond Williams' Cultural Materialism as a proposal of society's structure against Marx's historical materialism and argue that it is the emphasis on culture rather then the economic in Williams' works that allows him to identify the means of communication as a means of production.

But we must recognize a difference between the tangible nature of goods and the intangible nature of "communication." At one level, there exists a form of communication between the producers and the suppliers; at another level between workers and managers. There is also a level of communication that exists between the consumer and the producer. We must then recognize a distinction between *mass communication* and *localized communication.* The distinction between *mass* and *localized* is never made in Marx's work; the type of communication that is discussed in the work of Marx is ultimately related to that of mass communication. This is communication that appears on a grand scale in the productive process. We can say that *localized communication* is a sub-domain of *mass communication.* Without the effects of *localized communication,* or the manager telling the workers what to do, then there would be no effective *mass communication* or the dispersal of information from the workers as producers of a certain product, to various other groups including suppliers and consumers.

4   Williams on Base and Superstructure

In the exposition of Williams' discussion on the base and superstructure, we find the focus is on specific keywords that formulate the discourse. We are confronted in Williams work with a detailed discussion of *production,*

determination, base and *superstructure*. It is Williams's position that the base
and superstructural construction of society originally formulated by Marx has
been misconstrued by thinkers throughout the generations due in part to a
misunderstanding of Marx's use of particular forms of language. It was an
aspect of Williams's method to study the language of individual thinkers rather
then the abstractions that they posed (Eldridge and Eldridge 1994). As he
writes in *Marxism and Literature* (1977): "In the transition of Marx to Marxism,
and then in the development of expository and didactic formulations, the
words used in the original arguments were projected...as if they were precise
concepts, and...as if they were terms for observable 'areas' of social life"
(Williams 1977, 77). For Williams the description that Marx posed of the base
and superstructure edifice is no more than an analogy (Williams 1993); a linguistic expression of the structure of society which does not adequately por-
tray society. Such an expression merely provides a simplified variation of what
society is actually like. The letter to J. Bloch written by Engels in 1890 provides
grounds, for Williams, which lessen the usefulness of the formula of the base-
superstructure that Marx used (Williams, 1993). Of the formula provided by
Marx, Williams turns to a passage in *The Eighteenth Brumaire* to show that
Marx asserted rationalism to the superstructure which Williams's states
increased the complexity of the formula. He writes of this that "recognition of
complexity is the first control in any valid attempt at a Marxist theory of culture. The second control...is an understanding of the formula of structure and
superstructure" (Williams 1993). In the letter that Engels writes to Bloch, Engels
argues that any statement which reduces the social structure to the determined effect of the economic base has misconstrued what Marx and himself
meant and that any such reduction becomes "meaningless, abstract and
absurd...." (Engels 1890). Engels writes further that "the economic situation is
the basis, but the various elements of the superstructure...also exercise their
influence upon the course of the historical struggles and in many cases preponderate in determining their form" (Engels 1890, 475). Building from this,
Williams argues that Engels provides the complexity of the social structure,
which is needed in the development of a Marxist theory of culture and shows
Marx's formula to be just an analogy, in reality the structure is less absolute and
less clear. Williams does not fully follow Engels approach., He argues that
Engels' model falls into the same problem as Marx's chastising him for failing
to escape the formulaic approach in terms of levels: "Engels does not so much
revise the enclosed categories...as reiterate the categories and instance certain
exceptions, indrectnesses, and irregularities which obscure their otherwise
regular relation" (Williams 1977, 80). It is possible to argue at this point that
Williams is determined to move away from any Marxian theory of culture

that privileges the economic base over the superstructure. For Williams, "Marx...had correctly stressed the connection between culture and the economy, but had badly mistaken the nature of that connection. Culture and communication were to be understood as primary and not secondary components of the social totality, constitutive and not reflective in the maintenance and development of the social order" (Higgins 1999, 110).

Williams' objection to the base and superstructure analogy of Marxian theory is summed up in this passage which appeared in *Marxism and Literature*. He writes: "The social and political order which maintains a capitalist market, like the social struggles which created it, is necessarily a material production. From castles and palaces and churches to prisons and workhouses and schools; from weapons of war to a controlled press: any ruling class, in variable ways though always materially, produces a social and political order. These are never superstructural activities. They are necessary material production within an apparently self-subsistent mode of production can alone be carried on" (Williams 1977, 93). Of course, it is only logical to conceive of castles, palaces, churches and prisons as material production, despite their "superstructural activities," but we can immediately perceive a deficiency in Williams' argument. While it may be true that the "superstructure" has in the past been seen to be nothing more then a immaterial form of consciousness. This is a rejected claim in contemporary Marxian theory. As Terry Eagleton has pointed out: "there is a strong implication through...Williams' work that to label a phenomenon 'superstructural' is somehow to assign it a lesser degree of effective reality than an element of material production" (Eagleton 1989, 168). It may be perhaps that Williams, like Althusser, had in mind a Hegelian form of causality which expressed the idea that all phenomena of the social totality may be reduced to a particular form of essence. But unlike Althusser, who showed that Marx had moved past the Hegelian influence of his past, Williams' contends that the base-superstructure of the late Marx was still heavily invested in this form of effective causality. In Eagleton's mind all Williams' has done thus far is to re-invent the wheel. His criticism of an outdated model of the base and superstructure is more ritualistic then useful in any theoretical sense (Eagleton 1989). Williams' *Marxism and Literature*, like Althusser's *For Marx* and *Reading Capital* can be seen as "a return to the complex unity of Marx's original insight into the 'indissoluble unity' of the 'whole social process'" (Higgins 1994, 114) It is "the overcoming of the dichotomy between 'society' and 'nature'" (Williams 1977, 19) For Williams instead of the economy as the central concept of society, he has argued that it is culture at the centre "of modern thought and practice" (Williams 1977, 11). The term *culture* thus become a central concern of Williams, evidenced by his attempt to formulate a *Cultural Materialism* (See Williams

1977, 1993) and a *Sociology of Culture* (See Williams 1981). For Williams, "Marx... had correctly stressed the connection between culture and the economy, but had badly mistaken the nature of that connection" (Higgins 1999, 110). It was not that culture was a secondary attribute aligned with the superstructural elements such as the politico-legal, as some Orthodox Marxists were fond of saying, but that "culture and communication were to be understood as primary... components of the social totality" (Higgins 1999, 110). Cultural Materialism is the position that *Culture* should be recognized as both a social and material productive process and practice which identifies "the arts" as social uses of material means of production (Williams 1981). Following on from the German Romanticism of Herder and Coleridge, Williams sort to establish culture "as separate from and yet superior to both economics and politics" (Milner 1994, 45). Is this culturalism, however, not just simply a form of determinism, which privileges culture over economy? A reverse of the formulation of the Orthodox Marxists that Williams criticizes? Not necessarily. Though it appears as such, *determinism* in Williams is a quite specific meaning different from that which he seeks to criticize. The notion of *determination* plays a large role in Williams' work: "no problem in Marxist cultural theory is more difficult than that of 'determination'," he writes in a section of *Marxism and Literature* entirely dedicated to this keyword. He seeks to define determination, not as a "predicted, prefigured, controlled content," but moreso as content which sets the limits and exerts pressure (Williams 2005, 34). This is in keeping with his dislike of the technological determinism that he feels is present in the orthodox Marxist presentation. Once again we must point out a similarity that Williams shares with Louis Althusser. Both thinkers, rather than see determination as a process of control, saw it as a setting of limits. Both to some extent follow the Engelsian description of determination laid out in the letter to Bloch which we discussed above. Williams criticizes what he calls *abstract objectivity* in which the determining process is independent of men's will in the absolute sense that they cannot control it. This is the basis for the position of economism that was widespread in the 2nd International, furthermore Williams thinks this position as a philosophical and political doctrine is worthless (Williams 1977). Economism is rejected by Williams, but despite his words to the contrary, determinism still plays a role in his work. Williams asserts the primacy of culture within the societal structure, culture is no longer superstructural but becomes a basic process along with other determining elements such as the economy and politics. In order to escape from the *cultural determinism* that may be levelled at such a position as Williams, he connects his work with that of Antonio Gramsci, specifically the concept of hegemony. Hegemony in this sense refers to notions of dominance and subordination. This is to say that the dominant element of the societal structure does not "rule" over the other elements, as one might be persuaded to say in the sense of Orthodox Marxism, but that the dominant element necessitates the needs and wants of other elements of society and in those other elements recognizes its own needs and wants. In this sense, for Williams, the cultural, political and economic elements of the societal structure work co-operatively in the construction of society.

Under Williams model, due to theneglected way "material" is used in describing the "base" and "superstructure," the means of communication cannot properly be identified as a means of production. If we were to accept Williams model, then the use of *production* would be broadly defined to such an extent that the Marxian notion of *production in general* would become colloquially used to be defined as any type of *production*. Without a determining base, even one that "in the last instance" is never actually realized. Society becomes an open category, always being redefined. Instead in the following section, I will argue that the means of communication can be adequately identified as a means of production by applying the structural-Marxist formulation of society that was devised by Louis Althusser.

5   Althusser and the Means of Communication as a Means of Production

Unlike Williams, Althusser strongly recommends the model first proposed by Marx in the 1859 *Preface*. However, Althusser also takes into account the reaction by Engels, formulated in a letter to Bloch, to the point that the economy is the primary determinant of the social structure. Louis Althusser's reading of Marx overcomes the determination and economism that Williams also tried to overcome, but the benefit of Althusser's reading is that he does not fall into a deterministic mode of relying on culture as Williams did. Like Williams, Althusser's starting point is the importance of complexity in the Marxian social structure and Engels' letter to Bloch. For Althusser there is still the importance of the base-superstructure edifice, but in following Engels, Althusser argues fro the *relative autonomy* of the superstructural elements, of which the economy only determines in the last instance. Now at a glance this determination in the last instance seems to present an extrapolated version of Marx's determinism. However for Althusser, the type of determinism involved is one of setting limits. This is to say that the economy, in the last instance, determines the elements of the social whole that dominates in the social formation. This is not a fixed absolute, as Williams may contend, the dominant element "varies according to the overdetermination of the contradictions and

their unseen development" (Althusser and Balibar 2009, 357). We are interested in two points that arise from this firstly, the differences between *determination in the last instance* and *structures in dominance* and secondly, the role of
overdetermination. Williams' criticized the notion of *overdetermination* as
being a repetition of the basic error of 'economism' which is that it still relies
on the economy as a primary determinant within the social structure (Williams
1977). However before we get to deep into a discussion about *overdetermination,* we must discuss the difference between "*determination in the last instance*"
and *domination*. The category of *determination in the last instance* first becomes
known in the letter between Engels and Bloch that we have referred to throughout this chapter. Engels writes that "there is an interaction of all...elements in
which, amid all the endless host of accidents (hat is, of things and events
whose inner interconnection is so remote or so impossible of proof that we
can regard it as non-existent, as negligible), the economic movement finally
asserts itself as necessary" (Engels 1890). This is to say that where a causal connection cannot be found in regards to the elements of the social structure, it is
the economic base, which asserts itself as the determining force. Althusser
takes up Engels notion and expands it in regards to the structural reading of
Marx's social structure. One of the expansions that Althusser added to this
form of determination is that the *last instance* is never actually realized
(Althusser 2005). What Althusser is trying to do is apply an applicable form of
causal relation instead of the two past forms of causal relation (i.e. mechanical
and effective) which he sees as containing flaws. For Althusser, structural
forces are at work within social formations. Contained within these social formations are elements of the social structure which interrelate with one another
to determine the effect that the social formation has. This is understood in that
the effects of the social structure are determined not by something that lies
outside the social structure but by the elements of the social structure itself
(Althusser 2008). What Williams and the Orthodox Marxists had in common
was that they conceived of the base structure (whatever it may contain) as a
separate entity from the superstructure. Althusser remedied this by arguing
that the base and superstructure were elements of the same structure and that
it was the interrelationship between these elements that explained the social
structure.

    How does Althusser's structural theory succeed in identifying the means of
communication as a means of production, where Williams's theory failed? In
Williams' theory, as we have shown already, his problem was that he had pre-
supposed that the superstructural was combined of immaterial content that as
such, in arguing for the materiality of the superstructure, attempted to show
that the elements of the superstructure were just as much an aspect of material

production as was economic production. However, no one would disagree that the elements of the superstructure are material and that they themselves produce things. In Althusser's famous essay *Ideology and the Ideological State Apparatus* (1990), he argues for the materiality of ideology, which makes up the elements of the superstructure. For Althusser, "an ideology always exists in an apparatus" (Althusser 1990, 112) and he claims that ideology has a material existence. For Althusser, the notion of material exists in different modalities, which are all rooted in physical existence. So while ideology may not be "material" in the sense that Williams' palaces are material, they still nonetheless exist in a specific material modality. So while we may maintain that *ideology* as an imaginary relation to reality doesn't have material existence, Althusser wants to argue that the realization of these beliefs in action and practices confirm their materiality. We have certain relations to the real that require us to partake in certain practices within the material ideological apparatus. These practices can then be confirmed as the material existence of our ideological beliefs. In this sense the superstructure pertains to be a material structure. The practices of the social, legal and political ideologies are to be seen as the material existence of these ideologies. In Williams' case he argues that the means of communication can be understood as a means of production because of the sense in which "material" is used. But as I have just shown, there is no need to change the keyword of "material" if we just apply a structuralist thinking to the problem.

6   E.P. Thompson's Critique of Althusserian Marxism

Having given an overview of Althusser's position, I'll now attend to a critique of Althusser's Marxism by E.P Thompson (1978). Thompson's critique, as polemical as it was "moving from irony to caricature...to mere abuse" (Thompson 1978, 130) attributing Althusser's Marxism to a neo-Stalinism does provide good insights and has provided influential. Although Gregory Elliot has stated that Thompson's critique has less to do with Althusser and more to do with Barry Hindess and Paul Hirst (Elliot, 2009). Nevertheless we shall outline one particular criticism provided by Thompson in an attempt to over come it. For E.P. Thompson, Althusser and his Marxian methodology are unable to provide answers to questions about Culture (Communications) because the structuralism that Althusser endorses departs from Marx's historical method he writes that "Althusser (and his progeny) find themselves unable to handle, except in the most abstract and theoretic way, questions of value, culture – and political theory" due to in part the "structuralism of stasis" that departs from Marx's own historical method (Thompson 1978, 197). He further argues that Althusser's conceptual universe does not provide the adequate tools for the explanation of change. According to Thompson, Althusser' structuralism does not allow for transformations; historically or socially. "Structure, like a whale, opens up its jaws and swallows process up...process survives unhappily in the structure's stomach" (Thompson 1978, 283). This is to say that while processes may take place within the structure of society as elaborated by Althusser, they don't actually change the structure itself which remains a constant. However Althusser's structuralism is far from a static monolith as Thompson would like to suggest. The explanation of the structure, in Althusser's structural causality does not exist in a form of static. The relationship between the irreducibility of the base and the superstructure does not allow for the stasis that Thompson sees, it is the overdetermination of processes within the structure which Althusser saw, and by introducing concepts such as 'determination in the last instance and structures in dominance, he avoided the structures collapse into relativism. Anderson (1980) shows that Thompson's reading of Althusser does not show that Althusser put forward a definition of "the object of history" which unveils a dynamic structure: "For Althusser does attempt a more substantive definition of the object of history: a historical fact is one 'which causes a mutation in the existing structural relations'.... Thompson has overlooked what is the hinge of the definition he is attacking, the term 'mutation'. Althusser's formula puts an impeccable emphasis on *change*, rather than on stability as Thompson imagines it to do" (Anderson 1980, 14).

Althusser's structuralism is based upon the notions of *Overdetermination, determination in the last instance* and *Structures in dominance*. It is these notions which provide the dynamism within Althusser's system which is at odds with Thompson's allegations. For Althusser, as we showed above, the determination he speaks of one which exerts pressure on the particular elements, setting the limits by which the 'structure in dominance' is able to function. this Thompson misreads in Althusser and would very much agree with him, as he himself states that "Williams and I have been insisting for years of defining "determine" in its senses of "setting limits" and "exerting pressures" (Thompson 1978, 351). *Structures in Dominance* are not permanently fixed but vary according to the overdetermined contradiction (Althusser 2009). If it is true, as we believe it is, that Althusser's structuralism is one of dynamism and not one of stasis as Thompson believes, then we may also argue that Althusser's conceptual universe does provide us with the conceptual tools to judge and analyse change and further more allow us to grasp questions related to culture.

The contestation between Althusser and Thompson lies in the heated debate between that of structure and human agency. The debate is that of the primacy of structure or agency in the development of human behaviour.

We know from Marx that "it is not the consciousness of men that determines their existence, but their social existence that determines their consciousness" (Simon 1994, 211). For Marx it is the structure of the superstructure (ideology) that determines the consciousness of human behaviour. Althusser follows this presenting humanism as an ideology which manifests itself in the interpellation of the individual as a subject by the ideological state apparatus (Althusser, 1990). In contrast to this Thompson argues that while social structure may have an effect on human behaviour, its effect is weak "for any living generation, in any 'now', the way in which they 'handle' experience defies prediction and escapes from any narrow definition of determination" (Thompson 1978, 363).

The debate between structure and agency is far too large to cover adequately in this chapter. But let us try and think what we have already said back to the main argument of the piece. The internet, it cannot be denied, as proved to be a major cultural change in Western society. As such, human behaviour has itself changed in order to cope with such change. One is now always connected to the internet; the checking of emails is a daily (or even twice daily) occurrence. Contra Thompson, Structures of society do determine our behaviour, but I agree with Thompson to the extent that I do not think Structure is the only determinate of human behaviour. Given Althusser's structural causality as a dynamic structure, I do not think that it is claimable that structure determines every aspect of human behaviour. In many respects the debate between structure and agency is also a debate of nature or nurture.

The Internet as a Means of Communication and a Means of Production

The technological advancement of media and communications has been astounding since the publication of Raymond Williams' paper. In this last section, I want to argue that the means of communication that we have available to us via the Internet, such as Facebook and Google, are in fact a type of means of production, though not in the way that Williams would probably suggest. In Marx, the means of production are the unity between the tools of production and the materials of production. The tools of production are, or can be defined as things, which an agent will use on the materials of production in order to formulate a specific item of interest. In an economic situation, this item of interest, known as a commodity, would then be sold in the marketplace for a value. However, the type of process we have described does not only take place within an economic framework. Let us take as an example: the production of this book you are now reading. The authors are provided with two things: 1. The tools of production, by which we mean, in this case, conceptual tools such as Marx's theory of capital and Althusser's structural Marxism, the PC used to write the chapters contained in the book on, the books poured through in order to understand the fundamental components of each thinkers arguments and so on and so forth. 2. The materials of production, or the work of Raymond Williams. The author then uses his material and conceptual tools to develop the material of production into a product, or the book that now sits before you. Essentially, the author is not driven primarily by the capitalist commodity production, which Raymond Williams argued dominates society, of course we may argue that a reason to be published is in order to secure a position at an academic institution, but this is only a subset of reasons which play into the whole publishing culture of academia. This type of production is not only limited to the production of knowledge, which happens in academia, and the production of commodities that happens in the economy, but can also be applied to the idea of the means of communication that we have available to us via the Internet. Let me give an example of how the types of means of communication described above act as a means of production. In the use of Facebook, the user will gain access to this Internet forum by use of a computer, mobile phone or any sort of electronic device, which has access to the Internet. We have thus identified two forms of tools of production: 1) An electronic device linked to the Internet and 2) The Internet itself. Our task now is to identify the materials used in production. In this case the materials provided to be used by the tools of production are the voluntarily submitted information. Whether it is everything about you, including your hobbies, your likes and dislikes etc., or just a simply name and email address, what you provide Facebook with is raw materials, which are then used to produce a finished product, i.e. your Internet profile. I must admit that the use of the term "production" is broad in this sense, but I do not think that this denigrates that such Internet forums as "Facebook" can be identified as a means of production.

The internet as a means of communication is also a fast growing means of production. Following Alvin Toffler (1980) and Christian Fuchs (2012), I want to use the notion of a prosumer in the development of this idea. Prosumer, as the name suggests is a neologism of "producer" and "consumer." The Internet as a means of communication and a means of production has seen the growth of the prosumers. Fuchs (2012) has argued that while users of the Internet have seen to the growth of the commodity market of the internet based on their user activity, they have also recognized as content producers that "there is user-generated content, the users engage in permanent creative activity, communication, community building and content production" (Fuchs 2012, 43). As a means of production, the Internet, or in particular, web-based companies such as Google, Facebook and Youtube are able to take the raw material of information that is provided to them by the user and use that information to create new products, whether that be new online games designed to have the user invest time and money or simply a new addition to their integral system which gets such companies more users. We have briefly confronted the question of the Internet both as a means of communication and as a means of production, but can the Internet be a means of communication as a means of production.

We can also distinguish between the social means of production and the economic means of production. As Jacob Torfing has written: "Mass media are...engaged in the production of the fabric of everyday life as they organize our leisure time, shape our social behaviour and provide the material out of which our very identities are constructed in terms of class, race, nationality, sexuality and distinctions between 'us' and 'them'" (Torfing 1999, 210). In terms of social "means of production," sites like Facebook and the search engine Google are said by Eli Pariser to have formulated algorithms so that what you view on your specific page is informed by your interests and has even gone so far as to suggest that ideological viewpoints dissimilar to your own are filtered from your immediate view, what he called "filter-bubbles" (Pariser 2011). I call this a social "means of production" because the product generated by this algorithm working on your personal information generates an identify of yourself viewed by the world. In the same way we can understand the means of communication as an economic means of production, in which your personal information is used by advertisers of certain products to appeal to you. One needs simply to look at the front-page of their Facebook profile to be bombarded with advertisements that "you may like" according to Facebook. Fuchs (2012) has discussed this in relation to the advertising cookie *DoubleClick*. Purchased by Google in 2007, *DoubleClick* "collects and networks data about usage behaviour on various websites and sells this data" (Fuchs 2012, 46). This information allows companies to then target you with personalized advertising messages.

7   **Smythe: Blindspots, Audience Commodity and the Means of Production**

The role of advertising, both in the economic and cultural milieu of the capitalist mode of production was heavily analysed by Dallas Smythe. Smythe (1977) argued that when it came to mass media and communications, an inability to present "the economic and political significance of mass communication systems" presented a blindspot in "Marxist theory in the European and Atlantic basin cultures" (Smythe 1977, 1). As we mentioned above Google employs tactics of data mining in order to target the consumer of Google's product with advertisements that are produced in line with the consumer's interests. For Smythe, such advertisements are an aspect of the economic function of capital (Smythe 1977, 1981) In answering the question of what the form of the commodity of mass-produced, advertiser-supported communications are (Smythe 1977) the audience. According to Smythe, the advertisements that appear on television, Radio and (in our case) the internet are bought from the communicative industry in an attempt to build particular audiences of their specific product. Traditionally it was thought that advertisers bought space from the communications industry in order to advertise their products. It was understood that space was the commodity. (Meehan 1993) However if the commodity of advertisers and communications was space then space would be equal value no matter where the advertisers placed their advertisement. However this is not the case. The value of certain spaces of advertisement (i.e. Billboards, Television ads, Radio ads, Internet ads) is higher according to the space in which the advertisement occupies. In terms of the internet, A website with a high-traffic yield is capable of charging more for advertising then a website with a low-traffic yield. This presents us with the fact that while space is an aspect of the commodity that advertisers purchase, it is not the whole aspect. Smythe argues that what the advertiser is purchasing is the "services of the audiences with predictable specifications who will pay attention in predictable numbers and at particular times" (Smythe 1977, 4). This can be seen in respect to television and internet advertisement. For example, if I am watching a particular television show, advertisers who product may correspond to that particular show will press for that advertising space (i.e. A Cartoon show usually have advertisements about the toys of characters presented in the show). For Smythe, the audience becomes the commodity in the communicative industry as it is bought and produced, and sold, in various ways.

How can we understand this further in terms of the means of communication as a means of production? I showed in the previous section that the internet has seen the growth of the productive consumer; this is to say that while we as users of the internet consume its products, we also have the ability to generate products for the internet. An obvious case in this is the ability to join and create your own Facebook page. Why is this product? In creating your own Facebook page, regardless of what it is about, you use the means of production (i.e. information, computers, internet access) to produce something that others will use. It is these types of pages which generate much interest in Facebook and contributes much to its survival as one the largest social networking site. In introducing the work of Dallas Smythe, we also introduce a new level to the means of communication as a means of production. In this sense we can see the means of communication (Television, Radio, Internet etc.) as producing audiences through advertising. We may then seek to understand the means of communication as a means of production at the structural level, in which the level, which has been elaborated by Smythe, helps inform, the level of prosumers.

8   Conclusion

The Internet challenges the conception of industrial production that Marxist theory has been most comfortable with. It may be suggest that in our time, Marx's conception of the productive forces and relations of production may be better used to understand the productive processes of television, telecommunications and newspapers. But the Internet is not only a combination of these three processes, but expands upon them in new directions in terms of cognition, communication, co-operation, production, circulation, distribution, consumption. As a "virtual world," its capacity to participate with a materialist theory of production is still in need of much discussion and theorizing. The introduction of concepts such as *prosumers* may only account for a tiny amount of the projects that need to be actualized in relation to a Marxian theory of the Internet. Perhaps in a similar vein to *prosumers*, a concept of *promunication* (productive communication) needs to be thought out.

 The way forward in developing a theory in which one can properly address the issues raised by the communicative array of the internet is by submitting it towards a structural Marxist interpretation of society. While the economy is an element which is involved in the development of the internet, not only as a productive force but also as a politico-legal and cultural element, it is far from being a determining factor. I have discussed above the difference between *determination in the last instance*, an instance that never comes, and *domination*. This is the type of relation which occurs daily, hourly, minutely on the Internet. In respect to Williams, we may say that the dominating force of the Internet is culture. The vast majority of interactions between people are social interactions; whether they are via an online game, a dating website, or just friends communication for free using various types of freeware and software. But this is not to say that culture is a determining element of the internet. In the tradition of the structural Marxists, the Internet is overdetermined, but each interaction that takes place on the Internet is dominated by a different element, whether that be political, legal, economic or cultural. This cannot however be the final word on the subject, nor will it. What I have tried to provide in the chapter above is a foundation for further development of the idea that the Internet as a means of communication can be identified as means of production.

References

Althusser, Louis. 1990. *Lenin and Philosophy and other Essays*. New York: Monthly Review Press.

Althusser, Louis. 2005. *For Marx*. London: Verso.

Althusser, Louis and Etienne Balibar. 2009. *Reading Capital*. London: Verso.

Anderson, Perry. 1980. *Arguments with English Marxism*. London: Verso.

Cohen, Gerald A. 2000. *Karl Marx's Theory of History: A Defence*. Princeton: Princeton University Press.

Eagleton, Terry, ed. 1989. *Raymond Williams: Critical Perspectives*. London: Polity Press.

Eldridge, John and Lizzie Eldridge. 1994. *Raymond Williams: Making Connections*. London: Routledge.

Elliot, Gregory. 2009. *Althusser: The Detour of Theory*. London: Haymarket Press.

Engels, Friedrich. 1890. Engels to J. Bloch in Königsberg. Retrieved January 6, 2012, from http://www.marxists.org/archive/marx/works/1890/letters/90_09_21.htm.

Fuchs, Christian. 2012. Google Capitalism. *tripleC – Cognition, Communication, Co-operation: Open Access Journal for a Global Sustainable Information Society*. 10 (1): 42–48.

Higgins, John. 1999. *Raymond Williams: Literature, Marxism and Cultural Materialism*. London: Routledge.

Marx, Karl. 1994. *Preface to A Contribution to the Critique o Political Economy* in. L.H Simon, *Karl Marx: Selected Writings*. Hackett Publishing Company: Cambridge.

Marx, Karl. 1990. *Capital: Vol 3*. London: Penguin.

Marx, Karl. 1992. *Capital: Vol 2*. London: Penguin.

Marx, Karl. 1994. *Capital: Vol 1*. London: Penguin.

Meehan, Eileen. 1993. Commodity Audience, Actual Audience: The Blindspot Debate. In *Illuminating the Blindspots*, edited by Janet Wasko, Vincent Mosco and Majunath Pendakur, 378-397. Norwood, NJ: Ablex Publishing Corporation.

Milner, A. 1994. Contemporary Cultural Theory: An Introduction, second edition, University College London Press, London.

Pariser, Eli. 2011. *The Filter Bubble: What the Internet is Hiding from You*. London: Penguin.

Simon, Lawrence S., ed. 1994. *Karl Marx: Selected Works*. Cambridge: Hackett Publishing Company.

Smythe, Dallas W. 1977. Communications: Blindspot of Western Marxism. *Candian Journal of Political and Social Theory* 1 (3): 1-27.

Smythe, Dallas W. 1981. *Dependency Road: Communications, Capitalism, Consciousness and Canada*. Norwood, NJ: Ablex Publishing Corporation.

Thompson, Edward P. 1978. *The Poverty of Theory and other Essays*. London: Merlin Press

Torfing, Jacob. 1999. *New Theories of Discourse: Laclau, Mouffe and Žižek*. Oxford: Blackwell.

Toffler, Alvin. 1980. *The Third Wave*. New York City: Bantam Books.

Williams, Raymond. 1977. *Marxism and Literature*. Oxford: Oxford University Press.

Williams, Raymond. 1981. *The Sociology of Culture*. Chicago: University of Chicago Press.

Williams, Raymond. 1993. *Culture and Society*. London: Hogwarth Press.

Williams, Raymond. 2005. *Culture and Materialism*. London: Verso.

CHAPTER 17

Media and Power for 21st Century Socialism in Venezuela*

Lee Artz

1   Introduction

Objectively speaking, movements, classes, and media must challenge power to be revolutionary. One cannot govern from below. There can be no grass roots social transformation without replacing existing power. History has shown from Ghandi and Mandela to Daniel Ortega in Nicaragua and Lula in Brazil, neither the working class nor its charismatic representatives can secure any lasting accommodation with their patriotic capitalists. Negotiating better terms for the exploited while leaving the social relations of capital intact is not revolutionary, nor even defensible as pragmatic today. If freedom, democracy, and social justice are expected, there is no "third way" as Hugo Chavez and Venezuela realised after the media coup of April 2002.

In the 21st Century, it's either global capitalism, with more human suffering and environmental collapse or it's socialism with the working class and its allies building a democratic society of international solidarity. Venezuela provides a positive prime instance of this claim. In Venezuela, revolutionaries are changing society by taking power. This chapter attends to the features and contradictions in this historic process, turning to media practices in particular to illustrate the dialectic of state and revolution. This chapter also recognizes the need for revisiting and contextualizing the Marxist theory of the state, the role of the working class, and the relationship between culture and socio-economic relations under capitalist globalization of the 21st century. Marx and Engels wrote almost two centuries ago, while Lenin and Trotsky constructed and implemented Marxist theory in an isolated and underdeveloped, largely precapitalist country. Their collective contributions have been debated, defended,

* Much thanks and solidarity to Ana Viloria at MINCI (Ministry of Communication and Information, Wilfredo Vasquez at Catia TV, and Carlos Lugo at Radio Primero Negro for their time, insights, and dedication to democracy and social justice; thanks to Carlos Martinez for logistics and translation during visits with dozens of Venezuelan media workers. Travel grants from Purdue University Calumet made the field research possible.

and redefined in the subsequent decades by reformists and revolutionaries alike – from parliamentary social democrats insisting socialism would organically arise from mass democratic experiences to Maoists, fidelistas, and other focoistas fighting rural guerrilla wars to take power "through the barrel of the gun," the character of the state and state power has remained crucial to social revolution, both theoretically and practically. This chapter does not attempt to review and evaluate the claims and contentions from past or ongoing debates, rather it offers the Venezuelan phenomena as a concrete opportunity for observing class conflict in action. Without constant reference or elucidation, this chapter accepts the thrust of Antonio Gramsci's writings on hegemony, which seem to offer considerable clarification to understanding capitalist society since its modern, industrial development, including multiclass political parties, referenda elections, and commercialised mass media and popular culture.

Unless one is active in the solidarity movement or subscribes to radical journals, probably little is known about Venezuela and its inspirational project for social transformation. The US media quickly settled on two themes: democratic elections in Venezuela are suspect; elected Bolivarian officials from local to national are both dangerous and incompetent. Thus, former President Hugo Chavez (who died in 2013) was a caudillo, a populist dictator, hiding behind repeat show elections and bribing the population with social programs funded by oil wealth; the new President, Nicolás Maduro, (a former bus driver) is unqualified to lead but maintains an anti-democratic agenda evidenced by authoritarian attacks on private industry and the media, pushing policies that create inflation, shortages, and corruption. These themes express US disdain for all participatory democracy and (for audiences relying on US and UK commercial media) obscure the actual existing democracy of citizens and workers who overwhelming ratified a constitution with "obligations of solidarity, social responsibility, and humanitarian assistance." The real problem for US media and US capital is that Venezuela is demonstrating to the world that democracy indeed can work, but not through neo-liberal, market relations. Democracy needs socialism.

2   A Strategy for Revolution: Government Policy and Political Parallelism

The transition to socialism in Venezuela is a dialectical political process synthesizing objective conditions with subjective material possibilities. Initiated by the leadership of the former President Hugo Chavez and the United Socialist Party of Venezuela (PSUV) the Bolivarian socialist strategy (a hybrid of Marxism, Venezuelan revolutionary nationalism, and international solidarity) promotes the power and action of the working class and its allies as agents of social change. Since the first explicit pronouncement for socialism in 2006, the strategy has been to use the objective material power of the Bolivarian-led government to dismantle and break the capitalist state while expanding participatory democracy by the citizens – organizing and mobilizing "new forces and new passions" fettered by capitalist society (Marx 1867).

The Venezuelan strategy of a using the "state for revolution" proceeds along two intersecting avenues, with complementary tactics, creating a pincher movement on capitalism, the capitalist class, and capitalist social relations. First, the revolutionary leadership uses its position as the legitimate elected government to administer policies and practices that benefit the working class and frequently challenge capitalist social relations. Government power in the hands of Bolivarian socialists is used to undermine capitalist relations and advance socialist democracy, especially participation in decision-making. For every major proposal, the administration encourages public dialogue, mass communication, and mass public participation. Seeking public consent before action secures support for government policies. The ideological, political, and legal framework for such revolutionary policy and practice adheres to government decisions. The "socialist" government becomes a weapon against the "capitalist" state.

With nineteen successful elections in fifteen years, the leadership of the Bolivarian revolution (now organised in the PSUV), represents and relies on mass support for it programs and policies, which must be implemented involved citizen "protagonists," in Chavista terms. Since 1999, when 71% of voters approved a new Constitution and subsequently voted for representatives to the National Assembly, the Bolivarian movement has relied on a complex interactive process of public communication, program initiatives by and for social movements, and continuing confirmation of the legitimate political representation of the interests of the working class majority. Chavez and Maduro have used their executive powers as elected Presidents and the PSUV (and its organizational predecessors) has used its legislative power as elected representatives to create and implement new laws and policies (along local, regional, and national elections and referenda), while the courts and army have used their legal power to enforce and defend the new laws.

There have been many transformational new laws and policies, including land reform, housing reform, indigenous rights, widespread nationalizations (including in oil, steel, aluminum, electricity, telecommunications, and more), provisions for worker's control and ownership of production, creation of a social fund for education, health care, basic food subsidies, and other laws which benefit the working poor and middle classes. In almost every instance, laws, civil codes, and initiatives followed public debate and discussion organised through community councils or other venues. Although too often the PSUV, the social missions, and government agencies tend towards bureaucratic control, a countervailing process of political interaction and debate among class and community organizations expresses a revolutionary impulse. Structurally, social movements have indirect access to governing through the parliamentary process of "Legislator Pueblo," that allows citizens to propose laws directly to the National Assembly. In 2011, legislators approved a tenant's movement initiative, the Law on Renting, protecting tenants and small landlords from speculators and poor housing conditions (Robertson 2011). The National Assembly also passed a draft of a media worker's proposal on "Communications for People's Power" in 2012, to support the 1200 community media with increased licensing, funding, networking, and community control (Embassy 2012). For more than a decade, in law, policy, and enforcement, the Bolivarian government has resolutely advanced the interests of the working majority and undermined the interests of the capitalist elite.

Using direct government power has been coupled with a second complementary approach in the Venezuelan "state for revolution" strategy: parallelism. Recognizing that the existing national, state, and local government apparatus remains staffed by the old bureaucracy and technocrats, as well as a new a "boli-bourgeosie" of corrupt PSUV officials (Mallett-Ottrum 2013), the Venezuelan government, through both executive and legislative initiatives, continues to promote various popular missions parallel to traditional government institutions. Rather than confronting the old caste directly and instigating premature social conflicts, parallel institutions provide much needed social services, encourage participation, build consciousness, and establish new norms for solidarity and social responsibility. Organizing parallel institutions is the Bolivarian implementation of Marx's suggestion that the working class should "wrest power by degrees" (Marx and Engels 1998). Undoubtedly, parallelism is a useful strategy for establishing a new hegemony, creating leaderships, practices, social relations and ideology – a new culture of solidarity, collaboration, participation, and human needs before profits. While avoiding any direct confrontation with the existing capitalist state, parallel institutions, in the form of social missions, anticipate that any future attempts at abolishing or dismantling the missions would likely find engaged, confident, and experienced community activists unwilling to give up either their rights or powers. Such organised community action also challenges and curbs state and local officials reluctant or opposed to social change. Importantly, the missions provide vital human services to the working class, urban and rural poor, and underserved communities. The government has redirected income from oil rent and royalties to fund social service missions. Misión Robinson and Misión Rivas provide free public primary and continuing education to adults. With the help of Cuban volunteer doctors, Misión Barrio Al Dentro provides easy access community health care to millions. Misión Mercal has established neighborhood grocery stores across the country, providing affordable basic food supplies. There are many other federally supported programs in agriculture, land, housing, fishing, cooperatives, and independent community media. Democratic participation is the most striking characteristic of these government-supported missions and programs. Although participation is uneven across the nation, where active, democratically elected collaborative community councils ensure continuous dialogue with citizens. Significantly, more than 600 factory councils in primary industry control production, working conditions, and community relations.

The experiences and strategies of the Venezuelan revolution over the last ten years demonstrate the validity and value of several Marxist tenets which suggests how revolutionaries might use a "state for revolution" strategy: social being determines social consciousness; socio-economic structures frame political and cultural practices; and fundamental social change requires new social relations and structures. A capitalist state cannot do socialist tasks. So what's a revolutionary to do? Understand and wield historical materialism for revolution. With a clear strategy and flexible tactics, revolutionary movements can intentionally use the capitalist state to consciously dismantle that same state while simultaneously building a socialist "self-government of workers," in Marx's phrase. If used consciously to expand worker's control of production and politics, parallelism can help facilitate the transition from a socialist-leaning government to a socialist society led by the working class and its allies.

3   On the State

The state is not solely the government, nor does the government alone comprise the state, but using government power for revolutionary transformation to a new society, is not only viable, it may be a necessity for 21st century socialism. This is the big dialectic. A Marxist approach to society identifies what is materially present, where historical contradictions exist or may occur, and how conscious human intervention might influence developments. As expressed in countless essays and debates, the state has multiple, interactive components.

In general terms, the state organizes the social reproduction of social relations. We should speak of state power as the expression of dominant class relations and the state apparatus as the institutionalised political means for implementing and enforcing class relations. Additionally, state power depends on the population's hegemonic consent for dominant class leadership reproduced ideologically and culturally in common sense practices and everyday norms (Gramsci 1971).

State power thus consists of: (1) the forces and relations of production; (2) the state apparatus that establishes and enforces rules; (3) and the institutionalised cultural and ideological practices that legitimize class relations and norms. In class society, state power crystallizes relations between classes in institutional structures and expresses those class relations in policies. In other words, the state institutional apparatus (government) is a primary manifestation of the social division of labour expressed in the content and effect of government policies (Therborn 2008). Government policies in a capitalist state defend and reproduce market relations through laws, regulations, and enforcement. Meanwhile, in contemporary capitalist states, media and culture industries promote, reinforce, and reproduce ideological explanations and cultural practices appropriate and necessary for capitalism. A worker's government uses its power to advance socialist relations by enacting laws and policies that weaken and displace capitalist economic, political, and social relations – using the state apparatus for revolution – advancing and protecting the democratic interests of the working class majority.

In every instance, a state organizes social relations. A state is much more than just a collection of institutions or coercive agencies standing apart from and over a society. State power establishes, expresses and reproduces class relations through policies and practices – including cultural and ideological. A capitalist state apparatus uses its political and coercive powers to maintain and extend class relations and to break or obstruct any challenges to that rule. A capitalist state apparatus functions as a political manager and reproducer of class relations, including wage labour, private profits, and market tenets, while reflecting and reinforcing ideologies and cultural practices which legitimize capitalist relations, such as individualism, consumerism, authoritarianism, and spectatorship entertainment. Capitalism requires private, corporate ownership of production that secures profits from wages; depends on the legal and coercive protection of its governments; and the legitimation and consent provided by popular culture. Given this triad of state power, it is easier to recognize and comprehend a capitalist state that nationalizes industry while returning profits to the capitalist class, or a socialist state that reintroduces market relations while trying to protect worker's rights and quality of life.

Capitalism can function with state-run production, provided the market system with its wages and profits remains sacrosanct. Socialist states may even exist short term with small scale, atomised retail markets, provided the norms and practices of social production and social wealth are reproduced – although long term market relations tend to undermine solidarity, social responsibility, and collaborative relations (Lebowitz 2010) as Mészáros (1994) also observes in the Yugoslavian "socialist" market experience.

A capitalist state is marked by market mechanisms and managerial control of production, a government apparatus is comprised of party politicians, bureaucrats and technocrats, with entertainment and consumerism as cultural norms, if not pastimes. A socialist state would lead to collective participation, production by social appropriation and collective, democratic planning, while politics and culture would be characterised by public persuasion and participation in all cultural production and activity. In general terms, a state may be characterised by its tasks, personnel, and processes of decision and administration – its class character revealed by which class relations it defends, what rules and laws are created and enforced. A socialist government has less need for personnel because workers and community organizations initiate, evaluate, and implement policies and practices. A socialist state must have laws, but more importantly, in a socialist state, the government does not enforce, but the working class and other progressive social agents must realize and implement laws and policies on their own behalf – a perspective codified in the Venezuelan Bolivarian Constitution (Lebowitz 2006). Capitalist states encourage consumer atomization, privatization of social activities, and market rule: protecting the market, wealth, and the reproduction of private property and capital, by enforcing wage labour and private profits. Socialist states rely on human solidarity, collectivity, equality, participation, and public transparency: advancing public discourse and debate, public social ownership and collaborative, democratic decision-making. Lebowitz (2010) provides a lively, accessible summary of 21st century socialism as anticipated through the practices of Venezuelan communal councils.

Venezuela is a capitalist country. Bolivarian socialist Maduro is president. The socialist PSUV has a majority in the National Assembly. The Constitution proclaims participatory democracy. Missions, councils, nationalizations, and public service programs continue to expand. Still Venezuela is a capitalist country. Millions vote for Maduro, the PSUV, and socialism. Maybe most of eight million workers prefer factory councils. More than 30,000 workers may be members of worker's militias. Still, Venezuela remains a capitalist country. For now.

Michael Lebowitz (2010) calls Venezuela a "rentist" capitalist state, because the primary resource, oil, has been nationalised as state property since 1976 and global oil giants "rent" most of the oil fields from the government. Still, the classic explanation of capitalists exploiting labour power by providing wages while withholding surplus value as profit expresses dominant social relations in Venezuela. While no corporation "owns" the oil, the rent paid for using the oil fields and the royalties paid for extracting the oil does not interfere with wealth acquired in drilling, refining, processing, and distributing oil. Technically, rent and royalties is the Venezuelan government's share of surplus value, while capitalist social relations based on the wage labour production of a commodity for the market remain. Oil provides almost 80% of the exports and some 25% of the GDP for Venezuela. Venezuela has the fifth largest oil reserves and may have the largest oil shale fields in the world. With such oil wealth, development in Venezuela was distorted. Populations have been concentrated on the urban coast, agriculture has been neglected in lieu of food imports. In addition to oil production, Venezuela has other major industries, including: aluminum, steel, paper, concrete, auto assembly, textile, rice, retail food and beverage production, and media entertainment, among others (Enright, Frances, & Saaverda 1996).

   Until the 21st century, the Venezuelan economy was private, commercial, and capitalist. But capitalism has its internal contradictions of overproduction and class inequality. In short order, global capitalist actions ended the relative tranquility in Venezuela. Even as the wall fell in Berlin, signaling the triumph of capitalism for Western economists and the commercial media, the neoliberal policies of the Perez government led to mass unrest and working class resistance in Caracas. Beginning with Chavez in 1992, the Bolivarian project has articulated a new anti-capitalist direction of Venezuela. Venezuela may still be capitalist, but the government is not, and incursions elsewhere have begun. The capitalist state is now under siege.

4   Reproduction, Reform, and Revolution

Certain theoretical and practical questions arise from the above understanding of the state: Does the Bolivarian leadership have the commitment and/or power to implement socialist relations? What has the PSUV/Chavez government done and what will it do with its (government) power? What is the empirical evidence that government insitutions are maintaining and reproducing capitalist social relations, or is there evidence that government poiicies and actions have advanced working class interests and socialist relations? What are the conditions for change and how do policies and practices of the government promote collective action and working class power? Do policies and practices (including enforcement or lack of enforcement) maintain and protect exploitation and domination by the capitalist class? Capitalism creates surplus value through commodity production and the expropriation of wealth from labour power...it also must necessarily reproduce social relations with wageworkers, managers, owners and the economic, political, and cultural institutions that normalize those relations.

The big question is what social relations have been introduced or reproduced? What role has the PSUV government played in maintaining or protecting the capitalist class? What role has the Bolivarian leadership played in dismantling capitalist relations, private profit, and wage labour? Is the government advancing on capitalism/are capitalists organizing against government actions or complacent and sanguine about government policies? What role has the Bolivarian state played in promoting collective control of the production of social wealth? In other words, how are the three components of state power in Venezuela dialectically developing and what are various class forces doing to intervene in class relations and state power? Have capitalist relations of production (ownership, control, regulation, profit) expanded, been maintained, or curtailed? Has the state apparatus (administration, legislative, courts, and police) created laws, policies, and enforcements that protect capitalist relations or do they advance socialist relations? Have cultural and ideological practices been promoted or emerged that encourage collective collaboration, solidarity, citizen participation, creativity, and social justice or does consumerism, self-gratification, and passive spectatorship remain.

Even a cursory review of the political trajectory of the PSUV and social movements in Venezuela today indicates that a popularly elected revolutionary leadership is using its government power to consciously push against existing social contradictions and unleashing class conflicts that can only be resolved through concerted revolutionary class action. These conflicts are not orchestrated but are being systematically unearthed, providing impulses and opportunities for an organised working class to transform the social relations and replace the capitalist state, not just its government. Government policy and the Bolivarian leadership, including large sections of the PSUV, seem intent on extending and intensifying socialist relations across society: extending socialist relations through new nationalizations in more industries and services; intensifying new class relations by insisting on worker's control of production, establishing worker's militias to enforce decisions, and supporting social movement initiatives for accelerated land reform, housing reform, and media access. Despite being handicapped by a contradictory, cobbled-together political program (Fuentes, 2014), the government apparatus of Venezuela has extended socialist relations, creating space for new class relations, interfering with production for profit, against labour as a commodity, and for social intervention in the production of basic goods and services (as expressed in new laws on media, nutrition, production, and civil rights). Confrontations will come soon, because as VP Elias Jaua says: "without confrontation there can be no social gains" (Jaua 2011).

The strategy of "state for revolution" is a conscious process of building independent working class institutions with decision-making power and control. This strategy has three interrelated elements that conform to the three components describing state power presented above: in production and ownership; in political power; and in cultural norms. Chavez, Maduro, and the official program of the PSUV government declare socialism as its goal with worker's control of a nationalised means of production a first step. However, to be transformative this must be more than simply nationalization and government expropriation of industry. Significantly, in Venezuela, changing ownership of the means of production includes laws and policies for changing the relations of production through worker's councils, community councils, and worker's militias – not government control over production, but worker and community control to decide allocation of resources locally, regionally, and nationally. Of course, to be effective these laws and policies must be fully implemented.

The weekly three-hour television program, "Alo Presidente!" is one an iconic example of the government ideological commitment and persuasive campaign for 21st century socialism. More significantly, the popular programming on new public service television (ViVe TV, TVes, and Avila TV) and the hundreds of community radio and television stations organised by community councils indicate how democratic mass communication for a new socialist society permeates everyday life – media access, public discourse, and participatory communication – whatever the political consciousness of the programmers. Public access to media production, working class programming, and the development of a revolutionary culture expressed in mass media provides one venue to understand the trends and vibrancy of the revolutionary impulse.

5   Media in Venezuela

The changing ownership structure, production practices, and programming content in media in Venezuela illustrate the "state for revolution" strategy. The Bolivarian government has promulgated laws to curb the capitalist means of media production, expand working class access to the means of communication through laws which limit private ownership and privilege community social ownership, and thereby providing a public space for popularizing democracy, participation, and new social relations not based on advertising, profits, and audience markets. The narrative on community media in Venezuela is above all a prime example of class conflict, highlighting how the socialist government uses its power to nurture another site of power by establishing and promoting non-state institutions under worker's control for communicating a more socialist and humanist culture. Because the political economy of media in Venezuela reflects the social relations of the larger capitalist society, the incursions against commercial media and the burgeoning parallel community media also reveal the responsibilities and possibilities for the strategy using government power against state power, of creating a "state for revolution."

Historically, media in Venezuela have been commercial, private, and highly concentrated in a few hands (Golinger 2004). Commercial media still comprise more than 75% of all media operations. A small group of business families own fifteen television stations, including the large national broadcasters: Cinseros' Venevisión, Teleleven, RCTV (the Granier group), and Globovisión (Ravell's virulently anti-Chavista UHF and cable stations); and several regional stations. Supportive of successive conservative and neoliberal governments, these major media have been highly profitable, selling mass audiences to advertisers by producing mass entertainment programming from soaps to game shows and dramas. The Cisneros Group, owner of Venevisión, has become a significant second-tier global media corporation, with more than 70 media outlets in 39 countries, including DirecTV Latin America, AOL Latin America, Playboy Latin America, as well as beverage and food distribution (Coca-Cola and Pizza Hut in Venezuela, e.g.), and other cultural productions, including the Los Leones baseball team and the Miss Venezuela Pageant. Venevisión produces some 184,000 hours of telenovelas each year that are broadcast in 38 countries – more than exported by Argentina, Mexico, or even the famed Brazilian soap opera distributors. Six families own the six largest daily papers.

In general, commercial media and entertainment remain dominant and robust, exceeding paper, auto, and all agricultural production in net profits. Significantly, (with the exception of Venevisión and sporadically the news daily Últimas Noticias) commercial media are sensationalistic, oppositional, and at times even rabid in their attacks on Maduro, the social missions, communal councils, and worker's control of industry. In addition to the large commercial stations, there are a few national specialty broadcasters such as Vale TV, a Catholic, educational channel, Meridiano, a sports channel, La Puma, a music channel, and La Tele, an entertainment channel. The political economy summary reads as follows: consolidated private ownership of means of production; hierarchical production for profit from advertising-funded entertainment media; programs created and distributed to target audiences of consumers, replete with narratives and themes advancing capitalist social relations, reinforcing passivity, authority, and individual consumption.

6   Reaction and Revolution

These conditions of media production were dramatically challenged following the April 2002 coup, which was orchestrated under the leadership of major media, in particular the owners of RCTV, along with the Chamber of Commerce and the Catholic Church hierarchy (all in consultation with the US) (Golinger 2006). The coup leaders kidnapped Chavez, immediately "abolished" civil rights and the constitution, dissolved the National Assembly, shut down the only independent television station in the country, and broadcast cartoons for the duration of the coup on their own national networks. The people soon discovered the plot, however. The coup was short-lived – interrupted and blocked by mass civic action instigated by nascent community media in the hands of the more conscious sections of the Caracas working class, including low-power community radio and journalist-activists that printed and distributed thousands of flyers calling for mass demonstrations against the coup (Francia 2002; Sanchez 2012). In May, these activists created the on-line news site, Aporrea.org [American Popular Revolutionary Assembly], which has become an important clearinghouse for nationwide news and critique in support of revolution.

Hundreds of thousands came into the streets and surrounded Miraflores, the Presidential building, where the coup was headquartered. After President Chavez was rescued the people celebrated their success. The more conscious leaders had a more sober assessment of the relations of power, however. Perhaps they recognised that a Chavez government had not overcome the power of the capitalist state. Seventy-eight Caracas-area media workers met with Chavez and other government representatives demanding more public independent media – media for revolution – not only in policy but in practice.

Although the government-run VTV was nationally broadcast and available to all, community media workers pointed out the fragility of such concentrated mass communication. They insisted on community media outside the state, community media controlled by workers in communities. Government response was immediate. Within the year, Venezuela had a new formation for communication: the Ministry of Communication and Information (MINCI) launched its "strategic goal" to return the right of communication to the population, initiating independent community media while increasing the regulation and monitoring control over commercial media. MINCI was the state apparatus response to working class demands. With the legitimate power of the state apparatus (the government) in revolutionary hands, all three elements of state power were addressed. From its inception, the Chavez-led government passed laws and provided resources to revolutionize the political economy of the media, including the Organic Telecommunications Law of 2000, which established the right to community media (e.g., Article 12 states that every individual has a right to create a non-profit community station). The state apparatus acted to curtail capitalist relations in the media and to advance socialist relations. Media ownership changed a bit. Public ownership, as social ownership, was expanded, conceived as participatory and collaborative under direct popular control by citizens in their working class communities.

Meetings begun in 2002, however, led to a much clearer understanding, and a more pronounced emphasis on participatory community media production, codified in a new media law. First, the Open Community Radio and Television Broadcast Ruling in 2002 defined criteria for media production, prioritizing independently produced, community-based messages and programs. The 2004 Law on Social Responsibility for Radio and Television establishes the right of active participation and oversight by citizens in all media stages: production, distribution, and consumption of messages. The Partial Reform Law of Radio and TV Social Responsibility (2006) outlines media rights and interests "for the purpose of promoting social justice and contributing to the formation of the citizenry, democracy, peace, human rights, culture, education, health, and social and economic development" and "to promote citizens' active and direct participation" (MINCI 2006, 9, 14). Within the next few years, more than 300 FM radio and TV broadcasters were organised and licensed. By 2011, Venezuela was approaching 1200 community media outlets (Venezuela en Noticias 2012). The government provides equipment, technical resources and training using the Social Fund, established with revenues from the nationalised oil industry – simultaneously impinging on capitalist prerogatives over resources and turning those resources toward support for participatory democracy. Through licensing, the government provided space for public media – not the limited spectrum and low-wattage normally available to community media in most countries – but spectrum, power, and geography so "community" radio broadcasts reach 3 million in Caracas, for example. Using the "state for revolution," media production ownership, practices, and programming changed. Laws and licensing legitimised and empowered revolutionary voices by ensuring direct working class access and control. In law and in licensing, commercial, state, party, and religious officials are excluded from public media, while 70% of the production must be directly from community councils themselves.

A few examples may help illustrate how a socialist-led government may use its power to revolutionize the political economy of the media and its striking impact on cultural practices. The development and expansion of national public broadcasting is the most easily recognizable change to the Venezuelan media landscape. The programs and processes of program production underscore how a more democratic political economy frames cultural practice. In addition to TeleSUR, the cooperative satellite television venture of Venezuela, Argentina, Uruguay, Cuba and Bolivia (Artz 2006), and ANTV, the television channel of the National Assembly, three major DTH broadcastings stations have been established: TVes, ViVe, and Avila TV. These public broadcastings stations are primarily funded by subsidies from the Social Fund and "advertisements" for national social services. They are each independently run outside government direction, oversight, or even approval – highlighted by several shows highly critical of Chavez, Maduro, and the government. Production and programming practices demonstrate the dialectic of social being determines social consciousness, because becoming producers, editors, narrators, and videographers for the new society creates new human beings – their social awareness, their life being is prompted to develop by the explosion in consciousness and awareness of their own creativity, power, and experience of social contradictions. In dozens of conversations and interviews with producers, directors, and technicians (conducted in person in 2006 and 2009, and electronically 2010–2011) expressions of determination and desire for a new society reflected the cumulative experience of democratic participation and decision-making that emphasizes and privileges community, workers, women, indigenous, and the average citizen.

7   Public Media, Public Access

In 2007, the license to broadcast expired for RCTV, the largest private broadcaster in the country. CONATEL (National Telecommunication Commission) and MINCI reviews found that RCTV had violated and admitted violating numerous broadcasting laws (Wilpert 2007). Moreover, the new Constitution required expansion of public broadcasting, so Channel 2 was licensed to Venezuelan Social Television (TVes, pronounced "te ves" – meaning "you see yourself," in Spanish). RCTV continues its broadcast via satellite and cable, while Globovisión, Venevisión, and other private local stations maintain media opposition to the Bolivarian social project.

TVes became the first national broadcaster in the public interest and with public access (Ciccariello-Maher 2007). TVes is a publicly-run station with a

Board of Directors elected by unions and community organizations. Funded with $11 million from the National Assembly (and revenues for some social service advertising productions), TVes relies heavily on independent producers (PIN), journalists and community producers. Seventy-eight PIN s provide some 229 programs on TVes' yearly schedule. Meant to be "merely a conduit through which independent cultural production reaches the airwaves," according to Minister of Communication, William Lara (quoted in Ciccariello-Maher 2007), for the first time in national broadcasting history, TVes prominently features working class, women, and indigenous people. Although telenovelas were perfected by Venevisión and RCTV, TVes airs the first ever soap opera with a black lead. Documentaries of popular history are a regular fare on TVes (see http://www.tves.gob.ve).

Founded four years earlier, Vision Venezuela TV (ViVe) is almost exclusively dedicated to community productions. Independent, public, and cooperatively-run, ViVe is funded by the Social Fund and prohibits commercial advertising. Only 10% of programming is produced in-house, the remaining 90% of shows come from community videographers and documentarians (with specials on traditional peasant planting practices, indigenous musical performances, local community cultural activities, and investigative pieces on housing, utilities, and even religious events). More than 14,000 communities have been featured over the last 10 years, aired on some 40 half-hour shows each week. Given its community production focus, for the first time on national television, women, Afro-Venezuelans, and indigenous people are prominent. To ensure quality productions, ViVe has organised community-based training for video production through community councils and some worker's councils. The Bolivarian socialist project "created social missions with health care and education for the poor. ViVe will be the equivalent for television, where everybody regardless of class, colour, or beliefs can take part in the great political debate for socialism and the transformation of this country" (Sergio Arriasis, quoted in Wynter 2010).

ViVe is not public service broadcasting as advocated by the media reform movement in the US. No charity or "service" here, rather, ViVe is public access, public control, and public production of communication. ViVe even has mobile transmitting stations in each region of the country, along with courses to teach citizens broadcasting skills. A new social power has emerged as working class communities and individuals – directly participating and collectively collabourating – produce solidarity media and democratic cultural experiences. Vive programming includes: "Secretos de Familia" (historical traditions across generations), "Querencia Andean" (Andean cultural traditions), "Culturar de Dia" (arts and crafts reflecting Venezuela's cultural diversity) "Real o Media" (critques of media from Zulia) and many more (see http://wive.gob.ve/programacon for current programs). The creative producers featured on Vive represent new human beings, human agents consciously working in and for solidarity among working people and their allies.

One more important public broadcaster deserves mention for its connection to Venezuelan youth. Avila TV was originally launched in 2006 as part of a socialist communication initiative by the former Bolivarian mayor of Caracas, Juan Barretto.

Close to 400 twenty-thirty year olds produce, write, edit, film, and broadcast edgy, creative programming aimed at urban youth. Avila might be described as a station with hip-hop sensibility and socialist lyrics. A typical Avila broadcast day includes news, political talk shows, features on international and community issues, and telenovelas about Caracas working class families – but no commercials. Programming decisions are guided by an explicit commitment to a new social order, as expressed by one of the many articulate young producers, "We aren't trying to sell shampoo or name brands clothes, or any capitalist products for that matter. We are trying to stay true to our principles and combat consumerism" (Mellado 2009). Watching Avila TV, viewers quickly notice the style, the tone, the structure of programming. At times even the music feels argumentative, strident. Avila is "not like ViVe, they privilege discourse, we privilege the aesthetic" (Mellado 2009). For example, in the spring of 2009, Avila aired a weekly series called "El Entrompe de Falopio," about women and gender issues in the revolution. A year-long live program, "Voice, Face, and Struggle of the People," included one titled "Impunity," where hosts, guests, and audience members sharply criticised the government for granting amnesty to the 2002 coup leaders. Even the telenovelas have political overtones with not-so-subtle barbs at the opposition for undemocratic obstruction and the government for not championing working class interests and advancing socialism more quickly. High-quality documentaries, professionally and creatively produced, have included the widely acclaimed 2008 "El Golpe" (The Coup) and the 2009 feature, "200 years of Caracas: The Insurgent Capital of the Continent." The young producers at Avila have also aired shows on Afro-Venezuelans, indigenous cultures, and homosexuality – all topics ignored or taboo on commercial television (see http://avilapendiente.blogspot.com/ for more examples). Finally, Avila has been an integral part of RED TV (Education for the Revolution and Development of Venezuela), a city-wide educational project to bring classes in screenwriting, playwriting, and video production to the working class communities of Caracas. By 2010, fifty-five community councils in Caracas had media committees, where community members receive extensive training, mentoring and equipment – cameras, computers, and editing software for video production and post-production. Community media committees then have regularly scheduled spots on Avila's daily schedule for airing 10–15 minute video productions.

In 2013, two new public stations were launched, one by and for youth, the other TV Obrera (Worker's TV) directed by labour, both to appear on the news Open Digital Television system. On Venezuela public television, the lives and experiences of working class communities and community activists are valuable, valued, and shared – informing the nation of how and what new creative human beings can and will be with a revolutionary, democratic transformation of social relations.

As illustrated by these public media, the socialist government, nationally and locally, has created laws, provided resources, and prepared space for non-commercial, non-capitalist media production. In the vocabulary of the Bolivarian project, new "protagonists" can now fully participate in creating their own culture, their own stories, expressing their own interests. While they are making video, making television, making communication, they are also making new human beings. Lives and experiences of working class communities and community activists are valuable, valued, and shared – informing the nation of how and what new creative human beings can and will be with a revolutionary transformation of society from capitalism to socialism.

8   Community Media: Independent and Participatory

Complementing and historically and politically preceding these major broadcast ventures, community radio and television in Venezuela have a rich tradition of participatory communication. The seminal leader of all is Catia TV in Caracas, the first legal community television station in the country. Catia TV's slogan "Don't Watch TV, Make TV!" is inscribed on the outside walls of its broadcast studios and demonstrated daily by collabourative rotating teams of 4–7 community producers organised in ECPAI s (Independent Community Audiovisual Production Teams). Each ECPAI decides the topics, formats, aesthetics, and content for broadcast programs, "emphazing stories from the barrio, contradictions and changes, or not" (Vasquez 2009). Popular education and democratic participation lives in and through Catia TV, expressing its television production and programming with assemblies, events, and communication guerrillas: muralists, storytellers, oral historians, artisanal creators, and puppeteers. Its purpose "is to act as an organizing tool, where communities build their own audiovisual discourse..." (Catia TVe Collective 2006). Collaboratively teaching and learning creates dozens of ECPAI s.

Having knowledge of communication; having a critical analysis surrounding the conditions and social context in which an individual or
group must live; identifying the cultural and ideological values that effect
the group's or collective's vision; developing a understanding of reality
and how they act; associating learning with the collective construction of
knowledge; and identifying and analyzing [their] own practices. Catia
TVe Collective 2006

Beginning as the Simon Rodriguez Cultural Center, a volunteer-based
community-building project, showing film and video in vacant buildings in
the neighborhood, Catia TV eventually emerged as a media-based social
movement that expanded and organically developed through intimate interaction with the community. Even before the Chavez election in 1998, the cultural center was showing community-produced news and entertainment in
the community centers of West Catia. (An early leader of the Cultural Center
was Blanca Eekhout, past president of ViVe TV, and now Vice-President of the
National Assembly, extending the participatory radical social ethos into the
heart of public broadcasting and government decision-making, confirming in
practice the revolutionary impulse of the Bolivarian government.) Following
the national impetus to develop community media, Catia TV was licensed in
2000, and by the April 2002 coup was setting the standard for participatory,
democratic, public access television – a model to be emulated by hundreds of
community media launched after 2003. "The fundamental principle of Catia
TVe is to encourage participation within organised communities. Catia TVe
seeks community participation in the making of audiovisual productions
reflecting community struggles and demonstrating how to build networks
within the community".

The "objective is to build a media that the people want, with democratic
participation based on dialogue. As part of this objective and considering
that community media is a space for the people to exercise their power,
at least 70 percent of Catia TVe's programming must be produced from
within the community... Because Catia TVe is a television station connected to the working class...every Catia TVe participant has a minimum
political consciousness and social responsibility...Catia TVe shares a
space for communication with organised groups that come from various
communities in Caracas, as a way of protesting."Catia TVe Collective 2006

Dozens of community television stations now broadcast across Venezuela.
Not all are successful in integrating community participation with media

production. Petare TV, for example, was established without much community input and despite funding, technology, and training, it struggled from the lack of collaboration and organic connection to residents. Petare TV showed how government initiatives have little effect without participation and interest: Petare's communal council struggled to exist; a wave of Colombia right-wing immigrants created much social disruption. For a while, crime, unemployment, drugs, and atomization marked Petare daily life. Citizens were more intimidated than motivated. Thus, for several years, Petare TV became just one more station on the dial for neighborhood residents who had not yet internalised social responsibility or collective action. Remarkably, as of 2013, democratic activism against right-wing attacks in Petare appeared and the local TV station soon attracted many more participants. The lessons: disaffection and surrender are not key motivators for social change; neither governments or leaderships can impose participation or a new social order; socialism and the transition to socialism requires participation, initiative, time, aptitude, creativity, and an organic connection to the life of the community.

In contrast, Afro TV, in Balo Vento on the east coast of Venezuela, illustrates the cultural and social potential for community media led by community activists and linked to a politically awakening community. About 15% of Venezuelans are Afro-Venezuelan, the historic consequence of Spanish slavery and its cocoa plantations in the east. Balo Vento had long been neglected by central governments, relegated to continued exploitation by the remaining cocoa growers. Following discussion and ratification of the new Constitution that establishes Venezuela as a multiethnic, pluri-culture society, the government established a subcommission of African descendants in the National Assembly (Wilpert 2003). All education, health, and housing missions were extended to Balo Vento, along with the opportunity for public, independent, community media. Afro TV was the early regional media project launched by a handful of community activists. Their mission includes recovering their African past, expressing their cultural and artistic present, and organizing public dialogue on contemporary issues important to Balo Vento, such as land reform, development, and worker's control of cocoa production. In 2009, Afro TV was broadcasting 4–5 hours daily on a UHF signal. Afro TV is also available via the Internet (see http://vimeo.com/2990685, e.g.). Early programs included "Cimmarones," stories of slave rebellion, and "Que Es Eso," featuring local characters telling their life stories (Perdemo 2009). Afro TV, while modest in its operation, nonetheless illustrates the relationship between media access and community cultural experiences, the dialectical development of becoming new human beings through participation in creating one's one existence. In the words of MINCI Alternative and Community Media Director, Ana Viloria:

> Community media visibilises our faces, our voices, so we collectively
> know what we are doing connected to humanity. We become protago-
> nists...we make for ourselves the task of learning ideas and tools that are
> available for the political actor.
>
> VILORIA 2009

There are currently more than 100,000 community activists working with more
than 400 community radio and 40 television stations with some additional 800
broadcasters in various stages of preparation, production, training, licensing
and regular broadcasts. Community media have been a national priority for
MINCI since 2008, when it unveiled a new strategic plan for funding, training,
and licensing community media with national broadcast capabilities. By 2009,
community media reached 56% of the population. As already indicated, this
national program represents the continuing dialogue about communication
and the concerted interaction between government and working class communities to establish laws, practices, and democratic control over media in
Venezuela. An example of government intent, was Chavez's defense of CONA-
TEL's (National Telecommunication Commission) decision in 2008 to "recuperate" 32 private radio and 2 private television stations for violations of laws
on media monopoly, those "stations now belong to the people" who should
"control the strategic means of production" of communication in Venezuela
(Viloria 2009). At all levels, from officials to teenage producers, socialism for
the 21st century is articulated as a process for creating new social relations,
beginning with ownership and control over industry, including media that
contributes to a new social consciousness and new social being across classes.
Community radio illustrates this dialectical process of protagonist-initiated
development of political self-awareness and power.

9   Community Radio

At Radio 23 de Enero (broadcasting at 3000 watts in Caracas), community
council journalists and producers from the more than 50 social movement col-
lectives broadcast weekly programs of music, opinion, health, public affairs,
and news. Also in Caracas, teens, grandparents, DJ s, and investigative journalists collectively share the broadcast schedule at Radio Primero Negro, a station
with a long history of community organizing. More than 60 programs are aired
weekly by "students, housewives, unemployed, and members of community
organizations" (Lugo 2009) The station's community activists conduct regular
surveys and conversations with neighborhood residents to assure programs

meet the needs and interests of all, and to always recruit more participants for the station, offering training and the expertise of station technicians. Both of these "community" stations reach more than 1 million residents of Caracas – not your typical "community" broadcaster in the US or the rest of the North.

In Tumeremo, Bolivar, in eastern Venezuela near the Guyana border, Radio Minero is operated by working miners and community members producing their own news and programs. In Zulia, Maracaibo, the indigenous community broadcasts over Radio Yupa in their native language, with stories and topics drawn from their historic culture and everyday concerns. About 40 television stations, and hundreds of radio stations, now air countless inspiring stories by novices facing microphones for the first time and feeling the power of communication, directly experiencing the meaning of democracy and community (Labrique, 2011). Local stations have leaders, directors, and specialists on cultural, political, indigenous, and community issues, creating a "communication force" for revolutionary change (Viloria 2009).

Participatory journalism and participatory democratic production at ViVe, Avila, Catia TV, El Negro Primero, and other public and community media outlets reflect changing social relations. University and professionally trained journalists work alongside community correspondents and participatory journalists, constructing and distributing news and news reports that are accurate and timely, but much more democratic in framing and sourcing because they are not bound by the advertising needs or editorial dictates of a market-driven media. New norms of objectivity with partisanship serve the information and educational needs of the majority striving for democratic control over their lives (Rothschuh 1986). The goal of 21st century socialism as promulgated in word and deed in Venezuela exists (not to provide government largess and with patronizing welfare benefits) but for nothing less than to place the working class and its allies as protagonists in the process of restructuring social relations, including replacing the artificial norms of professional journalism, which pretend to separate facts from context.

Community and public media for 21st century socialism alter the practices and functions of media in line with human needs, so that a participatory socially-conscious media contribute to a new cultural hegemony of a creative, socialist humanity – challenging the hegemony of consumerism and neoliberalism – for a culture of cooperation, solidarity, and dedication to creating social justice and solidarity. In this mix, journalism of necessity becomes more vibrant, more alive, identifying facts, sources, and truths related to the real experience and conditions of the working class population.

In addition to community radio, television, and newspapers, the media battle in Venezuela has entered cyberspace. Early on media activists recognised the importance of Internet communication. Aporrea.org went on-line in

May 2002, bringing together dozens of journalist-activists linked to community councils, community media, and independent newspapers and journals. Working with and through the National Association of Community and Alternative Media (ANMCLA), Apporea.org has demonstrated the value of networking news and information among community media – one of the few means for countering commercial media dominance. Meanwhile, with more access, more resources, and more cultural capital, privileged youth and university students working with the conservative Primero Justica party, the right-wing foundation Futuro Presente, and other opposition groups have been developing coordinated attacks on the Bolivarian revolution using social media and the Internet. The conservative youth have been courted and funded by the U.S. State Department, Freedom House, the Cato Institute, and the National Endowment for Democracy, and other U.S. government and private agencies. With millions from the United States Agency for International Development (USAID), anti-Chavez youth and student groups have used Twitter, Facebook, blogs, websites, and email messaging to destabilize the government through rumor and agitation against social programs and social reform (Golinger 2010). The Venezuelan government has not ceded the terrain. In the last few years, the government has energetically extended Internet access to millions of citizens. In 2000, only 4.1% of Venezuelans had Internet access, in 2009, 33% had Internet access (Internet World Stats, 2009). In addition to the 8 million citizens who have Internet access, and in direct refutation of commercial media claims about Internet restrictions, the government has established 668 community-based Internet "infocenters" with free public access. In 2010, the Ministry of Science and Technology launched 27 mobile infocenters "which will travel to remote areas in the Amazon, Andean, and rural regions, guaranteeing free Internet services and computer training to citizens" who previously lack access to the technology (Golinger 2010). The Ministry also budgeted $10 million to build another 200 free cybercenters in underserved neighborhoods. In all, the current infocenters provide Internet to 2.5 million permanent users and up to 10 million visitors annually. As with all community media, the government is dedicated to participatory democracy, seeking to transfer operations and administration to community councils so citizens can collectively determine the technological needs of the residents.

Extending access to working classes and indigenous people is only part of the solution. As with other social projects, working class protagonists creating new social relations and more democratic communication forms will determine what a "socialist" Internet may look like, likely including some kind of a commons-based network (Fuchs 2012, 48) and the socio-cultural thrust of participatory social programs would suggest the Bolivarian revolution will so advocate, but at this point, beyond extending free public access and community administration it is not yet clear what the Venezuelan revolution will contribute to a more democratic, participatory Internet.

Government support for public and community media continues. A national alternative media network was established in 2012 to train community journalists, facilitate the sharing of news, and challenge commercial media dominance (Boothroyd 2012). In 2013, the network was expanded to the Bolivarian System of information and Communications with increased funding for further promoting public and community media as a means for advancing democratic communication and civic participation in the revolution (see http://www.sibci.gob.ve/ for details).

10   The Socialist Triangle

The trajectory of public broadcasting, community media, and participatory democracy with public access to media portends a new social function for media. Legalised, funded, and supported by the Bolivarian government in power, these independent community media may still be entertaining, but more importantly, they are participatory and revolutionary. These media air working class-generated narratives reflecting the collaborative creativity and shared experiences of those who aspire to write their own future history; these media broadcast messages, stories, and images of solidarity, collective action, participatory democracy, and communities in struggle for democracy, social justice, self-government, and working class leadership of society. As part of a larger revolutionary project for 21st century socialism, the Bolivarian government has used its power against the capitalist state, expanding sites for additional participation by the Venezuelan working and middle classes, women, youth, Afro-Venezuelans, indigenous populations, and others previously underserved and excluded, politically, socially, and economically. The Bolivarian government has unevenly but continuously been using its legislative, executive, and administrative power to direct Venezuelan national resources towards advancing working class control and democratic social relations.

The emerging popular community media represent what Michael Lebowitz (2010), following István Mészáros (1994, 2008), terms the "socialist triangle." Moving beyond the economist, determinist version of Marxism, which distorts historical materialism, Mészáros and Lebowitz understand the political economy of socialism to include: (1) the productive capacity and forces of society; (2) the social relations of "production" of humanity, understood as revolutionary human development that comes from the "simultaneous changing of circumstances and human activity or self-change" (Lebowitz 2010, 49); and (3) (in direct contrast to capitalist self-interest) the creation of communities of human solidarity – humans consciously working to meet the needs of the [global] community, including the "full development of the creative potentialities" of all humans (Mészáros 1994, 817). There is no doubt informed Chavez and seems to be appreciated by Maduro. Citing Mészáros, Chavez proclaimed in 2005 that Bolivarian socialism is creating "a communal system of production and consumption" (in: Lebowitz 2006, 108). In other words, socialism thus conceived includes nationalised industry to secure social wealth (removing capitalist ownership and exploitation of resources and labour), worker's control of production to institute democratic relations of production (ending production for profit without regard for safety, the environment or human needs and opposing state control over production), and democratic, participatory culture for determining how social wealth will be applied to develop humanity (replacing the culture of consumption,, hyper-individuality, ethnocentrism, and self-interest). Public and community media in Venezuela aspire to this "socialist triangle" in their public, social ownership of the means of media production, in the direct control over production and distribution of media by workers and community councils (without interference by the state or commercial media institutional control), and in the organic development of a culture of solidarity through collaborative, participatory production from and by the people themselves (as illustrated in Catia TV's ECPAI teams, Avila and ViVe communal documentaries, and community radio programming across the nation).

Public and community media in Venezuela illustrate the dialectic of creating a "state for revolution." As MINCI's Community Media Director Ana Viloria explains this is "an exquisite contradiction. The state is used to initiate new practices requiring direct working class control *outside* and *above* the state. The government did not impose, or implement. The government did not bribe or provide a gift, or even provide a service to the public. Rather, the [Bolivarian] government initiated a policy, provided funds [from the nationalised social wealth], while communal councils and worker's councils implement, direct, create and decide how to use media to communicate their own messages and ideas" (Viloria 2009).

One third of media broadcasts in Venezuela are now socially-owned with licensing collectively held by the media users themselves. These new media social relations are nothing like the vertical broadcasting and control prevalent in commercial media. These media do not broadcast to "receivers" or "audiences." These new media have established democratic relations of production, directed by workers and community organizations, functioning to develop class actions and advance a new social order. State power over communication (including private control and ownership and government regulation) is passing to organised worker and their constituents, as community media become organizing structures and practices undermining capitalist social relations, production norms, and ideology. Community media, in practice, transform individuals, communities, and social classes who directly experience the power of the power to communicate, the power of the power to democratically decide and implement. Community media, and their national public media counterparts, prepare the working class majority for the coming confrontation with capitalism (within Venezuela and from the us) by experiencing and communicating in production and programming new norms of class solidarity, collective ownership, and democratic practices.

11　The Reality of Power

This is no idealistic journey into possibility. The Venezuelan community media experience is an actual historical dialectic, based in the material reality of an unfolding revolution. In dialectical terms, the social consciousness of workers and their allies arrives before, simultaneously, and in interaction with existing social structures. The material dialectic of becoming is based on the consciousness informed by experience and possibility. Media workers, women, youth, indigenous people, and large sections of the working class, middle class, and unemployed are propelled by workers and communal control to imagine and create new social practices – in violation of the norms of class society that dictate power and control from bureaucratic institutions. New working class media practices include writing their own stories, producing their own programs, relying on working class sources, recognizing the integrity and value of working class experiences and knowledge, serving their communities and cultures, and connecting with other communities. These practices uncover real human potential, inspire further creative endeavors, as illustrated daily through TVes, ViVe, and Avila airing of communally-produced news and culture. Importantly, these multiple, but shared experiences have the potential to lead protagonists to new understandings, including the recognition that their access to communication and power can only be secured ultimately by establishing democratic social relations throughout society – not just in one plant or at one station. Their individual self-realization requires the collective societal realization of 21st century socialism.

In Venezuela, revolutionary voices are no longer compelled to cry out from the grass roots. Revolutionary voices now broadcast from the highest hilltops of the urban centers. Because resolute leaders in the Bolivarian government, from the president to the National Assembly are using the state apparatus for revolution, revolutionary voices have the power of communication, the power of direct action, the power of decision and control over production. In the process of democratic media production, social relations and social consciousness are being transformed.

Socialism, after all, is not just an ideology or a program. Socialism means new, revolutionary human beings with the power to realize the needs of all, using their own voices as power – not "speaking truth" to power (that impotent refrain of the powerless liberal) – but speaking working class power with the truth of an organised social movement, as collective agents of their own historic reconstruction. Community media are a vital, if insufficient, venue for creating new human beings as active agents of history, agents of communication who are no longer listeners, viewers, or spectators, but protagonists who make their own realities.

12   Two States: Dual Power in the Balance

Just as the nationalizations of steel, aluminum, and other industries have not replaced capitalism or its social relations throughout Venezuela and social missions have not replaced traditional political or social institutions, neither has the development of public and community media alongside an entrenched and still popular commercial media displaced the entertainment-based individual consumerist culture in Venezuela. Indeed, and contrary to the *New York Times*, the *Washington Post*, and US network television, media in Venezuela are diverse in form and substance, with commercial media being openly, and harshly critical of the Chavez government.

In other words, despite and because of the advances of the Bolivarian movement, there are currently two classes contending for power in Venezuela. The government represents the working class majority and is repeatedly using that power to organize and promote parallel institutions and sites for building political power and a new socialist culture.

At the same time, several wealthy families and their middle class managers remain as a part of a still powerful capitalist class with major interests in media, banking, retail and food production and distribution, and importantly in popular culture. Music, movies, television, fashion, and the discomforting familiarity of market relations encourage simple self-gratification, individualised mass entertainment, and consumerism. The capitalist class may be politically disoriented and divided, finding political unity difficult even with US guidance, but it continues to obstruct and resist social change, becoming increasingly desperate with every working class advance. Meanwhile, managers, shopkeepers, and middle class students and professionals are anxious and fearful, pummeled by the market, constrained by their small business mentality. Most are atomised and alienated from society, but many are attracted to the democratic impulses of the socialist reforms in education, health care, housing, and credit. In brief, Bolivarian socialism is growing; capitalism is under siege. A major confrontation is near.

13   Making Change by Taking Power

In the transition to socialism in Venezuela, the conflict between two states must be resolved. The future socialist state is embodied in the current Bolivarian government, parallel political and social institutions, including new media, changing social relations of production represented by worker's control of production, and the explosion of class consciousness and political organization of the working class. The weakened capitalist state relies on the prevalence of wage labour and market relations across the national economy and in global trade, its entrenched government bureaucracy, especially on the provincial and local level, ideologically reinforced by Venezuela's energetic consumerist entertainment culture and expressed through organised economic sabotage and media disruption campaigns, as exemplified in the 2014 protests. The future socialist state is pressuring the lethargic, but agitated capitalist state, featuring "elements of the new society with which the old collapsing bourgeois society is pregnant" (Marx 1871, 335). The capitalist class will not willingly relinquish its power to profit and exploit. There will soon be a war of movement, in Gramscian terms. There will be a battle of classes and their allies. Skirmishes like the media coup of April 2002, the oil management strike of December 2002, the daily obstruction by mid-level government officials, industrial sabotage, irregular border incursions by Colombia, continuous media incitement against government policies and over social problems like crime and housing, are but precursors to more organised civil unrest, including civil war. In February 2014, a section of the capitalist class disappointed with the PSUV's substantial electoral victory following Chavez's death, organised student protests against economic shortages and insecurity, calling for 'la salida' – the exit of President Nicolás Maduro. The violent protests echoed the 2002 coup and management strike, following a pattern of disruption, rumor and slander, and then concerted physical attacks against the Bolivarian revolution, especially government offices, social missions, and citizens deemed chavista supporters (Beeton 2014) – all mentored by US advisors (Weisbrot 2014; Zabludovsky 2014).

In fact, overshadowing the national and regional class conflict is the threatening presence and ongoing intervention of the United States, which continues to advise, finance, and intervene on behalf of the Venezuelan elite and larger U.S. interests (Benjamin 2006; James 2006; Weisbrot 2014). In 2012, U.S. President Obama asked for another $5 million for the opposition groups, adding to the $57 million they received in 2010 from the US and EU combined (Golinger 2011). As inroads are made into capitalist power, US intervention will surely increase in myriad ways. The immediate future in Venezuela will be an intense struggle between the old and the new.

Will the Venezuelan working class and its allies be prepared in consciousness and organization to withstand the onslaught, including the likely increasing intervention of the US? The strategy of "state for revolution" must anticipate the coming confrontation by resolutely building sites and experiences prompting the self-organization of the working classes (Ciccariello-Maher 2014). Some success can be noted: six million members of PSUV, twenty thousand community councils, hundreds of worker's councils in nationalised industry, thousands of social missions directed and staffed by tens of thousands of community activists, thirty thousand workers in popular militias, and hundreds of independent community media. The "state for revolution" continues to create opportunities for the working class and their allies to organize their own institutions, relations, and actions to fight for socialism. In action, the collective leadership of the state apparatus, the parallel working class institutions, and the independent political organizations seem to understand that their Bolivarian goals will realize 21st century socialism, only if they secure sufficient revolutionary power in a new state – with democratic, non-capitalist social relations, worker's control of production; direct, participatory political leadership and authority in law and policy; and socio-cultural practices for solidarity, democracy, and democratic communication.

The transitional phase to socialism became possible once the government began rejecting the capitalist class and undertook socialist goals, including writing laws and policies that opened avenues for new social relations, and putting the production of social wealth, including the production of media in the hands of the majority. Access to information and media production is a recognised human right in the Venezuelan Constitution (Articles 57–58, 65), the 2004 Law of Social Responsibility in Radio and Television declared the airwaves and radio spectrum a public good. CONATEL, MINCI, the National Assembly have only elabourated proposals for democratic media. The working class communities are the agents for implementing those proposals. The state apparatuses, such as MINCI exist to "solicit the people's involvement," because revolutionary leaders "know what we are doing is connected to humanity...so we put ourselves the task of learning that ideas and tools are there for political action" by the working class as protagonists of history (Viloria 2009).

By all available indications, using the "state for revolution" in the case of media suggests that public and community media have working class leaders stepping forward as protagonists in the revolution, markedly helping personalize the meaning of collective participation for media workers and their community bases – exemplified by each of the interviewees cited in this chapter. Yet, with a completely sober assessment, this may prove insufficient, because consumer culture is ingrained in Venezuela and seductive in complex ways. When ViVe TV showed indigenous Venezuelans speaking their own language with Spanish subtitles, nobody understood the political breakthrough, including many of the Chavistas (Sergio Arriasis, quoted in Wynter 2010). Fashion shows and beauty pageants remain popular, as do games shows and soap operas on commercial television.

Public and community media in Venezuela are constructing and broadcasting images for a new democratic socialist society, but with a growing awareness that new cultural identities cannot come from images or stories alone. A new socialist culture can only be created through political debates and battles for social justice, democracy, and new social relations that put human needs before private profits. The experiences of community media strongly hint at the real creative potential for humanity. Recognizing that objective material conditions frame possibilities for subjective intervention at opportune conjunctural moments has been a hallmark of historical materialism. In Venezuela, material conditions include oil resources, oil prices, class forces, lingering capitalist cultural norms and the likelihood of US intervention. Subjective conditions include the increasing organization and class consciousness of the working class and its allies, as well as concerted efforts to inform and persuade all of the benefits of international class solidarity, regional collaboration, and social justice.

Of course, even if understanding the dialectic of history and the contradictions within class society informs the Bolivarian leadership, it does not guarantee success. Nonetheless, Marxism has once again demonstrated its analytical and practical value for social change. Championing participatory democracy and implementing a "state for revolution" policy of government action and parallelism in social programs is a well-conceived strategy for winning socialism in the 21st century.

Those convinced of the democratic ethic of working class organization and the practical logic of historical materialism would do well to add their own subjective contribution to the efforts for 21st century socialism. Collectively raising more voices to defend, promote, and emulate community and public media in Venezuela will broaden awareness of an important historical lesson and increase the possibilities for its success. Community and public media in Venezuela are demonstrating an important strategic truth: social change can only be fully realised when working class protagonists for democracy have state power. Beyond Venezuela, others have a responsibility to recognize and organize our own power in acts of solidarity, mobilizing our own independent political power as working people are doing in Venezuela.

References

Artz, Lee. 2006. TeleSUR (Television of the South): Discarding Contraflow for Horizontal Communication. *International Journal of Media and Cultural Politics* 2 (2): 225–232.

Beeton, Dan. 2014, February 19. Violent Protests in Venezuela Fit a Pattern. Center for Economic and Policy Research. Accessed September 25, 2014. http://www.cepr.net/index.php/blogs/the-americas-blog/vient-protets-fit-a-pattern.

Benjamin, Media. 2006. US Intervention in Venezuela. *Common Dreams.* March 4. Accessed April 12, 2012.http://www.commondreams.org/views06/0304-20.htm.

Boothroyd, Rachel 2012, April 24. National Alternative Media Network Launched in Venezuela. *Venezuelanalysis.com* Accessed October 9, 2014. http://venezuelanalysis.com/news/6924.

Catia TVe Collective. 2006. Television from, by, and for the People. *Venezuelanalysis*, July 19. Accessed February 22, 2012. http://venezuelanalysis.com/analysis/1843.

Ciccariello-Maher, George. 2014, September 8. Venezuela at a Tipping Point. *Venezuelanalysis.* Accessed September 25, 2014. http://venezuelanalysis.com/analysis/10891.

Ciccariello-Maher, George. 2007. Zero Hour for Venezuela's RCTV. *Venezuelanalysis*, May 29. Accessed February 22, 2012. http://venezuelanalysis.com/analysis/2415.

Embassy of the Bolivarian Republic of Venezuela in the U.S. 2012, January 6. Community Media in Venezuela Gets Funding from Telecoms Authority. Retrieved June 6, 2012 from. http://venezuela-us.org/2012/01/06/community-media-venezuela-gets-funding-from-telecoms-authority/print/.

Enright, Michael, Antonio Frances, and Edith Scott Saaverda.1996. *Venezuela: The Challenge of Competitiveness.* New York: Palgrave, MacMillan.

Francia, Néstor. 2002. Abril Rojo—El Rescate de Chavez: Crónicas, analisis, documentos, entrevistas. Caracas: Imprenta Nacional.

Fuchs, Christian. 2012. Google Capitalism. *tripleC – Communication, Capitalism, & Critique: Journal for a Global Sustainable Information Society* 10 (1): 42–48. Accessed April 14, 2014. http://www.triple-c.at/index.php/tripleC/article/view/304.

Fuentes, Frederico. 2014, July 21. *Venezuelanalysis.com.* Accessed October 9, 2014. http://venezuelanalysis.com/analysis/10798.

Golinger, Eva. 2011. Money and Intervention in Venezuela. Wikileaks: U.S. Embassy Requests Funds for Anti-Chavez Groups. *Global Research.* Accessed April 10, 2012. http://www.globalresearch.ca/money-and-intervention-in-venezuela-wikileaks-us-embassy-requests-funding-for-anti-chavez-groups/25444.

Golinger, Eva. 2010. Internet Revolution in Venezuela. *Venezuelanalysis*, March 26. Accessed April 10, 2012. http://www.globalresearch.ca/index.php?context=va&aid=25444.

Golinger, Eva. 2006. The Chavez Code: Cracking US Intervention in Venezuela. London: Pluto Press.

Golinger, Eva. 2004, September 25. A Case Study in Media Concentration and Power. *Venezuelanalysis*, September 25. Accessed January 15, 2012. http://venezuealanalysis.com/analysis/710.

Gramsci, Antonio. 1971. *Selections from the Prison Notebooks of Antonio Gramsci.* Ed. and trans. Quintin Hoare and Geoffrey Nowell Smith. London: Lawrence and Wishart.

Internet World Stats. 2009. Usage and Population Statistics. Venezuela. Accessed April 17, 2012. http://www.internetworldstats.com/sa/ve.htm.

James, Deborah. 2006. U.S. Intervention in Venezuela: A Clear and Present Danger. Accessed April 12, 2012. http://www.globalexchange.org/sites/default/files/USVZrelations1.pdf.

Jaua, Elias. 2011. Without Confrontation There Can Be No Social Gains. *Venezuelanalysis*, July 20. Accessed February 22, 2012. http://venezuealanalysis.com/analysis/6366.

Lebowitz, Michael. 2006. Build It Now: Socialism for the 21st Century. New York: Monthly Review Press.

Lebowitz, Michael. 2010. The Socialist Alternative: Real Human Development. New York: Monthly Review Press.

Labrique, Laruent. 2011. Community Media Give New Face to Venezuela. Accessed January 16, 2012. http://presstv.com/detail/164807.html.

Lugo, Carlos. 2009. Personal interview at Radio El Primero Negro. Caracas, Venezuela. June, 2008.

Mallett-Ottrum, Ryan. 2013, July 13. Venezuela Government Continues Crackdown on Corruption. *Venezeulanalysis.com.* Accessed October 9, 2014. http://venezuelanalysis.com/news/9703.

Marx, Karl. 1867. *Capital. Volume One.* Accessed April 12, 2012. http://www.marxists.org/archive/marx/works/1867-c1/ch32.htm.

Marx, Karl. 1871. The Civil War in France. In *EngelsMarx Collected Works: Volume 23*, 307–359. New York: International Publishers.

Marx, Karl and Frederick Engels 1998. *The Communist Manifesto.* Originally published in 1848. New York: Penguin.

Mellado, Antonio. 2009. Personal interview at Avila TV, Caracas, Venezuela. June, 2008.

Mészáros, István. 1994. *Beyond Capital: Toward a Theory of Transition.* New York: Monthly Review Press.

Mészáros, István. 2008. *The Challenge and Burden of Historical Time: Socialism in the Twenty-first Century.* New York: Monthly Review Press.

Perdemo, Luis. 2009. Personal interview with Afro TV organizers in Caracas. Caracas, Venezuela. June, 2008.

Robertson, Ewan. 2011. October 29. Venezuela Passes New Leasing Law Proposed by Popular Initiative. Venezuelanalysis, October 29. Retrieved January 15, 2012. http://venezuelanalysis.com/news/6588.

Rothschuh, Guillermo Villanueva. 1986. Notes on the History of Revolutionary Journalism in Nicaragua. In *Communicating in Popular Nicaragua*, edited by Armand Mattelart, 28–36. New York: International General.

Sanchez, Martin. 2012. *Ten Years after the Coup: Alternative Media in Venezuela.* Presentation at DePaul University, Chicago. April 13.

Therborn, Goran. 2008. *What Does the Ruling Class Do When It Rules?: State Apparatuses and State Power Under Feudalism, Capitalism and Socialism.* London: Verso Books.

Vasquez, Wilfredo. 2008. Personal interview at Catia TV studios. Caracas, Venezuela. June, 2008.

Venezuela en Noticias. 2012. Community Media in Venezuela Get Funding from Telecoms Authority. *Venezuealanalysis,* January 8. Accessed January 9, 2012. http://venezuealanalysis.com/news/6731.

Viloria, Ana. 2009. Personal interview at the Ministry for Information and Communication (MINCI). Caracas, Venezuela. June, 2009.

Weisbrot, Mark. 2014, February 18. US Support for Regime Change in Venezuela is a Mistake. *Theguardian*.com. Accessed September 25, 2014. http://www.theguardian.com/commentisfree/2014/feb/18/venezuela-protests-us-support-regime-change-mistake.

Wilpert, Gregory. 2003. Venezuela's New Constitution. *Venezuealanalysis*, August 27. Accessed January 15, 2012. http://venezuealanalysis.com/analysis/70.

Wilpert, Gregory. 2007. RCTV and Freedom of Speech in Venezuela. *Venezuealanalysis*, June 2. Accessed January 15, 2012. http://venezuealanalysis.com/analysis/2425.

Wynter, Coral. 2010. Venezuela: Creating a New, Radical Media. *Green Left Weekly*, May 23. Accessed January 21, 2012. http://www.greenleft.org.au/node/44207.

Zabludovsky, Karla. 2014. February 21. Leopoldo Lopez Gives Venezuela the Image of the Revolutionary Who Has It All. Newsweek, February 21. Accessed January 15, 2012 from http://www.newsweek.com/2014/02/28/leopoldo-lopez-gives-venezuela-image-revolutionary-who-has-it-all-245568.html.

CHAPTER 18

Dallas Smythe Today – The Audience Commodity, the Digital Labour Debate, Marxist Political Economy and Critical Theory. Prolegomena to a Digital Labour Theory of Value

Christian Fuchs

1 Introduction

In 1977, Dallas Smythe published his seminal article *Communications: Blindspot of Western Marxism* (Smythe 1977a), in which he argued that Western Marxism has not given enough attention to the complex role of communications in capitalism. The article's publication was followed by an important foundational debate of media sociology that came to be known as *the Blindspot Debate* (Murdock 1978, Livant 1979, Smythe answered with a rejoinder to Murdock: Smythe 1994, 292–299) and by another article of Smythe on the same topic (*On the Audience Commodity and its Work*: Smythe 1981, 22–51). More than 30 years have passed and the rise of neoliberalism resulted in a turn away from the interest in class and capitalism and in the rise of postmodernism and the logic of the commodification of everything: Marxism became the blindspot of the social sciences.

The declining interest in Marx and Marxism is visualized in Figure 18.1 that shows the average annual number of articles in the Social Sciences Citation Index that contain one of the keywords Marx, Marxist or Marxism in the article topic description and were published in the five time periods 1968–1977, 1978–1987, 1988–1997, 1998–2007, 2008–2013. Choosing these periods allows observing if there has been a change since the start of the new capitalist crisis in 2008 and also makes sense because the 1968 revolt marked a break that also transformed academia.

Figure 18.1 shows that there was a relatively large academic article output about Marx in the period 1978–1987: 3659. Given that the number of articles published increases historically, also the interest in the period 1968–1977 seems to have been high. One can observe a clear contraction of the output of articles that focus on Marx in the periods 1988–1997 (2393) and 1998–2007 (1563). Given the historical increase of published articles, this contraction is even more severe. This period has also been the time of the intensification

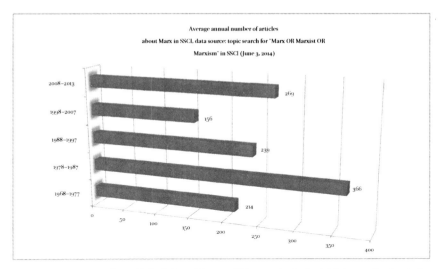

Average annual number of articles
about Marx in SSCI, data source: topic search for "Marx OR Marxist OR
Marxism" in SSCI (June 3, 2014)

FIGURE 18.1   *Articles published about Marx and Marxism in the Social Sciences Citation Index*

of neoliberalism, the commodification of everything (including public service communication in many countries) and a strong turn towards postmodernism and culturalism in the social sciences. One can see that the
average number of annual articles published about Marxism in the period
2008–2013 (269) has increased in comparisons to the periods 1988–2007 (156
per year) and 1988–1997 (239 per year). This circumstance is an empirical indicator for a renewed interest in Marx and Marxism in the social sciences as
effect of the new capitalist crisis. The question is if and how this interest can
be sustained and materialized in institutional transformations.

Due to the rising gap between the rich and the poor, widespread precarious
labour, and the new global capitalist crisis, neoliberalism and the silence about
class and capitalism have suffered cracks, fissures, and holes. Eagleton (2011)
notes that never has a thinker been so travestied as Marx and shows that the
contrary of what the common prejudices say about Marx makes up the core of
his works. But since the start of the global capitalist crisis in 2008, a relatively
large interest in the works of Karl Marx has developed. Slavoj Žižek (2010)
argues in this context that the recent world economic crisis has resulted in a
renewed interest in the Marxian Critique of the Political Economy. This is
also shown by the attention recently paid to Marx in the mainstream media.
Time magazine, for example, had Marx on its cover and asked about the
global financial crisis: What would Marx think? (*Time Magazine*, February 2,
2009). Hobsbawm (2011, 12–13) says that for understanding the global dimension

of contemporary capitalism, capitalism's contradictions and crises and the existence of socio-economic inequality, we "must ask Marx's questions" (p. 13). "Economic and political liberalism, singly or in combination, cannot provide the solution to the problems of the twenty-first century. Once again the time has come to take Marx seriously" (Hobsbawm 2011, 419). Given the importance of Marx for understanding, interpreting, and changing contemporary society, we should take Smythe's suggestion to develop a Marxist theory of media and communication very serious today. If we want to have a society and media oriented on human interests, then we need a Marxist theory of society and a Marxist theory of media and communication.

The task of this chapter is to explore perspectives for the Marxist study of media and communication today. First, I discuss the importance of taking a Marxist approach for studying media and communication (Section 2). Second, I give a short overview of the audience commodity debate and its renewal (Section 3). In Section 4, I analyze social media capital accumulation with the help of the notion of Internet prosumer commodification. Section 5 provides an overview of ideological changes that relate to digital media, perceived changes and the relationship between play and labour in contemporary capitalism (playbour). Section 6 presents a critique of criticisms of the digital labour debate. Finally, I draw some conclusions.

2 The Importance of Critical Political Economy, Critical Theory and Dallas Smythe Today

Dallas Smythe was a founding figure in the establishment of the Political Economy of Communications and taught the first course in the field (Mosco 2009, 82). He stressed the importance of studying media and communication in a critical and non-administrative way: "By 'critical' researchable problems we mean how to reshape or invent institutions to meet the collective needs of the relevant social community [...] By 'critical' tools, we refer to historical, materialist analysis of the contradictory process in the real world. By 'administrative' ideology, we mean the linking of administrative-type problems and tools, with interpretation of results that supports, or does not seriously disturb, the status quo. By 'critical' ideology, we refer to the linking of 'critical' researchable problems and critical tools with interpretations that involve radical changes in the established order" (Smythe and Dinh, 1983, 118).

In the article *On the Political Economy of Communications*, Smythe (1960) defined the "central purpose of the study of the political economy of communications" as the evaluation of "the effects of communication agencies in terms of the policies by which they are organized and operated" and the analysis of "the structure and policies of these communication agencies in their social settings" (Smythe 1960, 564). He identified various communications policy areas in this article. Whereas there are foundations of a general political economy in this paper, there are no traces of Marx in it. Janet Wasko (2004, 311) argues that although "Smythe's discussion at this point did not employ radical or Marxist terminology, it was a major departure from the kind of research that dominated the study of ass communications at that time." Wasko (2004, 312) points out that it was in the "1970s that the political economy of media and communications (PE/C) was explicitly defined again but this time within a more explicitly Marxist framework." She mentions in this context the works of Nicholas Garnham, Peter Golding, Armand Mattelart, Graham Murdock, Dallas Smythe as well as the Blindspot Debate (Wasko 2004, 312–313).

Later, Smythe (1981) formulated explicitly the need for a Marxist Political Economy of Communications. He spoke of a "Marxist theory of communication" (Smythe 1994, 258) and that critical theory means "Marxist or quasi-Marxist" theory (Smythe 1994, 256). He identified eight core aspects of a Marxist political economy of communications (Smythe 1981, xvi-xviii):

(1) materiality,
(2) monopoly capitalism,
(3) audience commodification and advertising,
(4) media communication as part of the base of capitalism,
(5) labour power,
(6) critique of technological determinism,
(7) the dialectic of consciousness, ideology and hegemony on the one side and material practices on the other side,
(8) the dialectics of arts and science.

Smythe reminds us of the importance of the engagement with Marx's works for studying the media in capitalism critically.

He argued that Gramsci and the Frankfurt School advanced the concepts of ideology, consciousness, and hegemony as areas "saturated with subjectivism and positivism" (Smythe 1981, xvii). These Marxist thinkers would have advanced an "idealist theory of the communications commodity" (Smythe 1994, 268) that situates the media only on the superstructure of capitalism and forgets to ask what economic functions they serve in capitalism.

In a review of Hans Magnus Enzensberger's (1974) book *The Consciousness Industry*, Smythe on the one hand agreed with Enzensberger that the "mind industry" wants to "'sell the existing order" (Enzensberger 1974, 10), but on the other hand disagrees with the assumption that its "main business and concern is not to sell its product" (Enzensberger 1974, 10): "Enzensberger's theory that every social system's communications policy serves the controlling class interest in perpetuating that system is of coruse correct," but to say that "the mass media and consciousness industry have no product" would mean to identify commodity production with "crude physical production" (Smythe 1977b, 200). Smythe (1977b) characterizes Enzensberger's views as bourgeois, idealistic and anarcho-liberal. For Smythe (1994, 266–291), the material aspect of communications is that audiences work, are exploited and sold as commodity to advertisers. He was more interested in aspects of surplus value generation of the media than their ideological effects. So Smythe called for analyzing the media more in terms of surplus value and exploitation and less in terms of manipulation. Nicholas Garnham (1990, 30) shares with Smythe the insight that the Political Economy of Communications should "shift attention away from the conception of the mass media as ideological apparatuses" and focus on the analysis of their "economic role" in surplus value generation and advertising. The analysis of media as "vehicles for ideological domination" is for Garnham (2004, 94) "a busted flush" that is not needed for explaining "the relatively smooth reproduction of capitalism."

Given the analyses of Smythe and Garnham, the impression can be created that Frankfurt School Critical Theory focuses on ideology critique and the Political Economy of Media/Communications on the analysis of capital accumulation by and with the help of the media. This is however a misunderstanding. Although wide-read works of the Frankfurt School focused on ideology (Adorno, Frenkel-Brunswik, Levinson and Sanford 1950, Horkheimer and Adorno 2002, Marcuse 1964), other books in its book series *Frankfurter Beiträge zur Soziologie* dealt with the changes of accumulation in what was termed late capitalism or monopoly capitalism (for example: Pollock 1956, Friedmann 1959). The Marxist political economist Henryk Grossmann was one of the most important members of the *Institut für Sozialforschung* in the 1920s and wrote his main work at the Institute (Grossmann 1929). Although only few will today agree with Grossmann's theory of capitalist breakdown, it remains a fact that Marxist political economy was an element of the Institut für Sozialforschung right from its beginning and had with Pollock and Grossmann two important representatives. After Horkheimer had become director of the Institute in 1930, he formulated an interdisciplinary research programme that aimed at bringing together philosophers and scholars from a broad range of disciplines, including economics (Horkheimer 1931). When formulating their general concepts of critical theory, both Horkheimer (2002, 244) and Marcuse (1941) had a combination of philosophy and Marx's Critique of the Political Economy in mind.

Just like Critical Political Economy was not alien to the Frankfurt School, ideology critique has also not been alien to the approach of the Critical Political Economy of the Media and Communication. For Graham Peter Murdock and Golding (1974, 4), the media are organizations that "produce and distribute commodities," are means for distributing advertisements and also have an "ideological dimension" by disseminating "ideas about economic and political structures." Murdock (1978, 469) stressed in the *Blindspot Debate* that there are non-advertising based culture industries (like popular culture) that sell "explanations of social order and structured inequality" and "work with and through ideology – selling the system" (see also: Artz 2008, 64). Murdock (1978) argued in the *Blindspot Debate* that Smythe did not enough acknowledge Western Marxism in Europe and that one needs a balance between ideology critique and political economy for analyzing the media in capitalism.

Smythe acknowledged himself the importance of ideology when talking about the "consciousness industry" (Smythe 1981, 4–9, 270–299). Although critical of Hans Magnus Enzensberger's works (Smythe 1977b), Smythe took up Enzensberger's concept of the consciousness industry and interpreted it in his own way. In contrast to the Frankfurt School, Symthe does not understand ideology as false consciousness, but as "system of beliefs, attitudes, and ideas" (Smythe 1981, 171). The task of the consciousness industry is for Smythe to make people buy commodities and pay taxes (Smythe 1994, 250). Its further task is to promote values that favour capitalism and the private property system (Smythe 1994, 251–253). One role of the capitalist media would be the "pervasive reinforcement of the ideological basis of the capitalist system," assumptions like "human nature is necessarily selfish and possessive. It has always been this way: You can't change human nature" (Smythe 1994, 251). So while Smythe criticized the Frankfurt School, he advanced and confirmed the importance of ideology critique himself. Robert Babe argues in this context that although Smythe stressed the need for a materialist theory of culture that sees audience power "as the media's main output" (Babe 2000, 133–134), his concept of the Consciousness Industry "is 'idealist' in Smythe's sense of the term" (Babe 2000, 134). The circumstance that Smythe took up Enzensberger's terminology and gave space to discussing the attempts of the media to ideologically distort reality shows that although he used fierce words against some represenatives of the Frankfurt School (idealist, bourgeois, etc.), he did not altogether dismiss ideology critique, but rather wanted to open up the debate for also giving attention to the media's capital accumulation strategies that are coupled to its role as mind manager.

A difference between the Critical Political Economy of Media and Communications and Critical Theory is that the first is strongly rooted in economic theory and the second in philosophy and social theory. Dallas Smythe acknowledged this difference: "While the cutting edge of critical theory lies in political economy, critical theory in communications has the transdisciplinary scope of the social sciences, humanities, and arts" (Smythe 1984, 211). Smythe defined critical theory broadly as "criticism of the contradictory aspects of the phenomena in their systemic context" (Smythe and Dinh 1983, 123) and therefore concluded that critical theory is not necessarily Marxist. The historical Critical Theory of the Frankfurt School has its roots in Marxist political philosophy, so the question is if one should really have a broad definition of the term "critical" that does not focus on systemic critique.

Robert Babe (2012) compares the works of Theodor W. Adorno and Dallas Smythe. He stresses that both worked out Marxist, political-economic and materialist analyses of media and culture. Smythe would have primarily been inspired by the opposition to monopoly capitalism, Adorno by the opposition to National Socialism. Whereas Smythe would have favoured quantitative analysis and would have stressed the impacts of dominative media on external reality and the capital/labour relationship, Adorno would have employed more qualitative methods and would have focused on the psychological implications of dominative media and the relationship of elites and non-elites. Babe sees Smythe as more policy-oriented and Adorno as more concerned about the improvement of individual lives. Smythe would have been more of an activist and optimist than Adorno. "Adorno and Smythe both complement and contradict one another in their political economy approaches. Smythe certainly fills some immense gaps in Horkheimer and Adorno's treatment of the culture industry by addressing market structures and historical details of the industries and firms. [...] Adorno, on the other hand, went beyond Smythe in treating the culture industry not just as the persuasion element of late ('monopoly') capitalism, but as harbinger and cause of future totalitarianism. [...] Adorno and Smythe, though, were totally agreed on one thing: control of the means of communication is an important basis of political power. Together they provide powerful analyses of the control function of the culture/consciousness industry. They constitute convincing counterweights to the limited-effects literature by Lazarsfeld, Schramm, Katz, and other mainstream American writers" (Babe 2012, 112–113).

The approaches of the Frankfurt School and of the Critique of the Political Economy of Media and Communications should be understood as being complementary. There has been a stronger focus on ideology critique in the Frankfurt School approach for historical reasons. For Horkheimer and Adorno, the rise of German fascism, the Stalinist praxis and American consumer capitalism showed the defeat of the revolutionary potentials of the working class (Habermas 1984, 366–367). They wanted to explain why the revolutionary German working class followed Hitler, which brought up the interest in the analysis of the authoritarian personality and media propaganda. As Communists and coming from Jewish families, Horkheimer and Adorno (as well as their colleagues) were directly threatened by the violence of National Socialism and therefore had to escape from Germany. The violent consequences of Nazi ideology may partly explain the relevance that the notion of ideology had throughout their lives in their works. The Anglo-American approach of the Political Economy of the Media and Communications was developed by people like Dallas Smythe and Herbert Schiller in countries that during the Second World War fought against fascism. Whereas North American capitalism was after 1945 based on liberal ideology, anti-communism and a strong consumer culture that certainly also had fascist potentials, German post-war capitalism was built on the legacy of National Socialism and a strong persistence of fascist thinking in everyday life and politics.

The lives of Smythe and Schiller themselves were not as in the case of Horkheimer and Adorno directly threatened by fascist regimes. But both showed a lot of concern about fascism, which shaped their thought. Vincent Mosco (2009, 83) writes in this context that contacts with anti-fascists that fought in the Spanish civil war had profound political effects on Smythe's thinking. Serving in the US army in World War II and working for the US government in Germany after the war had "substantial formative influence" (Mosco 2009, 85) on Herbert Schiller. The works of the American economist Robert A. Brady influenced both Smythe's and Schiller's thinking (Schiller 1999). Brady had contacts with Franz Neumann, a representative of the Frankfurt School who was in exile in the USA and just like Brady (1937) wrote an analysis of National Socialism (Neumann 1966). Brady was especially concerned with fascist potentials of capitalism, like in the form of media propaganda and public relations. Neumann (1966) stressed that National Socialism was a form of monopoly capitalism that was based on a leadership cult. Dan Schiller (1999, 100) argues that "Brady endowed the study of the political economy of communications with a critical intellectual legacy." The fascist threat was both a concern for German critical theorists and North American critical political economists.

Horkheimer's (1947) notion of instrumental reason and Marcuse's (1964) notion of technological rationality open up connections between the two approaches. Horkheimer and Marcuse stressed that in capitalism there is a tendency that freedom of action is replaced by instrumental decision making on the part of capital and the state so that the individual is expected to only react and not to act. The two concepts are grounded in Georg Lukács (1923/1972) notion of reification that is a reformulation of Marx's (1867) concept of fetishism. Reification means "that a relation between people takes on the character of a thing and thus acquires 'phantom objectivity', an autonomy that seems so strictly rational and all-embracing as to conceal every trace of its fundamental nature: the relation between people" (Lukács 1923/1972, 83).

The media in capitalism are modes of reification in a multiple sense:

- First, commercial media reduce humans to the status of consumers of advertisements.
- Second, culture is in capitalism to a large degree connected to the commodity form. There are cultural commodities that are bought by consumers and audience and user commodities that media consumers and Internet prosumers become themselves.
- Third, in order to reproduce its existence, capitalism has to present itself as the best possible (or only possible) system and makes use of the media in order to try to keep this message (in all its differentiated forms) hegemonic.

The first and the second dimension constitute the economic dimension of instrumental reason, the third dimension the ideological form of instrumental reason. Capitalist media are necessarily means of advertising and commodification and spaces of ideology. Advertisement and cultural commodification make humans an instrument for economic profit accumulation. Ideology aims at instilling the belief in the system of capital and commodities into human's subjectivity. The goal is that human thoughts and actions do not go beyond capitalism, do not question and revolt against this system and thereby play the role of instruments for the perpetuation of capitalism. It is of course an important question to which extent ideology is always successful and to which degree it is questioned and resisted, but the crucial aspect about ideology is that it encompasses strategies and attempts to make human subjects instrumental in the reproduction of domination and exploitation.

For Marx, the analysis of capitalism starts with the analysis of the commodity: "The wealth of societies in which the capitalist mode of production prevails appears as an 'immense collection of commodities'; the individual commodity appears as its elementary form" (Marx 1867, 125). Marx therefore begins the analysis of capitalism with the analysis of the commodity: its use value, exchange value, value, the labour embodied in it, the value forms of the commodity, including the money form (x commodity A = y amount of money). After this analysis, Marx turns in Chapter 1.4 (*The fetishism of the commodity and its secret*) of *Capital, Volume 1* to the analysis ideology as immanent feature of the commodity. The "mysterious character of the commodity-form" is that human social relations that create commodities are not visible in the commodity, but appear as "the socio-natural properties of these things". "The definite social relation between men themselves [take in ideologies] [...] the fantastic form of a relation between things" (Marx 1867, 165). Ideologies legitimatize various phenomena by creating the impression that the latter exist always and naturally and by ignoring the historical and social character of things. So for Marx, ideology and commodification are interconnected aspects of capitalism. A Marxist theory of communication should therefore, besides the focus on struggles and alternatives, have a double-focus on the role of media and communication in the context of ideology and commodification.

Smythe said that the "starting point for a general Marxist theory of communications is [...] the theory of commodity exchange" (Smythe 1994, 259). Adorno acknowledged that "the concept of exchange is [...] the hinge connecting the conception of a critical theory of society to the construction of the concept of society as a totality" (Adorno 2000, 32). Commodity and commodity exchange are crucial concepts for Critical Political Economy and Critical Theory. As the commodity concept is connected to both capital accumulation and ideology, both approaches should start simultaneously with the value aspects and the ideology aspects of media commodities.

Accumulation and ideology go hand in hand. An example: "social media." After the dot.com crisis in 2000, there was a need to establish new capital accumulation strategies for the capitalist Internet economy. Investors were reluctant to invest finance capital after the crisis as venture capital into digital media companies. So the discourse on "social media" became focused on new capital accumulation models for the Internet economy. Nobody knew if the users were interested in microblogs, social networking sites, etc. The rise of "social media" as a new capital accumulation model was accompanied by a social media ideology: that "social media" are new ("web 2.0"), pose new opportunities for participation, will bring about an "economic democracy," enable new forms of political struggle ("Twitter revolution"), more democracy ("participatory culture"), etc. The rise of new media was accompanied by a techno-deterministic and techno-optimistic ideology. This ideology was necessary for convincing investors and users to support the social media capital accumulation model. The political economy of surplus value generation on "social media" and ideology heavily interacted here in order to enable the economic and discursive rise of "social media."

Some scholars tends to say that Frankfurt School and the Critical Political Economy of Media and Communication are pessimistic, elitist, and neglect audiences (see for example: Hall 1986, 1988; Grossberg 1995/1998). They say that the concept of ideology as false consciousness makes "both the masses and the capitalists look like judgemental dopes" (Hall 1986, 33). Hall (1988, 44) criticizes Lukács (whose works have been one of the main influences on the Frankfurt School) by saying that the false consciousness theorem is simplistic (it assumes that "vast numbers of ordinary people, mentally equipped in much the same way as you or I, can simply be thoroughly and systematically duped into misrecognizing entirely where their real interests lie") and elitist ("Even less acceptable is the position that, whereas 'they' – the masses – are the dupes of history, 'we' – the privileged – [...] can see, transitively, right through into the truth, the essence, of a situation").

In other works, Hall advocated a different concept of ideology that is not completely unrelated to the one of the Frankfurt School. In their work *Policing the Crisis*, Hall et al. (1978) showed how the state and the media use moral panics about crime as "the principal ideological consciousness by means of which a 'silent majority' is won over to the support of increasingly coercive measures" (Hall et al., 1978, 221) and the establishment of a law and order-society. If both the mainstream media and the police argue for increasing law and order policies in the course of a moral panic, then they both legitimate the control process, a mutual enforcement of the "control culture" and a "signification culture" emerges (Hall et al., 1978, 76) so that "the mutual articulation" of the two "create an *effective ideological and control closure* around the issue" (Hall et al., 1978, 76). The media, just like the police, then act as "an apparatus of the control process itself – an 'ideological state apparatus'" (Hall et al., 1978, 76).

Colin Sparks describes the relationship between Stuart Hall's version of Cultural Studies and Marxism as "move towards marxism and move away from marxism" (Sparks 1996, 71). He argues that Hall in the 1970s engaged with structural Marxism, which culminated in the *Policing the Crisis*-book, and that then there was a "slow movement away from any self-identification with marxism" (Sparks 1996, 88) in the 1980s that was influenced by the uptake of Ernesto Laclau's approach. The resulting "distance between cultural studies and marxism" is for Sparks a "retrograde move" (Sparks 1996, 98). Vincent Mosco (2009) argues that Hoggart, Williams, Thompson, Willis and Hall "maintained a strong commitment to an engaged class analysis" (Mosco 2009, 233), but that later Cultural Studies became "less than clear about its commitment to political projects and purposes" (Mosco 2009, 229) and that therefore it is "hard to make the case that cultural studies has devoted much attention to labor, the activity that occupies most people's waking hours" (Mosco 2009, 214).

Hall in his criticism of Frankfurt School that can be read as self-criticism of his own earlier works misrecognizes that not all people are equally educated because in a class society basic and higher education is to a certain extent also shaped by class differences so that left-wing intellectuals tend to have more time and resources than white and blue collar workers for engaging in studying how capitalism works. Recognizing this circumstance means that ideology critique gives organic intellectuals a role in struggles because they have the potentials of "providing a map of the structure of domination and the terrain of struggle" (Garnham 1995/1998, 607). For Hall, the assumption that ordinary people are active and critical follows from the rejection of the manipulation thesis: "Since ordinary people are not cultural dopes, they are perfectly capable of recognising the way the realities of working-class life are reorganised, reconstructed, and reshaped by the way they are represented (i.e. re-presented) in, say, Coronation Street" (Hall, 1981/1988, 447). Lawrence Grossberg (1995/1998) argued that both Frankfurt School and Political Economy have a simple "model of domination in which people are seen as passively manipulated 'cultural dupes'" (616) and that for them "culture matters only as a commodity and an ideological tool of manipulation" (618).

In contrast to such claims, Dallas Smythe had a very balanced view of the audience: capital would attempt to control audiences, but they would have potentials to resist: "People are subject to relentless pressures from Consciousness Industry; they are besieged with an avalanche of consumer goods and services; they are themselves produced as (audience) commodities; they reproduce their own lives and energies as damaged and in commodity form. But people are by no means passive or powerless. People do resist the powerful and manifold pressures of capital as best they can" (Smythe 1981, 270).

Adorno, who is vilified by many scholars as the prototypical cultural pessimist and elitist, had a positive vision for a medium like TV. For television (in German: Fernsehen = literally: to watch into the distance) "to keep the promise still resonating within the word, it must emancipate itself from everything within which it – reckless wish-fulfilment – refutes its own principle and betrays the idea of Good Fortune for the smaller fortunes of the department store" (Adorno 2005, 57). Adorno frequently acknowledges the need and potentials of emancipation. In the case of TV, he points out that enabling watching into the distance beyond capitalism is a good fortune. This is indirectly a call for the creation of alternative media that question the status quo. Adorno also did not, as falsely claimed by many, despise popular culture. He was for example a fan of Charlie Chaplin and pointed out the critical role of the clown in popular culture (Adorno 1996). Even in the *Culture Industry*-chapter of the *Dialectic of the Enlightenment*, the positive elements of popular culture are visible. For example when Adorno writes that "traces of something better persist in those features of the culture industry by which it resembles the circus" (Horkheimer and Adorno 2002, 114). Adorno (1977, 680) in his essay *Erziehung nach Auschwitz (Education after Auschwitz)* wrote about the positive role that TV could play in anti-fascist education in Germany after Auschwitz. If one goes beyond a superficial and selective reading of Adorno, then one will find his deep belief in the possibility of emancipation and in the role that culture can play in it. English translations of Horkheimer's and Adorno's works are imprecise because the language of the two philosophers is complex and not easily translatable. But besides the problem non-German speakers are facing when reading Horkheimer and Adorno, there seems to be a certain non-willingness to engage thoroughly with the Frankfurt School's and Critical Political Economy's origins in order to set up a straw man.

Karl Marx (1867) titled his opus magnum not *Capital. A Political Economy*, but rather *Capital. A Critique of Political Economy*. Political Economy is a broad field, incorporating also traditions of thinking grounded in classical liberal economic thought and thinkers like Malthus, Mill, Petty, Ricardo, Say, Smith, Ure, etc. that Marx studied, sublated, and was highly critical of in his works. His main point of criticism of Political Economy is that it fetishizes capitalism. Its thinkers "confine themselves to systematizing in a pedantic way, and proclaiming for everlasting truths, the banal and complacent notions held by the bourgeois agents of production about their own world, which is to them the best possible one" (Marx 1867, 175). They postulate that categories like commodities, money, exchange value, capital, markets, or competition are anthropological features of all society, thereby ignoring the categories' historical character and enmeshment into class struggles. Marx showed the contradictions of political economy's thought and took classical political economy as starting point for a critique of capitalism that considers "every historically developed form as being in a fluid state, in motion" and analyzes how "the movement of capitalist society is full of contradictions" (Marx 1867, 103), which calls for the "development of the contradictions of a given historical form" by political practice (619) and means that Marx's approach is "in its very essence critical and revolutionary" (Marx 1867, 103).

Marx developed a Critique of the Political Economy of Capitalism, which sees critique as threefold process:

(a)   an analysis and critique of capitalism,
(b)   a critique of liberal ideology, thought and academia,
(c)   transformative practice.

To be precise, one should not speak of Political Economy of Media/ Communications, but of the *Critique of the Political Economy of Communication, Culture, Information and the Media*. Some authors realized this circumstance and stressed that what is needed is a "Marxist theory of communication" (Smythe 1994, 258), that critical theory means "Marxist or quasi-Marxist" theory (Smythe 1994, 256) and that "Critical Political Economy of Communications" is critical in the sense of being "broadly marxisant" (Murdock and Golding 2005, 61).

Robin Mansell (1995, 51) argues that Smythe engaged in establishing a Critical Media and Communication Studies that "had at its core the need to interrogate the systemic character of capitalism as it was expressed through the means of structures of communication" and that his focus was on exposing "through critical research the articulation of political and economic power relations as they were expressed in the institutional relations embedded in technology and the content of communication in all its forms" (Mansell 1995, 47). Robin Mansell points out the importance of a critical methodology in Smythe's approach. Smythe was interested in developing a "Marxist theory of communication" (Smythe 1994, 258) and argued that critical theory means "Marxist or quasi-Marxist" theory (Smythe 1994, 256). I therefore think that it is consequent and important to characterize Smythe's approach not just as Critical Communication Research – which it certainly also, but not exclusively was –, but as Marxist Communication Studies, which means a unity of theoretical/ philosophical, empirical and ethical studies of media and communication that is focused on the analysis of contradictions, structures and practices of domination, exploitation, struggles, ideologies and alternatives to capitalism in relation to media and communication. One should not split off the importance of Marx and Marxism from Smythe's approach and reduce him to having established a critical empirical research methodology. Janet Wasko stresses in this context that Marx's 11th Feuerbach thesis ("The philosophers have only interpreted the world, in various ways; the point is to change it") applied to the work and life of Dallas Smythe: "Analyzing and understanding the role of communications in the modern world might be enough for most communication scholars. But Dallas Smythe also sought to change the world, not only by his extensive research and teaching in academia, but in his work in the public sector, and through his life as a social activist" (Wasko 1993, 1).

In the German discussions about the Critique of the Political Economy of the Media, Horst Holzer (1973, 131; 1994, 202ff) and Manfred Knoche (2005a) have distinguished four functions of the media in capitalism that are relevant for the Marxist Critique of the Political Economy of the Media and Communication:

(1)   capital accumulation in the media industry;
(2)   advertising, public relations and sales promotion for other industries;
(3)   legitimization of domination and ideological manipulation;
(4)   reproduction, regeneration, and qualification of labour power.

Holzer and Knoche have provided a good framework that is, however, too structuralistic and lacks the aspect of struggles and alternative.

So building on and at the same time going beyond Holzer and Knoche, one can say that the task of a *Critical Theory and the Critique the Political Economy of Communications, Culture, Information and the Media* is to focus on the critique and analysis of the role of communication, culture, information, and the media in capitalism in the context of:

(a)   processes of capital accumulation (including the analysis of capital, markets, commodity logic, competition, exchange value, the antagonisms of the mode of production, productive forces, crises, advertising, etc.),
(b)   class relations (with a focus on work, labour, the mode of the exploitation of surplus value, etc.),
(c)   domination in general and the relationship of forms of domination to exploitation,
(d)   ideology (both in academia and everyday life) as well as the analysis of and engagement in
(e)   struggles against the dominant order, which includes the analysis and support of
(f)   social movement struggles and
(g)   social movement media that
(h)   aim at the establishment of a democratic-socialist society that is based on communication commons as part of structures of commonly-owned means of production (Fuchs 2011a).

The approach thereby realizes that in capitalism all forms of domination are connected to forms of exploitation (Fuchs 2008, 2011a).

So I am arguing for a combination of Critical Theory and Critical Political Economy. However, such an approach does not have to stay pure in terms of its theory connections, it is open for theoretical links, as my own drawing on certain concepts by authors such as Sigmund Freud, Pierre Bourdieu or Gilles Deleuze in this chapter shall show. My basic contention is that in establishing such links, it is important to maintain an analytical framework that stresses the importance of capitalism and class, i.e. that is guided by Marxist theory. In the next section, I will give a brief overview of one foundational debate in Critical Media and Communication Studies that has gained new relevance today: the blindspot debate, in which Dallas Smythe introduced the notion of the audience commodity.

3   The Renewal of the Audience Commodity Debate

According to Dallas Smythe (Lent 1995, 34), he first formulated the "'blind spot' argument about audience members' work for advertisers" (Lent 1995, 34) in 1951 in the article "The consumer's stake in radio and television" (Smythe 1951).

In this paper, Smythe asks what "the nature of the 'product'" (Smythe 1951, 109) of radio and television actually is. First, there would be a market for receivers. Second, "there is that product known as station time, and sometimes as audience loyalty (measured by ratings) which stations sell to advertisers. What is sold is a program for the audience (in whose continuing loyalty the station management has a vital interest), and the probability of developing audience loyalty to the advertiser. [...] In commercial radio and television, our Janus-like product is paid for twice. It is paid for once, as a producer's good, if you please, when the sponsor pays for its production. And it is paid for again, as a consumer's good, when the more or less predictable audience response results in the ringing of cash registers where the sponsor's product is sold to ultimate consumers" (Smythe 1951, 119). It would therefore be a myth that "radio and television programs are 'free'" (Smythe 1951, 110). Smythe here shows a clear concern for the role of advertising in commercial radio and television and the audience as a product. The notion of the audience commodity is already present in the 1951 article in an implicit manner, whereas Smythe formulated it more explicitly in the 1970s.

In 1977, Dallas Smythe argued that the "material reality under monopoly capitalism is that all non-sleeping time of most of the population is work time. [...] Of the off-the-job work time, the largest single block is time of the audiences, which is sold to advertisers. [...] In 'their' time which is sold to advertisers workers (a) perform essential marketing functions for the producers of consumers' goods, and (b) work at the production and reproduction of labour power" (Smythe 1977a, 3). David Hesmondhalgh (2010) remarks that also sleeping time can be seen as reproductive work time that recreates labour power. Smythe stressed this circumstance (not in the *Blindspot*-article, but later) when writing: "For the great majority of the population [...] 24 hours a day is work time" (Smythe 1981, 47).

Media content would be "an inducement (gift, bribe or 'Free lunch') to recruit potential members of the audience and to maintain their loyal attention" (Smythe 1977a, 5). Smythe (1977a; 1981, 22–51) introduced the notion of the audience commodity for analyzing media advertisement models, in which the audience is sold as a commodity to advertisers: "Because audience power is produced, sold, purchased and consumed, it commands a price and is a commodity. [...] You audience members contribute your unpaid work time and in exchange you receive the program material and the explicit advertisements" (Smythe 1981, 26, 233). Audiences "work to market [...] things to themselves" (Smythe 1981, 4). The "main function of the mass media [...] is to produce audiences prepared to be dutiful consumers" (Smythe 1994, 250). Work would not necessarily be wage labour, but a general category – "doing something creative" (Smythe 1981, 26).

Eileen Meehan (1984) argues that commercial media not only have a commodity message and an audience commodity, but also commodity ratings. She stresses the importance of the question "how do ratings and the ratings industry fit into the production of the commodity message?" (Meehan 1984, 217) for answering the question "what commodity is produced by mass communications industries?" (Meehan 1984, 216). Meehan (1993) says that ratings serve "to set the price that networks" can demand and that advertisers have "to pay for access to the commodity audience" (Meehan 1993, 387). It would depend on the used measurement technique how strongly the audience measurement industry over- or underestimated the audience size. The ratings industry would be highly monopolized and monopoly capitalists (like A.C. Nielsen) would set the standards of measurement. The ratings industry would have a preference for measuring a particular audience that is likely to buy and consume a lot of commodities, therefore "the commodity audience and commodity ratings are entirely artificial and manufactured" (Meehan 1993, 389). Chen (2003) has coined in this context the notion of the fictitious audience commodity. Meehan (2007, 164) stresses: "all television viewers are not in television's commodity audience and [...] some parts of the commodity audience are more valuable than others". Göran Bolin concludes based on Meehan's arguments that there is an "empiric fallacy of Smythe, Jhally and Livant, and Andrejevic, who see statistics as representative of reality" and says that "it is not the viewers who work, but rather the statisticians" (Bolin 2009, 357; see also: Bolin 2011, 37, 84). This claim might be too strong because it implies that the audience cannot be exploited by capital. But there is no doubt that the audience commodity is connected to the rise of the ratings industry that engages in setting prices for audiences. If the audience produces the value of the audience commodity, then the ratings industry sets the price of this commodity and thereby is central in the transformation of audience commodity values into prices. With the rise of commercial Internet platforms, audience ratings no longer need to be approximated, but permanent surveillance of user activities and user content allows the definition of precisely defined consumer groups with specific interests. It is exactly known to which group a consumer belongs and advertising is targeted to these groups.

Eileen Meehan (2002) points out that the audience commodity is gendered:

(a)   Employees who sell ads tend to be female and low-paid.
(b)   Advertisers and the advertising industry tend to base assumptions about the audience commodity on sexist values and so "discriminate against anyone outside the commodity audience of white, 18 to-34-year-old, heterosexual, English-speaking, upscale men" (Meehan 2002, 220). Focusing

on the connection of gender and class, patriarchy and capitalism, sex and money in the media is an important task that has faced both neglect and mutual interest on the side of feminists and political economists (Meehan and Riordan 2002). Valerie Steeves and Janet Wasko (2002) point out that socialist/Marxist feminism and Marxist political economy are natural allies, but that there has been a turn away from socialism and the interest in the connection of partiarchy and capitalism in feminism. They stress that it is an important task both for feminism and poltiical economy to not just focus on words, symbols and discourses of gender and the media, but to realize that "words, symbols, and discourses are important in shaping structures of inequality" (Steeves and Wasko 2002, 26).

Sut Jhally (1987, Chapter 2) argues that Dallas Smythe's notion of the audience commodity is too imprecise. Jhally says that advertisers buy the watching time of the audience as a commodity. His central assumption is that one should see "watching time as the media commodity" (Jhally 1987, 73). "When the audience watches commercial television it is working for the media, producing both value and surplus value" (Jhally 1987, 83). He says that the networks buy the watching-power of the audience (Jhally 1987, 75). Jhally argues that the audience watching time is the programme time and that advertising watching time is surplus time (Jhally 1987, 76). The audience's wage would be the programming (Jhally 1987, 85). "The programming, the value of watching-power, is the wage of the audience, the variable capital of the communications industry" (Jhally and Livant 1986/2006, 36). The question that arises is if watching time can be considered to be a wage equivalent in a society whose main structuring structures are money and capital.

So I disagree with Jhally's argument that the wage that TV viewers receive is the TV programme, that the necessary labour time is the watching of non-advertising programmes and that the surplus labour time is the watching of advertisements. You cannot live by watching TV, so watching TV is not an equivalent to a wage. Göran Bolin argues in this context: "It might be argued that what audiences get is television programmes, but if audiences are working, and if their salary is entertainment shows, how can they further convert this salary? The average viewer cannot buy food for the experience earned in watching an entertainment or any other television show" (Bolin 2005, 297; Bolin 2011, 37). Rather all watching time of commercial TV is surplus labour time. In the "digital labour"-debate, some people employ an argument that is related to the one by Jhally. They argue that Facebook does not exploit users because they receive free access to the platform as a "wage." There is a difference to Jhally because he maintains the notion of exploitation and surplus value, but both arguments ignore that money is the most important structure in capitalism that is privileged over all other structures and relations in terms of the power that it gives to its owners. Therefore Marx argues that in capitalism, money has a "social monopoly [...] to play the part of universal equivalent within the world of commodities" (Marx 1867, 162).

The human is, as Marx (1844) knew, a natural and a social being that needs to eat and to communicate in order to survive. In capitalism, the access to many means of human survival is organized through the commodity and money form: you can only get access to many of the necessary means of survival if you are able to buy commodities. And to do so, you need to get hold of money. And for largest share of people, this circumstance compels them to sell their labour power as a commodity in order to earn a wage that they can use in order to buy means of survival. The means of communication are part of the means of survival. If they are organised as public or common goods, then they can escape the money form and people do not have to pay in order to get access to them. Some means of communication, as e.g. most movies and popular culture, are organised as commodities that are sold. One can only get access by paying for them or by trying to undercut the commodity form (e.g. by downloading them without payment on the Internet). Internet platforms like Facebook and Twitter provide access to means of communication without selling access or content as commodity, yet they do not stand outside the commodity form, but rather commodify users' data. In return for the commodification of data, Facebook and Twitter provide a means of communication to its users. These means could be considered as being in-kind goods provided as return for the users granting the companies the possibility to access and commodify personal data. If the relationship between users and platform were organised in the form of a modern wage relationship, then the users would receive money in return for the commodification of their digital labour power. They could use this money for buying various means of survival. The difference to such monetary payments is that users on Facebook and Twitter do not receive a universal medium of exchange, but rather one specific means of communication. By giving users access to their platforms, Facebook and Twitter do not provide general means of survival, but rather access to particular means of communication whose use serves their own profit interests. This is not to say that I argue for payments to users of corporate Internet platforms that are advertising-financed. I rather argue for the creation of non-commerical non-profit alternatives that altogether escape, sublate and struggle against the commodity form.

The point I want to make is that the means of communication that Facebook and Twitter provide to its users are not simple means of survival and should not be analytically treated as such, but are rather also means of production for

the creation of value and profit. This circumstance arises from the simultaneous character of social media users as consumers of technological services and
producers of data, commodities, value and profit. The circumstance that the
means of consumption/communication provided by Facebook are not simple
means of survival, but that in this consumption all users during the full consumption time produce value for Facebook and Twitter, makes the argument
that service access is a form of wage inappropriate. If one buys a can of Coke
from parts of the wage one earns and drinks it, one does not produce value
(and as a consequence profit for Coca Cola) during the drinking/consumption
process, one rather for being able to drink the Coke has to pay money so that
Coca Cola realizes monetary profit. The consumption does not directly create
value for the company. On Facebook and Twitter, the consumption process of
the service entails all online communication and usage time. All of this time is
not only reproduction time, i.e. time for the the reproduction of labour power,
but at the same time labour time that produces data commodities that are
offered by Facebook and Twitter for sale to advertising clients. In the consumption process, the users not just reproduce their labour power, but produce
commodities. So on Facebook, YouTube, Twitter, etc., all consumption time is
commodity production time.

    The analytical problem that Smythe and Jhally in relation to TV radio, and
newspapers had to cope with was that consuming these media is a rather passive activity. Therefore they had to find a way to argue that this behaviour also
produces surplus value. Jhally's analysis that in the case of television watching
time is sold as a commodity, equals saying that the more watchers there are,
the higher advertising profits are generated. In the case of television, this part
of the analysis is feasible, but in the world of the Internet, the situation is different. Here users are not passive watchers, but to a certain degree active creators of content. Advertisers are not only interested in the time that users
spend online, but also in the products that are created during this time –
user-generated digital content and online behaviour. The users' data – information
about their uploaded data, social networks, their interests, demographic data,
their browsing and interaction behaviour – is sold to the advertisers as a commodity. Contrary to the world of television that Jhally analyzes, on the Internet
the users' subjective creations are commodified. Therefore, Smythe's original
formulation holds here that the audience itself – its subjectivity and the results
of its subjective creative activity – is sold as a commodity. The Internet is an
active medium, where consumers of information are as a tendency also producers of information. Therefore it is better to speak in the case of Facebook
and other corporate social media of Internet prosumer commodification
(Fuchs 2010). However, also television has today become digital and more

interactive so that audience commodification can take place in real-time and make use of consumer profiles and new forms of commerce (T-commerce, U-commerce, etc.) that further advance commodification (Andrejevic 2007, McGuigan 2012).

Brett Caraway (2011) claims that the audience is no commodity because "the activities of the audience are not under the direct control of the capitalist. Nor is it clear that the product of the labour of the audience (whatever that may be) is alienated from the audience" (Caraway 2011, 697). Capitalism uses the force of markets to coerce workers to sell their labour power: if you do not work for a wage, you are unlikely to survive. Whereas wage labour is coerced by the threat of physical violence (the threat is death because of the lack of being able to purchase and consume goods), audience labour is coerced by ideological violence (the threat is to have less social contacts because of missing information from the media and missing communication capacities that are needed for sustaining social relations). Audiences are under the ideological control of capitalists that possess control over the means of communication. If for example people stop using Facebook and social networking sites, they may miss certain social contact opportunities. They can refuse to become a Facebook worker, just like an employee can refuse to work for a wage, but they may as a consequence suffer social disadvantages in society. Commercial media coerce individuals to use them. The more monopoly power they possess, the easier it gets to exert this coercion over media consumers and users.

The product of the working audience is the attention given to programmes that feature advertising breaks. Access to audience attention is exchanged with money paid by advertisers to commercial media operators. The audience cannot control its attention itself because it does not own, create and control the commercial media, rather their labour and attention is alienated – others, namely the corporate media and their advertising clients, define and control the programme time. The same is true for Facebook and other commercial user-generated content Internet sites, on which user labour generates content and transaction data are surveilled and sold to advertising clients that get access to the attention of specifically targeted groups. Users of commercial social media platforms do not control and own their data, they are alienated from it. The labour that generates audience commodity is exploited because it generates value and products that are owned by others, which constitutes at the same time an alienation process. Digital labour is ideologically coerced. Being coerced, exploited, and alienated makes audience labour a class-in-itself.

David Hesmondhalgh (2010, 280) claims that "Smythe's account is crude, reductionist and functionalist, totally underestimating contradiction and struggle in capitalism" and that it "has totally lost its connection to pragmatic political struggle". Similarly, in a contemporary critique of Smythe's audience commodity theory and its application to digital media, Caraway (2011) argues that "Smythe's theory represents a one-sided class analysis which devalues working-class subjectivity" (696), gives "no discussion of wage struggles, product boycotts, or consumer safety" (700), and thereby conducts "audience commodity fetishism", in which "we are all now merely cogs in the capitalist machine" (700). Caraway's criticism of Critical Political Economy coincides with his celebration of the "creative energy residing in the new media environment" (706), which sets his analysis on par with social media determinists like Henry Jenkins, who argue that "the Web has become a site of consumer participation" (Jenkins 2008, 137) and that media are today a locus of "participatory culture" (Jenkins 2008). These criticisms are based on uninformed or deliberately selective readings of Smythe that ignore his focus on alternative media as counterpart to audience commodification. Smythe does not celebrate audiences as always rebelling and does not argue for social-democratic reformism that tolerates exploitation and misery. His analysis rather implies the need for the overthrow of capitalism in order to humanize society and the overthrow of the capitalist media system in order to humanize the media.

Dallas Smythe did not ignore the ability of humans to create alternative futures, which is shown by the fact that he engaged with the idea of an alternative communication system. For Smythe, political subjectivity is revolutionary subjectivity that aims at fundamentally transforming society and establishing an alternative media system. Critics like Hesmondhalgh and Caraway overlook this aspect of Smythe's approach. Mao wrote in 1957 about big-character posters (Dazibao, Tatsepao): "We should put up big-character posters and hold forums."[1] In 1958, he said:[2] "The Tatsepao, or big-character poster, is [a] powerful new weapon, a means of criticism and self-criticism which was created by the masses during the rectification movement; at the same time it is used to expose and attack the enemy. It is also a powerful weapon for conducting debate and education in accordance with the broadest mass democracy. People write down their views, suggestions or exposures and criticisms of others in big characters on large sheets of paper and put them up in conspicuous places for people to read."

When Dallas Smythe wrote in the early 1970s about communication in China in his article "After bicycles, what?" (Smythe 1994, 230–244), he took up Mao's idea of the big-character posters for thinking about how to democratically organize the broadcasting system. He spoke of a "two-way system in which each receiver would have the capability to provide either a voice or

---

1 http://www.marxists.org/reference/archive/mao/selected-works/volume-5/mswv5_65.htm.
2 http://www.marxists.org/reference/archive/mao/selected-works/volume-8/mswv8_09.htm.

voide-and-picture response. [...] a two-way TV system would be like an electronic tatzupao system" (Smythe 1994, 231–232). These thoughts paralleled the ideas of Hans Magnus Enzensberger's (1970) concept of emancipatory media use, Walter Benjamin's (1934, 1936/1939) idea of the reader/writer and Bertolt Brecht's (1932/2000) notion of an alternative radio in his radio theory.

Mao had the idea of a media system that is controlled by the people in grassroots processes and Smythe applied this idea to electronic media for formulating a concept of alternative electronic media. Yuezhi Zhao (2011) points out the relevance of Smythe's article and his ideas of an alternative non-capitalist communication system for China. Given a world dominated by the logic of neoliberal capitalism (both in the West and China), she stresses inspired by Smythe the importance of establishing communications and societies that are based on non-capitalist logic. Zhao (2007, 92) argues that Smythe raised the question 'After bicycles, what?' "in the context of China's search for a socialist alternative to capitalist modernity, with the hope that China would avoid the capitalist path of development." She says that although Smythe misjudged the political situation in China in the 1970s in a number of points, his intervention would continue to "offer a useful point of departure in analyzing not only the deployment and development of ICTs in China during the reform era, but also the broad path of China's post-Mao development strategy and its sustainability" (Zhao 2007, 96). The question one would have today to ask about Chinese media in Dallas Smythe's manner, would be: After mobile phones, what? (Zhao 2007). Whereas Smythe answered to the question 'After bicycles, what?', that China should create a media structure that favours "public goods and services [...] against goods and services for individual, private use" (Smythe 1994, 243), ICTs would not only serve capitalist purposes, but would "by their very nature" be social and allow "alternative uses," including collective political action (Zhao 2007, 96). The reality of ICTs in China would show the antagonistic character of these technologies as both means of domination and protest.

Dallas Smythe was fundamentally concerned with processes of commodification, which is reflected in his creation of the audience commodity category. Although he was critical of some other Marxist theories of culture, important elements of ideology critique and alternative media accompany his focus on the audience commodity. He was furthermore deeply concerned about social struggles for a better world and democratic communications. Smythe's work was connected to politics, e.g. he worked with unions for improving the working conditions of communications workers, gave testimonies and conducted studies in favour of public ownership of satellites, public service broadcasting and affordable universal access to telecommunications and spoke out against corporate media control and monopolization (Yao 2010). He also was involved in debates about the establishment of a New World Information and Communication Order and acted as public intellectual (ibid.). The claim that Smythe had no connection to political struggles, pragmatic or not, is therefore not feasible.

Janet Wasko (2005, 29) argues that "with the increasing spread of privatized, advertiser-supported media, the audience commodity concept has been accepted by many political economists, as well as other communication theorists." In recent years, this tendency has grown and there has been a revival of the interest in Dallas Smythe's works, especially in relation to the question if the users of commercial "social media" are workers and are exploited. Tiziana Terranova made an early contribution to the digital labour debate by introducing the notion of free Internet labour: "Simultaneously voluntarily given and unwaged, enjoyed and exploited, free labour on the Net includes the activity of building Web sites, modifying software packages, reading and participating in mailing lists, and building virtual spaces on MUDs and MOOs" (Terranova 2000, 33). Terranova connected the concept of free labour to the Autonomist Marxist concept of immaterial labour, but did not think of the connectedness to Dallas Smythe's notion of the audience commodity. Conferences like "Digital Labour: Workers, Authors, Citizens" (University of Western Ontario, 2009), "The Internet as Playground and Factory" (New School, 2009) and "Critique, Democracy and Philosophy in 21st Century Information Society. Towards Critical Theories of Social Media" (Uppsala University, 2012) have helped to advance the discourse on digital labour.

I have stressed in my works that Smythe's concept of the audience commodity is very suited for describing the exploitation of user activities by corporate platforms on the contemporary Internet and have in this context coined the notion of the Internet prosumer commodity (Fuchs, 2010, 2011a, 2011b, 2012a, 2009). Vince Manzerolle (2010) builds on this analysis and on Smythe's works for analyzing prosumer commodification on the mobile Internet, for which he uses the concept of the mobile audience commodity. Marisol Sandoval (2012) empirically analyzed the reality of Internet prosumer commodification and found that more than 90% of all analyzed web platforms used targeted advertising and the surveillance and commodification of users' data. A qualitative analysis of the terms and policies that legally guarantee Internet prosumer commodification show that they are "confusing, misleading, ideological, or even manipulative. [...] They try to create the impression that the only aim of these platforms is to provide to its users an attractive high-quality service and experience that allows them to produce their own media content and to connect with friends. The fact that these platforms are owned by commercial companies that aim at increasing their profits by selling user information and space for advertisements remains hidden" (Sandoval 2012, 164–165).

Vincent Mosco (2009) argues in a discussion of Smythe's audience commodity concept that digital "systems which measure and monitor precisely each information transaction are now used to refine the process of delivering audiences of viewers, listeners, readers, movie fans, telephone and computer users, to advertisers. [...] This is a major refinement in the commodification of viewers over the earlier system of delivering mass audiences and it has been applied to practically every communication medium today, including the Internet, where social networking sites like Facebook provide detailed information on users" (Mosco 2009, 137). Graham Murdock (2011) points out that Internet gifting organized by commercial platforms like Google "points to a more general incorporation of gift relations into the economy of commodities" that signifies "the intensification of exploitation" (Murdock 2011, 30–31). One "of the major tasks now facing a critical political economy of culture and communication" would be to argue the case "for a public cultural commons for the digital age" (Murdock 2011, 37).

Nick Dyer-Witheford argues that Smythe's analysis has today gained credibility because the "level of surveillance in the home tends toward that already experienced in the workplace, and the activity of the waged 'watchman' in the automatic factory, described by Marx, becomes integrally with the unpaid 'watching time'" (Dyer-Witheford 1999, 119). Interactive systems would enable "the compilation of comprehensive profiles of consumer behavior" that allows the "ever more precise targeting of consumers differentiated by taste and income" (Dyer-Witheford 1999, 118). He criticizes that Smythe would too "often assume that capital's intended exploitation of audience power is fully successful" (119) and says that activities like online piracy and alternative media are attempts to break capital's dominance.

Mark Andrejevic (2002, 2004, 2007) has applied Sut Jhally's (1987) analysis to reality TV, the Internet, social networking sites and interactive media in general. He says that there the accumulation strategy is not based on exploiting the work of watching, but the work of being watched. Andrejevic (2012) argues that the Marxian concept of exploitation needs to be updated for the online world ("exploitation 2.0") by realizing that on platforms like Google or Facebook "monitoring becomes an integral component of the online value chain both for sites that rely upon direct payment and for user-generated content sties that rely upon indirect payment (advertising)" so that "user activity is redoubled on commercial platforms in the form of productive information about user activity" (Andrejevic 2012, 84). "It is important to understand that the capture and sale of TGI [=transaction generated information] generates harm by supporting discrimination in markets in ways that capture consumer surplus" (Gandy 2011, 451). Lauer (2008) offers an analysis that is related to the one by Andrejevic.

Cohen (2008) argues based on Smythe that the "labour involved in the production of Web 2.0 content" is the production of "information, social networks, relationships, and affect". Coté and Pybus (2007) stress that one cannot speak of audience labour on the Internet, therefore they use the term "immaterial labour 2.0". Bermejo (2009), Couvering (2004, 2011), Kang and McAllister (2011) and Lee (2011) apply the notion of audience commodification to Google and search engines. McStay (2011) uses the audience commodity concept for the analysis of online advertising. Napoli (2010) stresses that audience commodification is being taken one step further online so that users even engage in taking over the work of advertisers by spreading advertising messages online to their contacts or by co-creating advertising content.

The more than 500 pages long *tripleC*-special issue *Marx is Back – The Importance of Marxist Theory and Research for Critical Communication Studies Today* that was edited by Christian Fuchs and Vincent Mosco (2012) shows the importance of Marx's works for critically understanding the media and communication today. It also shows a sustained interest in and relevance of Dallas Smythe's work, especially in the context of the digital labour debate. Several contributors stress that Smythe's audience commodity theory is very well applicable to digital labour on platforms like Facebook or YouTube (Ekman 2012, Fisher 2012, Hebblewhite 2012, Nixon 2012, Prey 2012, Prodnik 2012). Lee McGuigan and Vincent Manzerolle (2014) have edited the collected volume *The Audience Commodity in a Digital Age* that presents Smythe's classical Blindspot article as well as the responses by Graham Murdock, Sut Jhally/Bill Livant and Eileen Meehan together with new contributions by distinguished scholars such as Detlev Zwick/Alan Bradshaw, Graham Murdock, Jason Pridmore/Daniel Trottier, Lee McGuigan, Mark Andrejevic, Micky Lee, Philip Napoli, Vincent Manzerolle, Vincent Mosco, William Melody and Christian Fuchs that reflect on the relevance of the concept of the audience commodity in the age of digital media.

The discussion shows that Smythe's Marxist political economy of the media and communications has had a crucial influence on the digital labour debate. What the discussed approaches share is the analysis that digital labour is exploited by capital. The exploitation of digital labour involves three elements:

- Coercion: Users are ideologically coerced to use commercial platforms in order to be able to engage in communication, sharing and the creation and maintenance of social relations, without which their lives would be less meaningful.
- Alienation: companies, not the users, own the platforms and the created profit.

- Appropriation: Users spend time on corporate Internet platforms that are funded by targeted advertising capital accumulation models. The time spent on corporate platforms is the value created by their unpaid digital labour. Their digital labour creates social relations, profile data, user-generated content and transaction data (browsing behaviour) – a data commodity that is offered for sale by Internet corporations to advertising clients that can select certain user groups they want to target. The act of exploitation is already created by the circumstance that users create a data commodity, in which their online work time is objectified, that they do not own this data themselves, but that rather corporate Internet platforms with the help of terms of use and privacy policies acquire ownership of this data. Corporate Internet platforms offer the data commodity that is the result of Internet prosumption activity for sale to advertisers. The value realization process, the transformation of value into profit, takes place when targeted users view the advertisement (pay per view) or click on it (pay per click). Not all data commodities are sold all of the time, specific groups of data commodities are more popular than others, but exploitation always takes place at the point of the production and appropriation of the commodity and prior to a commodity's sale.

In Section 4, I will provide an analysis of how commodification works on corporate social media platforms. Section 5 will then analyse ideological structures that are associated with digital media. Analysing digital media thereby makes both use of the unity of the critical analysis of commodification and ideology critique that I argued for in Section 2.

4   Digital Labour: Capital Accumulation and Commodification on Social Media

For a deeper analysis of how the notion of the audience commodity can be applied for analyzing digital labour on "social media," we need to engage with Marx's analysis of capitalism. In the three volumes of *Capital*, Marx analyses the accumulation process of capital. This process, as described by Marx, is visualized in Figure 18.2.

  In the accumulation of capital, capitalists buy labour power and means of production (raw materials, technologies, etc.) in order to organize the production of new commodities that are sold with the expectation to make money profit that is partly reinvested. Marx distinguishes two spheres of capital accumulation: the circulation sphere and the sphere of production. In the circulation

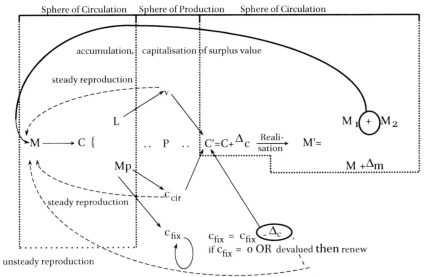

c_{cir} : raw- and auxiliary-materials, operating supply items, semi-finished products,
c_{fix} : machines, buildings, equipment; circulating capital: c_{cir}, v; fixed capital: c_{fix}

FIGURE 18.2   *The accumulation/expanded reproduction of capital*

sphere, capital transforms its value form. First money M is transformed into commodities (from the standpoint of the capitalist as buyer) – the capitalist purchases the commodities labour power L and means of production Mp. The process M-C is based on the two purchases M-L and M-Mp. This means that due to private property structures, workers do not own the means of production, the products they produce and the profit they generate. Capitalists own these resources. In the sphere of production, a new good is produced: the value of labour power and the value of the means of production are added to the product. Value takes on the form of productive capital P. The value form of labour is variable capital v (which can be observed as wages), the value form of the means of production constant capital c (which can be observed as the total price of the means of production/producer goods).

In the sphere of production, capital stops its metamorphosis so that capital circulation comes to a halt. There is the production of new value V' of the commodity. V' contains the value of the necessary constant and variable capital and surplus value Δs of the surplus product. Unpaid labour generates surplus value and profit. Surplus value is the part of the working day that is unpaid. It is the part of the workday (measured in hours) that is used for producing profit. Profit does not belong to workers, but to capitalists. Capitalists do not pay for the production of surplus. Therefore the production of surplus value is a process of exploitation. The value V' of the new commodity after production is $V' = c + v + s$. The commodity then leaves the sphere of production and again enters the circulation sphere, in which capital conducts its next metamorphosis: it is transformed from the commodity form back into the money form by being sold on the market. Surplus value is realized in the form of money. The initial money capital M now takes on the form $M' = M + \Delta m$, it has been increased by an increment Δm that is called profit. Accumulation of capital means that the produced surplus value/profit is (partly) reinvested/capitalized. The end point of one process M' becomes the starting point of a new accumulation process. One part of M', M_1, is reinvested. Accumulation means the aggregation of capital by investment and the exploitation of labour in the capital circuit M-C...P...C'-M', in which the end product M' becomes a new starting point M. The total process makes up the dynamic character of capital. Capital is money that is permanently increasing due to the exploitation of surplus value.

Commodities are sold at prices that are higher than the investment costs so that money profit is generated. Marx argues that one decisive quality of capital accumulation is that profit is an emergent property of production that is produced by labour, but owned by capitalists. Without labour, no profit could be made. Workers are forced to enter class relations and to produce profit in order to survive, which enables capital to appropriate surplus. The notion of surplus value is the main concept of Marx's theory, by which he intends to show that capitalism is a class society. "The theory of surplus value is in consequence immediately the theory of exploitation" (Negri 1991, 74). One can add: The theory of surplus value is the theory of class and as a consequence the political demand for a classless society.

Capital is not money, but money that is increased through accumulation, "money which begets money" (Marx 1867, 256). Marx argues that the value of labour power is the average amount of time that is needed for the production of goods that are necessary for survival (necessary labour time). Wages represent the value of necessary labour time at the level of prices. Surplus labour time is labour time that exceeds necessary labour time, remains unpaid, is appropriated for free by capitalists, and transformed into money profit. Surplus value "is in substance the materialization of unpaid labour-time. The secret of the self-valorization of capital resolves itself into the fact that it has at its disposal a definite quantity of the unpaid labour of other people" (Marx 1867, 672). The production of surplus value is "the *differentia specifica* of capitalist production" (Marx 1867, 769) and the "driving force and the final result of the capitalist process of production" (Marx 1867, 976).

Many corporate social media platforms (Facebook, YouTube, etc.) accumulate capital with the help of targeted advertising that is tailored to individual user data and behaviour. Capitalism is based on the imperative to accumulate ever more capital. To achieve this, capitalists either have to prolong the working day (absolute surplus value production) or to increase the productivity of labour (relative surplus value production) (on relative surplus value, see: Marx 1867, Chapter 12). Relative surplus value production means that productivity is increased so that more commodities and more surplus value can be produced in the same time period as before. "For example, suppose a cobbler, with a given set of tools, makes one pair of boots in one working day of 12 hours. If he is to make two pairs in the same time, the productivity of his labour must be doubled; and this cannot be done except by an alteration in his tools or in his mode of working, or both. Hence the conditions of production of his labour, i.e. his mode of production, and the labour process itself, must be revolutionized. By an increase in the productivity of labour, we mean an alteration in the labour process of such a kind as to shorten the labour-time socially necessary for the production of a commodity, and to endow a given quantity of labour with the power of producing a greater quantity of use-value. [...] I call that surplus-value which is produced by lengthening of the working day, *absolute surplus-value. In* contrast to this, I call that surplus-value which arises from the curtailment of the necessary labour-time, and from the corresponding alteration in the respective lengths of the two components of the working day, *relative surplus-value*" (Marx 1867, 431–432).

Sut Jhally (1987, 78) argues that "reorganizing the watching audience in terms of demographics" is a form of relative surplus value production. One can interpret targeted Internet advertising as a form of relative surplus value production: At one point in time, the advertisers show not only one advertisement to the audience as in non-targeted advertising, but they show different advertisements to different user groups depending on the monitoring, assessment and comparison of the users' interests and online behaviour. On traditional forms of television, all watchers see the same advertisements at the same time. In targeted online advertising, advertising companies can present different ads at the same time. The efficiency of advertising is increased: the advertisers can show more advertisements that are likely to fit the interests of consumers in the same time period as in non-targeted advertising. Partly the advertising company's wage labourers and partly the Internet users, whose user-generated data and transaction data are utilized, produce the profit generated from these advertisements. The more targeted advertisements there are, the more likely it is that users recognize ads and click on them.

The users' click-and-buy process is the surplus value realization process of the advertising company. This process transforms surplus value into money profit. Targeted advertising allows Internet companies to present not just one

FUCHS

advertisement at one point in time to users, but rather numerous advertisements, so that there is the production of more total advertising time that presents commodities to users. Relative surplus value production means that more surplus value is generated in the same time period as earlier. Targeted online advertising is more productive than non-targeted online advertising because it allows presenting more ads in the same time period. These ads contain more surplus value than the non-targeted ads, *i.e.*, more unpaid labour time of the advertising company's paid employees and of users, who generate user-generated content and transaction data.

Alvin Toffler (1980) introduced the notion of the prosumer in the early 1980s. It means the "progressive blurring of the line that separates producer from consumer" (Toffler 1980, 267). Toffler describes the age of prosumption as the arrival of a new form of economic and political democracy, self-determined work, labour autonomy, local production and autonomous self-production. But he overlooks that prosumption is used for outsourcing work to users and consumers, who work without payment. Thereby corporations reduce their investment- and labour-costs, jobs are destroyed, and consumers who work for free are extremely exploited. They produce surplus value that is appropriated and turned into profit by corporations without paying wages. Notwithstanding Toffler's uncritical optimism, his notion of the "prosumer" describes important changes of media structures and practices and can therefore also be adopted for critical studies.

Ritzer and Jurgenson (2010) argue that web 2.0 facilitates the emergence of "prosumer capitalism", that the capitalist economy "has always been dominated by prosumption" (14), and that prosumption is an inherent feature of McDonaldization. The two authors' analysis ignores that prosumption is only one of many tendencies of capitalism, but neither its only nor dominant quality. Capitalism is multidimensional and has multiple interlinked dimensions. It is at the same time finance capitalism, imperialistic capitalism, informational capitalism, hyperindustrial capitalism (oil, gas), crisis capitalism, etc. Not all of these dimensions are equally important (Fuchs 2011a, Chapter 5).

We have seen that Dallas Smythe's (1977a, 1981) analysis of the audience commodity has gained new relevance today in the digital labour debate. With the rise of user-generated content, free access social networking platforms and other free access platforms that yield profit by online advertisement – a development subsumed under categories such as web 2.0, social software and social networking sites –, the web seems to come close to accumulation strategies employed by capital on traditional mass media like TV or radio. Users who upload photos, and images, write wall posting and comments, send mail to their contacts, accumulate friends or browse other profiles on Facebook, constitute an audience commodity that is sold to advertisers. The difference between the audience commodity on traditional mass media and on the Internet is that in the latter case the users are also content producers, there is user-generated content, the users engage in permanent creative activity, communication, community building and content-production. That the users are more active on the Internet than in the reception of TV or radio content is due to the decentralized structure of the Internet that allows many-to-many communication. Due to the permanent activity of the recipients and their status as prosumers, we can say that in the case of corporate social media the audience commodity is an Internet prosumer commodity (Fuchs 2010). The conflict between Cultural Studies and Critical Political Economy of the Media (see: Ferguson and Golding 1997, Garnham 1995/1998, Grossberg 1995/1998) about the question of the activity and creativity of the audience has been resolved in relation to the Internet today: On Facebook, Twitter, blogs, etc., users are fairly active and creative, which reflects Cultural Studies' insights about the active character of recipients, but this active and creative user character is the very source of exploitation, which reflects Critical Political Economy's stress on class and exploitation.

Economic surveillance on corporate social media is surveillance of prosumers, who dynamically and permanently create and share user-generated content, browse profiles and data, interact with others, join, create, and build communities and co-create information. The corporate web platform operators and their third party advertising clients continuously monitor and record personal data and online activities. They store, merge and analyse collected data. This allows them to create detailed user profiles and to know a lot about the users' personal interests and online behaviours. Surveillance is an inherent feature of corporate social media's capital accumulation model (Fuchs 2012a, Sandoval 2012). Social media that are based on targeted advertising sell prosumers as a commodity to advertising clients. There is an exchange of money for the access to user data that allows economic user surveillance. The exchange value of the social media prosumer commodity is the money value that the operators obtain from their clients. Its use value is the multitude of personal data and usage behaviour that is dominated by the commodity and exchange value form. The corporations' surveillance of the prosumers' permanently produced use values, i.e., personal data and interactions, enables targeted advertising that aims at luring the prosumers into consumption and shopping. It also aims at manipulating prosumers' desires and needs in the interest of corporations and the commodities they offer. Whereas audience commodification in newspapers and traditional broadcasting was always based on statistical assessments of audience rates and characteristics (Bolin 2011), Internet surveillance gives social media corporations an exact picture of the interests and activities of users. The characteristics (interests and usage behaviour) and the size (the number of users in a specific interest group) of the Internet prosumer commodity can therefore be exactly determined and it can also be exactly determined who is part of a consumer group that should be targeted by specific ads and who is not.

In grounding the approach of a critical political economy of personal information, Oscar Gandy has introduced the notion of the panoptic sort: "The panoptic sort is a difference machine that sorts individuals into categories and classes on the basis of routine measurements. It is a discriminatory technology that allocates options and opportunities on the basis of those measures and the administrative models that they inform" (Gandy 1993, 15). It is a system of power and disciplinary surveillance that identifies, classifies and assesses (Gandy 1993, 15). The mechanism of targeted advertising on social media is the form of surveillance that Gandy has characterized as panoptic sorting: it *identifies* the interests of users by closely surveilling their personal data and usage behaviour, it *classifies* them into consumer groups and *assesses* their interests in comparison to other consumers and to available advertisements that are then targeted at the users.

Social media users are double objects of commodification: they are commodities themselves and through this commodification their consciousness becomes, while online, permanently exposed to commodity logic in the form of advertisements. Most online time is advertising time. On corporate social media, targeted advertising makes use of the users' personal data, interests, interactions, information behaviour and also the interactions with other websites. So while you are using Facebook, Twitter, YouTube, etc., it is not just you interacting with others and browsing profiles, all of these activities are framed by advertisements presented to you. These advertisements come about by permanent surveillance of your online activities. Such advertisements do not necessarily represent consumers' real needs and desires because the ads are based on calculated assumptions, whereas needs are much more complex and spontaneous. The ads mainly reflect marketing decisions and economic power relations. They do not simply provide information about products as offers to buy, but information about products of powerful companies.

Figure 18.3 shows the process of capital accumulation on corporate social media platforms that are funded by targeted advertising. Social media corporations invest money (M) for buying capital: technologies (server space, computers, organizational infrastructure, etc.) and labour power (paid employees). These are the constant capital (c) and the variable capital v_1 outlays. The outcome of the production process P_1 is not a commodity that is directly sold, but rather a social media service (the specific platforms) that is made available

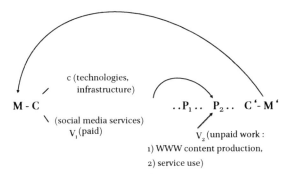

FIGURE 18.3   *Capital accumulation on corporate social media platforms that are based on targeted advertising*

without payment to users. As a consequence of this circumstance, management literature has focused on identifying how to make profit from free Internet services. Chris Anderson (2009) has identified 50 models of how an Internet service is given for free in order to boost the selling of other services or where an Internet service is given for free for one type of customers and sold to others. The waged employees, who create social media online environments that are accessed by users, produce part of the surplus value. The users employ the platform for generating content that they upload (user-generated data). The constant and variable capital invested by social media companies (c, v_1) that is objectified in the online environment is the prerequisite for their activities in the production process P2. Their products are user-generated data, personal data, social networks and transaction data about their browsing behaviour and communication behaviour on corporate social media. They invest a certain labour time v2 in this process.

Corporate social media sell the users' data commodity to advertising clients at a price that is larger than the invested constant and variable capital. Partly the users and partly the corporations' employees create the surplus value contained in this commodity. The difference is that the users are unpaid and therefore – in monetary terms – infinitely exploited. Once the Internet prosumer commodity that contains the user-generated content, transaction data and the right to access virtual advertising space and time is sold to advertising clients, the commodity is transformed into money capital and surplus value is transformed into money capital. A counter-argument to the insight that commercial social media companies exploit Internet prosumers is that the latter in exchange for their work receive access to a service. One can here however interpose that service access cannot be seen as a salary because users cannot "further convert this salary [...] [They] cannot buy food" (Bolin 2011, 37) by it.

For Marx (1867), the profit rate is the relation of profit to investment costs:

$p = s / (c + v)$ = surplus value / (constant capital (= fixed costs) + variable capital (= wages)).

If Internet users become productive prosumers, then in terms of Marxian class theory this means that they become productive labourers who produce surplus value and are exploited by capital because for Marx productive labour generates surplus value (Fuchs 2010). Therefore not merely those who are employed by Internet corporations for programming, updating and maintaining the soft- and hardware, performing marketing activities, etc. are exploited surplus value producers are, but also the users and prosumers, who engage in the production of user-generated content. New media corporations do not (or hardly) pay the users for the production of content. One accumulation strategy is to give them free access to services and platforms, let them produce content and to accumulate a large number of prosumers that are sold as a commodity to third-party advertisers. Not a product is sold to the users, but the users are sold as a commodity to advertisers. The more users a platform has, the higher the advertising rates can be set. The productive labour time that capital exploits involves on the one hand the labour time of the paid employees and on the other hand all of the time that is spent online by the users. Digital media corporations pay salaries for the first type of knowledge labour. Users produce data that is used and sold by the platforms without payment. They work for free. There are neither variable nor constant investment costs. The formula for the profit rate needs to be transformed for this accumulation strategy:

$p = s / (c + v_1 + v_2)$

s: surplus value, c : constant capital, v_1: wages paid to fixed employees, v_2: wages paid to users

The typical situation is that $v_2 = > 0$ and that v_2 substitutes v_1 ($v_1 = > v_2 = 0$). If the production of content and the time spent online were carried out by paid employees, the variable costs (wages) would rise and profits would therefore decrease. This shows that Internet prosumer activity in a capitalist society can be interpreted as the outsourcing of productive labour to users (in management literature the term "crowdsourcing" has been established, see Howe 2008), who work completely for free and help maximizing the rate of exploitation:

e = s / v = surplus value / variable capital

The rate of exploitation (also called the rate of surplus value) measures the relationship of workers' unpaid work time and paid work time. The higher the rate of exploitation, the more work time is unpaid. Users of commercial social media platforms have no wages (v = 0). Therefore the rate of surplus value converges towards infinity. Internet prosumer labour is infinitely exploited by capital. This means that capitalist prosumption is an extreme form of exploitation, in which the prosumers work completely for free. Infinite exploitation means that all or nearly all online activity and time becomes part of commodities and no share of this time is paid. Smythe (1994, 297) spoke of the commercial audience as "mind slaves", so we may speak of commercial social media users as online slaves. Marx (1867) distinguishes between necessary labour time and surplus labour time. The first is the time a person needs to work in order to create the money equivalent for a wage that is required for buying goods that are needed for survival. The second is all additional labour time. Users are not paid on corporate social media (or for consuming other types of corporate media), therefore they cannot generate money for buying food or other goods needed for survival. Therefore all online time on corporate social media like Google, Facebook, YouTube or Twitter is surplus labour time.

So one line of argument is that on the monetary level, users are infinitely exploited because they do not receive a wage, although platforms like Facebook make monetary profits. There is also a second line of argument: The Facebook platform is a means of communicative survival for users and a means of the capitalist production of value, commodities and profit. It is at the same time means of consumption and means of production. If the platform is considered as in-kind good provided to the users as means of communicative survival, then all costs that Facebook has for providing the platform can be considered as de-facto value of an in-kind good "paid" as means of consumption to its value producers. According to Marx, the value of a good is the sum of constant capital, variable capital and profit: V = c + v + p. In the case of the Facebook platform as good, there is no profit because it is not sold as a commodity. Rather, user data is sold as a commodity. Therefore the value of the Facebook platform is the sum of the invested constant and variable capital. This implies that one can consider Facebook's investment costs as constituting the "wages" of its users. In 2011, Facebook's total costs and expenses were 1.955 billion US$ and its revenue was 3.711 billion US$ (Facebook SEC Filings: Form S-1

Registration Statement). So Facebook made a profit of 1.756 billion US$ in 2011. If one accepts the argument that the Facebook platform is an in-kind good provided to the users and that therefore Facebook's investment costs form a wage-equivalent for means of consumption, then the rate of exploitation of the total Facebook work force consisting of paid employees and users is e = profits / investment costs = 1.955 / 1.756 = 1.113 = 111.3%. This means that the profits that Facebook makes are 111% times the monetary value of the investments it makes for services that are consumed by users as "wage-equivalent."

There are however some limitations of this second line of argument. In capitalism, money forms a monopolized generalized means of exchange. With the term wages, Marx means the price of wage labour expressed in monetary terms/the general equivalent of exchange. Marx considers the emergence of wage labour as a specific feature of capitalism. Wage labour is "double free":

(1)   Workers are not physically owned by capitalists like slaves, they are rather compelled to sell their labour power in exchange for a wage in order to survive.

(2)   This compulsion is based on the circumstance that they are "free" from/ not in control of the ownership of the means of production and capital.

So the notion of the wage in a capitalist society presupposes access to a general equivalent of exchange that can be spent for purchasing various commodities that have different use-values. Therefore Marx (1849) says that "wages are the amount of money which the capitalist pays for a certain period of work or for a certain amount of work. [...] The exchange value of a commodity estimated in money is called its price. Wages therefore are only a special name for the price of labour-power, and are usually called the price of labour; it is the special name for the price of this peculiar commodity, which has no other repository than human flesh and blood." Money is in capitalism the monopolized general equivalent of exchange. It has special relevance because it can be used for getting hold of most use-values. It is therefore not a straight forward argument to treat in-kind goods as wage-equivalents. The specific structures of capitalism privilege money as specific and general equivalent of exchange. The money logic therefore has special relevance. I nonetheless want to offer both interpretations of the "wage" of Facebook users for interpretation and discussion. No matter which interpretation one chooses, both versions imply that Facebook users are workers that are exploited.

Users spent 10.5 billion minutes on Facebook per day in January 2011 (Facebook, SEC Filings, Amendment No. 3 to Form S-1 Registration Statement). We can therefore make the following estimates about the value generated on Facebook:

Value generated on Facebook in 2011: 10.5 billion * 365 = 3832.5 billion minutes = 63.875 billion working hours per year.

Average working hours per year of a full-time worker: 1800.

Value generated on Facebook in 2011: 35 486 111 full-time equivalents of work.

The rate of exploitation is calculated as the ratio e = surplus labour time / necessary labour time = unpaid labour time / paid labour time. In the case of Facebook, all 64.99 billion working hours were unpaid, so the surplus labour time amounts to the full amount of labour time. Given that Facebook exploits more than 35 billion full-time equivalents of free labour or more than 60 billion hours of unpaid work time, it becomes clear that Facebook's business model is based on the outsourcing/crowdsourcing of paid work time to unpaid work time. Given that Facebook's profits were 1 billion US$ in 2011 (Facebook, SEC Filings, Amendment No. 3 to Form S-1 Registration Statement), it becomes clear that free user labour is at the heart of Facebook's business model. That the rate of exploitation is infinite means that no wages are paid, that all user labour is unremunerated and creates value. Free user labour is what Marx (1867) termed abstract labour, labour that creates value:

By abstract human labour, Marx means that aspect of labour in a commodity-producing society that makes commodities comparable and exchangeable: "Whether 20 yards of linen 1 coat or = 20 coats or = x coats, i.e. whether a given quantity of linen is worth few or many coats, it is always implied, whatever the proportion, that the linen and the coat, as magnitudes of value, are expressions of the same unit, things of the same nature. Linen = coat is the basis of the equation. [...] By equating, for example, the coat as a thing of value to the linen, we equate the labour embedded in the coat with the labour embedded in the linen. Now it is true that the tailoring which makes the coat is concrete labour of a different sort from the weaving which makes the linen. But the act of equating tailoring with weaving reduces the former in fact to what is really equal in the two kinds of labour, to the characteristic they have in common of being human labour. This is a round-about way of saying that weaving too, in so far as it weaves value, has nothing to distinguish it from tailoring, and, consequently, is abstract human labour. It is only the expression of equivalence between different sorts of commodities which brings to view the specific character of value-creating labour, by actually reducing the different kinds of labour embedded in the different kinds of commodity to their common quality of being human labour in general" (Marx 1867, 141–142).

Abstract labour is "abstract" because it is a dimension of labour, at which we have to abstract from the qualitative differences of commodities (their use-values) and see what they have in common, i.e. that they are all products of human labour and objectifications of a certain amount of labour, which makes them comparable and exchangeable in certain relations (x commodity A = y commodity B = ...): "If then we disregard the use-value of commodities, only one property remains, that of being products of labour. But even the product of labour has already been transformed in our hands. If we make abstraction from its use-value, we abstract also from the material constituents and forms which make it a use-value" (Marx 1867, 128). "A use-value, or useful article, therefore, has value only because abstract human labour is objectified or materialized in it. How, then, is the magnitude of this value to be measured? By means of the quantity of the 'value-forming substance', the labour, contained in the article. This quantity is measured by its duration, and the labour-time is itself measured on the particular scale of hours, days etc." (Marx 1867, 129).

At the level of values, we can say that the collective Facebook worker works almost 64 billion hours per year. The surplus hours and surplus work amount to 64 billion hours per year. Personal and social data is the product that is created in this work time. The more hours users work on Facebook, the more data they generate. The more hours users spend on Facebook, the more ads are generated and presented to them. So productive time is also advertising time (although not all advertising time, but only a portion of it, is turned into money profit).

From Facebook's balance sheet that was published at its stock market registration, we know that Facebook's profit rate 2011 = total profit/total costs and expenses = 1 billion / 1.955 billion = 51.2% (data source: Facebook Inc., SEC Filings Facebook, Form S-1 Registration Statement). This is a very high profit rate, especially in times of global economic crisis. Such a rate can mainly be achieved by the circumstance that Facebook has a low number of employees, 3976 at the end of June 2012,[3] but can without costs valorize the entire work time of its users for generating its commodity – data commodities. Infinite exploitation of the users (= no wage) allowed Facebook a profit rate of > 50% in 2011. The secret of Facebook's profits is that it mobilizes billion hours of users' work time (at the level of values) that is unpaid (at the level of prices).

Unpaid labour extends to different realms, such as Google, Twitter, YouTube, Baidu, LinkedIn, knowledge creation and reproduction, "reproductive labour" such as housework, care work, educational work, affective work, sexual work, etc. so that the human being in contemporary capitalism spends a lot of working hours every day in creating value for capital by abstract labour that is unpaid. We can therefore say that life has become a factory, factory life. The factory is not limited to the space of wage labour, but extends into everyday life. The secret of corporate social media's capital accumulation is that it mobilizes a

---

3   Data source: http://newsroom.fb.com/content/default.aspx?NewsAreaId=22 (accessed on September 17th, 2012).

huge number of unpaid workers, who engage in a tremendous amount of fully unpaid working hours that generate data commodities that are sold as targeted advertisements. There is a need to mobilize value production and to make it free labour at the same time in order for this capital accumulation to function.

Marx described a contradiction between value and labour time: the development of technological productivity reduces the labour time needed for producing a commodity due to technological productivity, but at the same time labour time is the only measure and source of wealth in capitalism: "Capital itself is the moving contradiction, [in] that it presses to reduce labour time to a minimum, while it posits labour time, on the other side, as sole measure and source of wealth. Hence it diminishes labour time in the necessary form so as to increase it in the superfluous form; hence posits the superfluous in growing measure as a condition – question of life or death – for the necessary" (Marx 1857/58, 706). The result of this contradiction is, as contemporary capitalism shows, unemployment and precarious labour. In contemporary capitalism, this contradiction takes on a second meaning and reality that is at the heart of corporate social media's capital accumulation model: Corporate social media capital tries to push down the costs of necessary labour (wages) to a minimum, but at the same time increases superfluous labour that is unpaid as productive labour that creates surplus value. The contradiction between necessary and superfluous labour takes on its specific form on corporate social media: paid labour is reduced, unpaid labour is increased, value generation is outsourced from paid to unpaid labour. The contradiction between superfluous and necessary labour is sublated so that a new quality emerges: value-creation is transferred to unpaid labour. At the same time, the contradiction is set at a new level and intensified because the propertylessness, poverty, and precariousness of labour on the one hand and the wealth of capital are intensified.

Michael A. Lebowitz (1986, 165) argues that Smythe's approach is only a "Marxist-sounding communications theory." Marxism would assume that "surplus value in capitalism is generated in the direct process of production, the process where workers (having surrendered the property rights over the disposition of their labour-power) are *compelled* to work longer than is necessary to produce the equivalent of their wage. Perhaps it is for this reason that there is hesitation in accepting the conception that audiences work, are exploited, and produce surplus value – in that it is a paradigm quite different to the Marxist paradigm" (Lebowitz 1986, 167). Media capitalists would compete "for the expenditures of competing industrial capitalists," help to "increase the commodity sales of industrial capitalists" and their profits would be "a share of the surplus value of industrial capital" (Lebowitz 1986, 169). Smythe's audience commodity approach would advance an "entirely un-Marxian argument with un-Marxian conclusions" (Lebowitz 1986, 170).

Lebowitz bases his argument on three specific assumptions that he claims to be inherent to Marx's works:

(1) That industrial capital is the central form of capital.
(2) That only work performed under the command of industrial capital is productive labour and creates surplus value.
(3) That only wage labour can be exploited.

The immediate theoretical and political consequences of this logic of argumentation are the following ones:

(1) Commercial media are subsumed to industrial capital.
(2) Slaves, house workers and other unpaid workers are not exploited.
(3) The wage and non-wage work performed under the command of media capital is unproductive work. Media companies cannot exploit workers because they create products and services that are part of the circulation sphere of capitalism.

The political question that Lebowitz's argument poses is if one wants to share the implications of a wage-centric theory of exploitation that unpaid workers cannot be exploited. Productive labour, i.e. labour that generates surplus value, is a complex, contradictory and non-consistent topic within Marx's works. In *Capital Volume 1*, Marx distinguishes different concepts of productive labour. In the narrower sense, the "only worker who is productive is one who produces surplus-value for the capitalist, or in other words contributes towards the self-valorization of capital" (Marx 1867, 644). This formulation does not imply that only a wageworker can be a producer of surplus value because there can be workers that produce for capital, but are unpaid, i.e. surplus labour time makes up 100% of their work time. In a second definition, Marx argues that for being considered a productive worker, "it is no longer necessary for the individual himself to put his hand to the object; it is sufficient for him to be an organ of the collective labourer, and to perform any one of its subordinate functions" (Marx 1867, 643–644). This means that productive labour understood this way implies that a worker, who contributes to a "social product" that is controlled by a capitalist and is the "joint product of a collective labourer" (Marx 1867, 643), is an exploited worker, no matter if s/he receives a wage for it or not. S/he is part of a collective or social worker. In a third approach, Marx abstracts from the capitalist production process and argues in Chapter 5 in the German edition and Chapter 7 of the English edition of *Capital Volume 1* that all work is productive because it creates products that conditions and results of work.

Given the first two understandings, there is no necessity to assume that Marx saw non-wage workers that contribute to capitalist production processes as "unproductive" and non-exploited. Leibowitz gives one interpretation of Marx's works and claims that this is the only possible interpretation and that one is not a Marxist if one does not share this interpretation. The common name for this logical procedure is dogmatism. Representatives of wage-labour dogmatism can certainly counter my argument by citing passages from the *Theories of Surplus Value* or *Capital, Volume 3*, where Marx argues that circulation workers, commercial workers in trade or servants are unproductive workers. But it remains a fact that in his most thought-out book, namely *Capital Volume 1*, that in contrast to *Volume 2* and *Volume 3* (that were edited by Engels after Marx's death) and the *Theories of Surplus Value* (that were unpublished notes) he authorized for publication and subsequently revised several times, Marx wrote passages that allow a non-wage labour-fetishistic interpretation of the concept of productive labour.

In contrast to wage fetishism, Marx argued that surplus labour – and therefore the concept of exploitation – is not specific for capitalism: "Capital did not invent surplus labour. Wherever a part of society possesses the monopoly of the means of production, the worker, free or unfree, must add to the labour-time necessary for his own maintenance an extra quantity of labour-time in order to produce the means of subsistence for the owner of the means of production, whether this proprietor be an Athenian kalos kagathon [aristocrat], an Etruscan theocrat, a *civis romanus*, a Norman baron, an American slave-owner, a Wallachian boyar, a modern landlord or a capitalist" (Marx 1867, 344–345). Marx argued that the slave performs 100% of his work as unpaid work: "With the *slave*, on the contrary, even that part of his labour which is paid appears to be unpaid. Of course, in order to work the slave must live, and one part of his working day goes to replace the value of his own maintenance. But since no bargain is struck between him and his master, and no acts of selling and buying are going on between the two parties, all his labour seems to be given away for nothing" (Marx 1865).

Although having different origins, contexts and theoretical implications, the works of Dallas Smythe and Autonomist Marxism share the criticism of wage-labour fetishism as well as the concept of a collective work force that contributes to the production of surplus value, is exploited by capital and is constituted in various spaces of capitalism, including the factory, the household, colonies of primitive accumulation and leisure.

In the context of a digital labour theory of value, it is not so easy to fix advertising in the realm of capital circulation and to reduce it to a relationship that is determined by industrial capital. Within the overall capitalist economy, the commercial media and advertising industries certainly take the role that they help other capitalists realize their profits, i.e. they spread messages about why specific commodites should be bought. But they form a capitalist industry in itself that accumulates capital based on the exploitation of work. For Marx, the notion of productive labour is primarily oriented on criticizing the exploitation process. And given that the media and advertising industry is oriented on profit making and makes use of the work of paid employees and unpaid users/ media consumers, it follows that this industry makes use of unpaid labour time for creating profit, i.e. the involved work "produces surplus-value for the capitalist" and "contributes towards the self-valorization of capital" (Marx 1867, 644) – which is Marx's definition of productive labour. In addition, in the digital labour context it is not so easy to say that media audiences are just media consumers and therefore located in the consumption and circulation realm because the consumption of digital media to a certain extent produces content, behavioural data, social network data and personal data that is commodified and sold to advertising clients.

Figure 18.4 shows the connection of the capital accumulation process of commercial digital media that are based on targeted advertising and the capital accumulation process of advertising clients. They both have their relatively

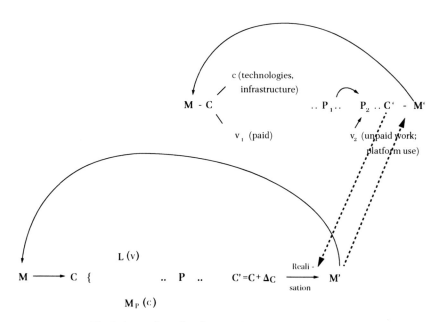

FIGURE 18.4   *The dialectic of social media capital accumulation and advertising clients'*
capital accumulation

autonomous capital accumulation processes that are based on the exploitation of abstract labour and are interdependent in the form of an exchange process M – C, in which advertising clients exchange their money for the access to
user data commodities.

Jhally (1987, 83) argues that "watching is an extension of factory labour"
and that the living room is one of the factories today. The factory is the space
of wage labour, but is also in the living room. Outside of wage labour spaces,
the factory is not only in the home – it is everywhere. The Internet is the all-
ubiquitous factory and realm of the production of audience commodities.
Social media and the mobile Internet make the audience commodity ubiquitous and the factory not limited to your living room and your wage work place –
the factory is also in all in-between spaces, the entire planet is today a capitalist
factory.

The contemporary globalization of capitalism has dispersed the walls of the
wage labour factory all over the globe. Due to the circumstance that capital
cannot exist without non-wage labour and exploits the commons that are created by all, society has become a factory. Reflecting this development, Mario
Tronti has coined the concept of the social factory: "At the highest level of capitalist development social relations become moments of the relations of production, and the whole society becomes an articulation of production. In
short, all of society lives as a function of the factory and the factory extends its
exclusive domination over all of society" (Mario Tronti, quotation translated
by and taken from Cleaver 1992, 137) "Now we have the factory planet – or the
planet factory, a regime that subsumes not just production, consumption, and
social reproduction (as in Fordism), but life's genetic and ecological dimensions" (Dyer-Witheford 2010, 485).

The social worker and the social factory are concepts that allow to go beyond
a wage-centric concept of value, labour and exploitation. In fact, especially
women, migrant workers, illegal workers, precarious workers, house workers,
home workers and the working class in developing countries have long been
facing the struggle of surviving in modes of production that feature non-, low-
and underpaid work. Especially neoliberalism has generalized the precarious
mode of work so that housewifized work that is insecure, low paid, temporary,
precarious, individualized, lacks social security, unionization, access to health
care and other welfare benefits, etc., has become the normality of work for
many. The concept of the exploitation of the social labourer who works in a
global social factory allows connecting Marxist political economy to feminism
and studies of race and post-colonialism. There is a global division of labour in
the organisation of knowledge work. And this division is class-structured, gendered and racist. There is an inherent connection of class, gender and race in

the capitalist mode of production. Dallas Smythe, Marxist Feminism and Autonomist Marxism have stressed that exploitation takes place beyond the confines of the traditional wage-labour factory, which opens up connections between these approaches.

Vincent Mosco and Catherine McKercher (2008, 62) stress that Dallas Smythe has "established a groundwork for" the research of voluntary, low paid and unpaid labour "by describing the extent of audience labor on the home through the sale of people's attention to advertisers. The connection of capitalism, patriarchy and racism has become ever more obvious in recent years, needs to be more analysed and can be a foundation for solidarity between the different exploited groups that we find in capitalism today." Harry Cleaver (2000, 123) argues that capital "tries to shape all 'leisure', or free-time, activities [...] in its own interests. Thus, rather than viewing unwaged 'non-labour time' automatically as free time or as time completely antithetical to capital, we are forced to recognize that caital has tried to integrate this tiem, too, within its process of accumulation. [...] Put another way, capital has tried to convert 'individual consumption' into 'productive consumption' by creating the social factory." Capitalist media and culture are shaped by a global mode of production, in which houseworkers and consumers shop for commodities, actively reproduce labour power and work as audience for the media, users generate a data commodity on the Internet, slave workers in poor countries extract minerals that are used for the production of hardware, low-paid children, women and other workers in Chinese and other manufacturing companies assemble the hardware of computers, phones and printers under extremely hard and dangerous working conditions, highly paid and overworked software engineers work for companies like Google, Microsoft etc., relatively low-paid knowledge workers in developing countries create, transform, process or edit cultural content and software for firms that are subcontractors to Western media and communications companies, a feminized low-paid workforce takes care of communications services in call-centers and other service factories, etc. The contradictory relations between communications workers in a global value chain pose the question: "Will knowledge workers of the world unite?" (Mosco and McKercher 2008, 13).

"The urban" is "one of the critical sites for contemporary struggle" (David Harvey, in: Harvey, Hardt and Negri 2009). "The metropolis is a factory for the production of the common. [...] With the passage to the hegemony of biopolitical production, the space of economic production and the space of the city tend to overlap. There is no longer a factory wall that divides the one from the other, and 'externalities' are no longer external to the site o f production that valorizes them. Workers produce throughout the metropolis, in its every crack and crevice. In fact, production of the common is becoming nothing but the life of the city itself" (Hardt and Negri 2009, 250–251). Commercial social media show that the Internet is simultaneously a playground and a factory (Scholz 2011). They lock "networked publics in a 'walled garden' where they can be expropriated, where their relationships are put to work, and where their fascinations and desires are monetized" (Scholz 2011, 246). Internet user commodification is part of the tendency of the commodification of everything that has resulted in the generalization of the factory and of exploitation. "Commodification presumes the existence of property rights over processes, things, and social relations, that a price can be put on them, and that they can be traded subject to legal contract. [...] In practice, of course, every society sets some bounds on where commodification begins and ends" (Harvey 2007, 165). Neoliberal capitalism has largely widened the boundaries of what is treated as a commodity. "The commodification of sexuality, culture, history, heritage; of nature as spectacle or as rest cure; [...] – these all amount to putting a price on things that were never actually produced as commodities" (Harvey 2007, 166).

The outsourcing of work to consumers is a general tendency of contemporary capitalism. Facebook has asked users to translate its site into other languages without payment. Javier Olivan, international manager at Facebook, commented that it would be cool to use the wisdom of the crowds.[4] Pepsi started a competition, in which one could win US$10 000 for the best design of a Pepsi can. Ideabounty is a crowdsourcing platform that organizes crowdsourcing projects for corporations as for example RedBull, BMW or Unilever. In such projects, most of the employed work is unpaid. Even if single individuals receive symbolic prize money, most of the work time employed by users and consumers is fully unpaid, which allows companies to outsource paid labour time to consumers or fans that work for free.

Value is a complex concept. Göran Bolin (2011) identifies economic value, moral value, news value, public value, cultural value, aesthetic value, social value, educational value, political value and symbolic/sign value as specific interpretations of the term. Marx shared with Adam Smith and David Ricardo an objective concept of value. The value of a commodity is for them the "quantity of the 'value-forming substance', the labour, contained in the article," "the amount of labour socially necessary" for its production (Marx 1867, 129). Marx argues that goods in capitalism have a dual character. They have a use value-side (they are used for achieving certain aims) and a value-side. There are aspects of concrete and abstract labour. Concrete labour generates the commodity's use value (the good's qualitative character as useful good that satisfies

---

4   http://www.msnbc.msn.com/id/24205912 (accessed on August 20, 2011).

human needs), abstract labour the commodity's value (the good's quantitative side that allows its exchange with other commodities in the form of the relationship x amount of commodity A = y amount of commodity B). Subjective concepts of economic value, as held for example by classical French political economists as Jean-Baptiste Say and Frederic Bastiat or representatives of the neoclassical Austrian school, assume that the worth of a good is determined by humans cognitive evaluations and moral judgements, they interpret the notion of value idealistically. They say that the value of a good is the value given to them by the subjective judgements of humans.

One problem of the value concept is that its subjective and objective meaning are often mixed up. As the moral value of capitalism is economic value, one needs a precise concept of value. To focus the meaning of the term value on economic value does not automatically mean to speak in favour of capitalism and commodification, it only reflects the important role the capitalist economy has in modern society and stresses commodity logic's tendency to attempt to colonize non-commodified realms. For socialists, an important political goal is a world not dominated by economic value. But achieving this goal does not necessarily need a non-economic definition of the value concept.

Marx made a difference between the concept of value and the concept of price. When we talk about the value of a good, we talk about the average number of hours needed for its production, whereas the price is expressed in quantities of money. "The expression of the value of a commodity in gold – x commodity A = Y money commodity – is its money-form or price" (Marx 1867, 189). Marx argued that the value and the price of a commodity do not coincide: "the production price of a commodity is not at all identical with its value [...] It has been shown that the production price of a commodity may stand above or below its value and coincides with it only in exceptional cases" (Marx 1894, 892). He also dealt with the question how values are transformed into prices. Chapter nine of *Capital Vol. 3* (Marx 1894, 254–272) is devoted to this question.

Information is a peculiar commodity:

- It is not used-up in consumption.
- It can be infinitely shared and copied by one individual without loosing the good itself. Several people can own it at the same time.
- It has no physical wear and tear. Its wear and tear is what Marx (1867, 528) called "moral depreciation": it is caused by competition and the drive of companies to establish new versions of informational commodities, such the newest version of the iPod or iPad or a new song by an artist in order to accumulate ever more capital and by the creation of symbolic difference

postulated by advertising and branding so that the older informational commodities appear for consumers to be "outdated."
• It can be easily and cheaply copied and quickly transmitted.
• It is a social good that reflects the history of social interactions and the history of knowledge.
• The value for producing the initial form of information is relatively high (it includes many hours of development costs), whereas starting with the second copy the value is relatively low (work time mainly is the time of copying and distributing the good).
• Information is, however, normally sold at a price that is higher than its value (measured as the amount of hours needed for its production). The difference between value and price is at the heart of profit making in the information industries.

An artwork sold at a high price makes use of the value-price-differential and the ideological belief of the buyers in the superiority of the artist. Similarly, branding can constitute a value-price-differential. It is an ideological mechanism that wants to make consumers believe that a commodity has a symbolic value above its economic value. Consumers' ideological belief in the superiority of a certain commodity allows companies to achieve excess-profit, a profit higher than yielded for similar use values. Related phenomena are financial assets that are sold at prices that do not correspond to the profits the underlying commodities are yielding. Marx (1894) speaks in this respect of fictitious capital and David Harvey (2005) of a temporal fix to overaccumulation that results in the deference of "the re-entry of capital values into circulation into the future" (Harvey 2005, 109) so that the difference between profits and asset price can result in financial bubbles. Just like there can be a difference between value and price of a commodity, there can be a difference between profit and financial market worth of a financial asset.

Bolin (2011) argues that in broadcasting, not audiences, but statisticians work. The advertisers would not buy audiences, but the belief in a certain audience value generated by statisticians that relatively arbitrarily measure audience ratings. "Audiences do not work; It is rather the statisticians and market executives who do" (Bolin 2011, 84). From a Marxist perspective (that Smythe employed), audiences' work time is the time they consume commercial media. The exact quantity of labour value can never be determined, therefore Marx said that the "individual commodity counts [...] only as an average sample of its kind" (Marx 1867, 129f). Audiences create the value of the commercial media commodity, whereas audience statistics determine the price of the audience commodity by approximating average audience numbers based on a sample of a certain size. Statistical workers are crucial in setting prices and transforming labour values of the media into prices.

On corporate social media, users create content, browse content, establish and maintain relations with others by communication, and update their profiles. All time they spend on these platforms is work time. The Internet prosumer commodity that an advertiser buys on e.g. Facebook or Google is based on specific demographic data (age, location, education, gender, workplace, etc.) and interests (e.g. certain keywords typed into Google or certain interests identified on Facebook). Thereby a specific group can be identified as target group. All time spent by members of this group on the specific social media platform constitutes the value (work time) of a specific Internet prosumer commodity. This work time contains time for social relationship management and cultural activities that generate reputation. One therefore needs to reflect on how economic value production by the media is connected to what Bourdieu termed social, cultural and symbolic capital (Bolin 2011). Users employ social media because they strive for a certain degree to achieve what Bourdieu (1986a, b) terms social capital (the accumulation of social relations), cultural capital (the accumulation of qualification, education, knowledge) and symbolic capital (the accumulation of reputation). The time that users spend on commercial social media platforms for generating social, cultural and symbolic capital is in the process of prosumer commodification transformed into economic capital. Labour time on commercial social media is the conversion of Bourdieuian social, cultural and symbolic capital into Marxian value and economic capital.

Marx (1894) stressed the difference between a commodity's value and price. The price of production of a commodity may lie above or below its value and in some cases coincides with its value. The value level measures the labour needed for the production of commodities in work hours, the price level measures for which amount of money a commodity is sold. The ratings industry transforms the value of the audience commodity into prices. Advertisements are linked to certain programmes because one expects specific kinds of audiences to watch certain programmes (or to read certain parts of a newspaper). The value of one specific programme that is interrupted by advertisements is the sum of the time all viewers spend viewing the programme (including the advertisements). It is impossible to measure this value exactly. Rather, as Marx (1894) knew, only approximations of the average value of a commodity are possible. If more viewers watch a certain programme because it is popular, then its value increases. This makes it likely that also the audience price will be higher because more advertisements will be watched. However, there is no automatic correspondence between value and price of the audience commodity: if one million young, urban middle class youngsters who can be expected to buy a lot of commodities watch one programme and two million elderly rural people watch another programme that has the same length, then the second audience commodity's value is higher. However, due to the expectation that young urban people are more consumption-oriented than elderly rural people, the first commodity audience's price (measured as amount of money that an advertiser needs to pay at a certain point of time in the programme slot for a specific advertisement length in order to reach a defined audience of a particular size) may be higher.

Once value has been created on Facebook by online labour, the resulting data commodities are offered to ad clients with the help of either the pay per click (CPC) or the pay per 1000 impressions (CPM) methods of payment. At his point of analysis, we leave the value-level and the commodity production-sphere and enter the price-level and the sphere of commodity sales. How is the social media prosumer commodities' price determined and how is value transformed into money profit? Advertising clients are interested in the access to specific groups that can be targeted with individualized advertisements that fit their interests. Access to this group and data about their interests (information about who is member of a specific consumer group that shares certain interests) are sold to advertisers. On Google and Facebook, advertisers set a maximum budget for one campaign and a maximum they are willing to pay for one click on their advertisement or for 1000 impressions (1 impression = a presentation of an ad on a profile). The exact price for one click or for 1000 impressions is determined in a automated bidding process, in which all advertisers interested in a specific group (all ads targeted at this specific group) compete. In both models, every user is offered as a commodity and commodified, but only certain user groups are sold as commodity. In the pay-per-click model, value is transformed into money (profit is realized) when a user clicks on an ad. In the pay-per-view model, value is transformed into money (profit is realized) when an ad is presented on a user's profile. The price is mathematically determined by an algorithm and based on bids. The number of hours spent online by a specific group of users determines the value of the social media prosumer commodity. The price of this commodity is algorithmically determined.

All hours spent online by users of Facebook, Google, and comparable corporate social media constitute work time, in which data commodities are generated, as well as potential time for profit realization. The maximum time of a single user that is productive (i.e. results in data commodities) is 100% of the time spent online. The maximum time that the same user contributes to profit realization by clicking on ads or viewing ads is the time that s/he spends on a specific platform. In practice, users only click on a small share of presented ads. So in the pay-per-click accumulation model, work time tends to be much larger than profit realization time. Online labour creates a lot of commodities that are offered for sale, but only a certain share of it is sold and results in profits. This share is still large enough so that companies like Google and Facebook can generate significant profits. Online labour time is at the same time potential profit realization time. Capital tries to increase profit realization time in order to accumulate capital, i.e. to make an ever-larger share of productive labour time also profit realization time.

According to Facebook, the price of an ad in a bid is determined by the number of people competing for a specific ad space/target audience, by ad quality and ad performance (source: Facebook Help Center, Campaign Cost and Budgeting= > Ads and Sponsored Stories). On Google AdWords, the price of an ad depends on the maximum bid that one sets/can afford and ad quality. Ad quality is based on an assessment of how relevant and well-targeted the text of an ad is (source: Google, video "AdWords: Control Your Costs"): the more targeted an ad, the lower the CPC cost. Google's quality score of an ad is based on the number of past clicks for the targeted keyword, the display URL's number of past clicks, the targetedness of the ad text and the number of past clicks for the ad (source: Google AdWords Help: Quality Score). Google offers like Facebook both CPC and CPM as payment methods. How exactly Google's and Facebook's pricing algorithms work is not known because they are not open source.

According to statistics, the most expensive keywords on Google are insurance, loans, mortgage, attorney and credit (http://techcrunch.com/2011/07/18/most-expensive-google-adwords-keywords/). The most viewed adds on Facebook are those from the retail sector (23% of all viewed ads), the food & drinking industry (19%), the finance industry (14%), the entertainment industry (11%) and the games industry (11%) (http://allfacebook.com/facebook-advertising-rates-2_b86020).

A study of Facebook advertising conducted by Comscore (2012) argues that:

- Users spend 40% of their Facebook time in the news feed, therefore exposure to adds is larger there than on brand pages.
- According to DoubleClick, click-through-rates are on average 0.1%.
- Many companies would today mistakenly see the number of fans on brand pages as main success indicator for online advertising.
- People exposed to Facebook ads are more likely to purchase products online or in stores than those who are no. The purchase ratio grows with the length of the advertising campaign. The study therefore suggests the importance of "view-through display ad effectiveness in a medium where click-through rates are known to be lower than average for many campaigns" (Comscore 2012, 3).

Time dimensions play a crucial role in determining the price of an ad: the number of times people click on an ad, the number of times an ad or target URL has already been viewed, the number of times a keyword has been entered, the time that a specific user group spends on the platform. Furthermore, also the bidding maximums used as well as the number of ad clients competing for ad space influence the ad prices. In the pay-per-view method, Facebook and Google earn more with an ad that is targeted on a group that spends a lot of time on Facebook. The larger the target group, the higher Facebook's and Google's profits tend to be. In the pay-per-click method, Facebook and Google only earn money if users click on an ad. According to studies, the average click-through-rate is 0.1% (Comscore 2012). This means that Facebook and Google tend to gain more profit if ads are presented to more users.

Generally we can say that the higher the total attention time given to adds, the higher Google's and Facebook's profits tend to be. Attention time is determined by the size of a target group and the average time this group spends on the platforms. Online time on corporate social media is both labour time and attention time: All activities are monitored and result in data commodities, so users produce commodities online during their online time. In the pay per view mode, specific online time of specifically targeted groups is also attention time that realizes profit for Facebook or Google. In the pay per click mode, attention time that realizes profit is only the portion of the online time that users devote to click on ads that are presented to them. In both cases, online time is crucial for (a) the production of data commodities, (b) the realization of profit derived from the sales of the data commodities. Both surveillance of online time (in the sphere of production) and attention time (in the sphere of circulation) given to advertisements play an important role in corporate social media's capital accumulation model.

According to Google Trends, Michael Jackson was one of the top trending search keyword on Google on June 27th, 2012. Using the Google AdWords traffic estimator (on June 27th, 2012) showed that by creating a campaign with a maximum CPC of 10 € and a budget of 1000 Euros per day, one can expect to attract 2867–3504 impressions and 112–137 clicks for total costs of 900–1100 Euros per day if one targets Google users who search for "Michael Jackson." In comparison, I used the same settings for the keyword "Cat Power" (an outstanding American indie rock singer, much less popular and less sought-after on Google than Michael Jackson). In a campaign that targets users who google "Cat Power," one can expect to attract 108–132 impressions and 3.9–4.7 clicks for total costs of 30.96-37.84 Euros per day. The profit that Google makes with the data commodity associated with the keyword "Michael Jackson" is much larger than the one it makes with the keyword "Cat Power" because the first is a more sought-after keyword. And that a keyword is popular means that users spend more collective usage time per day for entering the keyword and reading result pages than for other keywords. The example shows that popular interests, for whose generation and result consumption users spend more labour time on the Internet than for not-so popular keywords, tend to result in higher profits for Google than interests that are not so popular.

Marx formulated the law of value as saying that "the greater the labour-time necessary to produce an article, [...] the greater its value" (Marx 1867, 131). The law of value also applies in the case of commercial social media: The more time a user spends on commercial social media, the more data about her/his interests and activities are available and the more advertisements are presented to her/him. Users spending a lot of time online, create more data and more value (work time) that is potentially transformed into profit. That the law of value applies on commercial social media can also be observed by the circumstance that there are high prices for advertisements presented in the context of frequently searched keywords on Google. A lot of users spend their work time on searching for these keywords, i.e. the value (work time) underlying specific keywords is high. This makes the corresponding user commodity more precious (it is likely to be a large group), therefore its price can be set at a high rate.

That surplus value generating labour is an emergent property of capitalist production means that production and accumulation will break down if this labour is withdrawn. It is an essential part of the capitalist production process. That prosumers conduct surplus-generating labour, can also be seen by imagining what would happen if they would stop using Facebook or Google: The number of users would drop, advertisers would stop investments because no objects for their advertising messages and therefore no potential customers for their products could be found, the profits of the new media corporations would drop and they would go bankrupt. If such activities were carried out on a large scale, a new economy crisis would arise. This thought experiment shows that users are essential for generating profit in the new media economy. Furthermore they produce and co-produce parts of the products and therefore parts of the use value, value, and surplus value that are objectified in these products.

Not all prosumer work on social media is commodified (just like not all audience work is comodified). Work that contributes content, attention or comments to non-commercial non-profit projects (such as Wikipedia or alternative online news media, such as Indymedia, Alternet, Democracy Now!, openDemocracy, WikiLeaks, or the use of social media by NGO s) is work in the sense that it helps creating use values (alternative news, critical discourse etc.), but it is non-commodified work, it cannot be exploited, does not have exchange value and does not yield profit. Non-commercial non-profit online projects are expression of the struggle for a society and an Internet that is not ruled by the logic of commodities and exchange value. Although they are frequently precarious, the existence of alternatives shows that social media and media in general are in capitalism shaped by (a) class structures, (b) ideological "incorporation and legitimation" and (c) "gaps and contradictions" that constitute "cracks and fissures" that allow "currents of criticism and movements of contestation" (Golding and Murdock 1978, 353).

Corporate social media have an immanent connection to finance capital. Google's profits were 9.7 billion US$ in 2011 (SEC Filings Form 10-K 2011), whereas its financial market valuation (stock market capitalization) was 182 billion US$ on June 26th, 2012.[5] Facebook's profits were 1 billion US$ in 2011 (SEC Filings Form S-1 Registration statement), whereas its stock market capitalization was 70 billion US$ on June 26th, 2012.[6] This shows that the financial market values achieved on the stock market and the profits achieved by Internet prosumer commodification do not coincide. Companies like Facebook and Google are overvalued on the stock market, their profits do not match the high market values. This divergence phenomenon does not lie outside of the logic of Marxist theory, but was rather described by Marx (1894) in the analysis of fictitious capital in *Capital Volume III*.

For Marx, financial capital is based on the formula M (money) – M' (more money). "Here we have M-M', money that produces money, self-valorizing value, without the process that mediates the two extremes" (Marx 1894, 515, see also 471). Consumer credits, mortgages, stock, bonds, and derivates are all based on this financial type of accumulation. Finance capital does not itself produce profit, it is only an entitlement to payments that are made in the future and derive from profits or wages (the latter for example in the case of consumer credits). Marx therefore characterizes finance capital as fictitious capital (Marx 1894, 596). The "share is nothing but an ownership title, *pro rata,* to the surplus-value which this capital is to realize. A may sell this title to B, and B to C. These transactions have no essential effect on the matter. A or B has then transformed his title into capital, but C has transformed his capital into a mere ownership title to the surplus-value expected from this share capital" (Marx 1894, 597f). Financial investments in stocks and financial derivates are transformed into operative capital, but they are not capital themselves, only ownership titles to a part of surplus value that is expected to be produced in the future. "All these securities actually represent nothing but accumulated claims, legal titles, to future production" (Marx 1894, 599). The value of shares

---

5   http://money.cnn.com/data/us_markets/.

6   http://money.cnn.com/data/us_markets/.

is therefore speculative and not connected to the actual profits of the company, but only to expectations about future profits that determine buying and selling decisions of stock investors: "The market value of these securities is partly speculative, since it is determined not just by the actual revenue but rather by the anticipated revenue as reckoned in advance" (Marx 1894, 598, see also 608, 641). The result is a high-risk system of speculation that resembles gambling (Marx 1894, 609) and is crisis-prone (Marx 1894, 621). "Monetary crises, independent of real crises or as an intensification of them, are unavoidable" in capitalism (Marx 1894, 649).

Financialization is a crucial aspect of corporate social media platforms like Facebook and Google. Financialization is a mechanism that Marx described as important element of capitalism. User labour is the source of profit on these platforms. Finance capital invests in platforms like Facebook and Google because it has the expectation of high future profits. The new economy crisis in 2000 has shown that the difference between stock market values and actual profits can result, as Marx knew, in bursting financial bubbles that result in economic crises. Crises can have multiple sources (e.g. lack of sales = overproduction, underconsumption; class struggle that increases investments and negatively impacts profits (profit-squeeze); overaccumulation; crisis events that trigger large-scale sales of stocks and disappointed investment situations; combinations, etc.). The stock market values of companies like Google and Facebook are based on expectations how well these corporations will in the future be able to exploit users' and employees' labour and turn it into profit. The actual profit rates influence, but do not determine stock market investors' buying and selling decisions. The latter are determined by multiple factors and expectations, especially expectations about potential futures, which is the reason why Marx speaks of fictitious capital.

Capital has the inherent interest to maximize profit. For doing this, it will take all means necessary because the single capitalist risks his/her own bankruptcy if s/he cannot accumulate capital as a result of high investment costs, heavy competition, lack of productivity, etc. The wage relation is, as we have argued earlier, a crucial element of class struggle. Capital tries to reduce the wage sum as much as possible in order to maximize profits. If possible, capital will therefore remunerate labour power below its own value, i.e. below the socially necessary costs that are required for survival. The transformation of the value into the price of labour power and the difference between the two is, as Cleaver (2000) and Bidet (2009) stress, the result of class struggle. Labour legislation and an organized labour movement can struggle for wages that are higher than the value of labour power. If labour is, however, weak, e.g. because of fascist repression, capital is likely to use any opportunity to reduce wages as much as possible in order to increase profits. Neoliberalism is a form of govern-mentality that increases profits by decreasing the wage sum with the help of cutting state expenditures for welfare, care and education, privatizing such services, creating precarious wage-relations that are temporary, insecure and underpaid, weakening the power of labour organisations, decreasing or not increasing wages relatively or absolutely, outsourcing labour to low-paid or unpaid forms of production, coercing the unemployed to work without pay-ment or for extremely low wages, etc. It is a form of politics that aims at helping capital to reduce the price of labour power as much as possible, if possible even below the minimum value that is needed for human existence. The cre-ation of multiple forms of precarious and unpaid forms of work is an expres-sion of the class struggle of capital to reduce the costs of labour power. The result is a disjuncture of the value and price of labour power. Digital labour should be situated in the context of capital's actual struggle to reduce the price of labour power and potential resistance by the working class. The disjuncture between value and price of labour power is accompanied by a disjuncture of the value and price of commodities: The financialization of the economy has established stocks and derivatives that have fictitious prices on stock markets that are based on the hope for high future profits and dividends, but are dis-jointed from the actual labour values and commodity prices. Contemporary capitalism is a disjuncture economy, in which values, profits and prices tend to be out of joint so that there is a high crisis-proneness.

After analyzing the commodity and capital side of corporate social media, I will in the next section discuss changes in the relationship between play and labour relate them to the digital labour debate.

5   Ideology, Play and Digital Labour

Ideology takes on two distinct forms in relationship to contemporary digital media:

(1)   The presentation of social media as form of participatory culture and new democracy.
(2)   The hidden appearance of exploitation as play.

Ideological claims are not specific for what some term "web 2.0," rather also ear-lier claims about the Internet in the 1990s constituted a "Californian ideology" (Barbrook and Cameron 2001) that stresses individualism, personal responsi-bility, competition, private property and consumerism, lacks consciousness of inequality and exploitation and is in line with the basic ideas of neoliberalism (Fisher 2010). Neubauer (2011) stresses in this context the existence of a specific ideology of informational neoliberalism that combines the belief in the power of ICT s and neoliberal values.

The turn of the millennium saw a crisis of heavily financialized Internet companies. The "dot-com" crisis destroyed the hopes that the "Internet age" would result in a new age of prosperity and unhampered economic growth. In the years following the crisis, companies such as Facebook (2004), Flickr (2004) LinkedIn (2003), Sina Weibo (2009), Tumblr (2007), Twitter (2006), VK (VKontakte, 2006), Wordpress (2003) and YouTube (2005, sold to Google in 2006) were founded. They provide Internet services that are today among the most accessed web platforms in the world. They represent capitalists' new aspiring hopes to found a new capital accumulation model that is based on targeted advertising.

The rise of these platforms was accompanied by an ideology that celebrated these services as radically new and the rise of an economic democracy and participatory culture. Henry Jenkins (2008, 275) argues that "the Web has become a site of consumer participation" and has supported the rise of a participatory culture. Axel Bruns argues that Flickr, YouTube, MySpace and Facebook are environments of "public participation" (Bruns 2008, 227f) and give rise to "a produsage-based democratic model" (Bruns 2008, 372). John Hartley (2012) describes the emergence of a "dialogical model of communication" (Hartley 2012, 2), in which "everyone is a producer" (Hartley 2012, 3). His general argument is that with the rise of online platforms that support social networking and user-generated content production and diffusion, journalism, the public sphere, universities, the mass media, citizenship, the archive and other institutions have become more democratic because "people have more say in producing as well as consuming" (Hartley 2012, 14). Clay Shirky (2008, 297) says that "web 2.0" means the "democratization of production." Tapscott and Williams see the rise of a new economy they call wikinomics that results in the emergence of "a new economic democracy" (Tapscott and Williams 2006, 267).

Especially management gurus and cultural theorists have made the claim that user-generated content platforms have advanced a participatory economy and culture. They have helped to sell "web 2.0" as the "next big thing" that venture capitalists need to invest in. The hype turned out to be more about capital accumulation than democracy. The discussions about terms such as "social media" and "web 2.0" have started when Tim O'Reilly (2005) introduced the term "web 2.0" in 2005. Although Tim O'Reilly surely thinks that "web 2.0" denotes actual changes and says that the crucial fact about it is that users as a collective intelligence co-create the value of platforms like Google, Amazon, Wikipedia, or craigslist in a "community of connected users" (O'Reilly and Battelle 2009, 1), he admits that the term was mainly created for identifying the need of new economic strategies of Internet companies after the "dot-com" crisis, in which the bursting of financial bubbles caused the collapse of many Internet companies. So he says in a paper published five years after the creation of the invention of the term "web 2.0," that this category was "a statement about the second coming of the Web after the dotcom bust" at a conference that was "designed to restore confidence in an industry that had lost its way after the dotcom bust" (O'Reilly and Battelle 2009, 1). This means that the person, who coined the notion of "web 2.0" admits that it is an ideology aimed at attracting investors.

Web 2.0 enthusiasts tend to use the notion of participation in a shallow way, forgetting that it main use stems from participatory democracy theory, in which it signifies the control of ownership, decision making and value-definition by all (Fuchs 2011a, Chapter 7). Statistics such as the ownership structures of web 2.0 companies, the most viewed videos on YouTube, the most popular Facebook groups, the most popular topics on Google and Twitter, the Twitter users with the highest number of followers show that the corporate web 2.0 is not a democratic space of equal participants, but a space, in which large companies, celebtrities and entertainment dominate. They achieve a much higher number of followers, readers, viewers, listeners, re-tweets, likes, etc. than the everyday users (Fuchs 2011a, Chapter 7). If a claim about reality is disjointed from actual reality, then one commonly characterizes such a claim as an ideology. "Web 2.0" and "social media," conceived as participatory culture and participatory economy, are ideological categories that serve the interests of the dominant class. They ignore power structures that shape the Internet.

Claims about the power of "social media" are not only trying to attract business investments, but also have a hegemonic side in the life and thought of everyday users. Jodi Dean (2005) speaks in this context of Internet fetishism and argues that it is an ideology to assume that the Internet is inherently political and that "web 2.0" is a form of politics in itself: "Busy people can think they are active – the technology will act for them, alleviating their guilt while assuring them that noting will change too much. [...] By sending an e-mail, signing a petition, responding to an article on a blog, people can feel political. And that feeling feeds communicative capitalism insofar as it leaves behind the time-consuming, incremental and risky efforts of politics. [...] It is a refusal to take a stand, to venture into the dangerous terrain of politicization" (Dean 2005, 70).

But ideology not only takes on the form of overdrawn claims about the democratic implications of "social media." It is also present in the media production process itself, in which exploitation as social relation tends to be hidden in structures of play. The labour side of the capital accumulation strategy

of social media corporations is digital playbour. Kücklich (2005) first introduced the term playbour (play + labour). The exploitation of digital playbour is
based on the collapse of the distinction between work time and playtime. In
the Fordist mode of capitalist production, work time was the time of pain and
the time of repression and surplus repression of the human drive for pleasure;
whereas leisure time was the time of Eros (Marcuse 1955). In contemporary
capitalism, play and labour, Eros and Thanatos, the pleasure principle and the
death drive, partially converge: workers are expected to have fun during work
time and play time becomes productive and work-like. Playtime and work time
intersect and all human time of existence tends to be exploited for the sake
capital accumulation.

Capitalism connects labour and play in a destructive dialectic. Traditionally,
play in the form of enjoyment, sex and entertainment was in capitalism only
part of spare time, which was rather unproductive (in the sense of producing
commodities for sale) and separate from labour time. Freud (1961) argued
that the structure of drives is characterized by a dialectic of Eros (the drive for
life, sexuality, lust) and Thanatos (the drive for death, destruction, aggres-
sion). Humans according to Freud strive for the permanent realization of
Eros (pleasure principle), but culture would only become possible by a temporal negation and suspension of Eros and the transformation of erotic
energy into culture and labour. Labour would be a productive form of desexu-
alisation – the repression of sexual drives. Freud speaks in this context of the
reality principle or sublimation. The reality principle sublates the pleasure
principle. Human culture thereby sublates human nature and becomes man's
second nature.

Marcuse (1955) connected Freud's theory of drives to Marx's theory of capitalism. He argued that alienated labour, domination, and capital accumulation
have turned the reality principle into a repressive reality principle – the performance principle: alienated labour constitutes a surplus-repression of Eros. The
repression of the pleasure principle takes on a quantity that exceeds the culturally necessary suppression. Marcuse connected Marx's notions of necessary
labour and surplus labour/value to the Freudian drive structure of humans and
argued that necessary labour on the level of drives corresponds to necessary
suppression and surplus labour to surplus-repression. This means that in order
to exist, a society needs a certain amount of necessary labour (measured in
hours of work) and hence a certain corresponding amount of suppression of
the pleasure principle (also measured in hours). The exploitation of surplus
value (labour that is performed for free and generates profit) results not only in
the circumstance that workers are forced to work for free for capital to a certain
extent, but also in the circumstance that the pleasure principle must be additionally suppressed.

"Behind the reality principle lies the fundamental fact of Ananke or scarcity (*Lebensnot*), which means that the struggle for existence takes place in a world too poor for the satisfaction of human needs without constant restraint, renunciation, delay. In other words, whatever satisfaction is possible necessitates work, more or less painful arrangements and undertakings for the procurement of the means for satisfying needs. For the duration of work, which occupies practically the entire existence of the mature individual, pleasure is 'suspended' and pain prevails" (Marcuse 1955, 35). In societies that are based on the principle of domination, the reality principle takes on the form of the performance principle: Domination "is exercised by a particular group or individual in order to sustain and enhance itself in a privileged situation" (Marcuse 1955, 36). The performance principle is connected to surplus-repression, a term that describes "the restrictions necessitated by social domination" (Marcuse 1955, 35). Domination introduces "additional controls over and above those indispensable for civilized human association" (Marcuse 1955, 37).

Marcuse (1955) argues that the performance principle means that Thanatos governs humans and society and that alienation unleashes aggressive drives within humans (repressive desublimation) that result in an overall violent and aggressive society. Due to the high productivity reached in late-modern society, a historical alternative would be possible: the elimination of the repressive reality principle, the reduction of necessary working time to a minimum and the maximization of free time, an eroticization of society and the body, the shaping of society and humans by Eros, the emergence of libidinous social relations. Such a development would be a historical possibility – but one incompatible with capitalism and patriarchy.

Gilles Deleuze (1995) has pointed out that in contemporary capitalism, disciplinary power is transformed in such a way that humans increasingly discipline themselves without direct external violence. He terms this situation the society of (self-)control. It can for example be observed in the strategies of participatory management. This method promotes the use of incentives and the integration of play into labour. It argues that work should be fun, workers should permanently develop new ideas, realize their creativity, enjoy free time within the factory, etc. The boundaries between work time and spare time, labour and play, become fuzzy. Work tends to acquire qualities of play, whereas entertainment in spare time tends to become labour-like. Work time and spare time become inseparable. At the same time work-related stress intensifies and property relations remain unchanged (Boltanski and Chiapello 2007). Corporate social media's exploitation of Internet users is an aspect of this transformation. It signifies that private Internet usage, which is motivated by play, entertainment, fun and joy – aspects of Eros – has become subsumed under capital and has become a sphere of the exploitation of labour. Internet corporations accumulate profit by exploiting the play labour of users.

Luc Boltanski and Éve Chiapello (2007) argue that the rise of participatory management means the emergence of a new spirit of capitalism that subsumes the anti-authoritarian values of the political revolt of 1968 and the subsequently emerging New Left such as autonomy, spontaneity, mobility, creativity, networking, visions, openness, plurality, informality, authenticity, emancipation, and so on, under capital. The topics of the movement would now be put into the service of those forces that it wanted to destroy. The outcome would have been "the construction of the new, so-called 'network' capitalism" (Boltanski and Chiapello 2007, 429) so that artistic critique – that calls for authenticity, creativity, freedom and autonomy in contrast to social critique that calls for equality and overcoming class (37f) – today "indirectly serves capitalism and is one of the instruments of its ability to endure" (490).

Also paid creative industry work is becoming more like play today. Hesmondhalgh and Baker (2011) show the ambivalence of much creative industry work that is precarious, but cherished, because of the fun, contacts, reputation, creativity, and self-determination that it may involve. The difficulty is that labour feels like play and that exploitation and fun thereby become inseparable. Play and labour are today in certain cases indistinguishable. Eros has become fully subsumed under the repressive reality principle. Play is largely commodified, spaces and free time that are not exploited by capital hardly exist today. They are difficult to create and to defend. Play is today productive, surplus value generating labour that is exploited by capital. All human activities, and therefore also all play, tends under the contemporary conditions to become subsumed under and exploited by capital. Play as an expression of Eros is thereby destroyed, human freedom and human capacities are crippled. On corporate social media, play and labour converge into play labour that is exploited for capital accumulation. The corporate Internet therefore stands for the total commodification and exploitation of time – all human time tends to become surplus-value generating time that is exploited by capital. Table 18.1 summarizes the application of Marcuse's theory of play, labour and pleasure to corporate social media.

Some authors have criticized the main arguments advanced in the digital labour debate. In the next section, I present and discuss some of the points of criticism.

6   A Critique of the Critique of Digital Labour

David Hesmondhalgh (2010) argues that Internet labour is not exploited because there is much cultural work in society that is unpaid. "Most cultural

TABLE 18.1 *Pleasures in four modes of society (human essence, society with scarcity, classical capitalism, capitalism in the age of corporate social media), based on a table from: Marcuse 1955.* 12

Essence of human desires:	Reality principle in societies with scarcity	Repressive reality principle in classical capitalism	Repressive reality principle in capitalism in the age of corporate social media
immediate satisfaction	delayed satisfaction	delayed satisfaction	Immediate online satisfaction
Pleasure	restraint of pleasure	leisure time: pleasure, work time: restraint of pleasure, surplus repression of pleasure	Collapse of leisure time and work time, leisure time becomes work time and work time leisure time, all time becomes exploited, online leisure time becomes surplus value-generating, wage labour time = surplus repression time of pleasure, play labour time = surplus value generating pleasure time
joy (play)	toil (work)	leisure time: joy (play), work time: toil (work)	play labour: joy and play as toil and work, toil and work as joy and play
Receptiveness	productiveness	leisure time: receptiveness, work time: productiveness	Collapse of the distinction between leisure time/work time and receptiveness/productiveness, total commodification of human time
absence of repression of pleasure	repression of pleasure	leisure time: absence of repression of pleasure, work time: repression of pleasure	play labour time: surplus value generation appears to be pleasure-like, but serves the logic of repression (the lack of ownership of capital)

production in history has been unpaid, and that continues to be the case today. Consider the millions of people across the world, especially young people, who will, on the day you are reading this, be practising musical instruments, or, to use an example from an industry that I would call a leisure industry rather than a cultural industry, imagine how many young people are practising football or basketball. Now it could be argued that all this represents labour (defined here as the expenditure of effort, under some kind of compulsion; it will usually seem preferable to undertake some other more restful activity) which is vital to the realisation of surplus value in the music industry or the football industry. For this work helps to create a reservoir of workers, from whom these industries can draw" (Hesmondhalgh 2010, 277). Hesmondhalgh says that the claim "that contacting friends and uploading photographs on to Facebook represents some kind of exploited labour is, to my mind, more along the lines of arguing that we should demand that all amateur football coaches be paid for their donation of free time: not impossible to argue for, but hardly a priority – and accompanied by the danger that it may commodify forms of activity that we would ultimately prefer to leave outside the market" (278).

Hesmondhalgh mixes up two different types of activity:

(1)   hobby or private activities, in which labour power is reproduced, but no commodities are produced (like playing football or sleeping);
(2)   hobby activities, in which value is generated that is directly appropriated by capitalist companies (using commercial Internet platforms, watching commercial television, etc.).

Hesmondhalgh conflates different activities – reproductive activity that recreates labour power, but produces no commodity that is sold, and reproductive activities that recreate labour power and at the same time create an audience or Internet prosumer commodity. If a wage for either or both of these activities should be demanded (there are pro- and counter-arguments from a left-wing political perspective) is another (political) question, but Hesmondhalgh ignores the direct role of class, commodification and profit in the second type of activity.

The audience and digital labour are definitely exploited on corporate social media because three conditions of exploitation (Wright 1997, 10) are given:

(a)   the profit accumulated deprives the audience and users of material benefits (inverse interdependent welfare),
(b)   audience and users are excluded from the ownership of media organizations and the accumulated profit (exclusion),
(c)   capital appropriates the created profit (appropriation).

Pasquinelli (2009, 2010) argues that Google creates and accumulates value by its page rank algorithm. He says that Google's profit is a form of cognitive rent. Caraway (2011, 701) shares this analysis on a more general level and argues: "The economic transaction described by Smythe is *rent*. The media owner rents the use of the medium to the industrial capitalist who is interested in gaining access to an audience. The rental may be either for time (broadcasting) or space (print). It is the job of the media owner to create an environment which is conducive to the formation of a particular audience". Rent theories of the Internet substitute categories like class, surplus value, and exploitation by the notion of rent.

Marx (1867) showed that technology never creates value, but is only a tool that is used by living human labour for creating commodities. Therefore it is a technological-deterministic assumption that the page rank algorithm creates value. Marx (1894) argued that rent is exchanged for land and formulated the trinity formula that expresses the three aspects of the value of a commodity (Marx 1894, Chapter 48): profit (including interest), rent, wages. Profit is attached to capital, rent to land, and wages to wage labour. The three kinds of revenue are connected to the selling of commodities, land and labour power. Rent is obtained by lending land or real estates. Rent is not the direct result of surplus value production and human labour. No new product is created in the renting process. Rent indirectly stems from surplus value because capitalists take part of the surplus in order to rent houses, but it is created in a secondary process, in which surplus value is used for buying real estates. "First we have the use-value land, which has no value, and the exchange-value rent" (Marx 1894, 956). "Value is labour. So surplus-value cannot be earth" (Marx 1894, 954). Therefore using the category of rent for describing commercial media and Internet practices and their outcomes means to assume that activities on the corporate media and Internet, such as surfing on Google or creating content on YouTube or Facebook, are not exploited and are no form of labour. The category of cognitive rent is not useful for a critical political economy of the media and the Internet. The notion of the Internet prosumer commodity that is created by exploited knowledge labour is more feasible.

Adam Arvidsson formulates a critique of the digital labour hypothesis and of Smythe's audience commodity approach. "As a consequence, the labor theory of value only holds if labor has a price, if it has been transformed into a commodity that can in some way be bought and sold on a market. It is clear already at this point that it is difficult to apply the labor theory of value to productive practices that do not have a given price, that unfold outside of the wage relation" (Arvidsson 2011, 265). "The circumstance that digital labour has no price and that it becomes impossible to distinguish productive time from unproductive time" would make "it difficult to sustain, as Arvidsson (2006), Fuchs (2009a), and Cote and Phybus (2007) have done, that the Marxist concept of 'exploitation' would apply to processes of customer co-production" (Arvidsson 2011, 266–267). "But since 'free labor' is free, it has no price, and cannot, consequently, be a source of value" (Arvidsson 2011, 266–267). Arvidsson's conclusion is that digital labour is not exploited because it has no price (i.e. it is unpaid).

Digital labour is not the only work that has historically been unpaid, one can think also e.g. of housework or slave work. Marxist feminists have argued that houseworkers are an exploited colony of capitalist patriarchy that is locus of "ongoing primitive accumulation" (Mies, Bennholdt-Thomsen and Werlhof 1988, 6): they are unpaid, unfree and fulfil a function for capitalism. They are therefore locus of extreme exploitation. The argument of Marxist feminism is that "subsistence production – mainly performed through the non-wage labour of women and other non-wage labourers labourers as slaves, contracted workers and peasants in the colonies – constitutes the perennial basis upon which 'capitalist productive forces' can be built up and exploited" (Mies 1986, 48).

There is a crucial difference between classical slaves, houseworkers, and corporate Internet users because the first are repressed by physical violence (they are likely to be killed if they stop working), the second are partly coerced by physical violence and feelings of love and affection, whereas the third are ideologically coerced (they are compelled to use the dominant corporate Internet platforms in order to maintain social relations and reputation, if they stop using the platforms, they do not die, but are likely to be more isolated). But all three forms of labour produce value that is appropriated by others (the slave master, capitalists and wageworkers, corporations). They are unpaid. Others exploit all of their work time. Arvidsson's false assumption that exploitation is only present if a wage is paid downplays the horrors of exploitation and implies also that classical slaves and houseworkers are not exploited. His assumption has therefore problematic implications in the context of racist modes of production and patriarchy. It is furthermore interesting that Arvidsson criticizes himself for having shared the thesis of the exploitation of free labour in an article published in 2006.

iPhones, iPads, iMacs, Nokia phones etc. are "blood phones," "blood pads" and "blood Macs": Many smartphones, laptops, digital cameras, mp3 players, etc. are made out of minerals (e.g. cassiterite, wolframite, coltan, gold, tungsten, tantalum, tin) that are extracted under slave-like conditions from mines in the Democratic Republic of Congo and other countries. The existence of the Internet in its current dominant capitalist form is based on various forms of labour: the relatively highly paid wage work of software engineers and low-paid proletarianized workers in Internet companies, the unpaid labour of users, the highly exploited bloody Taylorist work and slave work in developing countries producing hardware and extracting "conflict minerals." Arvidsson's approach implies that unpaid Congolese slave workers that extract the material foundations of ICT s are not exploited, which has problematic implications.

Arvidsson's alternative to the labour theory of value is an idealistic and sub-jectivist concept of value – ethical value understood as "the ability to create the kinds of affectively significant relations" (Arvidsson 2005, 270) – that ignores the reality of material inequality, precarious labour, and gaps between the rich and the poor and assumes that everything in the contemporary economy has become affective.

Arvidsson (2011, 273) argues that I have come to the "absurd suggestion that Facebook users are subject to 'infinite levels of exploitation' since the exchange value of their labor is zero". In a comment on one of my digital labour articles (Fuchs 2010), Arvidsson and Colleoni argue: "If Facebook made a profit of $355 million in 2010 [...], this means that each Facebook user was a 'victim of exploi-tation of surplus value' to the extent of $0.7 a year, [...] hardly [...] 'a rate of exploitation that converges towards infinity' as Fuchs claims" (Arvidsson and Colleoni 2012, 138). Fuchs (2012b) provides a more detailed critique of Arvidsson's work. Arvidsson and his colleague mix up value and price. If 500 million people use a corporate platform that is funded by targeted adver-tising for an average of 90 hours a year (which is on average 15 minutes a day), then the value created is 45 billion hours of digital labour. All of this online time is monitored and creates a traffic commodity that is offered for sale to advertisers, none of the time is paid. 45 billion hours of work are therefore exploited. Exploitation is constituted by the unpaid work time that is objecti-fied in a commodity and appropriated by capital. To which extent the data commodity can be sold is a question of the transformation of value into profit. If not enough data commodities are sold, then the profit will be low. Workers are however also exploited if the commodities they create are not sold because value and surplus value of a commodity is created before it is sold. Arvidsson's criticism implies that exploitation is based in the sphere of commodity circu-lation and not in the sphere of commodity production. This assumption is absurd because it implies that workers, who create a commodity that is not sold (e.g. because there is a lack of demand), are not exploited. Arvidsson's criticism is based on a lack of knowledge of Marx.

Marx stressed the difference between a commodity's value and price: The measure of the substance of value of a commodity is the amount of hours needed for its production: "How then is the magnitude of this value [of a com-modity] to be measured? By means of the quantity of the 'value-forming sub-stance', the labour, contained in the article. This quantity is measured by its duration, and the labour-time is itself measured on the particular scale of hours, days etc." (Marx 1867, 129). "Every commodity (product or instrument of production) is = the objectification of a given amount of labour time (Marx 1857/58, 140)". Marx formulated the law of value as saying that "the greater the labour-time necessary to produce an article, [...] the greater its value. The value of a commodity, therefore, varies directly as the quantity, an inversely as the productivity, of the labour which finds its realization within the commodity. (Now we know the *substance* of value. It is *labour*. We know the *measure of its magnitude*. It is labour-time [...])" (Marx 1867, 131).

Price is not the same as value: "The expression of the value of a commodity in gold – x commodity A = y money commodity – is its money-form or price"(Marx 1867, 189). "Price is the money-name of the labour objectified in a commodity"(Marx 1867, 195–196). This means that values are determined at the level of working hours and prices at the level of money. Both are quantitative measures, but use different units of measurement. Value is a measure of the production process, price a measure of the circulation process (selling) of commodities. Labour is extended in time (and space) in the production process, in which commodities are created, and is transformed into profit (measured as a price in money) in the sphere of circulation, i.e. commodity markets, on which commodities are sold for certain prices. This means that *exploitation of labour takes place before the selling of commodities*. Even if a commodity is not sold, once it is produced, labour has been exploited.

When introducing the concept of brand value in an article that also mentions Smythe, Adam Arvidsson (2005, 238) immediately gives figures of brand values in US$, which shows that he thinks of value in terms of money (that signifies only the price of a commodity) and not in working hours (that signify the value of a commodity). The definition of brand value as "the present value of predictable future earnings generated by the brand" (Arvidsson 2005, 238) is not only circular and therefore absurd (definition of value by value), but also makes clear that Arvidsson defines value only at the price level ("earnings").

7   Conclusion

The global capitalist crisis has resulted in cracks, fissures and holes of neoliberalism and the logic of the commodification of everything. It has however not brought an end to neoliberalism, but a phase of uncertainty. There is a renewed interest in Marx's works, Critical Theory, Critical Political Economy class, and the critique of capitalism. Media and Communication Studies should see the sign of the times and build a strong focus on Marxism, class and capitalism.

The engagement with Dallas Smythe's works today is a contribution to the renewal of Marxist Media and Communication Studies.

Smythe spoke of the audience commodity and Jhally/Livant of watching as working for analyzing media commodification. Internet and media watching/reading/listening/using is value-generating labour, the audience commodity and the Internet prosumer commodity are commodities created by the work of watching/reading/listening/using. The audience produces itself as commodity, its work creates the audience and users as commodity.

We can summarize the main points of this chapter:

- Dallas Smythe reminds us of the importance of engagement with Marx's works for studying the media in capitalism critically.
- Both Critical Theory and Critical Political Economy of the Media and Communication have been criticized for being one-sided. Such interpretations are mainly based on selective readings. They ignore that in both approaches there has been with different weightings a focus on aspects of media commodification, audiences, ideology and alternatives. Critical Theory and Critical Political Economy are complementary and should be combined in Critical Media and Communication Studies today.
- Dallas Smythe's notion of the audience commodity has gained new relevance in the debate about the exploitation of digital labour by corporate Internet providers. The exploitation of digital labour involves processes of coercion, alienation, and appropriation.
- Corporate social media use capital accumulation models that are based on the exploitation of the unpaid labour of Internet users and on the commodification of user generated-data and data about user behaviour that is sold as commodity to advertisers. Targeted advertising and economic surveillance are important aspects of this accumulation model. The category of the audience commodity becomes in the realm of social media transmogrified into the category of the Internet prosumer commodity.
- Corporate "social media" and "web 2.0" do not imply a democratization of the economy and culture, but are rather ideologies that celebrate new capital accumulation models and thereby help to attract investors.
- The exploitation of the Internet prosumer commodity is a manifestation of a stage of capitalism, in which the boundaries between play and labour have become fuzzy and the exploitation of play labour has become a new principle. Exploitation tends to feel like fun and becomes part of free time.
- Critics of the digital labour debate conflate different work activities, tend to trivialize exploitation and to a certain degree misunderstand concepts like surplus value, value, price and rent.

Capitalism is highly contradictory today. The crisis is a manifestation of capitalism's objective immanent contradictions that it is unable to overcome. The reactions to the crisis are contradictory: they range from hyperneoliberalism (politics that want to intensify neoliberalism by implementing "socialism for the rich and banks" and privatizing and cutting public funding for welfare, education, health, etc.) to uproars, riots, protests, demonstrations and occupations (like the Occupy movement or the protests in Greece, Spain, and Portugal), and revolutions (like in Tunisia, Egypt, and Libya). These struggles and forms of politics reflect the subjective contradictions of capitalism in crisis times. It is the task of critical intellectuals today to engage in the academic and political struggle for a just world that is based on common goods and services, including the communication commons.

References

Adorno, Theodor W. 1977. *Kulturkritik und Gesellschaft II.* Frankfurt am Main: Suhrkamp.

Adorno, Theodor W. 1996. Chaplin Times Two. *Yale Journal of Criticism* 9 (1): 57–61.

Adorno, Theodor W. 2000. *Introduction to Sociology.* Cambridge, UK: Polity.

Adorno, Theodor W. 2005. Prologue to Television. In *Critical Models*, 49–57. New York: Columbia University Press.

Adorno, Theordor W., Else Frenkel-Brunswik, Daniel Levinson and Nevitt Sanford. 1950. The Authoritarian Personality. New York: Harper & Row.

Anderson, Chris. 2009. *Free. How Today's Smartest Businesses Profit by Giving Something for Nothing.* London: Random House.

Andrejevic, Mark. 2002. The Work of Being Watched. Interactive Media and the Exploitation of Self-Disclosure. *Critical Studies in Media Communication* 19 (2): 230–248.

Andrejevic, Mark. 2004. *Reality TV. The Work of Being Watched.* Lanham, MD: Rowman & Littlefield.

Andrejevic, Mark. 2007. *iSpy. Surveillance and Power in the Interactive Era.* Lawrence, KS: University Press of Kansas.

Andrejevic, Mark. 2012. Exploitation in the Data Mine. In *Internet and Surveillance. The Challenges of Web 2.0 and Social Media*, ed. Christian Fuchs, Kees Boersma, Anders Albrechtslund and Marisol Sandoval, 71–88. New York: Routledge.

Artz, Lee. 2008. Media Relations and Media Product: Audience Commodity. *Democratic Communiqué* 22 (1): 60–74.

Arvidsson, Adam. 2005. Brands. A Critical Perspective. *Journal of Consumer Culture* 5 (2): 235–258.

Arvidsson, Adam. 2006. *Brands: Meaning and Value in Media Culture.* New York: Routledge.

Arvidsson, Adam. 2011. Ethics and Value in Customer Co-Production. *Marketing Theory* 11 (3): 261–278.

Arvidsson, Adam and Eleanor Colleoni. 2012. Value in informational capitalism and on the Internet. *The Information Society* 28 (3): 135–150.

Babe, Robert E. 2000. *Canadian Communication Thought. Ten Foundational Writers.* Toronto: University of Toronto Press.

Babe, Robert E. 2012. Theodor Adorno and Dallas Smythe. Culture Industry/ Consciousness Industry and the Political Economy of Media and Communication. In *Revisiting the Frankfurt School: Essays on Culture, Media and Theory*, ed. David Berry, 91–115. Farnham: Ashgate.

Barbrook, Richard and Andy Cameron. 2001. Californian Ideology. In *Crypto Anarchy, Cyberstates and Pirate Utopias*, ed. Peter Ludlow, 363–387. Cambridge, MA: MIT Press.

Benjamin, Walter. 1934. Der Autor als Produzent. In *Medienästhetische Schriften*, 231–247. Frankfurt am Main: Suhrkamp.

Benjamin, Walter. 1936/1939. The Work of Art in the Age of Mechanical Reproduction. In *Media and Cultural Studies. KeyWorks*, ed. Meenakshi Gigi Durham and Douglas M. Kellner, 18–40. Malden, MA: Blackwell.

Bermejo, Fernando. 2009. Audience Manufacture in Historical Perspective. From Broadcasting to Google. *New Media & Society* 11 (1&2): 133–154.

Bidet, Jacques. 2009. *Exploring Marx's Capital. Philosophical, Economic, and Political Dimensions.* Chicago, IL: Haymarket Books.

Bolin, Göran. 2005. Notes from Inside the Factory. The Production and Consumption of Signs and Sign Value in Media Industries. *Social Semiotics* 15 (3): 289–306.

Bolin, Göran. 2009. Symbolic Production and Value in Media Industries. *Journal of Cultural Economy* 2 (3): 345–361.

Bolin, Göran. 2011. *Value and the Media. Cultural Production and Consumption in Digital Markets.* Farnham: Ashgate.

Boltanski, Luc and Eve Chiapello. 2007. *The New Spirit of Capitalism.* London: Verso.

Bourdieu, Pierre. 1986a. *Distinction. A Social Critique of the Judgement of Taste.* London. Routledge.

Bourdieu, Pierre. 1986b. The (Three) Forms of Capital. In *Handbook of Theory and Research in the Sociology of Education*, ed. John G. Richardson, 241–258. New York: Greenwood Press.

Brady, Robert A. 1937. *The Spirit and Structure of German Fascism.* New York: Viking.

Brecht, Bertolt. 1932/2000. The Radio as a Communications Apparatus. In *Bertolt Brecht on Film & Radio*, ed. Marc Silberman, 41–46. London: Methuen.

Bruns, Axel. 2008. *Blogs, Wikipedia, Second Life, and Beyond: From Production to Produsage*. New York: Peter Lang.

Caraway, Brett. 2011. Audience Labor in the New Media Environment. A Marxian Revisiting of the Audience Commodity. *Media, Culture & Society* 33 (5): 693–708.

Chen, Chih-hsien. 2003. Is the Audience Really Commodity? An Overdetermined Marxist Perspective of the Television Economy. Papers of the International Communication Association Conference 2003. http://citation.allacademic.com/meta/p_mla_apa_research_citation/1/1/2/0/8/pages112086/p112086-1.php.

Cleaver, Harry. 1992. The Inversion of Class Perspective in Marxian Theory. From Valorisation to Self-Valorisation. In *Open Marxism. Vol. 2*, ed. Werner Bonefeld, Richard Gunn and Kosmos Psychopedis, 106–144. London: Pluto.

Cleaver, Harry. 2000. *Reading Capital Politically*. Leeds: Anti/Theses.

Cohen, Nicole. 2008. The Valorization of Surveillance. Towards a Political Economy of Facebook. *Democratic Communiqué* 22 (1): 5–22.

Comscore. 2012. *The Power of Like2. How Social Marketing Works*. White Paper. http://www.comscore.com/ger/Press_Events/Presentations_Whitepapers/2012/The_Power_of_Like_2-How_Social_Marketing_Works (accessed on June 27th, 2012).

Coté, Mark and Jennifer Pybus. 2007. Learning to Immaterial Labour 2.0: MySpace and Social Networks. *Ephemera* 7 (1): 88–106.

Couvering, Elizabeth. 2004. New Media? The Political Economy of Internet Search Engines. IAMCR 2004 Paper. http://citeseerx.ist.psu.edu/viewdoc/summary?doi=10.1.1.129.1900.

Couvering, Elizabeth. 2011. Navigational Media. The Political Economy of Online Traffic. In *The Political Economies of Media. The Transformation of the Global Media Industries*, ed. Dwayne Winseck and Dal Yong Jin, 183–200. London: Bloomsbury.

Dean, Jodi. 2005. Communicative capitalism: circulation and the foreclosure of politics. *Cultural Politics* 1 (1): 51–74.

Deleuze, Gilles. 1995. Postscript on the Societies of Control. In *Negotiations*, 177–182. New York, NY: Columbia University Press.

Dyer-Witheford, Nick. 1999. *Cyber-Marx. Cycles and Circuits of Struggle in High-Technology Capitalism*. Urbana, IL: Universiy of Illinois Press.

Dyer-Witheford, Nick. 2010. Digital Labour, Species Being and the Global Worker. *Ephemera* 10 (3/4): 484–503.

Eagleton, Terry. 2011. *Why Marx was Right*. London: Yale University Press.

Ekman, Mattias. 2012. Understandig Accumulation. The Relevance of Marx's Theory of Primitive Accumulation in Media and Communication Studies. *tripleC – Journal for a Global Sustainable Information Society* 10 (2): 156–170.

Enzensberger, Hans Magnus. 1970. Baukasten zu einer Theorie der Medien. In *MedienkulturKursbuch*, ed. Lorenz Engell, Oliver Fahle, Britta Neitzel, Josef Vogel and Claus Pias, 264–278. Stuttgart: DVA.

Enzensberger, Hans Magnus. 1974. *The Consciousness Industry.* New York: Seabury Press.

Ferguson, Marjorie and Peter Golding. 1997. Cultural Studies and Changing Times: An Introduction. In *Cultural Studies in Question*, ed. Marjorie Ferguson and Peter Golding, xiii-xxvii. London: Sage.

Fisher, Eran. 2010. *Media and New Capitalism in the Digital Age. The Spirit of Networks.* New York: Palgrave Macmillan.

Fisher, Eran. 2012. How Less Alienation Creates More Exploitation? Audience Labour on Social Network Sites. *tripleC – Journal for a Global Sustainable Information Society* 10 (2): 171–183.

Freud, Sigmund. 1961. *Beyond the Pleasure Principle.* New York: Norton.

Friedmann, Georges. 1959. *Grenzen der Arbeitsteilung. Frankfurter Beiträge zur Soziologie, Volume 7.* Frankfurt am Main: Europäische Verlagsanstalt.

Fuchs, Christian. 2008. Internet and Society: Social Theory in the Information Age. New York: Routledge.

Fuchs, Christian. 2010. Labor in Informational Capitalism and on the Internet. *The Information Society* 26 (3): 179–196.

Fuchs, Christian. 2011a. *Foundations of Critical Media and Information Studies.* London: Routledge.

Fuchs, Christian. 2011b. The Contemporary World Wide Web: Social Medium or New Space of Accumulation? In *The Political Economies of Media. The Transformation of the Global Media Industries*, ed. Dwayne Winseck and Dal Yong Jin, 201–220. London: Bloomsbury.

Fuchs, Christian. 2012a. Critique of the Political Economy of Web 2.0 Surveillance. In *Internet and Surveillance. The Challenges of Web 2.0 and Social Media*, ed. Christian Fuchs, Kees Boersma, Anders Albrechtslund and Marisol Sandoval, 31–70. New York: Routledge.

Fuchs, Christian. 2012b. With or without Marx? With or without Capitalism? A Rejoinder to Adam Arvidsson and Eleanor Colleoni. *tripleC – Open Access Journal for a Global Sustainable Information Society* 10 (2): 633–645.

Fuchs Christian. 2009. Information and Communication Technologies and Society A Contribution to the Critique of the Political Economy of the Internet. *European Journal of Communication* 24 (1): 69–87.

Fuchs, Christian and Vincent Mosco, eds. 2012. Marx is Back – The Importance of Marxist Theory and Research for Critical Communication Studies Today.

Gandy, Oscar H. 1993. *The Panoptic Sort. A Political Economy of Personal Information.* Boulder, CO: Westview Press.

Gandy, Oscar H. 2011. The Political Economy of Personal Information. In *The Handbook of Political Economy of Communications*, ed. Janet Wasko, Graham Murdock and Helena Sousa, 436–457. Malden, MA: Wiley-Blackwell.

Garnham, Nicholas. 1990. *Capitalism and Communication.* London: Sage.

Garnham, Nicholas. 2004. Class Analysis and the Information Society as Mode of Production. *Javnost* 11 (3): 93–104.

Garnham, Nicholas. 1995/1998. Political Economy and Cultural Studies: Reconciliation or Divorce? In *TheoryCultural and CulturePopular*, ed. John Storey, 600–612. Harlow: Pearson.

Golding, Peter and Graham Murdock. 1978. Theories of Communication and Theories of Society. *Communication Research* 5 (3): 339–356.

Grossberg, Lawrence. 1995/1998. Cultural Studies vs. Political Economy. Is Anybody Else Bored with this Debate? In *Cultural Theory and Popular Culture*, ed. John Storey, 613–624. Harlow: Pearson.

Grossmann, Henryk. 1929. *Das Akkumulations- und Zusammenbruchsgesetz des kapitalistischen Systems*. Leipzig: C.L. Hirschfeld.

Habermas, Jürgen. 1984. *Theory of Communicative Action. Volume 1*. Boston: Beacon.

Hall, Stuart, Chas Critcher, Tony Jefferson, John Clarke and Brian Roberts. 1978. *Policing the Crisis. Mugging, the State and Law and Order*. London: Macmillan.

Hall, Stuart. 1981/1988. Notes on Deconstructing the Popular. In *Cultural Theory and Popular Culture. A Reader*, ed. John Storey, 442–453. Hemel Hempstead: Prentice Hall.

Hall, Stuart. 1986. The Problem of Ideology – Marxism without Guarantees. *Journal of Communication Inquiry* 10 (2): 28–44.

Hall, Stuart. 1988. The Toad in the Garden. Thatcherism among the Theorists. In *Marxism and the Intepretation of Culture*, ed. Cary Nelson and Lawrence Grossberg, 35–73. Urbana, IL: University of Illinois Press.

Hardt, Michael and Antonio Negri. 2009. *Commonwealth*. Cambridge, MA: Harvard University Press.

Hartley, John. 2012. *Digital Futures for Cultural and Media Studies*. Chicester: Wiley-Blackwell.

Harvey, David. 2005. *The New Imperialism*. Oxford: Oxford University Press.

Harvey, David. 2007. *A Brief History of Neoliberalism*. Oxford: Oxford University Press.

Harvey, David, Michael Hardt and Antonio Negri. 2009. Commonwealth: An Exchange. *Artforum*, http://www.thefreelibrary.com/Commonwealth%3a+an+exchange.-a0211807984.

Hebblewhite, William Henning James. 2012. "Means of Communication as Means of Production" Revisited. *tripleC – Journal for a Global Sustainable Information Society* 10 (2): 203–213.

Hesmondhalgh, David. 2010. User-Generated Content, Free Labour and the Cultural Industries. *Ephemera* 10 (3/4): 267–284.

Hesmondhalgh, David and Sarah Baker. 2011. *Creative Labour. Media Work in Three Cultural Industries*. London: Routledge.

Hobsbawm, Eric. 2011. *How to Change the World. Marx and Marxism 1840–2011*. London: Little, Brown.

Holzer, Horst. 1973. *Kommunikationssoziologie*. Reinbek: Rowohlt.

Holzer, Horst. 1994. *Medienkommunikation*. Opladen: Westdeutscher Verlag.

Horkheimer, Max and Theodor W. Adorno. 2002a. *Dialectic of Enlightenment*. Stanford, CA: Stanford University Press.

Horkheimer, Max. 1931. The State of Contemporary Social Philosophy and the Tasks of an Institute for Social Research. In *Critical Theory and Society. A Reader*, ed. Stephen E. Bronner and Douglas Kellner, 25–36. New York: Routledge.

Horkheimer, Max. 1947. *Eclipse of Reason*. New York: Continuum.

Horkheimer, Max. 2002. *Critical Theory*. New York: Continuum.

Horkheimer, Max and Theodor W. Adorno. 2002b. *Dialectic of Enlightenment*. Stanford, CA: Stanford University Press.

Howe, Jeff. 2008. *Crowdsourcing. Why the Power of the Crowd is Driving the Future of Business*. New York: Three Rivers Press.

Jenkins, Henry. 2008. *Convergence Culture*. New York: New York University Press.

Jhally, Sut. 1987. *The Codes of Advertising*. New York: Routledge.

Jhally, Sut and Bill Livant. 1986/2006. Watching as Working. The Valorization of Audience Consciousness. In *The Spectacle of Accumulation. Essays in Culture, Media, & Politics*, Sut Jhally, 24–43. New York: Peter Lang.

Kang, Hyunjin and Matthew P. McAllister. 2011. Selling You and your Clicks. Examining the Audience Commodification of Google. *tripleC* 9 (2): 141–153.

Knoche, Manfred. 2005. Kommunikationswissenschaftliche Medienökonomie als Kritik der Politischen Ökonomie der Medien. In *Internationale partizipatorische Kommunikationspolitik*, ed. Petra Ahrweiler and Barbara Thomaß, 101–109. Münster: LIT.

Kücklich, Julian. 2005. Precarious Playbour. *Fibreculture Journal* 5, http://five.fibreculturejournal.org/fcj-025-precarious-playbour-modders-and-the-digital-games-industry/ (accessed on May 29, 2011).

Lauer, Josh. 2008. Alienation in the Information Economy. Toward a Marxist Critique of Consumer Surveillance. In *Participation and Media Production*, ed. Nico Carpentier and Benjamin De Cleen, 41–56. Newcastle: Cambridge Scholars.

Lebowitz, Michael A. 1986. Too Many Blindspots on the Media. *Studies in Political Economy* 21: 165–173.

Lee, Micky. 2011. Google Ads and the Blindspot Debate. *Media, Culture & Society* 33 (3): 433–447.

Livant, Bill. 1979. The Audience Commodity: On the "Blindspot" Debate. *Canadian Journal of Political and Social Theory* 3 (1): 91–106.

Lukács, Georg. 1923/1972. *History and Class Consciousness*. Cambridge, MA: MIT Press.

Mansell, Robin. 1995. Against the Flow. The Peculiar Opportunity of Social Scientists. In *A Different Road Taken. Profiles in Critical Communication*, ed. John A. Lent, 43–66. Boulder, CO: Westview Press.

Manzerolle, Vincent. 2010. Mobilizing the Audience Commodity. Digital Labour in a Wireless World. *Ephemera* 10 (3/4): 455–469.

Marcuse, Herbert. 1941. *Reason and Revolution. Hegel and the Rise of Social Theory.* 2nd edition. London: Routledge.

Marcuse, Herbert. 1964. *One-Dimensional Man.* Boston, MA: Beacon.

Marcuse, Herbert. 1955. *Eros and Civilization.* Boston, MA: Beacon.

Marx, Karl 1844. *Economic and Philosophical Manuscripts.* London: Lawrence and Wishart.

Marx, Karl. 1849. *Wage Labour and Capital.* http://www.marxists.org/archive/marx/works/1847/wage-labour/index.htm.

Marx, Karl. 1857/58. *Grundrisse.* London: Penguin.

Marx, Karl. 1865. Value, Price and Profit. http://www.marxists.org/archive/marx/works/1865/value-price-profit/index.htm.

Marx, Karl. 1867. *Capital: Volume I.* London: Penguin.

Marx, Karl. 1894. *Capital: Volume III.* London: Penguin.

McGuigan, Lee. 2012. Consumers: The Commodity Product of Interactive Commercial Television, or, Is Dallas Smythe's Thesis More Germane Than Ever? *Journal of Communication Inquiry* 36 (4): 288–304.

McGuigan, Lee and Vincent Manzerolle, eds. 2014. *The Audience Commodity in a Digital Age: Revisiting a Critical Theory of Commercial Media.* New York: Peter Lang.

McStay, Andrew. 2011. Profiling Phorm: An Autopoietic Approach to the Audience-as-Commodity. *Surveillance & Society* 8 (3): 310–322.

Meehan, Eileen. 1984. Ratings and the Institutional Approach. A Third Answer to the Commodity Question. *Critical Studies in Mass Communication* 1 (2): 216–225.

Meehan, Eileen. 1993. Commodity Audience, Actual Audience. The Blindspot Debate. In *Illuminating the Blindspots. Essays Honouring Dallas W. Smythe*, ed. Janet Wasko, Vincent Mosco and Manjunath Pendakur, 378–397. Norwood, NJ: Ablex.

Meehan, Eileen. 2002. Gendering the Commodity Audience. Critical Media Research, Feminism, and Political Econmy. In *Sex & Money. Feminism and Political Economy in the Media*, ed. Eileen Meehan and Ellen Riordan, 209–222. Minneapolis, MN: University of Minnesota Press.

Meehan, Eileen. 2007. Understanding How the Popular Becomes Popular. The Role of Political Economy in the Study of Popular Communication. *Popular Communication* 5 (3): 161–170.

Meehan, Eileen and Ellen Riordan, ed. 2002. *Sex & Money. Feminism and Political Economy in the Media.* Minneapolis, MN: University of Minnesota Press.

Mies, Maria. 1986. *Patriarchy & Accumulation on a World Scale.* London: Zed Books.

Mies, Maria, Veronika Bennholdt-Thomsen and Claudia von Werlhof. 1988. *Women: The Last Colony.* London: Zed Books.

Mosco, Vincent. 2009. *The Political Economy of Communication.* London: SAGE. 2nd edition.

Mosco, Vincent and Catherine McKercher. 2008. *The Laboring of Communicaiton. Will Knowledge Workers of the World Unite?* Lanham, MD: Lexington Books.

Murdock, Graham. 2011. Political Economies as Moral Economies. Commodities, Gifts, and Public Goods. In *The Handbook of Political Economy of Communications*, ed. Janet Wasko, Graham Murdock and Helena Sousa, 13–40. Malden, MA: Wiley-Blackwell.

Murdock, Graham. 1978. Blindspots about Western Marxism. A Reply to Dallas Smythe. In *The Political Economy of the Media I*, ed. Peter Golding and Graham Murdock, 465–474. Cheltenham: Edward Elgar.

Murdock, Graham and Peter Golding. 1974. For a Political Economy of Mass Communications. In *The Political Economy of the Media I*, ed. Peter Golding and Graham Murdock, 3–32. Cheltenham: Edward Elgar.

Murdock, Graham and Peter Golding. 2005. Culture, Communications and Political Economy. In *Mass Media and Society*, ed. James Curran and Michael Gurevitch, 60–83. London: Hodder.

Napoli, Philip M. 2010. Revisiting "Mass Communication" and the "Work" of the Audience in the New Media eEnvironment. *Media, Culture & Society* 32 (3): 505–516.

Negri, Antonio. 1991. *Marx beyond Marx*. London: Pluto.

Neubauer, Robert. 2011. Neoliberalism in the Information Age, or Vice Cersa? Global Citizenship, Technology, and Hegemonic Ideology. *tripleC – Journal for a Global Sustainable Information Society* 9 (2): 195–230.

Neumann, Franz. 1966. *Behemoth. The Structure and Practice of National Socialism 1933–1944*. New York: Harper & Row.

Nixon, Brice. 2012. Dialectical Method and the Critical Political Economy of Culture. *tripleC – Journal for a Global Sustainable Information Society* 10 (2): 439–456.

O'Reilly, Tim. 2005. *What is Web 2.0?* http://www.oreilly.de/artikel/web20.html.

O'Reilly, Tim and John Battelle. 2009. *Web Squared. Web 2.0 Five Years On. Special Report.* http://assets.en.oreilly.com/1/event/28/web2009_websquared-whitepaper.pdf.

Pasquinelli, Matteo. 2009. Google's PageRank Algorithm: A Diagram of Cognitive Capitalism and the Rentier of the Common Intellect. In *SearchDeep*, ed. Konrad Becker and Felix Stalder. London: Transaction Publishers.

Pasquinelli, Matteo. 2010. The Ideology of Free Culture and the Grammar of Sabotage. In *Education in the Creative Economy. Knowledge and Learning in the Age of Innovation*, ed. Daniel Araya and Michael Peters. New York: Peter Lang.

Pollock, Friedrich. 1956. *Automation. Materialien zur Beurteilung der ökonomischen und sozialen Folgen*. Frankfurter Beiträge zur Soziologie, Volume 5. Frankfurt am Main: Europäische Verlagsanstalt.

Prey, Robert. 2012. The Network's Blindspot. Exclusion, Exploitation and Marx's Process-Relational Ontology. *tripleC – Journal for a Global Sustainable Information Society* 10 (2): 253–273.

Prodnik, Jernej. 2012. A Note on the Ongoing Processes of Commodification. From the Audience Commodity to the Social Factory. *tripleC – Journal for a Global Sustainable Information Society* 10 (2): 274–301.

Ritzer, George and Nathan Jurgenson. 2010. Production, Consumption, Prosumption. *Journal of Consumer Culture* 10 (1): 13–36.

Sandoval, Marisol. 2012. A Critical Empirical Case Study of Consumer Surveillance on Web 2.0. In *Internet and Surveillance. The Challenges of Web 2.0 and Social Media*, ed. Christian Fuchs, Kees Boersma, Anders Albrechtslund and Marisol Sandoval, 147–169. New York: Routledge.

Schiller, Dan. 1999. The Legacy of Robert A Brady. Antifascist Origins of the Political Economy of Communications. *Journal of Media Economics* 12 (2): 89–101.

Scholz, Trebor. 2011. Facebook as Playground and Factory. In *Facebook and Philosophy*, ed. D.E. Wittkower, 241–252. Chicago: Open Court.

Shirky, Clay. 2008. *Here Comes Everybody*. London: Penguin.

Smythe, Dallas W. 1951. The Consumer's Stake in Radio and Television. *The Quarterly of Film, Radio and Television* 6 (2): 109–128.

Smythe, Dallas W. 1960. On the Political Economy of Communications. *Journalism & Mass Communication Quarterly* 37 (4): 563–572.

Smythe, Dallas W. 1977a. Communications: Blindspot of Western Marxism. *Canadian Journal of Political and Social Theory* 1 (3): 1–27.

Smythe, Dallas W. 1977b. Critique of the Consciousness Industry. *Journal of Communication* 27 (1): 198–202.

Smythe, Dallas W. 1981. *Dependency Road*. Norwood, NJ: Ablex.

Smythe, Dallas W. 1984. New Directions for Critical Communications Research. *Media, Culture & Society* 6 (3): 205–217.

Smythe, Dallas W. 1994. *Counterclockwise*. Boulder, CO: Westview Press.

Smythe, Dallas W. and Tran Van Dinh. 1983. On Critical and Administrative Research: A New Critical Analysis. *Journal of Communication* 33 (3): 117–127.

Sparks, Colin. 1996. Stuart Hall, Cultural Studies and Marxism. In *Stuart Hall. Critical Dialogues in Cultural Studies*, ed. David Morely and Kuan-Hsing Chen, 71–101. London: Routledge.

Steeves, H. Leslie and Janet Wasko. 2002. Feminist Theory and Political Economy. Toward a Friendly Alliance. In. *Sex & Money. Feminism and Political Economy in the Media*, ed. Eileen Meehan and Ellen Riordan, 16–29. Minneapolis, MN: University of Minnesota Press.

Tapscott, Don and Anthony D. Williams. 2006. *Wikinomics. How Mass Collaboration Changes Everything*. London: Penguin.

Terranova, Tiziana. 2000. Free Labor. Producing Culture for the Digital Economy. *Social Text* 18 (2): 33–58.

Toffler, Alvin. 1980. *The Third Wave*. New York: Bantam.

Wasko, Janet. 1993. Introduction. In *Illuminating the Blindspots. Essays Honoring Dallas W. Smythe*, ed. Janet Wasko, Vincent Mosco and Manjunath Pendakur, 1–11. Norwood, NJ: Ablex.

Wasko, Janet. 2004. The Political Economy of Communications. In *The SAGE Handbook of Media Studies*, ed. John D.H. Downing, 309–329. Thousand Oaks, CA: Sage.

Wasko, Janet. 2005. Studying the Political Economy of Media and Onformation. Comunicação e Sociedade 7: 25–48.

Wright, Erik Olin. 1997. *Class Counts. Comparative Studies in Class Analysis*. Cambridge. Cambridge University Press.

Yao, Lin. 2010. Revisiting Critical Scholars' Alternative. A Case Study of Dallas Smythe's Praxis. Paper presented at the 2010 Annual Meeting of the International Communication Association.

Zhao, Yuezhi. 2007. After Mobile Phones, What? Re-embedding the Social in China's "Digital Revolution"? *International Journal of Communication* 1: 92–120.

Zhao, Yuezhi. 2011. The Challenge of China. Contribution to a Transcultural Political Economy of Communication for the Twenty-First Century. In *The Handbook of Political Economy of Communications*, ed. Janet Wasko, Graham Murdock and Helena Sousa, 558–582. Malden, MA: Wiley-Blackwell.

Žižek, Slavoj. 2010. *Living in the End Times*. London: Verso.

Index